CW01025303

JOSEPH SEVERN
A Life

Portrait in oils of Keats Reading, 1821–3, painted to exorcise Severn's memories of the dead Keats.

JOSEPH SEVERN

A Life

The Rewards of Friendship

SUE BROWN

OXFORD

UNIVERSITY PRESS

OXFORD
UNIVERSITY PRESS

Great Clarendon Street, Oxford ox2 6dp

Oxford University Press is a department of the University of Oxford.
It furthers the University's objective of excellence in research, scholarship,
and education by publishing worldwide in

Oxford New York

Auckland Cape Town Dar es Salaam Hong Kong Karachi
Kuala Lumpur Madrid Melbourne Mexico City Nairobi
New Delhi Shanghai Taipei Toronto

With offices in

Argentina Austria Brazil Chile Czech Republic France Greece
Guatemala Hungary Italy Japan Poland Portugal Singapore
South Korea Switzerland Thailand Turkey Ukraine Vietnam

Oxford is a registered trade mark of Oxford University Press
in the UK and in certain other countries

Published in the United States
by Oxford University Press Inc., New York

British Library Cataloguing in Publication Data
Data available

Library of Congress Cataloging in Publication Data
Data available

Typeset by SPI Publisher Services, Pondicherry, India
Printed in Great Britain
on acid-free paper by
CPI Antony Rowe, Chippenham, Wiltshire

ISBN 978-0-19-956502-3

1 3 5 7 9 10 8 6 4 2

For the Washington English History Buffs

Who first shared my pleasure

in the company of Joseph Severn

at the Villa Drusiana, Rome on

1 January 2000

ACKNOWLEDGEMENTS

Y first and greatest debt is to Grant Scott. From my earliest tentative approach, he, an established scholar in the field, welcomed me to the world of Joseph Severn. Since then we have exchanged many hundreds of emails and had a number of lively meetings, sharing and discussing our Severn finds. He has read and commented wisely on the first (and much longer) drafts of all chapters. The publication of his finely edited *Joseph Severn: Letters and Memoirs* in 2005 immeasurably eased my task and saved me many hours of work. But the debt goes deeper than that. Were it not for Grant's unfailing interest and encouragement this book might never have been finished.

One of the pleasures of writing it has been getting to know several of Severn's many descendants, each of whom hold rich stores of Severn material and remain keenly interested in the life of their famous forebear. Rose Wild, Katharine Mackenzie, and David and Ross Severn have all been very generous in the access they have given me. So, above all, has Lady Juliet Townsend, the daughter of Severn's previous biographer, Sheila, Countess Birkenhead, and of the second Lord Birkenhead, himself a distinguished biographer. I have spent many happy hours working in the congenial place where they worked, as Lady Juliet opened to me the riches of her mother's research archive on Severn and Ruskin, collections of family papers, and, a wonderful treat, Mary Newton's delightful sketchbooks of Severn family life. Juliet's enthusiastic encouragement of Keats scholarship (and much else) is a model for all owners of important private archives.

I have also benefited from the expert advice of Jack Stillinger on the composition of Keats's 'Bright Star' sonnet, Nick Roe on Keats's and Severn's journey to Rome, and the encouragement of Peter Vassallo at the University of Malta, Tim Webb at Bristol University and Roderick Cavaliero. At key stages I encountered the keen intelligence and biographical expertise of Jane Ridley and the practised editorial eye of Martin Shepherd. Many curators and archivists have helped me, chief among them Catherine Payling of the Keats–Shelley Memorial House, Rome; Mick Scott and Ken Page of Keats House, Hampstead; and Leslie Morris and her welcoming staff at the Houghton Library at Harvard where the principal collection of Severn papers is to be found; Mark Pomeroy at the Royal

Acknowledgements

Academy Archive; Iain G. Brown at the National Library of Scotland; Michael
Powell, the Manchester Cathedral Archivist at Chetham's Library (where, to
my astonishment, I worked at the table where Marx and Engels composed
the *Communist Party Manifesto*); Chris Pensa at Sotheby's; Tim Moreton at
the National Portrait Gallery; Angela Moore at the Flintshire Record Office;
Stephen Wildman at the Ruskin Library in Lancaster; Bruce Barker-Benfield
at the Bodleian Library; Doucet Fischer at the Carl H. Pforzheimer Collection,
New York Public Library; Elizaveta Renne at the Hermitage Museum, St Petersburg; Maxine Vermeire at the Royal Palace, Brussels; and many others have all
gone beyond the call of duty in assisting me. The staff of the London Library
have been ever-helpful, ever-tolerant.

At OUP I am grateful for Andrew McNeillie's immediate interest in the idea
of a new biography of Joseph Severn, Jacqueline Baker's firm, but sympathetic
guidance through the publication process, Claire Thompson's skill in getting
the book into production and Elizabeth Stone's meticulous copy-editing and
willingness to fit in with my timetable at a difficult period for us both.

I am indebted for the right to reproduce Severn art works and memorabilia
to Lady Juliet Townsend, Rose Wild, and Katharine Mackenzie, the London
Metropolitan Archive, the Houghton Library, Harvard, the National Portrait
Gallery, the Victoria & Albert Museum, the Art Gallery of South Australia in
Adelaide, the Reform Club and the Institut Royal du Patrimoine Artistique,
Brussels.

This is a book about friendship. The interest and support of many friends has
been essential to its making. If I acknowledge just a few it is because of the specific help they have given me in a whole array of tasks, from finding a publisher
to tracking down the christening record of Severn's illegitimate child, straight-
ening out IT muddles and helping prepare the illustrations. Mary Clapinson,
formerly Keeper of Western Manuscripts at the Bodleian, and her husband,
Mike, have been invaluable. So, too, have Ralph and Margaret Houlbrooke at
Reading University; Alice and Frank Prochaska at Yale; Jo and Elizabeth Carey;
Hazel and Andy Morgan; Tom and Sarah Bowring; Gray Standen; Neil Bennet;
Margaret de Fonblanque; Jill Webster; Charles and Griselda Drace-Francis and
Martin Haddon; and in Malta, where much of this book was written, David
Milne, Edward Warrington, and Paul and Bice Asciak.

In choosing a dedication I have preferred the living over the dead. But I think,
too, of someone who died far too young and who, like Severn, adored Rome. I
hope he would have enjoyed this book.

CONTENTS

Contents

LIST OF ILLUSTRATIONS

List of Illustrations

LIST OF PLATES

Portrait in oils of *Keats Reading*, 1821–3, painted to exorcise Severn's memories of the dead Keats. (Copyright National Portrait Gallery, London) Frontispiece

1 John Keats drawn by Severn in the winter of 1816–1817, the likeness of Keats which Charles Cowden Clarke admired above all others. (Copyright V&A Images/Victoria and Albert Museum, London)

2 Severn's miniature of Keats done in oils and watercolour on ivory and exhibited at the Royal Academy in 1819. (Copyright National Portrait Gallery, London)

3 Severn's miniature of his family, from left to right Charles, Tom, Sarah, Charlotte, Maria, his mother, Elizabeth, and father, James *c.* 1820. (Copyright City of London, London Metropolitan Archives)

4 Severn's night-time pen and ink sketch of the dying Keats, 28 January 1821. (Reproduced by kind permission of the Keats–Shelley Memorial House, Rome)

5 Self portrait in pencil of Severn seated at a keyboard *c.* 1823. (Copyright City of London, London Metropolitan Archives)

6 *The Fountain* painted by Severn in 1828. (Copyright IRPA-KIK, Brussels)

7 *Shepherds in the Campagna*, painting in oils, 1834, later bought by Gladstone. (Private collection)

8 *Shelley at the Baths of Caracalla*, portrait in oils, 1845, commissioned by Mary Shelley. (Reproduced by kind permission of the Keats–Shelley Memorial House, Rome)

9 *The Deserted Village*, 1857, Severn's last painting to be exhibited at the Royal Academy. (Reproduced by kind permission of the Art Gallery of South Australia, Adelaide)

ABBREVIATIONS

BL	British Library
DNB	*Dictionary of National Biography*, ed. Leslie Stephen and Sidney Lee, 22 vols (London: Oxford University Press, repr. 1921–2)
FO	Foreign Office
IGI	International Genealogical Index
Keats Circle	Hyder Edward Rollins, ed., *The Keats Circle: Letters and Papers and More Letters and Poems of the Keats Circle, 1816–1878*, 2 vols (2nd edn, Cambridge, MA: Harvard University Press, 1965)
LMA	London Metropolitan Archive
Letters	Hyder Edward Rollins, ed., *The Letters of John Keats 1814–21*, 2 vols (Cambridge, MA: Harvard University Press, 1958)
Letters and Memoirs	Grant F. Scott, ed., *Joseph Severn: Letters and Memoirs* (Aldershot: Ashgate, 2005)
Letters of Charles Brown	Jack Stillinger, ed., *The Letters of Charles Armitage Brown* (Cambridge, MA: Harvard University Press, 1966)
Life and Letters	William Sharp, *The Life and Letters of Joseph Severn* (London: Sampson Low, Marston & Co., 1892)
New Letters of Charles Brown	Grant F. Scott and Sue Brown, eds, *New Letters from Charles Brown to Joseph Severn* (University of Maryland Romantic Circles electronic edition, 2007, <http:/www.rc.umd.edu/editions/brownsevern>)
Memoir of Thomas Uwins	Sarah Uwins, *Memoir of Thomas Uwins*, 2 vols (London: Longman, Brown, 1858)
Nostrand	Sudie Nostrand, ed., 'The Keats Circle: Further Letters' (New York University: PhD dissertation, 1973)
Oxford DNB	*Oxford Dictionary of National Biography*, ed. H.C.G. Matthew and Brian Harrison, 61 vols (Oxford: Oxford University Press, 2004)
RA	Royal Academy
TNA	The National Archives, Kew

Introduction

WERE it not for Joseph Severn, John Keats would never have got to Rome in the autumn of 1820 and biographies of the poet would probably end with a couple of lame sentences: 'He died at the Hotel Villa di Londra, Naples on — October 1820. Nothing is known of his final weeks after he left England.' In fact, we know a great deal about Keats's last few months, for not only did Severn take care of him on the journey to Italy and help get him to Rome, he also reported regularly to London on his friend's physical, intellectual, and emotional disintegration in the period leading up to his death on 23 February 1821. These letters, which are virtually the only record of this time, paint an indelible picture of the trials of both patient and nurse at perhaps the most poignant deathbed in English literary history. They become all the more moving when we visit the place where they were written, the Keats–Shelley House in Rome.

Keats's sufferings are almost too painful to contemplate. He experienced a miserable death, half-starved, fighting for breath, weakened by frequent bleedings, and deprived of any sedatives to ease his sufferings. He was in such emotional turmoil that he could not bear to see the handwriting of his closest friend Charles Brown, his sister, or Fanny Brawne, the girl who obsessed him to the exclusion of almost everything else. On his deathbed, Keats, who had never had any interest in being an also-ran, came to believe that he had failed in everything that mattered: love, fame, and the making of great poetry. He was desperate to die and determined to be forgotten.

It is a relief to turn to the friend who nursed Keats and whose presence in the Keats–Shelley House is equally vivid. Severn's oil painting of Shelley, miniatures of Keats and his brothers, his famous sketch of Keats on his deathbed, and one or two letters give a clear sense of his character, a fallible, excitable young man who struggled to keep going. Nothing had prepared him for this, the harshest trial of his life. He had come to Rome expecting to advance his artistic career and assist his friend's recovery. Instead, for the last two long months of Keats's life he barely left their lodgings, sitting up for many nights watching over him, sharing his despair and dreading the inevitable outcome. But though we think of Severn in a tragic place, he was by nature irrepressible. He reacted to his terrible situation by taking out his fury on his landlady and 'these wretched Romans' with whom he had to negotiate his life in a language he barely understood. He wrote gossipy letters home, full of comforting fictions about his artistic activities and prospects. He played the piano in the room next to Keats's, trying to cheer them both with spirited performances of Haydn's symphonies. And he read aloud to the dying poet, even if he could not always keep his mind on the words in front of him. Twice he sketched Keats, once, as he said, to keep himself awake at night. It was then, too, that he wrote to Keats's friends in London.

Breathless and uncalculating, Severn's letters did not conceal his many domestic anxieties nor his consciousness of his failings as a nurse. Out of the clutter of his daily concerns, however, a compelling picture of Keats in his last days emerged. Others might have told what they saw differently. Severn lightened the grimness of the scene by his instinct for finding in Keats a quality he had himself: kindness. As Keats's world narrowed at the end, he turned to comforting his comforter. That, at least, was how Severn described him in his last exhausted days of suffering. Keats's solicitude for his deathbed companion and the grace of his dying words as recorded by Severn became an inseparable part of the poet's appeal to posterity.

For the Victorians, the friendship of Keats and Severn was a model of all that was noblest in the annals of selfless masculine companionship. When Severn died almost sixty years after Keats there was outrage that he had not been buried beside his friend in the Protestant Cemetery in Rome. The pressure for his reburial proved irresistible, and in March 1881 he was laid to rest in the same enclosure beneath a matching stone whose triumphant assertion that he had lived to see JOHN KEATS 'numbered among the Immortal Poets of England' tempered the bleak anonymity of Keats's own stone.

In the twentieth century, by contrast, Severn got a more mixed reception as Keats scholars lighted on inaccuracies in his reminiscences of the poet and misrepresentations of his place in the Keats Circle. Amy Lowell was the first to disparage Severn, shouldering him aside in her eagerness to stand next to Keats in his hour of need. Others, like Robert Gittings, as fine a Keats biographer as any, were so irritated by Severn's unreliability as a witness that they could accept little he said at face value. More recently, Severn has been misportrayed not just as a lightweight personality but as an equally modest artist, 'a wannabe painter' as described in the *Keats–Shelley Review*. Despite the publication in 2005 of Grant Scott's meticulously edited selection of Severn's letters and autobiographical pieces, which gives for the first time a sense of Severn's richly varied life and achievements, the debunking goes on, as in Stanley Plumly's *Posthumous Keats: A Personal Biography* published in 2008.

Remarkably, however, even the most critical hold back when describing Severn's time nursing Keats in Rome. Briefly, they raise him to a higher plane: as the deathbed companion, Severn undergoes a transformation before sinking back to his mundane self. This disjointed Severn, caught and ennobled in the spotlight at Keats's deathbed, owes much to the work of William Sharp, his first biographer. His *Life and Letters of Joseph Severn*, put together in fits and starts and completed in a great hurry in 1891–2, though long known to be unreliable has had an extraordinarily pervasive impact on studies of both Keats and Severn. For Sharp, much of the interest in Severn's life ended with Keats's death. Though he devotes many pages to the subsequent history and correspondence of members of the Keats Circle, and some to Severn's artistic career, his eleven years as British Consul in Rome are covered in just four. Nor is Severn's rich family life, which Sheila Birkenhead affectionately evoked in her subsequent biography of him, adequately covered. Sharp did a further disservice to his subject, too, by rewriting Severn's idiosyncratic but colourful prose, producing in the process overwritten accounts of key moments in Keats's life, which have brought down the wrath of Keats scholars on Severn's innocent head.

To focus on Severn's life exclusively in relation to Keats not only distorts that life and Severn's character but even obscures the nature of his time in Piazza di Spagna. Severn did not become a different being in his few last months with Keats. Knowledge of his early life and temperament deepens the impression we get from his letters that he was as unprepared as a man can be for what he found there. Though he had known death before, it was a reality he found almost impossible to bear. Optimistic as always, he came to Rome with a great deal still to prove, uncertain but ambitious, too. But in Piazza di Spagna in the winter of 1821, even Severn's optimism was blighted. His trial there was, in consequence, the more moving.

Severn won fame in a painful, unexpected place. His devotion to the dying Keats gave him new standing in the Keats Circle and in his later years made him a legendary figure. But a man cannot thrive, marry, and bring up a large family of unusually gifted children, as Severn did, simply on the memory of a celebrated friendship. He never lost his deep sense of indebtedness to Keats: even so, the 385 recently discovered letters he wrote to his wife contain just four references to the poet and she, of course, never knew him. Severn had a life to get on with, a way to make in the world. As his tombstone attests, it was full of interest and achievement, far from the attenuated existence lived in the shadow of poignant memories which has sometimes been assumed. In particular, Severn was a more successful and significant artist than Keats scholars suggest. The best-known part of his life is the story of an untried, volatile man who had to face tragedy and defeat before seeing his confidence in the genius of Keats vindicated as the poet won increasing recognition. But there is much more to Severn than that. Here is an ebullient man who recreated himself more than once, sometimes bruised by the world, but unstoppably exuberant and, whatever his vanities, generous-spirited and instinctively benevolent.

Here, too, is a man with a gift for friendship with extraordinary people. To have been 'The Friend of Keats' would have been sufficient glory for most men. But Severn could also claim friendship with other great contemporaries like Gladstone and Ruskin, Liszt and Mendelssohn, and many other leading artists and writers of his age. This biography sets out for the first time to explore the range of Severn's many friendships and the charm and kindness which drew men to him. Until now he has perhaps been best known as the man who did not shirk the obligations of friendship, travelling to Italy with the dying Keats when other, closer friends made their excuses; but, as this book shows, alongside the obligations of friendship, Severn would also come to know its rich and varied rewards.

CHAPTER 1

A Hazardous Childhood

JOSEPH SEVERN was a Cockney, born 'within the sound of Bow Bells' on 7 December 1793. It was the nearby clangour of the ten bells of St Leonard's at Shoreditch, however, which dominated his childhood. They hung in one of London's tallest spires, attracting ringers from far around for arduous feats. Not only was Severn christened at the church on Boxing Day 1793,[1] he also grew up within its sound and sight and regularly attended services there. Today, St Leonard's is a crumbling hulk where down-and-outs around its blackened steps contrast with City workers relaxing in its grassed-over graveyard on sunny weekends. Then, this massive red-brick barn with its white stone facings, was only sixty years old and as impressive inside as out for a restless child looking curiously about him. The stained glass in the sanctuary showed scenes from the life of Jacob illuminated in brilliant yellow light; below the fine organ case was a superb carved clock with the royal arms; wooden cupboards held loaves of bread for the poor of the parish; and, if he dared to peep at it, a terrifying funerary monument in white marble showed two skeletons cackling with glee as they split apart an oak tree. The paintings, done in 1792 by an apprentice to the King's History Painter, Sir Benjamin West, were easier on the eye. From the beginning, painting for Severn meant history painting.

St Leonard's stood at the junction of two old Roman roads. Here Old Street, leading on to Clerkenwell and the West End, met Hackney Road going off east towards Hackney and the villages beyond. From the north, Kingsland Road joined with Shoreditch High Street on its way to the City. Through this busy crossroads came livestock driven towards the markets and slaughterhouses of Spitalfields and Smithfield, timber from the docks for fashioning by local joiners, fresh produce bound for Covent Garden, and coal and other necessities for the fast-growing population of London, brought by road from wharves along

1 The junction in front of St Leonard's Shoreditch in 1810 including the charity school at which Severn may have been educated

the river. The constant traffic gave the young Joseph a sense of the immensity of London and of wider worlds beyond. As covered horse-drawn carts, closed carriages, and cabs delivering goods and people competed for right of way with animals and harassed pedestrians in the dust and stench of summer mornings and the muddy refuse of dark winter afternoons, he dragged his heels on his way to school or scampered across to find his friends in Hoxton.

In later life he described himself with some pride as 'an Hoxtontonian'. As with much of what he said, this was a partial truth. Though born in Hoxton, his parents decamped to Shoreditch when he was still a baby. While Hoxton remained as a focus of his youthful social aspirations, Shoreditch was the place which formed him. It had a turbulent history of rowdy independence, having developed just outside the reach of the City authorities. As James Burbage, the father of Shakespeare's actor-manager friend Richard Burbage saw, it was the ideal place for public entertainment. Burbage built London's first theatre there in 1576, establishing a theatrical tradition which flourished for three centuries. Rail though they might against the overcrowded tenements, unsanitary streets, and riotous inhabitants on their doorstep, there was little the City authorities could do to halt the growth of Shoreditch. By the time the Severns moved there in 1793 it was thriving as the heartland of artisanal London. Cabinet-makers, jewellers, ironmongers, clothiers, brewers, coalmen, candlemakers and many more conducted their businesses in workshops and small factories along Shoreditch High Street and in the courts and alleyways behind. On the fringes, orchards, market gardens, rough grazings, and tenter grounds for bleaching cloth offered some respite from the urban congestion until the developers moved in during the years of peace after the Napoleonic wars.

Mason's Court where Severn was brought up was the second turning to the left down Shoreditch High Street. A narrow alley led into a new construction of eight tenements built in rows of four facing each other across a courtyard. The Severns' home was the first of their own that James and Elizabeth had known since their marriage six years before. James's family were of West Country origin, where generations of Severns dwelt close to their eponymous river. His father, Joseph, however, moved to London where Severn family tradition had it that he was a schoolmaster and organist. Though he may well have been musical, the record shows a humbler occupation. When he apprenticed his fourteen-year-old son to a weaver, William Littel, on 6 December 1779, his occupation was entered in the Weavers' Company Court Minutes as 'cork cutter'. Nor could he afford the £10 premium Littel felt obliged to demand. That had to be paid from charity.[2]

If Littel was no better off than Severn, he could boast of Huguenot ancestors, probably some of those who crowded into London after the revocation of the Edict of Nantes in 1685 had deprived them of their religious freedom in France. Many became silkweavers in Spitalfields, living exhausting, noisy, impoverished lives in cramped quarters. Though William escaped to live south of the river in Southwark, his business did not thrive and he was regularly in arrears with his dues to the Weavers Company.[3] James Severn, his apprentice, was a handsome, ambitious youth who, like Thomas Keats and many another, won the classic reward of marriage to his master's daughter. At twenty-five, three years older than him, Elizabeth was perhaps in need of a husband, but she was far from plain and it is likely that the marriage had been planned for some time. Unusually, however, it was not the preliminary to joining his father-in-law's business. With Littel's son, William Joseph, treading on his heels there may not have been enough work to go around. Or James may have revolted against the tedious clatter of the weaver's life and its excessive hours. About the time that his marriage was settled, he determined to become a professional musician.

James and Elizabeth married at the fine Hawksmoor Church of St Luke's, Old Street, on 18 February 1787,[4] beginning their life together in Hoxton Town.

By then William Littel had also moved to Hoxton and probably kept house with his daughter and son-in-law until the regular arrival of children forced the Severns to seek a place of their own. Sarah was born two years after the marriage, Charlotte eighteen months later, followed by their first son, Joseph, in 1793. Four more children were born after the move to Shoreditch: Maria in 1797, Thomas in 1800, Thomas Henry in 1801, and Charles in 1806. Only the first Thomas failed to survive his infancy. At a time when infant mortality was as high as one in three in the poorer parts of London this was a tribute to the hardiness of the Severn stock,[5] the soundness of Elizabeth's nurturing, and the healthiness of life in Mason's Court. Indeed, four of the Severn children would live into their eighties, while their mother was eighty-eight when she died.

Mason's Court was the usual mix of residential and working accommodation in the alleys and backstreets of central London. Though it was made up of just eight buildings, there were many occupiers.[6] The Severns were well placed. Instead of some noisome trade on their doorstep, they looked out on a baker's yard 'letting in the perfumes of buns and ginger bread'.[7] Between the two rows of tenements ran a narrow grassy strip where children could bounce their balls and play and, behind, the Severns had their own garden with its water butt half-hidden among the bright red flowers on the runner beans climbing up the walls. A paradise for children, it was also a refuge for their mother, a place where she could settle her babies and stifle their crying when her husband was in irritable mood.

Temperamentally, James and Elizabeth were not well matched, she gentle and soft-hearted, he volatile and quick-tempered. Nor did they present a united front to their children. Elizabeth cultivated them behind his back, coaxing out their secrets and enveloping them in affection and concern. She was, Severn liked to think, 'an Angel' 'an image of Patience' and 'an intellectual guide'.[8] James, by contrast, could be harsh. He laid down petty rules: no house work was to be done in his presence and crying babies were to be banished to the garden. On occasion he ruled his domestic roost with his fists. Though Joseph had the privileged place of the first-born son, indulged by his mother, encouraged by his father, James would still knock him around or upturn the food and crockery on the table in sudden outbursts of anger. These were generally fuelled by drink, with the occasional heavy bout leaving him ill for days. Elizabeth learnt to put up with it, replacing the broken crockery without complaint, escaping into the garden and finding time to be with her children. She created her own space in the crowded house by staying up late while her husband slept off his excesses upstairs. Such times gave her a chance to find out about her children's exploits, bandage grazed knees and elbows or ease her son's growing pains as she massaged his spindly legs. Late into the night she darned and mended, often, as Severn remembered, passing her husband on the stairs as she went up to bed and he came down to start another day's work.

The habit of early rising was just one of the traits Severn inherited from his father. When not in his cups James was honest and hard-working, a man who provided for his family. There was always a roast on the table for Sunday dinner and a goose and a sirloin of beef at Christmas, followed by plum pudding. Though the basis of his trade was piano-tuning, he also developed a respectable business as a music master, a cut above the occupations of his neighbours.[9] Music came naturally to him as it did to his three sons, but both he and they worked hard at it, learning to read and write music and acquiring skills on a variety of instruments. Incensed though he was by the cries of babies, James never objected to the sound of his sons practising. Both Tom and Charles were to make a good living as professional musicians, playing, conducting, composing, and holding down positions as organists in big north London churches.[10] Joseph could easily have done the same. His taste in music was always more original than in the visual arts and he was a fine keyboard player into old age as well as an occasional composer.

As a music master, James Severn had an entrée into the homes of the better sort, professional people living in the outlying villages, or middle-class homes with good furnishings and pictures as well as daughters intent on accomplishment. Sometimes he took his son along to be cosseted and admired, which sowed the seeds of social ambition in the young Joseph. 'I longed for fame and notice', he later remembered, 'I never saw a great house or personage, without aspiring wishes even when I was a boy.'[11] James, too, developed aspirations. He began to collect pictures and sometimes made a little money from cutting up large canvasses to resell the smaller versions at a profit. His tastes were narrow, however. He turned down a 'Van Dyck' that was going cheap to save up for landscapes. (It was Joseph who retrieved the painting from the dealer, paying two shillings and sixpence to borrow it for copying.) Alongside his picture 'gallery', James also devised a crest, reflecting not just his ambition but the exigencies of family life. It showed a group of cormorants with their mouths open—singing perhaps, more probably waiting to be fed. Beneath it was the motto 'Severnot'.[12] These were the vanities of a man anxious to keep up a position, someone who needed, but did not always get, respect.

2 The family crest devised by James Severn, with annotations by Walter Severn

Clashes with his eldest son were inevitable. Joseph was a wilful and imaginative child. Though dominated by his father he was determined to stand up to him and venture out into the world. With his brother Tom he went west along Old Street to fly kites in the open fields beyond City Road,[13] or, crossing the St Leonard's junction to the north, he made new friends in Hoxton. Despite its later notoriety as a den of the most skilled thieves in London, when Joseph ventured into Hoxton it was a pleasant semi-rural area with fine new squares and terraces going up east of the High Street, like Charles Square, where his friend Frederick Catherwood lived. Another resident was Dr James Parkinson, a leading member of the congregation at St Leonard's where a plaque now records his discovery of the disease named after him. Joseph was a sociable, engaging child with many local friends. In later years he would pepper his letters from Rome with enquiries about them. Even so, he did not remember his childhood years as happy, describing them seventy years later as 'hard and cheerless' and darkened by 'ill health'.[14] Death, too, touched his young life more than once.

A child growing up in Georgian London was much more familiar with the deaths of friends and contemporaries than his counterpart today. There were illnesses which could not be treated, accidents in the street or at home, and frail young lives that never quite took root. Joseph would have known his first brother, the infant Tom, who did not long survive his birth. The death of a schoolfriend about the same time, however, was a much more traumatic memory. They had gone to swim at the gravel pits in Hackney, stripping off and splashing around. Neither was a strong swimmer, and the friend, a boy named Cole, soon got into difficulties in the deep, steeply banked pool. With no one to help, Joseph could only watch him desperately gulping for air as he drowned. It fell to him to break the news to the boy's parents, a tough ordeal for an eight-year-old child. It was not an incident he talked about in his later years though in his memoirs he vividly remembered the awful walk to the Coles's house, carrying the dead boy's clothes as proof of the horror that had overtaken them.[15] Not until his late seventies could Severn face death with any equanimity.

Five years later, his own life was at stake in an accident in the back garden of Mason's Court. He had invited some friends round for his birthday. The high point was to be the firing of a home-made cannon, in imitation no doubt of grander celebrations he had seen elsewhere. They made it up from the barrel of an old pistol, nailing it on to an old block of wood to hold it steady. Short of gunpowder they filled the gap with wadding. When lit, the shaky contraption blew up, projecting a nail into the corner of Severn's right eye. His mother rushed him to Dr Parkinson. After an excruciating half hour in the days before anesthetics, the twisted two-inch nail was extracted from the bone socket around Joseph's eye.[16] This was the first in a series of escapes from death in Severn's long life. Even as a child the experience convinced him that he was being preserved for greater things.

Severn's third childhood encounter with death was impressive rather than frightening. Far and away the biggest national event of his early years was the British routing of the French and Spanish navies at Trafalgar. Joy at the triumph was tempered by grief at the death in battle of England's greatest hero, Lord Nelson. Even so, crowds gathered in London to mark the victory. Joseph ran off to join in the hubbub along the river. Carried away with the excitement, and exhausted after hours of cheering, he slumped down in a street corner to sleep. His parents knew him well enough to guess where he had gone, and after an anxious search found him a mile away from Shoreditch. It is unlikely he avoided a beating when they got him home. A month later the preserved body of Nelson, which had lain at the Naval Chapel in Greenwich, was brought for burial at St Paul's. The highlight of the immense cortège, which wound its way for hours from Westminster pier to the City, was the huge funeral car. Joseph could not take his eyes off it. Back home he did a drawing, flooding the coffin with the same yellow light as in the stained glass at St Leonard's. Shortly afterwards, the musket ball which had felled Nelson was put on public display. This time Joseph tried a watercolour, painstakingly noting the differences between the piece of cloth which still adhered to it, the fragments of lace and torn epaulette, and the 'Depression in the ball from Striking against Iron'.[17]

Though we know where Severn grew up and went to church, he left no record of his schooling other than a passing reference to its 'dull monotony'.[18] Close by though they were, Haberdashers' Aske's and Christ's Hospital were beyond the reach of a jobbing music master, even for a favourite and talented child. Joseph probably passed his infant years at the free school for boys at Norton Folgate or the Shoreditch Charity School, neither of whose registers for the period survive. Though he got a grounding in reading and writing, arithmetic and science, it was a limited education and he remained acutely conscious of its weaknesses. As a teenager he did what he could to make up with enthusiastic, if haphazard reading of his own: later he would set himself to self-improvement in a more methodical way. It was at home, not school, that his childhood horizons expanded. James Severn's bent was for history and literature of the grander sort. He fed his son's imagination with heroic tales of the Englishman's long struggle for liberty. He took him to Westminster Abbey to admire the tombs of kings and queens and the monuments to famous Englishmen. He stumbled ominously around the hearth, poker in hand, demonstrating the walk of the ghost of Hamlet's father as he had seen it at the theatre. For a young child this was powerful stuff. When he began reading for himself he turned to history and the epic poem, not penny novels or lurid tales of crime.

His talent for drawing emerged at an early age and went well beyond the child's usual fascination with crayons and paper. His father, who liked to see his son bent over his work, encouraged him with drawing books, turning a blind eye when his son got up early to steal paper from his father's top drawer and copy designs from them.[19] James liked to show off his talented son, taking him along sometimes to the polite houses where he gave his music lessons. When Joseph was old enough, he walked with his father to the country villages away from the City, where he could sketch churches and picturesque buildings. At Tottenham, a good six miles from Shoreditch, a kind lady brought out a stool for the weary child to sit on, tempting him with cake to draw her thatched cottage. His true inclination, however, lay elsewhere. Though his father tried to interest him in landscape it was always people who appealed to Severn. His first production to attract the praise of friends and family as something out of the ordinary for a small child was a drawing he did of his father. The likeness was recognizable: not only that, but he had taken the unusual decision for a six-year-old of showing his father in profile. A proud James decided that the time had come to put his son in long trousers, an important milestone in any boy's life. He was rewarded by Joseph's striking depiction of him as the ghost of Hamlet's father (without the poker).

Musical skills of a high order were taken for granted in the Severn family. Joseph's ability to draw, however, marked him out as a prodigy. Brought together by the need to pacify an uneven-tempered parent, and admiration for their eldest brother, the Severn siblings were a cohesive unit. As a young man Joseph was closest to Maria, who idolized him. But he was also a hero to his two brothers, both of whom were much younger, Thomas by eight years and Charles, the baby of the family, by thirteen. Sarah, the eldest child, was at least as independent as Joseph, a New Woman before her time. Single until well in her thirties she might have been expected to stay at home, helping with the domestic chores and bringing up her younger brothers, as Maria was to do. But she chafed under the tyranny of her father, whose firmness and determination she inherited. In her mid-twenties she moved out, setting herself up as a landlady in Islington close to the pleasure gardens and therapeutic spa at Sadler's Wells. It was a pleasant part of town and, though she moved from time to time, it was always along the same agreeable road, Goswell Street. She was close enough to come home for Sunday dinner, if she chose, but far enough away to provide an alternative base for the Severn boys as they grew to manhood. Joseph moved in with her just before he became a full-time student at the Royal Academy. It gave him the luxury of a room of his own where he could paint, play his harpsichord, and entertain friends, or sit chatting to Sarah as she shared his dreams and ambitions. Charlotte took a more conventional route out of Mason's Court, marrying at the age of twenty-three and happily sinking herself in the domesticity of home, garden, and children with her husband, William Giles. In individual ways, each of the Severn children found an accommodation with a difficult parent. Though Thomas and Charles remained at Mason's Court for a time, they would laugh together over the vehemence of their father's opinions. Only Maria never moved away, mediating between James and Elizabeth, anxiously following every step of Joseph's career, distraught at his foibles and sometimes perplexed by his social progress.

Far away from home, Severn could sentimentalize his parents: his mother 'a guardian angel', his father 'noble and generous'.[20] It was harder at the time to escape the dualism in his father's character, the contrast between the drunken beatings and petty domestic tyrannies and the conscientious care of his family and nurturing of his child's imagination and abilities. In temperament they were not dissimilar, sharing the same volatility, the 'sudden enthusiasms, swift emotions, personal vanity with extremes of self-deprecation'.[21] Even in his thirties, Joseph was still trying to impress his father. But he chose to do it in his own way. Much as he wanted his father's approval, he rebelled against his authority. And the uncertainty of his father's reactions, the unpredictable swing from warm encouragement to violent conflict, marked him. When praised, Severn was always unreasonably elated, when criticized he despaired. For his sense of himself he would always depend on the opinion of others. In his letters from Rome he exaggerated his triumphs, setting himself up as the son of whom any man would be proud. At a safe distance the relationship prospered. But before then, there were some harsh passages.

When his schooling was done around the age of thirteen, father and son clashed over his future. Joseph had fantasies of a career as a great painter, James expected him to settle to a good trade and was prepared to make the sacrifice of apprenticing him. This meant that his eldest son would bring in little until he was in his twenties. Beyond that, however, James could not go: while most apprenticeships required a premium, his means would not stretch that far. Happily, he spotted a newspaper advert by William Bond, a well-established engraver in Newman Street near Oxford Circus, who was prepared to take on an apprentice without charge, provided he lived off the premises and was responsible for his own upkeep. James took his son along to Bond's workshop with some samples of his drawing and painting. A deal was quickly struck.

A Hazardous Childhood

In setting his son up to become a professional engraver, James Severn was following the example of many parents of artistically talented children. At the Royal Academy Schools Joseph would find several fellow students who had been apprenticed to engravers. Though it helped to develop a careful eye and a good line, most were glad to escape the business. Engraving, or 'stabbing copper' as Severn dismissively called it, was demanding work, requiring from the apprentice accuracy, skill, patience, and strict adherence to copying the original. None of this came easily to the impulsive young man. The relationship with Bond started well enough, however. Joseph was entranced to find in his studio original oil paintings of real quality, particularly some historical scenes by John Copley Singleton. For the first six months he drew copies and made Indian ink sketches, but then Bond started him on the real business of his training, engraving. What irked Severn as much as the long hours and the discipline of the work was the way it discouraged invention. In so far as it was an art (and in skilled hands it was always that), its virtue lay in its ability to transfer the creations of others to a different medium for ready dissemination. Metal plates were not to Severn's taste and, despite his claims, he was never a skilled engraver. What he liked was the feel of paint and brush, the freedom to invent and draw his own subjects. But by the time he got home in the evening to eat a cold supper after a twelve-hour day in Bond's workshop and a three-mile walk each way, he had little energy for original work.

He began to rebel against his master, keeping painting things in his drawer and making his own much freer watercolour copies when Bond was out of the way, or dreaming over the texts of epic poems. He turned up late for work, sometimes by as much as two hours, complaining about his wet feet and the long trek from St Leonard's to Newman Street. His route took him along one of London's two main east–west thoroughfares by Old Street, Holborn, and into the newly fashionable West End glittering with fancy shops, but though he lingered there, he had no money to buy what he saw. The seven-year apprentice-ship stretched ahead endlessly. Bond, as redoubtable a figure of authority as his father, had his own commercial reasons for keeping his apprentice at the graver and scorning his ideas of becoming an artist. Nonetheless, Joseph managed a finished drawing of his namesake interpreting the dreams of Potiphar's wife and could do a good likeness for friends. In the little spare time he had he also amused himself making a model theatre and painting sets and costumes.

Eventually he ran away again, from both home and work. He was friendly with the builder Richard Chapman and his family in Islington, and sometimes broke his journey to see them, occasionally spending the night there. This time, however, he woke determined not to go back to Bond's. Instead, he sketched the Chapman children as they rode the family donkey. For two weeks he stayed away, until his father and his employer found him out. Joseph showed them his sketches. Bond was dismissive but James was impressed. Perhaps remembering his own decision to turn to music, he persuaded Bond to allow his son the occasional day off to earn a little money painting portraits or to do original work. There was a price to pay: the time away from Bond's studio was added to the term of the apprenticeship. In the end, Severn served nearly eight years, a long time for an ambitious teenager who had no intention of becoming a professional engraver.

By the time he finished he was almost twenty-two, living with his sister Sarah in Goswell Street and making enough to keep himself in clothes and go out with friends. In his last year at Bond's he finally achieved his ambition of studying at the RA Schools. He enrolled as a part-time student, attending for a couple of hours in the evening in the Antique School and preparing himself for full-time admission. His father acquiesced reluctantly, proud of his son's talent but anxious about his professional future.

CHAPTER 2

The Royal Academy Student

Severn said little about his time in the Royal Academy Schools, and it is largely through Keats's letters and the memories of others that we catch glimpses of him in this formative period. Nor do the haphazardly kept minutes of the RA Council record his graduation from drawing casts in the Antique School to sketching models in the Life School and later copying pictures in the new Painting School. If we know little about Severn at this period, however, we know much about the institution, his teachers and best-known contemporaries, and the environment in which he learnt his craft. Severn was always a loyal RA man, proud of the fact that he had trained in one of the most prestigious academies in Europe; but his education there had its limitations. Even as a student he recognized the need to look elsewhere.

Having served his probation as a part-time student, he was required to submit chalk drawings of an antique cast, an anatomical figure and a study of a skeleton, and then, to secure his full-time admission, repeat the antique drawing under supervision. In addition, he had to furnish a testimonial on his morals and good character.[1] Relatives, friends, and students of existing Academicians could readily offer proofs, however fictive, of their soundness. It was more difficult for Severn. Working in Bond's studio on Newman Street, in the heart of London's artistic quarter, he saw the Academy's leaders going about their daily business, but could hardly approach Sir Benjamin West, the President, or Henry Howard, the Secretary, who lived nearby. Instead, he was steered towards James Northcote, one of the most venerable of the Academicians. Severn was thrilled by his first encounter with eccentricity masquerading as genius.

Northcote traded on the fact that he had been Sir Joshua Reynolds's apprentice. That, together with his training in Rome alongside Heinrich Fuseli, won him election to the Academy in 1786. He was a loyal member, regularly attending the Royal Academy Council meetings and showing at the annual exhibition, while he made his living as a portrait painter and book illustrator. His fund of stories about the old days particularly engaged Hazlitt, who published his *Conversations of James Northcote* in 1830. Miserly, sharp-tongued, and dishevelled—'a rat that had seen a cat'[2]—he kept up a bachelor establishment with his sister in a dirty, dilapidated house in Argyll Street where Severn sought him out. Twenty-five years later he told Ruskin about it:

He was shown into a room without chair table or comfort. Northcote came to him—and having talked a little— went to a cupboard—took out a sheet of paper—and a paintbox—water colours— mixed some black—took a brush, lay down all his length on the floor and wrote the letter required. Severn said he then a mere boy—was much astonished and set him down as a man of first rate genius.[3]

Bearing Northcote's letter Severn went to enrol on 24 November 1815. In his excitement he got his age wrong and was entered in the Register as twenty-two although he was still a few days short of that. The dreary years in Bond's studio had seemed even longer then they really were. Joining the Academy Schools full time brought both release and social uncertainty. It was a big leap from the dull but reliable drudgery of Bond's studio. Now, as never before, he had time to see friends, make music, go to the theatre or paint on his own account before lectures in the late afternoon and evening classes in the Schools. There were long vacations, too, at Christmas, in the late spring when the Academy concentrated its energies on its annual exhibition, and in the autumn. This gave him the chance to earn money from painting portrait miniatures and selling some of his sketches, though he was often behind on his rent for Sarah. Others of his fellow students were not under the same financial pressure. Though an artisan apprenticeship was not an uncommon preparation for the Academy Schools, amongst the eighty or so training alongside him were many whose admission owed more to the strength of their connections than their commitment to an artistic career.[4] To survive in this new setting he needed to show a confidence he did not always feel.

The Academy's premises at Somerset House were designed to impress. Gifted by George III and specially designed by Sir William Chambers in 1780 they formed a small but inspiring series of rooms. To the right of the door off the Strand was the entrance hall, dominated by copies of the massive Farnesi *Hercules* flanked by the Furietta *Centaurs*. Almost as formidable was the Academy's porter, Sam Strowger, who had his lodge there. A man of good country stock he owed his appointment to his prowess as a model. As porter, he kept as keen an eye on the Academicians as on the students and was not slow to point out the mistakes of either. 'Mr Fuseli haven't altered that leg yet, I see, as I told him yesterday was wrong' he was heard grumbling to one tyro.[5] He gave occasional suppers for the students, serving up the chickens he kept in his backyard, and though he fed them on the pieces of bread used in the Schools to clean off mistakes in pencil drawings, no one suffered any ill effects.

To the right of Strowger's lodge was the Life School, where the students drew from models, and ahead, the steep elliptical staircase leading on the first floor to the Antique School, the Lecture Room, with the names of winners of the RA's gold medals prominently displayed on boards, and the Library, with its collection of the paraphernalia needed to give authenticity to history paintings, alongside books and prints.[6] On the top floor was the glory of the Academy, the Great Room, in which its annual exhibitions and grand dinners were held. The compactness of the Academy's premises brought students and established practitioners into frequent contact. As Severn wandered into class in the Antique School he might see Turner or Lawrence emerging from the Lecture Room where the RA's Council met, or enjoy watching Strowger haranguing Fuseli.

The close link between masters and pupils followed the model of the continental academies. In two important respects, however, the Royal Academy was different: its membership was exclusive, allowing for only forty full Academicians, and the training it offered was free, a boon for bright but penniless young men like Severn. The costs of the Academy were met from admission charges to its annual exhibition of the work of its members, students, and those outsiders willing to brave the verdict of its hanging committee. Academicians were not only expected to show their best or most interesting work in the exhibition, but also required to involve themselves in the Academy's affairs, taking their turn on the RA Council and serving in the Schools as Visitors (a cross between teachers and inspectors). Its professors, too, except in anatomy, were drawn from their ranks.

In the years after the Academy's foundation in 1769, the commercial market for art in England grew rapidly. The annual exhibition at the RA became a leading event in the social calendar, attracting large crowds and more than covering the cost of running the Schools. It also played a major part in establishing the reputations of the Academy itself and the profession it personified.[7] Despite all the carping of those like Benjamin Robert Haydon, who failed to get elected, or John Martin, the popular painter of oversized melodramas who chose to show elsewhere, the Royal Academy succeeded in raising the status of artists in Great

Britain and providing the first formal system of training in painting, sculpture, and architecture. It also had an ambitious theory.

It was first enunciated by the Academy's founding President, Sir Joshua Reynolds, whose *Discourses* became the bible of every Academy student. In adopting continental theory on the superiority of historical painting over all other forms, Reynolds looked to the Academy to develop a new national school of painting which could challenge the French. This meant turning away from the naturalism of Hogarth and, later, devaluing the significance of the fine school of landscape painting which emerged in the early years of the century, led by Constable. It also meant encouraging students in the Schools to follow a dauntingly uncommercial path, striving for the grand manner and the portrayal of the ideal, with instructive scenes from the classics, history, and the Bible. As Reynolds explained it, art must be a public good, a way of revealing universal values rather than concentrating on the particular, a means of elevating not memorializing.[8] The history painter needed to be aware of tradition, too. The Greeks headed Reynolds's league of past masters alongside Michelangelo and Raphael, all of them artists who had benefited from enlightened patronage. The prospectus of the aspiring history painter was daunting. He must be widely read, knowledgeable about the classics of European literature, and familiar not just with the narrative of rousing historical events but also with the detail of period costume and settings.

The imaginative appeal of all this to the young Severn was undeniable. It fed his ambition, spoke to his love of the theatre, and encouraged him to go on with the sort of reading which, under his father's tutelage, he had enjoyed in Mason's Court or in the duller moments in Bond's studio. In his enthusiasm, he was hardly likely to spot the disjunction between Academy theory and practice— Reynolds himself made only limited attempts as a history painter, but earned a comfortable living producing portraits to order. Whatever the superior moral value of history painting, it still required large empty walls, long private pockets, and an elite of taste, independence, and social awareness. Though there were outstanding private patrons, the supply was limited. Only West, George III's history painter, was commercially successful. As the RA exhibition demonstrated year after year, what the English buyer most wanted was the satisfaction of pictures of himself, his family, his houses, his lands, and his animals. Or genre scenes. The most immediately successful product of the RA Schools was not in fact a history painter but David Wilkie, who judged the market well: 'The taste for art in our isle is of a domestic rather than a historical character', he shrewdly said. 'A fine picture is one of our household Gods and kept for private worship: It is an everyday companion.'[9] Wilkie's pictures were always the biggest hits at the RA Exhibitions. Quiet and comical, touching and lively, his finely finished, detailed scenes of everyday life told stories that engaged his audience. Severn loved them without perhaps realizing how effectively they undermined reigning theory at the Academy. Their 'Dutchness', which he specially admired, was not a quality Sir Joshua had advocated.

It would, of course, have been open to Severn to reject what he heard in Academy lectures. Some of his most successful contemporaries, including Edwin Landseer and C. R. Leslie, quickly made their mark by choosing less rarified courses. Nor was there any shortage of examples of the struggles in store for the history painter. William Hilton, a good friend of Keats, was always looking for patrons, despite his election as Associate RA in 1819, while Haydon, another member of the Keats Circle, noisily, but unavailingly, insisted on the obligation of the state to provide for historical painters as a compensation for the failings of the private sector. But far from rejecting RA orthodoxy on the superiority of historical painting, Severn embraced it. To set out to be a historical painter was to choose the loftiest way, to declare an ambition to be the best and live in worlds of heroic fantasy. As a student he had neither the inner artistic confidence nor the independence of taste to resist its siren call.

While Reynolds's theory, haltingly expounded by West, his successor as President, but brilliantly developed by Fuseli, was still dominant, students in Severn's day also sat at the feet of a glittering roster of professors. Though regular attendance at lectures was required for students who wanted to get on, it needed little compulsion to turn up for Fuseli, who became Keeper in 1804 and was also Professor of Painting from 1810; Turner, the Professor of Perspective for thirty years from 1807; Sir John Soane, Professor of Architecture; and John Flaxman, the first Professor of Sculpture from 1810 until his death in 1826. Sir Anthony Carlisle, the Prince Regent's Surgeon Extraordinary, was the only outsider, serving as Professor of Anatomy from 1808 to 1824. His lectures were always packed as students admired Chinese jugglers or guardsmen rippling their muscles and peered into the dinner plates holding human organs passed round for close inspection. West, too, still gave occasional Presidential Discourses, homespun in their wisdom but prescriptive in their observations on the use of colours or the grouping of figures in a composition. He took his responsibilities as President seriously, remaining accessible to students until his death in 1820, opening up his studio to them and offering encouragement and occasional financial help. As an American émigré who had been at the top of his profession in England for many years, he was a potent exemplar for the young of the rewards they might win in return for hard work, good public relations, and the knack of recognizing and repeating a successful formula in painting.

Turner's lectures, at least initially, attracted the greatest attention. Journalists, critics, art lovers, and Academicians all crammed in, leaving little room for the students. Arriving at the last minute, Severn was put out not to find a seat and appealed to Fuseli: 'Offer anyone of the audience a pot of beer, in exchange, and you will get a seat anywhere, and at once!' was the sardonic reply.[10] It was unkind. Though Turner lacked Fuseli's lecturing skills, the crowds came to see, not hear. (Stoddart, for example, the stone deaf Academician, regularly attended.) The attraction was the illustrations Turner prepared for his lectures, their colours glorious and fresh. Without them—for sometimes they got mislaid in cabs en route—he was at a loss. Regularly though he attended Turner's lectures, however, Severn remained respectful but mystified. Turner was not a painter a student could readily imitate.

The dominant influence on his training at the Academy was a very different artist, the Swiss Heinrich Fuseli. As Keeper, he presided over the regime of copying and drawing in the Antique and Life Schools; as Professor of Painting, he developed the discourse on artistic theory begun by Reynolds; and as a member of both the Council and the General Assembly, he was at the heart of RA decision-making. Severn was much in the hands of this idiosyncratic pedagogue. Early encouragement from Reynolds and a study visit to Rome helped Fuseli's rapid rise at the Academy, where he was chosen as a full member in 1780. By then his mature style was well established: big canvasses of heroic, classical or mythic figures or scenes of horror such as his best-known work, the mesmerizing *Nightmare* of 1781. His style was mannered, with overmuscled male torsos and sinuous, elongated, draped female figures, which made for striking but uncomfortable images, boldly drawn, and thinly coloured. Though he had his patrons, he was not a commercial success. The house and salary he was offered as RA Keeper in 1804 freed him from the need to seek out commissions: now he could bite the hand that had failed to feed him. His attacks on the art market were vitriolic.

On the face of it, his limitations made him an implausible Keeper and Professor of Painting. His oil-painting technique was always deficient: 'he used many of his colours in a dry powdered state', wrote his biographer, 'and rubbed them up with his pencil only, sometimes in oil alone, at others with an addition of a little spirit of turpentine, and not infrequently in gold size'. Although his chiaroscuro was admired, his colouring was not. 'I have found colour a coy mistress so I left her', Fuseli dismissively explained. He disdained the use of models for himself and had no truck with landscape painting: 'Damn nature— she always puts me out.'[11] He was foul-mouthed and irascible; domineering and often uncollegiate. Yet almost everyone agreed that the Academy had made a far-sighted choice in its Keeper and even enemies like Hazlitt and Coleridge could not deny that 'Fuzzly' was a 'genius'. His lectures were masterpieces of cultural cross-reference and artistic perception which enhanced the Academy's prestige. Nor did he teach as he painted: no 'School of Fuseli' ever developed at the Royal Academy.

By the time Severn first encountered him, Fuseli was already in his seventies but had the energy of a much younger man. His eyesight was sharp until the end; and if he seemed hard of hearing, it was only because he got bored listening to other people. Despite a tremble in his hands he painted and drew ambidextrously, using his left hand to correct student drawings, which he did with great force. Unlike West or Turner, Fuseli adored lecturing. A fellow student of Severn's remembered him preparing: 'snugly ensconcing himself in his upright lecture-cage ... turning a lozenge in his mouth by an effort which usually brought his lower lip in immediate contact with the tip of his nose, sipping from a glass of water, and beginning one of those beautiful discourses ... not one word of which was lost by those who attended the lectures'.[12] Severn would take his prized copy of Fuseli's lectures to Italy, lending it out judiciously and taking uncharacteristic pains not to lose it.

Fuseli began where Reynolds left off, with a more outspoken critique of the deplorable effects on artists of the privatization of art patronage. He attacked 'Modern artists' for 'partaking of the corruption of their audience, treat[ing] art as a commodity, and materialis[ing] the spiritual and the ideal by converting style to manner and means to ends'. Far above them soared the Greeks, Michelangelo, and Raphael. Influentially for Severn, Fuseli also admired Titian. 'He invented that breadth of local tint which no imitation has attained, and first expressed the negative nature of shade ... his eye engaged nature with Gold without impairing her freshness.' But Veronese, who was to become another of Severn's artistic heroes, aroused only contempt. Venice after Titian was no more than 'the splendid toyshop of the time'. Over-reliance on colour, Fuseli argued, had turned art into 'a mere vehicle of sensual pleasure. Manner failed to exert its power over the senses to reach the intellect and heart.'[13] It was not a mistake Fuseli was ever in danger of making, even as his teaching sent Severn off down a blind alley.

Fuseli held to Reynolds's hierarchical ordering of painting modes with history at the top, followed by portraiture, landscape, and still life. 'Face painting' earned particular condemnation as no more than 'the remembrancer of insignificance, mere human resemblance in attitude without action, features without meaning, dress without drapery, and situation without propriety'. Not only that, but the prevalence of portraiture had demeaned its social significance. It was 'no longer the exclusive property of princes, or a tribute to beauty, prowess, genius, talent, and distinguished character' but 'a kind of family calendar'.[14] Here was Academy theory at its most high-flown. Severn loved it.

Though some students found Fuseli intimidating—'Beware Fuseli' was the watchword in the Schools—he could also be kind-hearted. Severn always remembered him with respect and affection touched with amusement at the great man's eccentricities. In one important regard he was also an ideal instructor: his draftsmanship was immaculate and he distrusted cheap effects—there was never much hatching or careful shading in his work (nor in Severn's). 'It was no uncommon thing with him if he found in the Antique Academy a young man careless about the accuracy of his lines, and intent only upon giving a finished appearance to his drawing, to cut in, with his sharp thumbnail, a correct outline, and thus spoil in the opinion of the student, his elaborate work.'[15] In general, however, he was not an interventionist teacher. C. R. Leslie, one of his most successful pupils, remembered him coming into class in the evening 'and rarely without a book in his hand. He would take any vacant place among the students, and sit reading nearly the whole time he stayed with us.' 'I believe he was right', Leslie concluded, they 'were the better for not being made all alike by teaching'.[16] Wilkie, Haydon, Landseer, Etty, Eastlake, Leslie, and, in his own way, Severn were proof of the benefits of Fuseli's 'wise neglect'. In Severn Fuseli found a pupil who was not just ambitious but biddable: the East End swagger concealed an insecurity and willingness to learn. He was also high-spirited, handsome, and fun-loving, a young man who moved in literary circles and loved the theatre as well as more dubious night spots, a youth after Fuseli's heart.

Severn joined the Schools at a time of renewal. In the first decade of Fuseli's Keepership they were often empty and neglected. In 1816 a determined effort was made to renew the casts in the Antique School, victims, as Fuseli complained to the Council, of 'Frequent Mutilations of extremities, rupturing of limbs and even greater injuries', as well as the unwillingness of students to snitch on the culprits.[17] The Prince Regent donated casts of sculptures in the Vatican and a set of copies of the Elgin and Phigalian Marbles was ordered. The most significant new arrivals in this period, however, were paintings, which quickly led to the creation of a School of Painting at the Academy. Though this put the Academy ahead of all but one of its continental rivals, the need in England for a place where students could see and copy fine paintings was greater than abroad. In Europe, training at an academy offered regular access to royal or aristocratic collections; in London opportunities were limited. Apart from the annual exhibitions of Old Masters at the British Institution, which Keats and Severn regularly attended, needy students had few opportunities to see great pictures. Most were in private collections, where large tips to housekeepers and footmen were required, while visits to the auction rooms were inevitably serendipitous. The opening of the Dulwich Gallery in 1815 to house Sir Francis Bourgeois's bequest made great art freely accessible for the first time. The Gallery even offered to lend the RA a Poussin, Rembrandt, Rubens, Van Dyck, and Annibale Carracci. West added a Titian, a Guido, and a Giorgione, the Prince Regent sent Raphael's Ananias cartoon and the London goldsmith Thomas Hamlet his recently acquired *Bacchus and Ariadne* by Titian. These great paintings in the Academy Schools became the nucleus of the new School of Painting in 1815. Though the emphasis remained on copying rather than free expression, it offered a more varied range of subjects than the other Schools and a chance to learn about colouring and composition. Students quickly gravitated there.

None of the work Severn did in the Painting School has survived. We do, however, have an indication of how he fared in the Antique and Life Schools. An old Hoxton friend, James Birch Sharpe, invited him to do the plates to illustrate a book he was publishing, *Elements of Anatomy Designed for the Use of Students in Fine Arts*.[18] Sharpe was both a member of the Royal College of Surgeons and a student at the RA, where he enrolled in spring 1818.[19] Though the collaboration was not altogether happy, he and Severn were at one in their intense admiration for Fuseli. The *Anatomy* was published with a fulsome dedication to 'His exalted Genius . . . his kindness and condescension . . . His laudable Instruction in the Royal Academy of Art.' Severn's contributions, which he engraved himself, displayed the disposition of various groups of muscles as illustrated in well-known classical poses. There was 'a fighting Gladiator' and 'foot of Hercules', copied perhaps from the test drawings which he and Edwin Landseer had been required to do to secure their promotion into the Life School.[20] Sharpe did not acknowledge Severn's contribution, and in his memoirs Severn had some unusually acerbic things to say about him and his practice 'of every kind of obscenity' despite his genteel upbringing. (Was it perhaps Sharpe, the lusty, well-to-do medical student who first got Severn into the brothels?)[21] Severn later remembered that the book had failed to attract any notice.[22] Unfortunately, he was wrong. Haydon's organ, *Annals of the Fine Arts*, gave the plates, though not the text, an exceptionally hostile review, recommending students to ignore them as 'wretchedly bad' and 'ill engraved'.[23] Though Haydon always took an uncharitable view of Severn's work, in this case his criticism was not misplaced. Painstaking though the drawings are, the gladiator's head does not sit well on his unrealistically wide shoulders.

Despite Severn's hopes of a commission from the Czar of Russia, Sharpe was Severn's only patron as a student.[24] To try to get his work before the public he decided in December 1816 to take part in the showing at the British Institution of copies of the Old Masters in its special exhibition. Entrants were free to choose which work to copy. Unwisely, Severn opted for one of the most prominent, a Raphael cartoon, and found himself crowded out by Haydon and his 'school'. Two of the Landseer brothers and William Bewick hogged the space, producing full-size copies of the cartoons, while their master worked on a chalk of St Paul Preaching at Athens. In that company, Severn's effort went unnoticed. Even his name was misspelled in *Annals of the Fine Arts*. The following year he gave the exhibition a miss but was back in 1818 in the company of a new friend, Washington Irving, copying Guido's *Angel of the Assumption*.[25]

Irving was one of a group of Americans Severn got to know through the Schools. It included Samuel Morse, who failed as a history painter before winning immortality as the inventor of the electric telegraph; C. R. Leslie, with whom Severn became particularly close; and Washington Allston, their leader. Expatriates though they were, banding together under West's benevolent protection, they were not exclusive. Severn readily fitted in, coming round to their lodgings in Fitzroy Square to talk about art and play the piano late into the night. Allston's sophisticated technique in oils, which owed something to both Reynolds and the Italian masters, was a revelation. Severn watched him as he painted, 'constantly in tears', after his wife's sudden death in 1815. One of the pieces Allston was working on was *The Cave Scene from Gil Blas*, an atmospheric painting, counter-pointing the grotesque faces of the robbers with the calm full-frontal beauty of his heroine.[26] To divert him, Severn chatted about his brilliant new friend, John Keats. This piqued Allston's curiosity: he was one of the few who read the 1817 *Poems* and, perhaps, *Endymion*, soon after they were published, and delighted Severn by saying that he found in them 'crude materials of real poetry'.[27] In the autumn of 1818 Allston returned to America for good. He was elected an Associate of the Academy while at sea and considered for full membership a year later. Severn, who knew of the rule that Academy members should reside in the United Kingdom must have been puzzled, but, as he was discovering, consistency was not one of the Academy's virtues.

His friendship with Leslie continued after Allston's return to America. They were almost of an age and though Leslie grew up in Philadelphia, he had been born in Clerkenwell, less than a mile from Shoreditch. A group of wealthy art patrons in America spotted his talents and paid for him to return to England and attend the Academy Schools. By the time Severn joined, Leslie was well established, having graduated from the Life School where he won a silver medal to add to the one he had gained in the Antique School.[28] He exhibited historical and religious scenes in the RA Exhibitions in 1813, 1814, and 1816, but had the good sense to recognize his limitations. David Wilkie's success with genre paintings, an encounter with Hogarth's work at the 1814 exhibition at the British Institution, and a commission from Washington Irving for book illustrations, turned him towards light-hearted literary scenes. *Sir Roger de Coverley Going to Church*, an immediate success at the RA exhibition in 1819, was followed by incidents from Shakespeare, Sterne, and Cervantes; and the humour and sentimentality of all these found a ready audience. By 1821 he was an Associate of the Royal Academy: at the age of thirty-two he was elected as a full Academician. For all his success, he remained a modest, equable, and affectionate man, devout and graceful, and a good friend to Severn. If he lacked Severn's ebullience, he surpassed him in staying power. As students, they went to the theatre together, talked about art, read some of the same books, looked out for each other's interests, and compared notes on Fuseli. Leslie was less impressed than Severn: Fuseli's coarseness and uncertain execution were 'very fine in ghosts and witches' he thought, 'but very bad in gentlemen and ladies'.[29]

In later life, Leslie remembered only two of his contemporaries in the Schools, Severn and Edwin Landseer. Landseer was a prodigy from the time he was admitted at the age of thirteen with a silver medal from the Royal Society of Arts already in his pocket. His *Fighting Dogs getting Wind* shown at the 1818 RA Exhibition was bought by the most influential patron of the day, Sir George Beaumont, earning him the affectionate nickname from Fuseli of 'my little dog boy'. By the age of eighteen Landseer had earned £1,000: at twenty-four, like Turner and Wilkie before him, he was an ARA. Despite this brilliant early success, however, it was not Landseer but Severn who made the greatest impact on Leslie in their student days together. 'My father said', wrote Leslie's son, 'that Severn was regarded by his fellow students as a marvellous genius, certain of becoming one of the leading painters of his age.'[30] What gave him this aura of the coming man, the great artist in the making? No doubt his ambition and enthusiasm, his good looks (what Leslie described as his 'refined and regular' features)[31] and gifts as a raconteur contributed. He had, too, distinguished literary friends outside the usual predictable student circle. And he was a favourite of Fuseli's. Added to that was the bravado he had learnt in his teenage years. But there must have been more to it still, particularly in an arena where students constantly scrutinized each other's work. His miniatures of the time show his ability to create an atmosphere and catch a convincing likeness. Absorbed as he was in his art, he was also learning objectivity. He told a friend, Robert Seymour, that if he saw an old woman fall down in the street, he would sketch her rather than help her up. Nor was he distracted when he stumbled across the corpse of a murdered Jew late one night in the East End. Next morning he was back to make careful drawings for use in the court proceedings.[32]

Though Severn's apparent confidence and chirpy adaptability helped him prevail, he was not always happy in the Academy Schools. It was a demanding environment and Severn never thrived on competition. When his turn came to propose a toast at a congenial dinner with Keats and Charles Wells in 1818, Severn tellingly chose Peter Pindar, an unorthodox poet and satirist, best known at the time for his scurrilous attacks on the Academy.[33] In retrospect, too, he was aware of the deficiencies in his training and conscious that the imaginative appeal to young minds of the Academy's insistence on the superiority of historical painting had not been for the best. 'I may perhaps have been inclined since to undertake works that were rather the effect of love than skill, of enthusiasm than judgement. This may have been an evil for me', he ruefully concluded fifty years later.[34] Technically, he benefited from Fuseli's insistence on clarity of line and the long hours of copying in the Schools, a practice which he replicated when he got to Rome, but he learnt little of value about colour and composition and nothing at all about how to deal with patrons or manage a commercial career. Only portrait miniatures and a few sketches brought him any money as a student. Nor, for all his youthful glamour and the expectations of those around him, was he socially at ease in the Academy. Apart from Landseer and his brothers and the Allston circle, Severn looked outside the Schools for his friends.

In Hoxton he found three unusually talented young men, early proof of his gift for spotting and making friends with remarkable people. The first was Frederick Catherwood, six years younger but a good few rungs up the social ladder. Severn was, nonetheless, his mentor, encouraging him to attend the Academy Schools while he was still apprenticed to the architectural firm of Michael Meredith in Bishopsgate Road in the City. The Architecture School at the Academy was not then fully developed, and Catherwood was a restless man of many talents. Though he signed up as a probationer on 7 January 1817,[35] there is no record that he ever sought to become a full-time student. In the autumn of 1821 he would follow Severn out to Rome with an idea of pursuing his architectural studies independently. It was his first sortie in a lifetime of exotic wanderings, including epoch-making journeys in Central America where he penetrated the jungles to make superb watercolours of hitherto unknown Mayan temples.[36]

By comparison, Edward Holmes was a stay-at-home. He and Severn were kindred spirits, handsome and sociable, quick to fall in love, and brought together by their delight in music. Holmes's father, who lived in Hoxton, gave private musical parties, and it would have been natural for Severn, and perhaps his father, to be invited. The friendship brought him to the fringes of the Keats Circle, since Holmes had been at school in Enfield with Keats and his brothers and become a friend of the headmaster's son, Charles Cowden Clarke. As schoolboys, Holmes and Keats would creep out of their dormitory to sit together on the stairs, entranced by the distant sound of Charles playing Mozart, Arne, and Handel on the piano.[37] Holmes, who had a flair for literature, was apprenticed to a Fleet Street bookseller, but music remained his passion. He began to take lessons with Vincent Novello, the organist at the Portuguese Chapel, and attended Novello's musical evenings meeting Leigh Hunt, Hazlitt, Lamb (who always had a soft spot for 'the bonny Holmes'),[38] and Shelley, as well as Keats. He became increasingly indispensable to the busy Novellos and in 1823 joined their household. In time he would become the leading mid-Victorian music critic and the first biographer of Mozart in English.

Though they kept in life-long touch, Severn knew Holmes best when he was still suffering in his Fleet Street apprenticeship. It was a relief to get together in the evenings and make music. They chose an adventurous repertoire: Gluck, Mozart, Haydn, and 'that heavy-arsed Harmonist', J. S. Bach, at a time when many found his works hard going. Holmes strummed on Severn's harpsichord as he painted, before they sauntered up to the Islington Road for 'suppers...with that fiery faced, red nosed old woman that was always tormenting us with accounts of the State of her Bowels'.[39] No doubt when they could get away, they talked of more enticing women. Holmes was so often infatuated with women that his friends nicknamed him 'Young Werther' after Goethe's love-struck suicidal young hero.[40] Occasionally, Keats joined them in Severn's lodgings on Goswell Street,[41] or Holmes's cousin, Robert Seymour, walked over from his room in Canonbury Tower on the far side of Islington.

Seymour was a gifted but melancholic young man. He too had been miserable in his apprenticeship to a pattern-drawer in Smithfield. Severn cheered him up, admiring the miniatures he produced as a teenager, and encouraging him to think of an artistic career. As a successful student at the RA, Severn must have seemed a glamorous figure to the struggling, fatherless Seymour, though he was not above asking for the younger man's opinion on his entry for the Academy's Gold Medal competition in historical painting. In turn, Severn got Seymour started on an oil painting which he exhibited at the Academy in 1822. In the next decade Seymour developed into an outstanding illustrator. In 1835-6 he prepared a set of 'Cockney sporting plates' for Chapman and Hall, who commissioned the then unknown Charles Dickens to provide some accompanying text. And so *Pickwick Papers* was born. The narrative opens in the very street where Severn lived, Goswell Street, where Mr Pickwick has his comfortable lodgings with his ever-hopeful landlady, Mrs Bardell. As the book took the world by storm, so Goswell Streets proliferated. But Seymour took no pleasure in the success of *Pickwick Papers*. In a fit of depression triggered, in part, by the way Dickens had commandeered his creation, he committed suicide in 1836, leaving his widow and children to the care of the still unmarried Edward Holmes.[42]

Holmes was probably the man who introduced Severn to William Haslam, a key figure in the chain of friendships which led eventually to Keats himself.[43] For Severn the new friendship with Haslam was an attraction of opposites. Haslam had trained as a solicitor and by 1819 held a responsible position looking after the legal business of a leading wholesale grocer. He was steady and practical, level-headed and mature, a man who lived in the demanding commercial world, and the sort of friend on whom others relied. Though Haslam was possibly as much as five years younger, Severn recognized in him a potential counsellor in times of trouble. Haslam, for his part, enjoyed Severn's high spirits, liked his optimism, admired his artistic talents, and did his best to overlook his disorganization. A deep, but increasingly anxious love for John Keats would cement the friendship.

William Sharp, Severn's first biographer, says that it was with Haslam that Severn went to the theatre on the memorable night of 31 May 1816,[44] though it is in fact more likely that his companion was Leslie. Mrs Siddons, in a rare return from retirement, was playing a favourite role, Queen Katherine in *Henry VIII* at the Haymarket Theatre. Connoisseurs of her performances thought her now past her best: her voice less resonant, her gestures, famous for their imperious stateliness, forced. Severn, however, who had never seen her, was overwhelmed. Forty years later he still remembered 'the Juno-like' brow, 'the large black lustrous eyes', 'that deep touching voice whose tones whether loud and impassioned or soft and pathetic, were like the finest music', and her affecting changes of mood from public queen to private victim, from royal splendour to the calm and resignation of death. 'The lovely Miss Foote' played Anne Boleyn. 'She was fair', Severn recalled, 'and might well have been the real Venus of the antique world, as Mrs Siddons would then have as certainly been the Juno.' Even Leslie, who had seen Mrs Siddons in her prime, was entranced.[45]

Severn's euphoria was not just a response to what he was seeing. Having waited in a huge crowd to get into the theatre, he was knocked down once the doors were opened in the surge of patrons forcing their way to the pit through a narrow passage. Only as they thinned out was his unconscious body discovered, 'flattened like a pancake', with the oranges in his pocket squeezed to a pip. He was lifted over the heads of the audience to the front of the pit to give him some air. From there he watched the performance in a daze.[46] By the end, both he and Leslie were so excited that they hit on the idea of making portraits of the actors. Leslie used his connections, unsuccessfully, to try for an appointment with Mrs Siddons. Severn aimed lower, but did no better. Attending at the stage door he left a note begging for the honour of doing a portrait of Maria Foote. Her father turned him down in no uncertain fashion:

Sir,

There is at this time, a New Play Rehearsing and getting up at Covent Garden, which engrosses my Daughter's attention and time, so much that it is totally out of her power to comply with your request at present

I am Sir Your Obt. Servt,

Samuel Foote

The grandiloquent signature took up a good half of the page. Severn was probably more amused than dismayed by this rejection. Foote's letter, with the ink faded and the paper mottled, is the earliest of the many hundreds of letters he kept by him for the rest of his life.[47] He contented himself with a number of drawings of Mrs Siddons in characteristic poses done from memory. From the proceeds of their sale he bought paints, canvas, brushes, and a palette and made a start on his first oil painting.[48] Not for the last time, a narrow escape from death spurred him forward.

CHAPTER 3

Painter and Poet

Just as Severn was inclined to think Providence had protected his young life from all its hazards, so he never doubted it had put him in the way of the first of the great friendships of his life. About the time he joined the RA Schools he was introduced to a young medical student at Guy's Hospital, John Keats. The course of their subsequent friendship has been haloed in romance, casting a retrospective glow over the whole of their association. A comparison between Severn's later reminiscences and the mosaic of fragmentary references in contemporary letters, however, suggests a different kind of friendship: hero worship and persistence on one side, affection and companionability on the other, and a shared interest in music and the visual arts. Though Severn was one of the earliest members of the Keats Circle, he stood some way off centre in the lively group of friends united by their admiration for Keats. Nonetheless, he had a distinctive place. His artistic interests and ambitions gave him standing. He was likeable, too, and his susceptibility, verging on haplessness, was appealing. In Severn's company Keats could relax. He was one of the few friends with whom Keats never quarrelled, a sign perhaps of their lack of real intimacy before Keats's final months. Nor, as Keats's life expanded, bringing new and grander contacts, did they lose touch. There was always a place for Severn in the Circle, even if it was not that of the inevitable deathbed companion. Until the last days, Keats was always much more important to Severn than Severn to Keats.

Providential though their friendship was for Severn, it was not surprising that they should have met as young men in London. They moved in overlapping circles. Edward Holmes was the key. Through him Severn met Haslam and, probably, Charles Cowden Clarke, and began a life-long friendship with the Novello family whose musical evenings Keats attended. Though any of these could have introduced Keats to Severn, the honour fell to Haslam. It happened so naturally that Severn could never quite remember the details. Sometimes he placed the first meeting in 1813, at others in 1817: the one, when Severn was still confined to Bond's studio and Keats was an apprentice apothecary in Enfield is too early; the other, as the dating of Keats's letters to Severn shows, too late.

They probably first met in the spring of 1816 when Severn was enjoying the new freedoms of student life. 'A new world was opened to me', he later wrote, 'and I was raised from the mechanical drudgery of my art to the hope of brighter and more elevated courses.' From the beginning he sensed something out of the ordinary in Keats: 'At my first acquaintance with him—he gave me the compleat idea of a Poet.'[1] If true, it was a striking perception, for at the time Keats was not an obvious star. He lived south of the river in the Borough, unhappily pursuing his training at Guy's Hospital. There he served as a dresser to the bloodily incompetent surgeon 'Billy Lucas', worried about exams coming up in the summer, and dreamt in the stench of the lecture theatre about writing poetry. He was about to publish his first poem, 'On Solitude'. He read it to his new friend at their second meeting. Severn hit on its only distinguishing feature, the image of 'the deer's swift leap' startling 'the wild bee from the fox-glove bell'.

If Keats had little to show as a poet when Severn first met him, his appearance was more indicative of what was to come. Even in medical school he cultivated an eccentric, romantic look. He wore his hair long with almost feminine soft chestnut curls ('like the rich plumage of a bird', according to one friend, Benjamin Bailey),[2] affected open-necked shirts and a black ribbon at his neck. It was a way of proclaiming his artistic intentions, but also a reflection of his insecurity. He wanted to stand out, but at only an inch above five feet, he was almost a foot shorter than his younger brother, George, whose robust build, early loss of hair, and general air of competence led many to assume he was older than John. Anxieties about his looks were also one of the causes of Keats's unease with women. As he told Fanny Brawne three years later, when comparing Severn's winning features with his own, 'I hold that place among Men which snub-nos'd brunettes with meeting eyebrows do among women.'[3]

In this he misjudged himself. Severn was not the only one of Keats's friends to testify to his attractive physical presence: his body compact but strong and well proportioned, his hair fine but growing thickly, his face with its wide full mouth striking. It was Keats's eyes, however, they all remembered best: 'large and luminous' (Barry Cornwell), 'dark and sensitive' (Leigh Hunt), 'softened into tenderness' or beaming 'with a fiery brightness' (Bailey). Haydon got carried away in his description of 'the inward look' of Keats's eyes, 'perfectly divine,

like a Delphic priestess who saw visions'.[4] Severn also tried rather too hard
to remember their special quality when he talked of 'the hazel eyes of a wild
gypsy-maid in colour set in the face of a young god' or 'the wine-like lustre
of Keats's eyes just like those of certain birds which habitually front the sun'.
He was closer to the mark in describing them as 'falcon eyes'. With his por-
traitist's interest in physiognomy, he also left the best idea of Keats's manner,
'a characteristic backward pose (sometimes a toss) of the head', though when
reading or deep in thought 'his chest fell in, the head bent forward as though
mightily overburdened, & the eyes seemed almost to throw a light before
his face'.[5]

In the winter of 1816–17, when Keats and his two brothers had moved north
of the river to settle in Cheapside, closer to their guardian Richard Abbey's
counting house in the City, Severn attempted to catch this likeness. Charles
Cowden Clarke remembered the sketch being completed in just a few minutes.
Though only $4^{1}/_{2}$ inches by $3^{1}/_{4}$, the image is powerful, showing the long wavy
hair, the forward lean of the head, the prominent nose and short upper lip, the
generous mouth and, above all, the intensity of Keats's gaze seen in profile.
Indeed, so intent is the look in Keats's eye that it is tempting to think he
is listening to music, or, as Severn later persuaded himself, concentrating on
Shelley reading his preface to *Alastor*. What he had actually caught was Keats's
keen engagement with everything around him even when, as on this occasion,
it was simply the company of friends. No doubt, Severn enjoyed showing off
his new-found Academy skills. The sketch is in black crayon on the standard
blue-grey paper used by Academy students, and there is more than a touch of
Fuseli about the dream-like image. He gave it to Keats who in turn gave it to
Leigh Hunt, who kept it above his work table. Clarke preferred this image of
Keats to all others.[6]

One of the earliest of Keats's surviving letters, written to Severn on 1 November 1816, gives a glimpse into the nature of their friendship at this stage. The
salutation, 'My Dear Sir', is a little formal, and the occasion no more than the
cancellation of a planned walk in the country, but the letter bursts with news
of Keats's most recent success: 'I know you will congratulate me when I tell
you that I shall breakfast with Haydon on Sunday.'[7] Seven weeks later Keats
invited Clarke and Severn to get to know another young poet, John Hamilton
Reynolds, he had met a few days earlier at Haydon's studio. Though Keats still
kept up attendance at Guy's Hospital his poetic career was moving ahead: he
was now a regular at Haydon's; Clarke had taken him to Hampstead to meet

Leigh Hunt; and he had written and published his first indisputably great poem 'On First Looking into Chapman's Homer'. Quite possibly, he recited it at the dinner with Severn and Reynolds on 17 December.[8] Severn was astonished by 'the spirit and completeness' of Keats's first mature sonnet, 'the poetical fire' of his 'illustrious friend'. Now he had 'a really live poet' at his elbow: it was 'a tip top felicity'.[9]

Four months after this, in March 1817, Keats published his first book of poems with a hastily written sonnet dedication to the radical Leigh Hunt, which, in a viciously polemical age, got him into trouble. Severn received his own inscribed copy, though the punning dedication was wry: 'The Author consigns this Copy to the Severn with all his heart.'[10] Far from making Keats's name, the *Poems* of 1817 caused only aggravation. Sales were minimal, notices, except those of friends, were slow in coming and mostly damning. Severn had mixed feelings about the collection. Though it gave 'a good idea of his beautiful character', he came to see that the publication was premature: the poems 'were not fit things to offer to the world'.[11] At the time, however, he was more concerned that, after the exhilaration of their early friendship, he was losing touch with Keats.

Severn was never short of friends in and out of the Academy. Even so, he was not prepared to forego his friendship with Keats. He had hoped to impress him by completing and exhibiting his first oil painting on a subject from Keats's favourite poet, Shakespeare. Act III, Scene 2 of *Midsummer Night's Dream* gave him the idea for a double portrait of Hermia and Helena, 'Two lovely berries moulded on one stem'. But the picture was hung in an obscure corner and lost its Shakespearian tag, and Keats never got to the gallery to see it:[12] bruised by the failure of his 1817 *Poems*, he was anxious to move on and took himself away from London to start on his next major project, an epic poem.

Keats was passive about initiating friendships. In the early days he left it to his brother, George, to bring new members into the Circle. Charles Brown, later to become the closest of all Keats's friends, thought that the secret was to leave the poet free to come and go as he chose. After their first meeting on the Hampstead Road, Brown played hard to get: 'I succeeded in making him come often to my house by never asking him to come oftener...We quickly became intimate.'[13] Lacking Brown's assurance, Severn chose a more anxious route. He complained not to John but to George, who replied robustly with a warm invitation to visit Hampstead where he and his brothers now lodged with the postman, and the news that John and his youngest brother, Tom, were temporarily in Canterbury. Apologetically, Severn wrote again. George was yet more boisterously reassuring:

Have the goodness never to complain again about being forgotten. How many invitations have you received from me? How many have you answered? to the former question may be answered 'a dozen'; to the latter 'not one'! . . . John will be in town again soon. When he is, I will let you know and repeat my invitation.[14]

Severn's persistence was an indication of the treasure he feared to lose, for Keats was, indeed, an exceptional friend. When Richard Monckton Milnes collected reminiscences of Keats in the 1840s in preparation for a biography, this was the quality everyone praised. Reynolds wrote that he was 'the sincerest Friend,— the most loveable associate,—the deepest listener to the griefs & disappoint- ments of all around him, that ever lived in the tide of times'. Benjamin Bailey, who had good reason to know, remembered that 'he was uniformly the apologist for poor frail human nature & allowed for people's faults more than any man I ever knew . . . especially for the faults of his friends'. Severn, too, vividly recalled Keats's instinctive sympathy, his ability to feel himself into the situation of his friends, a quality which illuminates his letters. The identification was so strong that, as Severn remembered, Keats unconsciously mimicked his friends' ways of speaking when talking of them.[15]

As an orphan, friends were a compensation for the family Keats increas- ingly missed. Even when his two brothers were still living with him in April 1818, he told Reynolds 'I could not live without the love of my friends.'[16] He delighted in their individuality, enjoyed their successes, accepted their faults and, despite an occasional prurience about their sex lives, was not censorious. He also defended them pugnaciously and was angry on their behalf if they were slighted or ill-treated. Only when they let him down, did he turn against old friends.

Once Keats was well started on his new poem, *Endymion*, and could return to London to get on with Book II in the summer of 1817, the friendship between Keats and Severn entered its most rewarding phase. After a morn- ing's composition, Keats relaxed with friends. Severn's later memory of 'almost daily intercourse'[17] at this period is probably an exaggeration, but they saw a good deal of each other, visiting museums and exhibitions, enjoying convivial evenings, and going for long walks on the Heath and beyond. It was a stiff four- mile pull for Severn up the Highgate turnpike road to Caen Wood or across the fields to Hampstead, but his early experience of walking with his father had kept him trim. A flavour of their walks together survives in William Sharp's reworking of an original account by Severn:

Nothing seemed to escape him, the song of a bird and the undernote of response from covert or hedge, the rustle of some animal, the changing of the green and brown lights and furtive shadows, the motions of the wind—just how it took certain tall flowers and plants—and the wayfaring of the clouds: even the features and gestures of passing tramps, the colour of one woman's hair, the smile on one child's face, the furtive animalism below the deceptive humanity in many of the vagrants, even the hats, clothes, shoes, wherever these conveyed the remotest hint as to the real self of the wearer . . . Certain things affected him extremely, particularly when 'a wave was billowing through a tree', as he described the uplifting surge of air among swaying masses of chestnut or oak foliage, or when, afar off, he heard the wind coming across woodlands. 'The tide! The tide!' he would cry delightedly, and spring on to some stile, or upon the low bough of a wayside tree, and watch the passage of the wind upon the meadow-grasses or young corn, not stirring till the flow of air was all around him, while an expression of rapture made his eyes gleam and his face glow.[18]

For an artist, even one then as little interested in landscape as Severn, Keats's quickness of response to the natural world was an education.

At other times Keats came down into the City, as on one Sunday in August 1817 when he spent the day with Clarke and Severn at Clerkenwell. They strolled around the neighbourhood with its odd mix of small workshops, big breweries, charitable institutions, and prisons, graced by the spire of the recently refurbished St James's Church on Clerkenwell Green. Back in Clarke's lodgings Keats pulled out his manuscript of *Endymion* and began reading aloud as his friends exchanged appreciative glances over some of the finer passages like the 'Hymn to Pan' in Book I. He also recited a long section from Book II on the Bower of Adonis, looking up from his text 'with conscious pleasure' when he came to the lines describing the descent and ascent of the silver car of Venus.[19] Though he greatly admired Keats's later work, *Endymion* was the poem to which Severn always felt closest. He adored its lush Romanticism and what he thought of as its Greek spirit. He was always teasing out new meanings or being reminded of how well it reflected the character of the young poet. In the months after Keats's death it was the book he turned to most often and the one which inspired more of his paintings than anything else by Keats. It was also the poem about which Severn felt most proprietorial, especially in relation to the description of 'Bacchus and his train' in Book IV.

Keats's description is not an exact depiction of the scene in Titian's *Bacchus and Ariadne*, but clearly owes much to it. Severn liked to claim the credit for drawing the picture to Keats's attention. This was probably when it was exhibited at the British Institution in 1816, the year before Keats began his epic.[20] Keats may also have seen it again when it was on loan to the RA. Even if he only refreshed his memory of it in 1817 by looking at engravings, Severn, having studied it in the Schools, would have been on hand to talk knowledgeably about it. Not only did the painting inspire one of the best-known passages in *Endymion*, but 'Bacchus and his pards' would also appear in the 'Ode to the Nightingale'.

By 1817 Keats was moving in the London literary world and happy to introduce his friends to the leading lights he was getting to know, including the two dominant influences on his early poetic development, Leigh Hunt and Benjamin Robert Haydon. They quickly appreciated Keats's extraordinary potential and competed for his attention. Severn had reservations about both of them.

Hunt, born in 1784, the son of an American Unitarian Minister and the nephew by marriage of Benjamin West, wrote poems from an early age and, later, with his brother John, edited the *Examiner*. The independent stance of this journal in a repressive age led to both brothers serving their time in prison for what was no more than fair comment on the follies of the Prince Regent. Hunt emerged in February 1815 with the standing of a champion of the freedom of the press, a radical following, and heavy debts. He was the first to publish a poem by Keats, soon followed by an article in the *Examiner* predicting great things for Reynolds, Keats, and Shelley. For a time Keats was in thrall. Hunt was a man of charm and generosity, suave and cultured, self-confident if sentimental, brave and loyal. At his house, Keats found fine books, busts of Hunt's literary and political heroes, drawings by Raphael and Michelangelo, a lock of Milton's hair, albums of engravings, music, and a great deal of talk about politics, religion, and art.

Haydon, initially a great friend of Hunt's, was a more vigorous presence. As the son of a Plymouth book and print seller, his early life had been more of a struggle, but by industry, determination, and an unshakeable belief in his own genius, as well as help from Fuseli, he forced his way into the Royal Academy Schools in 1805, when he was nineteen. Two years later he made himself famous showing a canvas six feet by four of *Joseph and Mary*. His second grand painting, *Dentatus*, sold for 210 guineas; his next, *The Judgement of Solomon*, for 600. But, like Hunt, he was soon in financial difficulty. The deeper he got into debt, the more he spent on his art, buying ever bigger canvasses and loading them with paint. His painting did not improve. He had the energy and ambition of a history painter but not the originality, while his relish for controversy made him enemies at the Royal Academy—his bid for election as ARA in 1810 was rejected. If his hatreds were strong, so too were his enthusiasms, which were, by contrast, enlightened and infectious. He was overwhelmed by his first encounter with the Elgin Marbles, drawing them incessantly, taking casts, and campaigning vigorously and sometimes counterproductively for their purchase by the government.

Hunt and Haydon were opposite poles of attraction for the young Keats. Hunt gave him the idea of the artist as aesthete, Haydon the artist as hero. Where Hunt was graceful, Haydon was strenuous. Intellectually, too, they were far apart: on religion Hunt's deism ran up against Haydon's muscular Christianity; in literature Spenser was Hunt's greatest love, for Haydon it was Shakespeare. And while Haydon relished the continuing power of classical Greek culture, whether in Homer or the Elgin Marbles, Hunt was happier with the romance of Greek mythology or the fantasy world of Tasso and Ariosto. Increasingly, Keats gravitated towards Haydon's intellectual world (except in religion) but grew tired of his egotism and nonchalant insensitivity in failing to repay loans Keats could ill afford. The breach with Hunt, as Keats sought artistic independence, was more painful. Hunt was hurt but, given the extraordinary quality of the poetry Keats was writing only eighteen months later, the friendship was restored. Hunt was one of the few to whom Keats turned in his last months in England. By then Haydon was little more than a nuisance.

Severn was uncomfortable with both these Titans. He was, of course, impressed by them but could not get beyond some elementary prejudices. He was suspicious of Hunt's political radicalism, and even more alarmed by his free thinking on religion. And he was concerned about their impact on Keats. Severn had his own treasured idea of his friend, the ready-made young poet, gentle, fanciful, and gay, a man living in a world far removed from the unsettling speculations of Hunt and his circle. While Keats thrived on uncertainty, believing it essential to the making of poetry, Severn was always troubled by it. What for a time engrossed Keats disturbed Severn. In retrospect he came to blame Hunt for setting Keats on the road to despair and even cultivating 'the hatred rather than the love of mankind'. In time, Severn would congratulate himself on the fact that Keats had been entrusted at the end to one 'who was not, in any way in this manner of training'.[21] Nor, for all Hunt's charm and generosity, did Severn think him a good influence on Keats's poetic development. He blamed him for his uncritical admiration of the younger man's work, his 'excess of enthusiasm' which had encouraged Keats to publish immature work. In particular, he mistakenly believed that it was Hunt's insistence on frequent publication which led Keats to abandon *Hyperion* in 1819, and publish a magnificent but incomplete fragment. Beyond that, Severn saw Hunt as responsible for 'a kind of mawkishness' in Keats's work, which disappeared only when Keats went to live with Brown late in 1818.[22]

Severn might have been expected to feel more sympathy with Haydon, the historical painter with something of Fuseli's bravura, if not his establishment success. In the debates on religion which plagued the Hunt–Haydon circle, Severn stood on the same side as Haydon. He shared his suspicion of Shelley; both delighted in music; and both worshipped Keats. Yet Haydon never took to Severn, finding him insufficiently combative and mistrusting his connection with the Academy. In so far as Haydon noticed him at all, he thought him a lightweight. Comments on his work in *Annals of the Fine Arts*, which Haydon controlled, were always brutally dismissive. Perhaps, Severn was the unnamed 'noodle' that Keats brought to Haydon's studio in May 1818. The visitor 'expected we should all be discussing Milton & Raphael etc', Haydon wrote, and was disconcerted when they broke into a concert. 'The wiseacre sat by without saying a word, blushing and sipping his wine as if we meant to insult him.'[23] While the first half of the description certainly suggests Severn, only an uncharacteristically abashed Severn would have held back from a concert. But he was always ill at ease in Haydon's company. He approved of his insistence on the importance of hard work ('hard work and fagging', wrote Severn, 'is the virtue of the poor man & without it very few men rise to distinction') and applauded the results (Haydon had 'a true genius for history painting'), but found himself 'almost frightened' by Haydon's 'excessive vanity & presumption' and his assumption that he had 'a right to the amplest patronage'.[24] And when it came to appreciating classical Greek culture Severn looked to Keats, not Haydon, as his guide.

Nonetheless, Haydon introduced Severn to one of his and Keats's great idols, Wordsworth—or so Severn later said, leaving in his memoirs a lively account of the occasion when Keats again recited his 'Ode to Pan':

he did [it] with natural eloquence and great pathos & being finished we all looked in silence to Wordsworth for his praises on the young poet—After a moment['s] pause Wordsworth coolly remarked 'a very pretty piece of Paganism' & with this cold water thrown upon us we all broke up.

On the same occasion, a discussion developed between Haydon, Hunt, Wordsworth, Reynolds, and Keats, on the virtues of a vegetarian diet. (Haydon's strident advocacy was later discredited when he was seen slipping out of a chop house.) Hunt, much under the influence of Shelley's passionate commitment to vegetarianism:

> most eloquently discussed the charms & advantages of these vegetable banquets—he showed us the cauliflowers swimming in melted butter, the peas the beans never profaned with animal gravy, in the midst of his rhapsody, the Venerable poet Wordsworth begged permission to ask a question 'If they ever met with a caterpillar, that they thanked their stars for this delicious animal food.'[25]

These are good stories and Severn enjoyed telling them. According to an account written thirty years later in Haydon's voluminous diary, however, only he and Wordsworth's friend Tom Monkhouse were present when Keats recited the *Hymn to Pan* on 16 December 1817.[26] Nor does Haydon record a supper involving himself, Wordsworth, Keats, Leigh Hunt, Reynolds, and Severn. Most probably Severn heard about these occasions from Keats, who spent a good deal of time in Wordsworth's company over Christmas and New Year. At first he was daunted by his encounters with the great man, finding him starchy and on his dignity. But they saw each other several times and, as the relationship warmed, Keats's excitement rose. After one supper, he made a detour on his journey home to tell Severn all about it, no doubt with his usual lively imitations of Hunt and Wordsworth.[27] He told it so well that Severn could almost think he had been there.

Severn's account of meeting Shelley is more trustworthy. Hunt brought them together in 1817. The conversation quickly turned to religion. Keats, who had heard too many debates of this kind, might have been bored without Severn's innocent plunge into the argument.

> Shelley, in our first interview, went out of his way to attack me on my Christian creed. He repeated to Leigh Hunt the plan of a poem he was about to write, being a comparison of the Blessed Saviour with a mountebank, whose tricks he identified with the miracles. I was shocked and disturbed and breaking in upon his offensive detail, I exclaimed 'That the fact of the greatest men having been Christians, during the Christian period placed the religion far above such low ridicule.'

They set about 'enumerating on our fingers the great men who were Christians, and the few who were not'. It was a quantitative, not a qualitative argument, which quickly got on to Shakespeare as Shelley and Severn traded quotations. Shelley chose *Measure for Measure*; Severn, showing off in this distinguished company, picked on 'the utterances of Portia, Hamlet, Isabella and numerous others'. Keats, perhaps half from amusement but also out of loyalty to his friend, declared him the winner, as did Hunt, while Shelley, according to Severn, said that 'he would study the subject and write an essay upon it'. Keats, who was always wary of being patronized by Shelley, would not have been unhappy to see Severn getting the best of the argument. Severn, on the other hand, though deeply suspicious of Shelley's political and religious views, was impressed by his striking presence:

His manner, aristocratic though gentle, aided by his personal beauty. Fine, classical features, luxuriant, brown hair, and a slightly ruddy complexion, combined with his unconsciousness of his attractive appearance, added to his fine exterior. He expressed himself in subdued accents, which commanded attention from their mental character.[28]

Severn's willingness to invent some of his meetings with great men raises the question of just how close he really was to Keats. Of the handful of letters from Keats which survive, most are short, friendly but businesslike. That in itself is not particularly significant. If they saw each other frequently, there was no need for lengthy correspondence. But Severn was not one of the friends Keats wrote to when he was away from London. Nor is Severn always mentioned in the long journal letters to George and Georgiana Keats he wrote after their emigration to America in the summer of 1818, where he liked to include some lively gossip about mutual friends. Similarly, when Keats returned briefly to London from Winchester in September 1819 and, in a desperate attempt to avoid the lure of Hampstead and his new love, Fanny Brawne, sought out his friends in town but found 'no-one around' except James Rice, he had not thought to look up Severn.[29] When he does appear in Keats's life, it is sometimes as an afterthought. Despite his association with the writing of *Endymion*, Keats did not give him a copy when it was published in May 1818. It probably needed a reminder from Severn himself to trigger the quick note to his brother Tom as Keats was about to leave for a walking tour with Brown a month later, asking him to arrange with the publishers for Severn to call on them for his free copy.[30] Nor, in the great crisis of his life, did Keats confide in Severn his all-consuming passion for Fanny Brawne, though others, like Brown and his neighbours, the Dilkes, knew at least something of it.

Nevertheless, it was a durable friendship. By November 1819 the spare bed at Wentworth Place had become what Keats described to Severn as 'your little Crib', where he could sleep for nine hours and spend the rest of the day chatting with his friend as he painted in the backgrounds to his miniatures. And Keats came to Severn's lodgings, sitting next to him for many hours, humming along as Severn played.[31] There was a comfortable familiarity between them, a geniality which left their friendship untroubled by the disappointments and frustrations which sometimes turned Keats against Brown or the Dilkes, distanced him from Reynolds, and, for a time, Hunt, or produced the rupture with Bailey and disillusionment with Haydon. By 1819 Severn was the only one of his earliest friends whom Keats saw regularly. He was also one of the few to know all Keats's siblings, including his young sister, Fanny, who was rarely released from Abbey's oppressive guardianship in Walthamstow. So, too, Severn was one of the first to be introduced to Mrs Brawne and her three children. He flirted with the eldest, Fanny, as he would with any pretty girl, and she responded. Though there was nothing in it for either of them, the watching Keats, acutely conscious of the superiority of Severn's looks, was morosely jealous. It was Fanny, however, who had to bear the brunt of Keats's pain, while Severn continued to see the Brawnes and became particularly fond of the admirable Mrs Brawne.

As the only artist in the Keats Circle, Severn was asked to use his talents to record some of its principal members. Five portraits survive, of John, George, and Tom Keats, Reynolds and Leigh Hunt. The memorable sketch of Tom is the only certain visual record: a teenager trying to look like a man, fine-featured, a little melancholy and self-absorbed. By contrast, the miniature of George, which may have been painted as a keepsake for John before his brother left for America, shows a substantial presence, with gleaming eyes and sensuous mouth. Here is a man with his eye on the far horizon, about to venture forth to seek his fortune. Keats liked the portrait and used to prop it up in front of him as he wrote to his much-missed younger brother on the far side of the Atlantic. Only the upper lip he thought not quite right.[32] The miniature of Reynolds is a more sophisticated affair, even though the hands and arms are awkwardly done. The face is not poetic but stands out strongly against an indeterminate background, robust, even a little brutal about the mouth. By comparison, Severn's miniature of Hunt, unfinished though it is, shows, with its luminous eyes, a more refined presence than the chubby, pugnacious face recorded by Haydon in a portrait in 1821. Hunt's eldest son, Thornton, thought Severn's the best of all likenesses of his father.[33] Keats knew how well his friends liked having their faces captured by Severn. Indeed, he berated himself for once assuming that that was the only reason they went to see him.[34]

3 Severn's miniature of George Keats which Keats set before him when writing to his brother in America

4 Severn's water colour sketch of Tom Keats, the only certain likeness of Keats's youngest brother

In the winter of 1818–19 Severn finally secured his major objective, the chance to paint a miniature of Keats. He took great pains, working on ivory, trusting that the association between poet and painter would reflect credit on them both. The result was the most frequently reproduced image of Keats ever painted, but also the one which has been most degraded through inferior copies and engravings. Unlike the miniatures of George Keats and Reynolds, it is not a naturalistic portrait. Severn set out to paint a poet, his right hand resting on a Shakespeare folio, his mouth a little open, his eyes (the best feature) inspired. Though the hands in some versions are, once again, poorly done, Keats was happy to give the miniature as one of his leaving presents to Fanny Brawne when he sailed for Italy, and friends, including George Keats, Charles Dilke, Jane Hood, the sister of Reynolds, and Richard Woodhouse, all asked Severn to make copies, while Charles Brown made his own.[35]

While his role as unofficial court painter gave Severn a secure place in the Keats Circle, he never claimed intellectual parity with Keats. Conscious of his inadequacies, he was grateful for Keats's grace in finding ways of 'apparently making me an equal to himself'. Though two years older than Keats, he happily accepted him as mentor, 'receiving such intellectual gifts with a warm feeling of gratitude & on his part the generosity of imparting his poetical gifts, his taste in the arts, his knowledge of history, his most fascinating power of communicating all these'.[36] Unlike Dilke, Haydon, and Hunt, Severn was not dogmatic. Keats appreciated this quality. His comment that Severn was 'the most astonishingly suggestive innocent' he had ever met was not unkindly meant.[37] Nor did Keats have the monopoly in their intellectual interaction. Severn could claim a part in developing both Keats's visual sense and his love of music.[38]

Hunt was the first to encourage Keats to see poetry and painting as sister arts. His education in the visual arts continued under Haydon, a gifted teacher who owned many fine drawings and engravings. Haydon also first took Keats in March 1817 to see the Elgin Marbles in their new home at the British Museum, pointing out their anatomical sureness and communicativeness. In the presence of such greatness Keats was left feeling 'like a sick eagle looking at the sky'.[39] He went back often to see them. Not surprisingly, he sometimes chose to go in the less demanding company of Severn, who had the good sense not to disturb his friend when he once came upon him alone in the gallery, absorbed in contemplation. The plaster casts Severn copied in the Antique School at the Academy were mostly Roman, and though he had heard Fuseli enthusing 'De Grekes were Godes', it was from Keats that he acquired his sense of the Greek spirit: 'the Religion of the Beautiful, the Religion of Joy, as he used to call it. All that was finest in sculpture—and, as I came to see directly or indirectly, all that was finest too in painting, in <u>everything</u>—was due to that supreme influence. "I never cease to wonder at all that incarnate Delight", Keats remarked to me once: nor do I either now that in inferior measure I too see something of what he saw.' He 'made me in love with the real living Spirit of the past. He was the first to point out to me how essentially modern that Spirit is: "It's an immortal youth", he would say "just as there is no Now or Then for the Holy Ghost".'[40] For Severn, this all sat comfortably alongside a conventional Christian faith: Keats, by contrast, saw the pagan world with the passion of the initiate.

Severn always enjoyed talking about pictures and sharing his enthusiasms. Both he and Keats admired Titian and Salvator Rosa and enjoyed a turn together round the treasures of the recently opened British Museum, engrossed by their first sight of a Sphinx 'of a giant size, & most voluptuous Egyptian expression'.[41] The development of Keats's visual sense and its impact on his poetry has been fully examined:[42] less has been written about his interest in music. A man who could be kept awake all night by a Mozart tune was clearly far from indifferent to this art.[43] At times Keats even fantasized about becoming a composer. 'I well remember his telling me that, had he studied music, he had some notions of the combinations of sounds by which he thought he could have done something as original as his poetry', Benjamin Bailey, a perceptive commentator on the musicality of Keats's verse, recalled.[44] Lack of technical proficiency held Keats back, but though he had no skill as a performer, his ear for music was keen. Mary Cowden Clarke, daughter of Vincent Novello and eventual wife of the man whose keyboard playing had delighted Keats as a schoolboy, remembered him at her father's musical evenings. He sat, one leg crossed over the other, leaning forward, his head resting on the organ, listening intently. Afterwards, there were jokes and puns with Leigh Hunt. Holmes remembered Keats describing a fugue to Hunt as 'like two Dogs running after one another through the Dust'.[45] But Keats came for the music and tired of Hunt's witticisms. More rewarding were his sessions with Severn. He respected not just Severn's performing skills but his taste in music, recognizing its sureness even in the appreciation of then little-known composers, like Henry Purcell, whose Shakespeare settings Keats particularly enjoyed. It was probably Severn, too, who taught Keats to admire Gluck, one of whose arias was the inspiration for the passage in *Hyperion* depicting the coming of Apollo.[46]

[47]

Though Keats could not play, he could make a musical noise. At the 'concerts' he hosted for his friends, each chose an instrument to imitate in performances of familiar pieces. Lubricated with alcohol and good cheer, they could keep going for hours, as Keats did with Charles Wells and Severn from four until ten early in the New Year of 1818, coining puns in breaks in the boisterous music-making.[47]

In literature, Severn necessarily took more of a back seat, though he could sometimes surprise Keats with the results of his avid teenage reading:

One day he came to me full of the finest idea that poet ever had which he said Leigh Hunt was then writing—It was a comparison of Nature's effects striking on an elegant mind to Memnon's image of music at the suns rays—I told him he would find it in Akenside (a Poet he so hated that he would not look in him) & I quoted the whole passage to his great surprise.[48]

In another case Severn's literary tastes were apparently ahead of Keats, a fact which shamed Keats into making an important literary discovery. Though an early admirer of Milton, his appreciation cooled when he came under the spell of Spenser. As Severn recalled:

Keats was abusing Milton to me & a fd. whose name I forget, but who was rather stern [it sounds like Bailey who did indeed claim credit for introducing Keats to Milton]—I had expressed my great admiration & delight in Milton, when this fd. turning to Keats said 'Keats I think it a great reproach to you that Severn should admire and appreciate Milton & you a poet should know nothing of him, for you confess never to have read him, therefore your dislike goes for nothing'— after this Keats took up Milton & became an ardent admirer and soon began the Hyperion.[49]

More usually it was Severn who followed Keats, absorbing his love of Spenser, worshipping Shakespeare, delighting in his friend's rapid poetic development, and relishing the times when Keats read his compositions aloud to him as in January 1818 when he recited his sonnet 'On Sitting Down to Read King Lear Once Again'.[50] Later that year Severn felt confident enough in his judgement of Keats's poetry to remonstrate with him over the decision to abandon *Hyperion*. But he chose the wrong argument. By assuring Keats that *Hyperion* was the equal of *Paradise Lost* he only bolstered Keats's resolution not to write a poem 'that might have been written by John Milton, but one that was unmistakably written by no other than John Keats'.[51]

Though Severn and Keats kept in regular touch in 1818, Keats was increasingly moving into the orbit of a new friend, Charles Brown, whom he had met the previous summer. He was preoccupied, too, by the illness of his youngest brother, Tom, and George's plan to marry and try his fortunes in America. In June Keats and Brown accompanied the newlyweds to Liverpool and then set off on a demanding walking tour in the north. Haslam, and perhaps Severn, kept an eye on the ailing Tom left behind in Hampstead. By the middle of September Keats was back, ill and exhausted. We have Severn to thank for the nice story that he sank blissfully into a comfortable chair at Mrs Dilke's with a quotation from *Midsummer Night's Dream*, 'Oh Bottom Bottom thou art translated'.[52]

Keats persisted alone in nursing his brother while Haslam fretted that his long seclusion with a tubercular patient, for such Tom now clearly was, might prove fatal. The young brother whom Keats believed had always understood him best, died peacefully early in the morning on 1 December. He quickly moved in with Brown at Wentworth Place, where he saw more of the Brawne family, who had been Brown's tenants and now lived close by. Mrs Brawne was a widow with three surviving children, Fanny, aged eighteen, Margaret, and Sam. Keats was increasingly taken with Fanny, 'beautiful and elegant, graceful, silly, fashionable and strange'.[53] For a time poetry and love went hand in hand, with Keats launched on the greatest passion of his adult life and on his richest period of poetic achievement.

For Severn, too, the end of 1818 and beginning of 1819 was a critical period. In September he contracted typhus and, once again, came close to death.[54] The experience led him to take stock and set his sights higher. He would enter some of his work for the 1819 exhibition at the Royal Academy and put in for the top student prize, the Gold Medal for Historical Painting. For the exhibition he submitted a retouched version of *Hermia and Helena* and the miniature of *J. Keats Esq*. Both were accepted by the hanging committee at the RA, a sign that he was beginning to make his mark. Keats, however, worried about the apparent self-importance of having his portrait exhibited at the Academy. He set out his objections firmly, if tactfully:

My dear Severn,

Your note gave me some pain, not on my own account, but on yours—Of course I should never suffer any petty vanity of mine to hinder you in any wise; and therefore I should say, 'put the miniature in the exhibition' if only myself was to be hurt. But, will it not hurt you? What good can it do to any future picture—Even a large picture is lost in that canting place—what a drop of water in the ocean is a Miniature. Those who might chance to see it for the most part if they had ever heard of either of us—and knew what we were and of what years would laugh at the puff of the one and the vanity of the other I am however in these matters a very bad judge—and would advise you to act in a way that appears to yourself the best for your interest. As your He[r]mia and Helena is finished send that without the prologue of a Miniature. I shall see you soon, if you do not pay me a visit sooner—there's a Bull for you.

Yours ever sincerely,

John Keats[55]

It was the closest they ever came to a quarrel. Keats's anxiety was understandable, given the brutal kicking he had experienced in September from both *Blackwood's* and the *Quarterly Review* for daring to present himself to the world as a poet. Severn had much less to lose. In the absence of an outright prohibition he went ahead. Neither need have worried: the miniature was unnoticed. The examination picture for the Gold Medal was another matter, however. It would be displayed at the Academy, and reviewed in the press: this time Severn's work would not escape scrutiny.

The subject announced by the Academy for the prize painting was a hackneyed one, Una in the Cave of Despair as described in Book One of Spenser's *Faerie Queene*. Academy rules were strict: the painting was 'To consist of not less than three figures. The size of the cloth to be a common half length, viz. four feet two inches by three feet four inches; the principal figure to measure not more than two feet in height, nor less than twenty inches.'[56] Severn thought it a good sign that the lines he had to illustrate were from one of his favourite poets. Spenser describes his heroine, Una, seizing a dagger from the hands of the suicidal Red Cross Knight who is overcome by the horrors he has seen in the Cave of the Giant Despair. Keats knew the passage well and quoted it from memory to Severn, but though they must have talked about how to treat the subject, the poet did not see the work until it was finished.[57]

Severn laboured over his painting for almost a year. He was determined to be ambitious. Far from confining himself to three figures he introduced five, including a corpse, and then added a horse. With a large canvas to fill, he was obliged to sell his watch and some books to buy painting materials. Neither he nor Sarah could afford a fire in his room and so, despite the bay window, it was dark in the winter months. In the lighting of the main figures within the gloom of the Cave and in the introduction of an internal source of illumination, he drew on his memories of Allston's *Cavern Scene from Gil Blas*. The predominant influence, however, was that of Fuseli's favourite painter, Michelangelo. Severn's rear view of a horse was a straight lift from *The Conversion of St Paul*, while the sleeping giant is reminiscent of the recumbent figures at the base of the tomb of Guiliano de' Medici.[58] Yet the overall effect is far from monumental: there is a conventional depiction of a blonde Una with a wealth of pale drapery and a mustachioed knight holding his dagger in a theatrical pose similar to the gladiator's in Severn's engraving for Sharpe's *Anatomy*. The giant, though in shade, is the most striking feature as he rests his feet on the corpse of an earlier victim. Severn had a good model for the carefully worked bare legs and feet: his own shivering limbs in the cold grey light of his room as he peered at them in a misted looking glass.[59]

He painted on in the gloom as a distraction from the first major crisis of his adult life: he was about to become a father. He was not even sure the child was his, and the mother refused to take any responsibility. There was no shortage of institutions, unappealing though most of them were, for unwanted babies in Regency London. They could be left in the capacious basket outside the Foundling Hospital in Coram Fields or consigned to orphanages and workhouses. Severn chose a different route. Poor art student though he was, he determined to provide for the child himself and secure a good home for it. He discussed his predicament not with Keats but the more worldly Brown, who may well have reinforced his doubts about the infant's paternity. Brown told Keats about the child and he, in turn, passed the gossip on to George and Georgiana in America, writing in code in deference to his dual audience:

Severn has got a little Baby—all his own let us hope—He told Brown he had given up painting and had turned modeller. I hope sincerely tis not a party concern; that no Mr—or **** is the real Pinxit and Severn the poor Sculpsit to this work of art—you know he has long studied in the Life-Academy.[60]

Though Life Academy was slang for a brothel, it seems unlikely that Severn would have accepted responsibility for a child engendered there. Given her unwillingness to bring up her own child, the mother was, most probably, one of the loose-living young women Severn would have met on the fringes of the theatres he frequented in Islington or Covent Garden. While a few of his friends knew about his troubled emergence as a father, he took great care to keep Mason's Court out of the secret. Henry, as his son was called, was taken to be brought up by foster parents, the Roberts family.

Now, as at other difficult times in his life, painting was a welcome distraction. By the end of October 1819 *The Cave of Despair* was finished and he was keen for friends to come and see it. For once, Keats failed him. Though Severn had been the only friend to look in on him earlier that month when Keats spent a miserable few days in Westminster, now that he was back in Wentworth Place, he felt too weary and listless to make a special trip to Islington. But he countered with a promise that he would go with Severn to see his picture once it was installed at the Academy.[61]

Severn got his picture to Somerset House by the deadline of 1 November. Two weeks later he returned with his two fellow competitors to make an oil sketch under the watchful eye of Fuseli. Five hours were allowed to tackle 'Ulysses addressing the shade of Ajax in Tartarus'. Peering around Severn could see his classmates struggling. Unhappy though he was with his own effort, Fuseli praised its tone. The sketches were then pinned underneath the paintings of *The Cave of Despair* ready for inspection. This was a promising sign. In 1815 the entries for the Gold Medal for painting had been so poor that the Academy dared not show them.[62]

Severn now renewed his pressure on Keats. Though Keats was preoccupied with sorting out his family's financial affairs, he agreed to come early enough one morning to catch Severn in Goswell Street and go with him to the Academy. In return, he joked, he expected Severn to accompany him 'to see a Poem I have hung up for the Prize in the Lecture Room of the Surry Institution'. But the humour was forced. 'You had best put me into your Cave of Despair', he concluded, wearied by his journeys into the City and fruitless struggles with his guardian.[63] At the Academy Keats said all the things that a loyal friend should. If Severn's painting did not win, it would still be the most honourable of the failures.[64] Two other people Severn was keen to impress proved much more recalcitrant. His father refused to have anything to do with *The Cave of Despair*, seeing it as a presumptuous waste of time and money. William Bond also needed a good deal of persuasion before he came to the Academy. Once there, however, as Severn recalled, 'he opened his copper eyes to the fact that I was sure to be a great painter & that I had a splendid future before me'.[65]

On 1 December the General Assembly met to decide whether the Gold Medals for Historical Painting, Historical Sculpture and Architectural Design should be awarded. Having voted in favour, the Academicians then marked their preferences on the ballot forms which remained sealed until 10 December, when the names of the winners would be announced.[66] Rumours flourished as word leaked out that this year, unlike 1815 and 1817, the Gold Medal for painting would be awarded. Though Severn was picked in the press as a likely winner, he was far from confident.[67]

The biennial prize-giving ceremonies at the Royal Academy were the major event in the Schools calendar, with distinguished guests invited in the hope that something might catch their eye as patrons. It was an evening for boisterous high spirits, the long-haired students in their everyday coats, vigorously slapping the backs of the prize-winners and treating them to noisy suppers with steaks and porter at nearby pubs and chop houses after the ceremony.[68] Reynolds had begun the custom of making a major presidential address after the prizes had been handed out. Though West was too ill to attend in 1819, seventy of the eighty members of the student body turned up. Fuseli took charge, handing out the medals and then delivering what the RA Minutes described as 'some admonitory observations'.[69]

Severn's name was the first to be called. As the winner of the top student prize, he was presented with the Gold Medal for Historical Painting and copies of the Presidential Discourses of Reynolds and West. He was probably too euphoric to pay much attention to Fuseli's dash of professorial cold water in the speech which followed. Though none of the entries was 'an unequivocal pledge of genius', Fuseli commented, all showed 'sufficient indication of capacity which, if guided by diligence may, at more or less distant periods, lead to respectability, and even to excellence'. He then turned to the subject of the Historical Painting, unable to resist telling his audience how he might have approached this typical Fuselian subject.

[It] fluctuates between the extremes of pathos and of terror, and in some respects even borders on horror and caricature; and perhaps required more discrimination than could be expected of young men of fervid fancy, anxious to avoid the imputation of tameness, by allowing preponderance to the pathetic beauties of Una over the horror of Despair

His conclusion was judicious: 'the Academy's real motives for granting premiums [are] to consider them rather as encouragements and stimuli to further exertions, than as rewards due to your present achievements'.[70]

But if Severn still had a long way to go, he was conscious that night only of how far he had already come. He had not overreached himself. He had been right to rebel against his father's circumscribed ambitions for him. Instead of going to the chop houses to celebrate, he hurried through the thick snow, with the heavy gold medal safely stowed away, to find his family in Mason's Court. His father had not waited up for news. Though Severn placed the medal in his hands James was too befuddled to react. He would talk about it in the morning. And so Severn left him 'to chew the cud at his leisure'.[71] It did not come easily for James to admit he had been wrong in trying to hold his son back from prizes that were his to grasp. Joseph's fight for parental approval had still not been won.

CHAPTER 4

The Warm South

In the early months of 1820 Severn and Keats saw less of each other, even as each wrestled separately with the same question: whether to go to Italy. For Keats, it was a fate he resisted as long as he could; for Severn, a challenge he lacked the confidence to take up. Everything he had learnt at the Royal Academy underlined the importance of studying in Rome. For Reynolds, West, Fuseli, Allston, and many others, a visit there had been the turning point in their artistic lives. With Napoleon finally defeated in 1815, Europe was once again open for travellers and, as Severn knew, the traffic in British artists going to Rome had quickly resumed. Thomas Lawrence, the obvious successor to West as President of the Academy when the time came, made a triumphal visit in 1819, and was quickly followed by Turner. There was a steady trickle of students, too, some paying their own way, others supported by patrons or taking on copying tasks. In recognition of the changed circumstances, the Academy revived its travelling scholarship in 1818. Though he could have studied anywhere in Europe, Lewis Vulliamy, its first recipient, who had won the Gold Medal for architecture in 1813, chose to go to Rome.

The scholarship, which was only open to Gold Medal winners, was awarded in rotation between the three disciplines of painting, sculpture, and architecture. In 1821 it would be the turn of painting. As the only Gold Medal winner for painting in eight years, Severn was the obvious candidate. Indeed, he told his friends he too would soon be off to Rome, the Mecca of any aspiring history painter. Charles Brown, who enjoyed penning instructive homilies for young minds to ponder, explained the situation to Master Henry Snook, Dilke's nephew, on 11 February 1820:

I must tell you about Mr Severn . . . He is a young Artist, who lately strove with his fellow students for a gold medal, which the Royal Academy gives annually for the best historical painting; the subject was fixed to be the Cave of Despair as described in Spencer's poem; it was Mr Severn's <u>second</u> attempt in <u>oil</u> colours, and therefore it might have been supposed he stood no chance of success, and yet he won it!—it has been so much approved of that he will have his expenses paid for three years during his travels on the Continent & his Majesty is to furnish him with letters of recommendation. What think you of this? I tell it you as proof there is still some good reward in the world for superior talent; now and then a man of talent is disregarded, but it is an error to believe that such is the common fate of true desert.[1]

The muddle in this account probably reflects Severn's own exuberant talk about his prospects. The medal was not awarded annually; nor did the scholarship automatically go with it; and there were no royal letters of introduction. But the most serious flaw in Brown's account is that not only had Severn not won the travelling scholarship in February 1820, he was not even working towards it. Instead, he was about to withdraw from the Academy and revert to that form of artistic activity which his training had taught him to despise—'face painting'.

Why did Severn fall so far and so fast from his high ambitions? In one of his later autobiographical memoranda he says only that after December 1819, 'A certain degree of pride was popped into my head & for the first time there seemed a chance for me, but only seemed, for the solid pudding never showed & all I got was such an amount of ugly envy that I was obliged to forsake the R.A.'[2] It is not difficult to imagine his boastful, high spirits getting on the nerves of his fellow students. Taken as a whole, they were not a charitable lot.[3] There may have been accusations of favouritism by Fuseli and jealousy of Severn's familiarity with some of London's leading literary figures. Perhaps, too, rumours had got around of his illegitimate child. The Academy rules required high standards of morals and Severn may have worried that Henry's existence might be used against him if he applied for the travelling scholarship.

His visibility as the Gold Medal winner left him exposed. Though some in the press took satisfaction from the fact that they had predicted Severn's success, *Annals of the Fine Arts* complained when *The Cave of Despair* was hung in the summer exhibition: 'we are sorry that of all their students such as this should be their best. Their regulations drive the able from their schools, and humble mediocrity is all that is left to them.'[4] Keats and the new Academician William Hilton attended a dinner at which Hilton's brother-in-law, Peter De Wint, and other artists with Academy connections poured scorn on the painting. Keats fiercely defended Severn before storming out. Wisely, he said nothing about the incident to his friend for many months.

Severn never throve in a hostile atmosphere. He needed the good opinion of others to counteract his inner uncertainties. In 1820 he could not persevere in the face of ridicule from his fellow students. Nor was there anywhere further for him to go in the Schools. The travelling scholarship was the only prize left to win. He might have withdrawn to work on his submission for it. Unlike Haydon, however, he was not driven to become a history painter regardless of the personal cost. Nor was he a man to journey alone to Rome. He had scarcely travelled outside London and never been to sea. He also had a child to maintain. So he turned back to the sort of thing which had helped him pay his way as a student: doing portraits and miniatures. In *Annals of the Fine Arts* for 1820 he identified himself in the index of artists as a painter of miniatures, rather than a history painter. In the first half of 1820 he almost disappears from view. Were it not for his friendship with Keats we might know as little about him now as we do about most of the other gold medallists in the first decades of the nineteenth century.

1820 also began badly for Keats. Creatively, he was exhausted after the supreme achievement of the astonishing year up to September 1819 in which he had produced much of his greatest work. In the last fourteen months of his short life he wrote only one more new poem, the uneven 'To Fanny', a plea to be free of his passion and soar again into the realm of poetry. In love for the first time in his life, he struggled in an agony of dependence, jealousy, frustration, and delight. His finances, too, were seriously depleted. George's early business affairs in America had not prospered. In January, he arrived back in England to get Tom's inheritance settled. Three weeks later he left with his own and most of Keats's share. Keats was hurt.

On 3 February, after a damp journey back from town sitting on the outside of the coach, Keats coughed blood for the first time. 'I know the colour of that blood,' he told Brown, 'it is arterial blood ... that drop of blood is my death-warrant; I must die.'[5] He remained ill throughout February and much of March, unable to open letters from friends. He fretted over whether Fanny, who now lived next door at Wentworth Place, would pop in or leave a Good Night note to put under his pillow, and wore himself down trying to reduce the tensions between the possessive Brown and the attentive Fanny. And he began to contemplate the likelihood of his death, aware more than ever of the beauty of the natural world. To James Rice, himself ill and in low spirits, he wrote: 'how astonishingly does the chance of leaving the world impress a sense of its natural beauties on us ... I muse with the greatest affection on every flower I have known from my infancy.'[6] Lying awake at nights he discounted what he had achieved, longing for Fanny and regretting that he had not had the time to make himself remembered as a poet.

A new specialist, Dr Bree, was invited to give his opinion at the beginning of March. A less restricted diet and the prescription of some mild sedatives improved Keats's health enough to enable him to walk into town for the grand unveiling of Haydon's *Christ's Entry into Jerusalem*. Its size and ambition caused a sensation. Keats found himself in good company both in the painting (where he was depicted in the crowd together with Wordsworth, Voltaire, Newton, and Hazlitt) and at the launch, where he chatted with Hazlitt in a noisy corner. Severn also went to see the painting and shared the general enthusiasm, later recalling it as a 'fine work . . . the animal was most wonderfully painted as to attract the eye before any other object in the picture for the painter had actually kept a donkey in his study for several days'.[7]

In the spring Keats revived a little and began preparing his next volume for publication. The collection was a rich one: the six great Odes, the three books of the unfinished *Hyperion*, 'The Eve of St Agnes', 'Lamia', and 'Isabella'. He was nonetheless under great pressure. Brown wanted to let his half of Wentworth Place earlier than usual and get the Irish housemaid who was carrying his child off the premises. Keats was not well enough to go on another walking tour, and to be separated from Fanny was now a torment. Brown did what he could to sort out Keats's arrangements over the summer, asking George Keats for £200 to finance a holiday in Italy, borrowing £50 on Keats's behalf and paying the first week's rent for lodgings in Kentish Town. Keats sailed with Brown as far as Gravesend and returned to his solitary rooms in Wesleyan Place, a modest two-storey house close to Parliament Hill Fields.

He had little to occupy him. While Mrs Brawne could occasionally look in, it was more difficult for Fanny. Most of his friends were away or engrossed in their own affairs. Though the Hunts were close by and kindly, they were, as always, harassed with domestic troubles. He longed to see Fanny but doubted whether he had the strength. During his troubled week in Westminster the previous October, Severn was the only friend who had sought him out. Now, too, he loyally kept in touch, enjoying the brisk walk from Islington to Kentish Town and going off with Keats for rambles on nearby Hampstead Heath. Though Keats was feeling increasingly dissatisfied with many of his friends, he did not discourage Severn's visits. A greater contrast in temperaments at this time, however, is hard to imagine. While Keats was jaded and ill, Severn's prospects were looking up. His gossip and kindly interest may momentarily have distracted Keats from the great obsession of his life. He said not a word about Fanny, but did talk about the possibility of going to Italy to avoid another winter in England. If this idea set Severn thinking, he made no plans.

The one letter of Severn's that survives from the summer of 1820 suggests he was beginning to make a successful career as a miniaturist. He has, he tells Haslam, been off on 'a face-making expedition' to Hampton Court, Teddington, and Richmond. Next week he will come to Deptford to rework his miniature of Haslam's new wife. He is currently finishing five miniatures, all on commission: 'my reputation is increasing most largely and nobly—and I hope soon to reap much profit'. 'I am glad to be going this way altho' it takes me entirely from my other Painting,' he concludes, adding tantalizingly, 'but soon I begin and continue until the end of the Year', suggesting that he had not altogether given up hope of painting a submission for the travelling scholarship.[8]

The main point of his letter was to keep Haslam informed about the state of Keats's health. On 22 June, while trying to get to see his sister in Walthamstow, Keats had another small haemorrhage, followed by a more serious one that evening. Since he could no longer live alone, the Hunts took him in. Their noisy, chaotic household was not the best place for an invalid, though he stayed for seven weeks of the stiflingly hot summer. Severn went to see him two weeks after the attack, despite his quaint concerns about the contaminating effects of Hunt's presence: 'most certainly his body cannot be in better hands—but for his soul—altho' I can see in Keats such a deep thinking—determined—silent spirit—that I am doing him the greatest injustice to suppose for a moment that such a man as L- H- can ever taint him with his principles now—or even school him with his learning'.[9]

Mrs Gisborne, who saw Keats at Hunt's, reported his listlessness and pallor to Shelley who then wrote to Keats tempering his tactless reference to his 'consumptive appearance' with an invitation to spend the winter staying with the Shelleys among the restorative wonders of Italy.[10] Severn, too, was shocked by the sight of his friend and, for once, Keats opened up to him about the nature of his illness: '[he] now reminds me of poor Tom—and I have been inclined to think him in the same way—for himself—he makes sure of it—and seems prepossed [*sic*] that he cannot recover'. Severn's own view was a characteristic triumph of determined optimism over observation: 'now I seem more than ever

<u>not</u> to think so and I know you will agree with me when you see him'. But although Severn reassured Haslam that he would try to visit Keats twice a week, he had seen him only once in the two weeks after his move to the Hunts.[11]

Keats's *Lamia, Isabella and Other Poems* came out in the last week of June and was widely and mostly favourably reviewed. Severn loved the poems, especially 'Lovely Isabel—poor simple Isabel', and was confident that it 'would even please the Million', an accurate, if premature judgement.[12] Despite its critical success, the volume sold only moderately. Keats had too much else on his mind to care overmuch. By then his doctors were insisting on a move to Italy. He broke the news to Fanny in one of his bitterest letters, dreading the prospect of separation.

'Tis certain I shall never recover if I am to be so long separate from you . . . if you still behave in dancing rooms and other societies as I have seen you, I do not want to live . . . I cannot live without you, and not only you but chaste you, virtuous you.[13]

By the beginning of August he still found it 'almost impossible to go to Italy'. Isolation and illness made him misanthropic. He no longer wanted to have anything to do with friends like Brown and Dilke. All his thoughts centred on the unbearable pain of parting from Fanny:

Suppose me in Rome. Well I should there see you as in a magic glass going to and from town at all hours . . . The world is too brutal for me. I am glad there is such a thing as the grave. I am sure I shall never have any rest till I get there.[14]

It was probably her reply to this last terrible letter, which got mislaid in the Hunt household. Keats received it two days after its arrival, already opened. He could take no more and set off up the hill to Hampstead, ending up on the doorstep of the house he had thought about all summer, Mrs Brawne's in Wentworth Place. She, bravely, defied convention and took him in. For the next month, which he thought of as the happiest of his life, he revelled in her maternal tenderness with the faithful Fanny constantly in his sight. Hunt looked in regularly and Taylor came to talk about Italy. There were few other visitors. Haydon called to offer Christian consolation and fuss over the return of a book Keats had borrowed. He was quickly dispatched. It is not certain that Severn came.

However intense, Keats's happiness was bittersweet. He could stay with the Brawnes only because his early departure for Italy was now confirmed. On the day after his arrival, he sent out a flurry of short letters, setting the wheels in motion. He tried to reassure his sister, closeted in Walthamstow, that his illness was 'not yet Consumption . . . but it would be were I to remain in this climate all Winter'.[15] To Taylor he wrote that 'This Journey to Italy wakes me at daylight every morning and haunts me horribly. I shall endeavour to go though it be with the sensation of marching up against a Battery.' He wrote the next day, enclosing a simple will.[16] He also told Brown of his plans, but heard nothing in return.[17] Towards the end of August, when the weather had turned suddenly cold, he wrote again, pressing Brown to go with him to Rome, where he would be in the good hands of 'Dr Clarke'. 'I ought to be off at the end of this week, as the cold winds begin to blow towards evening,' he pathetically wrote, 'but I will wait to have your answer to this.'[18] It did not come as Brown tramped the Highlands, catching up with his post only sporadically.

At the end of the month Keats had another haemorrhage. He was now too ill to travel, but had no other option. He could not stay with the Brawnes: they could not go to Italy with him. They knew nothing of 'abroad' and formally, at any rate, had no connection with Keats, while Mrs Brawne had two younger children to protect. The fact that they considered the journey at all was a mark of how close they had grown in Keats's time with them. Now, as Fanny understood, he must leave to spare her the pain of watching him die.[19] Amongst the leaving presents he gave her was Severn's miniature. Hessey and Taylor, Keats's publishers, made generous arrangements to fund the journey and a winter in Italy, based on the putative value of Keats's existing and future copyrights and the hope that George would make good his promise to send £200 when he could. Keats received £30 in cash and a credit line of £120 was opened for him in Rome. A passage was booked on the *Maria Crowther*, which was due to sail at the end of the second week in September. Desperately ill, Keats was nevertheless to travel alone, trusting that Brown would eventually follow him. It was a shocking prospect.

Haslam, whom Taylor had entrusted with making some of the practical arrangements for the journey, thought up a better plan. He tried it out on Keats on his last evening in Hampstead on Tuesday, 12 September. The next morning he went to see Severn. Their conversation changed Severn's life. He loved to recall it:

One day a mutual [friend] William Haslam said to me 'as nothing can save Keats but going to Italy why should you not try to go with him for otherwise he must go alone & we shall never hear anything of him if he dies—will you go I answered "I'll go" but you'll be long getting ready Keats is actually now preparing, when would you be ready? "in three or four days" I replied & I will set about it this very moment.[20]

Severn later embellished what is already a fine story to the point of absurdity by claiming that he had gone at six hours' notice. It has been suggested that even his claim that he had only three to four days in which to prepare was excessively boastful since the *Maria Crowther* did not sail till Sunday, 17 September.[21] For once, however, Severn was not exaggerating. At the time Haslam spoke to him the *Maria Crowther* was expected to sail on the Friday or Saturday. It was not until later on the Wednesday, when Keats had already moved to town to be ready for off, that Taylor learnt that 'the Vessel . . . does not sail till Sunday morning' and passed the news on to Haslam.[22] Severn had just over three and a half days in which to settle his affairs, pack up, and prepare for Italy.

The two most important decisions of his life—to go to Rome with Keats and, eight years later, to marry—were both taken apparently on impulse. Each turned out well. But in this case there are signs that Severn took more persuading than he later admitted.[23] To Haslam the idea of Severn accompanying Keats made good sense. Severn was the only one of the Circle who was apparently free and fit to go. His friendship with Keats was of long standing, as was his devotion. He had been attentive to him in the summer and what Hunt later described as Severn's 'great animal spirits [and] active tenderness' seemed the perfect attributes for the companion of a seriously ill man.[24] Not only that, but a few months earlier Severn had been telling everyone he was about to go to Rome. As Haslam discovered, however, there were loose ends to tie up. Severn was responsible for the maintenance of his son but could not rely on making a living in Rome. He explained the problem to Haslam, who agreed to take on the cost of supporting Henry until Severn was able to repay him.[25] There was also the worry that by travelling to Rome he might debar himself from the scholarship. The qualifying picture had to be submitted in London and the Academicians might look askance at the presumption of an applicant who had already made his own way abroad. Henry Howard, the Secretary of the RA and a Gold Medal winner in 1790, had done exactly that and seen the picture he submitted from Rome rejected.

Whatever the risks, there were still compelling reasons for Severn to go. Rome was the obvious next step in his career if he was to become a historical painter. There he would have Keats to himself and get him away from the friends he saw as a harmful influence. Together they would recreate the happy days of their early friendship, going to the galleries and discovering the artistic riches of Rome. If Severn was too insecure to go on his own, the prospect of being there as 'the companion of Keats' was dazzling. And there would be the joy of seeing him restored to health. In the adrenalin rush of his decision to go, Severn swept aside the difficulties. He already imagined their triumphant return, Keats strong and untroubled, Severn the friend who had stood by him, securely placed at the centre of the Circle. There was even the prospect of Brown joining them in a comradely male trio. Though Severn knew that Keats was ill he shielded himself from dwelling on the fact, relying on the doctors' view that a winter in Italy would keep consumption at bay.

It was Shelley, in the introduction to *Adonais*, who first launched the myth of Severn's selflessness in going to Rome with Keats:

He was accompanied to Rome, and attended in his last illness by Mr Severn, a young artist of the highest promise, who, I have been informed, 'almost risked his own life, and sacrificed every prospect to unwearied attendance upon his dying friend'.

Richard Monckton Milnes burnished the story further in his *Life and Letters of John Keats*. 'Entirely regardless of his future prospects', he wrote, 'and ready to abandon all the advantages of the position he had won, Mr Severn at once offered to accompany Keats to Italy.'[26] The reality was more nuanced. There was, as Severn later admitted, a strong element of self-interest in his precipitate decision.[27] But if he was far from selfless, he was devoted. The thought of being of service to Keats emboldened him to attempt something that had seemed beyond his reach.

Having found a way round the unthinkable idea of losing touch with Keats in Rome, Haslam, with his practical good sense and knowledge of Severn's unbusinesslike habits, supplied his friend with thick bank paper on which he could keep a daily journal for circulation amongst Keats's friends. In their relief that Keats would not travel alone, few paused to consider whether the highly strung, impressionable young Severn would be able to cope in a foreign land with the possible agony of Keats's illness and eventual death. Only Reynolds, in a letter to Taylor, criticizing those like the Brawnes and Hunt who had done most for Keats in recent months, was ready to say what others shied away from and question his aptitude for the test ahead. 'Severn', he wrote on 21 September, 'will much like the voyage, & greatly pleasure Keats, if I mistake not: though he is scarcely the resolute, intelligent or cheerful companion which a long voyage and a sickly frame so anxiously call for.'[28] Taylor, by contrast, was delighted at

Severn's willingness to go. It has, he wrote to Haslam, 'given me the greatest Pleasure', adding 'and to Keats it is most cheering'.[29]

In the short time available there was much for Severn to do. A harsher reality began to cloud his optimism: he had to tell his family of his decision. His mother was sympathetic, sharing his confidence that this would be the making of him as an artist and understanding his wish to speed the recovery of his brilliant young friend. But though Severn wanted his father's approval, James would not yield. He knew Joseph's excitability and fondness for 'Castels in the air'. He also had a respect for authority and feared that by appearing to pre-empt the Academy's decision on the travelling scholarship, his son might offend the Academicians and deprive himself of a reward which was his for the taking. He was concerned, too, that Joseph was giving up a promising career. Above all, he could not bear the thought of losing his favourite child. The more vehemently his father tried to talk him out of it, the more determined Severn was to go. 'I had no ear to his reasons,' he later remembered '& as I had certainly the virtue of the donkey, obstinacy in the highest degree, so my plan went on preparing.'[30]

His mother and sister Maria set about getting his clothes ready, and he went to his lodgings to pick up his painting things and some books. A disorganized folder of drawings and engravings was left with his family, as too was *The Cave of Despair*, which his mother would delight in showing off to visitors. Most of his books, his harpsichord, and some paintings he left behind with Sarah, in expectation of a fairly early return. And he visited the Roberts family to explain the arrangements he had made for the continuing support of Henry, now just over a year old, and give them Haslam's address. He applied for a passport and put together what money he could for the journey, collecting £25 for a miniature of 'a lady in a white satin bonnet and feathers'. If correctly remembered, this was a large sum for a miniature and a measure of how successfully his career was developing.[31] The bulk of the money for his time in Italy, however, was to come, as Haslam would have explained, from the credit line opened up for Keats in Rome. Severn could repay his share and the cost of Henry's maintenance from 'face painting' or from the travelling scholarship if he won it.

Like any RA student going to Italy, Severn also called on the President of the Academy in his studio in Russell Square. Sir Thomas Lawrence had held the post for only five months, having been elected on the day of his return from Italy ten days after the death of West on 10 March. As a brilliant young painter Lawrence's plan to study in Italy had been blocked by his father. Fortuitously, this saved him from a hazardous career as a historical painter and turned him to portraiture, a genre in which he became the most successful practitioner in the country. By the time he finally got to Rome in 1819 he could command 1,000 guineas a portrait.[32] The Eternal City left a lasting impression on him and, as President of the RA, he would do much to encourage young painters to study there. Severn's situation had piquant parallels with his own as a young man and so he readily wrote out a letter of introduction to Canova and another to 'some old German artist' who had made copies of the Michelangelos in the Sistine Chapel.[33] It is unlikely, however, that he knew Severn well since he had been abroad when *The Cave of Despair* won the gold medal. So he tested him out, inviting his views on the latest of his many portraits of George IV which stood on the easel in his studio. Severn took the invitation at face value, speaking out about the unnaturalness of the king's uncreased red coat. Lawrence corrected him, explaining that it was the royal tailor's task every morning to cut out any folds and sew up the cloth. Even the young Severn realized his mistake, though he was smart enough to draw the right conclusion: 'I was struck with my unfashionable ignorance & at my presumptuous remark but it showed to me how much I had to learn.'[34] Lawrence, for his part, was left with reservations.

Severn still had to face his greatest challenge, saying goodbye to his family. He would take with him to Italy, in a specially made travelling case, a miniature of them he had painted on ivory, perhaps at the time of Charlotte's marriage. It charmingly shows everyone in a characteristic pose: Charles in full face, young and expectant, Tom, with a strong resemblance to his father, playing at a keyboard, James looking 'benevolent and generous', the qualities Severn most admired in his father, his mother a little plaintive, his three sisters all individually characterized, despite the family likeness between them and similarities of dress. As Keats watched enviously, Severn would set it in front of him on his table in Rome chatting to each in turn.[35] It became a consolation for the bitterness of his leave-taking from his father.

The *Maria Crowther* was due to sail at first light on Sunday, 17 September. It was after midnight when Severn got to Shoreditch to pick up his trunk and say goodbye. His youngest brother, Charles, was already in bed. Tom was to accompany him to the boat. Some neighbours looked in to witness the excitement of this momentous departure for Rome. While his mother and Maria anxiously fussed over the final packing of his trunk, his father brooded drunkenly in a chair:

The time being near for my departure my eldest brother & I tried to lift up the trunk but twas beyond us & so I asked my Father to help us he rose up in a fury, dashed my trunk to the ground & swore that I should not go but as I attempted to go & take leave of my youngest brother, my father stopped the doorway & on my attempting to pass, in his insane rage he struck me a blow which fell me to the ground—my brother amazed at this indignity to me at once held back my raving Father—we all passed a dreadful moment even the neighbours who had come to wish me good bye.[36]

This was the last time Severn saw his father. Once again he had rebelled: once again he had sought and failed to win his father's approval. The manner of their parting was so terrible that Severn did not refer to it in letters home for another seventeen years, and even so only obliquely. By then his father had been dead for four years and the breach long since healed. At the time, however, Severn feared from his father's vehemence that he might never recover and worried about the toll on his mother. It was three months before he heard from Haslam that all was well at home.

The stunned brothers trundled in the dark through the silent streets on their way to Tower Dock.[37] Severn had felt liverish for several days. Now he was totally downcast. He was not surprised as he went on board to overhear a lady politely enquiring 'which of them was the dying man' as she scrutinized Keats and Severn.[38]

Though they left at 7 a.m. after their sleepless night, the departure for Italy was protracted. Taylor, Haslam, and Richard Woodhouse, together with Tom, came on board, sailing on the morning tide. Severn stood with his brother on deck but at Gravesend, where the friends stayed for a midday meal, uncharacteristically kept to his cabin. He was preoccupied with the family crisis and his parting from Tom, who got off the boat as soon as it docked. 'It was not a little painful to me', he later apologized. Keats summoned him up at 4 p.m. to say goodbye to one of his oldest and staunchest friends, Haslam, and to Taylor and Woodhouse. In his confusion, Severn had left his passport behind. Haslam set off to arrange to get it sent to Gravesend the next day.

Once the visitors had gone they relaxed after the emotions of parting. They liked the captain and his cat and even 'this little Cabin with 6 beds and at first sight every inconvenience—in an hour was more endeared to us—and to our every purpose—than the most stately Palace', wrote Severn valiantly trying to cheer himself up.[39] Mrs Pidgeon, who had boarded the *Maria Crowther* at Tower Dock as the companion to a young invalid who was to join them next day, presided good-humouredly at the tea table. Desperately short of sleep, both

Keats and Severn fell into a doze. Severn dreamed he was in odd places: firstly, a cobbler's shop and then, half-drunk, in a wine cellar. They went early to bed and slept soundly. During the night an incoming boat from Scotland arrived and moored within hailing distance. In it was Brown, answering Keats's summons too late to join him.

John Taylor thoughtfully sent Fanny Keats an upbeat account of her brother's health a few days later. It 'was already much improved by the Air of the River and by the Exercise and amusement which the sailing afforded . . . his friends have the satisfaction to think that from the time he leaves England he will probably have to date the commencement of many pleasures, and Benefits not the least of which, they trust, will be his Restoration to perfect health'. Haslam had a similarly cheering story to tell Fanny Brawne.[40] Keats knew otherwise.

On Monday morning Severn and the captain went on shore to buy essential supplies. Though Gravesend was a regular place for provisioning it had little to recommend it: 'the streets are narrow and dirty and the shops are like those of a village, except the spirit-shops which seem to thrive best. The women are anything but pretty', noted William Bewick, another voyager to Italy six years later.[41] Severn was lucky in his purchases, picking up the bottle of laudanum Keats wanted, and a supply of apples and biscuits. The kind-hearted captain, Thomas Walsh, with the prospect of two invalids on board, looked, unsuccessfully, for a goat to provide fresh milk on the voyage. Perhaps he was lucky not to find one. Goat's milk, declared another invalid on his way to the south, was 'of little use, unless a man have the stomach of a sailor'.[42]

At six in the evening Severn's passport arrived and two hours later the last passenger, Miss Cotterell, came on board. She was young and pretty but obviously consumptive. For Keats, who had been 'full of waggery' all day, it was a shock to confront another hopeless case despatched on the long sea journey to Italy. Both he and Severn did their best to cheer her up, competing for her attention with puns and jokes, 'his gold to my tinsel' as Severn reported. He quickly sketched a small, joking self-portrait for his sister Maria, his cheeks stuffed full of beef and tongue, and sat up on deck till midnight painting a 'Moonlight scene from the Sea'.[43]

The *Maria Crowther* cast off that evening and at last, it seemed, they were under way. Next morning they were in the Channel, discovering what seasickness was. Though he was never a good sailor, Severn became a believer in the restorative value of a sea voyage and the benefits of a good clear-out. All four of them lost their breakfasts on Tuesday morning, Keats 'in the most gentlemanly manner'. Severn took longer to recover and had to lie down, but not before he had helped to bring round Miss Cotterell, who had fainted. At this point Keats (who sometimes thought of becoming a ship's surgeon) 'ascended his bed—from which he dictated surgically—like Esculapius of old in baso-relievo'. He ordered them all to bed with no more than a cup of tea. They slept in their clothes, 'Keats the King—not even looking pale'.[44]

It had started well. The strains in the ill-assorted company showed only as conditions worsened. By Wednesday morning they were well along the Channel and breakfasted on deck in bright sunshine off Brighton. Keats sensed the storm coming as the wind swung round, blowing from the south-west against the ship's course. They retired to their cramped cabin as the captain persevered. By mid-afternoon the storm was at its height with water pouring through the skylight and their trunks rolling around on the floor of the cabin. Severn eventually struggled on deck to see the spectacle. He was less alarmed than he might have been by his first storm at sea: 'the ship's motion was beautifully to the sea—falling from one wave to the other in a very lovely manner—the sea each time crossing the deck and the side of the ship being level with the water—this when I understood—gave me perfect ease—I communicated below—and it did the same'. At dusk, however, a leak in the side of the cabin opened up with water flooding in on books, clothes, and Severn's writing desk. The captain gave up and, turning around, ran with the wind, the vessel shuddering and groaning as they were blown back twenty miles to Dungeness. Severn tried to reassure the ladies cowering in their bunks, 'the pumps working—the sailes squalling the confused voices of the sailors—the things rattling about in every direction—and us poor devils pinn'd up in our beds like ghosts by day light'. Only Keats was calm and 'himself all the time'. When Severn called out to him 'here's pretty music for you', he quipped back with a line Severn knew from a Thomas Arne song 'Water parted from the Sea'.[45]

At Dungeness, Severn sent off his first instalment of the journal letter. It was, as an amused Haslam commented, when forwarding it to Taylor and Hessey 'an original indeed'.[46] Boisterous and vivid it reads like a *Boy's Own* adventure story, but beneath the bravado Severn was becoming increasingly anxious. His postscript struck a different note. Having assured Haslam that 'we are like a Quartett of Fighting Cocks this Morg' and that he himself was 'better that [*sic*] I have been for years' he sent his love to his family and an apology for his letter:

When you read this you will excuse the manner—I am quite beside myself—and have written the whole thing this Morning Thursday on the deck after a sleepless night and with a head full of care—you shall have a better the next time.[47]

He was beginning to understand quite what he had undertaken.

For two days they were becalmed at Dungeness. Delighted to be on dry land, Severn crunched over the shingle bank to admire the ten-foot waves crashing on the beach and contemplated the horizon so intently that an Excise man questioned him. Severn had no clear explanation for why he was there and was lucky to be allowed to leave: 'his suspicion that I was looking out for contraband...let down all the high romance which the sublime waves had inspired'.[48]

And so it was back to the crowded cabin and its querulous occupants. Though the captain, who slept there, was obliging, Keats, a reasonably experienced sailor, was beginning to question his seamanship. Both Severn and Keats were sick of Mrs Pidgeon, who was no use in a crisis and abdicated responsibility for Miss Cotterell to them. Severn tried to cheer himself up with the thought that it was a good thing for Keats to travel with another invalid: each compared symptoms with the other and far from trying to gain sympathy by claiming to be the more poorly of the two (as Severn's mother would have done) both had the satisfaction of believing the other was worse. But the presence of another invalid, however vulnerable and charming, weighed on Keats and brought practical problems, too. With the porthole closed, Miss Cotterell fainted: when it was open, Keats had a coughing fit. Mediating between the two was Severn.[49]

It took them another week to get as far as Portsmouth, where they put in for twenty-four hours to refit and revictual. Once again, they went ashore, this time calling on Henry Snooks, the son-in-law of Charles Dilke's parents in Chichester, who lived just ten miles away. Keats knew the Snooks' mill-house well: he had written most of *The Eve of St Agnes* there, and the Snooks were in regular enough touch with the elder Dilkes to know that Brown was staying with them. In the twelve days that Keats and Severn had been beating up and down the Channel, Brown had arranged his affairs in London and gone to Chichester for a holiday. These were not the actions of a man actively preparing to follow Keats to Italy. Brown's closeness now offered Keats an excuse for pulling out of the voyage. Severn, too, had had enough. They talked about giving up, while Severn distracted himself with a careful pen and ink drawing of an acacia in the Snooks' garden. It was Keats who, stoically, chose to go on. As he wrote to Brown about London, 'what should I do there? I could not leave my lungs or stomach or other worse things behind me.'[50] Severn could not let Keats travel alone. Neither could turn back. To the dismay of friends in London who assumed they had got out of the Channel over a week before, it was Brown, of all people, who broke the news from Chichester of their overnight stay with the Snooks. He had not seen Keats, but breezily welcomed his reported 'antipathies' to the captain and Mrs Pidgeon and his 'anger' at the inconveniences of the journey as a good sign of recovering vitality.[51]

They set sail again with a fair wind on the afternoon of Friday, 29 September, floating gently past the Isle of Wight. By now both of them were miscounting the days. On Saturday (which Keats misdated 28 September) off Yarmouth he settled to writing letters, fearful that if he left it any longer it would be too late. Only one, to Brown, survives and even that was never posted.[52] It was intended as his last letter to his closest friend, charging him to take care of Fanny after his death:

> The thought of leaving Miss Brawne is beyond everything horrible—the sense of darkness coming over me. I eternally see her figure eternally vanishing. Some of the phrases she was in the habit of using during my last nursing at Wentworth Place ring in my ears. Is there another life? Shall I awake and find all this a dream? There must be; we cannot be created for this sort of suffering.

To Brown himself he could only bequeath the hope that 'you will never be as unhappy as I am'. Though writing letters exhausted Keats, it was better than battling 'contrary winds'.[53] As they edged their way slowly along the Channel the captain allowed his 'ill temper'd and weary' passengers two more opportunities to get away from each other and the sea. They landed briefly at Studland Bay and again at Lulworth Cove. Here in the sunshine Keats's spirits briefly picked up. 'For a moment', Severn remembered, 'he became like his former self. He was in a part that he already knew, and showed me the splendid caverns and grottos with a poet's pride as tho' they had been his birthright.'[54]

What happened next, back on ship, was later transformed into a favourite episode in nineteenth-century literary history. Keats took out his much-loved copy of Shakespeare's *Poems* and wrote out on the flyleaf opposite 'A Lover's Complaint' a poem he had composed over a year earlier, the sonnet beginning 'Bright Star, would I were steadfast as thou art'. Tender, but exact, 'Bright Star' represented Keats's feelings for Fanny Brawne at their gentlest, even as love was juxtaposed with death. Severn watched the poet writing. In time he persuaded himself he had seen Keats composing. His reminiscence was influential, turning 'Bright Star' into Keats's 'Last Sonnet'. Inaccurate though this was, the description held a kind of truth. Keats's act of writing down 'Bright Star' (with some small changes from the earlier version) as the *Maria Crowther* waited to get into the Portland Lanes and leave England behind, was his last recorded encounter with his own poetry, even if not quite 'the very last poetical effort the poor fellow ever made'.[55]

The tedious journey pursued its course as they moved out of the Channel. The cramped dark cabin remained a test of endurance. Keats slept on one side of the horseshoe, in the top bunk. Severn was below, fearful when he heard nothing from above that his friend had died. Alongside them was the captain: a curtain divided the tiny space shielding the two ladies from view, though it was pulled back to enable Severn to revive Miss Cotterell from a faint. No doubt, he enjoyed ministering to a pretty young lady under Keats's watchful eye. He went on deck when he could, painting, reading, or looking at the limited horizon: in a small boat like the *Maria Crowther* it was never more than 'a little circle of water, seven miles all round'. Even for those in good health, the monotony was hard to take. 'Your bones ache with lassitude and <u>ennui</u>, you tumble and toss and roll about. A game of chess is dull, draughts are stupid. Shakespeare is too much, Milton hard to understand. Your Italian grammar you cannot bear to look at', wrote another traveller.[56] Keats attempted to divert himself with Byron's *Don Juan* but quickly threw it down: the mocking account of a shipwreck in Canto II got on his nerves.[57]

In the Bay of Biscay they were pummelled by a storm for three days and almost sank, or so the captain told them once they were safely through. Off Cape St Vincent it was calmer, but then there was a new scare as a cannonball shot past the stern window, fired from a Portuguese man-of-war. The captain, fearing pirates, had done his best to ignore the larger boat. They were interrogated through a speaking tube, confirmed that they had seen no other vessel and allowed on their way. Soon after, they were stopped by a British warship, which informed them that the Portuguese were on the lookout to intercept ships and men going to fight for the liberal cause in Spain. In the dank cabin, stinking and airless, Keats became increasingly morose. Though he made an effort for Miss Cotterell, he saw no point in dragging out his physical and emotional misery. The bottle of laudanum bought in Gravesend became the focus of a struggle. It was not, as Severn had thought, for medicinal use,[58] but Keats's planned means of doing away with himself when he could take no more. A shocked Severn refused to hand it over. In time the crisis passed, but Keats did not forget the unopened bottle.

Passing through the Straits of Gibraltar into the calmer waters of the Mediterranean he seemed rather better, recovering his appetite after days of meagre nourishment in the Atlantic. Severn was entranced by the coast of Barbary 'lit up with the Suns first rays' and made two fine watercolour sketches of the scene.[59] The respite for Keats was short. After two days he had his fourth big haemorrhage, followed by fever and heavy perspiration. Without a ship's doctor he could not be bled: this probably aided his survival. On 21 October, three weeks after they had got out of the Channel, they sailed into the Bay of Naples. Despite all his anxieties Severn was impressed, taking in the prospect with a painter's eye and a musician's ear:

On the right was the range of Appenines with Sorrento to the left the splendid city of Naples, terrassed up & up with gardens & vineyards, in the centre Vesuvius with its clouds of smoke opening & extending all along the horison, the clouds edged with golden light, then the lovely deep blue sea making the foreground. All this was an inchantment with the people surrounding our ship with their guittars & songs & no end of delicious fruits in great abundance grapes peaches watermelons & plums.[60]

Like any northerner, Severn was entranced with his first encounter with the warm south. Before them was an ancient landscape rich with classical associations which Keats had long yearned to see.[61] But now he gazed at it with 'a staring haunted expression', incapable of responding. Though 'it looks like a dream' he could make no connection with 'the thousand novelties around' him. His disassociation from the brilliant scene confirmed his alienation: he had ceased to be 'a citizen of this world'.[62]

Even the longed-for release from the *Maria Crowther* was denied them, with their worst ordeal of the voyage still to come. The captain was informed that as typhus had been reported in London at the time of their sailing, they must spend ten more days on board to observe the six-week quarantine rule. Hemmed in amongst a tier of shipping, the port crowded by the presence of other boats in quarantine and some of the British fleet showing the flag in an attempt to deter the Austrians from attack, life on board the *Maria Crowther* was intolerable in the sultry heat. Their position was made worse when a Lieutenant Sullivan and six ratings came aboard from one of the British ships to offer friendly greetings. They too were immediately quarantined. In all, there were now almost twenty people confined to a heavily loaded cargo ship of not more than eighty foot in length. Miss Cotterell's brother, a naval lieutenant, sent them fresh produce and flowers to ease the wait, and eventually he too came on board. Keats 'thought up puns in desperation' but they were often bitter. Severn was at his wits' end. Looking at his friend's 'poor shattered frame', he realized how close Keats had come to dying at sea. Away from the rest of the company Severn broke down in tears, relieved that they had survived thus far but fearful for the future.[63]

He sent Haslam a miserably overwrought account of the journey. This was the first news that friends in England had received since Brown's bullish account from Chichester. Severn recounted the horrors of the voyage and their effect on Keats, 'the many privations coming in the want of fair winds—nice provisions—airing of beds—and—made him impatient—this brings on fever—and at times he has been very bad—but mind you I think from these things—for our passage has been most horribly rough—Keats has lived through it—but it is a wonder—no way could be worse for him.' And on his letter stumbled, with a brief account of their journey once they were out of the English Channel, 'we skipped the rest in 3 weeks—though quick not well', to Keats's recovery in the Straits of Gibraltar followed by his breakdown. And here Severn had to break off to catch the courier. His postscript was even more disquieting: 'Keats now is in a doubtfull state—I cannot guess what this climate will do.' Haslam was so upset by the letter that for a time he could not bear to show it to anyone.[64]

Keats's own letter from quarantine was more considered. Though his health had not improved, it was not worse. As he disarmingly told Mrs Brawne, 'I would always wish you to think me a little worse than I really am . . . If I do not recover your regret will be softened; if I do your pleasure will be doubled.' But despite the brave talk, the real purpose of his letter was to say a last goodbye to Fanny. Twice he sent his love to her, and there were touching messages to her sister and brother and an affectionate sign-off for Mrs Brawne. Having finished his letter, he picked up his pen again, squeezing into the tiny space at the end a desperate 'Good bye Fanny' and adding his favourite sign-off to her 'god bless you'.[65]

Finally released from the *Maria Crowther* on 31 October, they remained in Naples for a week, slowly recovering from the horrors of the voyage and staying modestly at the Villa di Londra, the simplest of the three hotels patronized by English visitors. Once in their rooms they settled again to writing letters, Keats to Brown and Severn to Haslam and his sister, Maria. The letter to Brown was a yet more anguished version of the one Keats had written off the Isle of Wight. Even when he tried to get away from the subject of Fanny he always came back to it within a couple of sentences:

The persuasion that I shall see her no more will kill me . . . I should have had her when I was in health, and I should have remained well. I can bear to die. I cannot bear to leave her . . . There is nothing in the world of sufficient interest to divert me from her for a moment.[66]

Alongside Keats, Severn sat writing to Haslam, doing his best to counter the impression left by his letter from quarantine. Since they had both got this far despite all the privations of the voyage 'May I not have hopes of him?' They were 'now breathing in a large room with Vesuvius in our view'. There were friends in Naples and good accommodation, even if the weather had turned cold and wet. Keats, Severn reported, showing how pitifully little he still knew of his friend's true state of mind, 'has become calm'. At this point in his letter he broke off. Keats wanted to talk to him.[67]

Severn always reacted to trouble by trying to maintain his cheerfulness. By the end of the voyage Keats was finding his friend's apparent high spirits wearing. He complained to Mrs Brawne that though Severn 'is a very good fellow' 'his nerves are too strong to be hurt by other people's illness'.[68] Relations between them were probably at their worst in the close quarters of their enforced quarantine. In Naples they began to understand each other better. The change began on the evening of 1 November when, for the first time, Keats told Severn something of the obsessive secret at the heart of his life.

Next day Severn reported carefully to Haslam, 'He told me much, very much, and I don't know wether it was more painful for me or himself—but it had the effect of much relieving him.' In later life Severn came to cast the tragic story of Keats and Fanny Brawne as a conventional tale of a happy marriage thwarted by illness, 'fortune on her part, fame on his'.[69] But in Rome certainly, and probably in Naples, too, Keats spoke of his unbearable sexual frustration, his fear of losing her to others, and the pain of separation. Severn was now something of a man of the world and had his own losses to count. He did his best to calm him, but was amazed not just by the revelation of Fanny's significance but by the hysterical intensity of Keats's feelings. 'If I can but cure his mind I will bring him back to England—well—but I fear it can never be done in this world', he told Haslam.[70] Until then, Severn had never thought much about Fanny Brawne. She was a young, apparently light-hearted girl, whose deepest interest was fashion. From now on she would be Keats's 'widowing love'.

At 9.30 next morning Keats was still sleeping when Severn resumed his letter to Haslam. He kept the detail of the confidences entrusted to him secret, concentrating instead on a racy account of the voyage: Mrs Pidgeon 'a most consummate brute', the captain 'a good-natured man to his own injury', the 'black hole' of their cabin, and the 'infernal set' of men on the Portuguese man-of-war. By the time he had finished Keats was awake and 'very much better'. 'We are in good spirits and I may say hopeful fellows', Severn concluded. Keats 'made an Italian pun today': it was a good portent for the rest of their journey. To Maria he wrote a short note begging for news from home, claiming that he was now in perfect health, and confident he would bring Keats safely back. He signed off with his usual talisman in bad times 'think of me as ever happy any where'.[71] He was determined to convince his family he had been right to come to Italy.

Lieutenant Cotterell drove them around and showed them the sights. Naples was noisy, colourful, and pungent. On his first visit, Severn got little pleasure from it. He walked off to catch a glimpse of King Ferdinand but found he had the face of a goat. Keats stayed behind, engrossed in that gloomiest of English masterpieces on the theme of sexual obsession, *Clarissa*, as the rain rolled down the windows of their lodgings. They had thought of staying in Naples a little time but Keats was anxious to finish the long travelling ordeal and meet Dr Clark in Rome. He hated the air of reactionary authoritarianism in the Neapolitan Kingdom which Ferdinand, 'La Bomba', had only retaken from the Napoleonic forces six years before and which was now at risk of falling to the Austrians. While Severn took things at face value, admiring a striking force of royal troops, Keats reckoned correctly that, for all their finery, they would not fight when the time came. (The Austrian army walked into the city only five months later.) But both were taken aback when they went to the superb San Carlo Opera House and found that what they had taken for two finely painted soldiers were real, their muskets at the ready in case of any disturbance in the audience. Keats had seen enough. On 6 November they obtained their visas from the British Legation and the Papal Consul General on the following day. Lieutenant Cotterell hosted a farewell dinner for them, at which Keats made a supreme effort to be sociable and amusing.

For the last stretch of their journey to Rome,[72] they chose the cheapest and slowest form of transport, the *vettura*, 'a sort of buggy on four wheels, drawn by a single horse'.[73] Terms were agreed in advance with the driver, including the cost of food and lodging. This left them in the hands of the *vetturino* and his contacts along the way. 'Accommodation at the wayside inns was', Severn remembered, 'villainously coarse and unpalatable, from which Keats suffered more than I did.'[74] Their experience, if no better, was not worse than that of other travellers along the same road. All were struck by the contrast between the romance of the scenery and the wretchedness of the inhabitants. Henry Mathews, who followed the same route two years earlier, remembered the half-naked inhabitants at Fondi scrambling eagerly 'for the orange peel which fell from our carriage'; Mrs Jameson in 1820 'the many begging friars—horrible specimens of their species'; and Lady Morgan the shoeless soldiers begging for coins. The women were 'bold coarse Amazons', the men 'had a slouching gait and looked at us from under their eyebrows with an expression at once cunning and fierce'.[75]

Since the horse or mule pulling the *vettura* was only rested, not changed, at night, the journey was slow, with the *vetturino* doing his best to conserve the strength of his beast. Three miles an hour was the usual rate, and as the horse rarely worked up to 'an equivocal amble' they did not reach Terracina until 12 November.[76] At this sluggish pace, it was more enjoyable to walk, as Severn chose to do for much of the way, relishing the fresh air, enjoying the sea views, and picking the wild cyclamen, sweet myrtles, and other flowers which grew in profusion along the roadside. On the first part of their journey the scenery was 'worthy of paradise' as the road wound through orange and olive groves from Mola di Gaeta, picturesquely sited by the sea, then up to the mountain fastness of Itri where the cold autumn air must have been a trial to Keats. From Itri they descended to Fondi and on to Terracina, perched dramatically on cliffs above the sea. Wild flowers were the only things which gave Keats any pleasure in the monotony of the small cramped carriage jolting painfully slowly along the roads.

Itri, the birthplace of Fra Diavolo, Fondi, and Terracina, were the heartlands of the bandits. Though soldiers were stationed along much of the Appian Way in huts hastily assembled from straw and brambles with their arms piled in front, they were so poorly paid, sickly in the malarial atmosphere, and demoralized that it was widely assumed they connived with the robbers. Another traveller, Selma Martin, was shocked at seeing them eating a dead horse by the roadside.[77] From Terracina the *vettura* went up through Velletri, with its filthy inn, and on into the Alban Hills. Now, in their inexperience, they seemed scarcely aware that they were travelling on the most dangerous road in Italy. The *vetturino*'s fear of bandits may explain why their journey took even longer than usual. Most managed it in four days; this one took up to a week. Perhaps the *vetturino* was cautious about travelling in other than good light, or he may have spun the journey out to increase his cut from the stopping places along the way. Almost certainly, Keats's poor health meant late starts in the morning to add to the long waits in the midday sun to refresh the horse. In Rome, Dr Clark, who had been alerted to their departure from Naples and knew the hazards of their route, began to get anxious.

Happily, Severn and Keats did not attract hostile attention, though they may have gone for a whole day without food after Mola di Gaeta.[78] From the Alban Hills, they trundled on into the desolate stretches of the Campagna, flat and dank with the odd ruin of a villa, the great arches of the ancient aqueducts projecting across the plain towards Rome, and decaying monuments lining the road. Flocks of sheep and goats grazed where they could, alongside herds of buffalo. Eel-catchers pursued their solitary business. The melancholy of the picturesque scene, which was later captured in one of Severn's favourite paintings, made less impression on him now than the colourful but incongruous sight of a cardinal in a large crimson cloak. 'He had an owl tied loosely to a stick, and a small looking-glass was annexed to move about with the owl. The whole merit of this sport', Severn perversely observed as the pile of small edible corpses mounted, 'seemed to be not shooting the owl. Two footmen in livery kept loading the fowling pieces for the cardinal, and it was astonishing the great number of birds he killed.'[79] For twenty-five miles they travelled through the Campagna on the big flat stones of the straight Appian Way towards Rome. Severn was elated. He felt infinitely better than he had when he left England.

They entered Rome through the San Giovanni Gate. Above it in an iron cage was the blanched skull of an infamous highwayman.[80] Beyond was one of the more deserted areas of Rome, frequented only by a few herdsmen driving their cattle and a clutch of tourists armed with guidebooks in 'a scene of magnificent desolation, and of melancholy yet sublime interest'. This made the sight of the Coliseum looming up ahead of them yet more striking: huge, mossy, and tumbledown with myrtles, fig trees, and wallflowers growing along the ledges, 'alone in its solitary grandeur'.[81] And so by the Arch of Constantine, past Trajan's Column, up the noisy crowded Corso, along the narrower Via Condotti and finally into Piazza di Spagna. They had been almost two months on the way.

The *vetturino* deposited them at Dr Clark's house in the square directly across from No. 26, a lodging house where Clark had arranged rooms for them, recently vacated by another English doctor. James Clark, a young Scotsman of thirty-two and newly married, had been established in Rome for little more than a year but was already the leading physician in the English community. His sympathetic bedside manner would eventually take him to the heights of the medical profession in England, with a baronetcy, a fellowship of the Royal Society and a grace and favour residence at Bagshot provided by his employer, Queen Victoria. In 1820, after a short but adventurous career as a ship's surgeon, he specialized in the treatment of consumptive patients. Earlier that year he had published his first book with the cumbersome title *Medical Notes on Climate, Diseases, Hospitals, and Medical Schools in France, Italy and Switzerland; comprising an Inquiry into the Effects of a Residence in the South of Europe in Cases of Pulmonary Consumption and Illustrating the Present State of Medicine in Those Countries.* It was probably this book which had attracted the attention of Keats's London doctors to his qualifications for taking care of their patient in Rome. Indeed, they may have met Clark when he was in Britain in August for his marriage in Edinburgh. Certainly, he was remarkably well prepared for his interesting new patient. He had read the *Edinburgh Review* notice of *Lamia, Isabella and Other Poems* and, despite its limited sale, acquired his own copy.[82] If his expectations ran high, he was not disappointed. Keats was, he immediately saw, 'too noble an animal to be allowed to sink without some sacrifice being made to save him'. 'I feel very much interested in him', he reported to London. But something about the chatty, excited Severn grated on the doctor, a great believer in the benefits of calm for convalescents. 'He has a friend with him who seems very attentive to him', he wrote several days after their arrival, 'but between you and I is not the best suited for his companion . . . I suppose poor fellow [Keats] had no choice', Clark concluded, perhaps on the basis of inside information from London.[83]

This initial assessment would change as Clark saw more of Severn in the weeks that followed.

CHAPTER 5

Piazza di Spagna

Though Severn and Keats were both abroad for the first time in their lives, and well over a thousand miles from London, there was much about the area around Piazza di Spagna to make them feel surprisingly at home. As they leant out of the windows to watch the throng on the square they would have heard emphatic English voices amongst the excitable Italian cries, for here in the liveliest quarter of Rome the British had taken possession. As they sauntered down to the end of the Via Babuino, with its artists' shops and mosaicists' galleries, they could not avoid the huge travelling coaches of the milords in the Piazza del Populo, announcing the presence of their owners in town. There were tribal bases in the quarter, too: the Caffè Inglese at No. 85 on the Piazza or the tearoom reserved for the English at the Caffè Greco. Severn reported home to his father that it was 'almost like London' with 200 British in town. More probably there were 2,000 (but Severn often got in a muddle over numbers).[1] The English made no attempt to downplay their presence, bustling about as they would in a market town with the assizes in session, flashing their money around and demonstrating their mastery by bursting into their national anthem in inappropriate places, like the top of the dome of St Peter's.[2] Confident in the superiority of their ways, they knew it was only their presence which kept some of the most noisome native habits in check. Keats, however, looking around him with a curious eye, lighted on a small fountain and amused Severn by describing it as a corner watering in revenge for all the watering in corners.[3] Like Shelley and Byron before him, who had both lodged in Piazza di Spagna, Keats was not disposed to accept the pretensions of his compatriots in Rome. Nor did he seek out their company.

In Rome Severn remained an early riser, stepping out to enjoy the morning air to the jangle of small bells as flocks of goats and the occasional cow were led into the Piazza to provide fresh milk on demand. As the day wore on, he cast a practised eye over the Italian models touting for custom on the Spanish Steps. They offered a wider range than in the Academy Schools. Alongside the classical heroes were Madonnas, kings, philosophers, and saints hoping to catch the attention of the painters and sculptors whose studios were concentrated in the neighbouring streets. In the evenings, as the crowds drifted away and the splashing of water in the Barcaccia fountain scarcely disturbed the unnatural quiet of Piazza di Spagna, he might just have heard the sound of the nuns in the church of the Trinità dei Monti at the top of the Steps. Their singing was of famous purity.

The tall house at 26 Piazza di Spagna, painted a deep Roman red and known as the Casina Rossa, occupied one of the best situations on the square, to the right of the Spanish Steps and above the Barcaccia. A saddler's and a stables were just a few doors away, as was the trattoria which prepared and sent out meals for lodgers in the neighbourhood.[4] Conveniently, too, Dr Clark was just across the square. Severn also had good reason to think he had found a congenial landlady in Angela Angelletti, a forty-three-year-old Venetian widow. 'Colonel' Finch, later a friend of Severn's, stayed with her in 1815 and subsequently kept up a flirtatious correspondence with this 'lively, smart, handsome little woman' who knew about drawing and engraving and had a taste for the fine arts. Another demanding English traveller had been equally impressed a few months earlier. After a dispiriting search for lodgings, John Mayne could hardly believe his luck when he lighted on an apartment in 26 Piazza di Spagna with a 'large cheerful and well-furnished' sitting room and linen 'furnished and washed, and everything for our housekeeping supplied'.[5] When Severn and Keats came to Rome, Angelletti lived with her daughter, son-in-law, and a serving woman in the back rooms on the main floor. Like many landladies after the war she had refurbished her lodging house to attract the new influx of foreign visitors. While most made only cosmetic improvements, she was thoroughgoing. A vacancy on the *piano nobile* where Keats and Severn were to stay, gave her the opportunity to 'furnish it as nicely as possible for visitors', offering 'comfortable accommodation for two friends or a family'.[6] As Severn would discover, however, the quality of the furnishings was a mixed blessing. Nor did the relationship with Angelletti develop as smoothly as he might have expected.

At the time he and Keats moved in, all her rooms were filled. Beneath them was an elderly Englishman, Thomas Gibson, with a French valet, and above an Irishman and an Italian army officer, each with an Italian servant. To have servants was a luxury Keats and Severn could not afford. Though they lived on the best floor, they fended for themselves with sporadic help from Angelletti's maid, whose habit of appearing unannounced disconcerted them. As best they could, they kept themselves to themselves. When Keats took to his bed, Severn had no one to call on for help with the menial chores of nursing an increasingly sick man.

Their lodgings did not come cheap. Faced with a rent of nearly £5 each a month, both worried about the expense, reasonable though it was for the location.[7] In all they had three rooms. A small windowless entrance lobby curtained off from the landlady's quarters led into a good-sized well-furnished salon with a window over the square. To the right of the salon, through a connecting door, was a smaller corner room, narrow but high-ceilinged with windows looking onto the Piazza and the Steps. This, in turn, led into a tiny but passably lit room where Severn set up his painting things. Keats took the middle room which had the only fireplace in the apartment and an unusual coffered wooden ceiling painted with *trompe l'oeil* white flowers with golden centres. Severn made up his bed behind a curtain in the salon. He was in earshot of his friend in case of night-time emergencies.

The relief of arrival at the end of a punishing journey was immense. Now they could make arrangements to settle in for the winter and spring. Like most British travellers, they presented themselves at Torlonia's, one of the two banks transacting business for visitors. Torlonia, a self-made man who had bought his grand title of Duke of Bracciano, was an expert money-man, consoling travellers for his ruinous exchange rates and high interest by offering balls and receptions at which his guests vented their snobberies about his Jewish origins.[8] But it was Keats's disinclination for grand entertainments, rather than snobbery, which kept Severn away from these set-piece occasions in his early months in Rome. Later he would become a regular. For now he preferred to be with Keats. Though one or two people made unavailing enquiries about Keats's whereabouts, few of the expatriates in Rome knew that a young English poet had arrived with his friend, a promising young painter.

The initial dealings at Torlonia's were straightforward. On 15 November they accepted the bank's calculation that the £120, deposited for them in London by John Taylor, was worth 552 *scudi*. They withdrew 92, advised that if they made few but large withdrawals the transaction charges would be lower. A week later they came back for another 100 *scudi* and on 26 December Severn withdrew a further 100, leaving less than half the sum painfully collected together by Taylor and Hessey to cover the costs of a spring convalescence in Italy. As reports of the transactions reached London, Taylor became increasingly alarmed.

Important as their landlady and banker were, the key person for Keats in his early days in Rome was Dr Clark. The doctor is now best known for his egregious misdiagnoses in a number of high-profile cases, but though these included that of Keats, Severn always had the highest respect for him. To those like him, with basically strong constitutions, Clark gave sound advice on diet and exercise. It was patients with life-threatening conditions who suffered from his misdiagnoses.[9] What he had to say after a few days' watching and talking to Keats was remarkably similar to what Keats's London doctors had said nine months before: there was little wrong with his body, the problem lay in his mental agitation. Some 150 years later, the distinguished medical man Lord Brock would dismiss this as a 'rubbishy assessment' and 'medically poor'.[10] But in 1820 Clark had few, if any, diagnostic tools or effective medicines when treating consumptive patients. In their absence he concentrated, as he was to do for most of his career, on treating the patient rather than the disease. Clark prided himself on his spirit of pragmatic enquiry. His study of tubercular patients, *The Effects of a Residence in the South of Europe in cases of Pulmonary Consumption*, was a pioneering work based on interviews with physicians and patients together with descriptions of the places around the Mediterranean most favoured by English doctors when sending patients south in search of recovery. It also served to enlarge Clark's clientele, and concluded that Rome and Piazza di Spagna, in particular, were the best places in Europe for the treatment of consumptives. The climate was mild and moist and, despite the northerly Tramontana in January, a patient was less exposed to harsh winds than in Nice, Marseilles, Hyères, Pisa, or Naples. For invalids coming to Rome, Clark was full of sensible advice. Ancient ruins and modern churches should be avoided as cold and damp. St Peter's, however, was a fine place to visit on rainy days so long as patients travelled in a close carriage and ladies took the precaution of wearing 'thick-soled shoes to protect them against the cold marble floors'.[11] Regular exercise on the Pincio at the top of the Spanish Steps was also recommended for all but the wettest of days.

Clark's prescription for consumptive patients—gentle exercise, fresh air, residence in an equable climate, the avoidance of harsh winds, some entertainment and relief from anxieties—would have served for many convalescent conditions and, in the absence of anything more specific, was not unhelpful to Keats. In other respects, however, though he followed well-established British medical opinion, Clark's practice was harmful. Like Dr Rodd in London, he went in for heavy bleeding and put his patients on a harshly restricted diet (those same 'pseudo victuals' that would have starved a mouse, which Keats complained about in February 1820).[12] By contrast, Italian practice was more enlightened: Roman doctors bled their English patients only on demand, and then took as little blood as possible.[13] Some of them had also noticed signs of infectiousness amongst their consumptive patients and, unlike Clark, took steps to counter it.

The doctor reported his findings about Keats to London, in a well-intentioned and reassuring way: Keats's 'mental exertions and application' were 'the sources of his complaints', which seemed chiefly 'situated in his Stomach' (indigestion is not uncommon in tubercular patients). Though Clark had 'some suspicion of disease of the heart and it may be of the lungs', he confidently predicted that 'If I can put his mind at ease I think he'll do well.'[14] Tactfully, too, he set about doing his best to mobilize the friends in London to relieve Keats of any money worries and talked up the benefits of enabling him to buy or hire a horse. Though it has the look of ignorance dressed up as medical erudition, the insistence of Keats's various doctors in 1820 that it was his mind, rather than his body, that was diseased is striking. Obviously, the extent of Keats's mental agitation was far easier to observe than any internal physical deterioration. Even so, there was clearly something exceptional in Keats's case. His late letters to Fanny Brawne, his conduct at Hunt's, and the 'last' unsent letter to Brown give us a sense of how impassioned, unreasonable, and overwrought he could be as illness took hold of him in 1820. Severn, all unprepared, had to cope with the full force of this as best he could. Witnessing Keats's mental disintegration was infinitely more painful than dealing with his physical collapse. Severn had worshipped Keats's 'beautiful mind'; he despaired over its ruin.

Though Keats was always his own best diagnostician, as a fellow professional he respected Dr Clark's opinion, reporting his assessment to Brown a few days later without any commentary of his own. And, as Clark recommended, he hired a horse, though at £6 a month it was rather more than they could afford. On it Keats, the ostler's son, went off for slow jogtrots with a friend they had got to know as they strolled on the Pincio. Severn delighted in every sign of Keats's improving spirits. Keats knew that he was simply passing the time as he waited for death.

Instinctively, he sought the company of fellow invalids, getting to know Lieutenant Isaac Elton, one of the many consumptives who had come to Rome on his own in search of a cure. This was a relief for Severn, frustrated by the slow pace of the convalescents as they ambled around. He could wave them off on gentle rides out through the Porta del Populo and along the Tiber or into the fields beyond the Pincio gardens, while he took more energetic walks around Rome. He went back to the Coliseum, climbing up to a high ledge to pick wallflowers to bring back to Keats. He made his way across the city to the Vatican, marvelling at the Raphaels in the Stanze and, at last, seeing the Michelangelo frescoes in the Sistine Chapel. These were the masterpieces on which his imagination had fed as a student at the Royal Academy. The excitement of seeing the real thing awakened his artistic ambitions as he dreamed of a grand career. No doubt he came back and described what he had seen to Keats. Physically stronger though he was, emotionally Keats could not face the challenge of seeing these iconic images, well though he knew them from engravings.[15] Severn, however, was unafraid of their power and wrote to Sir Thomas Lawrence early in January volunteering to make full-size copies of the Raphaels. Lawrence, still with doubts about Severn, did not take up the offer.[16]

On good days Severn walked with Keats and Elton along the Pincio, the most fashionable place in Rome to see and be seen, watching the crowds of promenaders and admiring the views of Rome from the terrace, with the dome of St Peter's prominent in the golden light of late afternoon. Keats did not disguise to Brown that his life in Rome was a 'posthumous existence', but it was not unpleasant. In the Elysian Fields of the elegiac city, he found a welcome disassociation from the stresses and hurts of life in London.

A reminder could quickly provoke a petulant reaction. One of the highlights of the daily parade on the Pincio was the appearance of Princess Pauline Borghese, Napoleon's sister, with her retinue of admirers. She lived apart from her husband, entertained royally, and, apart from her poor taste in lovers, was most notorious for the semi-nude statue Canova had made of her. She was always a figure of interest to British visitors, 'as smart and pretty a little bantam figure as can be imagined' despite her faded beauty. Keats, however, was enraged by her routine coquetry in ogling Lieutenant Elton, a painful reminder of another 'petite and graceful figure' with 'a tendency to the Cressid', now free in Hampstead to flirt with taller men.[17] His anger obliged them to take their walks elsewhere. Severn was happy to humour his friend. They could always fall back on the print shops on Via Babuino or stroll along the Corso when Keats did not stay at home reading. It was a 'dull' but agreeable enough life, even if Keats felt guilty about his inability to explore Rome to the full with Severn.

For Severn it was enough to have Keats to himself. He delighted in his friend's inventiveness. They had their dinners brought in from the trattoria in the Piazza. Mrs Eaton, another English traveller at this time, found the meals good but expensive.[18] Keats was less fortunate. His weakened digestion revolted against the ill-prepared food foisted on the apparently inexperienced young Englishmen. Severn never tired of telling (and embellishing) the tale of Keats's response. At its simplest the story ran:

'Twas a joy to me to see Keats improve from day to day, the winter being very fine he walked every day & was even like himself but our drawback was in the very bad dinners, so that Keats said to me 'Severn I have found out a way of having good dinners' but he would not tell me how— When the porter came with the Basket Keats opened it & seeing that it was the same horrid mess as usual he opened the window & quietly & deliberately emptied out on the steps each plate. This done he closed the basket & pointed to the Porter to take it away—Sure enough this was a masterpiece more eloquent than words as in half an hour we got an excellent dinner, & so on every day.

This was the Keats Severn relished: pugnacious and inventive, funny and worldly-wise. As he said, 'To be in Rome with Keats was in itself an event, independent of Rome and all it meant to me.'[19]

Along with better dinners, they had music, too. It was Keats who suggested they hire a piano. At 7 *scudi* a month it was cheaper than the horse and, in the end, amply paid for itself. Severn was delighted with the chance to keep up his keyboard skills. Dr Clark sent over a pile of music. Keats picked out a transcription of some symphonies by one of Severn's favourite composers, Haydn. Perhaps he played the 'Surprise' Symphony, emphasizing the contrast between the quiet introduction to the slow movement and the fortissimo crash which follows, to bring a smile to Keats's wan face. Keats listened intently and immediately got to the heart of the music: 'This Haydn', he told Severn, 'is like a child. You never know what he is going to do next.'[20] Severn kept the piano on until the end of his time at 26 Piazza di Spagna. Even during the most difficult periods he still played, consoling himself and soothing Keats as he lay in bed listening through the open door.

Severn was increasingly optimistic about his friend's recovering health and spirits, resolutely ignoring any contrary signs. Though Keats toyed with the idea of starting a long poem about Sabrina (the tutelary goddess of the River Severn), he was too weak to face the emotional challenge of writing poetry. Even reading it was too disturbing. He threw down a copy of Alfieri's poems after working his way through a few melancholy lines. With no creative future of his own, he turned instead to Severn's, devoting his limited energy to salvaging something from the wreckage of the journey to Italy by getting his friend well started there. This was, as Keats recognized, part of the bargain they had made in setting out for Rome together: Severn was there not just as the companion of an invalid but as an aspiring historical painter. Keats saw the need to harden and prepare him for the difficulties ahead. At first, he had been irritated by Severn's uncritical high spirits, but bit by bit he took an increasing interest in his friend's future, repaying him for his kindness with his own foresight. It was not the dependent relationship Keats wanted: he would have preferred Brown's worldliness and manly cheer. But though he was more candid about his feelings for Fanny in his letters to Brown than he could ever be with Severn, he no longer pressed him to come. In place of the friendship with the man whose handwriting he could scarcely bear to see, so strongly did it remind him of all he had left behind, he turned to Severn, accepting the role of senior partner, protecting his companion from his naivety and charting a course for him in a potentially hostile world.

Severn's first step on the way was to present the letters of introduction Lawrence had supplied. Canova, however, was temporarily out of town. Dr Clark suggested that he call instead on John Gibson, the doyen of the British sculptors in Rome. Gibson had learnt his craft the hard way, progressing from a strict, religious Welsh-speaking education in North Wales to schooling in Liverpool and apprenticeship first to a cabinet-maker and then in a marble statuary. He quickly attracted a wealthy local patron, William Roscoe, the author of a biography of Lorenzo de Medici which made a deep impression on Severn in the Academy Schools. Gibson himself eschewed the Academy. His sights were always set on Rome. A subscription of £150 was raised for him in Liverpool. With that and a small commission he set off in September 1817, knowing neither French nor Italian.

Rome did not disappoint. Canova took him into his studio and two years later he got his first major commission for a work in marble from the Duke of Devonshire. Others followed. Gibson was soon established and returned to England only occasionally. He adored Rome, glorying in the early morning sunshine as he walked to the Caffe Greco for breakfast 'inspired with a feeling of daily renovated youth and fresh enthusiasm'. He was a gentle, generous-spirited if careful man, a lifelong bachelor who kept his strongest emotions for his sculptures. But he was sociable and did much to promote a collegiate feeling amongst the British artistic community. For him Rome, unlike London, was the place where a sculptor was on his mettle to do his best in an atmosphere of friendly rivalry.[21]

Severn could not have hit on a more encouraging choice for his first taste of contemporary artistic life in Rome. Gibson was a model of all that was best there, as he soon discovered. Arriving at Gibson's studio at the same time as Lord Colchester, Severn instinctively turned away. But Gibson drew him in, paying equal attention to his visitors as they viewed his works. 'I was so much struck by this generous consideration towards a poor and unknown young artist like myself, that I thought, 'if Gibson, who is a great artist, can afford to do such a thing as this, then Rome is the place for me'.[22] To be treated as equal to a noble lord, and a rich patron at that, was an event far outside Severn's experience. It gave him a sense of what were to be the great prizes of artistic life in Rome: the association between artist and patron, and the way in which artists supported one another. For the first time, too, he glimpsed the social as well as the material rewards that could be his in this new environment. Though Gibson was only three years his senior he already had the confidence of the established artist but was still close enough to the struggles and aspirations of a young man, coming, like himself, from an unfavoured background, to offer a warm welcome. It was the start of a lifelong friendship. Severn rushed home to tell Keats about the meeting. Keats, who worried that he was holding him back in Rome, was delighted by this 'treat to humanity'. Excitedly, they settled down together to plot Severn's artistic future.

First was the picture Severn was required to submit in the summer if he was to gain the Academy's travelling scholarship. To be sure of meeting the deadline he would need to send it off by the end of the spring. Keats was determined that Severn's responsibilities as a nurse should not get in the way. They discussed possible subjects. Something in the grand manner was needed, heroic, historical, and morally unambiguous. Severn chose a classical subject, looking to Greece rather than Rome: Alcibiades, the fifth-century Athenian politician and warrior. Though Severn was the painter, it was Keats, the poet, who had the keenest sense of Alcibiades' physical presence: 'when a Schoolboy the abstract idea I had of an heroic painting was what I cannot describe. I saw it somewhat sideways, large, prominent, round and colour'd with magnificence, somewhat like the feel I have of Anthony and Cleopatra. Or of Alcibiades, leaning on his Crimson Couch in his Galley, his broad shoulders heaving with the Sea.'[23] Severn chose a more conventionally inspirational pose. He would paint Alcibiades at the point of death facing up to his assassins, their spears poised, their murderous intentions temporarily checked by the radiance of his nobility.[24] Virtue under pressure in classical garb was designed to appeal to conventional Academy tastes in historical painting. And the idea of defiance in the face of animosity was in both Keats's and Severn's minds in the autumn of 1820.

Severn set to work in his cramped studio off Keats's bedroom, sketching out his picture on the standard half-length canvas used for *The Cave of Despair*. In the excitement of new creation, he tended to overlook the problems he had made for himself by flouting Academy rules and travelling to Rome before he had won the scholarship. Keats tried to bring him down to earth, reminding Severn that the Academicians were touchy about the observance of their rules. His Gold Medal success had aroused ill feeling, while his determination to aspire to the highest rank and become a history painter exposed him to the spiteful machinations of 'a host of Tradesmen in Art'.[25] Now was the moment for Keats to tell Severn the story of the dinner with William Hilton and Peter de Wint, which he had so far kept to himself. The conversation had turned to Severn's *Cave of Despair* and the Gold Medal. 'Some one scornfully explained that the picture was very inferior, but that as the artist was an old fellow, and had made frequent attempts for the prize, the Council had given the medal out of pity and not for any merit.' Having waited in vain for the expected rebuttal, Keats hastily defended Severn ('as they well knew, I was a young man...the picture was my first attempt for a prize of any kind') before storming out. He recounted the incident vividly to the avid Severn: 'with his ready sympathy, he placed himself in my position. Although small of stature, yet on these occasions of acts of meanness, he seemed to rise to a larger stature, and the effect was a marvellous contrast to his charming manner when he was tranquil.'[26]

As Keats had foreseen, the incident made a powerful, even exaggerated, impression on Severn. It became one of the favourite stories in his repertoire. He liked to tell it not only as an example of Keats's fierce loyalty to his friends but also of the meanness of London artistic life. Over the years the story changed. When Severn's spirits were low, it confirmed his belief that all the world was against him. In the short term, however, with Keats on hand to put it in context, it had the salutary effect of encouraging him to get on with *Alcibiades* and not take the Academy's forbearance for granted, however well motivated his decision to accompany a sick friend to Rome.

With Keats's health apparently improving, Severn began to make new friends in Rome. Perhaps through Gibson, or on his own account as a fellow Academy

student, he contacted Lewis Vulliamy, who had won the Gold Medal for architecture in 1813 and the travelling fellowship in 1818.[27] Vuillamy was confident
that Severn would succeed him when his own scholarship ran out in July.
Another artist with whom he became increasingly friendly was the young sculptor William Ewing, who lived conveniently close in the Piazza and looked in
regularly.[28] Inevitably, too, Severn quickly came across Seymour Kirkup, the
most engaging of all the young painters in Rome with 'an eager love of new
acquaintances' and 'sudden admiration of them'.[29] Five years older than Severn, Kirkup had preceded him as a student at the Royal Academy. Weak lungs
and independent means led him in 1816 to Italy, where he remained for the rest
of his very long life. Another friend was Thomas Campbell, the sculptor, more
than twenty years older and close to the painter Charles Eastlake, who was away
from Rome at this time.

Most exciting of all, on Canova's return to Rome Severn finally presented his
letter of introduction to the man he had last seen at a distance in the Academy
Schools in 1815.[30] Canova's premises were more like a factory than a studio,
reflecting his huge commercial success and the amount of work he and his
assistants had on their hands. Like other callers on the great man, Severn walked
through a number of rooms containing blocks of marble in various states of
preparation and half-finished statues, to find Canova's studio at the end of the
building 'far from the din and bustle of less-inspired workmen' with the master
himself 'habited in his nankeen jacket and yellow slippers'.[31] He got the usual
kindly welcome and, as he later boasted to his father, 'shared a pot and a pipe'
with 'the Marquess'. Generous as always, Canova wrote out a note to the papal
authorities recommending that Severn be allowed to do copying in the Vatican
Galleries.[32]

In the excitement of his initial engagement with the artistic community in
Rome, Severn sometimes neglected his duties as a correspondent to Keats's
friends back in London. Haslam, deeply troubled by Severn's downbeat
accounts from Naples of Keats's health at the end of their sea voyage, waited
anxiously for the next report from Rome. Having heard nothing by 4 December,
he sent a stern reminder:

Why have you not kept your diary? I ask you solemnly for no one thing on earth can give such
satisfaction at home as such minute detail as you set out with [in the shipboard journal]—if you
have discontinued it—in God's name resume it, and send it regularly to me—rely that however I
may see fit to circulate it—I will zealously preserve each section (Number it, or letter it, that I may

do this unerringly)—and write on <u>Bank Post Paper</u> so that you may possess the entire whenever you call upon me for it—<u>do this</u> Severn, tho' at some sacrifice of your inherent dislike of order—and of obligation to do a thing—do it, if but because I ask it.[33]

In 1821 the shortest interval between writing a letter from England to Rome and getting a reply was six weeks. This led to some unhappy disjunctions as Keats's health fluctuated. A more positive account from Severn would produce cheering, gossipy letters from friends in reply, arriving inopportunely just after Keats had had a relapse. By the time Haslam's reprimand arrived, close to Christmas Day, it was badly out of joint. Severn was overwhelmed with cares: keeping a diary on bank post paper was far from his mind. 'Pray, my dear fellow don't ask me for journals,' he begged Haslam in reply, 'every day's would have been more or less like this.'[34] In any case, he had not been quite as disorganized as Haslam assumed. He had indeed written and slipped out on 9 December to post the letter in the course of his early morning walk.[35] He returned at 9 o'clock to find Keats waking and unusually cheerful, 'when in an instant a Cough seized him, and he vomited near two Cup-fuls of blood'.[36] Inevitably, Severn called Dr Clark and, as inevitably, Clark bled Keats, taking away another eight ounces of blood. It was what both expected him to do. As an apothecary's apprentice Keats had himself bled patients often enough. But bleeding weakened the patient just at the point where he most needed strength to fight infection. And Clark compounded his unintended savagery by putting Keats on a starvation diet designed to cut the flow of blood to his stomach: an anchovy and a piece of bread was now his daily ration.

Keats's collapse came as a complete shock to Severn. Its suddenness haunted him for the rest of his life. There was always, he thought, something inexplicable about it. Slowly, he came to recognize that the nature of his friendship with Keats and his task in Rome had altered. He had set out confident that Keats would be a resource to him in Rome, the mentor who would open his eyes to the glories around them, advise him on his future career, enhance his standing there and in London, and keep him steady. Now the situation was reversed: it was Keats who was totally reliant on him. Severn was about to be tested physically, mentally, and emotionally in a way he had never foreseen. Painfully, he rethought his relationship with Keats. 'I had made sure of his recovery when I set out', he confided to Haslam, 'I was selfish and thought of his value to me—and made a point of my future success depend on his candour to me.'[37]

Piazza di Spagna

From 9 December on, however much Severn tried to persuade himself otherwise, there could no longer be any doubt that Keats was dying. His respite in the autumnal beauty of Rome had not lasted even a month. The brief flicker of hope that he might again write poetry or go back to London was over. Still in shock at the suddenness of Keats's collapse, Severn faced an immediate and harrowing test. Keats's reaction was to end his miserable existence as quickly as possible. Weak though he was, he struggled out of bed insisting 'This day shall be my last.'[38] Severn knew all about hiding the breakables when his father came home in a drunken temper, and immediately took preventive action. He put away the knives, razors, and scissors, and then, to Keats's intense irritation, kept a close watch on him. The next morning Keats coughed up blood again and was again bled by Clark. He was by then so weak that he allowed Severn to calm him and even read out a little from the English newspapers. And he began to accept the intimate nursing that would now be part of his companion's regular care. In the next week Keats had five more attacks and, as difficult as anything for Severn, was in agony from starvation. While Clark had prescribed the absolute minimum (though he arranged for his wife to prepare it), Keats pressed Severn to give him more. Severn gave way but then worried endlessly over whether he had done more harm than good, convinced that another attack on 16 December was the result of exceeding Clark's draconian regime. 'You cannot think how dreadful this is for me,' he told Brown, 'the Doctor on the one hand tells me I shall kill him to give him more than he allows—and Keats raves till I am in a complete tremble for him.' In the end, Keats saved Severn from his desperate dilemma, bowing to the doctor's judgement and putting up with the constant pangs of hunger.

Reporting the dismal scene to Brown, after eight nights sitting up with no one to help him, Severn sent his regards to Mrs Brawne, remarking 'little did I dream on THIS when I saw her last in London'. Though he liked to compare Keats's agonies with his mother's bouts of acute indigestion, the truth was that he knew nothing at first-hand about nursing a terminally ill man. Had he been aware of the steady progression of the dying patient from self-pity, to anger and, eventually, acceptance, his ordeal would have been eased. Though he clearly charts this course in his reports of Keats's last weeks, Severn had no idea what to expect.[39]

Whether as nurse or patient, Keats always hated the sick-room. Although he had insisted on caring alone for his dying brother in 1818, he found Tom's

[91]

presence unbearably oppressive: 'his identity presses upon me so all day that I am obliged to go out…and plunge into abstract images to ease my self of his countenance his voice and feebleness'.[40] A few months later, staying with Rice on the Isle of Wight, when they were both ill, they fell into a morbid depression, making each other worse. In 1820 Keats was himself the patient. Brown, who nursed him, discovered that he was unable even to touch letters from friends and resented seeing him writing or reading. Even Fanny Brawne, about whose nursing Keats never complained, knew and accepted his 'savage malevolence' when ill. But the trials of caring for Keats were tempered by his awareness of the demands he placed on his friends. Brown submitted readily because 'his instinctive generosity, his acceptance of my offices, by a glance of his eye, a motion of his hand, made me regard my mechanical duty as absolutely nothing compared to his silent acknowledgement…It was an innate virtue in him to make those who most obliged him the most obliged, without effort, without a thought, well nigh magical.' 'Something like this,' Brown recorded, 'Severn, his last nurse, observed to me.'[41] In the initial stages of Keats's illness, however, when self-pity and anger were at their height, there were few consolations.

It was not the practical tasks that most troubled Severn. Carrying them out was a distraction from the emotional pressures. He found Rome 'a savage place for invalids', damp and cold indoors in winter, comfortless and short of basic facilities (the primitive sanitary arrangements in their lodgings must have been a particular trial). 'These wretched Romans have no idea of comfort,' he complained, 'here I am obliged to wash up—cook and read to Keats all day.'[42] But he preferred, as did Keats, to look after things on his own, with occasional help from Ewing, and, from time to time, Keats, no doubt remembering his own ordeal with Tom, obliged Severn to go out even though it meant leaving him alone. And Severn was now strong enough to sit up for nights in a row, taking the opportunity, while Keats slept, to write to friends in England at his table in the room next door.

It was a relief from the spectacle of Keats's mental disintegration. Half-starved, weakened with frequent bleeding and lack of oxygen, and, as it seemed, frustrated in everything he had ever sought to achieve, Keats experienced the misery of his dying as intensely as he had known the joy of living. At times he was deranged, keening over his failures, pushed to 'malevolence—suspicion—and impatience', obsessed by his persecutors in London or even convinced that someone there had tried to kill him. His spirit was broken, his fortitude gone, 'his voracious imagination colouring everything' and strengthening a conviction that his fate lay in the hands of 'a malignant being'. Severn reported Keats's decline to Taylor and Brown in the desperate night-time letters of a weary and oppressed watcher:

> his mind is worse than all—despair in every shape—his imagination—and memory present every image in horror so strong that morning and night I tremble for his Intellect. The recollection of England—of his 'good friend Brown'—and his happy few weeks in Mrs Brawne's Care—his Sister and brother—O he will mourn over evry circumstance to me whilst I cool his burning forehead—until I tremble through every vein in concealing my tears from his staring glassy eyes.—How he can be Keats again from all this I have little hope.

Severn recognized that he too was under strain: 'I may see it too gloomy', he confessed to Brown, 'since each coming night I sit up adds its dismal contents to my mind.'[43] Instinctively optimistic, Severn learnt to accept death with equanimity only towards the end of his own very long life. Now he was on his own facing the harshest of all realities, something that even he could not imagine away. His volatile spirits plummeted. Not for a moment, however, did he deviate from his belief in Keats as 'the most noble-feeling and brightest genius to be found in existence'.[44] Devotion kept Severn going. He complained about much, but scarcely ever about Keats.

By Christmas Eve Keats had been bedridden for nearly three weeks. Clark, who must have begun to doubt his own initial diagnosis, took the precaution of inviting in an Italian doctor, who confirmed the likelihood of consumption. And so Keats and Severn celebrated Christmas Day together, both of them aware that it was Keats's last. For once, the rigours of Dr Clark's dietary restrictions were lifted and there were mince pies baked by Mrs Clark and Severn's favourite, plum pudding. Keats could still make some striking puns, grim though they were. When Severn, in a burst of letter-writing the previous day, had told him he was writing to his publisher, Keats called out: 'Tell Taylor I shall soon be in a second edition—in sheets—and cold press.'[45] Perhaps Severn read to Keats; they had been working their way through *Don Quixote* and had Scott's romance *The Monastery* to hand. He also studied a Bible that Lieutenant Elton had just given him to help him through the long nights. Later on, it would become the Severn family Bible, recording key events in his and his children's lives.[46] For now it was a more poignant resource. He went through the Old Testament, noting in pencil in the table of contents the Books he had read. The tribulations of *Job* he 'read attentively', but this well-thumbed Bible also falls open more insistently than most at Psalm 142, 'David's Comfort in Time of Trouble'. Now that he needed it, Severn was discovering a modest, but consoling faith he had scarcely known he possessed.

CHAPTER 6

'Thanks Joe'

To the end of his life Severn never walked past 26 Piazza di Spagna without a shudder, and much that he had seen and heard there he put out of his mind as too painful to remember. In later days, he refashioned what he had witnessed into a 'good death', remembering a Keats who found religious consolation at the end, who retained his 'elasticity of mind' and whose greatest concern was for Severn's well-being rather than his own. Severn's contemporary accounts, written in the middle of the night when he was tired and close to breakdown, tell a harsher, more convincing story. They were anxiously read, copied, and circulated amongst the friends in London.[1]

These letters are quite different from any others Severn wrote. Normally, he said a great deal about himself. He was also a calculating correspondent. The purpose of a letter, as he saw it, was to cheer reader and writer. This gave a jauntiness to his letters, which his friends enjoyed. In Rome, however, he faced the challenge of reporting accurately on the state of Keats's health, and there was rarely any good news. His short, sometimes incoherent sentences, as he stumbles from one anxiety to another and back, have an immediacy that vividly conjures up Keats's sickroom while the hysteria and self-pity of his accounts are relieved by his occasional unexpected eloquence and eye and ear for the telling detail. The despondency of his letters, however, struck friends accustomed to his buoyancy. As Fanny Brawne remarked to Fanny Keats about Severn's letter from Naples to Haslam, 'From your brother I never expect a very good account, but you may imagine how lowering to the spirits it must have been when Mr Severn who I never imagined it was possible for anything to make unhappy, who I never saw for ten minutes serious, says he was so overcome that he was obliged to relieve himself by shedding tears.'[2]

Apart from short extracts from three of Dr Clark's letters, everything we know about the last three months of Keats's life comes from Severn's letters and reminiscences. If others had watched by Keats's bedside they might have described things differently, but despite Severn's later reputation for unreliability, no one has challenged his telling of Keats's dying.[3] His account has the ring of authenticity, which Clark's letters corroborate as well as attesting to Severn's devotion. Keats's agonies in the face of what looked like total defeat are almost unimaginable; it is easier to associate with Severn's accounts of his frailties, uncertainties, and efforts to keep going. Out of the clutter of his domestic concerns and daily anxieties, unmediated by attempts to craft a more elevating scene, a moving image of Keats *in extremis* emerges. Isabella Jones, an old flame of Keats, who was shown Severn's letters by Taylor, protested that 'one's best feelings are checked by an elaborate account of sweeping rooms—making beds and blowing fires'. In berating 'Mr Egotist's Productions', however, she missed the point.[4] There was nothing grand and Romantic about Keats's end. Severn told it as it was, putting no distance between us and the tragedy.

The visit of the Italian doctor on Christmas Eve brought new problems. Most probably it was he who tipped off Angelletti to the fact that one of her lodgers was dying of consumption. For her this was very unwelcome news. In Italy at that time consumption had many of the same social connotations as Aids in the 1980s. Even Paganini, for all his fame, was forced out of his Naples lodgings in 1818 when his tuberculosis flared up.[5] Consumptive patients were put in separate wards in Roman hospitals, with spare beds piled high with the linen of other sufferers, returned by their families fearing that it was infectious. Dr Clark considered the practice barbaric, 'originating in the old and almost obsolete opinion of the contagious nature of this disease', a notion 'maintained by the vulgar ... to the injury of the unfortunate patient'.[6] Angelletti knew better and needed to keep on the right side of the authorities. Under local regulations, the wallpaper and furnishings of a consumptive's room had to be burnt after death. The cost of refurbishment would fall on Severn, who knew as little as Clark about the infectious nature of tuberculosis. Though Haslam had been briefly concerned about the risk of infection Keats was running in his confinement with his tubercular brother, Tom,[7] in Rome Severn was guided by Clark. It never crossed his mind that the local regulations might be sensible precautions. Nor, until after Keats's death, was he troubled by the thought that he might have put his own life at risk through his long seclusion with Keats. For Signora Angelletti and her maid, however, handling the sheets of a consumptive was no light matter. Severn had no sympathy for their worries. All his anger at Keats's decline was displaced into fury at the landlady's determination to observe the hygiene requirements and get her compensation. Dr Clark's huffy contempt for local attitudes and practices only reinforced Severn's rising bitterness against her.

He was furious when 'this old Cat' told him she had notified Keats's condition to the police. Such official notification left no room for doubt: Keats was dying. Having absorbed that thought, he had to think about the cost of the redecoration. Less than half of the initial £120 remained at the banker's, though he still had £70 in cash.[8] After 26 December 1820 he made no more withdrawals for over two months but grew increasingly anxious about Angelletti's impending bill. It was not a worry he could share with Keats. For a man who relied on the support and counsel of others, this was a harsh predicament.

For a brief period early in the New Year an exhausted Keats grew calmer. Severn made the most of the respite. He had been looking forward to writing to Mrs Brawne, but only when he had some good news. Now he did his best to persuade himself that Keats was, somehow, improving. The strain of manipulating bad news into good was evident in a desperately contradictory letter, even as it prepared Fanny and her mother for what was to come:

I said that the first good news I had should be for the kind Mrs Brawne. I am thankful & delighted to make good my promise—to be at all able to do it—for among all the horrors hovering over poor Keats this was the most dreadful and I could see no possible way and but a fallacious hope for his recovery. But now thank God I have a real one. I most certainly think I shall bring him back to England—at least my anxiety for his recovery and comfort make me think this—for half the course of the danger has arisen from the loss of England—from the dread of never seeing it more.

But Severn's evidence for Keats's recovery was as paradoxical as could be:

Now he has changed to calmness & quietude, as singular as productive of good, for his mind was certainly killing him. He has now given up all thoughts hopes or even wish for recovery—his mind is in a state of peace from the final leave he has taken of this world and all its future hopes. This has been an immense weight for him to rise from. He remains quiet & submissive under his heavy fate. Now if anything will recover him it is this absence of himself.

Despite Mrs Clark's generosity, both Keats and Severn were short of female sympathy in Rome. Writing to the kindly, maternal Mrs Brawne, Severn rattled on, telling of his cleverness in outwitting the landlady and penning a touching self-portrait of his frustrations as a nurse:

For Three weeks I have never left him…What enrages me most is making a fire I blow—blow—for an hour—the smoke comes fuming out—my kettle falls over on the burning sticks—no stove—Keats calling me to be with him—the fire catching my hands & the door bell ringing—all these to one quite unused and not at all capable—with the want of every proper material come not a little galling—But to my great surprise I am not ill, or even restless nor have I been all the time—there is nothing but what I will do for him—there is no alternative but what I think and provide myself against—except his death—not the loss of him—I am not prepared to bear that.

Now that Keats was calmer, Severn decided that a change of scene would speed his recovery and create an opportunity to freshen up his room. Moving Keats into the salon, however, was not straightforward. Preoccupied as he was by the threat of the damages he would have to pay for the destruction of anything Keats had touched, he needed to get him there without anyone knowing. To add to his difficulties, he could not explain the situation to him. He thought up a plan which just about served, barricading the door to the Angelletti apartments, then making up a bed on the sofa in his room and carrying Keats through. Pretending that he was going out for dinner, he closed the door to Keats's room behind him, swept and aired it, and changed the sheets, telling Keats later that the servant had done this while he was out at dinner. Clearly, the story did not add up, but as a bemused Keats 'could not tell the why & the wherefore there it ended'.[9] Severn also found a solution to the problem of keeping a light burning through the night—sometimes as he watched he dozed off, waking to find the candle burnt out and struggling in the dark to light a new one: he rigged a thread between one candle and another. Keats, who may have watched Severn setting this up, was entranced as one candle stuttered out and another leapt into flame. 'Severn Severn here's a little faery lamplighter actually has lit up the other candel', he called out in appreciation.[10]

Though Keats had watched Severn enviously as he studied his new Bible, he would not let him read it aloud: 'you know Severn I cannot believe in your book—the Bible—but I feel the horrible want of some faith—some hope—something to rest on now—their [*sic*] must be such a book—I know that is it—but I can't believe it—I am destined to every torment in this world—even to this little comfort on my death bed'.[11] He looked for substitutes, asking for *Pilgrim's Progress* and Mrs Dacier's *Selections from Plato*. Above all, he wanted Jeremy Taylor's *Holy Dying*. To Severn's grief, it seemed that the book was not to be had in Rome, though Clark, who was also troubled by Keats's alienation from the consolations of religion, went on searching. In mid-January he found a copy. Severn began to read it aloud. For Keats, Jeremy Taylor had previously seemed a forbidding presence, first encountered when he went to stay with Benjamin Bailey in Oxford in September 1817. The solemn young Bailey had a stern portrait of the seventeenth-century divine above his desk. He 'always looks', Keats said, 'as though he were going to give me a rap with a Book he holds in a very threatening position.'[12] Now he was to discover in Taylor much that he needed.

The Rule and Exercise of Holy Dying, first published in 1651, is a sombre and demanding work. It offers no consolation to the dying unbeliever, other than the certainty of an end to earthly sufferings. But nor does it contain any of the pious cant Keats so much disliked. The sonorous prose, the range of classical, literary, and historical allusions, and the richness of metaphor held his attention as he listened to Severn hesitantly reading Taylor's severe meditations on the fragility of life, the inevitability of death, and the need to accept and prepare for it:

A man is a bubble . . . he is born in vanity and sin; he comes into the world like morning mush-rooms, soon thrusting up their heads into the air and conversing with their kindred of the same production, and as soon they turn into dust and forgetfulness: some of them without any other interest in the affairs of the world, but that they made their parents a little glad, and very sorrowful: others ride longer in the storm . . . and then peradventure the sun shines hot upon their heads, and they fall into the shades below . . . But if the bubble outlives the chances of a child, of a careless nurse, of drowning in a pail of water, of being overlaid by a sleepy servant, or such little accidents, then the young man dances like a bubble empty and gay . . . to preserve a man alive in the midst of so many chances and hostilities is as great a miracle as to create him . . .

Since we stay not here, being people but of a day's abode, and our age is like that of a fly, and contemporary with a gourd, we must look somewhere else for an abiding city, a place in another country to fix our house in, whose walls and foundation is God, where we must find rest, or else be restless for ever.

'Consideration of the Miseries of Man's Life', 'Remedies against Impatience', 'Advantages of Sickness' ('In sickness, the soul begins to dress herself for immortality'), so Severn read on. Towards the end of the book were prayers he recited over Keats. Taylor's superb language held Keats's attention well enough for Severn to read it to him morning and evening for several days. Though it did not persuade Keats of the reality of a Christian afterlife, its solemn periods accorded well with his steady contemplation of death. He now desired it 'with dreadful earnestness'.[13]

Keats's frustrations at the end were unbearable. Time, he believed, had not allowed him to write the poetry that would have secured his immortality. Though loving and being loved by Fanny Brawne, he could neither consummate his passion nor marry her. He had only a modest reputation as a poet, except among his friends, and no commercial success. He had no money and was separated from what little family he still had. And Brown, his closest friend, was far away. Severn shared Keats's anguish, hiding from him his own anxieties, but the strain sometimes showed. At first he stumbled through Taylor's magnificent prose, his mind on other things. Keats watched him anxiously: ' "Severn I can see under your quiet look—immense twisting and contending—you don't know what you are reading ... what is it puzzels you now—what is it happens"— I tell him that "nothing happens—nothing worries me beyond his seeing—that it has been the dull day".—getting from myself to his recovery—and then my painting and then England.—and then—but they are all lies—my heart almost leaps to deny them.'[14]

Amongst all his other troubles, Severn had a major concern he could not share with Keats: money. Learning of their large withdrawals at Torlonia's, Taylor, who worried that Keats had fallen into his usual habit of lending to others what he needed for himself, put a stop on the account. Severn was appalled. He estimated that he needed £100 to £150 to pay for redecoration after Keats's death, as much as the whole amount that Taylor had been able to put together for the journey to Italy and the cost of their stay in Rome. At some stage Dr Clark would have to be paid too; and there were outstanding bills for coaches and the hire of the horse. He could, he thought, earn the money by 'face-painting' for English tourists in Rome, but as he could hardly leave Keats unattended he had no opportunity to follow this up. Nor, since he was failing to make headway with *Alcibiades*, could he rely on the prospect of an eventual income from the travelling scholarship.

He first hinted at his money worries in his letter to Mrs Brawne on 11 January. Four days later he felt almost overwhelmed by anxiety and wrote to the 'oak friend' Haslam, fretting back and forth between his financial problems, his anguish over Keats's mental state, and his determination to remain strong. Ultimately, the anxiety over money was less than his pain at Keats's lack of composure, at his unreceptiveness to spiritual comfort:

this noble fellow lying on the bed—is dying in horror—no kind hope smoothing down his suffering—no philosophy—no religion to support him ... O! my dear Haslam this is my greatest care—a care that I pray to God may soon end—for he says in words that tear my heartstrings— 'miserable wretch that I am—this last cheap comfort—which every rogue and fool have—is deny'd me in my last moments—why is this—O! I have serv'd everyone with my utmost good—yet why is this—I cannot understand this'—and then his chattering teeth—if I do break down it will be under this.—but I pray that some kind of comfort may come to his lot.—that some angel of goodness will lead him through this dark wilderness.

Severn was still objective enough about his dismal situation to wonder, on the flap of the letter where he always scribbled what was uppermost in his mind, whether Haslam should 'have harrowing things like this' and to caution him 'Not a word at my Fathers.'[15]

While Dr Clark quietly set about sorting out the misunderstanding between Taylor in London and Torlonia's in Rome, volunteering to keep Severn solvent in the meantime, Keats deteriorated further. By the end of the month he had moved from self-pity to anger. Once again, he tried to persuade Severn to give him the bottle of laudanum. What was the point of allowing his sufferings to go on and on? They could only get worse and it was Severn who would have to nurse him. Drawing on his medical knowledge and his experience with his dying brother, he described the future course of his illness in detail, with the wasting away and severe diarrhoea that would accompany it. It was in both their interests that he should die now: it would free Severn to get on with his prize picture; and it would end Keats's agony. Severn never found it easy to disagree with Keats. He appeared to acquiesce, but put himself beyond temptation, handing over the laudanum to Dr Clark. Unwittingly, he was depriving Keats of the sedative that would have eased his dying.

Keats was bitterly angry with both of them. When Severn made coffee the next morning, he twice threw it back at him. This Severn could handle. He had learnt from his mother's example the power of unprotesting propitiation, and cheerfully brewed a third cup. A shamefaced Keats quietly accepted it, turning his anger on Clark. 'How long is this posthumous existence of mine to go on', he challenged the doctor whenever he appeared, with a look so intense that the silent Clark could not return it.[16]

Sitting up in the middle of the night around this time, desperately trying to keep awake, Severn hit on the idea of sketching his friend. It was the second drawing of Keats he had attempted in Rome. The first, which has never previously been reproduced, was done after Keats took to his bed. Even so, it shows a powerful figure and though the eyes are large and pleading, the mouth is still full. One hand lies open in a characteristic Baroque gesture of supplication. As Severn worked on it he may still have felt hope, but having begun to ink in his outline, he quickly abandoned the sketch. Perhaps he was distracted. Perhaps Keats lost patience holding the pose. Late in January there was no resistance. Severn's sepia drawing shows a defenceless Keats in a feverish sleep, his head outlined against the dark shadow on the wall cast by the light of the candle. His hair is matted with sweat and the eyelashes moist, the mouth grimaces in pain, the prominent nose stands out from an emaciated face. In this image of a dying man the poet is unrecognizable even from the earlier sketch, let alone the sturdy-faced young man in Severn's miniature done just over two years before. At the bottom he wrote the date and time 'Jan. 28th. 3 o'clock Mg' and then seemed to dismiss it noting 'Drawn to keep me awake.' He was never the best judge of his own work. In his exhaustion he had produced the least calculated but most powerful of all his drawings.[17]

By the end of January Severn had pretty well broken down under the physical strain of many nights watching and days attending to Keats's needs, as well as the emotional cost of sharing his friend's anguish. Keats saw how close Severn had come to the edge. Despite his dislike of strange faces, he suggested bringing in a nurse. Dr Clark made the necessary arrangements and from now on things improved for Severn. He could go for walks, or see members of the English artistic colony. He even began to make tentative plans for his life after Keats's death. There was talk of a studio which might be vacant and of the possibility of a commission from a visiting art lover, Sir William Drummond. And whether Severn knew it or not, Dr Clark's opinion of him had steadily improved. As he reported back to London, Severn's attentiveness to Keats was remarkable.[18]

Though Severn was not the friend Keats had chosen to have with him at the end, in observing him Keats discovered a power of endurance, a kindness, and devotion which he valued. Now that there were few things he could think of with any composure, he concentrated on his approaching death and Severn's situation. Frustrated in everything else, he went back to his first calling as a healer. From his sickbed he watched and worried over Severn, sensing his moods and anxieties, concerned that his illness was holding back Severn's artistic career in Rome, and conscious that 'you are induring for me more than I'd have [for] you'.[19]

Apart from his 'little but honest religion' which helped keep him going, Severn had another resource denied to Keats. He was a member of a large and loving family. Though Haslam had told him that his father was more reconciled

5 A previously unpublished pen and ink sketch by Severn of Keats in Rome together with lists of the books Severn and Keats had with them there

to his journey to Italy and that all were well at home, he had heard nothing directly. The silence weighed on him. He set the miniature of his parents and five siblings on his table, where Keats had admired it, and in his gloomier moments gossiped away to it, imagining himself far from the Piazza di Spagna and back home in Shoreditch.

On 21 January he began a letter to his youngest sister, Maria, which was to be the longest he had so far written. It is an extraordinary letter, just as full of ebullient accounts of his triumphs as the letters he wrote in far happier times. A classic in the self-censorship of letters home, it told only a small part of the story. But it acted as Severn's safety valve, the place where he could rediscover his usual exuberance and get away from an overwhelmingly painful situation. He said as little as possible about Keats and nothing at all about the awful circumstances in which he had parted from his father. Instead, he imagined himself at home for Sunday lunch, late, but warmly welcomed:

O! here he is, here he is. 'See the conquering hero comes, peel your turnips, pick your plums, wines prepare and dishes bring, round the table make a ring, see the dog's tail Joe advance' . . . O! the English welcome I always had at my dear Father's table, the kind and loving faces I always saw, the happy, contented look of my father when I visited him and the oftener the more happy he seemed, the anxious tender-hearted look of my mother with all her kind inquiries, then the good-natured laugh of my dear Maria and eye looking at me from head to foot to see that her Joseph was all neat and clean, hearty Tom looking at me and some new Music at once, eating his dinner and playing at the organ at the same time, and the good Charles giving me his seat. O! this is woven round and round my heart.

And so the letter went on, propelled by homesickness and the need to escape. Just as he had told lies to cheer Keats, now he presented himself to his family not as he was but as he thought they would have liked to see him. He took the letter up again three weeks later with an extravagantly cheerful account of himself, bearing up well, or so he said, as he waited for Keats to die and working on *The Death of Alcibiades*. For his family's benefit, he assumed that the travelling scholarship was his for the taking, resolving that he would do his 'best to be away from you three years. Three years! O! how can I bear it! For I am sometimes thinking that I have gained all I can here for my painting, but I must be in the wrong.' As he explained, 'I am writing to keep up my spirits.' The boastfulness was part and parcel of the process.

Three days later he was glorying in the mild weather: 'in our houses we have roses blowing, when I know you have nothing but your bellows blowing'. It was to become a familiar pun in family letters. His other reflected his daily preoccupations in the sickroom. Chamber pots, he wrote, were the only decent musical instruments in Rome: 'it is astonishing what a fine tone is produced by kicking them. If a few were put together they might make "a Chamber-Organ".' It was a poor sort of pun and the letter tailed off. He was still waiting to hear from home; but not until 19 February did a letter from Maria arrive.[20]

Other letters, however, did come. They were a solace to Severn, a torment to Keats. Mrs Brawne wrote to Severn with generous concern, reminding him to eat well to keep up his strength and sympathizing with him over the Italians' 'want of feeling'. Brown sent an ill-judged, gossipy reply to Keats's letter to him of 20 November, chivvying him for his self-pity. 'If I were in Severn's place, and you insisted on ever gnawing a bone, I'd lead you the life of a dog. What the devil should you grumble for? Do you recollect my anagram on your name? How pat it comes now to Severn! My love to him and the said anagram, "Thanks Joe!" ' Haslam did his best to steady Severn while confessing that he could not accept the thought that Keats was dying. 'If I know what it is to love, then truly I love John Keats.'[21] As Brown began to realize the true state of things in Rome his tone quickly changed. He longed to hear that Keats's suffering was ended but could not bear the idea of his death. 'He is present to me everywhere and at all times—he now seems sitting by my side and looking hard in my face,—though I have taken the opportunity of writing this in company,—for I scarcely believe I could do it alone.' Brown now became the most regular of Severn's correspondents, not waiting to reply to his letters, transferring to Severn the support he could no longer offer Keats. 'I feel towards you as a brother for your kindness to our brother Keats.'[22]

For Severn, letters were the only thing 'to break this dreadful solitude'. For Keats, they were unbearable physical reminders of all he had lost. Brown had warned Severn he would be enclosing a marked letter from Fanny Brawne to Keats and that he should think carefully about whether to show it to him. Severn forgot the warning and, thinking to please Keats, handed over Brown's letter—another in the familiar handwriting fell out, reviving all Keats's old anguish. He could not read it. Even a glance at it 'tore him to pieces'. At first he wanted it laid on his heart when he was buried, together with a letter from his sister. Then the bitterness and frustration returned and 'he found many causes of his illness in the exciting and thwarting of his passions'. Severn talked him round: 'I persuaded him to think otherwise on this delicate point.' For a few days he asked his friend for books. Severn piled up all those he could find round Keats's bed. Briefly they acted like 'a charm', but then that too failed.[23]

It was an unusually fine, mild winter.[24] In his walks, while the nurse kept watch, Severn relished the sight of fruit trees in blossom. Though the cold Tramontana blew from the north, the skies were brilliantly clear. Returning from one of his walks he bounded up the steep stairs at Piazza di Spagna to share his delight with Keats at the first signs of spring. It was a bad mistake. For Keats spring was a time of renewal, both in the natural world as he watched 'the silent growth of flowers', and in his own creative powers. Severn's news was a devastating shock. Keats had hoped to die before spring came. Now he grieved that he could not see it almost as much as he dreaded any stirring of new vitality in himself. 'He talks of the grave as the first rest he can ever have. . . . The thought of recovery is beyond everything dreadful to him.'[25]

Keats had finally come to acceptance. For Severn, this was an immense relief. As he reported to Brown on 14 February:

Little or no change has taken place since the commencement of this,—except this beautiful one, that his mind is growing to great quietness and peace. I find this change has its rise from the encreasing weakness of his body; but it seems like a delightful sleep to me,—I have been beating about in the tempest of his mind so long.[26]

They talked about what was to go on Keats's tombstone. In December Keats had instructed Severn to tell Taylor he did not want any notices published after his death, nor any memorial or engraving of his picture. Now he shocked Severn by insisting that his epitaph should be no more than 'HERE LIES ONE WHOSE NAME WAS WRIT IN WATER'. While Severn shuddered at its desolate anonymity, Keats slept peacefully or lay in bed looking up at the painted flowers on the ceiling, and comforting himself by thinking about his grave. In 'The Eve of St Agnes' he had portrayed the old bedesman shuffling past the effigies of the long-dead knights and ladies entombed in the church and feeling for their imagined aches in the coldness of their icy hoods and mails. But for Keats himself the grave now meant freedom from anguish and the comfort of the natural world: his name carried away on the water, his body lying snug in the cool earth.

He sent Severn off to find out about the Protestant Cemetery where he would be buried, and was so delighted with everything he heard that he sent him back to look again and tell him more.[27] What Severn found was one of the most picturesque places in Rome: little more than a field, where sheep and goats grazed, with a huddle of fine tombs in the shadow of the great white funeral pyramid of Caius Cestius. Wild flowers grew there—daisies and violets as in a tranquil English churchyard. Keats was enchanted: he lay quiet, feeling the flowers growing over him, his sense of the physical world as keen as ever. He held in his hands for consolation the white carnelian which Fanny Brawne had used to cool her fingers when she was sewing: its smoothness and weight calmed him. It was 'the only thing left him in this world clearly tangible'.[28] He was very ready to die.

The arrangement with the new nurse had settled down and for a couple of hours a day Severn could work at chalking out his picture or trying to pick up Italian.[29] There were occasional visitors, too. Ewing looked in to help Severn or searched the city to find an ice jelly to soothe Keats's throat.[30] Even as Keats lay dying a young Spanish radical and literary man, Valentin de Llanos, who was in

Rome that winter, came to see him. (Astonishingly, he would later marry Keats's sister Fanny and live for a while in his old home at Wentworth Place.)[31]

Beyond the narrow sickroom, potentially momentous events were going on in Rome. They troubled Severn less than they might have done. There were rumours of uprisings against La Bomba's authoritarian rule in Naples and fears that his disorganized troops would march on Rome to plunder it before the Austrians arrived to restore order in the Neapolitan Kingdom. Some of the English panicked and left; others packed up in readiness for an early departure; yet others decided it was safer to stay and avoid getting entangled in the march of opposing armies. Though there were rumours that the pope would flee, in the end he remained. Severn had no choice but to stay with Keats. He heard the papal forces rumbling their artillery through the Piazza on the way to Porta San Giovanni. He had little confidence in their efficacy. 'Rome might be taken with a straw—it is only defended by its relics', he told Brown. 'If the Austrians do not arrive in time our P's and Q's are likely to be altered.' A month later, to the delight of the foreigners in Rome, the Austrians did indeed arrive, bivouacking just beyond the Porta del Populo, on their way to Naples, 'a magnificent and impressive scene' as one relieved British tourist found.[32] By then events in the external world scarcely impinged on Severn.

All that was left for Keats was to prepare Severn. On 19 February, four days before his death, he counselled him. Throughout his illness he had plotted its course, always one step ahead of his doctors. Now, remembering his brother Tom's death, he accurately predicted his own last moments:

He told [me] not to tremble for he did not think he would be convulsed—he said—'did you ever see any one die'—no—'well then I pity you poor Severn—what trouble you have got into for me—now you must be firm for it will not last long—I shall soon be laid in the quiet grave—O! I can feel the cold earth upon me—the daisies growing over me—O for this quiet—it will be my first'—when the morning light came and still found him alive—O how bitterly he grieved—I cannot bear his cries.[33]

Severn escaped by resuming his long letter to Maria. At last, he had heard from home with just the sort of family chitchat he wanted. His spirits soared as he gossiped on about meeting 'the Marquess Canova', his certainty that he would 'go very far beyond any painter I have seen so far', his plans for a series of paintings on Good Queen Bess's reign modelled on Raphael's pictures in the Stanze, descriptions of his delicious Roman meals ('maccoroni. It is like a dish of large white earth worms made of Flour with butter etc, very good'), the dowdiness of Roman matrons, and the superiority of all things English. Next day he lost himself again in his letter home with a lively account of the journey to Naples ('what I enjoyed most was the storms ... waves as long as your Shoreditch'); a rehashing of the familiar complaint of British visitors to Italy and elsewhere in the nineteenth century ('O! how I wish the English had this country. What a fine account they would turn it to. It is thrown away upon these idle beasts of Italians'); and an account of his skill at putting the natives down ('I should have liked father to hear me blow up a fellow just now in Italian. I gave it him in style'). About Keats he was almost offhand: 'Poor Keats cannot last but a few days more', he remarked. 'I am now quite reconciled to his state, yet I fear that I shall feel the miss of him.' He then nonchalantly corrected himself: 'But here everybody is kind so that I shall not feel it.' It was the purest wishful thinking.

Even as an attempt to justify his trip to Italy to a sceptical family, this over-stepped the bounds, as he well knew. Two days later he apologetically explained to Haslam: 'I have at times written a favourable letter to my sister—you will see this is best.' Now when he had no good news to tell Haslam and could not resort to the inventions offered to his family, Severn had little to say. In comparison to the packed four sides sent to Maria, he managed to fill only two and a half for Haslam, the writing large and looped, the letter signed with an inappropriate flourish. It cheered neither writer nor reader, despite Severn's pathetic plea at the end 'Think of me my dear Haslam as doing well and happy as far as—will allow.' 'Farewell—God Bless you', he concluded with unusual solemnity.

He had sat up with Keats for three nights, expecting the worst, holding him upright, afraid he would suffocate, frightened by the change in him. He could not paint and might well lose the travelling scholarship; but there was one great consolation and on this Severn was suddenly eloquent: 'Poor Keats keeps me by him—and shadows out the form of one solitary friend—he opens his eyes in great horror and doubt—but when they fall upon me—they close gently and open and close until he falls into another sleep—the very thought of this keeps me by him until he dies—and why did I say I was losing my time—the advantages I have gained by knowing John Keats—would to gain any other way have doubled or trebled the time—they could not have gained' he concluded incoherently, but tellingly.[34] He watched again on through the night of the 22nd. On the 23rd Dr Clark told him that the end was very close.

Perhaps it was the nurse who noticed a change in the late afternoon and called Severn, who was resting after the previous night's vigil. Keats, too, knew the change in himself. 'Severn—S—lift me up for I am dying—I shall die easy—don't be frightened—thank God it has come.' Severn helped him up to ease his breathing. But Keats was now too weak to cough away the phlegm that filled his throat and his breaths were slow and difficult. He sweated feverishly. Severn kept his head close until Keats begged him to move away. 'Don't breathe on me. It comes like ice.' But still Severn held him as the light faded and the hubbub outside in the Piazza quietened. He did not call Dr Clark. There was no need. He heard the bells sounding the hours around Rome as Keats held his hand tight for comfort. The breaths came more slowly. Just after 11 they stopped so gently that at first Severn thought Keats was sleeping.

Initially, he was consoled by the peacefulness of Keats's face as it relaxed in death, but then became distraught at the sight of the still, cold hands, an image which was to haunt him for months.[35] Someone, probably the nurse, ran across the square to fetch Clark, who now showed his mettle as a doctor. His immediate concern was with Severn. Clark tried to persuade him to rest, but to no avail. His high hopes of accompanying Keats to Italy had come to nothing, he had lost the friendship of the most extraordinary man he had ever known, and seen him worn out by the frustration of every ambition, consigning himself to permanent anonymity. His own future in Rome was full of anxiety, and he was physically and emotionally exhausted. Now that there was no longer any need to 'be firm' he broke down. Clark took him away the next day to his own house, where he and his wife did their best to take care of him. It was Clark, too, who set about the practical arrangements consequent on Keats's death, which Severn was too distraught to handle.

On Saturday, casts were made of Keats's face, hands and feet, probably by Gherardi, Canova's mask-maker. The eyes are sunken, the face emaciated, the nose painfully sharp. Severn eventually sent the wax mask back to Taylor but kept a plaster copy by him for the rest of his life. Clark then informed the Roman authorities of the death of a consumptive patient and persuaded them to keep out of the house until Keats's body had been removed for burial. On the Sunday, he, Dr Luby, and an Italian surgeon carried out an autopsy. Though it can only have confirmed what they had known since Christmas, they were appalled at what they found: 'they thought it the worst possible Consumption—the lungs were intirely destroyed—the cells were quite gone'. For Severn it was another sleepless night. While Keats was still alive, the need to get through each day saved him from thinking too deeply about the loss to come. Despite all he had witnessed, he was totally unprepared for his friend's death. Even two weeks later he found that 'the recollection of poor Keats hangs dreadfully upon me—I see him at every glance'.[36] He cut some locks of his hair and placed the unopened letters from Fanny Brawne and Fanny Keats inside the winding sheet over his heart.

The funeral was set for early on the Monday morning. This was the customary practice for burials at the Protestant Cemetery, to avoid offending local sensibilities. Some melodramatic accounts have subsequently been written of Keats's interment in a darkness lit only by flickering torches. He was, in fact, buried at 9 a.m. in the early light of a February morning in Rome. Nor was the practice of dawn burials immutable. Eight months earlier a young girl, Amy Synnot, had been buried at midday out of consideration for the advanced age and poor health of her father with a troop of cavalry at the ready 'in case any insult should be offered'.[37] In Keats's case there was another reason for completing the funeral early. Carnival, the most riotous of all the Roman festivals was in its third and busiest day on 26 February, and it was important to get to the cemetery and back before the streets off the Piazza filled with crowds waiting for the celebrations to begin at midday on the Corso. There the shops were full of carnival masks and costumes, balconies were decked with canopies, and scaffolds in place for onlookers who could not get a seat in the double rows of chairs set out on the pavements. To avoid this gaudy display, the modest funeral procession would have taken the back streets parallel to the Corso. Severn was too broken to be aware of the unusual bustle in the quarter.[38]

Though he later told Taylor that 'many English requested to follow him', Keats's funeral cortège was small, with just nine mourners. Only four had known Keats; the two doctors Clark and Luby, Ewing, and Severn himself. Though Richard Westmacott, a leader amongst the convivial young British sculptors in Rome, was there, the painters were not represented. Seymour Kirkup was in bed with flu. Nor did Vuillamy attend. In his place another young architect, Ambrose Poynter, came with his friend and travelling companion, Henry Parke, a favourite of Sir John Soane.[39] Wolff, the English chaplain at Rome, read the funeral service and, no doubt, behaved with the same 'unremitting kindness and attentiveness' as at little Amy's funeral the previous year. Few as the mourners were, they had mostly come out of fellow-feeling for Severn rather than Keats, of whom they knew little. Standing at the graveside Severn was acutely conscious of being 'the only personal friend present from amongst the little band of devoted friends the poet had left behind'.[40] To be there at all was a major effort. Clark, not Severn, remembered one of Keats's last wishes and instructed the gravediggers to lay turfs covered in daisies over the grave.

Severn and Clark returned through the festive streets to find that, in their absence, Signora Angelletti had brought in the police to begin the process of condemning everything in Keats's room. This triggered some difficult bargaining, largely handled by the doctor, who succeeded in getting the bill for reparations cut by half.[41] But it was Severn who saved the hired piano and with it the fine furnishings in the salon. Clearly Angelletti baulked at having to burn someone else's valuable musical instrument. And so both sides found it convenient to agree that Keats had never been in the salon. Perhaps because she felt small-changed or perhaps because it was her usual practice, she tried another way of squeezing money out of Severn. 'I had scarcely payd the shameful demand' for refurbishment, he remembered, 'when the brute of a landlady sent to me to pay for the crockery broken in my service & I was amused to find a long table covered with the broken crockery of what must have been all the parish.' Not for nothing was he a Cockney. 'I assumed to be in a mad rage & with my stick I dashed and smash'd everything that was on the table & singular enough I frightened the vile creature of a landlady & I never heard anymore about the crockery.'[42] In an exceptionally long life, this is the only recorded instance of Severn ever using physical violence. All the accumulated frustrations of the last few months lent power to his elbow.

His recovery was slow. On the day after the funeral he tried to write to Brown but had to give it up. A second attempt was barely completed before the weekly post left for England. The description of Keats's death is almost identical in both drafts. Severn was, he confessed, 'broken down from four night's watching, and no sleep since, and my poor Keats gone. ... They take such good care of me here—that I must, else, have gone into a fever. I am better now—but still quite disabled. ... I will try to write to you everything next post; or the Doctor will ... I cannot get on.' On the reverse of his first draft he drew a mourning figure, head bowed, eyes covered. The overlarge toes and massive arms suggest the undigested influence of the Michelangelos he had admired in the Vatican. But if his drawing skills had temporarily deserted him, his fractured prose was eloquent. Few subsequent writers have strayed far from his description of Keats's death.[43]

A week later, by writing a little at a time, he managed a fuller letter to Taylor, describing the days before Keats's death, his last hours, and the funeral. By then

(6 March) 'these brutal Italians' had almost finished the destruction of every-thing in Keats's room and the remaking of the windows, floor, and a door. The public burning of Keats's clothes and bedding in the Piazza was a humiliation to both Clark and Severn, and on it Severn focused all his sense of hurt and anger at Keats's death. The act was carried out without finesse. Handling the possessions of a dead consumptive was, in Roman eyes, a hazardous business fit only for 'savage brutes' who expected to be well paid for the risks they ran. 'These wretches . . . have inraged me day after day—until I trembled at the sound of every voice', he told Taylor.[44] But he saved Keats's books and papers, his pocketwatch and signet ring from the blaze. And letters came from England designed to bring him comfort.

Taylor wrote early in February apologizing for the stress which the stop-page of the account at Torlonia's had caused. Now he confirmed that, through Clark, he had arranged for all Severn's expenses to be covered and the account unblocked. He added the welcome news that Severn could have access to a further £100 if he needed it. James Hessey, Taylor's Evangelical publishing partner, sent two long, well-meaning letters, preaching not only the consolations that religion could bring to Keats and Severn but also the pressing need to save Keats's soul from eternal damnation. The proffered advice on how to effect a deathbed conversion arrived too late—fortunately. It came from a world far removed from Keats's sickroom.[45]

By contrast, Leigh Hunt made a superb effort of imaginative sympathy in thinking himself into both Keats's state of mind and Severn's painful situation. His letter, written on the back of another from Brown, takes up just one side with only minor corrections. If this suggests Hunt's usual mellifluous facility, that would be wrong: there is not a word too many nor any excess of sentimentality. Hunt was not the man to bring Keats conventional religious comfort, even if he had been open to it, but he had a sense of the meaning of immortality which was close to that which Keats had felt after Tom's death. He also understood Keats's overwhelming sense of failure at the end, the conviction that he had fallen short in everything that counted: love, fame, and the making of great poetry. And, as at earlier times of sickness, Keats had turned away from the comfort of friends, unable to read their letters or think about them. Unpromising ground though this was in which to offer consolation, Hunt found it.

He was himself beset with money troubles, worried about his brother John who faced yet another trial for libel, and he was ill. So, too, was his wife, though her long struggle with tuberculosis gave him the confidence to try to assure Keats he might still recover:

If he cannot bear this, tell him—tell that great poet and noble-hearted man—that we shall all bear his memory in the most precious part of our hearts, and that the world shall bow their heads to it, as our loves do. Or if this again will trouble his spirit, tell him we shall never cease to remember and love him, and, that the most sceptical of us has faith enough in the high things that Nature puts into our heads, to think that all who are of one accord in mind and heart, are journeying to one and the same place, and shall unite somehow or other again, face to face, mutually conscious, mutually delighted. Tell him he is only before us on the road, as he was in everything else; or, whether you tell him the latter or no, tell him the former, and that we shall never forget he was so, and that we are coming after him. The tears are again in my eyes, and I must not afford to shed them.

For Severn, too, Hunt hit on an idea full of comfort:

we are sensible [that your spirits] must have been greatly taxed. But whether our friend dies or not, it will not be among the least lofty of our recollections by-and-by, that you helped to smooth the sick-bed of so fine a being.

   God bless you, dear Severn[46]

Though the letter arrived several weeks after Keats's death, it greatly consoled Severn. He treasured it for the rest of his life, showing it to friends, making copies and ensuring its place in Monckton Milnes's biography of Keats. It also gave direction to his own uncertain sense of himself, for it was Hunt who first correctly predicted a future he had not foreseen when he set out for Italy with Keats. For all its anguish, his time of trial in Piazza di Spagna would later bring him rich rewards.

CHAPTER 7

'The Most Striking Year of My Life'

S EVERN always had remarkable powers of recovery. Little by little after the catastrophe of Keats's death he righted himself. He made new friends; he worked hard; he tried to take care of himself; and he began to look around him in Rome. He liked what he saw and found congenial people. Even as Keats was failing he had decided he wanted to remain there. His encounters with the works of the Great Masters renewed his ambition as a painter; in Rome, unlike London, he knew he could improve. And he quickly came to love the place. He had arrived there with fewer preconceptions than the usual traveller. He brought no overhang of schoolboy Latin, no compulsion to puzzle out old inscriptions or identify the sites of favourite scenes from the classics. In so far as he had any sense of ancient civilizations, he identified with Greek, not Roman, culture. He had some idea of what he might find in the Vatican or Capitol museums (though the reality, much more powerful than copies and engravings, overwhelmed him), but had thought little of landscape. Now he saw everything with a receptive eye: the city and its surrounding countryside became an inspiration. While some saw Rome as a melancholy place, where a race of pygmies conducted a subfusc existence among the ruins of an heroic past, Severn delighted in the coexistence of present and past. For the first time, he got an inkling of a relationship between landscape, nature, and people which would later take his painting in new directions.

He was seeing the city at the best of times, in an exceptionally fine Roman spring. As he went for a walk each day in the early morning sunshine, he was astonished by the flourish of new life in its ancient setting: 'It was a look of nature that I had never even dreamed of ... I could almost see the wild flowers grow, such progress they made in a single day & this being contrasted with the old antique walls & marbles, on & about which I watched the vegetation in its Italian luxury, in its brilliant freshness & perpetual novelty.'[1] Three years earlier,

Shelley had felt the same delight in 'The bright blue sky of Rome and the effects of the vigorous awakening of spring' as he climbed high up on the mossy ruins of the Baths of Caracalla, notebook in hand, to compose *Prometheus Unbound*.[2] Twenty years later Severn set out to recapture the sensation in *Shelley Composing Prometheus Unbound in the Ruins of the Baths of Caracalla*. The poet is in open-necked shirt, straw hat at his side, and fresh-blooming flowers at his feet, an innocent figure at home among the verdant relics, inspired by the freshness of the natural world and the quaint remains of an unthreatening past.

Severn's first letter home after Keats's death was to his mother, the only occasion on which he wrote directly to her from Rome. Though the writing is shaky, he did his best to reassure her, fixing on those details of his existence which might make it more accessible to his family in Mason's Court. The letter is much thumbed. No doubt it was passed around, discussed, and frequently conned by Severn's mother anxiously trying to imagine a life so far outside her own experience. He chose a good day on which to write and mostly kept up a brave face, describing a life of exemplary discipline and well-regulated diet. He was up at 7.30 every morning for breakfast 'with a kind friend'; walked for three hours a day; painted for eight; and read or studied Italian for two. He had also taken to the local diet. As a newly converted Italophile he could now dismiss English fare. 'I dine at a Palace (for every place is a Palace here) at 1 o'clock—have a bottle of wine which costs 3 half pence—I have not tasted beer for 4 months—this Wine is glorious compared with your muddy Beer.' In the evenings he contented himself with a bun and a couple of cups of coffee. He was, he said, 'looking quite fat and formidable'. He was 'a lucky dog', 'this place—the manner of living—everything seems to agree with me.—I am more equal to my studies than I was in England ... If I go on as I do now you will not very soon have me back again', he warned his mother.

On Keats, however, he could not write with equanimity. 'I cannot get him out of my head—never shall out of my heart—never—I often drop a tear to his memory ... I cannot write any further about my poor friends death—I cannot bear to think on it.'[3] Optimist though he was, as he laboured under Keats's dying charge to his friends to connive in ensuring his oblivion, Severn could not be confident that he would be remembered outside his immediate circle. He was caught, too, by conflicting feelings. He missed the poet's lively presence at the same time as he was obsessed by images of Keats dead. When he did something new and enjoyable he thought of the pleasure it would have given Keats. When the weather was changeable or he was depressed about his painting, 'then comes

Keats—Keats—to my mind I can see his poor face—and his poor still hands and I am no longer master of myself'.[4]

The self-styled 'Colonel' Robert Finch caught Severn on a bad day a few weeks after Keats's death and picked up a grim story.[5] Finch had a chequered past but a rich wife. He hung around in Italy, living in style, currying favour with influential friends and cultivating a showy, pedantic connoisseurship. A busy-body, and, on occasion, a liar, it was inevitable in the intimate Anglo-Roman society that he would come across Severn. Finch was also friendly with John and Maria Gisborne, who were anxious on their own and the Shelleys' account to know more about Keats's last days. They asked Finch for information. Though he had never met Keats he was happy to oblige. In working up a melodramatic account of what Severn told him, Finch characteristically curried favour with the living at the expense of the dead.

He began with a short account of Keats's passage to Italy 'brooding over the most melancholy and mortifying reflections; and nursing a deeply-rooted disgust to life and to the world, owing to having been infamously treated by the very persons whom his generosity had rescued from want and woe'. In the last bedridden days, said Finch, Keats's 'passions were always violent, and his sensibility most keen. It is extraordinary that proportionally as his strength of body declined, these acquired fresh vigour; and his temper at length became so outrageously violent, as to injure himself and annoy everyone around him.' In contrast, Finch had nothing but good to say about Severn, introducing him, with a typically heavy flourish, as 'a young painter who will . . . one day be the Coryphaeus of the English school'. 'He left all, and sacrificed every prospect, to accompany and watch over his friend Keats. For many weeks previous to his death, he would see no one but Mr Severn, who had almost risked his own life, by unwearied attendance upon his friend, who rendered his situation doubly unpleasant by the violence of his passions exhibited even towards him, so much, that he might be judged insane. His intervals of remorse too, were poignantly bitter.'[6]

By the time Shelley received Finch's tittle-tattle from Gisborne in the middle of June he had almost finished *Adonais*, his elegy on the death of Keats. Though he said that had he seen Finch's 'heart-rending account' sooner, he would have been unable to complete his poem, it was, in fact, exactly what he wanted, a confirmation that Keats had been the victim of the reviewers. Now he could add a preface attacking those critics who had 'hooted' Keats 'from the stage of life'. Finch's account of Severn also had its uses for here, by contrast, was an exemplar of 'the virtuous man'. Thus Severn's own overwrought witness, amplified by Finch's mendacity as messenger, unwittingly laid the foundation stone of his future renown as the devoted deathbed companion.

The way in which he had nursed Keats had already brought him acclaim in Rome. William Ewing and Seymour Kirkup had seen it for themselves and, no doubt, talked about it to their friends, as would Dr Clark as he made his rounds. Some, like Clark, knew and admired Keats's work. For most who did not, the romance of the story was enough: the promise of a young poet, who was beginning to make his name, cut short at the age of only twenty-five, and the willingness of his friend, a Gold Medallist at the RA no less, to subordinate his artistic ambitions to caring for the dying man. Severn was an attractive addition to resident English society in Rome; the circumstances of his first few months there only added to his appeal.

In all, there were a dozen British artists in Rome. The sculptors were more engaging than the painters. Alongside their presiding genius, John Gibson, was Richard Westmacott, who had arrived the previous year. His father was an Academician with a busy practice in London which he would eventually join. Lively and sociable, young Westmacott was a natural leader as well as a prankster. He and Severn had fun conducting mock séances to the irritation of Kirkup, already leaning towards spiritualism. Ewing, another sculptor, was stiffer and less confident. His best work, Severn thought, was done in the painstaking art of carved ivory. The most graceful of the sculptors was Richard Wyatt, as adept with his guitar as his mallet, while another, Thomas Campbell, went out of his way to be helpful to Severn.

Charles Eastlake, the leading British painter in Rome, had entrusted the care of his studio to Campbell when he returned to England on family business in the winter of 1820-1. At 12 Piazza Mignanelli on the southern flank of Piazza di Spagna, it was one of the best in Rome. When Severn found lodgings high on the Pincian Hill at 43 Via San Isidoro, Campbell offered him the use of the empty studio. But Eastlake returned in May, sooner than expected, and was put out to find a stranger at work in his prized quarters. Severn was sent packing, 'my tail between my legs'.[7] It was an unpromising start to what would become, from an artistic point of view, the most important of all Severn's friendships in Rome.

While Eastlake would become his artistic mentor, his closest friend was the painter Seymour Kirkup. Generous, shrewd, wise, and witty, Kirkup helped

Severn find his feet in Rome. He had arrived soon after Eastlake, a friend and classmate at the Royal Academy. His father was a diamond merchant and so he had no difficulty financing his stay in Italy. This made life easy but blunted his ambition. Though he had come to Rome intending to be a historical painter his efforts were spasmodic. His opinion on artistic matters, however, was worth having. He regularly contributed a lively 'Letter from Rome' to *Annals of the Fine Arts* and kept up a correspondence with Lawrence, Haydon, and others in London. Kirkup was more thoroughly at home in Italy than his fellow-artists, living with an Italian girlfriend, Maria, and never fretting over whether to return to England to pursue his career. Italy was his natural habitat. Now his familiarity with Rome, sociability, love of music, and delight in female company made him the ideal companion for Severn, as he struggled with loss and loneliness. They breakfasted together most days; Kirkup gave him 'a splendid paint box with everything'; installed a piano for Severn to play; and took up his cause. Though he could never replace Keats, 'his noble mind—his learning—his taste—and his good heart remind me of Keats—every one here seems to love him—and have something good to say of him ... this good little fellow—(for he is just the same size as Keats) has done me most essential service', Severn told Haslam.[8] Kirkup was also on comfortable terms with British aristocratic society in Rome and well placed to introduce his new friend to potential patrons. Though the age of the Grand Tour was coming to an end in the 1820s, a new elite kept Rome as their base, welcoming old acquaintances and visiting collectors wintering there.

The two leaders of British society were the Duchess of Devonshire and the Countess of Westmorland. The Duchess, a widow, senior in both rank and age, was the principal artistic patroness. She was close to the Vatican, which relied on her to bring the British to heel when they behaved disrespectfully in church. She paid for excavations in the Forum, held 'conversazioni' and kept a list of the 'clever men' at Rome, like Charles Eastlake. Nor did she ignore newer talents. She sent her carriage to pick up Severn and returned with him to his lodgings where she made encouraging noises. But though Severn told Sarah that, improbably enough, the Duchess reminded him of his mother and 'her kindness and condescension to me are very great', it was Lady Westmorland 'I look up to most'.[9]

Through her mother's uncle, Jane Huck-Saunders had inherited a huge fortune and gone on to marry John Fane, the 10th Earl of Westmorland in 1800. He was forty-one, she just twenty. For all his rough manners, he had a distinguished career in government serving as Lord Lieutenant of Ireland from 1789 to 1795 and later as Lord Privy Seal. Though her marriage gave the new Countess an entrée to the highest political and social circles it was not happy. After producing two sons and a daughter as well as looking after five stepchildren, she abandoned them all to set up independently in London. It was a bold move, destined to fail. She could attract raffish company—Byron first saw Caroline Lamb in her house—but not compete with the sober establishment of her stepdaughter, the Countess of Jersey. Her anomalous social position and the determination of her husband to have her committed for irresponsible conduct, forced her to spend much of her time abroad. Here she flourished, living in style in Rome in the winter of 1814, during the brief period in which English travellers to the Continent could feel secure again with Napoleon in Elba.

As one of the few wealthy hostesses around, she attracted distinguished visitors to her dinners, concerts, and balls. Samuel Rogers and the archaeologist Charles Cockerell were both regulars,[10] impressed by her powers as a conversationalist, brilliant, witty, and cultured, if exhausting. She had a genuine eye for artistic ability. Like the Duchess she picked out Eastlake as a coming man. In the winter of 1820–1 she restlessly cast around for new interests and, encouraged by Kirkup, found one in Joseph Severn. When she chose, she could be immensely kind and welcomed the challenge of a new cause to champion. She appreciated his looks, they shared a love of music, and she was taken with the romance of his tragic arrival in Rome.[11] To his astonishment, Severn soon found himself the protégé of the imperious and unstable but stylish and influential Countess.

Other aristocratic patrons also took an interest in him. He went to dinners with Lord Colchester and Lord and Lady Ruthven and got to know Lord William Russell, the younger brother of the 5th and 6th Dukes of Bedford. A pleasant, but ineffectual widower, he idled his time away on the Continent, consorting with artists on behalf of the 6th Duke, a substantial patron of the arts who lived high on the hog at Woburn Abbey.[12] Even more gratifying was Severn's first encounter with Sir George Beaumont, who was in Rome for the winter. Exposure to Rome's artistic masterpieces had made Severn conscious of the need to 'revolutionize' his approach and improve his technique.[13] He would take his easel to the museums and copy paintings that caught his eye. One day as he worked on an oil sketch of Rubens's *Romulus and Remus* in the Capitoline, painting 'with outrageous boldness' in an attempt to free up his brush,

Beaumont came over to talk to him. Severn, who knew of his friendship with Joshua Reynolds, peppered him with questions about the great man. Beaumont was delighted to reminisce and invited Severn to dinner.[14]

Later, Severn would work hard to acquire the patina of a gentleman. In his early months in Rome he could still be gauche at set-piece occasions. At Sir George's he found that the guest of honour was Samuel Rogers. Banker, poet, and art collector, Rogers was in Rome for the first time since his visit of 1814, which had inspired his long poem, *Italy*. Embellished with engravings by Turner, this became one of the great nineteenth-century bestsellers. Rogers himself was a throwback to the previous century, living a splendid bachelor existence in his richly furnished house on St James Place, adorned with the choicest art works. He knew everyone who mattered, took a delight in the exposure of human frailty, and relished waspish gossip, concealing beneath his tough old carapace a more permeable heart. He was in characteristic form at Beaumont's dinner, complaining that 'he had been twice applied to by Keats for money & that there [were] so many of these needy poets and aspirers that he could only shut his door'. Severn plunged straight in, suggesting he had mistaken one poet for another. Rogers stood his ground. 'This made me "flare up" as I knew it was a falsehood ... Keats was not only far removed from such "mean acts" as he called them, but also ... had no occasion being in possession of a small competence & I finished by expressing my regret that one Poet should thus speak of another.' Rogers liked Severn's spirit and gracefully withdrew the accusation. Beaumont was also impressed and invited Severn to stay at the house he was renting at Tivoli. There, he reminisced about Reynolds and Gainsborough, Romney, Lady Hamilton, and Nelson with a charm that enchanted Severn. 'I had a vivid picture of the world then rapidly passing away', he remembered. His only regret was that 'poor dear Keats' was not with him to enjoy these new friends. Unlike those Keats had known in London, they 'had the cherishing qualities, the embalming of suffering minds, they knew how to fall back upon hope'.[15]

Both Byron and Shelley, in Rome in 1817 and 1819, were dismissive of the English society they found there. Byron criticized 'the second-hand Society of half-pay economists—no pay dandies—separated wives, unseparated <u>not</u> wives,—the Starke—or Invalid—or Forsyth—or Eustace or Hobhouse travellers—as they are called according to their Manual' and kept out of their way. Shelley, equally well placed to cock a snook at aristocratic society, complained, 'The manners of the rich English are something wholly insupportable,

& they assume pretences which they would not venture upon in their own country.'[16] Severn, who lacked their elitist measuring standard, was far more susceptible to the attractions of his new social context. In the English aristocratic society in Rome he found his ideal. It was not just their taste and learning, or their generosity and openness to newcomers, but their moral character. They were practical and positive, a group of people who loved their neighbours instinctively and without cant. 'I soon found myself', he later wrote, 'in the midst not only of the most polished society, but perhaps the most Christian in the world I mean in the sense of humanity or cheerfulness of living rather for others than ourselves. This was a "treasure trove" to me as a young Artist.'[17]

Given the peccadillos of some of its members, his assessment may sound starry-eyed. But Severn was not the only one to recall the 1820s in Rome as a golden age. The tough-minded art critic and blue stocking Elizabeth Rigby, who later married Charles Eastlake, wrote in similar vein in her memoir of her husband. 'There was, no doubt, a higher tone in Rome half a century ago than there is or can be now', she concluded as Thomas Cook tours proliferated:

The magical city was more difficult of access, wealth was more exclusively in the hands of the better bred and educated, and people went for a longer time and with a more definite purpose. If, therefore, the Anglo-Roman aristocrats prided themselves on the exclusiveness which is now of the past, they admitted, in self-interest, the acknowledged votaries of letters and arts within the circle. And, generally speaking, all were seen to advantage in a city where learning, taste, and enthusiasm were the order of the day.[18]

This was the environment Severn had been taught at the Royal Academy to see as the perfect setting for historical painting.

He also saw a connection between the grace of the English community in Rome and the *genius loci*. The beauty of the climate, the attractiveness of the Italians, and their surroundings and a freedom from northern inhibitions liberated everyone to behave at their best. His early grasp of the interplay between Italian grace and English good breeding was encapsulated in a potentially unpleasant incident, which he later wrote up at length in his memoirs. He had been at dinner with the Ruthvens who, with their friends, were keen to see what progress he was making on *Alcibiades*. They set off up a narrow footpath towards the Pincio walking in file, the ladies at the front and Severn at the rear. He was horrified to spot higher up on the path a 'Roman gentleman' voiding his bowels and froze with embarrassment at the ladies' coming exposure to this unseemly encounter. Both parties carried it off well. The ladies continued their advance, the gentleman 'not in the least changing his position ... called up a most gentlemanly smile & took off his hat & made a distinct bow to each Lady with so much ease & grace & then to each of us gentlemen'. They passed on without comment. For Severn it was a striking lesson in the inhibiting effects of 'our Northern notions'. 'No doubt the English people I had been accustomed too [*sic*] would have made a difficulty, if not a row ... the ladies would have fainted and so on.' Here he found instinctive good manners on both sides in a distinctly unpromising situation. The defecating man became his talisman: 'if I had been an Ancient Roman I should have had to make a statue to him for the temple of the Goddess Fortune & it would have added to the various positions of the ancient Statues'.[19]

By late May English winter residents were moving on. Most years they left for Naples after the Easter festivities, but this time had already stayed longer than usual to enjoy the fine weather. William Ewing, too, the only one of Severn's new friends who had known Keats, was returning to England. Severn gave him a letter of introduction to Leslie and wrote to Taylor and Brown.[20] Left behind in Rome Severn, for one of the few times in his life, enjoyed solitude. 'During the hot weather the place is almost deserted,' he told Sarah, 'a great number of persons die—so that the place is thinned of people.' She had been so excited by his accounts of life there, with every house a palace and living cheap and agreeable, that she planned to join him. He was anxious to put her off. An English lady, he explained, could not live like a bachelor. She 'must have £400 a year at least ... you must have your servants—cooks—coach—or there is nothing for a lady here ... you can't walk about the places—you must ride'.[21] So Sarah remained where she was, as did Severn. The summer was cooler than expected. He worked hard on *The Death of Alcibiades*.

It was an ambitious composition. Anachronistically, he depicted Alcibiades as the epitome of the patriotic hero 'his face full of pain and fury for his country's wrongs', facing up to a hail of arrows from his enemies, his house on fire behind him. The assassins were Fuselian creations, one 'covering his neck and face from the sight of Alcibiades sword', another 'starting away with two blazing torches in his hands his face full of horror', and a third, having missed his mark, 'full of malicious disappointment'. In the bright Italian light, his palette was becoming bolder: 'the effect and colour is very new and strikes the eye much', he told Sarah. By early July the painting was virtually finished.[22]

Working on it had helped ward away gloomy reflections on the death of Keats. 'I am still completely unnerved when I look upon poor Keats's death, it still hangs upon me like a horrible dream', he told Brown in the letter he sent by Ewing early in May. While painting he could 'abstract himself' from his grief.[23] It was not only Keats that he missed but the support of his friends. Though he had faithfully conveyed Keats's dying wish for an anonymous tombstone, the responsibility of settling the epitaph was not one he could shoulder alone. He put the problem to one side, waiting to hear what friends in London thought. Apart from John Taylor, they took their time to get their minds round Keats's terrible legacy. In March, Brown had written saying how emotionally unprepared he was for the news of Keats's death. As the friend who had failed to answer Keats's call, he now worried about Severn. 'My solicitude seems transferred from him to you.'[24] It was not an idle promise even if, for a time, it appeared so.

From Taylor, Severn received a cordial but business-like letter, confirming that he could draw on the further £100 which had been collected to settle Clark's bill, pay Keats's funeral expenses and cover the cost of the redecorations at Piazza di Spagna. The rest of the letter was more awkward. Despite Keats's prohibition, Taylor had decided to write a memoir and wanted Severn's help. He had reasonable grounds for seeing himself as Keats's executor. He also had on his hands most of the original stock of Keats's last volume. While he believed that an account of Keats's short life was his due, as a commercially minded publisher facing hard times Taylor also wanted to stimulate interest and sales. Only Severn could provide all the details of Keats's last days. Taylor set out what he wanted: 'any particulars of our friend's life and conversation, giving me as nearly as possible the identical words used by him', a portrait done from life and a sketch of the grave, together with the death mask.[25]

Severn replied quickly on 16 May with a confused statement of his financial position. He would, he said, be obliged to draw on the whole of the £50 (not the £100 mentioned by Taylor) to repay a £30 cash advance from Dr Clark. The rest would go towards Keats's funeral expenses, for which he still did not have a precise account, ('here the English are looked upon as so great and honest—that they are very rarely applied to for money'). Subsidizing Severn's living expenses in Rome had not been the intention of Taylor's donors, but

Severn sweetened the pill by explaining that when he and Keats had set out together for Italy they had agreed that Severn would be responsible for one-third of their joint expenses. He had kept an account and would, he said, repay his share to Taylor, but not before the winter. This mix of scrupulosity and casualness would become typical of his financial dealings in Rome. Four years later he had still not repaid Taylor.[26] Nor was he straightforward about the memoir. His initial reaction appeared positive: 'I am very happy at what you tell me about your intended memoir of Keats—his beautiful character will astonish people—for very few knew it.' Though he was still too troubled to set down his own memories, he promised to pack up Keats's papers and send them to Taylor the following week.[27] But for over two months he did nothing and when he finally got round to arranging for them to go to London they went to Brown not Taylor.[28] It was a decision with significant consequences.

Why did Severn not make good his promise? He had every reason to be grateful to 'the good Mr Taylor',[29] who had kept him afloat in Rome, written regularly, and been punctilious in offering advice on Keats's epitaph. Nor was Severn concerned about going against Keats's prohibition of a memoir: it had been issued when Keats was at his angriest. Perhaps, too, Severn was unaware that in London, Brown was creating every obstacle he could to Taylor's initiative, persuading Hunt, Dilke, and Richards not to cooperate and deriding the publisher as 'a mere bookseller—somewhat vain of his talents, and consequently self-willed' and a man who 'neither comprehended [Keats] nor his poetry'.[30] Severn scarcely knew Taylor. Even if he had known him better, however, he would still have sent Keats's papers to Brown, for Severn clung to what he believed Keats wanted, that Charles Brown should be the arbiter in everything affecting his posthumous reputation. But he did his best to keep in with all the parties, writing warmly to Taylor and encouraging Brown to collaborate with him on the memoir. It was a characteristic Severn operation: muddled, but fundamentally good-hearted. It meant, however, that there was no early memoir. Brown continued to guard his territory, Taylor postponed the writing and eventually gave up. For nearly thirty years Keats was barely known as anything other than the tragic victim of the critics conjured up in Shelley's *Adonais*.

In later life Severn remembered the summer of 1821 as a time of calm and healing. The heat was less trying than he had feared, he was teaching himself Italian by studying the guidebooks, and he was happy to stay close to Keats's grave. His letters of the time suggest more volatility. He was sometimes ill and fretted over the lack of guidance from London on the epitaph. As consolation he went to the cemetery now and again to visit the mound under which Keats lay. He described it to Haslam:

I walkd there a few days ago and found the daisies had grown all over it—it is one of the most lovely retired spots in Rome—the Pyramid of Caius Cest[i]us and the Roman Walls are in the same place . . . you cannot have any such place in England—I visit the place with a most delicious melancholy—which on many occasions has relieved my low spirits—when I recollect that Keats in his life had never one day without ferment or torture of mind and body—and that now he lies at rest in a grave—with the flowers he so much desired upon him—and in a place such as he must have form'd to his mind's eye—with no other sound than a few simple sheep and goats with their tinkling bells—this is what I feel grateful for—it was what I pray'd might be—I did pray most earnestly that his sufferings might end there was not one grain more of comfort for him in this world . . .[31]

On another occasion, or so he recalled many years later, he went in the evening and found a shepherd sleeping there with his dog and a flock of sheep and goats round him. A shaft of moonlight picked out his face. Here was the personification of Keats's *Endymion*, the shepherd in love with the Moon.[32]

Though he was often out of sorts during his solitary summer in Rome, Severn was thinking more calmly about Keats. He borrowed a copy of *Endymion* from Dr Clark to remind himself of happier days. 'I begin to think of him without pain', he assured Brown in July, 'all the harsh horror of his death is fast subsiding from my mind—sometimes a delightfull glance of his life about the time when I first knew him—will take possession of me and keep me speculating on and on to some passage in *Endymion*.' To his delight he came across people in Rome who knew and admired Keats's poetry. It gave him the opportunity for 'many most agreeable conversations about him'.[33]

A couple of months after Keats's death he began a new portrait of him in oils. In this attempt at exorcism he wanted to drive out of his mind the persistent memory of the dead Keats. He chose to paint him as he had last seen him at Brown's house: a neatly dressed young poet, book on his knee, head in hand, his elbow resting on a chair at his side, absorbed in reading. The door to the garden is open; the atmosphere calm and happy. Severn's memories of the scene included Keats's prized print of Shakespeare on the wall and his habit of leaning on a chair arranged at an angle to his own.[34] He laboured at a major disadvantage, however, since he had by him only his impression of the death mask and the casts of Keats's dead hands and feet. While they helped him work out the exact proportions of Keats's features, they constantly took him back to the image he was trying to erase. Brown did his best to help, sending his lively drawing of Keats done in Shanklin in 1819, but the picture remained unfinished at the beginning of 1822: 'the face is too like him in the last half year of his life— but it reminds me of him much'.[35] He had caught the pose but not the likeness of the living Keats. He needed a copy of the life mask Haydon had made before he could finish his picture.

Severn's peace of mind was easily disturbed. In July there was a crisis. He had thought himself well on course with *The Death of Alcibiades* to meet the Academy deadline. Taylor had spoken to Hilton who told him the picture was required by September. Surprised though he was that the submission date had apparently been put back, he adapted to the more extended timetable.[36] Meanwhile, Maria kept watch at the Academy. Looking in one day she found a notice announcing that submissions must be made by 12 August, more than a month earlier than Severn was expecting. The news revived all his old paranoia about the enmity of the Academicians and Hilton, in particular. He detected a plot to deprive him of the travelling pension. Though his new-found friends and patrons were away from Rome, in London he could still mobilize an array of support from family and friends. He set about marshalling it, excitedly duplicating arrangements.

Ensuring the safe passage of goods from Rome to England, and artworks in particular, was not easy in 1821. They could be delayed by bad weather, held up at customs, stored or damaged in warehouses or mislaid en route. The British Consul in Rome, John Parke, kindly offered to send *Alcibiades* by King's Messenger. Still damp, the picture was rolled, packed in a canister and despatched to Ancona to meet the messenger while Severn's family were instructed to retrieve it from the Under Secretary of State's office and arrange for its framing, stretching, and varnishing. Haslam was also put on the alert. The instructions multiplied as the picture failed to catch up with the King's Messenger and Severn lost track of it.[37]

Added to the difficulties of getting the picture to London was Severn's anxiety about how the RA would receive it. On 17 July he wrote to Brown telling him the story of the Hilton dinner and Keats's warning to watch out for enemies at the Academy. Now Severn wanted Brown to approach Taylor and get him to use his influence on Hilton, recalling, in improbable language, what he claimed Keats had said:

'I am sure Hilton will take up your case on my account—now promise me you will do this—I have been long brooding over it and think this damned H—will keep you without your Pension—or try to do so—I know he will—so that this cu[r]sed dying of mine—will have been to your loss'—this was but a short time before his death.[38]

Brown leapt into action, showing those qualities which had made him indispensable to Keats. He contacted the family and William Bond in an effort to locate the missing picture; he mobilized friends to write to Severn and cheer him up; he wrote more frequently himself and got in touch with Taylor, despite the coolness between them. Shrewdly he also advised Severn against misjudging Hilton. Taylor, he told him, had said Hilton was not even present at the dinner to which Keats referred: it was his partner, de Wint, who had made the disparaging remarks.[39] The reminder was opportune. Hilton was known for his kindness. Indeed, had Severn thought about it, he was living in part on his charity. When Taylor approached Hilton, he made the sensible suggestion that James Severn should write to the RA Council explaining the delay and begging their indulgence.

Now Severn's father was determined to do his best by his son. In the summer heat and dust he toiled through the streets, enquiring after *Alcibiades* in unfamiliar government offices, and then on 10 August wrote to the Royal Academy asking them to defer their decision on the scholarship. The Council met on 30 August with Lawrence in the chair and Wilkie and Hilton amongst the five members present. They agreed to do nothing until 'the arrival of Mr Severn's Picture'.[40] Howard, the RA Secretary, wrote to tell Severn he was the only candidate and Lawrence assured Lady Westmorland, who had written on Severn's behalf, that the Academy appreciated his reasons for leaving for Rome so precipitously.[41]

As *Alcibiades* continued to elude a King's Messenger Severn almost lost interest. Brown wrote preparing him for the worst and advising him to abandon history painting:

The English are not worthy of the sacrifice of a man's whole life. Can you not read a lesson in the fate of our unhappy Keats? If you continue to study portraits, both in miniature and in oil, crowds will be led by vanity to your door, and you be rich and at ease in your mind: but if you were to paint a work like the 'Transfiguration', lo! Now—you must be poor in purse, and (what is worse) poor in spirit, and kick your heels in a great man's antechamber, and be favoured thro' your life with broils and anxieties.[42]

From Sarah he received a less palatable letter. She had always had a sharp tongue: this was a 'rattler',[43] ticking Severn off for all the troubles he had put his father to over the summer. But there was more to it than a lost picture. The Severn family was still recovering from an unexpected visit. Somehow, the arrangement with Haslam over young Henry's maintenance had broken down. The Roberts, his foster parents, turned up unannounced at Mason's Court in August, demanding the arrears due to them. It was the first that the Severns knew of the existence of Joseph's child.

Maria sent her brother an anguished letter. Mortified, he begged Brown to take charge of the affair and ensure that the Roberts ('they are most honest and deserving people') got paid. Above all he wanted them kept away from his family: 'pray look to this for me—I am fretted about it beyond measure—mind I have taken it out of my sister's hands—and begd her not to say or think of it more'.[44] For once, Maria did not obey her brother. She reported that Henry was 'going on well and is taken the greatest care of' but said nothing about her determination to have him christened. For a baby to remain unbaptized in the East End of London was a sure sign of illegitimacy.[45] To avoid this stigma she and probably Sarah made arrangements, not at St Leonard's Shoreditch, but the more out-of-the-way Church of St James on Pentonville Road. Here, close to Goswell Street, Henry was brought for baptism on 10 October. The child's parents were recorded as 'Joseph and Martha Sevarn', and Severn's profession shown as 'Artist', an exotic occupation by comparison with the cordwainers and printer in adjacent entries in the register. Though the misspelt surname could be a clerk's error, Martha sounds like an all-purpose female name chosen for the occasion. Whoever the mother was, it is most unlikely she attended her son's christening. No doubt Severn's stay in Rome was advanced as an explanation for the absence of both parents. After the ceremony Henry returned to the Roberts family. Sarah and Maria had done their duty by him. Nor did they make heavy weather of their brother's indiscretion. While at least one letter home that autumn was suppressed by his family, in what remains there is only the briefest hint that could relate to the incident.[46]

Having got through a difficult summer, Severn was cheered in September by the arrival of his Hoxton friend, Frederick Catherwood. Without a scholarship or any commissions, and having made no headway at the Academy Schools, Catherwood adventurously decided to study architecture on his own in Rome. There he picked up what he could in the company of other architects like

6 The christening record for Severn's illegitimate son, Henry, at Pentonville Chapel in the Parish of St James Clerkenwell on 4 October 1821

Henry Parke, Joseph Scoles, and Thomas Donaldson, a lifelong friend and later founder member of the Royal Institute of British Architecture.[47] Severn was delighted to show him the sights in 'mighty Rome', including Keats's grave. Although it was autumn the grave remained 'covered with grass and flowers...quiet and undisturbed—the place where he lies is one of the most romantic I know', Severn wrote to Brown, enclosing a sketch of the site. The visit inspired him with an idea for a small monument to Keats, 'a Greek seat—with his solitary lyre standing against it'.[48]

Catherwood was the first person Severn had seen since he left England who knew his family and could bring news of them. They got on well and planned to move together to a set of rooms being vacated by a Russian artist: '2 Studys 2 sitting rooms 2 bedrooms and a view all over Rome' for just £1 12s a month. Lady Westmorland had other ideas. She was contemplating an expedition to

Egypt and wanted Severn as her resident artist. He knew that Catherwood's skills were far more apt for the task and succeeded in diverting her attention to his friend. In no time at all, Catherwood was installed as 'Lord and Master' and, possibly, something more, at the Palazzo Rospigliosi where Lady Westmorland insisted on having someone to protect her from her servants.[49] At the end of the season, however, he was ready to move on, setting off for Sicily and Greece and finally arriving on his own in Egypt in 1824.[50] In his first test of managing Lady Westmorland Severn had handled things dexterously, keeping his independence but still obliging her. In October he went with his patroness for a week to Civita Vecchia to finish a miniature of her.

Meanwhile *Alcibiades* continued its uncertain course towards London. By the end of October, the King's Messenger was insisting that he had already delivered it to the Academy. 'A search was ordered and a tin case, all bent double and without any direction or intimation as to whom it belonged was found. It was opened, and lo, my "Dying Alcibiades"!'[51] On 31 October the Council agreed to lay it before the General Assembly. By then the picture was in a bad way. Leslie varnished it and did what he could to buff it up. The General Assembly met on 1 December. They were not unanimous in awarding Severn the scholarship, even though he was the only candidate. Fourteen voted in favour but as many as six against. Perhaps they were defending Academy rules: Severn had failed to get his submission in on time and pre-empted their decision by going to Rome on his own initiative. The Council was deputed to settle the details.[52]

Here Severn got much more favourable consideration. The scholarship was backdated to August when Vulliamy's term expired, and he was awarded £40 for the travelling expenses he had already incurred. All this was Hilton's doing. He knew better than anyone why Severn had left for Rome in such a hurry. Respecting Academy rules weighed little with him compared to the comfort Severn had been to Keats. When he got to hear of Hilton's role Severn was duly grateful; though sadly, in the succeeding years, he fell back on the old canard of Hilton's enmity, which made a good story.[53]

He had to wait three weeks for news of his success. With or without the scholarship, however, he had decided to prove himself as a historical painter. While he worked on the portrait of Keats in the autumn for his private satisfaction and painted miniatures to pay his living expenses, his major endeavour was *Alexander the Great Reading Homer*. He chose a vast canvas, 9 feet by 7, and began in serious fashion with a sketch in oils and a full-size cartoon. This was the painting, he hoped, which would make his name and fortune.

Early in December he received a letter from Shelley in Pisa enclosing a copy of *Adonais*. Clearly, Shelley had only a vague recollection of any previous meeting with Severn ('Dear Sir' his letter begins and ends rather formally 'Your most sincere and faithful servant'), though he offered a hospitable invitation to meet if Severn were ever passing through Pisa with 'the pleasure of cultivating an acquaintance into something pleasant'.[54] This made Shelley's glowing tribute to Severn in the Preface all the more unexpected. While *Adonais* reflected Shelley's genuine grief over Keats's death and belated recognition after the publication of the 1820 *Poems* of his measure as a poet, Shelley was also intent on portraying him as the delicate, sensitive artist persecuted to illness and death by the malice of the critics. The result, since *Adonais* was better known throughout the 1820s and 1830s than Keats's own work, was to perpetuate an image of a feminized Keats, 'a pale flower', weak and suffering.[55] Initially, Severn was less concerned with the misleading impression of Keats's nature which Shelley had given to the world than with the obscurity of his poetry. He was, of course, pleased about the existence of 'a tribute to poor Keats's memory' and found 'many beauties' in *Adonais*, some even finer than in Milton's elegy *Lycidas*, but his old anxieties about Shelley's restless mind were easily revived. 'Is it not a pity', he wrote to Brown, 'so much beauty should be scattered about— without the balancing of lights and shades—or the oppositions of Colours.—in this poem there is such a want of repose.—you are continually longing to know what he will be at.'[56]

He could not help but be impressed by the Preface, however. Here Shelley set up a deliberate opposition between the viciousness of the critics and the selflessness of Keats's last friend. He would, of course, wrote Shelley have the 'recompense which the virtuous man finds in the recollections of his own motives'. But then he found more to say about the young Severn:

His conduct is a golden augury of the success of his future career—may the unextinguished Spirit of his illustrious friend animate the creations of his pencil, and plead against Oblivion for his name.

Shelley had eloquently crystallized Severn's sense of his debt to Keats. Blinded by tears, he chalked the words up on the wall of his studio.[57]

For the rest, he remained in despair. 'I had desponded a little, for every night and morning this pension arose in my poor head the first and last thing. Yet no letter came. In the days I kept up my spirits by hard painting and never thinking of it.' By Christmas Eve, however, with no news from the Academy and far from home at the festive season, he felt sorry for himself. He went to have supper with his fellow artists but was too downcast to notice Westmacott's suppressed excitement over a letter from his father in London. Halfway through the meal the young sculptor called for a toast, 'Here's Severn, the representative of the R.A., and success to him.' Severn was overwhelmed, receiving the congratulations of his friends, exactly as he imagined his father would be doing in Mason's Court. On Christmas Day letters arrived from Henry Howard confirming that Severn had won the travelling scholarship and from Maria telling of James Severn's satisfaction at his son's success. Kirkup gave a celebratory dinner with 'a plum pudding that could only be equalled by my Mother's' and 'plenty of music'. For his family's benefit, he wildly exaggerated the size of his pension. £390 over three years somehow became 'nearly £500.0.0 ... £10 a year more than any other student has had' and the travelling expenses were doubled from £40 to £80.[58]

He was in sentimental mood when he sat down to write to his family on Boxing Day. Now, as he compared his present success with his early struggles, he saw his father as

the ground work of all these fine things ... no one knows so well as myself what he has felt for me—what he has suffered—above all that he could hardly find room to hope such a noble station in life—such a glorious prospect for me. Particularly where great fortune fine education—rank— and all the powerfull things have been against me—when I went first to the Academy a poor fellow without a soul to incourage me or a friend to cheer me except this dear Father and his little home of comfort and peace! How could he—or how could I—hope for me to be in Rome as the Representative of the Royal Academy with a pension—and such a prospect before me as perhaps no other man can boast.[59]

1821 had been an extraordinary year for Severn. It began in despair and ended in triumph. He had faced the most severe test of his life and come through— if only just—to discover a world of delight in Rome and access to a society beyond his imagining. Surrounded by greatness it was all too easy to believe that he, too, was touched by it. Thanks to the pension his immediate future was secure and he was sure now that he had the makings of a great artist. Thinking back on the ups and downs of this 'the most striking year of my life',[60] Severn was, more than ever, convinced that Keats had been the instrument of a benevolent Providence. Without him, he would never have got to Rome nor won the respect of patrons for the way he had cared for his friend. But the debt went much deeper. Keats had opened his mind not just to poetry but to nature and art. However improbable the friendship given their intellectual disparity, it had persisted, inspiring him as an artist and winning him honour. At the beginning of 1822 when the sense of loss was still keen and with it a gratitude for all that Keats had given him, he was certain that his new-won standing in Rome was essentially a tribute to his dead friend: 'you would be astonished' he told Taylor, 'at the interest the Nobility have taken in my affairs.—but I know it is as the Friend of Keats'.[61] He had found the essential identity of his life.

CHAPTER 8

The RA Pensioner

T HE award of the travelling scholarship reignited Severn's ambitions. 'I find such quietness—such time and desire, since everything help it— to proceed in my occupations.—that I shall ever bless the day I came here', he wrote to Brown on New Year's Day 1822. Less happily, it also confirmed his determination to be a history painter. The Academy would expect no less. Already he was thinking beyond *Alexander Reading Homer*, and had done a sketch for the first of a grand series of scenes from English history: 'The Britons proclaiming Arthur—King—when the Romans took their final leave of Britain' (as he imaginatively entitled it). They were to be painted 'in the Rubens style' and 'unite the Composition and pure expression of Raffaele to Romantic subjects'.[1]

The Academician William Collins, who arrived in Italy fifteen years after Severn, older and already established, had some sharp things to say about the impact of Italy on unformed artistic personalities. As his son, the novelist Wilkie Collins, recalled, it was his 'decided opinion that no artist ought to come to Rome until he had gone through a long course of severe study in his own country and had arrived at an age where his judgement was matured, as the great works there were of a nature either to bewilder a young unpractised student, or to possess him with the dangerous idea that from seeing such pictures only he had become at once the superior of his fellow-labourers at home'.[2] Given his susceptibility and the splendour of what he saw in Rome, it was not surprising that Severn initially succumbed to these temptations. Impressionable though he was, however, he was also perceptive and looked with a fresh eye at the work of a controversial group of German painters, the Nazarenes.

Despite his distaste for the Nazarenes' passion for Italian primitives, he was attracted by their delight in the Italian landscape, climate, and people and shared their idealization of Rome as the centre of medieval Christendom. It was the irresistible call of the south to the northern spirit and an impatience with strict academic training which had brought them to Rome in 1810. They settled eventually in the monastery of San Isidoro, living a congenial collegiate life and affecting the long coats and shaggy beards which earned them their nickname. The arrival of Peter Cornelius in 1811 gave new impetus to their work. When they won a commission from the Prussian Consul, Bartholdy, for a cycle of scenes of Joseph's life in Egypt, Cornelius insisted that they use fresco, by then almost a lost art. They found an old workman to teach them the technique and discovered in themselves the dedication for a demanding discipline.[3] Severn, who lived round the corner from Overbeck, the only Nazarene still at San Isidoro in 1821, loved the result: 'I could look at their pictures for ever.— it is said to be bad taste in me—but I care not.'[4] Others were not so sure: Eastlake had reservations while Wilkie would dismiss them as wrong-headed and anachronistic.[5] But Severn stayed true, enjoying Overbeck's melancholy company and the group's love of music. It was he who in 1827 introduced William Dyce, later known as 'the English Nazarene', to Overbeck. This fraternization with foreign artists marked Severn out. Though all congregated at the Caffè Greco and kept an eye on each other's work, the nationalities kept separate tables. In the cosmopolitan Roman art market they were all competing for patrons.

By comparison with the Italian, French, and German artists, the British were at a disadvantage. While the Italians got together at St Luke's Academy and the French gloried in a comfortable, well-regulated life at the Villa Medici, an offshoot of the Academy in Paris, the British had no one place where they could meet apart from the cafés, and nowhere of their own where they could study. They also lacked the tradition and sense of identity which bolstered the French presence in Rome. English painters had come in the late eighteenth century and been mesmerized. Though he painted little there, Reynolds stored up an encyclopaedia of visual images which informed his theory and practice for the rest of his life. Fuseli, too, discovered his own idiosyncratic vocation in Rome. In so far as a distinctive English painting style developed in Italy, however, it was in landscape, though of a distinct kind. For the generation fed on a love of Claude, it was the classical associations of the Italian countryside that appealed, not the vibrant colouring of contemporary life. During the twenty-year interruption for war, the tradition, such as it was, died out. The young painters who reached Rome after 1815 came with their heads full of Academy theory. Intent on becoming historical painters, they began by ignoring the life around them and going no further back than Michelangelo and Raphael for their artistic inspiration. Meanwhile, French history painters confidently held the field in Rome, while the Italians were the most visible and the Germans found their own distinctive way. Lawrence's triumphant visit in 1819 did something to raise the profile of the British artists in Rome as well as convincing him of the benefits for the young artist of a period of study there. Turner soon followed, and, though he was less visible, produced a mass of work. Other RA luminaries, like John Jackson, Francis Chantrey, and Christopher Moore, came in their train. While their distinguished presence reflected glory on the small British artistic community, the artists who lived in Rome remained to be judged not on the merits of occasional visitors but on what they could do themselves.

Severn was dismissive about his colleagues, at least in his letters to his father. While he thought the Italians and French 'very great in History' (though after a few more months exposure to the Italians, at any rate, he began to think them strong on design but weak on colour), he found the English 'but poor fellows—they are really nothing . . . Historical Painting is scarce known to the English painters here—they have no learning in the Art—no imagination. . . . If I like', he told his father, 'I may be a God in Painting here compared with the others . . . the English here look to me to come up with [the French and Italian history painters.]'[6] The statement was not quite as extravagant as it sounds. The British painters who had made it to Rome by 1821 were not a distinguished group, and of them all only Eastlake and Severn were to make a name for themselves—unlike the sculptors, most of whom had successful careers. In the succeeding years, however, the painters were enlivened by the arrival of more accomplished artists such as William Etty, Thomas Uwins, and Penry Williams, and extended visits by Collins, Wilkie, and Turner.

In 1821 only Eastlake and Kirkup, among the first to come after the Napoleonic wars, were reasonably established. John Bryant Lane, another of the early arrivals, supported by Lord Dunstanville, had turned up with the intention of executing a historical painting that would astonish the world. He embarked behind closed doors on *The Vision of Joseph*, which moved ahead even more slowly than Haydon's *Christ's Entry into Jersualem*. The eventual disaster of its unveiling and Lane's exclusion from the papal territories on grounds of blasphemy was still in the making when Severn arrived. James Atkins, who came to Rome two years after Lane, was another historical painter with an aristocratic patron, in his case the Marquess of Londonderry. Richard Evans, quarrelsome and unclubbable, had had to look more widely for support. In London he painted backgrounds and some of the drapery for Lawrence's portraits before he got a commission from John Nash for Raphael copies for his newly built house in Regent Street. To help him get to Rome Lawrence also paid him to do copying in the Vatican. Richard Cook, another undistinguished member of the colony, was, like Kirkup, able to pay his own way.

Whatever their talents, they formed enough of a nucleus to be conscious of the disadvantages under which they operated in Rome. With no School of their own they were obliged to beg occasional admission to the Italian and French academies to keep up their drawing skills. The Italian academies were already crowded and it went against the grain to fall on the mercy of the French. Though Eastlake had an open invitation to work there, others were outraged at 'the oppressive idea of owing any part of our education, as artists, to the liberality of foreigners, and more particularly to the French, who cherished against us at that time all the smothered resentment of a baffled enemy'.[7] There were, nonetheless, practical advantages in cooperating. Italian models, though good, were expensive. Most of the English artists had come through the Academy Schools and knew the benefits of studying together as a break from the loneliness of their studios. For educated visitors coming to Rome, the world capital of art, the absence of an English academy was shameful, depriving the nation's artists of their rightful place in a society of foreigners which, in all other ways, the British confidently dominated.[8]

Earlier attempts to organize such an institution proved fitful. An Academy set up by sixteen English and Scottish artists in 1750 lasted only five years, and though the more substantial British presence in Rome in the late 1780s campaigned successfully to ensure that works of art could be exported duty-free to the United Kingdom, by 1817 there was neither the energy in Rome nor the interest in London to capitalize on the pope's offer of suitable premises for a British academy. What tipped the scales four years later was the presence of Eastlake, Severn, and Westmacott. Together they brought leadership, drive, and enthusiasm to the idea of matching the French in Rome.

It began simply enough in December 1821 as a way of sharing the costs of a model one evening. Just 'under a dozen' of the painters and sculptors attended the first session, with only Lane, true to his misanthropic form, keeping away. Expectations were high. 'Who knows but that our little beginning may lead in time to something of consequence', Westmacott reported enthusiastically to Colonel Finch.[9] Eastlake kept Lawrence in touch with developments.

Richard Evans was another who later claimed credit, and it is likely that in their early days the artists gathered in his studio.[10] By March 1822 they were meeting in more splendid premises, Severn's new lodgings at 18 Via San Isidoro, on which he had had his eye since the previous autumn. In Rome Severn always chose spacious quarters which he could rent out or share with friends. Now he had six rooms, three on the sunny side and three, including his studio, 20 by 30 feet, with a northern light. Opposite it was his 'library' and beyond that his bedroom with a view 'all over magnificent Rome'. And there were balconies and an observatory too. The Academy began to meet in a large room next to his studio, paying him £9 a year (or so Severn told his father). He had already acquired a skeleton and was expecting a corpse 'from which we are determined to be perfect in Anatomy' after dissecting it in one of his 'lofts'.[11]

By the end of March he had completed thirty-two figures in his evening studies: a year later he had added fifty more. 'How delighted my Father would be', he told Sarah, 'to see the first and the last—what a progress I have made.'[12] Working alongside his fellow artists boosted his confidence: 'no one can approach me in these Academy studies,' he boasted to his father, 'when the Academy breaks up of an evening the artists all come around me to look at the evening's work— and what I enjoy is that I can draw in every style'.[13] It was not, as he knew, the whole story. He was more aware than he admitted of the need for improvement and conscious that he could only achieve this by learning from better artists than himself: 'to know a parcel of inferiors is the sure way to become vain and proud and selfish and to go back from oneself'.[14] One name among the artists in Rome is rarely mentioned in his letters home: Eastlake. Severn, who got to know him well in the nascent academy, discovered a thoughtful, self-aware, proficient artist who dominated the British colony in Rome in the 1820s.

Charles Locke Eastlake, born within a few days of Severn, had had an altogether easier route to Italy. The son of a successful Plymouth solicitor, he went to a good local grammar school and, briefly, Charterhouse. He chose the RA Schools rather than university, however, after spending time as Haydon's first pupil. Admitted to the Academy in March 1809, Eastlake attended assiduously, taking careful, if critical, note of Fuseli's lectures. As an aspiring history painter he laboured for two years on *The Raising of Jairus's Daughter*, studying authentic backgrounds and working his way through a thirty-four-volume history of Jewish funeral rites, in Latin. His next work was a portrait of Napoleon on board the *Bellerophon* in Plymouth harbour waiting to be transported to St Helena. Having seen a sketch Eastlake had done of him, Napoleon obligingly came out to stand on deck while Eastlake painted from a nearby boat. Five Plymouth gentlemen paid the phenomenal sum of 1,000 guineas for the painting, which they then toured around the country. One way and another, Eastlake did well out of Napoleon. The sale gave him the money to set off for the Continent just at the time when Napoleon's exile was opening it up to young artists and adventurous travellers. He left in September 1816, arriving in the fortuitous company of a young Prussian tutor, Carl Bunsen, who would soon become a major cultural force in Rome.

In Italy Eastlake's spirits expanded. He came for a year but stayed for fourteen. Shy and old beyond his years as a youth, he now moved more confidently in society, enjoying the easy commerce between patron and artist in Rome and the company of the cognoscenti. He quickly developed an interest in landscape, spending hours in the sun sketching at Tivoli as he revolutionized his palette. Where Eastlake led, others followed. He set both trends and standards in the British artistic community and liked nothing better than talking about art and discussing technique. Lesser lights found him aloof. Others, like Uwins, Etty, and Severn, whose opinions he valued, owed much to him. In 1821 Eastlake was the only one of the painters to get a commission from Sir George Beaumont. It was for a portrait called *Sonino Woman tending a Wounded Brigand*. Though the subject was a curious one for the priggish young Eastlake, it was of a piece with his fascination with the darker side of Italian life. His translation of Bartholdy's *History of Secret Societies in Southern Italy*, published in 1821 by John Murray, kept his name before the British public. Nor, despite his dread of a return to the London art market and the parochial demands of its patrons, did he neglect the kingmakers at the Academy. In the meantime he moved in Roman society with a sureness which Severn learnt only by degrees, but was conscientious about the well-being of his fellow students.

With Eastlake's leadership and Severn's enthusiasm the small 'Academy' flourished. Though Lane and Evans remained prickly, Severn praised the openness of the rest, their respect for each other's opinion and willingness to take criticism of their work: 'the Friendship among the English Artists in Rome is a thing talked of here by all'. At carnival that year they made their presence felt, behaving badly, pelting each other with confits, joining in the battle of the tapers, kicking up a row in the theatre, and breaking down the partitions between the boxes.[15] The drollery could have artistic consequences. Eastlake was almost certainly present on the evening they were disturbed in their studies by a cry from Severn's old housekeeper that there were thieves in the house.

Their model leapt down from his dais and set off down the street wielding a big stick. 'It turned out to be a mistake—but the family who live under me were much alarmed.—and a Lady Countess who is a beautifull Musician—stood at the door wringing her hands in great frights and crying.' In his haste, the model had forgotten to put on his clothes. He returned shamefaced and naked to the relieved laughter of Severn's distinguished neighbours.[16] The vision of the heroic nude model in action stayed with Eastlake. Three years later, with a commission from the Duke of Devonshire, he chose as his subject the Spartan warrior Isidas, rushing naked but god-like from the bath to take up arms against the Thebans. The painting was a sensation at the Academy exhibition in 1827 and, despite Eastlake's absence abroad, won him election as an Associate of the Royal Academy.[17]

Useful and agreeable as it was, the young academy was always likely to aim higher than a self-help club for British artists in Rome. In the summer of 1822 Sir William Hamilton, the art-loving British Consul in Naples, was persuaded by Westmacott to make a donation to the new body, and Severn, who was in Naples over the summer and early autumn, was deputed to collect it.[18] Hamilton's support did not come without strings. He wanted it to lead to the establishment of a permanent institution and looked to the artists in Rome to mount an appeal there and in Florence and Naples to raise an endowment. The suggestion led to a lively debate. Some, like Evans, resented the prospect of living on charity. Others thought longingly about the equipment it would buy; casts, a skeleton, and seats and lights of their own. When the Duke of Devonshire gave a further £100 Severn began thinking of the grander possibility of finding a home for the academy. But Eastlake urged caution and the money was deposited at Torlonia's while they worked out what to do. Establishing an academy in Rome would not be easy when none of the artists knew how long they would stay there. The answer seemed to lie in securing some form of authorization from the Academy in London for their continued existence. As the RA travelling pensioner, Severn was asked (or perhaps volunteered) to write on behalf of the group to the President.

He wrote with feeling about the need for a regular establishment: 'we wish to prevent to others a recurrence of the inconvenience which we have indured at our beginning in Rome. Bad models—bad places—and a difficulty of admission are the drawbacks we have obviated by this Academy.' Conscious of the differing views of his fellow artists, however, Severn could only throw out vague suggestions and look for guidance from Lawrence and the Academicians on whether they should try and raise a public subscription ('Some few of us fear to have our quiet disturbed by any Public interference'). He also angled for what he described as 'the sanction' of the RA, a mark of recognition which would give the body in Rome enough status to look the French and Italian academies in the eye. 'At present as Englishmen we cannot meet together without being noticed;—and it is a little pain—tho' no interruption—that the place and manner of our meeting—should not be more in character with the English Nation.'[19] Much as Lawrence welcomed the initiative of the British artists in Rome, his reply was careful. He had not yet had the opportunity to put Severn's letter before the General Assembly, nor could he suggest a plan 'in ignorance of many local circumstances which must materially influence [its] arrangement'. A notoriously poor financial manager himself, Lawrence urged 'Prudence and Moderation' but hoped 'that in some way or other, though on a more limited scale, the English Academy at Rome may yet vie in real usefulness & Dignity, with the other foreign Institutions of that beloved City'. There was both a sweetener and a sting in the tail of his reply to Severn. Lawrence would give £50 to the new Academy, 'payable to the order of my greatly esteemed Friend Mr Eastlake to whom I beg the kindness of you to present my best Regards'.[20]

Eastlake quickly picked up the hint that Lawrence would rather do business with him. Now both he and Severn kept up the correspondence. It was their first exercise in bureaucratic management. Eastlake's letters show that he already had the makings of a masterly arts administrator; Severn's, in best copper plate, brim with enthusiasm but expose his unfamiliarity with high politicking at the Royal Academy. Despite Lawrence's caution, he came up with ever more ambitious schemes, suggesting the acquisition of a building with studios and accommodation for twelve or even twenty young artists selected by the Academy in London to come to Rome for four years, with extra space for exhibitions of the work of the British artists every one or two years.[21] Lawrence did not reply.

The subscriptions to the infant Academy accumulated: £200 came from the British Institution and a £50 annual grant from the RA (the maximum it was allowed to give to any one cause in a single year). Even Eastlake began to think of permanent premises ('if we were afraid at first of doing too much we [are] now afraid of doing too little').[22] With so much in the bank some bureaucracy was needed. Severn became an unlikely treasurer and Eastlake secretary to a committee including Gibson, Westmacott, Kirkup, Lane, and Evans. Trustees were appointed in London to manage the subscriptions; a circular was prepared in Rome and published in the *Literary Gazette*; and George IV, prompted by Lawrence, contributed £200 from the Privy Purse. Still nothing was done about a home for the academy. As a much more modest measure, admission to the drawing school was made free. Even that annoyed those concerned about lowering the entry standard.

A crisis arose when Eastlake discovered that they were getting far less than they might on their deposits at Torlonia's. He explained the problem to Lawrence:

> Mr Severn has hitherto been treasurer but it is no ill compliment to him to say he is fitter for the artist's portfolio than that of the accountant, as much might be said of many others. To remedy such evils in future it has been judged best to appoint a respectable person, for a proper compensation, to direct the difficult department we have none of us time or ability to undertake.[23]

Lawrence sympathized with Severn's frailties, though in lofty style: 'believe me you could not have written to a Correspondent more quick to see the difficulty of converting Artists into men of business than myself . . . I cannot wonder therefore if Mr Severn has failed to realise his own intentions of making the best possible Treasurer, and finds to the cost of the latter, that the man of Taste and Fancy is not so easily subdued.'[24]

A year later the British Academy was on a secure financial footing. Its relationship with the Royal Academy in London, however, remained delicate. Though Lawrence was ready to refer to the Royal Academy as 'the parent body', the connection between London and Rome was kept deliberately vague. While the organization in Rome aped some of the practices of the Royal Academy, such as the appointment of Visitors, of whom Joseph Gott was the first, it could not use the prefix 'Royal' nor call itself a branch of the Academy in London. For those with ambitions the lack of transparency was cause for anxiety. Eastlake claimed to speak for all his brother artists, but clearly had himself in mind when enquiring of Lawrence in December 1823 whether the Academy's reservations about the new body in Rome might debar its members from eventually becoming Academicians. More fundamentally, however, the arm's length relationship maintained between the Roman and London academies was indicative of a lack of cultural confidence and suspicions about the greater ease of life in Rome. Ultimately, the British would never lay claim to match the pretensions of the French in the world's art capital. Nor would the Academy extend its formal protection to those with the good fortune to be in Rome, where, in the Italian sunshine, patrons were numerous and, it was thought, less demanding than at home.

The Academy in Rome kept going after a fashion into the twentieth century but never regained the exuberance and sociability of its early days.[25] With Severn's withdrawal from the management of its affairs it lost some of its early spirit and ambition. By the time his RA pension came to an end in 1824 the evening classes had outlived their usefulness for the founder members. Now they found inspiration outdoors and the collegiate support and advice they needed in more informal groupings or in the company of the established artists coming to Rome.

In the spring of 1822, however, the pleasure of the evening gatherings in Severn's lodgings and the high jinks at carnival were an agreeable antidote to his labours on *Alexander Reading Homer*. He persisted with it for two and a half long years. Fortunately, as the RA pensioner, he could learn his craft slowly and, as with *Alexander*, make mistakes. In 1825 he decided to paint it over. Momentarily, he thought of another classical subject to fill the large canvas, 'Priam supplicating Achilles', but was easily dissuaded by his friend Thomas Uwins, who urged him to play to his strengths and paint women instead.

With £130 a year from his scholarship, Severn was comfortably off in Rome. Another young man about town, Henry Coxe, calculated in 1815 that a gentleman could easily live there on £150 a year provided he did without a carriage.[26] As the RA pensioner and frequenter of aristocratic drawing rooms, however, he was conscious that he needed to keep up a certain style. Not only had he moved into grander lodgings, he also enjoyed evenings at the opera and invested in new clothes. 'You must know', he told his brother Tom 'that I am quite a Buck at last—I found myself too singular in not being so that when I dine out I look as smart as any.'[27] But though he was able to settle some of his family debts—in July he arranged for £30 to go to his sisters 'to acknowledge their kindness'—Taylor remained unpaid and Haslam was still not being reimbursed for the costs of young Henry's maintenance.[28]

A sketch done about this time by Seymour Kirkup more than confirms Severn's description of himself as a young buck. As affectionately drawn by his friend, Severn's regular features show to their best: well dressed, bright-eyed, curly-haired and almost feminine, he has the glamour of a matinée idol. The portrait contrasts with a self-portrait, probably done around the same time, of a less confident, more questioning figure seated at a keyboard.[29] Making it in

Rome had been a struggle, but by July 1822 Severn was confident enough to pass on his accumulated wisdom to his brother Tom to help him find a quicker way to acceptance in the best society. Spelling, writing, a knowledge of geography, good manners, and correct grammar were all the hallmarks of a gentleman he assured his brother, encouraging him to apply himself.[30]

It cannot have come as a surprise to his family in the spring of 1822 to learn that Joseph was in love and had hopes of making an advantageous marriage. Marriage as a means of social advancement was unusual among the young British artists in Rome. Some, like Gott, who came to live with Severn later in the year, arrived with an English wife and family in tow and struggled to support them there. Others, like Gibson and Etty, were lifelong bachelors or, as with Uwins and Eastlake, bided their time before enjoying the comforts of marriage in late middle age. Yet others struck up liaisons with local girls. There was no disgrace in Seymour Kirkup openly living with his Maria. There were even rumours that Eastlake had some romantic involvement, while the shy William Ewing may have had a girlfriend in Rome: 'If you ever see Vittoria . . . tell the poor girl I do not forget her', he begged Severn in a postscript to his letter after his return to England.[31] Though Severn, who was never happy without female company, could have set up with a mistress, he chose a different route. Perhaps his experiences in London made him wary of further involvement with the demi-monde; certainly, in the social circles in which he now moved he saw an opportunity. If there was not passion, there was affection in his new relationship. For over two years he played the part of the lover.

His object was Maria Erskine, the younger of two daughters who lived with their widowed mother in Rome. She came of Scottish gentry and was the niece of the Lord Elgin who had brought back the Marbles from Greece. Severn was smitten from the first: 'I said to myself "Take care Master Joe, you will lose your heart, you had better not trust yourself with them." ' He admired the sisters' English beauty and cultivated manners while their mother was a kindly, Christian lady with a welcoming home.[32] In the spring of 1822 he was seriously ill with digestive problems, which kept him in bed for several days under the care of Dr Clark after he had collapsed in the street. Consoled by regular airings in the carriages of Lady Westmorland and Mrs Mostyn, the daughter of Samuel Johnson's great love, Mrs Piozzi, he decided to follow Dr Clark to Naples for the summer. Mrs Erskine invited Severn to accompany them on the journey. Together they braved the dangers of the Appian Way, sitting up drinking tea to keep awake when a wheel on their carriage broke in the Pontine Marshes.

7 Portrait of a young lady, Maria Erskine (?), done in pencil on the reverse of Severn's self portrait

They peered warily at enormous toads 'loathsome beings' crawling around in the malarial swamps, and talked. By the time they reached Naples he was 'desperately in love' and confident of Mrs Erskine's approval. He had made 'a lucky hit'.[33]

Initially, he stayed with Lieutenant Cotterell, learning that, after a brief rally in the Neapolitan sunshine, his sister had died not long after Keats. Then Severn moved up to the Monastery of San Martino to escape the heat in the city, making copies of the Ribera frescoes. He might have painted the stupendous view of the Bay of Naples from the terrace but was shocked to discover that he needed a permit from the Neapolitan authorities. Instead, he moved on to share the summer quarters in Sorrento of John Crawford, one of his supporters in Rome. The Erskines quickly followed.

For Severn it was a momentous summer. He found a new direction in his art, he was in love, and twice again came close to death. While bathing off Sorrento he was only saved from drowning by some fishermen; and then, on an expedition to Paestum, narrowly escaped being shot by bandits. He and the Erskines had gone by sea with a manservant to carry their picnic up to the temple precincts. Here Severn set up his easel and began sketching. He noticed some ruffians taking potshots at a marker knocked into one of the columns of the Temple of Neptune and politely asked them to move on. Though they still hovered, squinting critically at his canvas and eyeing the picnic, Severn took time to notice that the porter had disappeared. Alarmed, he shepherded his ladies down the rocky incline to the shore where they found him cowering in the boat. Safely home, they soon heard accounts of the same bandits smashing the palette of a French artist in his face the previous day. On the next, two English visitors, travelling ostentatiously by road, were killed by them in a shoot-out. Severn could only ruefully conclude that he and the Erskines had escaped the same fate because 'the Brigands thought I was a poor painter & these my Mother and sisters'.[34]

Though Naples was 'hot enough to roast St Lawrence without a fire' and the Neapolitans no more than 'dogs and idiots' except in their love of music, the landscape of the Bay of Naples delighted him: 'its Gardens—its Mountains—Grottos and the Sea—an Inchantment which would restore anyone to health', with Sorrento 'one of the loveliest places under the heaven's—cool and abounding in romantic scenery'. It tempted him to try some landscape sketches, thinking about the pleasure it would give his father and musing equivocally to Tom on the new direction in his painting. 'This beautiful place has changed many history painters into landscape painters—I hope it will not be my case. The scenes are irresistible—I must try my hand.'[35] Sitting on the terrace of Crawford's house in Sorrento with a view of Naples and Vesuvius 'and a sky ever without cloud' he also produced a series of watercolours. Two, a portrait of Falstaff and another of Rosalind and Celia, were inspired by Shakespeare, one by Dante, and a fourth by Keats, 'Some Greek Shepherds Rescuing a Lamb which is being carried off by an Eagle' from the 'Hymn to Pan'. In Rome, where he returned at the beginning of November, he worked it up into an oil painting (which would become his father's favourite picture) and painted a double portrait from *As You Like It* with the Erskine sisters as his models. And he wrote a duet to sing with Maria, choosing as his text the Act II love scene in *Romeo and Juliet*. Though his romance had still not come to a conclusion, his hopes remained high and he continued to spend happy, domestic evenings with Mrs Erskine and her daughters: 'it would be a great thing for me to be allied to a Noble family who would care for me & help me through the World'.[36]

Severn also created a family life for himself by inviting Gott to share his lodgings. Joseph Gott, seven years older than Severn, and a Yorkshire man, had been apprenticed to John Flaxman. Though he joined the RA Schools as early as 1805 and won a silver medal the following year, he then withdrew, returning in 1819 when, alongside Severn, he won the Gold Medal for sculpture. Lawrence encouraged him to go to Rome, giving him a small pension to get him started. Gott moved into Via San Isidoro with his wife and two daughters while Severn was in Naples. He was a gentle man much liked by the circle in Rome (the Duchess of Devonshire had a particular fondness for him) and a sympathetic companion for Severn. Bravely, he avoided the neoclassical style favoured by Gibson, Wyatt, and Westmacott, sticking to his own more intimate ways and working on superb terracottas of animals and children. Severn was sure that Keats would have been 'so much pleased' with Gott's sculptures. Mrs Gott was a welcome addition too: she 'prepares all the Meals in the house and we all eat together.—this is like being at home to me—we have an English pudding every day'.[37] Like many new arrivals, however, Gott quickly came down with a low-grade Roman fever and was unable to work for four months. Severn, too, was often ill with a recurrence of gastric troubles. The winter was 'a horrible one'.[38] He struggled with his pictures of *Falstaff* and *The Greek Shepherds*, hoping they would be ready in time for the RA exhibition in 1824, and lacking the energy to apply himself to much else. In particular, despite some optimistic promises to Brown, he had still not put up a headstone on Keats's grave.

The long delay was highlighted when Severn got involved early in 1823 in Shelley's burial rites. Shelley had drowned in a boating accident in the Bay of Lerici on 8 July 1822 on his way home from Leghorn, where he had gone to greet Leigh Hunt and his family on their arrival in Italy. Hunt had come to set up a new publishing venture, the *Liberal*, with Shelley and Byron. As with so many of his domestic arrangements, his journey was disorganized. He, his six children, and pregnant wife, Marianne, took seven and a half months to get from London to Leghorn. With Shelley's death, the point of their journey was destroyed almost as soon as they arrived, leaving Hunt to persevere on the new publication in the increasingly uncongenial company of the less-than-committed Byron. Both attended the cremation of Shelley's remains on the beach at Viareggio dramatically choreographed by a relative newcomer to the Shelley circle, Edward Trelawny. Mary Shelley wanted her husband's ashes interred in the same grave in the Protestant Cemetery in Rome as their much-loved son, William or Will-mouse, the enchanting, blue-eyed, fair-haired child whose sudden death in Rome in 1819 had blighted their stay there. The urn was brought to Leghorn and consigned to a merchant in the town who sent it to his business agent in Rome, John Freeborne, a wine merchant and acting British Consul. It remained in his vaults for the rest of the year having arrived at an unpropitious time. Fraught negotiations had gone on in 1821 with Cardinal Consalvi over the lack of protection for the Protestant Cemetery. While he refused to spoil the view of Caius Cestius's Pyramid by enclosing the old ground and forbade the planting of any more trees, agreement was eventually reached on opening a new walled cemetery alongside the old. The original site closed to further burials in August 1822. Shelley's ashes could not now be placed in his son's grave.

Troubled by the delays, Hunt thought naturally enough of Severn. As he winningly wrote to him: 'You have nothing, dear Severn, but funeral tasks put upon you; but they are for extraordinary people and excellent friends, and I hope all our prospects will brighten again before we join them.'[39] Severn promised to arrange things as soon as he could leave his sickbed and for once acted with despatch. By 10 January 1823 he and Freeborne had secured permission from the authorities to exhume William's body and rebury it with Shelley's ashes in the new cemetery. The committal was fixed for 21 January and attracted a small but distinguished turnout. It did not, however, go to plan. William's grave was identified, the gravediggers opened it, only to find the skeleton of a full-grown man. While they might have searched further, Severn gave up in deference to the crowd of 'respectful but wondering' Italian onlookers.[40] Shelley's ashes were buried on their own in the new cemetery.

Though he was anxious to shield Mary Shelley from the knowledge that they had failed to find William's remains,[41] and irritated by his wrangles with the Roman bureaucracy, Severn had reason to feel he had done well in an awkward task. He was quickly disabused when Edward Trelawny turned up. Severn scarcely knew what to make of the man who had spent the last few months reinventing himself. After an undistinguished naval career and life on a moderate private income, Trelawny became friendly with Thomas Medwin in Switzerland. He followed him to Pisa in hopes of meeting Medwin's cousin, Shelley, and another of his heroes, Byron. Both were planning to build boats and welcomed Trelawny's experience of the sea. More surprisingly, Mary Shelley also took a liking to him, delighting in his fantastical tales of his service with a privateer. It was Trelawny who broke the news to her when Shelley's body was washed up, comforting her in the bleak time that followed. He also undertook to go to Rome on her behalf to oversee the work on her husband's tombstone.

He arrived in April and quickly overturned all Severn's conscientious arrangements. He disapproved of the resting place chosen for Shelley and immediately set about having the much-travelled ashes reburied in a more prominent site which conveniently left room for his own eventual interment alongside. Though the stone he finally chose was a flat marble slab with Shelley's dates grandly carved in Roman numerals, for a time Trelawny toyed with one of Severn's ideas for Keats's grave: a bas-relief of the poet in Greek costume with half-strung lyre seized by the three Fates. Severn and Gott worked up a drawing which Trelawny appeared to like, but then 'the pair of Mustachios' disappeared. Not only that, but he had also dismissed the epitaph which Severn and his friends had painfully put together for Keats. Severn was, by turns, bemused, amused, and irritated by Trelawny's masterful tactlessness. He described him in unusually colourful but critical terms as 'a mad chap', 'great, glowing and rich in romance', 'Lord Byron's jackal', 'a cockney corsair', and an 'odd fish'. Cross though he was, he was intrigued and energized too.[42]

Despite all the complications in the burial of Shelley's ashes, the relative speed with which everything was settled in the opening months of 1823 could only serve as a reproach over Severn's long delay in putting up Keats's tombstone. He had told Brown the previous December that he had already given directions for its making. In January he reported that it should be finished the same week as Shelley's interment.[43] Yet the permission to erect the stone was not granted till 8 March and in April he was still discussing the wording of the epitaph with Trelawny. Not until 1 June was he able to tell Haslam 'I have just put up the Tomb to poor Keats.' Illness and depression in the spring held him back and the drawings he needed from London to help with the design of the stone did not arrive until October 1822. Even so, it is difficult to resist the feeling that something more was involved. Until his last years Severn was never reconciled to death. It was 'like the approaches of Old Age in the shape of Human misery. I bear these things poorly.'[44] He was even more averse to its memorialization. When an adored infant son died in an accident in 1837, he managed to get him buried close to Keats in the old cemetery; but never put up a stone. Even more tellingly, it was seven years before he placed a headstone on his wife's grave.

In the case of Keats there were practical as well as psychological hurdles. For the visitor to the Protestant Cemetery today walking along well-signed paths towards Keats's grave on the edge of the old cemetery, it is hard to recapture the grimness of his plea to his friends for an anonymous tombstone. Severn chafed at its harshness more than anyone, reluctant to see it set in stone. He wanted to celebrate Keats and further his fame, not consign him to oblivion. Others of Keats's friends also struggled. How far were they bound to respect his dying wishes? Might they add their own commentary? Only John Taylor appreciated the poetic aptness of Keats's chosen words. 'If I had seen the epitaph in an English country churchyard I should immediately have recognized it as the grave of a poet', he told John Clare.[45] Severn never had much doubt that more was needed, but in such an important matter he could not act alone. In May 1821 he pressed Haslam to get Brown 'to write me the inscription'. Brown, faced with an exceptionally difficult task, delayed. By the beginning of July, Severn was threatening to put up the stone without an epitaph.[46] Brown, who had been vainly hoping that Hunt would relieve him of his responsibility ('he could word it with feeling and elegance'), was now provoked into action: 'an epitaph' he told Severn, breaking through the impasse, 'must necessarily be considered as the act of the deceased's friends and not of the deceased himself'. So, while respecting Keats's wish for anonymity he diffidently proposed: 'This grave contains all that was mortal of a young English poet, who, on his death-bed, in bitter anguish at the neglect of his countrymen, desired these words to be engraved on his tomb-stone: HERE LIES ONE WHOSE NAME WAS WRIT IN WATER.'[47] Severn, distracted by his travails over the RA pension, did not reply till the following January: 'I liked the inscription much.—and it shall be done exactly.'[48]

As he delayed over finalizing the visual elements of the gravestone, Severn's doubts grew. The anonymity irked, the reference to neglect was too final. 'You seem to have anticipated so', he complained to Brown late in 1822, buoyed by his encounters in Rome with Keats's admirers.[49] If nothing else, surely Keats's name, age, and the date of his death should be recorded. Brown steadied him, recalling Keats's injunction and reminding him that initially he had liked the epitaph, as had Hunt, Dilke, and Thomas Richards.[50] And there the matter rested until Trelawny erupted on to the Roman scene. He was for scrapping Brown's draft altogether and replacing it with a quotation from *Adonais*. In a letter to Mary Shelley he was particularly dismissive about the reference to 'the neglect of his countrymen'.[51] Nor did the epitaph say anything about the cause of Keats's death as established by Shelley. Severn knew how little the critics had mattered to Keats in the end by comparison with his own sense of failure. Nonetheless, he went along with what was becoming the conventional wisdom. Without consulting Brown he changed 'the neglect of his countrymen' to 'the malicious power of his enemies': he also added the date of death of the anonymous young poet.

If the wording on the tombstone was always problematical and became an increasing embarrassment to Severn as Keats's fame grew, the visual elements were never controversial. Here Severn took responsibility, suggesting an idea whose appropriateness was immediately accepted by Keats's friends. It grew out of his constant rereading of *Endymion* in the spring of 1821 and harked back to an evening he had spent with Keats and, perhaps, Brown, in Hampstead. He explained his ideas in two letters to Haslam in the summer of 1821. The tombstone was to be 'like a Greek altar' with 'a delicate Greek lyre with half the strings broken—signifying his Classical Genius—left unfinished by his early death'. More specifically, he explained, the 'Greek lyre—very simple—with four of the strings broken...was Keats's idea a long time back in England', referring Haslam to a drawing he had made 'at Keats's request' in Brown's copy of *Endymion*.[52] Though this has sometimes been taken to mean that Keats designed his own tombstone, more probably Keats was thinking of the sort of frontispiece he would have liked for his poem.[53] The lyre which Severn drew for him resembles the Elgin Lyre which they would have seen together in the British Museum. Given Keats's interest, Severn went back to make more accurate drawings of it. It was these that he needed from England to help him design the tombstone. By 1823 he knew *Endymion* inside out and as he and Gott worked on the design he must often have thought of the lines in Book 3 about the breaking of a lyre: 'straight with sudden swell and fall / Sweet music breathed her soul away, and sighed, / A lullaby to silence'. In the image of the broken Greek lyre on Keats's tombstone Severn succeeded in bringing together poetry, music, and the visual arts. It reminded him of his happiest times with Keats, softening the awfulness of his friend's insistence on anonymity.

CHAPTER 9

'Searching for Fame and Fortune'

Having, at last, put up Keats's tombstone Severn could face Charles Brown. In London, he had known him less on his own account than as Keats's friend and landlord, the man who set the domestic rules at Wentworth Place. At difficult times, however, he had also found Brown a man in whom he could confide, and they had grown closer as a result of Keats's death. Now their relationship would warm into the most supportive of all Severn's many friendships.

Brown was a restless fellow, always ready to up sticks and make a new life elsewhere. As a young man he had briefly been in business in Moscow, a time reflected in the libretto he wrote for the comic opera *Narensky* put on at Drury Lane in 1814. He inherited from an older brother a reasonable competence which enabled him to build Wentworth Place with a friend from his school-days, the government clerk and literary man Charles Dilke. There Brown led a dilettante life, working up schemes with Keats for making their literary fortunes. He had a head for business; and usually took his responsibilities as Keats's closest friend seriously, nursing him, raising his spirits, hosting claret parties for friends, lending him money (of which he kept careful account), preserving his work, and collaborating with him on a play.

Both Brown and Severn were always happier living with others. After Keats's death Brown was at a loose end and anxious to get his son, Carlino, far away from his mother, Abigail O'Donaghue, the serving girl at Wentworth Place. Severn encouraged him to come to Italy. He arrived in Pisa in August 1822 where he hung around with the Hunts, Mary Shelley, and Lord Byron, who, in a passing show of interest in the *Liberal*, invited him to become a contributor. For the present, Brown was not ready. When the ill-matched party moved off to Byron's palazzo in Genoa, he stayed behind, learning Italian, husbanding his resources, getting to know his son, Carlino, and having fun with the local girls.

Pisa, however, was only a staging post towards Florence. He moved there early in 1823, waiting for Severn to join him.

Severn set off in June in the company of the Finches. Abandoning their carriage in Perugia, the 'Colonel', his wife, and sister-in-law embarked on a short walking tour of unfashionable Umbria. Dressed in rough clothes with knapsacks on their shoulders they bemused the inhabitants of Gubbio. Some thought them pilgrims, others pedlars. Severn had no doubt that Finch looked like a man with a weight of sins to confess: for himself, as soon as he opened his knapsack, the locals crowded around to buy his silk handkerchief. At Citta di Castello they caused a stir, being welcomed (or so Severn claimed), as the first English visitors ever and offered a civic reception. The 'Colonel' kept everyone talking late into the night but the townsfolk were up early enough next morning to escort their exotic visitors on the first mile of their walk to San Sepulcro, where Severn, no fan of painting before Michelangelo and Raphael, saw nothing worth recording. Their next objective was St Francis's remote retreat at La Verna.[1] Severn was enthralled by the wild landscape: 'masses of stone 400 feet high—standing on nothing hanging out in the Air—with immense trees striding from the very edges—and with such an atmosphere of coolness that (June 19th) we saw no Snakes, Lizards or any animal of the Sun . . . There are 80 Monks—savage—beastly devils.'[2] They quickly regained their carriage, arriving in Florence in high style and good spirits.

For Severn the reunion with Brown brought the pleasure of being able to talk about Keats for the first time in nearly three years with someone who had known him intimately. 'I have not shaken hands with one mutual friend of mine & Keats's since I left England', he had plaintively written to Brown the previous autumn, 'you cant think of this my dear Brown—at least not feel it'.[3] He would now become Brown's proxy for Keats. Just as he had looked out for Keats, so, too, Brown became Severn's eyes and ears, spotting potential trouble-makers, distinguishing friend from foe. With this masculine assertion went an appetite for domestic management. While Severn was off looking and copying in the galleries, Brown, always a hearty trencherman, cooked up stews and rich English puddings. If this hints at some gender confusion, in practice, it had more to do with Brown's recognition of his limitations. Though he could just about earn a living from writing, he was happiest as the handmaid to the creativity of others. In Keats's case there had been no need to talk up his genius. Given Severn's uncertainties beneath the salesman's patter, however, Brown was always ready with reassurance and encouragement.

[154]

Though Brown was the more assertive, it was not an unequal partnership. Severn had been in Italy longer and was beginning to make a name for himself in a way that Brown could never hope to manage. Severn, not Brown, determined their movements in the nine months they spent together. Severn also had the advantage of a much more straightforward relationship with Keats. He had done his best by his dying friend and won renown on the strength of it. Brown had to live with the thought that in the end he had failed his friend. Yet there was no rivalry between Severn and Brown over who had the best claim to be the friend of Keats. Severn accepted Brown's possessiveness about the poet's reputation, deferring, however reluctantly, to his long caution over how to honour the poet's memory.

Florence, which became Brown's favourite Italian perch, was a gentler, cleaner city than Rome, its climate less demanding, its accommodation cheaper. The respite from the drama and grandeur of Rome as well as what to British eyes was the gloom of a death-haunted city, was welcome. In Florence, away from the oppressive presence of the Church, the free-born Englishman could relax and feel at home under the welcoming eye of the enlightened Dukes of Tuscany. Brown was not alone in rating their rule the best in Europe.[4] Most English travellers stopped there on the way to and from the south. Some stayed. In 1823 Hunt estimated there were two hundred of them. Though this was a far smaller number than in Rome, in the more intimate, less cosmopolitan society of Florence they stood out: the name for a foreigner there was 'Inglese'. They could find Reading sauce and Woodstock gloves in the shops, read the latest English novels in the circulating libraries and, between times, enjoy select masterworks in the Uffizzi, though few lingered over Botticelli or Fra Angelico, Benozzo Gozzoli, and Massaccio. In Florence, as in Rome, the British made their own society. Brown quickly established himself at the centre of a lively cultural circle. Severn, who joked that 'none but a fat man—who loves Wine & has his trousers short' could like Florence,[5] was tempted by the society rather than the place. Rome was where his life lay. He returned to Florence only once after 1823. But Brown's preference for Florence and Severn's for Rome were never impediments to their continuing friendship.

He had expected to find Lord Byron and Trelawny in Florence in June 1823. Indeed, he had grandly told his family that he was going there at Byron's invitation. They reacted with alarm at the notorious company he was keeping and, in return, received a lecture about his new friends: 'great minds deeply learned in Art and Nature ... You greatly mistake to think I shall be injured by their

bad principals—we never talk of [anything] but Poetry & Painting & Music—
they are Men sought after by all the great English who come—but they wont
be seen.' What he did not tell Sarah was that, in the end, only Trelawny had
been in Florence. 'I did four sketches of him', he reported and then corrected
the 'him' to 'them'. After this, he was obliged to keep up the lie that he had
met Lord Byron in 1823, later even embellishing it with the detail of how he
lent his copy of *Adonais* to Byron who returned it with his favourite passages
marked.[6]

With Trelawny soon gone to meet Byron and set out for Greece, Severn
settled to the rhythm of Brown's well-ordered household and the routine of
daily visits to the galleries, looking and copying, searching out backgrounds
and costumes, striving after a fusion of the Gothic and Romantic. Even an
expedition to Vallambrosa with Brown and the Finches only briefly diverted
him. While they continued on three more days of walking, sketching, and
comparing monkish fare, Severn walked back the sixteen miles to Florence,
arriving at midnight.[7] His head was full of his next big painting. The idea for
it had been buzzing around since his student days when Leslie read to him
from William Roscoe's *Life of Lorenzo de' Medici*, a seminal work which gave
many their first sense of the energy and appeal of the Renaissance world. Severn
was seized by the scene of the attempted assassination of Lorenzo. In Rome he
conflated it with Raphael's *School of Athens*, which shows Plato and Aristotle
in the company of both their own and Raphael's distinguished contemporaries.
Now Severn dreamt of a painting which would not only include Michelangelo,
Leonardo, Raphael, and the Medicis, but Byron and Hunt too.

He broke off for a quick trip with Brown to Pisa to catch up with Carlino,
who had been left with an Italian family while his father settled into Florence.
The charming miniature Severn made of the child must have reminded him that
he had no similar memento of his own son. They also visited the Campo Santo.
The collection of frescoes on the walls of its cloisters, sadly badly damaged in
the Second World War, were one of the great glories of Italian art. Keats who saw
them in one of Haydon's books of engravings, awarded them his highest seal of
approval: they had given him the finest treat outside Shakespeare. Ruskin also
would put them on a par with the Sistine Chapel and Tintoretto's paintings
in the Scuola di San Marco in Venice, while for the pre-Raphaelite Brotherhood they were unsurpassed. But Severn was 'disappointed' by these tre- and
quattrocento masterpieces. Though he dutifully made a couple of sketches,
he chose the more reassuring figures: a bearded prophet and a Madonna and

child,[8] closing his eyes to the ferocious power of the Last Judgement and a graphic Triumph of Death, where good and bad angels fight for the souls of the newly departed dead, as the living hold their noses against the stink of decaying flesh.

Venice was a different matter altogether. 'Next to Heaven' it was the place he most longed to see.[9] They set off on 24 August, travelling with William Etty, who brought with him Richard Evans, whose rough edges were happily smoothed in La Serenissima. Though they had been together in the Schools, Etty started to make his mark there only about the time Severn withdrew from the Academy. *The Coral Finders* was a success at the exhibition in 1820: the following year *Cleopatra* did even better. This gave Etty the confidence to make his second venture to Italy. He arrived in Rome in the summer of 1822, moved on to Naples, and then returned in October, enjoying the company of fellow painters in the new Academy. Though he allowed himself to relax in Rome, he had not lost his anxieties about foreign parts, keeping himself up to the mark with salutary maxims: 'Don't drink too much tea', 'Sir Joshua says, Always have your porte-crayon in your hand', 'Avoid above everything, the loose habits and vicious manners of the Italians.'[10] Much as he enjoyed the company of the English artists in Rome, Etty's ultimate objective was always Venice, which he reached in November 1822. He stayed for most of the following year, working out the secrets of the Venetian Masters' glazing techniques, making superb copies of Titian, Veronese, and Tintoretto, preparing himself to become, as he hoped, the first great English history painter and acquiring the richness of tone which would in time see him honoured as 'the English Titian'. Even Eastlake, with whom Severn had hoped to see Venice, could not have been a better guide to its glories than Etty, homely, awkward and unfavoured, but full of carefully acquired insights.

Severn, with his love of colour, was overwhelmed. Venice was a 'Paradise of Art—where Painting is abstracted into itself—and the Painters are like Giants— in mind and body . . . all full of splendour and fresh nature which to me are a new element'. Studying the harmony which the Venetian School had achieved between portraiture and landscape set Severn thinking and quickly erased his interest in sketching 'Gothic' costumes and interiors in Florence. Though Titian was his main focus, he also discovered Tintoretto.[11] Long before Ruskin directed English visitors to Venice to what would become the well-worn track of 'James Tintoret', Severn and Etty delighted in a master rarely mentioned at the Academy. Energetically, 'the canvas-gentry' looked and copied in the Academia in the morning and in churches in the afternoons, while Brown prepared boiled legs of mutton with caper sauce and carrots and other un-Venetian fare. He could not wait to get out of 'this stinking, gnat-tormenting city'.[12]

He had agreed to spend the winter in Rome with Severn. They stopped in Florence for a few days on the way so that Severn could meet the Hunts and commiserate with them over their miserable time with Byron in Genoa. Whatever Severn's thoughts about Hunt's malign influence on Keats, he could not resist his charm. In the three years since they had seen each other, Hunt had lost the two friends whose genius he most admired, while Severn had buried them both in the Protestant Cemetery. 'It was a joyful meeting for LH and Severn and we all chatted of and concerning our old friends in England as prodigiously as you can imagine', Brown reported to London.[13]

They set off for Rome with a visible, if uncharacteristic reminder of Hunt, his second and most troublesome child, John. Even those who admired Hunt baulked at getting too closely involved in his chaotic domestic arrangements. Byron had found it an ordeal in Genoa, revolted by the sight of the 'six little blackguards', 'dirtier and more mischievous than Yahoos' putting their sticky fingers all over things which had belonged to Shelley. Some of the Hunt children, particularly their eldest son, Thornton, benefited from the free rein they were given in their early days. John was different. His superficial suavity, a caricature of his father's manners, barely concealed 'a savage temper and criminal subtlety'.[14] Brown, a devotee of Rousseau, took a fancy to the challenge of trying to reform him. Hunt, though relieved at the prospect of having Johnnie off his hands for six months, honourably warned of what might lie ahead. But Brown wanted to try out his theories before Carlino came to join him in Florence the following spring. Cleaned up and unnaturally quiet and polite, the twelve-year-old set off for Rome. For Severn, too, it was an experiment. He was being encouraged by Brown to bring Henry to Italy. Now he could find out for himself what was involved in bringing up a young boy.

Johnnie made an odd addition to the bachelor establishment in Rome. William Ewing, attracted by the new British Academy, had managed to raise the funds to get back to Rome. Together with the American painter William West, the nephew of Sir Benjamin, he joined Severn and Brown at the Via San Isidoro. Brown managed the household, putting everyone on a solid English diet of rump steaks, soups, stews, hashes, boils, and roasts and later in the year nursed Severn through an attack of jaundice. All too frequently, Brown ended up quarrelling with his friends. Severn was different: 'I think him a quite perfect fellow', Brown wrote. 'He has a generous way of thinking on all occasions and an independence of spirit that I seldom saw equalled.' Indeed, his only irritating fault was his comical mix of English and Italian: 'Vieni qui let's have a look at the costumi d'Esperanza; ecco! What think you of questo? Come pare? Pare a me bravo assai; but how do you piace it?'[15]

The bracing presence of Brown left its mark on Severn. His letters home became more assertive. Sarah, who was enterprisingly trying to teach herself Latin, got nothing for her pains but a ticking off. She would, Severn complained, do far better to 'write plain and distinct English'. But the asperity of this Brownite didactic tone was softened by his determination to pay off his debts to Sarah. Brown had cast a critical eye over his domestic accounts and shown him how to cut costs. Brown's methodicalness also rubbed off on Severn. He polished off *Alexander* and got *Greek Shepherds* ready to go to London. Encouraged to try his hand at writing, he sent Sarah a touching account of that staple scene of horror for English Protestants in Rome, a nun taking the veil. Severn focused on the human drama. The victim was 'a young Princess of great beauty' who 'went through the Catechism with a delicate faltering voice', before the abbess and 'some other nasty old Frumps' denuded her of her fine clothes and jewels and cut off her lovely long hair. 'O! I felt as though I was between the Scissors every time they closed', he confessed.[16]

Brown filled up his days without quite fitting in at Rome. He failed to interest a small private theatre company in putting on *Otho the Great*, the tragedy Keats had written to Brown's scenario, and, as an amateur, he was refused admittance of right to the Academy. He took his revenge in an article in *The Examiner* later that year, 'Actors and Artists at Rome', letting the London art world know that attendance at the Academy was in free fall, 'seldom exceeding 5 and sometimes as low as 1 or 2'.[17] No doubt, he was also a stirrer in a quarrel with the Finches over the 'Colonel's' right to his title. Severn wrote up the incident in a way more fitted for Johnnie Hunt than his two younger brothers who received a veritable sermon on the importance of truth-telling. 'Think what a pitch—to have not one word believed—to be left almost desolate—and yet to have the most splendid ability—fortune—everything—and not one friend—for in our station of life it is worse', he warned Tom.[18] As the breach with the Finches deepened, Johnnie looked for his opportunity to cause dissent in the bachelor household. He overheard Severn criticizing Ewing's lack of gentlemanly address and passed the comments on to the sensitive subject. Though Ewing stopped the child in mid-flow, he had heard enough. Johnnie was packed off back to Florence with a suitcase full of dirty clothes. Ewing also moved out. It was a sad break, which took time to repair, in a friendship begun at Keats's bedside.[19]

Though Severn did not neglect the Erskines in the spring of 1824, his romance did not progress and Brown was only too ready to warn him of the dangers of domesticity for an artist. In July he told his family the match was off. He abandoned the idea of marriage reluctantly. 'I cannot think but I am born for a Domestic life and in its comfort I am another being', he reflected to Sarah.[20] Though no longer a suitor, he continued as the devoted family friend, using Maria as a model for Miranda in a scene from *The Tempest*, and planning to share a house with the Erskines in the summer in the Alban Hills.

If Brown's presence in Rome brought out an uncharacteristic briskness in Severn's personal dealings, his advice on artistic matters was all to the good. It encouraged Severn to take a shrewder look at his future and prepare for the time after his pension ran out in the summer. He was only 'a poor fellow searching for fame and fortune—and they will not come without much seeking'. Technically more proficient though he now was, he still needed to earn his living as an artist, reduce expenses on models and materials, secure commissions, and sell pictures. So he abandoned *Lorenzo de Medici* in favour of a more marketable *Mother and Child*, capitalizing on what he had seen in Venice by including 'a beautiful landscape'.[21] The change of strategy worked. In June he got his first commission. It came from Thomas Erskine of Linlathen, a pious Scottish lawyer and cousin of Mrs Erskine, on his first visit to Rome. He had been taken by a sketch he had seen, *Cordelia Sitting by the Bed of King Lear*, and commissioned Severn to turn it into an oil painting for £50. Lady Westmorland too talked of a commission for six scenes from *Quentin Durward*. And he could always pick up 20 guineas from visiting English gentry for a quick portrait of 'a Gentleman on Horseback taking a farewell of his brother—with a Dog'.[22]

In May 1824 Brown returned to Florence. Severn would see him only three times again, and visit Florence only once.[23] Despite their physical separation, the friendship continued. Brown wrote regularly with gossip about mutual friends in Florence, shrewd advice on Severn's artistic career and health, recipes and gardening lore and arrangements for the regular traffic in goods and borrowed books and paintings between Rome and Florence. He was always the first person Severn turned to for advice on both professional and personal matters and, together, they pondered their obligations to Keats. In 1826 money was unexpectedly found in the Keats children's inheritance. Brown immediately submitted a bill to George Keats for John's unpaid expenses in 1819–20. Coaches, doctors bills, wine, and even 'sundries', all were included. But the petty-mindedness of the gesture was redeemed by his immediate offer to lend what had been 'miraculously torn from the fangs of Chancery' to Severn. It was a characteristic Brown proceeding. He went to some lengths to get the money not because he needed it, but because it was owing to him, and then immediately made it over to a friend with limited means, his 'dear Severn'.[24]

Severn's visit to Venice had left him eager to apply the lessons he had learnt there. In July 1824 he set out for L'Ariccia to study landscape outdoors and paint *The Vintage*. It was the start of a breakthrough not just in his own career but in the direction taken by the English painters in Rome. L'Ariccia was the smallest of the three hilltop villages in the Alban Hills just twelve miles out of Rome on the Appian Way. Together with its neighbours, Genzano and Albano, it had long been a favourite haunt for painters. They were attracted not only by its densely wooded hills and the beauty and stillness of Lakes Albano and Nemi in their deep volcanic craters, but also by the local girls and their distinctive costumes. The flower festivals and candlelit processions brought crowds from Rome, and the summer air was pure and gentle. In the 1770s British landscape painters knew the area well. Thomas Jones wrote of 'The hills gently swelling—Turrets and Cupolas are seen emerging from their tufted Summits—and the prospect terminated either by a vast expanse of Sea, the flat Campagna losing its horizon in the Atmosphere—or the rugged Appenines whose lofty Summits are covered with Snow.' While some, like Eastlake, preferred the more demanding landscape round Tivoli, which they associated with Poussin, gentler souls like Severn were happier with the more intimate Claudian look of the country around Albano. Increasingly, in the 1820s and 1830s a cosmopolitan company of young artists summered there. In the evenings they congregated on the square opposite the graceful Bernini church of Santa Maria dell'Assunzione at a tavern owned by the genial Signor Martelli, whose ugly, bad-tempered daughter was the mainstay of the business. Here they could smoke, play cards, show off their work or sing around an old spinet. Though they sat up late, William Bewick, who was there in 1828, found them out in good time next morning, the Germans equipped with straw hats, umbrellas, portable seats, walking sticks, leather pouches of wine, and sketchbooks, the French with little more than their cigars and 'the greatest nonchalance and grace imaginable'.[25]

Severn would later play a full part in the fraternizing and take his turn at the spinnet accompanying 'ballads, songs, and reminiscences of the opera'.[26]

His first stay was rather different as he enjoyed the domestic comforts of Mrs Erskine's rented house. He was intent on trying something new, painting not just the landscape but the local people too. He wanted to catch them not in some picturesque anecdotal pose, or Claude-like, aping their classical forebears as adjuncts to the landscape, but in the age-old productive communal activity of gathering and pressing the grapes at harvest-time. It was a more innovative approach than might now appear after the decades in which the London market was flooded with scenes of happy Italian peasants at their labours. It also went beyond the whimsical reportage of contemporary Italian genre painting. And it had a larger purpose than Eastlake's bandit scenes, whose popularity became an embarrassment to him. Severn's vision was more wholesome and less distanced. In *The Vintage* and *The Fountain* which closely followed, he brought together his happiest feelings about Italy, including his admiration for feminine beauty. The faces Severn painted in the vineyards of L'Ariccia reminded him of those he had seen on antique vases or in classical sculpture. He added a further layer of association by including a wild boar, the enemy of the harvest in Psalm 80. Essentially, however, it was the poetry and vitality of the present, not the past, that he sought to capture, choosing scenes attuned to his temperament: humane and joyous, pastoral and ideal. He worked quickly on his new painting. It engaged him in a way that history painting had never done. Lawrence, who had admired the women of Genzano, was immediately struck with the aptness and originality of Severn's conception when he heard about it.[27]

Outdoor painting brought a technical revolution. In composition *The Vintage* derived from Severn's study of Poussin and Titian: in technique he learnt from Eastlake. Painting under bright Italian skies required a different palette. Hunt saw the difference on his arrival in Italy: 'You learn for the first time in this climate, what colours really are. No wonder it produces painters. An English artist of enthusiasm might shed tears of vexation, to think of the dull medium through which blue and red come to him in his own atmosphere, compared with this.'[28] Eastlake had carefully worked through the implications, noting the way the Italian Masters had used shade only as a way of displaying form, or done without it and set conflicting colours side by side without the dark chiaroscuro favoured by English painters. White highlighting, needed to make an impact in northern light, was also ugly and redundant in Italy. Accordingly, he brightened his palette. While the self-aware Eastlake conducted a long correspondence with a sceptical Lawrence on the subject and was ever-anxious that what looked right in Rome might appear garish on London walls, Severn plunged in with less regard for Academy tastes. His colouring became increasingly controversial. In the summer and autumn of 1824, however, in his first major exercise in outdoor painting he had no doubts: he would follow Titian. 'Now that I have been studying from Nature in her own Pavillion—the open Air,' he enthused to Finch, 'I seem not to have half looked at Titian's works.—In my "Minds eye" while I am here in the wide presence of Nature, they appear the greatest and deepest felt works in our Art—he must have produced these works from a religious intercourse with God.'[29]

Initially, however, things did not go according to plan. The three Erskine ladies did not succeed in making the local women come to him to be painted; and the trinkets he had brought from Rome attracted only the least favoured. So he put it about that his real purpose was to find a wife. He soon had a queue of the finest beauties competing for his attention, emboldened by rumours that foreigners did not beat their wives. Here was what he wanted, examples of 'that elevated & abstract beauty of antique sculpture in the living people'.[30] His new work was tragically interrupted by the death of Mrs Erskine from a high fever. It all happened so suddenly that he was unable to call in a doctor. Nor could her daughters accept that their mother was dead. As they hung over her body, putrefying in the summer heat, it fell to Severn to bring in a local carpenter to make a coffin and remove the corpse to lie overnight in a cooling vineyard. He and the two exhausted girls set off for Rome before dawn, arriving at the Protestant Cemetery at 8 o'clock. Severn prevailed on a friend to read the committal lines. While her elder sister bore up bravely, Maria was hysterical and had to be carried to the waiting carriage. Severn stayed behind to keep an eye on an unkempt lot of gravediggers 'gazing at us like wild beasts'. He felt responsible for the disaster, blaming himself for the failure to get medical help and scarcely able to face the Erskine girls. He tried to make amends by painting a small portrait of their mother as they waited impatiently for their uncle to come and take them back to the security of England and English doctors.[31] His romance with Maria was now well and truly over.

For a while, Mrs Erskine's death seemed an even worse calamity than Keats's. But friends reassured him: Brown blamed Maria's hysterics as 'love spite', Eastlake 'laughed' him 'into good health again', and three friends went back with him to L'Ariccia and 'talked and charmed me out of all low spirits'. He soon recovered his buoyancy, painting hard and, on Sundays, serving up 'a nice morsel of Haydn, Mozart or some old thorough bass fellow' as he played the organ at Mass.[32] By the time he returned to Rome he had finished twelve whole-length figures in oils. He opened his studio to show them off: their originality impressed. For the first time his work was making an impact in Rome.

The declaration of a Holy Year in 1825 curtailed the usual busy social round and left Severn free to work on *The Vintage* uninterrupted. News of the picture was getting around. Though he began it without a commission, he soon attracted the interest of his first important English-based aristocratic patron, Lord William Russell, the Duke of Bedford's younger brother. Kirkup had first introduced them in 1821 when Russell bought an oil sketch of *Alexander the Great*, encouraging Severn to think he might eventually take the completed work. Now, once again, Russell was interested. Bedford had already put together a distinguished sculpture gallery at Woburn Abbey where the choicest piece was Canova's *Three Graces*. Now he planned a gallery of the best of English contemporary painting and deputed his brother to help him identify suitable works. Russell was a fussy and unconfident patron, always trying to second guess his elder brother's intentions. Though he confirmed the commission for Severn in August 1825 he jibbed at the price (150 guineas), the size of the picture, its colouring, and finish. Anxious though he was to please an important new patron, Severn conceded only on the last point. When *The Vintage* reached England, Leslie, once again, polished it up to match the standard of the rest of the company in the gallery: Landseer, Wilkie, Callcott, Collins, Hayter, and Eastlake, all of them far better known than Severn.

In learning to cope with Russell, Severn was sustained by the advice of a new friend, the painter Thomas Uwins. Eleven years older than Severn, Uwins came from a similar background, having served his apprenticeship in Pentonville, just down the hill from Goswell Street. He first made his name as a book illustrator before turning to portraiture in Edinburgh. Though successful at both, Uwins nourished an ambition to become a history painter and so set out for Italy. He arrived in Rome late in October 1824 and was quickly beguiled. He received a warm welcome from the English artists and immediately recognized in Eastlake 'a very good painter', 'a profound thinker', 'a man of most extensive learning and acquirements', and 'of sincere piety and . . . most exemplary conduct'. But while he was to think it 'the greatest honour to have made such a man my friend', it was Severn whom he got to 'love as a brother' in Italy.[33]

Uwins called in at Severn's studio as he was working on *The Vintage* in the winter of 1824. Leaning on the artist's shoulder he offered some frank criticisms. At this period Severn was always ready to take well-intentioned advice. He had long known and admired Uwins's work as an illustrator: 'how many books I have bought when I was a "young shaver" for the elegant frontispiece by "T.U."' he wrote to him in the summer of 1827 when Uwins needed cheering up. The debate between them continued in a lively correspondence once Uwins moved to Naples. They argued about realism versus idealism in landscape and about taste. Uwins worried about some small boys Severn had introduced which reminded him of 'the frivolities of Boucher'.[34] Severn stood his ground. He had checked out the details of his harvest scene with his housekeeper, Teresa. Brown joined in, assuring Severn that his boys were 'a touch of poetry'.[35] Though Uwins was the older and more established man, in this correspondence it is Severn who emerges as the senior partner. One evening in Rome he even faced down the combined weight of Gibson, Eastlake, and David Wilkie. They thought his figures would stand out better if he lowered the brilliance of his sky. Severn refused, rightly in the opinion of Lady Compton, a gifted amateur artist. 'I supposed it was a great raw extent of ultramarine,' she wrote to Severn when *The Vintage* went on display at the RA Exhibition in 1827, 'whereas it is as beautiful & glowing a piece of blending as those admirable old masters used to put behind the head of a Madonna.'[36]

While Severn could usually rely on support from Lady Compton, he also received an indirect compliment for *The Vintage* from an infinitely more demanding source, William Hazlitt. Hazlitt arrived in Rome in March 1825 midway through a tour of Italy with his second wife, Isabella. He travelled extensively, admiring the art works in Turin, Parma, and Bologna and spending two agreeable months in Florence in the company of Brown, Hunt, Kirkup, and Landor. He asked for a letter of introduction to Severn from Brown, and Severn's was one of the first studios he visited in Rome, finding the painter surrounded by sketches of Alban beauties.[37] Despite high expectations on both sides, however, the relationship did not prosper. Nor did Hazlitt take to Rome. He was one of the few who stayed for less, not more time than he had intended, hurrying north to Venice. It was not, he wrote, 'the Rome I expected to see'. Raphael and Michelangelo disappointed, while the City was 'an almost uninterrupted succession of narrow, vulgar-looking streets where the smell of garlic prevails over the odour of antiquity'.[38] His disaffection spilled over into his article 'The English Students at Rome'. But though it reads like a commentary on all the excesses of Severn's early letters home, its conclusion brought a surprising vindication of the soundness of the new direction in his painting.

Hazlitt's essential argument, shared by many of the grandees at the RA, but rarely expressed with such psychological insight, was that Rome was 'of all places the worst to study in'. There were too many distractions and too many inducements to an illusory sense of superiority: 'you look down as it were from this eminence on the rest of mankind—and from the contempt you feel for others, come to have a mighty good opinion of yourself'. Instead of painstakingly learning his craft, the English artist in Rome spent his time visiting galleries and working up ideas for grand canvases. Accurately, if unkindly, Hazlitt described the to-ing and fro-ing that went on in the English artistic community:

Then comes a new secret of colouring, a new principle of grouping, a new theory, a new book . . . Then a picture is to be copied as a preparation for undertaking a given subject, or a library to be ransacked to ascertain the precise truth of the historical facts or the exact conception of the characters . . . Then again friends are to be consulted; some admire one thing, some another; some recommend the study of nature, others are all for the antique; some insist on the utmost finishing, others explode all attention to minutiae.

But 'Nothing remarkable was ever done . . . by dreaming over our own premature triumphs or doating on the achievements of others.' Even the energy the English did work up in Rome was over the wrong things: gossiping about the attentions cardinals paid to pretty young girls; scheming to reform Italian institutions on the model of British ones; mugging up Gibbon in preparation for speechifying at the Academy; or plotting the management of patrons. In Hazlitt's eyes, the much-vaunted social cohesion of Anglo-Roman society was no more than presumptuous self-importance.

Though it caused inevitable offence to the artistic colony in Rome, Hazlitt had astutely anatomized the pitfalls in the way of aspiring artists in the world's art capital.[39] Eastlake studiously avoided them. For most of the 1820s Severn, too, navigated round them, increasingly aware of the need to avoid seeing Rome with an untutored eye. When Vincent Novello thought of sending his gifted son, Edward, there rather than to the Schools, Severn advised against the idea. Rome, he wrote, was only for those with a clear grasp of art history and the beginnings of an independent artistic identity.[40] It was a truth he had learnt the hard way after three years of dead ends. Irritated though he was by Hazlitt, he could find consolation in the conclusion of 'The English Students at Rome'. Hazlitt's advice was uncompromising: 'go to Genzano, stop there for five years, visiting Rome only at intervals, wander by Albano's gleaming lake and wizard grottos, make studies of the heads and dresses of the peasant girls in the neighbourhood, those Goddesses of health and good temper, embody them to the life, and show what the world never saw before.'[41] Severn had anticipated Hazlitt.

The contrast between his new-found source of artistic energy and labours on more conventional subjects showed when he turned back to *Cordelia*, for which Thomas Erskine had already paid him £50. Now it had become a chore. By the time it was finished at the end of 1826, Erskine, whose eye for art in Italy had been developing in the meantime, had lost interest. Brown drew a sensible moral: 'Always suspect that that which you do with the greatest difficulty is least adapted to your genius.'[42]

As the Holy Year of 1825 drew to a close, some of the stars of the Roman social scene returned. The most dazzling was always Lady Westmorland, who launched a busy round of balls, dinners, musical evenings, and tableaux vivants at Palazzo Rospigliosi. Standing more quietly in the background was a Scottish ward she had acquired to be her companion, the beautiful but shy Elizabeth Montgomerie, half-sister to the Earl of Eglinton. Artists, too, were making their way to Rome. In November David Wilkie arrived in the company of Hilton, together with Thomas Phillips, another Academician, who would become famous for his portraits of Romantic writers. While they stayed only briefly, Wilkie planned to winter in Rome and refresh his artistic career.

He approached the prospect with his usual caution, suspicious of the degenerate Italians, apprehensive that Dr Clark would not be sufficiently interventionist, fearful of the pilgrims still around and careful of his expenditures. But he quickly warmed to the place, appreciated the generous welcome he received from the British artists (he had always been one of Severn's heroes) and was more impressed by them than he had expected. By the start of 1826 he was even enjoying himself in society. Despite his frailties and fear of expense, he was persuaded to get into costume for Torlonia's fancy dress ball, the highlight of the carnival season. After anxious consultations with Severn and Westmacott and a trawl through Rome's pawnshops and backstage theatre wardrobes, he settled on a Van Dyck costume. The stars of the evening, however, were his friend, George Rennie, as Don Quixote with Severn as Sancho Panza: 'The two upon horses galloping about, played it to the life.'[43]

Seductive though he found the high jinks of Anglo-Roman society, Severn's success never effaced the memory of the young poet whose sickness first brought him there. Much as he admired his new patrons and aristocratic friends and the way they had accepted him, his deepest sense of gratitude was still to Keats. In the middle of exuberant accounts to his family of how well he was doing ('Tell my dear Father, that about me, all his cares are at an end—my fortune is made—if I please . . . he will yet see me equal with anyone'), he could still break off to reflect on his debt to Keats. 'I have now been in Italy for five years,' he wrote to Tom in November 1825, 'it seems impossible—Betwixt you and I—certainly I have gained more from poor Keats, who is dead and gone than from any other source—he introduced [me] to all the learned men I know—and helped me on in my painting by his own great mind—and then his Friendship and death are so interwoven with my name that it will ever be an honor to me.' A year earlier he had told Maria, 'my coming with Keats and friendship for him—will be a never fading Laurel . . . You would be surprised, how often it is mentioned to me—and how I am pointed out as the friend of the Poet Keats—It was the work of Providence for my good both in mind and fortune—I can never cease to remember it, and be thankful to God—for turning to good what I began so carelessly—it was a risk indeed.'[44]

Uncomfortable though he remained about the epitaph on Keats's tombstone Severn was always glad to take friends and visitors to the grave. In the autumn of 1826 he was, at last, able to show it to Charles Dilke. Dilke and his son were in Rome with Brown on a tour of Italy. Old friends though Brown and Dilke were, Brown preferred Severn's company in Rome, staying with him at his lodgings while the Dilkes went to a hotel. They came together at Keats's grave united in sad memories. Brown always claimed to be far more moved by the sight of Piazza di Spagna than Keats's burial plot, 'the living man was a stranger to it, and it only contains a clod like itself', but on this occasion he had to walk away to hide his tears. Dilke, too, struggled to keep his composure. It was his son, Wentworth, reflecting the emotion of the adults, who broke down, convulsed in sobs. Moved by the scene, Dilke, ever a scrupulous judge of men and motives, wrote glowingly to his wife about Severn and 'the very charming little monument' he had raised to Keats. 'Severn then a poor young artist, who, though comparatively successful, lives, as he himself told me, on half a crown a day, including his servant's wages, and at that time had little—but hope—raised this monument, and never would allow Brown to pay part of the expenses of it. I always liked Severn, and shall like him the better as long as I live.'[45] He asked Severn to arrange to get a copy of the background to Raphael's *Madonna of Foligno*. Severn knew just the man, an expert German copyist who would do the work for a reasonable price.

As Brown and the Dilkes moved on to Naples, Wilkie returned. Severn organized his usual Christmas Day dinner for the English artists, with Wilkie as guest of honour. He was in exuberant mood. *The Vintage* was to be exhibited at the next RA Exhibition and a companion piece, *The Fountain*, had already been commissioned by Prince Leopold of Saxe-Coburg. He went to some trouble over the dinner, producing a haggis as a surprise for the guest of honour. It was quickly demolished in a noisy evening: 'what was wanting in wit was amply made up in laughter'.[46] Amongst the guests was another visitor to Rome, William Bewick, a pupil of Haydon's and briefly a contemporary of Severn's in the RA Schools. He arrived in the autumn with a commission from Lawrence to make copies of the Prophets and Sybils in the Sistine Chapel. In London he had been friendly with Keats and Hazlitt and it was natural that he should now gravitate towards Severn. For years he kept a glowing memory of his friend there: 'as honourable and dear a fellow as ever breathed, with a noble and generous spirit, and the feeling of a true gentleman'.[47]

News of the success of the dinner put the Scots on their mettle to outdo the English tribute. They planned a grand affair. Fifty guests were invited, with the Duke of Hamilton in the chair. Eastlake and Lane represented the English, Camuccini the Italians, and Thorwaldsen the sculptors. Wilkie responded to the Duke's toast to the Academy with a heartfelt tribute to the British artists in Rome. He had admired what he found there, telling his friends back home to forget Hazlitt and not underestimate the seriousness of their efforts.[48] He picked out three works as the best of what he had seen. Each, he predicted, would bring credit to the artistic community in Rome when shown at the next Exhibition. At the head of the list were the two acknowledged leaders, Gibson and Eastlake, with *Psyche Borne by the Zephyrs* and *The Spartan Isidas*. Alongside them in honour Wilkie set *The Vintage*.

After five years of 'searching for fame and fortune', Severn had arrived.

CHAPTER 10

Love, Marriage, and Persecution

Back in Shoreditch, Joseph's ebullient accounts of his triumphs in Rome were the stuff of dreams, a fantasy unimaginably come true. References to lords and ladies, palaces and carriages were casually tossed off while Tom was offered an introduction to a prince (and advice on how to address a Royal Highness). Charles began to learn Italian with an idea of coming to Rome to complete his musical education.[1] In London he and Tom welcomed their brother's friends, putting on an impromptu piano duet for Ewing and quizzing Catherwood about Rome, while Severn's mother delighted in showing off *The Cave of Despair*.[2] Maria, however, resigned to staying at home to look after her parents, had time to reflect on her brother's letters and worry that he had outgrown his family.

A thoughtless reference in a more than usually buoyant letter of December 1825 led to a two-year silence. He had, yet again, promised to come and see them, but only if he could get some commissions: 'if not, why I won't come back—... only think of that now—and for a man of my kidney who used to be always sighing to come back to his "Mamma". Now I don't care a fig—and why should I—for if I "play my cards well" my fortune is made.'[3] When Maria did write again, she accused him of having changed. He could not deny it though he reminded her that he had always 'sighed in secret after greatness and distinction'. 'If you were to see me figuring away in high society,' he told his father, 'you would not know me for your son Joseph.'[4] But he was not ashamed to let his family know he had got where he was by constant effort and careful calculation. 'I make a point' he wrote to Sarah from Florence in 1823, 'never to know anyone who is not superior to me in fortune or ability—in some way or other—that I may still be raising myself and improving, even in moments of pastime—Tell Tom this.'[5]

In 1827, the family was brought closer to his distant world when *The Vintage* finally arrived in England. The only picture they had seen since his departure for Italy was *Greek Shepherds*, with its vividly un-English sky. When it failed to sell at the British Institution Exhibition in 1825 James Severn happily put it in his 'gallery'. *The Vintage* was different. It was the first picture of Severn's at the RA Exhibition since 1820 and already in the possession of a ducal patron. Tom and Charles rushed off to Somerset House to see it, returning several times. They came home full of their brother's triumph: 'Old Joe I could worship you for it. It has set London on fire', wrote Tom. James Severn, too, went to have a look and was 'Thunderstruck'. Though Joseph's mother had not ventured out of the East End for ten years, she and Maria put on their best bonnets to brave the fashionable crowds at the Academy. They stared in astonishment, dabbing their eyes in front of Joseph's painting of a scene so remote from their own lives.[6]

Far away though he was from them, changes at home unsettled Severn. The most dramatic were in Sarah's life. In 1827 she upped and married without a word to her parents. A year later she was dead.[7] Close as Severn and his eldest sister had been, it was the finality of death which troubled him most: 'Here am I, at this distance from my home, settled, perhaps <u>never</u> to return; and yet in that home I cannot bear the least change—even a garden (where I played when a boy) being built upon caused me to shed tears when I heard it.'[8] He was almost as troubled by his siblings' marriages. Tom was the first, marrying an old sweetheart, Caroline Plumstead, in November 1825. Yet more disconcerting was the news in January 1828 that Charles, last seen as a schoolboy, also wanted to marry. Once again Severn reflected on his anomalous bachelor state.

A year after his romance with Maria Erskine had petered out, he was fancy-free and susceptible. Charles Brown picked up a rumour in the summer that he had been 'wounded in the Wars of Venus' and gone off to the seaside to recover.[9] Though this might just imply that he had been dabbling in the lower end of the market, more probably his hopes had been dashed in another society match, for by the end of the year he was writing off women in high life as 'cats'; 'when I do chuse it won't be there', he assured Tom.[10] But would he ever 'chuse'? Two years later he was still uncertain: 'I am more and more convinced that I am better alone, as I am such an odd creature—I have thought much of it—have seen two other dear and beautiful lassies, and have been in love too—but somehow or other I am so full of second thoughts that I think I shall be content to be married to painting all my life.' At the beginning of 1828 he was even surer: 'I am too aspiring for the limits of a married life, nor am well enough of[f]— When I marry it shall be to increase my fortune as well as my happiness—it shall be for great talent or fortune, and certainly never for mere love or beauty—So you will easily see that I am like to be an old Bachelor.'[11]

With sales and commissions mounting, he lived comfortably. In June 1824 he moved from Via San Isidoro down into town at 22 Vicolo de Maronitti, taking over the upper floor of what had once been a monastery. Now he had two rooms, each 28 feet in length, where he could display his pictures and work in 'the most capital study in Rome', a book room, bed room, spare room and accommodation for his servants. For a couple of years he shared his apartments with Captain Baynes, a retired veteran of the Napoleonic wars, who amused himself with gentlemanly pursuits as an amateur actor and painter.[12] By 1826 he was on his own again and thinking about an idea which had long been maturing in his mind, a reunion with his son. Brown, who volunteered to meet Henry at Leghorn and help him on his way to Rome,[13] kept up a constant bombardment. A year later, Severn had determined to get his son to Italy. While Charles might have accompanied Henry, however, his new romance in London dampened his interest in Rome, and it was not easy to think of an eight-year-old getting to Italy by himself. For the time being nothing came of the plan.

Severn was not, in any case, short of infant company. In 1823 he took on a new servant, Teresa Bartholomei, who moved in with her husband, Giovanni, and two sisters who were replaced over time by a growing band of children. He was delighted with his new housekeeper. She was 'very clever and willing', had learnt to 'cook in our English taste', and, best of all, was scrupulously honest. He talked to her about his painting, consulted her about Italian life, and enjoyed her company. 'I hope that I may never lose them,' he told Tom when they had been together for four years, 'I pay them just a shilling a day, not finding anything but lodging and fire—for they work—wash—wait and go out on errands and in short are always at my command.'[14] Brown was so impressed he got himself a serving woman too.

Anglo-Saxon visitors to Rome often remarked on the more equal relationship that prevailed between master and servant and the lack of servility in the Roman populace. The cultured American visitor George Ticknor, for example, was amused at the way servants took part in the occasional dinner parties given by the impoverished Italian aristocracy, hanging around in their decrepit liveries in drafty dining rooms, nodding and chuckling appreciatively at the more amusing remarks of the guests.[15] But Severn's lack of precision in his dealings with Teresa and Giovanni would come back to haunt him. For now, with their help, he kept up a style which he estimated would cost him £500 a year in London. With an expensive German pianoforte and elegant furnishings, he was 'spoiled for England, unless I become very rich and can keep a large house when I return'. For an English artist in Rome, he lived in fine, independent style.[16]

If he felt under pressure from his family to marry, there was none from his friends in Italy. Looking at Hunt's struggles to provide for an overlarge family or Gott's anxieties about the effect of his ill health on his ability to keep his wife and children in Rome, Severn was only too aware of 'the pram in the hall' as an impediment to creativity. For much of the time he moved in bachelor circles: Brown's brief marriage to Abigail O'Donaghue in London left him ineligible for further marital adventures; Eastlake had other preoccupations, though there were times when he worried that he had left marriage too late; Gibson was disinclined; Etty and Uwins were wedded to the perfecting of their artistic skills; Westmacott, with the prospect of eventually joining his father's studio, was happy to enjoy his freedom in Italy (even if he knew at heart that both he and Severn were Benedicks);[17] and though Kirkup was rarely without a girlfriend, he succeeded in postponing marriage until the age of eighty-seven.

In the meantime the artists in Rome were in and out of each other's studios, showing them off to visitors from England such as the former Maria Graham, who turned up for a second honeymoon in 1827 on the arm of the distinguished Academician Augustus Callcott and was squired around by Eastlake and Severn.[18] Or they talked about art late into the night in the cafés or each other's homes, having largely abandoned the Academy to the more mediocre talents who came to Rome in the second wave of post-war enthusiasm. (Penry Williams, who arrived in 1826, was a notable exception.) And they danced attendance on their patrons and patronesses, went to balls and soirées or enlivened the company at genteel supper parties.

The most tireless hostess was Lady Westmorland. Though a patrician, she never disdained the company of the more established artists. Eastlake, Gibson, Kirkup, and Severn were all favourites. While Gibson and Eastlake were men anyone would have been proud to show off and Kirkup had the charm of a long-standing friend, Severn had other uses. He was her Master of the Revels, and sometimes her Lord of Misrule. When she wanted to show off her skills at a musical evening he was her partner at the keyboard. (She told a nervous Severn not to worry as they struggled with the tricky Overture to *The Marriage of Figaro*, 'if we play together I shall be the person looked at—nobody will look at you'.)[19] He was in demand, too, advising on costumes and headdresses for fancy dress balls. Lady Henrietta Monckton Milnes was directed to him in the winter of 1831 and delighted by the 'correct and beautiful' Greek costume he devised for her daughter.[20] He also played a key role behind the scenes at Lady Westmorland's spectacular evenings of tableaux vivants.

She generally chose works of the Old Masters, recreating them with living representations of familiar figures, sophisticated backgrounds, soft lighting, and sometimes music to enhance the mood. Severn described one to his family: 'we had a St. Cecilia by Raffaele, and Angels in the Clouds sang Novello's "Lauta Maria"—there were seven figures—all the ladies of the greatest beauty in Rome have appeared in these pictures and I have been Commander in Chief'. Henry Fox, who took part, saw it differently: 'The scene behind the scenes was dreadfully tedious, and a sad exhibition of vanity and ill-humour.' The noise of the backstage rows penetrated to the expectant audience seated the other side of the picture frame with the curtains closed, adding to the fun. At one point, Severn flounced out after a disagreement over how to recreate the effect of flame in an angel's hand. On another evening Lady Westmorland boxed his ears. Quietly, amongst the disorder, her ward, Elizabeth Montgomerie, adjusted costumes (she loved fine fabrics) or rouged the cheeks of the dwarf brought in to help recreate Van Dyck's *Charles I*.[21]

Though Lady Westmorland might call him 'that little goose Severn' in aristocratic company, she continued to promote his career and helped seal Prince Leopold of Saxe Coburg's purchase of *A Young Woman with her Child in a Cradle* in 1828, one of Severn's rare bandit pictures.[22] She was also a go-between in the commission for *The Fountain*. In 1827 she astonished Severn by choosing one of his pictures for a tableau. 'I owe you a pleasure' she graciously assured him in front of the assembled company. For Severn, escorting her from time to time to balls and dinners, and thinking of her resemblance to Elizabeth I, she was 'a Queen'. In the summer of 1826, despite an invitation to Florence, he preferred to paint studies for *The Fountain* in the famous inn, the Villa di Cicerone, at Mola di Gaeta where he joined her party, which included Elizabeth Montgomerie. They amused themselves recreating the imprint of monsters' feet on the sands to terrify the local fishermen and then travelled to Naples together, where he saw Uwins and again stayed with Lieutenant Cotterell.[23]

For Lady Westmorland, always looking for new entertainment, the relationship flattered her vanity. By now he had become 'rather dandyish—spruce certainly'. It was, however, a far less equal relationship than Severn suggested in letters home. 'Her ladyship shows me more and more attention. I am taken by her to the most magnificent fetes and introduced to the highest people who buy my pictures and treat me as a Gentleman', he told Maria. But his description of a dinner party in December 1827—'there were eighteen people and a fine turn out it was, we had "God Save" and "Rule Britannia"'—needs to be compared with Fox's account of the same event: 'The company very numerous, but very ill sorted. Lady M Deerhurst, Mrs Dennis, Jenks, Miss Daniel, Colgar, "Capt" Roberts...Severn, Eastlake, Gibson and several others even of lesser note or likelihood. The dinner was very long. Conversation did not thrive, though Lady Westmorland tried to make it general, but it would not do.'[24]

Nor did Lady Westmorland involve Severn in her obsessive feud in 1827 and 1828 with the scandalous *ménage à trois* of Lord and Lady Blessington and the Count d'Orsay. She pursued it so relentlessly that her friends in Rome tired of her embattled histrionics and started to cut her. Severn, too, was beginning to see a different side of his patroness. He had always known that she was capricious and controlling. He had also seen at first hand the disorder in her household with a constant to-ing and fro-ing of servants. One gave up because he could no longer stand the strain of being summoned in the small hours to drive her into the Campagna to admire the water buffalo; another was asked to identify a missed caller on the basis of his resemblance to 'a fine Murillo'; and all were frequently harangued. She was rarely up in the mornings and often kept the company waiting at dinner parties. Now Severn saw a darker side to these eccentricities. Her ward, Elizabeth Montgomerie, who stood in for her while she dallied over her toilette, and was privy to all her moods, was, he discovered, absolutely terrified of her. And Severn had become increasingly fond of Elizabeth.

He first met her when he and Eastlake went to pay their respects to Lady Westmorland on her return to Rome in late 1825. Reserved and serious, beautiful rather than pretty, she did her best to entertain them while Lady Westmorland got herself ready. They were surprised to meet her there and a mystery always hung around this gentle addition to the unruly Westmorland household. Elizabeth Montgomerie was, in fact, the illegitimate daughter of Archibald Montgomerie, the heir to the Earldom of Eglinton. She was born in Palermo in 1803 in the same week that her father married the eldest daughter of the 11th Earl of Eglinton, Lady Mary Montgomerie. Though Elizabeth's mother is unknown, family tradition has it that she was a close friend of Archibald's new wife.[25] The marriage was a dynastic one, designed to bring back lands entailed through the female line. The bride was just sixteen, the groom thirty, a slight, but agreeable man, with a respectable army career with the Royal Glasgow Regiment. He was overtaxed, however, when asked to stand in for his chief, Lord William Bentinck, the British Minister at the Sicilian Court and Commander-in-Chief in the Mediterranean. His health broke down under the strain. He died in 1814 at Alicante as he and his complicated household tried to get back to Scotland.

Archibald's widow quickly escaped, marrying a well-known, but extravagantly rich roué, Sir Charles Lamb, and taking with her the income from the entailed estates. Their joint fortune supported a life mostly spent racketing around the Continent. Her father-in-law took over the upbringing of her sons, Hugh and Archibald, and, as there was nowhere else for her to go, Elizabeth remained with them. A maiden aunt, Jane, was on hand to help. Lady Jane doted on Archie, as in his rougher way did the old 12th Earl. When Hugh died in 1817, Archie became heir to the extensive, if heavily indebted, Eglinton lands and one of the oldest and most glamorous titles in Scotland. Two years later his grandfather also died, leaving the estates in the hands of trustees until Archie reached his majority. Though still a schoolboy at Eton, he challenged them to increase his allowance. As they cogitated, his mother offered to pay all her son's expenses for four years on condition that he left Scotland. A heartbroken Lady Jane moved out of the castle, marrying a neighbour, John Hamilton, and settling in a house on the estate at Rozelle.[26] With her father dead, a mother she had never known, and the legitimate parties tussling over the Eglinton inheritance, Elizabeth's position was precarious.

Lady Westmorland's offer to make her a ward and take her to Italy must have seemed opportune. The gesture was a characteristic mix of generosity and selfishness. While Rome might serve as a finishing school for Elizabeth and introduce her to good society, Lady Westmorland would have a companion who could deal with servants and entertain her guests while she kept them waiting. Elizabeth had little choice in the matter and learnt by slow degrees the extent of her protectress's domestic tyranny and violent emotional makeup.

Thinking about it later, Severn was chivalrous enough to say that he was in love with Elizabeth from the first moment he saw her.[27] If so, he took time to realize it, though they were often thrown together at Lady Westmorland's entertainments or in odd encounters while he waited on her Ladyship's plea-sure. For Elizabeth, Severn had the romance of being an artist and a gaiety that was missing from the Palazzo Rospigliosi. He was older, too, confidently settled in Rome, and kind. Severn, admiring her beauty with a painter's eye, could not help but think of her as a possible model. Shy and uncertain, she was not, despite her upbringing in a castle, one of those 'cats' in society he had sworn to avoid. She probably first came to his studio in Lady Westmorland's carriage with messages from the Countess, but then he persuaded her to come more secretly to sit for him. It was not an easy outing for a well-brought up young girl, dodging the hazards of beggars and filthy streets. She was intrigued by his studio, but shocked by the state of his painting cap which she undertook to refurbish. He persuaded her to model for his painting *A Venetian Warrior Taking Leave of His Wife*. While she was the lady, the knight was a self-portrait. The subject matter added a frisson to their secret meetings.

He would slip little notes in her hand when they met at Lady Westmorland's, tightly folded squares and triangles or narrowly twisted strips of paper inviting her to come again or offering to squire her at balls.[28] By the summer of 1827 he was confident she would have him if only he could overcome his own objections to marriage ('yet really this is such an opportunity that I waver').[29] He went off to Naples sure that he would see much of her there. Once again nothing came of it. His new romance was following a familiar course.

Engrossed in her feud with the Blessingtons, Lady Westmorland scarcely noticed the comings and goings of her ward. If she heard some gossip about unauthorized absences, she took little notice. And so the surreptitious visits to Severn's studio continued, terrified though Elizabeth was that her guardian would get to hear of them from her servants. She was desperate to get away. Miss Mackenzie, a mutual friend, who knew of the private reign of terror at the Villa Rospigliosi, had always taken an interest in her fellow Scot and approved of her friendship with Severn. Perhaps, Severn thought, she might take Elizabeth in, but she was about to leave for Genoa while Miss Leach, another friend who might provide a refuge, was in Subiaco with her brother. What finally broke the impasse and tipped Severn over into committing himself to marriage at the age of thirty-five was not love, nor even social ambition, but pity. The most obvious way out of all Elizabeth's problems was marriage. Once she was his wife, Sev-ern could protect her. The thought of leaving her as she was, vulnerable and unhappy, became intolerable.

8 Sketch for *A Venetian Warrior Taking Leave of His Wife*, for which Elizabeth Montgomerie modelled during her secret courtship by Severn

Though Elizabeth was already twenty-five and without a clear future, she never found it easy to make up her mind and stick to a settled course. Confident though Severn had been the previous summer that she was more interested than he in marriage, in the end she took some persuasion:

Love, Marriage, and Persecution

Dear Miss M.,

I purposely kept away—your want of confidence annoys me—Yet I will tell you that I have to impart something which secures your freedom from Lady W. for ever. Your doubts are unworthy of you, more as I have ever shown myself your true friend, and once more say, I can insure you against all, even from Lady W. and Anna, down to the petty tattlers, but all rests in your faith of my word and power, you have no cause to doubt the one or the other, and my pride is to have them credited—I still hope to see you here this morning and still to call myself

Yours

J.S.

His postscript was an ultimatum: 'These are the last words about you, that I shall write, or say, or read.' She gave in, on condition that Lady Westmorland was not told until the marriage arrangements had been finalized. She and Elizabeth would be in Florence at the end of September, staying with Lady Westmorland's stepson, Lord Burghersh, the British Minister there. If Severn visited Brown at the same time they could be married, away from the prying eyes of gossips in Rome.

Having made the arrangements, Severn told Lady Westmorland he was getting married. It was not a well-considered interview. She was intrigued by his news and made lots of guesses about the identity of his bride. For once, she was way off the mark. When he finally named her ward 'she evinced great coldness'.[30] Nonetheless, she kept up appearances, delivering Elizabeth herself to the altar of the church at the British Mission, and signing her name, predictably full of curlicues, in the marriage register alongside Lady Burghersh, a niece of the Duke of Wellington, and Seymour Kirkup.[31] After that Severn and his bride were on their own.

Lady Westmorland had had time to brood on her conversation with Severn. When she had asked him about his host in Florence, he, remembering Brown's republican principles, flippantly told her that Brown would not want to know her. She was outraged: while Severn thought himself good enough to aspire to the hand of the daughter of an heir to an ancient title, she was not considered good enough to meet his friends in Florence. Though she was happy to invite artists to her table, as husbands they were less certain quantities. Relationships between artists and society girls which might just pass in Rome were differently viewed back home. (Even the most prosperous artist of the day, Sir Edwin Landseer, was to find that, though he might father most of the Duchess of Bedford's children, it was out of the question to marry her when the Duke died.) Though it never crossed Severn's mind, there was probably some sexual pique, too, in Lady Westmorland's bitter reaction to the marriage. She had held him in her ambit, confident of his devotion, while behind her back he had been making love to a much younger woman she thought of as little more than her dogsbody. It was on Elizabeth rather than Severn, however, that she first vented her spleen, writing to Severn hinting darkly, if ludicrously, at Elizabeth's impure past. Severn was outraged. Though she had hinted at a reconciliation, he resolved on a cut.[32]

Lady Westmorland took a long slow revenge. Back in Rome she first tried unsuccessfully to keep the new Mrs Severn out of society. This only increased Severn's determination to show off his bride. Despite their astonishment at his marriage, Lady Compton and Henry Fox, now a sworn enemy of Lady Westmorland, were delighted by it.[33] Eastlake, ruminating yet again on his own unattached state, thought Severn had 'been very fortunate, if good fortune can ever attach to the word marriage … But Severn was married without much consideration,—like all else that happens to him, and he is even happier than before. It was difficult for him to be <u>much</u> happier, but he has really reason to be so.'[34]

Severn was never a calculating man. His natural buoyancy made him ready to take risks. The first was his decision to go to Italy with Keats; the second to marry Elizabeth Montgomerie. In both there was compassion, compassion for the desperately ill friend about to travel on his own to Italy, and compassion for the tyrannized Elizabeth with no obvious protector. There was, too, a belief in his own ability to set the world to rights, to bring Keats home to health and happiness, to take care of a vulnerable young woman. And self-interest as well. Risky though both decisions were, they turned out favourably. His experience with Keats in Rome was the making of him; his discovery of domesticity with Eliza and their children gave him the greatest satisfactions of his life. His bachelor friends grew tired of hearing of his newfound bliss. 'Mecca, Loretto, and the hoary temples of India will lose their worshippers', wrote Trelawny in envious exasperation, 'and even St Peter's toe be left green with mould; all worship being transferred to Mrs Severn.'[35]

The battles for social acceptability in Rome, however, took their toll on the health of the newlyweds. Seymour Kirkup, understanding, as he did, the characters of both Severn and Lady Westmorland, wrote a wise letter, advising Severn to keep his head down:

Now you've enough to do, & to think of without distracting your attention in a war that does you no credit in any respect. For I can assure you however people appear to side with you to your face, they do not do so entirely behind your back & it is the way of the world. What you call an attack on Mrs S. is of no consequence as she is above harm but certainly in part your own fault. You <u>were</u> both out of order in your secret meetings at your lodgings—you have acted irregularly & you have since exasperated her to declare it . . . You'll be having a family to provide for soon & let that thought keep you from making enemies . . . it is not necessary in your station to do everything that is highly spirited for the sake of éclat.

Where you have been wrong (all are so sometimes) you will do yourself no credit by contesting—& when you are right the world will not thank you for defeating a Lady.[36]

Severn would have none of it. His pride was up. 'The winter of 1828 was all war between us.'[37]

In the spring he had sacked Teresa, becoming increasingly weary of the encroachments of her growing family on his living space.[38] At the end of the year, her husband, Giovanni, began legal proceedings, alleging that he had been employed by Severn and claiming back-pay from 1823. Lengthy affidavits signed by a number of workmen claimed that they had overheard Severn making a verbal commitment to Giovanni while they were working at Severn's premises. At first he did not take the case seriously. A check through his records showed that he had been in Venice at the time. When the judge asked for a private meeting with him, he was confident that he had 'foiled those rogues'.[39] But, unlike his opponents, he failed to take his opportunity to bribe the judge. They submitted revised evidence; the judge ruled in their favour; and Severn was ordered to pay over £100 in damages.

Shrewd friends like Thomas Uwins advised him to settle. He would not get justice in the papal courts against these 'tools of a much higher power', he wrote, hinting at the general suspicion that Lady Westmorland was financing the plaintiffs. 'A merchant or a man of leisure may sometimes try a contest with rogues; it will take the one but little out of his business, and be only an amusement and occupation to the other; but an artist, whose time is his estate, and whose head and fingers are the only effects in his banker's hands, for him to treat with lawyers or put himself in opposition to knaves, is worse than madness.'[40] Others, like Finch and Lady Compton, wanted the Severns to continue. He did not need encouragement. 'Finding myself in this dilemma and in a foreign country, and rather than be robbed by such a judge and such a set of vagabonds, I determined to make a stand. Having, moreover, along with ample leisure, plenty of patience and a calm temperament' (wrote Severn years later in a self-portrait none of his intimates would have recognized), 'I got in order the most formidable opposition.'[41]

He appealed to the English Cardinal in Rome, Thomas Weld, who had the case transferred to a higher court. Again the sentence was confirmed. By now Severn's legal troubles were a *cause célèbre* in the foreign community in Rome. James Cobbett, the son of the great English Radical, who was visiting Rome with his sister, Anne, wrote it up in scandalized terms, in an otherwise sympathetic account of life in Italy published in 1830.[42] There was talk of the British community getting together to pay Severn's fine and then creating a stink in the English papers. Kestner, the Hanoverian Minister, who acted on behalf of the British, took the matter up with the pope and was joined by Bunsen, now the Minister at the Prussian Legation.

Severn's case and the attention it aroused came at a sensitive time. A revolt against papal rule in Romagna in February 1831 was followed by uprisings in Parma and Modena. The Austrians moved in to reinstate the old order. The French followed, opportunistically seizing the papal port at Ancona. Though Britain had no official standing in Italy, Palmerston, its vigorous new Foreign Secretary, could not sidestep the issue. He put pressure on both the French and Austrians to withdraw, while encouraging them to work with him to persuade the pope to address some of the worst abuses of his administration. He also appointed a special emissary, Sir Brook Taylor, who had recently served as British Minister in Berlin. Taylor arrived in the spring of 1831 with a remit to persuade the pope to abandon the Inquisition in Romagna, appoint laymen to judicial tribunals, and release some of the rebels. Severn's court case was timely grist to Taylor's mill. He took it up with the Vatican as an example of the way in which the corrupt operation of the courts was bringing discredit on the papacy. The solution he brokered, however, quickly fell apart when court proceedings resumed. Nor did Taylor succeed in his larger objectives: though the French and Austrians withdrew, there was no reform. By the end of 1832 absolutist rule had returned to Romagna; and the prisons remained as full as ever.

It took a British insider, Monsignor Acton, the supplest of the English Catholics in Rome, to find a way of bringing Severn's trial to an acceptable conclusion. Born in Naples, but educated at Cambridge before his training in Rome for the pontifical public service, Acton had been appointed an assistant judge in Rome in 1828. He advised Severn to refuse to pay the fine but let the bailiffs distrain against his property by taking some of his pictures, which he could then redeem with some suitably showy object. The RA Gold Medal proved ideal for the purpose.⁴³ Meanwhile Acton negotiated privately with Giovanni Bartolomei, persuading him to settle for half the sum the courts had awarded him. The case had taken three years and, when his own legal fees were included, cost Severn £95.

Indecisive though the outcome was, Severn always saw himself as the victor. A natural Palmerstonian, he was defending not only his own rights but those of all foreigners in Italy. He had, however, lost some of his illusions in the process. In place of his innocent enjoyment of the honesty of the Italians when treated according to British standards, he had come to see a darker side of life in Rome. (This was reinforced by his involuntary attendance at the public execution by mallet of a young Italian, who had been falsely accused of murdering a Roman prelate.)⁴⁴ The search for justice also put strains on his and Elizabeth's health and drained some of his artistic freshness and creativity. Even so, his spirited challenge to the corruptions of papal administration had won him new admirers. Thirty years later it would bring him a rich reward.

One of the friendships cemented by the trial was with Thomas Weld, Rome's least likely cardinal. For much of his life Weld had been a typical English country squire, living with his wife and daughter on the family's estates in Dorsetshire, a well-respected member of a leading Catholic gentry family. In 1815 his wife died and three years later his only daughter married her second cousin, Lord Clifford of Chudleigh. Left on his own, Weld made over his estates to his brother and was ordained priest in 1821. In 1826 he travelled to Rome to be with his daughter. Pius VIII who, like his predecessor, Leo XII, was keen to make an English cardinal as a sign of his long-term ambitions for the Catholic community in England, knew he had a catch on his hands. Weld was made cardinal in 1830. Though he advised on matters relating to the Catholic Church in England (with a good deal of help from the brilliant young Rector of the English College in Rome, Nicholas Wiseman), he was not a strenuous member of the Curia. Nor was he minded to change his native ways. The Roman populace were scandalized by the sight of a cardinal in all his finery taking a daily airing in his carriage with a handsome young woman, little imagining that she could be his daughter. Even more shocking, he used the small red umbrella carried at the back of cardinals' carriages to protect the Sacrament, as a parasol for his granddaughter. A frequent dinner guest, gallant with visiting English ladies, he moderated his behaviour in only one respect. He had enjoyed playing the French horn, often with Severn accompanying him on the piano.

As this was judged an unseemly instrument for a cardinal, he was obliged to desist.[45]

Weld belonged to the tradition of the old English Catholic families who kept their heads down and did not proselytize. It was an attitude Severn approved. His own secure, undogmatic Anglicanism reinforced his suspicions about the increasingly confident Anglo-Catholic community in Rome in the 1820s and 1830s. At its heart was the English College in Rome, reopened after the Napoleonic Wars as a training school for priests preparing to reconvert England. It quickly became a spiritually intense, doctrinally pure focus of Catholic sentiment for the British in Rome. Both Lady Westmorland and Richard Monckton Milnes teetered on the brink of going over. Others proved yet more susceptible. Wiseman, who was appointed rector in 1828 and his deputy, Dr Baggs, regularly regaled Severn with lists of their 'converts'—or 'convicts' as Severn called them. Though they met often and Wiseman was a gifted musician and connoisseur of the arts, Severn was always wary of him, distrusting his intellectual allure, as well as his missionary zeal. For Severn, like Weld, religion was a private joy and comfort, not to be talked about overmuch. It was a question of manners too: 'A real gentleman cannot be a bigot.'[46] Severn devoted long passages in his reminiscences of this time in Rome to cloak and dagger tales of attempts to entrap unsuspecting English visitors. In one, he only narrowly escaped fighting a duel over some of Dr Bagg's gossip recounted to a rich but dissolute young artist from Yorkshire named Dean, another of the 'convicts'. Though Severn expected Weld to disapprove of his part in exposing Dean's impious habits, their affable relations continued unchanged. They were, after all, both gentlemen: neither paraded their religious convictions.

Ineffective though Weld had been in resolving Severn's legal problems, he found an appropriate way of compensating him. He commissioned an altarpiece on a subject Severn had been contemplating since 1827, *The Infant of the Apocalypse Being Saved from the Jaws of the Dragon* (as in chapter 12 of the *Book of Revelations*). He worked on it for the next seven years, inspired by what he had seen in Venice, and, briefly, going back there in 1833 to refresh his memory. Both the Virgin Mary, modelled on Eliza, and St John of Patmos, are richly coloured Titianesque figures. Between them is a less convincing object, the multi-headed dragon, displaying its toothy jaws: student of Fuseli though he was, Severn was never good at ferocious subjects. Even so, this work in progress commanded a prominent place in his studio in the 1830s, impressing both casual visitors and potential patrons.

Another friendship strengthened by the court case was with Carl Bunsen, the Minister at the Prussian Legation, and an opposite pole of attraction to Wiseman. He had first arrived in Rome in 1816, intending to pursue philological studies. Despite all his doubts about the worth of the diplomatic life, he became increasingly involved in the affairs of the Prussian delegation. By 1824 he was its head, juggling diplomatic despatches with vain attempts to puzzle out Etruscan scripts, and winning a Europe-wide reputation for his archaeological and textual researches. Though a champion of Protestantism, he never underestimated Rome's dual attractions at the heart of the classical and Catholic worlds. He reacted to the pull of Catholicism with energy, importing a German chaplain and reviving Sunday morning services at the Prussian Legation chapel where Severn was organist from 1830. He celebrated the tercentenary of Luther's break from Rome, revived the German liturgy, and vigorously took up the interests of the non-Catholics in the burying ground by the Caius Cestius Pyramid. Protecting the cemetery was a cause close to his heart: three of his children were buried there (ten, however, survived).[47]

Bunsen was an Anglophile. The English, he thought, were 'the best worth knowing in Rome'.[48] He and his young Welsh wife alternated their twice-weekly at homes between their German and British friends, with Fanny delighting the company with her performances of native folk songs. The highlight of their hospitable family calendar was always their celebration of Christmas, mixing simple German piety with sparkling decorations and a tree in a way which would not become familiar in England until Prince Albert's arrived nearly two decades later. The Severns were regular guests at these festivities.

Marriage changed Severn's social circle. He now saw less of his artist friends and more of a genteel circle of art lovers and patrons. Henry Fox forgot his earlier snobberies once Severn had a well-bred wife. Joseph and Eliza also saw much of the Finches, until the Colonel's sudden death in 1830 ('a worthy man, tho' a bore' was Kirkup's reaction).[49] Lady Compton, who wintered in Rome, was delighted to welcome a fellow Scot to her artistic evenings. Genteel in her origins, she had been adopted by Sir Walter Scott, who helped engineer a good marriage for her. She was proud of her famous connection, setting some of her guardian's poems to music and performing them for her friends. Severn introduced her to Keats's work.[50]

Robert Pemberton Milnes, a wealthy Yorkshire squire and father of Keats's first biographer, who travelled in Italy in 1831, was surprised by the number of British he found there, shrewdly guessing that they remained from a mix of pride and poverty: 'here they are somebody at home they will be no-body'. Women, too, flourished as patronesses of the arts: 'every city, as with the ancients, has its Divinities'.[51] If Lady Compton, Lady Coventry, Fox's mother-in-law, and Lady Westmorland were the tutelaries in Rome, there were lesser goddesses, too, like Miss Leach and the Hon Frances Mackenzie. Miss Leach's principal concern was her brother, the naturalist William Leach, who had suffered a breakdown after a stint as Assistant Keeper at the Natural History Department in the British Museum. Severn first met them at L'Ariccia in the summer of 1824 and was fascinated when Leach ran to his sister with an insect 'no bigger than the head of a pin' concealed in his hand. 'I thought William you had already got that in your collection' she objected. 'Yes,' he said, 'six months ago I found the male which I have by me, but this is the female.' While he sought out small insects, she looked for lame ducks, caring for a mentally disturbed young Russian artist and lingering at the bedsides of the sick.[52] Absent-minded and disorganized but kindness itself, she took drawing lessons from Severn. Like everyone else in his comfortable but uncritical new circle, she adored his work.

Frances Mackenzie was made of sterner stuff. Proud though she was of her parentage—her father, Lord Seaforth was head of his clan, Colonel of the Seaforth Highlanders, Governor of Barbados and a Fellow of the Royal Society—she and her five sisters had been left with a diminished future when he died in 1815, heavily in debt and broken by the death of his son and heir. Bravely, she struck out for Rome, one of the pioneering wave who settled there after the end of the Napoleonic Wars. Though an early engagement to the Danish sculptor Thorwaldsen did not survive his liking for simple working-class living, she fascinated cultivated English bachelors of limited sexual energy. Both Crabb Robinson and Uwins were devotees: 'there is a lofty, ladylike bearing about her, accompanied with so much sweetness and good sense, that to be commanded by her is happiness . . . mind, mind alone is the talisman with which the Mackenzie of Seaforth compels the obedience of her Votaries'.[53] In Rome she laid on imaginative entertainments, accompanied visitors on their rounds of the studios or tours of the Vatican, corresponded with them after they left, and exercised a moral and social authority in the British community which even Lady Westmorland accepted. But it took her almost ten years to effect a reconciliation between the Severns and their former patroness. In the meantime her own friendship with the Severns flourished. She was godmother to their third son; and went with them to the Alban Hills in the summer. A passionate lionizer, she lived in the best place in the world for it, proof that a bluestocking Scottish spinster could lead a richly fulfilling life in Rome.

Despite all their troubles in the early years of marriage, Joseph and his Eliza were supremely happy together. Once having brought himself to the point of marriage he never regretted his leap from bachelorhood. He delighted in designing costumes for his wife to wear at evening parties and, though he was disappointed by her lack of interest in music, she compensated with her fascination with his painting. She learnt to mix his colours, while he taught her to paint. In time, she would do the backgrounds to some of his pictures and varnish them for exhibition. The children, too, came quickly, Claudia in 1829, Walter a year later, Ann Mary in 1832, and Henry in 1833. In all the hundreds of letters he sent his wife, Severn, like most Victorian husbands, never said a word about sex and was, Elizabeth liked to claim, uncomfortable talking about love. When they were apart, however, his reticence disappeared: 'all my care and passion for women are centred in you', he wrote to her from Venice in 1833, 'being a husband & a lover has made me a better painter'. And from London in 1838, 'my mind is in a ferment about you ... I had no idea you were so completely a part of my being.'[54]

She and Joseph, or 'Severn' as she liked to call him to his 'Molly', had few secrets. He told her about his illegitimate son in London and she, doubtless thinking of her own parentless childhood, agreed to incorporate him into her growing family. On the point of leaving for Italy, however, young Henry died. It was a mark of Elizabeth's acceptance of Severn's first unseen son that they honoured his memory by naming their next boy child after him. And she was there to comfort her husband in a time of trouble he could not widely share. Brown, always at his most supportive in a crisis, was another of the few who had known about Henry. Sensitively he consoled Severn: 'if your boy was not to live, how happy it is for you that he did not first arrive in Rome and personally link himself tightly to your affections ... thank God! You have no recollection of him but as a baby, which he had long ceased to resemble.'[55]

After eighteen months of marriage Severn could not imagine his situation otherwise. 'The change in my life is very favourable to my pursuits—I cannot be happier.—My dear wife was made for me in the stati[o]n that I am in—she is an invaluable help to me', he joyously told Brown.[56] Even the trial, he persuaded himself, had been all for the best. Having come through that, he and Eliza 'had the most complete happiness and enjoyment that it is possible for human creatures to know—prosperity, friendship, the best and most entertaining society, no end of brilliant gaieties when we wished them, [and] our love for each other and our children'.[57]

Early in 1830 they bought a ten-year lease on an apartment in Via Rassella. It seemed they were settled in Rome for good.

CHAPTER 11

'Everybody's Man and a Very Obliging Creature': Severn in his Roman Prime

B
Y the early 1830s the close-knit group of British artists who had arrived in the aftermath of the Napoleonic wars was dispersing. John Lane slunk away embittered after the disastrous unveiling in 1828 of his *Joseph's Dream*. Richard Evans took his quarrels back to Birmingham, persecuting Sir Thomas Lawrence with complaints about old colleagues.[1] More of a loss to Severn was Seymour Kirkup, who went to Florence in 1824 and stayed.[2] Richard Westmacott, too, left to join his father's busy sculptural practice in London. Most significant of all, Eastlake, reluctantly but finally, left Rome in July 1830, knowing he could make his way in the British art establishment only if he returned to England. He would cast many wistful backwards glances in the following years. A year later, Thomas Uwins was also gone. Though based in Naples he had always stayed in close touch with the artists in Rome, especially Severn. While newcomers like Penry Williams and his friend William Havell, the landscape painter, were quickly absorbed and made their mark socially and artistically,[3] Severn's loyalties were to his earliest friends in Rome. Of them only John Gibson and Richard Wyatt, William Ewing and Joseph Gott remained, all sculptors.

The greatest loss, as everyone admitted, was Eastlake.[4] His presence in Rome had given lustre to the artistic community there and, after his election *in absentia* as an Associate Academician in 1827, he was yet more conscious of his responsibility to ensure that its claims to recognition did not go unnoticed in London. Eastlake was Severn's mentor in the period of his greatest artistic development, the established artist full of technical insights and painterly awareness. He enjoyed Severn's optimistic, expansionist temperament, so different from his own more careful nature: 'you are one of those people destined to be & to think yourself happy whatever becomes of the rest of the world, so that good fortune & contentment in your case never surprize me', he wrote enviously after his return to London.[5] He admired the originality of Severn's art and its distinctive feeling in Italian genre scenes. Their 'truth of circumstance, situation, incident and costume cannot fail to interest many'.[6]

Eastlake's natural authority, Severn's geniality, Westmacott's enthusiasm, Kirkup's wry kindness, and Gibson's generosity were at the heart of the new British school of artists in Rome in the 1820s. Their mutual supportiveness, as well as their artistic achievements, impressed newcomers like Wilkie and Bewick and kept Etty and Uwins in Rome far longer than they had intended. Uwins could hardly believe his luck in finding himself 'in the very centre of my artistical friends, enjoying with them a community of goods, and having everything supplied me the instant the want is communicated with a primitive simplicity and kindness that is like nothing so much as the fabled golden age of the poets'.[7]

In Rome not only did the artists direct buyers to each other's studios, they also hung their friends' work alongside their own to attract the eye of patrons. When he went to Florence in 1828, Severn took with him an oil sketch of his *Venetian Warrior Taking Leave of his Wife*. Kirkup put it on his wall, where it attracted the admiration of Sir Matthew Ridley, an enthusiastic collector of Italian paintings, and led to a commission from Lord Lansdowne for the completed work. Similarly, after his return to England, Westmacott displayed *The Falconer* in his house when it failed to sell at the British Institution in 1831 and then got it into a new exhibition.[8] In London Eastlake, too, remained a loyal friend. In 1828, when he returned briefly for the RA Exhibition, he got Severn a commission; in 1832 he sponged and polished *Italian Vintagers Returning* with his silk handkerchief; in 1833 he had *Sicilian Peasants Singing the Evening Hymn to the Virgin* moved to a place where there were fewer 'white' pictures to show up its yellowness; and in 1834 went out of his way to check the hanging and finish of *Shepherds in the Campagna*.[9] Uwins, Westmacott, and Eastlake all sent Severn regular reports on the annual exhibitions, recognizing his need to keep in touch with the London art world and get a sense of how his pictures looked in cooler English light.

'The Roman party', as Uwins called them, continued to be seen as a group, making a distinctive showing at the Academy with their genre scenes.[10] Interest in their work, coupled with the continuing passion for Byron and a general enthusiasm for Italy, encouraged a flood of imitative pictures, mostly produced in England and to English tonal prescriptions. Samuel Prout, for example, built a successful thirty-year career as an Italian artist on the basis of a single short stay in Rome in 1824. The early 1830s were the peak years of this fascination with all things Italian at the RA. In 1832 the exhibition was dominated by Turner's *Childe Harold in Italy*, Uwins showed his *Neapolitan Saint Manufactory*, which won him election as ARA, and Penry Williams exhibited *The Procession to the Christening: A Scene at L'Arricia*. Eastlake followed in 1833 with genre scenes and, in 1835, a reworking of his *Peasants' First Sight of Rome*. Severn, too, concentrated on Italian scenes in these years, showing *The Fountain* in 1830, *Italian Vintagers* in 1832, *Sicilian Peasants* in 1833, and the following year *Shepherds in the Campagna*.

Without their own dealers, the artists in Rome looked to the annual exhibitions at the Academy and the British Institution as a key way of promoting themselves. Exhibiting at Somerset House kept their name before the British public; it gave patrons the pleasure of seeing work they had already bought or commissioned, on show in a prestigious setting; and, for those with ambition, it was a way of qualifying for election as an Associate of the Academy. From 1827 until 1857 Severn showed his best work there in most years, doggedly trying to maintain his reputation. After the success of *The Vintage* in 1827 and *The Fountain* in 1830, he was usually hung on the line in the 1830s and in the best rooms.

It was not only his regular patrons who looked out for his work, he had attracted a critical following as well. Thackeray, who wrote art criticism for *Fraser's Magazine* under the pseudonym of Michael Angelo Titmarsh, had a soft spot for Severn. He liked his straightforwardness and sentimental appeal, the charm of his rich colouring and poetic sensitivity. What Severn lacked in technical finish he more than made up for in sincerity: 'I never can look [at his pictures] without a certain emotion of awe—with that thrill of the heart with which one hears country children sing the Old Hundredth, for instance. The singers are rude, perhaps, and the voices shrill; but the melody is still pure and godlike.'[11] Uwins, too, encouraged Severn not to be deflected from his course: 'for the credit of England', he wrote, 'you will continue to pursue out your own distinct and original feelings, uninfluenced by the jargon by which you will be assailed'.[12]

Other friends were becoming more critical, however, trying to warn Severn that his work did not show to advantage at the RA Exhibition: his palette was too dark and rich; his work lacked finish; his figures were sometimes poorly proportioned.[13] From a distance it was hard for Severn to judge. Rather than taking his chances before a fickle public he had, in any case, always preferred working for an established circle of well-heeled buyers, 'the lesser ambition of painting for a private gallery where my Patrons tell me my pictures look better than those of the exhibition'.[14] Most of these patrons he had found in his own studio.

The studio system contributed much to the buoyancy of the Roman art market by putting painters and sculptors in direct touch with enlightened cos-mopolitan private patronage. Buyers in Rome were in impressionable mood and, inspired by the artistic riches around them, apt to be more expansive in their commissions. There was still a cachet to pieces bought in Italy. That they had ventured to Rome to acquire their art works rather than picking them out at the annual scrimmage at Somerset House marked out their owners as men of taste and aspiration. By doing the rounds of the studios they could strike up personal relationships with artists, dropping in to see a commissioned work in progress, having an input into subject, treatment, and composition if the artist were compliant, and getting a sense of his oeuvre and personality.

The studio system suited Severn well. Here he could present not just his work but himself. He was an engaging talker and there was much to talk about: his early struggles and the drudgery of Bond's studio; the Gold Medal at the RA; and the romantic story of his arrival in Italy with a young and dying poet. He could also tell the stories behind his paintings and reassure hesitant buyers with casual references to his growing list of royal and aristocratic patrons. Puffery was Severn's way of keeping up his spirits. In Rome, unlike England, it was not out of place. He was obliging, too, and well settled in Italy, full of advice for visitors about what they should see and where they might get good lodgings, together with curious stories of the oddities of local life. And he was always happy to knock off a quick portrait as a souvenir of a visit to the world's art capital.

Most were captivated: a few like Henry Fox in the early days wearied of his salesman's patter. 'He is rather a pretty artist, but a provoking little cox-comb', he wrote disdainfully in his diary, 'cursed with a false idea of having been born a natural genius, and for ever detailing the singular traits and peculiarities of his own extraordinary temper and character.'[15] But Severn had learnt from experience that honesty did not pay. 'I used to think it necessary to point out all the defects of my things, and to those who knew nothing about it', he told Uwins. 'Now, I let the innocent souls find out the defects, which I find a great advantage.'[16] Or again, 'I believe only in putting the shoulder to the wheel...it is better to have vanity than genius.'[17]

British art lovers in Rome followed a regular route round the artists' quarter. First was the studio of Thorwaldsen, the acknowledged leader after Canova's death, followed by a call on Gibson or Eastlake. They then directed visitors to Severn as the next most established English artist in Rome. Maria and Augustus Callcott did the circuit in 1828, liking what they saw in Severn's studio and returning for a second visit, when Severn obligingly took them to the studios of other British painters in Rome.[18] From the amount of work on show it was obvious he was much in demand. At the beginning of 1827 he had nine pictures on order, a year later he had eleven on hand, and by April 1829 was refusing further commissions for the time being to allow him to concentrate on the seventeen already on his list.[19] And so it went on for most of the 1830s. He acquired a reputation as a man from whom it was hard to get a picture because he was so busy.[20]

His fame rested on the breakthrough of *The Vintage* and its companion piece, *The Fountain*, which now hangs in the Royal Palace at Brussels. Even under grey northern skies it is a striking picture, more Veronese than Titian. The colours, bright reds, pink, and orange are daringly bright but richly harmonious, too, while the carefully composed groups of women listening to a piper, filling water jugs or walking companionably away convey a generous feeling of tranquil enjoyment. *The Fountain* is a positive picture, less brittle than Uwins's Italian scenes, gentler and more wholesome than Eastlake's stiffer compositions. Not only do the women (all of them beauties) interact with each other, but the carefully painted Etruscan figures on the base of the fountain underline their relationship with the past. Eastlake had no doubt it was Severn's best work so far,[21] while William Havell, a perceptive but often harsh critic, was full of praise: 'the figures in cool, quiet shadow have so much purity of tint, and the oppositions of cool and warm colours are so gentle and true, that they are quite equivalent to the most brilliant contrasts...I had not a conception before how far mere daylight shadow could be carried without dullness.'[22] Cecilia Powell in her definitive study of the impact of Turner's encounters with southern Italy has even suggested that *The Fountain* influenced one of Turner's major works, *The View of Orvieto*.[23]

Severn continued to mine the Italian vein in the 1830s.[24] *Shepherds in the Campagna*, an atmospheric portrayal of an old shepherd and his family huddled together amongst their flocks in the melancholic wastes of the marshes outside Rome, was the freshest of his inspirations. In many ways, it is a complement to *The Fountain*. This time the figures are all male, apart from a colourful portrayal of Eliza in rich peasant costume, dandling the young Walter on her knee. But while *The Fountain* is a joyous picture *The Campagna* is sadder and more poetic, lit by the dying sunlight of a late afternoon catching the whiteness of the hilltop villages in the distance as a pale moon appears to the right. Others of Severn's Italian scenes were more repetitive. The competition, too, was becoming stiffer. If Turner had always been *hors de concours*, Uwins was beginning to make a reputation with his more censorious take on Italian life; Penry Williams and William Havell were successful entrants to the field; and the public was always ready for Eastlake's occasional representations of Italy. It was the proliferation of English imitators, however, which left the market saturated by the end of the decade. 'How long are we to go on with Venice, Verona, Lago di So-and-so, and Ponta di What-d'ye call'em?' Thackeray complained in 1840.[25]

Severn's range, however, was broad. Many of his best paintings in the 1830s had a literary inspiration. In 1830 he produced on commission for Finch, *Ariel on the Bat's Back*, with the last rays of the setting sun illuminating the glowing figure of Ariel in a vast expanse of golden light against a dark landscape. Even in the basement of the Ashmolean, where it now resides, it has a Titianesque resonance.[26] Finch was so pleased with it that he upped the price from £30 to £50. A more substantial inspiration, though it proved harder to sell, was Severn's *Rhyme of the Ancient Mariner*, painted in 1833 but not shown at the RA until 1839. Thackeray judged it 'a noble performance, and the figure of the angel with raised arm awful and beautiful too. It does good to see such figures as these ... they belong to the best school of art.'[27] Severn turned to Keats for artistic inspiration only once in this period, painting an *Isabella and the Pot of Basil* when he was marooned in the countryside outside Rome in 1837. While Keats's name was still obscure, Bulwer Lytton, another artistic inspiration, was a bankable proposition. By far the most successful novelist between the death of Scott and Dickens's maturity, Lytton, who was in Rome in the winter of 1833–4, ostensibly recovering from a breakdown and trying to mend his disastrous marriage, readily fell into his usual workaholic ways. Leaving his wife to take care of herself, he completed *The Last Days of Pompeii* and made a start on *Rienzi, Last of the Tribunes* in just four months. Severn never thought much of *Rienzi*, but was happy to capitalize on its success in his painting.

Severn's attraction to such scenes was all part of the hankering which never left him for the grand manner. Having completed his *Revelations* altarpiece, he immediately began sketching another, *The Three Maries at the Tomb*, and thinking of following it up with *The New Jerusalem*.[28] By the late 1830s he was again talking of himself as an historical painter, though a far less innocent one than in his early years in Rome. Now he could bring his mastery of genre painting to historical canvases. *The First Crusaders in Sight of Jerusalem*, the most popular of the four paintings he showed at the Academy Exhibition in 1838, included not only the historical figures referred to in Tasso's epic *Jerusalem Liberated*,[29] but a religious procession he had come across by chance when painting in the early morning at Tivoli.[30]

Throughout the 1830s he accumulated a loyal circle of patrons, including Sir Thomas Redington, Major Richard Sykes, and Sir Matthew Ridley. His work also entered a number of royal collections. In addition to Prince Leopold, the Grand Duke Alexander of Russia, an avid if calculating patron, ordered a copy of *The Roman Ave Maria* in 1840, which now hangs in the Hermitage. Through his Danish artist friend, Ferdinand Thoming, Severn sold to the royal family in Copenhagen.[31] In Britain the Queen bought some of his *Vintage* studies while her aunt, the Duchess of Cambridge, chose a version of *The Campagna* in 1840.[32]

No new visitor to Severn's studio was ever more favourably impressed than the young William Ewart Gladstone, who first came to Rome in 1832. Gibson, in his usual way, led Gladstone and his elder brother, John, across the road from his studio to Severn's on Monday 16 April, an auspicious day for Severn and the start of the second most rewarding friendship of his life. Gladstone recorded in his careful travel diary, 'enjoyed the visit much both from the man and from his works ... All his works are full of poetry: & of a higher <u>class</u> in this respect save any I have seen in Rome, either in painting, or Sculpture, except only Thorwaldsen's—if even those.' The personal relationship quickly flourished. After a tour to Naples the Gladstone brothers returned to Rome, enjoying 'a very pleasant evening' of music-making at the Severns and calling in again on their last day. Severn's 'pictures lose nothing on a second visit', he noted.[33]

Gladstone met Severn at a formative point in his life. Having won a brilliant double First at Oxford, he was travelling in Europe while he waited for a parliamentary seat in the forthcoming general election. Rome was the high point of his Grand Tour. He came not only as an accomplished Classical scholar, but as a man deeply interested in religion and keen to learn about art. While his father was a perceptive collector whose tastes ranged unusually widely for the period, young Gladstone was conscious only of his deficiencies. 'I never had any discrimination in pictures,' he confessed to his diary, 'Yet I should love to learn.' And learn he did, preparing for each visit by reading detailed descriptions in guidebooks and noting the points he was expected to admire. Many of his reactions were conventional. He looked for elevating subjects, dismissing the narrowness of Gibson and Wyatt's neoclassicism ('sublimity of conception' was no longer to be found in 'mythological subjects').[34] He appreciated devotional feeling, admired correct perspective, and the mastery of technical difficulties,[35] and enjoyed works with literary associations. Though some of Gladstone's contemporaries scoffed at his aesthetic tastes or decried his pedantry, his eye was more original than they allowed. Over the years he built up a varied and, in part, distinguished art collection.[36]

In Rome on his first visit he did all the things educated English tourists usually did amongst the 'splendour, poverty and filth'. He attended one of Torlonia's evening parties, finding it 'as dull as we deserved'; he watched a young girl taking the veil; he went to hear the nuns singing at Trinità dei Monte; he got to know the Bunsens; he visited the Protestant Cemetery; he tried unavailingly to meet the biggest celebrity in town, Sir Walter Scott; he 'lionized' in the company of Richard Monckton Milnes, the intimate at Cambridge of his idolized schoolfriend Arthur Hallam; he associated with the British artistic community ('It is very gratifying to see the English lay claim to so large a share of the talent of Rome in the fine arts'); and he diligently toured all the usual sights. Rome both fascinated and repelled him. Alongside the glories of its history and art and the city's melancholy beauty was the squalor of life under a corrupt, repressive papal temporal authority. 'Who can visit such a place of "beauty and decay" without feeling that it opens his mind to what he never knew before', he mused.[37]

As a souvenir of his first visit to Rome, Gladstone commissioned Severn to paint his portrait, though he was diffident enough not to mention the fact in his diary.[38] This, the earliest portrait of Gladstone,[39] now hangs in a dark corner of the Reform Club. It was one of the quick face-painting jobs done for visitors on the Grand Tour which helped supplement Severn's income in the 1820s and 1830s. He places Gladstone against a background he would often have used for portraits of this kind, sitting in a book-lined room admiring a fine illuminated text. The pale, good-looking, clear-eyed face, appealing if rather anonymous, is that of the scholar, the trappings those of the young aristocrat. This is the young Gladstone as Old Etonian aesthete.

Six years later he returned to Rome arriving in moonlight at the Porta del Populo and experiencing a familiar confusion of intense emotions. When Severn put himself out to please Gladstone in 1832 he could have had little idea of his future eminence. Now, 'the rising hope of the stern unbending Tories' in Macaulay's famous phrase, was making his mark in politics. His artistic tastes had also developed, to include Cimabue and Bellini.[40] Gladstone's loyalty to Severn as man and painter, however, was unchanged. He was delighted when he and his friend John Manning, the future cardinal, ran into the artist at the Vatican. Severn always loved showing friends around the galleries. Gladstone, who liked to feel privy to the insights of insiders, noted his comments, idiosyncratic though they were. There was the absence of 'sacerdotal characteristics' in the sculpture of the Trojan priest Laocoon and the father's apparent lack of concern for his sons (a characteristic Severn observation this); the suggestion that the left thigh and leg were 'on the whole the finest part of the work'; the over-tight helmet of the Minerva Medica ('too much for the character'); and the excellence of the statue of Demosthenes.[41]

When Gladstone called at 152 Via Rassella, the completed *Revelations* altarpiece dominated the studio: 'a bold effort . . . a new subject fierily conceived and executed'. Alongside it stood Severn's current major work, *Rienzi in the Forum*. There was also the 'very beautiful' *Roman Ave Maria* to admire. No doubt Severn pointed out the charming portrait in its corner of Eliza with the young Walter, a sturdy little fellow in a Roman tunic. Four days later Gladstone came back bringing Lord Carnarvon and Sir Stephen Glynne, an old schoolfriend he had met up with in Italy. A couple of weeks after that, he returned again with the Glynne family. In this company he was particularly susceptible, enthusing in his diary: 'How much has been painted within the last two hundred years which is of a higher order than Severn's Saint John?' This was high praise, but Gladstone was in excitable mood that day.

Though he wrote up his visit to Severn's studio in his diary, he said nothing about the most momentous event of 3 January 1838. In the evening he walked with Catherine Glynne in the moonlit Coliseum and attempted a proposal of

9 Severn's portrait of William Ewart Gladstone done in oils in Rome in 1832. The earliest known and previously unpublished portrait of Gladstone

marriage. He had already been rebuffed twice, and harshly, by two young aristocratic women he hardly knew, so he went about it circuitously. His intended was so bewildered by his circumlocutions that she could not be certain of his drift. But she did not reject him. Three days later he wrote to her and, back in London, they were soon engaged, the prelude to a long, unconventional but exceptionally happy marriage. The conjunction between his morning visit to Severn's studio and Gladstone's realization that he might, at last, have found a wife, may well have influenced the warmth of his subsequent feelings towards him. In Gladstone's mind, Severn was always associated with the place and the time in which his imaginative horizons had opened not only to new aesthetic possibilities but also to the prospect of personal happiness. The romantic memory of Severn in his glory days in the 1830s would sustain Gladstone's indulgence towards him and his family for forty years.

In Rome they enjoyed each other's company. Both had an eye for the picaresque nature of Italian life. Severn talked of the 'great ferocity inherent in the national character' and instanced two women he had seen being carted off to prison 'of whom one brandished in triumph a large handful of hair as she passed along', Gladstone of the squalor of the passport office, despite its 'Corinthian capitals of Pentelic marble rolling about [the] dunghills'.[42] Severn quickly persuaded himself that Gladstone was attracted to him because of his connection with Keats. For once, he underestimated his own appeal both as man and artist. Though Gladstone was a voracious reader, there is no mention of Keats in the 25,000 works by more than 4,500 writers he recorded in his diary. Nor, though he read most of Richard Monckton Milnes's works soon after publication, did he get round to his best-known book, the biography of Keats, until 1873. It was Shelley whom Gladstone read assiduously, not Keats, and Shelley was the poet who drew him to Severn.[43] For Gladstone, Keats's world of sensibility lacked robustness and intellectual stimulation, while his devotion to the pagan world of mythology was, like Gibson's neoclassicism, outmoded. If Severn talked to Gladstone about Keats (and it is hard to imagine he did not) he said nothing that his hearer thought worth recording in his diary, and though Gladstone visited the Protestant Cemetery, he was one of the few not to be struck by Keats's grave.[44]

Severn made a similar, but less excusable mistake with another visitor to Rome, Sir Walter Scott, far and away the most popular living writer. It was nearly thirty years before he wrote down his memories of their encounters. By then, frequent retelling of the tale had turned it into melodrama. In Rome, Severn recalled, thanks to his connection with Scott's ward, Lady Compton, they breakfasted together daily. Scott's grief at Lady Compton's early death was overwhelming: 'he would stop short to lament her unlooked-for death in tears & groans of bitterness, such as I had never before witnessed in any one—his head sunk down <on his heaving breast> & the tears made channels down his waist-coat'. Severn attempted to divert him by bringing him pictures and sketches, including his portrait of *Keats Reading*. Though Scott seemed uninterested, Severn chatted on about his friend and the way his growing fame as a poet was putting to shame the vicious attacks of the critics. Astonishingly, he was unaware that J. G. Lockhart, Scott's son-in-law, had been a prime mover in *Blackwoods Magazine*'s onslaught on the Cockney School of poets. 'I became bewildered at seeing Miss Scott turn away her face already crimsoned with emotion. Sir Walter then falteringly uttered these words "Yes, yes, the world finds out these things <u>for itself at last</u>" and taking my hand closed our last interview for he was taken seriously ill the following night & I never saw him again as his physician hurried him away from Rome.'[45] The suggestion that Scott's guilt over the death of Keats hastened his own last illness shows how little Severn really knew of the famous writer.

By the time Severn met him, he was a broken man, working against the odds to pay off debts incurred in the crash of his business partners. Recently widowed, suffering from the effects of three strokes, and accompanied by two quarelling children, he was travelling in the Mediterranean in 1831–2 not just in search of health but in hopes of making money. A happy stay in Malta was followed by a difficult journey to Naples which evoked the most poignant memories of Lady Compton[46] before he moved on to Rome. There he rallied enough to visit places associated with Cardinal Henry Stuart, the younger brother of Bonnie Prince Charlie. But when his daughter, Ann, insisted on going to the Protestant Cemetery to search out the grave of a Scottish kinswoman, Scott stayed in his carriage. It was not guilt that kept him away from the graves of Keats and Shelley but limited mobility. And lack of interest. Only one of the younger poets counted for Scott: Byron.

What Severn took to be a significant admission of responsibility for Keats's early death was no more than a politely dismissive way of closing down a tiresome conversation.[47] Though Severn's later account of the affair is one of his most egregious attempts to put himself centre stage at pivotal moments, it also reveals his eagerness in the 1830s to find the green shoots of Keats's growing fame even in stony places. It was inconceivable to Severn that a great writer, whom both he and Keats admired, could not be interested in Keats. He told the story of Scott's visit to Richard Woodhouse, who was in Rome soon afterwards on his way to Florence. Woodhouse set him straight about Scott's family connection with Lockhart. Most probably, too, he told Brown about the affair when they met. Incidents of this kind may well have given Brown pause for thought when Severn assured him, as he regularly did, that the time had come to do more to promote Keats's fame. Knowing his friend's big-hearted enthusiasms, Brown was usually dismissive. Though Severn might misread the motives of his visitors, however, he did not mislead Brown about the growth in their numbers.

One of the first was Arthur Hallam who, as Maria Callcott's diary of her stay in Rome in 1828 shows, moved in the same circle as Severn.[48] The teenage Hallam was already a poet. His contacts with Severn would have contributed to his early interest in Shelley and Keats and fanned his enthusiasm for republishing *Adonais* the following year. Though Shelley was the cult figure amongst the Apostles, the elite private debating society at Cambridge University, from 1829 to 1831, Hallam and his friend Tennyson, an occasional Apostle, were quietly drawn to Keats. Like the young Browning, Tennyson discovered Keats for himself, saying simply 'he's wonderful'.[49] The influence was immediately apparent in his first book of poems published in 1830. In part, Keats's fame rose on the back of Tennyson's after a period in which his poetry was largely unavailable except in the occasional anthology. His personality, too, was being misrepresented. The impression of the vulnerable young poet left by *Adonais* was amplified by Hunt's brief account of Keats in *Lord Byron and Some of His Contemporaries*, published in 1828. Though best known for its virulent score-settling over his unhappy time with Byron in Genoa, Hunt also found room for an affectionate, but patronizing portrait of Keats: modestly born, brilliantly gifted but insecure, the victim of ruthless, partisan critics, oversensitive and in delicate health. Both Severn and Brown loathed this 'milk and water' Keats.

In 1829 Galignani in Paris published a pirated collection of the work of Coleridge, Shelley, and Keats. It contained much of Keats's best poetry but the seventy-five pages devoted to it compared with 224 and 275 for the other two, and its place at the end of the volume, confirmed the impression given in the short memoir which preceded the selection. Here was a poet of immense promise but incomplete achievement: 'had he lived he might have worn a wreath of renown which time could not easily have withered'. But the poetry was there to be read; and the memoir contained a touching description of Keats's grave. Severn, too, got a favourable mention: 'a valuable and attached friend of the poet' and now 'an artist of considerable talent well known since in Rome'.[50]

Galignani's edition set Brown thinking about his responsibility to set the record straight. He started out on his long-promised biography in workman-like fashion, trying to fill the gaps in his knowledge of Keats's early years by tracking down Charles Cowden Clarke and William Haslam. He also wrote to Fanny Brawne seeking permission to include two poems that referred to her though without naming her. His letter reached her at a tragic time, a few days after the horrific death of her mother in a fire. She did not forbid publication, however, much as she dreaded the pain of reliving the emotion of her life with Keats.[51]

Charles Dilke was consulted and tartly enquired what Brown meant to do with the profits. Severn, by contrast, was delighted that 'a true tribute . . . such as I have ever long'd should be done' was to be paid to Keats, now that there was the added urgency of countering the impression of Hunt's 'whining, puling boy'.[52] He promised to set down some memories of Keats, provided they were not published as such, 'as I feel they must contain invectives against many persons whose enmity or even notice I am little anxious to have'. He had no qualms about claiming the right to produce the frontispiece, however, and would engrave a portrait of Keats himself. Could Brown ask Fanny Brawne for the loan of his original miniature of Keats? Honourably, Brown refused, given the risk that it would be lost en route. And so Severn contented himself with working from the copy which Brown had made.[53] As for the proceeds from the venture, he never had any doubt: 'Now I have thought a good deal of it, and am going to propose that we erect a monument to his memory here in Rome . . . I have consulted Gibson, who says that for £200 something very handsome may be made.' For its design he harked back to the ideas which Trelawny had thought of appropriating for Shelley's grave in 1823: a bas-relief showing 'Keats sitting with his half-strung lyre—the three Fates arrest him—one catches his arm—another cuts the thread—and the third pronounces his end . . . as the gravestone is so unworthy of him, and so absurd (as all people say), and as the spot is so beautiful, I hope you will agree to it'.[54] Severn also sent some lively impressions of Keats as a young man, revelling in the opportunity to recall the happiest days of their friendship. His 'invective', which was confined to Hunt, was restrained by Brown's standards.[55]

Despite promising beginnings, neither book nor monument made progress. Brown got sidetracked into a dispute with Dilke over George Keats's financial dealings with his brother. Though the quarrel was patched up for a while when Brown stayed with Dilke in London in 1833,[56] other distractions arose. Brown began a study of Shakespeare's *Sonnets* and helped his new housemate, Trelawny, rewrite his autobiography, *Memoirs of a Younger Son*, which would become a bestseller. Brown took credit for prefacing each chapter with poetical quotations, including a generous selection of Keats, some of it previously unpublished. But it was crab-like progress towards establishing Keats's fame. Faced with the enormity of his responsibility, Brown, for all his devotion, created one obstacle after another.

In Rome, Severn became impatient. He accused Brown of wasting time 'rewriting the lies of that Vagabond Trelawny' and threatened to write the life himself if Brown would not, 'which I am sure will make you look about you'.[57] Yet Severn's pressure never overcame Brown's inhibitions. Brown lacked Severn's optimism, worrying about acting prematurely and failing to do Keats justice. In part, too, it was a question of place: in Rome Severn got to know more Keats enthusiasts and had a higher visibility as the friend of Keats and guardian of his grave. But Brown also got his share of devotees. Richard Woodhouse, the gentlest and most discerning of all Keats's friends, spent seven weeks in Florence in 1832, charming Brown out of his 'funny odd dislike' for him, showing him the fine plaster medallion of Keats which he had commissioned from Girometti and extracting a promise from Brown 'to write the life of Keats in my quiet country nook during this winter'.[58] Still Brown did nothing.

By contrast, the steady stream of visitors to 152 Via Rassella anxious to learn more about Keats were eagerly welcomed. They came from Cambridge, New England, as well as Cambridge, England. The pirated Galignani edition was frequently reprinted in America where a literary coterie at Harvard in the early 1830s took to Keats with the same devotion as the Cambridge Apostles. Thomas Gold Appleton was only the first of many venturing across the Atlantic who sought out Severn, spending 'several hours' with him 'in most agreeable conversation. He told me a thousand things about Keats.'[59] Though he was gratified by this admiration for Keats in distant worlds, it was the Cambridge Apostles who changed Severn's idea of the poet. Arthur Hallam was followed by Richard Chenevix Trench in February 1830: 'My only introduction to him was our common admiration of Keats ... of whom he is never tired of speaking, when he finds one who listens with gladness.' A bookish, melancholic young man and occasional poet, Trench was still searching for the vocation which would in 1861 take him to one of the thorniest heights of Anglicanism as Arch-bishop of Dublin. Responding to his audience, Severn stressed Keats's final struggle to find salvation. 'Shelley and Hunt had deprived him of his belief in Christianity, which he wanted in the end, and he endeavoured to fight back to it, saying if Severn could get him a Jeremy Taylor, he thought he could believe.' He also primed Trench for what he would find at the Protestant Cemetery. Keats's epitaph 'is worded harshly towards his persecutors, who deserved not even such commemoration as that upon his tomb', Trench commented to a friend. 'Moreover, they who wrote it erred from the intention of any epitaph whatever.'[60]

Another visitor saw the grave and its anonymous epitaph with a more cynical eye. Henry Crabb Robinson, a friend of Coleridge and Wordsworth, had the unusual distinction of having recognized Keats's genius while he was still alive. He disapproved, however, of Keats's wish for an anonymous grave, finding 'a very small stone placed erect with an inscription—already nearly effaced. It had the affectation of not containing a name.' Astutely he sensed its potential to create a cult. But he was very ready to excuse his new friend, Severn: he 'deserves honour for his generous friendship and in causing this monumental stone to be put, probably did what his friend wished him to do'.[61] In the same winter Severn had more opportunities to talk about Keats with an initiate, Richard Monckton Milnes. The most irrepressible of the Cambridge Apostles, he was in Rome with his parents, coming under the spell of Wiseman and the English College, relentless in his socializing and newly avid for the warm south. He had come to Keats indirectly through *Adonais* and now talked at length with Severn about him.[62] He was rewarded with a snippet from the manuscript of *Lamia*. From Rome Milnes went to Florence and a chance meeting with Brown on the terrace of Walter Savage Landor's bare but magnificently sited villa at Fiesole. If Brown could not write about Keats he could certainly talk about him. Milnes was entranced.

Two years later, in 1834, another Apostle, who had been particularly close to Milnes, arrived in Rome with four of his Cambridge friends. This was Stafford Augustus O'Brien, a witty, energetic, light-hearted young Irish man and a good amateur actor. Severn readily took part in their play-reading of *The Merchant of Venice*. This gave him an idea: why not put on the unpublished play on which Keats and Brown had collaborated, *Otho the Great*? O'Brien, whose voice reminded Severn of Keats, was just the man to play Ludolf, the role originally written for Edmund Kean.[63] All that was needed was the script. Severn wrote to Brown in high spirits, reminding him how keen he had been to launch the play in Rome in 1823. But now even the offer of an Easter Sunday lunch of lamb and green peas prepared by Eliza could not tempt Brown, nor yet the eagerness of the five 'young men of rank...devoted admirers of Keats good actors and handsome young men'. Protective as always about anything that bore on Keats's reputation, Brown had shown the manuscript around a little since 1823. Even Landor had been critical. 'I am afraid it is not so good as you and I imagine', Brown wrote glumly, sidestepping Severn's assertion that 'The time has come, and I fear the time may pass. These young men read and recite Keats to me until I think him more beautiful than ever.' If Severn wanted the manuscript he would have to come and fetch it himself, Brown unhelpfully volunteered.[64]

The failure to put on *Otho the Great* in 1834 was only a secondary defeat in the string of reversals Severn experienced in his long campaign with Brown to be doing something about Keats.[65] Far more serious were the delays over the biography and the monument. As Severn saw it, the two were linked. Only a true account of Keats's life could counter the impression Hunt had given of a lack of manliness: a fitting monument would show that Keats was not just a man but a gentleman too. The nature of Keats's admirers proved that his poetry was best fitted for the appreciation of an elite of birth and culture. As he told Brown in 1834, excited by the enthusiasm of O'Brien and his friends, 'if he is not the Poet of the million he is more. For I would say that, judging of the talents of his admirers and their rank as scholars, that his fame is a proud one.'[66] This was in tune with Arthur Hallam's high-minded assessment. Shelley and Keats, he wrote in 1831, were 'poets of sensation rather than reflection. Susceptible of the slightest impulse from external nature, their fine organs trembled into emotion at colors and sounds and movements, unperceived or unregarded by duller temperaments.'[67] If Keats had become a gentleman poet, so Severn was a gentleman artist. A fine monument would make the point.

By 1836 Severn planned to approach Milnes for help with collecting subscriptions for a monument that Gibson would sculpt, 'either to be placed here or in England—tell me what are your thoughts', he pressed Brown, 'but don't tell me you set your face against it, for so I will have it—I can collect a handsome sum—I am an Artist myself, and a fine work I'll have'.[68] Brown, now back in England, and at last pulling together his memories of Keats, was unmoved. If Keats's fame was to become universal it would be through his poems not a monument put up by his friends. He had found rereading

Keats's letters and poems a painful process. Having heard his authentic voice again he was now convinced that the only change needed to the gravestone was to eliminate everything other than Keats's chosen epitaph.[69] And so Brown and Severn pulled in contrary directions, and so the simple stone remained.[70]

Unremarked by Severn, Keats's grave was acquiring a permanence all of its own. The desolate anonymous epitaph with its reference to 'malicious enemies' had an unstoppable Romantic momentum. Located on the edge of the unfenced old burial ground, it was, as it still is, a potent place of pilgrimage. Flowers were plucked from the grave, pressed, and sent back across the Atlantic, while descriptions of the site proliferated in the magazines. Keats's chosen words put his growing band of admirers under an obligation to ensure that his desire for oblivion was drowned out in the chorus of their own devotion. To change the small stone with its hard-to-read inscription, lying close to other reminders of extinguished early hopes in a community of the dead who were in, but not of, Rome, was becoming unthinkable.

Severn never stopped trying to revamp Keats's grave. His persistent lobbying for a monument was a tribute to his generous spirit and deep indebtedness to Keats. But it was also a mark of the conventionality of his taste in an age where monuments and funerary pomp were becoming integral to memorialization of the dead. Tasteful though Severn's ideas in the 1830s were for replacing Keats's stone, they were too grand for the old cemetery. Apart from 'Colonel' Finch, who earned himself a 302-word epitaph in Latin outlining his many virtues, elegiac simplicity reigned amongst its broken columns and coffered tombs. The alloy of self-regard was creeping into the gold of Severn's devotion to the memory of Keats. As he complained to Brown in 1836, the absence of a monument was a reproach to his own position as not only the most visible guardian of the heritage, but a well-known artist in his own right: 'something is look'd for from me, and something I will have'. By then his ideas about the form of the memorial had developed, too:

I have thought to have the beautiful profile of Girometti's on the upper part, surrounded with architectural flowers in the Greek style... I'll do nothing without you except your denial—with that I'll have nothing to do... I have the right, as Keats's last friend, and also as an Artist, to the management—After the Monument is up, I'll plant the most beautiful Laurels and Cypresses ever seen, and attend to the keeping them fresh to the extreme days of my old age—For I feel that I owe much to the name of Keats being so often linked with mine, it has given the Public an impression which has ensured me a good career, much as it was denied to him.

Happily, Severn's candour took the edge off his vanity: 'Now I dare say that you will think all this very vain on my part, and throw cold water upon me and that, but no, I am too old to be damped by you—You may encourage me to anything, but I won't be put down. Keats shall have a fine Monument—and I will produce fine historical works worthy of his friend.'[71]

Though Severn's artistic achievement never came close to matching that of Keats, he was not overestimating his eminence in Rome in the early 1830s. After Eastlake left he was the senior British painter. He was also at the heart of Anglo-Roman society, the indispensable *homme d'affaires*, helpful, practical, and knowledgeable in the ways of Rome, or, as William Dyce found, 'everybody's man and a very obliging creature'.[72] When Trelawny wanted exemption from quarantine for his three-year-old daughter arriving from Greece, he looked to Severn to intercede with the Roman authorities.[73] When Eastlake was out of town worrying that he might miss the imminent arrival of Turner in September 1828, he entrusted Severn with the task of ordering up a canvas for him ('it must be prepared with the purest <u>white</u>—this was his wish').[74] Severn was the man he also called on to organize the British showing at the international art exhibition at the Capitol in 1830 thought up by the papal authorities as a way of mending the ill-feeling between the local Italian painters and their foreign rivals. They did not altogether succeed. Severn's *Ariel* was banned from the exhibition on the grounds of indecency, though the semi-naked spirit is sexless enough. Cardinal Weld explained that the Vatican had confused Ariel with Uriel, identifying the bat with the devil and then assuming that the peacock's feather held by Ariel was a slur on papal ostentation.[75] By then Severn was familiar with the suspicious confusions of the Roman censor. It made a good story for his visitors. Crabb Robinson especially enjoyed it.

Inevitably, given his associations, literary as well as artistic visitors sought his help. Bulwer Lytton was astonished to discover, as he worked on *Rienzi*, that Gibbon's *Decline and Fall* was on the prohibited list in Rome. Severn had a quiet word with Cardinal Weld, who gave him a dispensation to lend his prized copy.[76] Artists, too, benefited from Severn's generosity. When Uwins needed a new set of paintbrushes, he turned to Severn.[77] And when the newly married Samuel Palmer arrived on honeymoon in November 1837, bewildered and anxious about money, it was Severn who organized the pass for the Vatican that enabled his wife, Hannah, to start on the copying which would finance their visit. Similarly, when William Collins came to Rome, Severn offered him space in his studio and helped him get the best models. In Severn the generous collegiate spirit of the 1820s had survived. Alongside him he now had Eliza, charming visitors with her grace and old-fashioned good manners. She could be practical as well. When George Richmond's wife, Julia, found herself giving birth unexpectedly in the middle of the night, it was Eliza who was hastily called in to help.

William Richmond, relying on his parents' memories, later described Severn in his heyday in Rome: 'his geniality charmed every member of the Roman society … Severn would do his utmost to render a year's sojourn in the Eternal City pleasant, and having great tact and considerable accomplishments, his house likewise became one of the centres where were to be found the foremost men and women of the day.'[78] Though the Richmonds and Severns were to become firm friends, in private George and Julia enjoyed making smug comparisons between the free and easy way in which the Severns brought up their children and their own stricter regime. But Richmond's fondness for the strap and the relentless piety forced on his children produced far less happy results than Severn's benevolent laxity. No Severn child ever ran away from home like Severn himself and the young William Richmond.[79] Nor did he maintain his authority with his fists as his father had. He was determined to give his children as different a childhood from his own as he could.

They ran in and out of his studio, enjoying the thrill of a father who earned his living in a much more interesting way than most, or helping their mother mix his paints. Both he and Eliza were determined that they should love the arts as much as they did. 'I trust that music & painting will be among the talents they will show to console my old age', he wrote to Vincent Novello's wife, whose children were also outstandingly talented.[80] He drew endless sketches of them in his notebooks, their heads bowed over a piece of paper with pencil or brush in hand, or engrossed together at the table sharing a book. And in the summers they enjoyed the cooling air of the Alban Hills. He described one of their journeys up the rough road to Subiaco to Brown: 'my four little ones in two hampers on the mule, my wife on another, and I on foot to look after the well-being of the party'.[81] Eliza, too, sent a charming unpunctuated letter, introducing her 'chicks' to the grandmother in London who had not yet seen them, to cheer her in her widowhood: Claudia 'a very clever nice little thing'; Walter 'a very fine funny little dog' and his father's favourite; Mary 'very pretty'; and Henry, white-haired and blue-eyed who, at only twelve months, 'carries chairs about the house with as much ease as a great London porter would do' (at least in his doting mother's eyes). 'We are very happy,' she assured her mother-in law, 'at least I am for I am very fond of painting and enter into all Joseph's pursuits with as much pleasure as he does himself.'[82]

The following year their fifth child, Arthur, was born. The Severns had arranged some distinguished godparents for their children. Arthur's ceremony, organized by Miss Mackenzie at the Villa Poniatowski, surpassed them all, for Wordsworth came and presented the silver mug from which he had drunk the baby's health. The poet was in Rome in the early summer of 1837 with Crabb Robinson. Though Robinson thought him 'the greatest man now living' in England,[83] they were not ideal travelling companions: Wordsworth was dour and overbearing with foreigners and insisted on early nights; Robinson was endlessly chatty and curious and often up until the small hours. Both spent a good deal of time with the Severns, as well as Bunsen, Gibson, and Augustus Hare. Miss Mackenzie, who was never likely to let such prizes slip through her fingers, brought along Lady Westmorland to one of the dinners. 'She must have been rather pretty in her youth', Robinson mercilessly noted.[84] Wordsworth took a particular liking to Severn, admiring his energy and dedication to his art: 'why he is out in the open air at five in the morning with his Wife and children when she is well enough, returns at 7, paints all day and does not stir out again till an hour or so after sunset', he approvingly wrote to his sister.[85] Severn sometimes had Wordsworth to himself, taking him to the Vatican and Doria Pamphilj galleries and chatting to him in his studio as he painted his portrait.[86] He jumped at the opportunity to correct the record on Keats in an influential quarter. 'He informs us that the foolish inscription on his tomb is to be superseded by one more worthy of him. He denies that Keats's death was hastened by the article in the *Quarterly*. It appears that Keats was by no means poor, but was fleeced by Haydon and Leigh Hunt.'[87] In return, Wordsworth, though jaded and anxious to be off from Rome, went out of his way to grace Arthur Severn's christening and make himself agreeable. His presence there was an occasion treasured in Severn family history and eventually recorded on Arthur's tombstone. In all the future years of financial hardship, the christening mug from which Wordsworth drank was one treasure that never went to the pawnbroker's.

In 1837 Severn was at the peak of his happiness in Rome. His order-book was full, he delighted in his family, he was sought-after by the most interesting visitors. Everyone thought him at least ten years younger than he was (not that he could remember his age).[88] And, it seemed, he was on the way to seeing Keats valued at his true worth. If the seeds of his eventual professional decline were already apparent to some of his colleagues, they did not trouble Severn. 'They want me to put down my name to become a member of the R.A. of London,' he told Brown, 'now I don't know—they may refuse me, and I am going on so well as to fame & fortune that I am not inclined to alter my course.'[89] His hand would be forced sooner than he expected.

1. John Keats drawn by Severn in 1817, the likeness of Keats which Charles Cowden Clarke admired above all others.

2. Severn's miniature of Keats done in oils and watercolour on ivory and exhibited at the Royal Academy in 1819.

(Copyright National Portrait Gallery, London)

3. Severn's miniature of his family, from left to right Charles, Tom, Sarah, Charlotte, Maria, his mother, Elizabeth, and father, James *c.*1820. (Copyright City of London, London Metropolitan Archives)

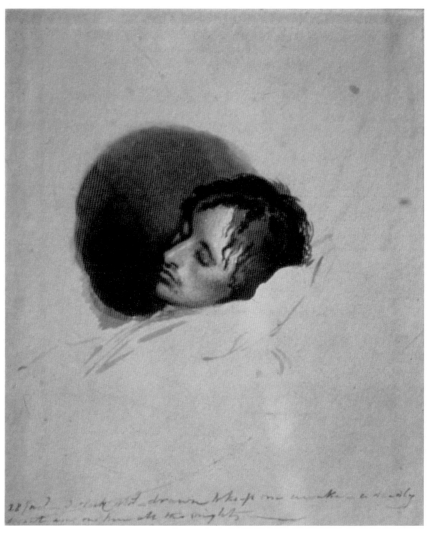

4. Severn's night-time pen and ink sketch of the dying Keats, 28 January 1821. Severn wrote underneath: '28 Jan^y—3 oclock Mor^g—drawn to keep me awake—a deadly sweat was on him all this night'

5. Self portrait in pencil of Severn seated at a keyboard *c*.1823.
(Copyright City of London, London Metropolitan Archives)

6. *The Fountain* painted by Severn in 1828. (Copyright IRPA-KIK, Brussels)

7. *Shepherds in the Campagna*, painting in oils, 1834, later bought by Gladstone. (Private collection)

8. *Shelley at the Baths of Caracalla*, portrait in oils, 1845, commissioned by Mary Shelley. (Reproduced by kind permission of the Keats-Shelley Memorial House, Rome)

9. *The Deserted Village*, 1857, Severn's last painting to be exhibited at the Royal Academy. (Reproduced by kind permission of the Art Gallery of South Australia, Adelaide)

CHAPTER 12

∽

Going Home

In the summer of 1837 both private and public tragedies darkened the Severns' feelings about Rome. On 15 July Eliza, always fondest of her last-born child, laid Arthur down for a nap. While she chatted in the next room about his winning ways, the toddler caught his head in the rails of his cot and choked to death. Though the Severns were lucky to lose only one child, it hit Eliza hard. Two months later she could still tell Maria only the bare facts. Alongside spiritual resignation was guilt: 'it was an accidental death which our foresight could have prevented and we are reconciled to it as the will of God'. Still in a daze, the family left to spend their summer in Olevano. Their nursemaid organized their get-away, anxious to get them out of Rome where cholera had been taking hold since June. They buried Arthur in the Protestant Cemetery close to Keats: there was no time to put up a stone.[1]

The great Roman cholera outbreak of 1837 was an apocalyptic moment in the British engagement with Rome, giving tangible effect to the association many made between the death-haunted city and the corruptions of an alien Church. Six years later when Mary Shelley went there, the subject was still eagerly discussed. She collected together the memories of her compatriots to add to what the Severns had told her in London, producing a Gothic tale of papal disregard, administrative incompetence, popular superstition, and ghoulish practice, lightened only by examples of British heroism. An elderly general who lived on the floor beneath the Severns died, as did a British sculptor named Barlowe, who rented their coach-house. Severn himself, who made a quick trip to Rome in October to check on the safety of their property, heard horrifying stories of corpses flung from the windows of houses and an unbroken series of carts trundling along from sunset until two or three in the morning taking the dead for unceremonious burial in hastily dug ditches outside the city walls.[2] Only the British redeemed themselves, opening up a convalescent hospital and dishing out 'blue pills'.[3] Some 15,000 people, one-tenth of Rome's population, died as typhus and starvation followed on the cholera.

At Olevano, sealed away from the outside world, the Severns were safe, if short of money. They reverted to the simple life, sustained by gifts of provisions from the locals 'pass[ing] our time very pleasantly amongst the peasantry, wandering through their beautiful vineyards'.[4] Away from his studio Severn painted small, saleable pictures of the local beauties: the occasional arrival of fumigated letters from Rome was a reminder of the horrors they were missing. In November, with the cholera abating and the evenings growing chill, they returned. There Severn found a letter from Brown anxiously begging for news. His reply described their melancholy homecoming: 'our house which within presents every painful remembrance of our dear angel and without doors reminds us of friends snatched off by the Cholera ... Our return to Rome was after an absence of 20 years instead of a few months ... the pallid countenances all seemingly sunk in years—the vacant streets and the gloom.'[5] Rome took many years to recover from the cholera epidemic. The decline in the number of visitors and patrons hit the artistic community hard. After two years without a sale, Gott took his family back to England in 1839. Two of his four children had died in the aftermath of the epidemic.[6]

Severn, too, was in financial trouble. Though in writing to Brown he blamed his stock of unsold pictures (£1,000 worth) on the effects of the cholera and the general flight from the city, he had already told his brother Tom in the spring of losses of £700.[7] Cardinal Weld's death earlier that year had lost him one of his most generous patrons. His heir, Lord Clifford, may have insisted on a price far below the £1,000 Severn expected for the *Revelations* altarpiece. Nor were the Severns economizing. Eliza had not lost the taste for fine clothes, carriages, and hospitable entertainment born of her upbringing at Eglinton Castle. Severn, also, liked to cut a good figure. In 1836 and early 1837 he lent Bunsen more than he could afford for the construction of the Protestant Hospital in Rome. Only a stern reminder about the embarrassment if he failed and an extension of the payment period saved face all round.[8]

Quick though he always was to deny the accusation, Severn was never a good business manager. Effective in talking potential patrons into giving him commissions, he shied away from making them settle up. (Prince Leopold took three years to pay for *The Fountain*.)[9] In his willingness to please, he could also get in a muddle over the details of a commission, assume a sale where only polite interest was intended or take on too much and fail to meet deadlines. Dilke was a case in point: the warm feelings he developed towards Severn on his visit to Rome in 1826 had a bitter aftermath. The Raphael copy Severn had promised to organize failed to materialize despite several reminders from Brown, who, assuming it was close to completion, arranged to pay for it from a joint account he held with Dilke. Dilke was not the man to overlook a botched transaction. When Brown stayed with him in 1833, he got an earful about Severn's underhand dealings. It was ten years before Severn completed the picture. His 'grazioissimo' letter accompanying it failed to soften Dilke's indignation, and so relations remained frosty for several years. Whatever his own failings, however, Severn was confident that his wife, with her 'shrewd Scotch head', made up for them. She was the closest thing he had to an agent thinking of ways of drumming up sales and patrons and working on her aristocratic connections. There was a price to pay. Though Eliza was as fertile as her husband in dreaming up new ventures, like him she lacked staying power. And she fortified his reliance on a narrow circle of buyers. As a result, Severn missed the rising tide of interest in collecting art amongst successful businessmen and industrialists.

Penry Williams was more astute. Steadily, he overtook Severn as the leading British painter in Rome and quickly attracted patrons among the new commercial buyers who valued polish and precision and appreciated straightforward sentiment.[10] He returned to England in 1837 for the RA Exhibition, put on a good show, and picked up commissions. It was made clear to him at the RA annual dinner that he would be made an Associate if he returned home.[11] The condition was important. That year Turner and F. L. Chantrey led a move to amend the Academy's Statute 1 to exclude non-resident artists from both associate and full membership. In Eastlake and Wilkie's absence, the Council approved the change, which was primarily directed against the British artists in Rome. Chantrey had been there in 1819 and not enjoyed himself, while Turner felt no obligation to the British artists there once Eastlake had returned. William Collins, who was in Italy at the time, was outraged by the Academy's decision, comparing it unfavourably with the close links which the French Academy maintained with its outpost in Rome. 'It checks the ardour of English artists here, and deprives the Exhibition of a very interesting class of works, which can be better done here than in England', he complained to Wilkie. 'English artists, who are the best at Rome, should be members of the Royal Academy.'[12] Both Wyatt and Williams were well up to the required standard he wrote (but said nothing about Severn).

Williams plumped for a life in Rome, where he was never short of patrons, sat on the committees, was popular with the Germans and Italians, and remained happy and prolific for nearly fifty years. If he had stayed a bachelor, Severn might have followed a similar course, with little pressure to return to England. As a family man, however, he could not afford the freedoms of Gibson and Williams to pursue their careers where they chose. Now Severn spent his evenings with his wife and children or in society, missing out on the comradely artistic get-togethers at the Caffè Greco which Samuel and Hannah Palmer found so invigorating. Nonetheless, he was aware of the competition from Williams, always looking a little askance at him as a latecomer to the 1820s artistic community: 'a painter (landscape & figure) of wondrous merit, but a mere painter, without any of the thing in Painting but paint, but in this he is super excellent', he wrote to Kirkup.[13]

While Williams and Gibson continued to welcome compatriots, in the 1830s Severn had become more distanced from the new British artists. He turned out for the set-piece occasions like the annual artistic expedition by donkey to the Caves of Cervara,[14] but found the newcomers lacking the ambition of their counterparts in the 1820s. 'They too frequently break down in bowls & billiards and if generous, in Guittars—and generally leave Rome in raffish resplendence, as Italian Dandies. My slender acquaintance with any of them has been thro' letters of recommendation and always with the comparison and loss of such fellows as Eastlake and yourself', he told Kirkup in 1833. He was not the only one to sense a falling-off in the quality of the British artists in Rome. Richard Chenevix Trench, who returned in 1835, was even more censorious than on his first visit: 'I cannot imagine the great artists of other times living as they do, or so laying waste their powers, going so much into barren society, and giving themselves so little to fruitful solitude.'[15] Severn's separation from the new wave of painters cashing in on enthusiasm for Italian costume pictures increased his readiness to detect the machinations of enemies in Rome. Weld's death before the *Revelations* altarpiece had been placed in San Paolo left him with an uphill struggle against the Italian art establishment. There was a wider animosity, too. In November 1837 he blamed this on the fact that he was the only English painter in Rome still getting commissions for historical paintings. In 1839, when he had a number of pictures on hand, the Duke of Sutherland, a passionate collector of Italian scenes, was in Rome and made enquiries about purchasing a Severn picture. Someone, unhelpfully, told him that none was finished.[16]

He could still, however, recreate the old comradely spirit for friends of friends in England like George and Julia Richmond. They arrived early in November in the company of Samuel Palmer and his bride, Hannah, the daughter of the painter and engraver John Linnell.[17] They made an odd-looking pairing: the one couple socially adept and prosperous; the other often taken for tinkers in their homespun clothes, with Palmer's pockets bulging with nuts. Despite appearances, Palmer was the senior partner as the founder of a group of painters and engravers who called themselves 'the Ancients' and spent the summer of 1827 together in the village of Shoreham in Kent, inspired by this pastoral paradise. In 1831 Palmer lent Richmond £40 to elope to Gretna Green and marry Julia Tatham. Marriage and the need for a reliable income turned Richmond away from Blakeian idealism to the profitable grind of portrait painting, but the hankering after greater things remained. He and Palmer planned a sabbatical in Rome, but Palmer refused to go without Hannah. Though her parents opposed the marriage, the prospect of profit won the day. Hannah took with her sets of the engravings her father had produced of the Michelangelos in the Sistine for colouring, and planned to make new copies of the Raphaels in the Stanza. This time, it was Richmond who loaned Palmer £300 to pay for his marriage and the trip to Italy.

While the Palmers lived happily, but economically, in a single room up three flights of stairs at the top end of Via Quattro Fontane, swathed in extra layers of clothing against the damp Roman winter, the Richmonds attended soirées at Torlonia's and suppers at Miss Mackenzie's, and, thanks to introductions from Severn, began lifelong friendships with Gladstone and Henry Wentworth Acland. A contemporary of Ruskin and Charles Newton at Christ Church College, Oxford, Acland arrived in Rome in the spring of 1838, on an extended tour of the Mediterranean. His parents, Sir Thomas and Lady Acland, had become friendly with the Severns the previous winter, and so it was natural that Severn, who was 'kindness itself', should introduce their son around.[18] Though the Severns saw more of the Richmonds than the Palmers, they offered help to both, recommending lodgings, taking them to the Vatican to get passes for copying, and conducting them on a tour of the studios. Anxious to improve his drafting skills and work on his colouring in oils, Richmond attended the British Academy.

He quickly got commissions while Palmer made only one sale and had to rely on Hannah's copying. She had set her heart on doing the Titian–Bellini *Feast of the Gods*. Severn knew the painting well—it clearly influenced the composition of *The Fountain*—and undertook to plead her cause with Vincenzo Camuccini, who had it in his jealous charge. Sensing perhaps that he had little to fear from this apparently modest competition, the Italian relented: 'he could not refuse a small watercolour by an English lady'. Palmer seized a 'tambarine' and 'performed a Bacchic dance' when he learnt of Severn's successful intervention.[19] In Rome and, later, Naples, Palmer's feeling for colour ran riot. Richmond was more cautious. There were long discussions with Severn, reminiscent of earlier days with Eastlake and Kirkup, on the vexed question of light and shade and the merits of transparent or opaque underpainting. Richmond was reluctant to abandon his use of grey or lighten his shadows. Severn, the advocate of a conjunction of transparent bright colours, encouraged him to study Veronese. After a day at the Borghese Palace examining the Veroneses Richmond attempted a head without 'the grey foundation'. But in three weeks he had reverted to English ideas of opaque chiaroscuro using 'black with the local colours for shadows'. The appreciation of Veronese which Severn had taught him, however, bore fruit in a conversation with a sceptical Ruskin in 1842. Ruskin had thought Veronese tame by comparison with Rubens. ' "That may be," said Richmond, "but the Veronese is true, the other violently conventional . . . compare the pure shadows on the flesh, in Veronese, and its clear edge, with Rubens' ochre and vermillion, and outline of asphalt". No more was needed. From that moment, I saw what was meant by Venetian colour', Ruskin wrote of this crucial conversation.[20]

Severn's talks with Richmond about colouring were indicative of how far his practice now diverged from that in England. In the summer of 1838 he had the chance to judge for himself. At last, he made his return to London for the annual RA Exhibition. Much hung on the visit. He needed to make a strong showing to revive his career; he wanted to assess his chances of securing election to the RA; he had to make enquiries about schools for his two boys; and, at long last, see his mother and brothers and sisters. Tom had warned him in 1831 that his father was failing.[21] Briefly, Severn thought of going with Brown to England in 1833, but, instead, chose Venice. In July, the father he had not seen since their last brutal quarrel died. By then the days in which Severn was driven by the need to impress his father and secure his approval were long past. After his marriage he kept in looser touch with his family in London, concentrating his efforts on supporting Eliza and the children in Italy.

He and Eliza planned the visit to England carefully. He picked out four of his best paintings of the 1830s and got them to the Academy in good time for the

Exhibition. They showed his range: a study for the *Revelations* altarpiece, a new version of *Ariel*, a historical painting, *The First Crusaders in Sight of Jerusalem*, and a genre scene, *The Finale of a Venetian Masque at the Summer's Dawn*. He also took his paints and brushes in readiness for portrait commissions, the small paintings he had done at Olevano the previous summer, and a sketch for a new history painting, *Rienzi*. His visit coincided with the coronation of the young Queen Victoria, which Eliza hoped he would get a commission to paint. Though she was now set on a return to England, Severn was less convinced. The 1838 visit would be a trial run, a chance to sniff the air of artistic London and find out how his family might fare there. He stole quietly away, saying nothing to the children, and this time accomplished in fourteen days a journey which had taken eight fraught weeks with Keats in 1820. He was still a poor sailor, however. After twenty-four hours on the steamer from Civita Vecchia to Leghorn he felt '90 years old, and without the soul of a flea'. But soon he was enjoying the treasures of the Louvre for the first time and six days later crossed the Channel: 'it was an affecting sight to me coming upon the English shores, after such an absence'.[22]

Eliza had told him not to show his face in the West End until he had been kitted out by a London tailor. While his new clothes were being made he stayed with his family, first at Charles's house and then at Tom's. The excitement was immense as Charles, whom he did not recognize, knocked over the chairs to get at him and Tom, 'big fellow as he is', lifted him up and held him tightly. Maria he found 'much changed' after the twenty-year gap. All of them wondered anxiously about the effect of his return on his mother, but the seventy-six-year-old Mrs Severn 'received' her favourite child 'with calm dignity, she is younger looking than ever, her mind quite clear'. He had been away for a quarter of her life.

For all that Severn had written over the years about his desperation to be with his family, he stayed in the East End only a couple of nights. Even before the tailor had done his work, he walked over from Shoreditch to the West End, following the drearily familiar route of his apprentice days to Bond's studio. Bond was still there, shook hands with Severn, and remarked how little he had changed: it was the first of many proud moments on his 'Coronation visit'. He next bumped into the Marquess of Northampton, who invited him to meet his brother-in-law, Charles Scrace Dickins, and daughter, Marianne. In no time he had commissions from them and a cheque for £50, as well as the news that Thomas Spring-Rice, the Chancellor of the Exchequer and a Trustee of the

National Gallery, would pay £100 for *Ariel*. They took him off to Westminster Abbey to see the preparations for the coronation and find a good place for the ceremony, where Charles would sing in the 700-strong choir.[23]

Elated by these early successes, he was condescending about what he saw in the exhibition. Though Uwins had warned him about the harshness of the London art world, Severn was slow to recognize how much had changed. In his absence in Rome, William Mulready had emerged as the dominant painter of literary scenes done in the grand manner, while another very popular painter, Daniel Maclise, was the star of the 1838 Exhibition with five well-liked history pictures. Severn lived with his memories of exhibitions twenty years before and was only interested in painters whose work he knew. Now he found 'a sad, sad falling off—Wilkie and Leslies works grieved me, but for Eastlakes I could have cried over it, so fond I was of him.—the want of taste is extraordinary'. By comparison, he told Eliza, his *Crusaders* stood out 'like an honest man in the midst of sycophants—Uwins said of it that now I had no occasion to come to England'. Uwins, who went out of his way to 'trumpet' Severn around London, was as determined as ever that the British artists in Rome should get their due.[24]

The competition for commissions of the coronation scene, however, proved too intense. Though Severn had the nice idea of painting the moment when the Queen started up to help the elderly Lord Rolle who tottered as he backed away after paying homage, it was John Martin who executed it, to great popular acclaim. The official commission went to the Queen's favourite, George Hayter, a man whom Severn, familiar with his scandalous private life in Florence, thought in every way 'such a bad painter'.[25] Leslie also got a commission direct from the Queen. Severn consoled himself with his success at the exhibition. Sir Thomas (or 'Lord' as Severn called him) Redington not only bought *The Crusaders* but also commissioned *Rienzi* and ordered a copy of *Ariel*. His enthusiasm as a patron delighted Severn: 'he says I must pursue History painting because I have a genius for it, and nobody comes up to me'.[26]

There were dinners and speeches: at the annual dinner of the Artists' General Benevolent Institution Wilkie complimented him on his standing as a history painter while Sir Thomas Acland proposed a toast to the artists in Rome, to which Severn replied. At the Academy dinner on 31 July, he was given a place of honour opposite the President and toasted by Uwins 'in a very beautiful speech . . . full of all the facts about Rome that could interest them'. Severn replied 'in good style, & pleased them very much'.[27] Though Pickersgill, one of the Academicians who had supported the change in RA rules to exclude non-resident artists, made some sour remarks to Severn, he could dismiss him as no more than a 'face painter'.[28] At heart, however, he was less insouciant, looking anxiously for signs of whether he would be elected to the RA if he returned. By 13 August he was fairly sure: 'they wish to have a painter as well as a sculptor in Rome', he reported overlooking Penry Williams's prior claim. Two weeks later he had convinced himself. 'The Royal Academy will elect me no doubt, which will ensure you £300 a year should I make my exit', he promised Eliza, thinking of the generous pension provision for the widows and orphans of RA members.[29]

His literary friends in London gave him a warm welcome. Samuel Rogers invited him twice to his select breakfast parties, where he met Mary Shelley, Caroline Norton, and Crabb Robinson, telling them the tale of Keats's fury over Hilton's failure to defend him after his Gold Medal success. He also became involved in the agitation to extricate Thorwaldsen's statue of Byron from the Customs House where it had languished for six years while Westminster Abbey declined to find room for it. This brought him once again into the orbit of Edward Trelawny, whose portrait he painted in oils.

Some old friends, however, were neglected. Brown had taken the trouble to come from Plymouth to see the RA Exhibition and sent Severn an enthusiastic account of how his pictures were looking. ('Imagination, which we rarely see nowadays in painting, is in your painting; not a dreamy one, like Fuseli's, but one that makes your treatment of a subject gain imperceptibly on the beholder.') Though Brown fully expected to see Severn and assumed he would look up Haslam and Thomas Richards, Severn saw none of them. Instead, he moved to the fine house in Putney which the Radical MP John Temple Leader shared with Trelawny, talking of schemes for Gibson to do a marble group of Keats and Shelley. Brown wearily said nothing about it in his reply. Not surprisingly, he was cross: 'You puzzle me with your unadvised comings, your threatened goings, and your unthought of stayings.' He was quick to defend himself, too, over Severn's charge that he still dilly-dallied over Keats biography. 'You do me injustice in thinking I am remiss or lukewarm. His memoir has been long ready, and I am anxious it should be published.' But there were problems over copyright. Perhaps, Brown suggested, Severn who had talked of 'stirring up ... for a new edition' of Keats and Shelley, could find a publisher to sort them out. Though Severn had told Brown it was 'shamefully unjust that you all on the spot do not pull together & catch this nice moment for Keats', he did no more himself than chat to Trelawny about 'the beautiful engravings' they might include in the collection of Keats and Shelley.[30]

In place of the Keats Circle, Severn cultivated politicians and potential patrons. He hung on at Putney waiting to paint a portrait of Thomas Spring-Rice. Acland, the MP for North Devon, took him to the House of Commons three nights running where he bumped into Gladstone. Now that the busy young politician had started collecting, he was on the look-out for bargains and asked Severn whether any of his work at the exhibition remained unsold. Severn followed up with a polite and expeditious letter. It was five years, however, before Gladstone made his first Severn purchase, the oil sketch of the *Revelations* altarpiece.[31] Yet amongst other friends and acquaintances he met in the House was one who would play a dominant part in his life, Macdonald Lockhart, the Tory MP for Lanarkshire, and an old Scottish connection of Eliza's whom he 'salute[d] very kindly'. Others, too, had warm memories of his wife. Richard Monckton Milnes's sister, Lady Galway, saved a coronation medal for her 'which she caught in the scramble in the Abbey'; Samuel Rogers sent his regards ('he remembers you well at Lady W.s'); and his bachelor friends drank her health at their supper parties.[32] Now, too, Eliza's nemesis, Lady Westmorland, wanted news of her old ward.

She and the Severns had been brought together the previous year by Miss Mackenzie. Severn took in his stride Lady Westmorland's plea to let the past lie: Eliza, remembering the miserable times trailing around behind her guardian and her unpredictable temper, was still mistrustful. In London Lady Westmorland, as always, kept Severn waiting. When they finally met, she was out to be agreeable to her former protégé—and make mischief, as she chatted on for hours. Flirtatiously, she asked Severn to play for her. Listening appreciatively, she told him, as in the old days, that his true gift was for music not painting; and fixing her gaze on him, observed that he was far too young and handsome to be let loose on his own in London. She would write and warn Eliza. Severn knew her well enough by now: 'I suspect the old devil . . . was only spying upon me . . . How little she knows me after all, how narrow minded and disposed to stir up a row in any way.'[33] But if she could no longer harm them, she could, and later would, help them.[34] Now that he had no doubt of his ability to handle her, Severn enjoyed showing himself off in the smart surroundings of Brook Street where he was staying with the nephew of 'Colonel' Finch's widow, Seth Thompson, the Severns' doctor in Rome.

Going Home

From time to time he went back to Shoreditch. Both his brothers were doing well in the music world and he was proud of them, but 'going to see my family is like going to another world'. Just as in Rome he had thought longingly of Shoreditch, now in London his thoughts flew to his wife and children in distant Olevano. 'What would I give to be eating your nice Macaroni with that dear Capelli [a scholarly Italian they had met there] with us & his large dog under the table—& my wandering out to meet you and Walter & Hal.' The longer he was away, the more homesick he became: 'you are never out of my thoughts' he told his wife at the end of August. 'It seems to me years & years since I saw you, everything sickens on my sight without you.' Only the need to make his fame and fortune in London kept him away.[35]

Quite how much she would have to spend as a result of his efforts must have puzzled Eliza, pursued as she was by an officious clerk at Torlonia's complaining about their overdraft, and dispirited by his long absence. 'Borrow what you need from Gibson', Severn told her more than once, confident that his earnings in London would more than cover any short-term debts.[36] If not quite the triumph he presented to his family, the 'Coronation visit' had, indeed, been a solid success. Though he had fallen below his target of one thousand 'yellow boys', *The Crusaders* was off his hands as were most of his Olevano pictures, he had orders for *Rienzi* and copies of *Ariel* and *The Roman Ave Maria*, and had painted five portraits. All in all, he reckoned he had made £800 (over £50,000 in today's money). He had also cemented relationships with existing patrons and picked up on potentially important friendships with Acland and Gladstone.

His feelings about a permanent return to London, however, remained ambivalent. The noise and constant distractions, the soot ('how ladies keep themselves clean I cannot tell') and dingy light, the vast distances and constant 'fagging about', all were a trial compared to the simplicity of life in Rome. Prices for art works were shockingly low and he was out of sympathy with prevailing fashions: 'there is so little true taste or knowledge of Art, everything is recommendation & jobbing'. He was having to lower his sights: 'if I were driven out of Rome I could beat them all here, and perhaps succeed, but only in Portrait I fear'. Walter's school prospects, however, were looking good. Severn was sure he could use his connections to get him into the Blue School or the London University School where 'the children of the nobility go'.[37] By 18 September he was on his way back, travelling with Captain Baynes through Brussels, Cologne, Munich, Verona, and Bologna, marvelling at the art works on the way. He returned home on 'an autumn day that belonged to paradise . . . Rome surpassed herself in beauty'.[38]

Invigorated by his visit to London, he worked hard over the winter, completing *Rienzi* and starting his copy of *The Roman Ave Maria*. Though he sent *Rienzi* to the 1839 Exhibition along with *The Ancient Mariner*, he did not go himself. Eliza's health had again broken down and she spent the summer in the first of her many 'cures', at Casciano dei Bagni. Severn hated the separation and worried about the expense, but was cheered by his sale of a copy of *The Roman Ave Maria* to the Grand Duke Alexander of Russia and news from Eastlake and Uwins of the reception of his pictures at the Exhibition.[39] 'The impression you made last year has made people ready to carp at you', Eastlake judiciously wrote. 'Had you not exhibited your "Ancient Mariner", which is greatly admired, you would hardly have held your own for the "Rienzi" is not so great a favourite.' Severn was ready to admit that the orange light and green shade did not work well together but was consoled by Uwins's enthusiasm for *The Ancient Mariner*: 'No picture of yours exhibited in London has ever excited more attention or called forth more admiration from all whose opinions are worth having . . . In truth this picture stood alone.'[40] It was the sort of work which might win him election to the Royal Academy.

As Eliza took the waters, Severn looked after the children, pondering a return to England and thinking about the darker side of life in Rome. He wrote to her about a violent quarrel in the street outside, which had ended in murder. 'O what vile people, we'll get out of it & never let our children know such things.'[41] In the autumn they retreated to their rural paradise in Olevano where he painted a new version of *The Fountain*. In May 1840 Eliza set off with the boys for England to get them into schools and prepare for her husband's return. Again, he made a good showing at the RA Exhibition, with a well-finished Raphaelesque portrait, *Portia with the Casket*, *The Witches Cavern*, a scene from Bulwer Lytton's *Last Days of Pompeii*, and a version of *The Roman Ave Maria*, together with the *Isabella* he had painted in Olevano in 1837.

His separation from Eliza in 1840 was longer and more troubling than that in 1838. In Rome he felt jaded, 'painting pictures which I shall never sell'. Lady Coventry was 'all dinners', the Mandevilles, who had failed to give him a commission, 'all religion', and a brother and sister-in law of his friend Colonel Palliser disappointed: 'he's a Clergyman & his wife a cold Saint . . . [he] assured me you might live very cheaply in London by wearing second hand cloaths bought of the Jews'. Only his girls gave him undiluted pleasure. Claudia read

10 Self portrait with chalk highlights *c.* 1840

Goldoni aloud to Mary and played piano duets with her father while Mary had started to draw. Watching her, he began to wonder if she would not 'turn out the most talented of all'. Psychologically, he was readying himself for his return: ''tis wonderful now that I have made up my mind how all the English feelings that have been lurking within my inmost heart during these 20 Years now expand & sustain me . . . however great my passion for my painting & Italy has

11 Severn family group in chalks *c.* 1840. From left to right: Mary, Walter, Henry, Claudia, and Eliza

been . . . yet now it changes to the love of my children . . . I long to breathe the free air of England, see my children grow up Englishmen.'[42]

Eliza's movements in Britain were a sign of strains to come. 'I only see you with a silver spoon in your mouth', he wrote in January as she moved on from one aristocratic house to another. But she did set up his first important portrait commission after his return with a famous beauty and old friend, Lady Wilhelmina Stanhope, and engineered a loan of £150 from her half-brother, cash-strapped though he was after the extravagance of the Eglinton Tournament the previous August. She was less successful with the boys' schooling and agonized over where to live in London: perhaps Park Lane (Severn thought he could manage the £200 annual rent) or Piccadilly (too noisy and expensive, he replied). Nor could she make up her mind on whether to go back to Rome to help wind up their affairs and bring the girls to England. 'It seemed so funny to me', wrote Julia Richmond to her husband, 'to hear Mrs S making arrangements in the morning to set off instantly as she said to Rome, in the middle of the day accepting invitations at the distance of a week, and in the evening saying she should go to Scotland in a few days, & sometimes making a fourth determination to take lodgings for the boys & herself & remain in London till Mr S came to England . . . never was there a woman who required the wise direction of a husband as she does.'[43]

Perhaps Lady Westmorland's poisonous warning about the danger of a handsome, unsupervised husband, began to work on Eliza. There was a row in December over his new picture, *Angelica Being Rescued by Ruggiero from a Sea Monster*. He planned to paint from the nude and had found a respectable widow who would attend his studio with her daughter, the model. Eliza put her foot down, appealing to the solemnity of their marriage vows. Severn was outraged: 'it would be impossible that I could do a thing that would create or raise suspicion in your mind . . . if I ever heard that you ever believed or even listened to anything against me on this ground, even the <u>shade of a doubt</u>, I think I should never forgive you'.[44] He did not protest too loudly. For all the sins of his youth and the vanities of his old age, the sensuality of his middle years was firmly centred on Eliza.

In November George Richmond returned to Rome with his brother, Tom, coming every morning to work at Via Rassella and sometimes dropping in of an evening to exchange unflattering stories of Italian life or talk about the London art world. He was in tetchy mood, missing his wife, disliking Italian food, and giving way to his habitual hypochondria. Severn's breezy confidence irritated him. 'Severn is round and complacent as ever talking of doing everything and as far as I can see making very little progress towards each great achievement.'[45] In public, however, they put on a genial united front, or so it seemed to yet another young man bearing a letter of introduction who presented himself at Severn's door in mid-December. By then, Severn had got tired of such visitors, complaining to Eliza: 'there seems no end to those of Artists—30 at least'. Only one had been worth the trouble, 'a Mr Swinton'.[46] He must have guessed what the newcomer, toiling up to his door, was about and, though Richmond half-recognized him, the two continued breezily down the stairs. But the lanky, red-haired youth, too shy to interrupt them, was sufficiently interesting for Severn to comment that he had the look of a poet. The caller doggedly continued up to Severn's door and left the letter of introduction Henry Acland had supplied. Though the visitor kept a detailed diary, he said nothing of the incident. Over forty years later, however, he described it with vivid Proustian recall:

his door was at the right of the landing at the top of a long flight of squarely reverting stair,—broad, to about the span of an English lane that would allow two carts to pass; and broad-stepped also, its gentle incline attained by some three inches of fall to a foot of flat. Up to this I was advancing slowly,—it being forbidden me ever to strain breath,—and was within eighteen or twenty steps of Mr Severn's door, when it opened and two gentlemen came out, closed it behind them with an expression of excluding the world for evermore from that side of the house, and began to descend the stairs to meet me, holding to my left. One was a rather short, rubicund, serenely beaming person; the other, not much taller, but paler, with a beautifully modelled forehead, and extremely vivid, though kind, dark eyes.[47]

Of all the extraordinarily gifted men Severn was to know well, this was the most extraordinary: John Ruskin. Their destinies were linked in ways which neither could have imagined in December 1840. It was Severn's as yet unborn son who would marry Ruskin's ward and cousin, Joan, and, after a fashion, care for him in his last terrible years at Brantwood. And it was primarily to delight Joan that Ruskin wrote this account of his first unsuccessful attempt to meet her father-in-law.

However bored with letters of introduction, Severn was not likely to ignore one from Henry Acland. He called round and met Ruskin and his parents at their lodgings, while Ruskin followed up with a visit to Richmond, whom he had already met in London in September.[48] An expedition was arranged to see Tasso's study and garden at St Onofrio's and visit the Vatican. Obliging though his hosts were, Ruskin sensed their reservations. In particular, he had failed to be impressed by the Raphaels in the Stanze: '[I] looked very reverently at whatever I was bid. Of Raphael, however, I found I could make nothing whatever. The only thing clearly manifest to me in his compositions was that everybody seemed to be pointing at everybody else, and that nobody, to my notion was worth pointing at.'[49] Richmond was appropriately severe in his private comments, describing the new acquaintance to Julia as 'a very delicate subject indeed' and complaining in his diary, 'he has too much of the amateur and a good deal of theory that he must either look under or over before he can appreciate the fine things for they are not to be enjoyed through it'.[50] Richmond would revise his view: Severn always kept his mistrust of Ruskin's artistic theory.

Rome was never close to Ruskin's heart. On his first visit, he struggled to retain his freshness of perception. The Eternal City assailed him with the deadening insistence of received opinion and, as the centre of an alien religion, it repelled. Nor did its classical past and Renaissance riches appeal. The pope was 'an ugly brute', the cardinals 'dirty', St Peter's, both inside and out, ill-proportioned, the Coliseum the ugliest thing he had ever seen, Italians, apart from the boys, universally unattractive, and 'the noisy streets and dark churches' 'a plague'. As for the Vatican choir's castrati (a name he shied away from using), they might perhaps be heard, but should certainly not be seen.[51] The city fell into place only as he discovered the great vantage point on the Janiculum with vistas of sunlit snow-capped mountains beyond the mass of ruins. And he delighted in a picturesque corner with a jumble of marble and broken brick. A shopkeeper lent him a chair and brought out a brazier to warm him as he sketched it. He came across Shelley's tombstone unexpectedly when he visited the Caius Cestius Pyramid and 'was surprised into tears almost', though he quickly recognized that the grave of Keats, a poet he knew far less well, was in better taste. He clambered up on the rocks of the Trevi Fountain and revelled in some 'Turner clouds'. But still he could not shake off the perception that Rome was a city haunted by death.[52] Irritatingly opinionated though Severn and Richmond found him, they were charmed by his parents who offered their usual hospitable welcome. 'My father and mother's quiet out-of-the-wayness at first interested, soon pleased, and at last won them', and they were happy to join in 'consultation as to what was best to be done to bring me to anything like a right mind'.[53]

The contrasting diaries of Christmas and New Year kept by Ruskin, Richmond, and Ruskin's cousin, Mary Richardson, are supplemented by Ruskin's vivid later memories and Richmond's letters to his wife. Only Severn is silent about his new friends. On his first call on the Ruskins on the evening of 11 December, he was in typical mood. 'He gave me a scandalous account of Italians, blaming them for want of generosity and everything mean in conduct; says that truth is absolutely a thing unknown and unthought of.' Four days later he dropped in again and obligingly offered to teach Ruskin how to read music. Before they could start, Ruskin fell ill with a fever, spending his Christmas Day in bed in his 'melancholy room with a cat, and three chimney tops by way of view'. Severn and the Richmond brothers had a happier time, sharing Christmas dinner, lovingly toasting their absent wives, and staying up talking until midnight.[54]

Although John was still confined to his room, Severn and Richmond made up 'a very pleasant evening' with Mr and Mrs Ruskin on 26 December, when Severn was the most likely source of 'some interesting stories of apparitions'.[55] Their happiest time together, however, came at dinner on 1 January 1841. Severn told story after story. Ruskin wrote some down and regretted he had not recorded more. Mary Richardson, too, delighted in Severn's gusto as a raconteur. The high point of the evening was his account of the priest at Albano explaining to his congregation why so few had come to Rome in the Holy Year in 1825: 'the winter was late, the roads were bad, the pilgrims were coming— "towards the end of April, you will be certain to see numbers; and in May, all the roads will be covered; but for June! Whew-ew-ew"—finishing with a prolonged whistle and extension of hands, expressive of infinite multitude! . . . The effect of this climax was indescribable . . . it set us all into such a fit of laughing that we could not recover from it for some time', Mary wrote in her diary. Almost as much fun was Severn's story of the priest chastising his congregation for their devotion to Punch. Pointing to a crucifix he had admonished them: 'that is the true Punch; there is the Punch that will last you through eternity'.[56]

Dutifully sceptical of some of Severn's stories though the young Ruskin was, he took a great liking to the man: 'Clever and droll' was how he first saw him. Ruskin also spotted the essential Cockney in Severn, despite the Roman overlay. Though *Blackwood's Edinburgh Magazine* had used it as a term of abuse, 'Cockney', as in Severn's case, could also refer to 'the upbeat, bright-as-a-button, never-say-die spirit of the born Londoner taking the world in his stride, whatever his lack of social standing'.[57] Twelve years later another familiar English prototype came to Ruskin's mind when he saw a singer at the opera 'in a brass-buttoned coat, with the most good-humoured English farmer-like look conceivable . . . he put me more in mind of Mr Severn than anybody I can recollect'.[58] But good company though he was over the festive season, Severn's thoughts were with his wife and whether she would return. By the beginning of January he was begging her not to brave the treacherous winter travelling conditions through France. His warning was too late: she had already set off, leaving London on 29 December, travelling alone by road and reaching Rome on 18 January 1841.[59]

In the few weeks that remained to them there, Severn faced his last fight with the local artistic establishment to get his *Revelations* altarpiece into the showy new church of San Paolo fuori le Mura, built on the ashes of its burnt-out predecessor. Weld's death left Severn without a champion in the senior reaches of the Catholic hierarchy in his fight with Camuccini, who wanted to keep San Paolo as a preserve for the best of contemporary Italian sacred art (including his own). Camuccini, who proved remarkably solicitous over the preparations for Severn's departure,[60] offered to take charge and get the altarpiece hung after Severn left. Severn's suspicions intensified when he talked the problem over at a farewell dinner with the German artists. They advised him to speak to Cardinal Tosti, who was responsible for the oversight of San Paolo. Severn found Tosti unexpectedly helpful and his architect even more so. Having hauled his painting over to the church early one morning, he persuaded the architect that it should go, not in the sacristy, but more prominently, on one of the bricked-in arches dividing the newly built transept from the nave where building work continued. Returning home, Severn was amused to discover that Eliza had been visited by Camuccini's wife, full of apologetic explanations that since no architect in Rome was available, the picture would have to be handed over to her husband for him to arrange its installation. Eliza enjoyed letting the discomfited Baroness know where her husband and his picture were.[61]

The installation of the altarpiece in San Paolo became a *cause célèbre*. Crowds flocked to see it, astonished that a foreigner, and a Protestant at that, had found his way into Rome's most prestigious ecclesiastical project. It was a triumph Severn loved to enlarge on: 'not only had I sympathy at having overcome serious obstacles, but I had what was in the Italian eyes the greater glory of having defeated the priests, from Monsignor Wiseman downwards and so, in some measure, having assisted the cause of Italy and the Italians'.[62] If that was overdoing it, still Severn's triumph was noticed as far away as Berne, where Bunsen was delighted to hear of Camuccini's discomfiture.

Leaving Rome was not easy. In Eliza's absence, Severn had gone to the Doria Pamphilj Gardens planning to paint some backgrounds. He was soon lost in nostalgic family memories: here Walter and Henry had played amongst the haycocks while Eliza sat in a tree reading Miss Mackenzie's copy of 'Philip of Actium'. Here, too, at the age of four Mary had suddenly found her feet and begun to run around. He picked some of the famous anemones that grew there, enclosing them in a letter to Eliza.[63] 'Dear old Rome' for all its darkness was full of affecting memories. He paid a last visit to Keats's grave in the Protestant Cemetery and happened on a pair of young lovers kneeling hand-in-hand in front of the stone. As Ruskin might well have thought, this sounds like one of Severn's tall stories (though a good subject for a picture, which it soon became). The image epitomized the effect of twenty years in Rome on his feelings about

Keats. The old anguish of the terrible weeks in Piazza di Spagna had dissolved into a sunny vision of Keats as the poet of tender romance, the idol of the young and untroubled.

Severn, Eliza, Claudia, Mary, and the Italian nursemaid, 'Baglia', set out for England in late February, arriving on 15 March. There would be many nostalgic glances to the good times in Rome, and his secure social position there. Ruskin, adopting some of his subject's geniality, left a memorable portrait of Severn in his Roman prime:

> there is nothing in any circle that ever I saw or heard of, like what Mr Joseph Severn then was in Rome. He understood everybody, native and foreign, civil and ecclesiastic, in what was nicest in them, and never saw anything else than the nicest; or saw what other people got angry about as only a humorous part of the nature of things. It was the nature of things that the Pope should be at St Peter's, and the beggars on the Pincian steps. He forgave the Pope his papacy, reverenced the beggar's beard, and felt that alike the steps of the Pincian, and the Araceli, and the Lateran, and the Capitol, led to heaven, and everybody was going up, somehow; but might be happy where they were in the meantime. Lightly sagacious, lovingly humorous, daintily sentimental, he was in council with the cardinals to-day, and at picnic in Campagna with the brightest English belles to-morrow; and caught the hearts of all in the golden net of his good will and good understanding.[64]

Life for the Severns would never be quite so confident again.

CHAPTER 13

The Passion for Fresco

I T was a sign of how little the Severns knew of London in 1841 that they took up residence in Mayfair, an area far beyond their means. For Severn the choice was a statement of intent: he would live not among artists, but close to aristocratic patrons and Eliza's friends and acquaintances. Though he still saw old friends like Uwins and the Richmonds, he did not seek new contacts, pursuing his career on his own terms, reluctant to change his style, concentrating on a narrow circle of familiar patrons and lacking the suppleness and critical self-awareness which had helped Uwins through a difficult re-entry to the demanding London art market. In the next twenty years in London, Frederick Leighton, who had first made his name in Rome, was the only new artist who caught Severn's eye, as he mostly kept his distance from Dyce, Maclise, and the rising stars of the Pre-Raphaelite Brotherhood. His failure to secure election as an Associate at the Royal Academy also left him outside the artistic establishment.[1] In London he would become embattled and increasingly insecure.

Though his artistic life was poorer than in Rome, he enjoyed re-establishing old friendships with what remained of the Keats Circle. And there were rewards within his family. In the summer of 1842, they moved from Mayfair to Westminster, setting up at 21 St James Street across the road from Buckingham Palace. The Pallisers, whom they knew from Rome, lived next door (there was much to-ing and fro-ing between the Severn and Palliser children), Bulwer Lytton, as productive as ever, was over the garden wall, and the Dilkes just round the corner. Walter was enrolled at the nearby Westminster School. Henry, a less robust boy, was mostly educated at home. On 14 August 1842, the family was completed with the arrival of twins: Arthur, named after the infant who had died in 1837, and Eleanor.

To outward appearances, Severn's new career began well. He settled to a mix of activities which promised both financial and artistic rewards: portrait painting to pay the bills, Italian genre scenes to keep his name before the public at the Academy Exhibitions, and grander projects for private satisfaction. His first portrait commission in London from Lady Wilhelmina Stanhope was a good way of announcing the expansion of his calling. Though at £50 the price was low, the prestige of the commission was high. Lady Wilhelmina was a celebrated beauty, famed for her wit and cleverness, her artistic ability and distinguished royal and political connections. Lady Marianne Alford followed with a commission at £100 and Severn had two profitable years at the RA Exhibition in 1841 and 1842, selling Italian genre scenes. In 1843 he exhibited a portrait, paid for by subscription, of the recently arrived Prussian Minister, his old friend Bunsen. Commissions to paint Gladstone and Richard Monckton Milnes followed and were included in a book of engravings of leading politicians of the day, where Gladstone's extravagant suiting makes more of an impact than the conventionally Byronic face.[2] Severn supplemented his income with a few guineas for teaching aristocratic ladies to paint in oils or arranging tableaux vivants in smart London houses. In all he made nearly £600 in 1842.[3] Coupled with Eliza's allowance of £100 from the Earl of Eglinton, this should have been enough. Already, however, the Severns were falling behind.

Unlike Uwins, in his first three miserable years back in London, Severn had no capital to help him through re-entry.[4] Again, unlike Uwins, he failed to win the official recognition of his peers. Always a modest man, Uwins had been surprised to be elected to the Academy within a year of his return. Severn was more confident about his chances. His nicely varied body of work in the 1838 and 1839 Exhibitions gave him a good claim for consideration. In 1840 he made a trial run from Rome; but Turner stepped in to object on the grounds of his non-residency. Even so, two Academicians voted for him, perhaps as a way of registering their continuing opposition to the 1837 rule change.[5] When Severn's name was again proposed in 1842, there was no technical impediment to his election. Now he would be considered on his merits. In the first round, he and Thomas Creswick, the landscape painter, topped the poll. In the run-off between them Creswick was elected with thirteen votes to Severn's eleven. Almost invariably, the RA General Assembly elected the runner-up to the next vacancy. On this occasion, there were two more slots to fill. Extraordinarily, Severn got neither. Hollins, a now obscure Academician, emerged from nowhere to top the second poll, when Severn's vote fell to two, and the third vacancy went to Francis Grant, a future President of the Academy. By then only one Academician was still voting for Severn. Neither the General Assembly minutes nor contemporary diaries and letters explain his dramatic reverse. Clearly, there was influential opposition to his advancement, compounded, perhaps, by the openness of the Academy's voting procedures. For the run-offs, two ballot boxes were set up on a table in front of the President, who handed a cork ball to each member as he came to vote.[6] Severn's enemies must not only have voted ostentatiously for his rivals but voiced their opposition, too. Turner may well have led them though he was not Severn's only critic at the Academy. Men like Pickersgill were not going to admit someone who had built his artistic reputation in Italy. As important, Eastlake was away and unable to lead a show of support by 'the Roman party'. In the end, even Severn's friends deserted him. Having paid their dues in the first run-off for his generosity in Rome, Etty and Collins turned back to the claims of London colleagues. Only one (surely Uwins) stayed loyal. Severn's name remained on the Academy list of candidates for the next ten years: in all that time he never won a single vote. His failure set him apart from Eastlake, Etty, and Uwins who had each been elected on their return from Italy. He continued to strive for the honour, unaware of how strong the hostility towards him in some quarters was, and conscious only of the exhausting 'battle and toil there is about everything' in the London artistic world.[7]

Away from the capital he energetically pursued his new career as a portrait painter, working old patrons hard and spending a month or two each autumn in their country houses fulfilling commissions. In 1843 he was at Bettisfield Park in Shropshire with Sir John Hanmer, in 1844 at Stamford Hall in Leicestershire with Lady Braye, in 1845 he paid his first visit to Eglinton Castle, in 1846 and 1847 it was the turn of the Countess of Warwick at Gatton Park, Surrey, and in 1848 he enjoyed the baronial splendour in which Sir Thomas Acland lived on his estate at Killerton in Devon. However great the challenge, he persisted in his attempts to produce flattering likenesses. His old friend James Birch Sharpe, who had come into money and acquired a country estate, was encouraged to set the seal on his gentrification with a series of family portraits. Severn travelled to Malvern in 1844 where Sharpe's daughter and son-in-law were taking the waters. Mrs Ellis was not a tempting proposition. Graceless and fidgety, she 'yawned and yawned' at sittings while Severn struggled in front of this 'hippopotamus'. Her husband had 'queer things' to say about the result but paid up 60 guineas, while Severn got away from his ordeal with a quick scramble before breakfast to the ridge of the Malvern Hills and an eighteen-mile Sunday walk to Worcester to get a close look at the River Severn and muse on his forebears.[8]

But he still hankered after greatness, a masterwork on which he could 'rest his fame'. For more than a decade he had been thinking of an altarpiece depicting the three Marys approaching the empty tomb on Easter Sunday morning. He showed Gladstone a sketch in Rome in 1838 and continued to tinker with it in London, though he knew that, without a patron, he could not embark on a project that might cost him £500 in time and materials. Sir Thomas Acland suggested that he work up a list of subscribers each paying £10 who could present the painting to a suitable church. Severn turned to the patron he had courted most assiduously since his return to London: Gladstone.

Though heroically engaged in a root-and-branch overhaul of the customs tariff at the Board of Trade, Gladstone was not slow to respond to Severn. Back-breakingly hard though his ministerial work was, he still found time to develop his artistic tastes and looked to Severn for advice. Together they went to the enforced sale of the art collection of the silversmith Thomas Hamlet, who, in happier days, had lent Titian's *Bacchus and Ariadne* to the RA Schools. There were long conversations too, sometimes with Bunsen, about fresco, an art form in which some of the Nazarenes who had returned to Munich were attracting wide attention.[9]

Gladstone was clearly marked out for a great future. Severn liked to keep him informed about his artistic progress, occasionally canvassed his support for jobs in the arts establishment, and managed to sell him some of the pictures he had admired in Rome, including the oil sketch of the *Revelations* altarpiece, the large version of *The Campagna* and *Sylvia*. Though he was an obliging patron (when Severn was in a tight corner the cheques came quickly), he could also drive a hard bargain. Severn begged him not to let it be known he had paid only £40 for *The Campagna*. Little though he paid for it, Gladstone was particularly fond of the painting, judging it amongst Severn's best works, 'a very characteristic one and valuable on that account'.[10] He was also, at least initially, an eager collaborator in the subscription for *The Holy Sepulchre*. He put himself, his father, and sister-in-law down for £10 each while Mrs Gladstone solicited contributions from her friends. He even talked of installing it in the new church he and his friend James Scott-Hope were building as part of a school for the sons of Episcopalian clergy at Glenalmond in Scotland.[11]

Severn gathered other distinguished subscribers, including the Duke of Sutherland, Ruskin, Bunsen, and Monckton Milnes. In 1844 and 1845 he collected over £200 from them and at one stage even contemplated painting a copy to satisfy the rival claims for its placement from the Scottish party led by Gladstone and the London party of Sir Robert Inglis.[12] Ultimately, however, there were never enough subscribers and, as Severn painfully learnt, English ecclesiastical architecture, unlike Italian, did not lend itself to painted altarpieces: side altars were few and 'all the new churches are made with a large window at each end'.[13] Through the 1840s he spent time and money on *The Holy Sepulchre* he could ill afford. By 1848, when it was nearly finished, he was in serious financial difficulty. He turned to Gladstone, picking up an earlier suggestion that the existing subscribers might be invited to double their contributions. But now Gladstone was less compliant. He would double his own subscription but not invite others to do so.[14] As Gladstone's tastes developed in the 1840s, his enthusiasm for Severn as an artist, though never as a man, declined, overtaken by his growing appreciation of the work of William Dyce. It was Dyce, not Severn, whom Gladstone consulted about the layout and decoration of the church at Glenalmond where he was not about to compromise his carefully thought-out church architecture to make room for *The Holy Sepulchre*.[15] At 19 feet by 12, it was Severn's largest work, but not his best. Its failings were not for lack of inspiration. Though the joy of the Resurrection was at the heart of Severn's Christian faith and feminine constancy one of his favourite themes, the altarpiece is old-fashioned, Italianate, and poorly composed.[16]

In 1843 he may have felt he could afford this artistic indulgence. His prospects were, apparently, about to be transformed, as the state prepared to spend unprecedented amounts of money on history painting and in a medium, fresco, about which he could claim to be more expert than most of his London competitors. In 1834 the old Houses of Parliament burnt down. The porter at the Academy immediately saw its significance. 'Now, gentlemen, now you young architects, there's a fine chance for you', he announced, inviting them to admire the blaze.[17] Though architects were the first to benefit, they would not be the only ones. In an open competition for designs in 'the Gothic or Elizabethan style' Edward Barry, with covert help from Augustus Pugin, emerged as a popular winner, with detailed plans for a massive Perpendicular palace. The choice of style had both practical and symbolic importance. The new palace not only needed to fit in with the unscathed medieval Westminster Hall and the Abbey across the road, but also recall the period in which, as historians were now teaching, the foundations of British liberty were laid. A powerful lobby developed for decorating the pseudo-medieval architecture at Westminster with its counterpart in painting, fresco.[18]

While Barry and Pugin kept tight control over the building and its magnificent furnishings, the artwork was entrusted to the newly established Royal
Fine Arts Commission. Its work became a text-book example of the inability
of committees, however well funded, to inspire great art. Twenty years later,
with the painting scheme for the new Houses of Parliament in disarray and
some of the few frescoes that had been put up already peeling from the walls, it
was hard to imagine why enthusiasm for a long extinct art form had swept the
arts establishment in the 1830s and 1840s. Its origins were diverse. A House of
Commons Committee looking into ways of encouraging arts and manufactures
in England in 1835 had reported favourably on fresco as craftsmanship. In the
1840s Prince Albert's activities as patron, connoisseur, and arts administrator
made German art as fashionable as Italian had been in the previous decade and
directed attention to Peter von Cornelius's experiments in fresco in Munich.
British visitors to Italy were also starting to appreciate the Italian primitives.
Wilkie returned from his European travels passionate about fresco: 'he recom-
mends all the young men to turn their attention to it', Uwins told Severn in
October 1834. The discipline and dedication it required were thought to give
it moral authority: here was a medium well suited to the aspirational intent of
the new Houses of Parliament. Supported by ample funding and placed on the
empty walls of Britain's most important new building, fresco would, at last,
establish a tradition of history painting in the grand manner.

A Parliamentary Committee, chaired by Sir Benjamin Hawes, examined its
role in 1841. Two expert witnesses, Dyce and Eastlake, made a strong impression. Both could talk knowledgeably about fresco, drawing on their experiences
in Italy and Germany. Dyce, superintendent of the recently created Government
School of Design, advocated getting a group of painters together to enable them
to learn the technique in local conditions. Eastlake was more bullish. He saw no
reason why English artists should not do just as well at fresco as the Germans.
Nor was the lack of experience in the medium a problem: 'Ability, if wanting,
would of necessity follow.'[19]

The Royal Fine Arts Commission, under the chairmanship of Prince Albert,
was set up in November 1841. Hard though he tried to avoid it, Eastlake was
drafted in as secretary.[20] Of all the positions he accepted in the mid-Victorian
art world, this was the most invidious. As the only professional artist associated
with the Commission, he was the target for much jostling over the unparalleled
amount of money waiting to be handed out. Severn was not the only friend he
lost in his over-cautious management of a hapless project.

Initially, the Commission chose to organize a number of competitions aimed at discovering the extent of native talent and expertise in the new medium. In April 1842 it invited competitors to submit cartoons 'in chalk or the like' with figures at least life-size on any subject taken from English history, Spenser, Shakespeare, or Milton. Three prizes of £300, three of £200, and five of £100 were offered.

Severn wasted no time in staking his claim as a leading advocate and practitioner of the newly fashionable art form. He rushed off to take a look at Westminster Hall, under the excusably mistaken impression that this would be the first place to be decorated. It was perfect for fresco. His youthful ambitions revived: once again he saw himself painting a cycle of key moments in British history. In 1821 he had thought of Julius Caesar and Good Queen Bess: now it was Richard II's confrontation with Watt Tyler. He wrote to Gladstone to sound him out about his chances of getting a commission to paint a fresco cycle in Westminster Hall. Gladstone referred him to Hawes, who suggested a start in a more modest setting. Severn's enthusiasm was undampened: 'my whole mind is bent on introducing the grand style of Art, and I care not what sacrifices I make to it'.[21] He arranged to give a lecture on fresco to the Royal Institute of British Architects. Dilke knocked it into shape for publication in the *Athenaeum* on 9 April 1842. Two more articles followed in May and August.[22]

The Commission's decision to organize an open competition for fresco painters rather than relying on a small number of artists with known expertise was an unpleasant shock. Competitions, Severn protested to Gladstone, were fine for 'good manufactures' but not for great art. What was needed was money for a 'steady sincere and genuine band of artists, who shall have as much care & love for art as they have a knowledge of it'.[23] Self-interested though this was, it hit on one of the flaws in the Commission's approach: its reluctance to commission individual artists and give them long-term support to develop facility in an unfamiliar and demanding medium. But Severn could not afford to turn his back on a share of 'the great employment'. In autumn 1842 he worked on his cartoon submission for the competition.

His *Athenaeum* articles had already established his expertise. As Dilke wrote in introducing them, Severn was not only the 'devoted, self-sacrificing friend' of Keats, but through his contacts in Rome with the Nazarenes a man 'intimately acquainted, not only with the greatest works of the greatest masters in fresco, but with the whole history of the late arrival of the art'.[24] Much of what Severn said followed Eastlake's line in his reports for the Royal Fine Arts Commission.

Both argued that, because large oil paintings reflected light in awkward ways, the medium was unsuitable for historical works in public places. The gift of the English artists for watercolour, however, boded well for their abilities at fresco, while the superior incidents of British history would make it even more successful in England than in Germany. More discursive than argumentative, enthusiastic rather than critically aware, Severn talked up the new medium with aplomb. It was a 'manly' art: it would establish the historical style of painting which Reynolds had hoped to see; it would instruct and inspire; and put painting where it belonged, alongside poetry and philosophy in the national canon.

Severn also seized his opportunity to attack some pet hates: the artificiality of French historical painting; Lawrence's diversion of English painting from grandeur into 'fashion'; and booksellers who debased the painter's art with demands for cheap engravings and book illustrations. Inadequate state support had left artists distractingly dependent on the vagaries of private patrons. 'The English artist', Severn wrote with feeling 'is obliged to make an expensive tradesmanlike figure—this not only takes up half his time, but it takes up all his money.'[25] Now painters must lift their sights, forget history painting derived from theatrical scene-painting and the literalness of 'Dutch painting', and aspire to the elevated beauties, fine colouring, and authority of fresco. As always the cheerful salesman, Severn also outlined two complete schemes he hoped to complete himself, on the lives of Richard II and King Alfred. And though it seemed that the argument had already been lost, he continued to press the merits of the old Italian studio system as the best way of fostering skill in the new technique. Fresco would give artists 'the sustained though moderate reward of years of constant employment, instead of the intoxicating, lottery, chance system of the present day. We shall now have the excellent old Italian plan of master and scholar.'[26] It was a heady prospect.

Severn's articles were noticed. The Marquess of Ormonde sent a copy of the first to Prince Albert, while Bunsen asked for extra copies to send to 'Royal Personages' in Germany.[27] Indulgent though he was towards Severn's enthusiasm, however, Ruskin, for one, was not convinced. 'I don't want to damp him,' he wrote to his father 'but it is monstrously absurd in him to speak of inoculating England with the love of <u>Fresco</u> as if that were all she wanted, and men could be sublime on a wall who were idiots on canvas.' And to Severn himself Ruskin sent a long critique of the poverty of British art and public life in the industrial age: 'It is not the love of fresco that we want ... You want a serious love of art in the people, and a faithful love of art in the artist, not a desire to be a R.A., and to dine with the Queen: and you want something like decent teaching in the Academy itself.' 'I never hear one word of genuine feeling issue from any one's mouth but yours, and the two Richmonds', he added to soften the blow.[28]

While Ruskin let Severn down lightly, Haydon was brutal behind his back. He had never had any time for Severn. Now he detected this unheroic light-weight camping on ground he had staked out for himself. With his old pupil Eastlake in charge of the new state patronage, Haydon expected to play a key role in the decoration of the Palace of Westminster and was already practising fresco technique on the wall of his painting room.[29] The announcement that artists would be chosen through competition stoked up his insecurities. 'As to Joseph Severn of Rome', Haydon wrote to Kirkup in Florence, 'what a twaddle it is ... The only thing he was ever fit for was a wet-nurse to Keats. It is to be regretted he did not advertise the continuance of his calling.' Anxious to humour Haydon and get him away from polemic and back to painting, Kirkup replied in the same scurrilous vein: 'Leave writing to the snobs and penny-a-liners ... Look what a hand Severn has made of it. Is it advisable to proclaim to the world that painters have had no schooling? ... It was a mere puff to draw attention and get a job.'[30] But while Severn was to be bruised, it was Haydon who would be broken on the wheel of the Royal Fine Arts Commission's endless deliberations.

In the first competition, the top prizes went to a mix of rising stars like George Watts and Charles Cope and experienced fresco practitioners like J. C. Horsley and J. Z. Bell. Severn, who claimed to be the only 'long standing Artist' among the winners, got one of the five £100 prizes for his cartoon, *Queen Eleanor saving the life of her husband by sucking the poison from the wound of Edward I*.[31] This is an Italianate composition, the clutter of carefully drawn objects around the wounded monarch being in the manner of old-fashioned 'authentic' English history painting. All submissions were anonymous, and though East-lake might have guessed many of the originators, there was concern that two Academicians, Pickersgill and Henry Howard, now the Professor of Painting at the RA, won nothing. To spare ruffled feelings, both were included in a supplementary list of prize-winners. The most prominent casualty, however, was Haydon, who had submitted a cartoon of 'Edward the Black Prince'. Though Eastlake gave him advance notice of his failure, it did no good. Haydon complained to everyone that his old pupil had become the creature of the establishment.

Even for those more favoured, success in the first competition was not what it seemed. To win was almost as invidious as to lose. *The Times* generally approved of Severn's cartoon, while Lady Holland told her son, Henry Fox, that Severn's cartoon 'is reckoned to be the best'. But there were accusations of favouritism and Haydon's hand was detectable in a sour attack in *Britannia* which appalled Ruskin's kind-hearted father. Severn's cartoon was 'the product of an ignorant and unimaginative mind...he has exhibited in the Royal Academy, but his pictures have always been lost amid the host of mediocre performances with which they have been properly classed'.[32] Nor did the £100 prize and £30 for the reproduction of his cartoon in a book of engravings of the winning entries cover Severn's costs. Most dispiriting of all, no work followed. Despite the huge attendances at the exhibition of the winning cartoons in Westminster Hall in the summer of 1843 and the popular enthusiasm as they toured the country, the Royal Fine Arts Commission held back from handing out any commissions.

Another exhibition followed in the summer of 1844, aimed at discovering whether British artists could not only design but execute fresco. No prizes were offered and no subjects set. Artists were simply invited to submit specimens of fresco work in small portable frames. The only incentive lay in the Commission's characteristically convoluted promise that the submissions 'taken together with [the competitors'] larger compositions in drawing which they have exhibited or may exhibit, and with other existing evidences of their talents, may enable us to proceed to the selection of artists for the decoration in fresco of certain portions of the palace'.[33] Severn was ill and struggled to meet the new deadline. His attempt, *The First English Bible as it was allowed to be read by the People in the Church Porches during part of the Reign of Henry VIII*, was not a success and, for once, he was ashamed to see it exhibited in Westminster Hall.[34] He was not among the six well-known artists that the Commission then invited to produce designs for the decoration of the House of Lords Chamber, though, having plucked up its courage to assign a theme to each of them, the Commission followed up with the extraordinary step of announcing a further open competition in 1845 for cartoons on precisely the same subjects. Severn lost out again, making the tactical mistake of choosing *The Baptism of Ethelbert*, which Dyce had been invited to design. The Commission's next competition contradicted everything it had so far said by inviting submissions in oils. Though Pickersgill now came into his own, Severn's *Allegorical Portrait of Her Majesty Queen Victoria as Victory* did not please.

Although he had not won a prize since the first competition, the Commission remained indulgent towards him. Perhaps Eastlake felt guilty about his failure to support Severn in the Academy elections in 1842. Perhaps, too, the Commission, with old friends like the Duke of Sutherland, Lord Lansdowne, Sir Robert Inglis, and Samuel Rogers amongst its members, was grateful for his early advocacy of fresco, even as its own commitment faltered. Two pieces of patronage were steered Severn's way: a small commission for work in a summer house in the gardens of Buckingham Palace and a fresco in the Upper Waiting Hall in the House of Lords.

Eastlake had always argued that private patronage must follow public if a tradition of fresco painting was to be established. Prince Albert obliged by making a recently constructed pavilion available as the site for experiment. In the central room, a number of established artists were invited to paint scenes from Milton. Eastlake, characteristically, took the most difficult spot, working in his own light above the fireplace: most of his colleagues began their efforts in the privacy of their own studios. Apart from Maclise, few of them knew much about fresco technique. Etty could not get on with it at all and quickly threw up his commission. Uwins, too, found fresco 'a very roundabout and imbecile process that requires the head to be done without the body, and the trunk without the members'.[35] Landseer kept to familiar subject matter, producing a ferocious conglomeration of animals, at odds with the vaunted serenity of fresco. Uwins was staid and Leslie domestic, while Eastlake's reluctance to assume artistic direction of his colleagues led to duplication of subject matter. The central room in the Buckingham Palace Summer House was a failure.

In the two smaller adjoining rooms things went more smoothly. One, 'The Classical', was left in the hands of Agostine Aglio, an old Italian fresco painter brought in to teach the technique to the bemused English stars. The other, 'The Romantic Room', was dedicated to one of Victoria's favourite authors, Sir Walter Scott. Amongst stucco medallions of his heroines, characteristic landscapes and bas-reliefs decorated with plaster swags of flowers, eight small lunettes were left above the frieze for scenes from the novels. Severn just scraped in. Townsend (who had won a £200 prize in the 1843 competition), Stonhouse, and Richard Doyle were each given two scenes to paint, while Severn and James Doyle got one. Severn's, however, was one of the most successful. When a book of coloured engravings of the Summer House frescos was published in 1846 it was the wall containing Severn's fresco of Edith Plantagenet from *The Talisman* that was chosen to give an idea of the pleasing ensemble of the

Romantic Room.[36] He received £37 for his work and later reproduced it at the front of a book of his engravings published in 1855, proudly identifying it as 'in the possession of HM The Queen'.

His other commission proved less happy. In August 1845 the Commission invited six artists to submit fresco designs on the English poets for the House of Lords Upper Waiting Hall. All of their choices, apart from J. R. Herbert, had been prize-winners, though Severn was the only one of the £100 winners to get a commission. Just as the artists already working in the Lords Chamber struggled to make the pale virtues of fresco tell against the richness of Pugin's furnishings and the clashing lights of stained-glass windows, so the painters in the Upper Waiting Hall were given an impossible challenge. Damp and dark, it was a poor place for fresco, with the spaces reserved for paintings tightly crammed against each other high up in the corners. Two were left vacant while the Commissioners struggled to decide which poets to admit to their pantheon in addition to Chaucer, Spenser, Shakespeare, Milton, Dryden, and Pope. The instructions given to the artists were unusually airy. They were to sort out amongst themselves who illustrated which poet but desired to 'act in concert as regards the size of the nearest figure or figures and the style of design, so far as the various epochs which may be selected and the character of the Poets respectively may permit'.[37] Each artist must then submit 'a small sketch or design' for the Commission's approval. At £400 for each fresco, however, the price was good.

Severn secured the right to do a scene from one of his favourite poets, Spenser ('Amasea's Despair'). He submitted his sketch early in 1846. The Commissioners approved the general conception but were concerned that 'the two nearer figures (lying on the ground) might be better composed'. Three months later when he put in a revised drawing, Eastlake's tone was sterner: the Commissioners 'still observe in his drawing defects which they trust to find removed in the Cartoon which he will execute'. Was this an authorization to press on? Severn was not sure. Desperate for ready cash, he put in for half his fee and got £100. Before hiring models for the cartoon he submitted another revised drawing. The verdict came quickly: 'while acknowledging the merit of various parts of the design the Commissioners regret that they are not prepared to recommend its execution in fresco'. He was to be paid off with a further £100.[38]

Severn was distraught at the 'dishonour and degradation' of being rejected and 'the odium & hostility of Artists' which would result. He wrote to Sir

Robert Inglis begging to be allowed to submit a cartoon, dragging in everything he could think of: the vagueness of the original commission, his record in winning 'the respect & even Royal Patronage of foreigners' and the presence of a German fresco student in his studio. In Rome he might have talked his patrons round, but not in London. On 11 June 1847 Eastlake wrote that he was 'directed to intimate that the correspondence on the subject . . . may be considered at an end'.[39]

Severn had muffed his chance in 'the great employment'. Perhaps he was lucky. Though work in the Upper Waiting Hall was not completed until 1854, the frescos there were the first to deteriorate. Set on wooden frames with a narrow unventilated space between them and the outer wall, the damp seeped in from behind as London dirt and building dust accumulated on the front. After only four years 'flesh tints became painfully livid, greens disappeared, blues and browns changed places . . . The ground itself . . . blistered, became loose and disintegrated.'[40] And as the frescos in the Upper Waiting Hall bit the damp so too did the public's enthusiasm for the new medium.

In 1862 the Commission wound itself up. Only Dyce, who produced a series of paintings in the Queen's Robing Room on the life of King Arthur, came close to finding the spirit of the Italian masters. Maclise, responsible for the largest wall paintings in the New Palace, was obliged to resort to the new technique of isinglass, watercolour with a wax overlay, in his minutely detailed epics of the death of Nelson and Wellington at Waterloo (darkened though they now are). Some of the most popular frescos were those of Edward Ward. Colourful and anecdotal, if a little stretched on the long walls of the House of Commons corridor, Ward's frescos, originally executed as oil paintings, harked back to the theatrical scene painting Severn had decried. Their instructive way of telling the national story was quickly taken up by the engravers and influenced a generation of school history textbooks.[41] Far from liberating artists from the demands of the booksellers, as Severn had hoped, the great fresco experiment, ultimately, turned artists into illustrators. The last and ostensibly best opportunity of establishing that native school of history painting in the grand manner which Reynolds had advocated, the Academy had promoted, and Severn had yearned after, ended in failure. Severn was only one of the casualties. Without any commission, Haydon continued to produce historical scenes for the new Houses of Parliament. But the public had lost interest and his exhibition of them was a disaster. In the stifling heat of the summer of 1846, having failed to shoot himself, he cut his throat.[42]

Late in 1847 Severn had an unexpected opportunity to recover his reputation. A summons came to meet Lady Warwick at one of her country houses, Gatton Park in Surrey. There he found an old Roman friend, Charlotte Monson, who introduced him to her mother-in-law, the 'singular and determined' Countess. She led him into a replica of the Orsini Chapel in Rome which her recently deceased and much-lamented son, Lord Monson, had built. He had hoped that Cornelius would fresco it: now her family were pressing her to whitewash it over. Though she wanted to complete the work as a tribute to her son, she was, she said, short of funds. Severn found this romantic, if implausible, story irresistible. He offered to do the work for the cost of the materials and labour needed to prepare the plaster, reckoning that the project would bring him future commissions.

It got off to a sticky start. Severn's first thought was the graceful one, familiar from the work of the Old Masters, of depicting Lord Monson surrounded by architectural drawings in the fresco on the wall above the entrance. He sketched out his idea and showed it to Lady Warwick, who promptly fainted. Though devoted to the memory of her son, his was a name not to be mentioned. Raphael was quickly substituted for 'Him' in the design, and, at last, Severn got his opportunity to reproduce *The School of Athens*, if only in miniature in his fresco.

Together with John Porter, the local plasterer, he set about learning to do fresco on a large scale. Initially they made mistakes. When his first morning's work failed to dry, he instructed a footman to put a scuttle of hot charcoal near it and returned from church to find the scaffold smouldering. A year later, on his second visit he had an anxious time with one of his female heads who 'sulk'd' for a morning 'all putrid and scaly'. He 'flung a tumbler of water in her face' and the colour began to show. After many more tumblers 'lo! and behold she came to herself & blushed the perfection of painting'. He set himself perspective challenges too in choosing to make the wall above the entrance look curved and introducing a variety of *trompe l'oeil* effects. The fake marble pillars and pretend cupola in the ceiling kept twelve workmen busy under his direction. He liked to think he was following the early masters of fresco as he prayed for answers to his technical problems and put in long days on the scaffolding.[43]

The scheme went well. In its first phase in the autumn of 1846 he recreated his design from the Buckingham Palace Summer House, above the painting of Raphael. He returned in October and November 1847 to decorate the spandrels. He chose four female figures, representing Lady Warwick's 'persevering virtues' in completing her son's work: Penelope for Patience; Queen Eleanor for Fortitude; and Queen Esther for Prudence. His fourth choice, Ruth for Meekness, had little to do with his patroness. It was Eliza who modelled for this idealized view of the quiet good temper he looked for in his wife. She visited him for the odd day out in the country, bringing the boys. It was a distraction from her trials in London juggling the bills and appealing to Severn to press his employer harder for money. He, by contrast, had the pleasure of handing the wealthy Countess into dinner whilst thinking up ways to help her save money on her fresco schemes. While he waited for his work to dry he delved into old books in the library. In one he found a version of the 'concert' which took him back thirty years to rowdy evenings with Keats and his friends. He copied it out as a 'Game for My Dear Monkies'.[44]

Severn's fresco work at Gatton Park survived much longer than the Buckingham Palace Summer House, which fell apart in the 1860s or the frescos in the Chamber of the House of Lords which were boarded over, lasting until 1934 when the Orsini Chapel was destroyed by fire.[45] Only a colour photograph from the turn of the century survives to give an idea of the impressive ensemble of *trompe l'oeil* marble pillars, coffered dome, and fine fresco of Raphael above the entrance. In the 1880s Severn's youngest son, Arthur, visited the Chapel incognito and found the frescos 'looking as if they were painted yesterday ... one of the figures up high between the arches, is so exactly like my Mother that it gave me quite a start' he told his wife. He asked the 'nice housekeeper' if she knew who the artist was and was obligingly told 'Severnus Fessit' as she pointed to Severn's details facetiously rendered in Latin.[46]

While Arthur was a knowledgeable, though not unbiased judge, another caller was more objective. In June 1850 Eastlake visited Gatton Park and sent Severn an agreeable, if nuanced letter of congratulation. Though his warmest praise was reserved for the architecture of the Chapel he found the frescos 'well adapted to it' and commented, carefully, that 'the side where the figure of Raphael is introduced almost produced illusion at a distance'.[47] Eastlake had a professional interest in examining one of the very few private fresco schemes completed in Britain, but there was a more immediate reason for his visit. Severn had applied to the Commission to work on the two still vacant compartments in the Upper Waiting Hall in the House of Lords, submitting designs for scenes from Scott and Pope. Perhaps Eastlake's compliments on Gatton Park were designed to soften the blow he knew was coming. On 27 July he wrote in his official capacity to tell Severn that the Commissioners had still not decided whether to admit Scott to their Poets' Corner. 'As regards the sketch in illustration of Pope, they are not prepared to recommend its adoption. I am, Sir, Your Obedient Servant, C. L. Eastlake.'[48]

It was the last letter from Eastlake that Severn kept and almost the end of one of his most important friendships. Later that year, as Eastlake climbed ever higher in the art establishment, Severn wrote to congratulate him on his election as President of the Royal Academy, 'touch[ing] nicely', as he thought, 'on his indifference & my hope that the term of my penitence was up whatever my faults may have been & which I was ignorant of '. Though he received 'a kind and warm letter' in reply,[49] there was no more that Eastlake could do for his old lieutenant. Now, as the breach widened, Severn, like Haydon before him, nursed a sense of hurt. In time he would enjoy Kirkup's potshots at Eastlake behind his back, mocking the time he spent learning his after-dinner speeches by heart and passing on unkind gossip about the reported strains between him and his wife.[50] It was a sad end to a friendship warmed in Rome by Eastlake's fondness for Severn's genial adventuring and Severn's respect for his mentor's integrity and fine artistic judgement.

By the 1850s Eastlake was far beyond Severn's power to wound. His accumulation of the top jobs in the Victorian art establishment continued. To his fretful task as Secretary to the Royal Fine Arts Commission, he added not only the Presidency of the RA in 1850 but the Directorship of the National Gallery in 1855. Others of Severn's old friends were also rising high: Leslie was appointed Professor of Painting at the Academy in 1847 and always stood well with the Queen. So too did Uwins who, prior to his appointment as Keeper at the National Gallery, was made Surveyor of the Queen's Pictures in 1845. Perhaps, he speculated, the Queen had given him the post because he was one of the few who had not lobbied for it. Severn certainly had, turning as usual to Gladstone, who had taken up his cause. Though he had twice failed to get the job himself, Severn was delighted that it had gone to Uwins, sending him a warm letter of congratulation from Eglinton Castle. Much as he rejoiced in Uwins's overdue success—'you were always left behind a hundred others, your competitors, whom I did not care a straw for'—he could not help reflecting on his own faltering course. 'Our fates now reverse . . . your London career has gently been inclining to the better . . . I fear mine is tending all the wrong way.' It was a rare moment of self-doubt, a recognition that his return to England was not working out. Socially, too, Severn found himself in no man's land. Though he always took an innocent delight in writing to his mother and friends from the houses of his aristocratic hosts, he was not at home at Eglinton Castle, despite the family connection.

He and Eliza had both been anxious about this, his first visit to Eglinton Castle. Since they could not repay the £150 loan Eliza had negotiated in 1841, it had been agreed that Severn should work off the debt by painting a portrait of the Countess of Eglinton and her infant son, Lord Montgomerie. Affable, extravagant, and popular amongst the racing world and in the London clubs, the Earl of Eglinton had made an unlooked-for marriage in 1841 to the widow of a naval officer, Theresa Cockerell, one of the eight illegitimate daughters of Viscount Newcomen. A handsome woman who knew how to live in style, she bore the Earl four children and supported his turn to Conservative politics. Her pathological jealousy of any woman under seventy (including the servants), however, made the Earl's life a misery.

Severn approached his delicate task at Eglinton Castle nervously. His anxieties centred on his lack of the essential appurtenance of the gentleman, a seal. In Malvern, staying with the Ellises, he had been obliged to borrow his host's: it was not a favour he could beg at Eglinton Castle. He discussed the problem with Eliza in the autumn of 1844, remembering that amongst the few effects he had taken charge of at Keats's death was a fine example. Though Severn cherished his memories of Keats, he was not sentimental about his personal effects and had few qualms about breaking up his seal and using the gold and crystals around the edge to pay for its transformation into a Severn seal.[51] So armed, he presented himself at Eglinton Castle intent on making a good impression on Eliza's relations. Despite the fiasco of the Eglinton Tournament in 1838 and the debt of £40,000 with which it had saddled him,[52] the Earl continued to live in fine style on his ancestral estates. Severn did his best to join in the hearty outdoor pursuits of Victorian country-house society. He went hare-coursing, watched the many games of curling on the ice, and tried to feel at ease among Eglinton's fabulous collection of armour, but drew the line at gambling, retreating to a quiet corner in the little-used library. Only when bad weather kept the company indoors did he really enjoy himself as they made up an impromptu orchestra—the Earl on the tongs and poker, the Countess on the draft board and Severn banging away with gusto on the door.

The painting went well, and Severn later exhibited his portrait of the Earl's wife and heir at the 1845 Exhibition. A place had been reserved for it over the fireplace in the drawing room at Eglinton Castle, and he was on his mettle to come up to an Angelica Kauffmann portrait on the opposite wall. For once he whitened his palette to match her flesh tones. The further commissions which would have brought in money did not come, however. The Earl, he was told, hated being done, and while Lady Eglinton delighted in showing him her jewels valued at £40,000, she made it clear that the £30 he had suggested for a portrait of her young daughter was excessive. The longer he stayed the less comfortable he was. Though the Earl implied the family connection between them by calling him 'Severn', at times he felt little more than a tradesman and was not introduced to Eglinton's guests at dinner. This could lead to embarrassments. Some, like the Coventrys he had known well in Rome, but now could not acknowledge. Stoically, he promised Eliza to 'submit to it all as it comes'.[53] At Eglinton Castle, as in the London art world, he was now out of his element. Only in the wider world was he about to receive his due.

CHAPTER 14

The Friend of Keats

I N later years Severn happily contributed to the myth that his main reason for returning to London in 1841 was to ensure a biography of Keats got written. He said as much to Charles Dilke in 1859: 'Keats memoir was my first great object in coming to England.'[1] By then his artistic career was in decline. Putting a brave face on his reverses in his twenty years in London, he clung to the one unquestionably successful project with which he had been closely associated in this period, Richard Monckton Milnes's *Life and Literary Remains of John Keats* published in 1848. But if he had not come back from Rome in 1841 on Keats's behalf, his arrival was certainly opportune. The momentum was, at last, gathering for the publication of a full account of Keats's life and character. 'Severn has arrived just in time for you has he not?' wrote Charles Brown to Milnes on 29 March when sending him the manuscripts of Keats's poems he still held.[2]

The Severns arrived just as Brown was about to leave. Tiring of Plymouth and anxious to see his son settled, Brown's attention was caught at a public meeting by the promise of a fresh start in remote New Zealand. He signed up with the New Plymouth Company to become a settler in Taranaki Bay. The prospect left him unable to accept the Severns' invitation to share a house with them on their return. They had not seen each other for ten years and now corresponded less frequently, but the bond of friendship remained strong. Brown was tempted by the invitation, if obliged to put his son's interests first. By the time he wrote to welcome the Severns home the following March, Carlino had already embarked for New Zealand. Brown would follow in May.[3] In preparation, he handed over to Milnes not only his Keats manuscripts but his 'Life of Keats'.

Finished in 1837, it had been on his hands ever since. He tried some publishers but got no takers, falling back on the familiar, but increasingly untenable argument that Keats's fame was not yet sufficient to justify a biography. Early in 1841, however, William Smith published an edition of Keats's poems based on the Galignani text, and *The Morning Post* asked to have another look at Brown's manuscript. By then there was not enough time to see it into print before he sailed. Having chased other claimants from the field, however, Brown recognized his responsibility to find a biographer for Keats before he emigrated. He made a wise choice in Richard Monckton Milnes, poet and literary man, socialite, traveller, and politician. Though Milnes had never known Keats the man, he had long admired him as a poet. Nor, happily, had he been involved in the disputes and accumulated dislikes which tore apart Keats's Circle after his death. In handing over his 'Life of Keats' as the basis for the new memoir, Brown did his best to tie Milnes's hands in the use he made of it, instructing Milnes not to soften the attacks on the critics nor lessen the agony of Keats's last days.[4] A quick glance at the text showed Milnes that he still had much to do.

Brown's 'Life of Keats' was a major disappointment. Though it contained two touching accounts of iconic moments in Keats's life—the composition of 'The Ode to a Nightingale' and his recognition in the lamplight that he had coughed up arterial blood, his 'death warrant'—Brown's text was little more than a memoir of his own friendship with Keats. He had talked of approaching William Haslam for information on Keats's early years but had not troubled to do so, while his quarrels with Dilke, George Keats, and Reynolds denied him access to papers that would have given a much fuller idea of Keats's life and character in the period before Brown knew him. As a result, he gave a very narrow view of Keats's friendships. Brown himself and, towards the end, Severn, were presented as the only friends of consequence while the names of all others, apart from Hunt, were blotted out with ostentatious 'XXXX's. If this was one way of repaying old scores, Brown's attacks on the reviewers was another. Keats, he attempted to show, had been hounded to death by the critics. To make the point, one-third of the 'Life' was devoted to Keats's sufferings in Italy. All his most intimate letters to Brown after he left England, together with some of Severn's increasingly desperate accounts of Keats's miseries, were incorporated. It was a way of berating Keats's enemies: perhaps, too, it was Brown's attempt to transfer to them his residual guilt for failing to be with Keats in Rome. Though he had insisted on writing 'The Life', thinking about Keats or reading his poetry was troubling: 'As soon as I begin to be occupied with his Ms poems, or with the Life I have written, it forcibly seems to me, against all reason . . . that he is sitting by my side, his eyes seriously wandering from me to the papers by turns, and watching my doings. Call it nervousness, if you will; but with this nervous impression, I am unable to do justice to his fame.'[5] In the end, Brown proved unequal to the great task he had reserved for himself.

Though Severn was the only witness of Keats's final agony, he had none of Brown's inhibitions. He had known Keats for longer, too, and was anxious that the world should know of the poet's high spirits as a young man and his solicitous tenderness towards his friends. When Milnes sought Severn's opinion on Brown's 'Life' Severn consulted Dilke. Though he came out of the 'Life' well, he knew that it would not do. As he explained to Dilke, he had read Brown's text 'with pain, with anguish', it was 'not fit for publication, altho' it is the truth but it is not <u>all the truth</u>'. Milnes would need to start again 'working up Brown's material as dismal & cool colours to set off the bright & gay'. Dilke was only too happy to concur: 'No friend either of Keats or Brown's—no judicious friend I mean—could be a consenting party to its publication', he wrote before settling to a long list of Brown's distortions and insensitivities.[6] Relieved to know that his doubts were shared, Severn arranged an early meeting to discuss what help they might offer to Milnes.

Though he had lent a loyal ear to Brown's accounts of his quarrels with surviving members of the Keats Circle, Severn had always stood aside from them. Living in Rome it was easier to do, but it was also his nature to try to get along with all but his most obvious enemies. Some members of the Circle, like Reynolds, Bailey, and Rice, he had never been particularly close to and had no cause to dislike; with others, like Taylor, he avoided rows by dealing with them obliquely. Dilke was now ready to overlook his annoyance over Severn's dilatory production of the Raphael copy, while Severn was more than willing to pay what he assumed was the price of cooperating with Dilke. He would accept his, rather than Brown's view, of the probity of George Keats's financial dealings with his brother (not that he had ever understood the ins and outs of the arcane dispute). He also sent a cordial letter to Taylor soon after his return, apologized to Haslam for his failure to see him in 1838, and contacted Charles Cowden Clarke and Edward Holmes. This flurry of activity at a time when he was working to establish himself as an artist in London, had a distinct purpose. '<u>I am distressed at the divisions of Keats friends which at every turn are unjust & hurtfull to his fame</u>—Milnes I trust will <u>unite</u> all these.'[7] With Brown now far away, Severn did everything he could to help Milnes bring the Circle back together again.

Picking up the friendship he had first established with Milnes in Rome in 1832 was easy. Milnes proved keen to cultivate Severn's company. He commissioned his own portrait from him in 1842, admired the picture he had painted of his last sight of Keats's grave, and a few years later bought *The Cave of Despair*. Although it had little more than curiosity value, he hung it in one of his reception rooms and enjoyed showing it off at his grand parties.[8] Only in one quarter did Severn's approach fail: Fanny Brawne refused to see him. By 1841 she had been eight years married to a man, Louis Lindon, twelve years her junior, who knew very little about her relationship with Keats. She was the mother of two sons and spent much of her time abroad. She had not seen Severn for over twenty years and would have guessed that he would want to talk about the old days and perhaps borrow the Keats miniature that she kept locked away. Her long struggle to leave a painful past behind her was hard won. When Brown had approached her in 1829, before her marriage, about his plans for a biography and his hope that she would agree to the publication of some poems and a letter referring to her, she had replied equivocally. She would not stand in Brown's way: if it were possible to establish Keats's fame and vindicate his name, she was obliged to 'make that sacrifice to his reputation that I do now to your kind motives'. But, clearly, she would rather the question had never arisen: 'I fear the kindest act would be to let him rest for ever in the obscurity to which unhappy circumstances have condemned him.' Nor did she want to share Keats with the rest of the world. 'Without claiming too much constancy myself I may truly say that he is well-remembered by me and that satisfied with that I could wish no one but myself knew he had ever existed.'[9] Twelve years later she was no keener to talk about Keats than she had ever been to anyone except his sister. While she would always appreciate what Brown and Severn had done for her old lover, she wanted to keep her distance. In 1841 Severn respected her decision: it only underlined the tragic intensity of Keats's and Fanny's feelings for each other. The failure to meet, however, had unfortunate consequences six years later.

Others were happier to pick up the reigns of old friendship. The Dilkes were always glad to see Severn in Westminster. On one evening he took round his two elder daughters. For Mary, in particular, an evening's conversation about Keats was a special treat.[10] She adored his poetry and loved to hear about the romance of her father's connection with him. Hard-pressed though he was in the City, Haslam, too, was keen to see Severn, who wrote apologizing that 'the labour of making a kind of beginning' in London had led to his neglect of 'one of my dearest friends'. Now that 'R M Milnes M.P.' was 'preparing' 'a memoir and splendid edition' he was anxious to have his 'advice and help'. 'I contribute all I that I am able, and I am sure you will have gratification in doing the same', he wrote.[11] He also encouraged Milnes to get in touch with Haslam directly and dashed off a collection of anecdotes, mostly about Keats in Italy, together with examples of his punning.[12]

Having got a sense of the task ahead of him in 1841 and 1842, Milnes put it on one side for three years. Though *The Life and Literary Remains of John Keats* was to be by far his best-known work, at times he could be surprisingly insouciant about it, dismissing it as no more than 'the biography of a mere boy'.[13] In the summer of 1842 he set off for a lengthy tour to Turkey and Egypt and, on his return, began trying to make his mark in politics as a radical campaigner for improvements in the condition of the working classes, despite his Tory party affiliation. Late in 1843 he took serious steps to launch himself on a diplomatic career, but was dissuaded by his good friend Gladstone. In 1844 he began writing for the Whig *Edinburgh Review*. Such was the quixotic character of Richard Monckton Milnes and the range of his talents and interests. His gifts were many, his achievements fewer. The expert compiler of the most famous collection of Victorian erotica who was also the persistent, but disappointed suitor of Florence Nightingale, is not an easy man to pigeon-hole. Many adored him; others found him insufferable. Generous, inspirational, gossipy, and sometimes irresponsible, he was not a man for the long haul. His literary activities were largely confined to review articles, poetry, travel reminiscences, and political pamphlets. The sustained effort required to write the first full life of Keats did not come readily to him. Once he had made a serious start in 1845, however, he applied himself with grace and skill to securing the cooperation of what remained of the Keats Circle, and encouraged its members to write down their memories of the poet. Though he was sometimes careless over details and allowed letters to be mistranscribed, his literary sympathies enabled him to produce a rounded portrait of Keats and do justice to the concerns of his friends. Severn, who had enough of his own worries to occupy him during Milnes's fallow period, bided his time between 1842 and 1845, waiting for the biographer to pick up his pen.

While Severn's artistic connections in London were now limited—in April 1845 he asked for George Richmond's comments on one of his cartoons, telling him 'you are the only friend I have who gives me a sincere & carefull opinion',[14]—he was a welcome guest in literary and diplomatic society. Now in London, the Bunsens maintained their splendid Christmas celebrations in their fine premises at Carlton House Terrace: it was a highlight of the year for the Severn children who also looked forward to the delicious boxes of nuts and raisins which James Ruskin sent over at the festive season. Ruskin, too, kept in touch with Severn, treating him to a private view of Turner's filthy but inspiring studio in November 1841 in the apparent absence of the great man, and going with him to the RA in February 1844. Severn was also able to build on the musical connections he had made in Rome. Mendelssohn came to Buckingham Gate and showed off his virtuoso keyboard skills for the Severns and their friends.[15] A good piano was a necessity Severn always maintained.

The richness of his literary connections made him a welcome guest at dinner. In May 1846 the publisher Moxon invited him to meet Browning and Tennyson, who on this occasion quizzed him about Shelley, while Browning was delighted to see Severn's portrait of *Keats Reading* and satisfy his curiosity about its subject.[16] The Severns also grew closer to Mary Shelley. By 1843 the friendship had ripened to the point where she was able to ask Eliza for letters of introduction to their friends in Rome, which she visited in the spring of that year with her son, Percy. Eliza's letters to Captain Baynes, Lady Coventry, John Gibson, Mrs Colyar, and a local Italian artist, Garofolini, transformed what had been a dispiriting visit to Italy into a heart-warming stay which revived her old love of Rome despite its sad associations. After the snubs she had endured from Anglo-Italian society in Florence, she began to use her letters of introduction in Rome with increasing confidence and found a hospitable welcome. It was, as she said, a tribute to the affection which old friends there still felt for the Severns. She went out of her way to see *The Infant of the Apocalypse*, writing it up in her published account of her travels as 'a beautiful composition' which 'shews to great advantage'. Privately, she told Eliza that it was 'much the best of the three there'.[17] Severn thought so too, mortifying though it was to him that he could never quite get the credit he deserved in London for surpassing Agricola and Camuccini on their home territory.

In April 1844 Percy Shelley came into his inheritance on the death of his grandfather Sir Timothy Shelley. Much depleted though it was, both he and his mother were now free of the old man's grim attempts to block the growth of his scandal-ridden son's poetic reputation. Sir Percy, who had scarcely known his father, wanted a portrait of him. Severn was the obvious man to paint it. But the commission was a delicate assignment. Only one portrait of Shelley existed, done by Amelia Curran in Rome in 1819, and though she lent it to Severn to help guide him, Mary Shelley was not satisfied with it.[18] A bust done in 1836 by Marianne Hunt, who had known Shelley only at the end of his life, though a better likeness, showed a melancholy, defeated figure. Severn had a more upbeat idea of the young Shelley, remembering his 'fine presence', 'tall, elegant, but slender figure', 'his restless blue eye', 'personal beauty & fine classical features', 'luxuriant brown hair and a slightly ruddy complexion'.[19] Vivid though this image was, it was nearly thirty years since he had seen him, and Mary Shelley was a demanding judge.

She and Severn must have discussed the setting for the portrait, though the idea of showing Shelley amongst the ruins of the Baths of Caracalla composing *Prometheus Unbound* looks like a typical Severn inspiration. He had a gift for matching sitter to background and throwing light on their character and situation. In 1846 he painted a touching portrait of Anne Matthew, the wife of Sir George Buckly, the Governor of the Bahamas. Her wistful West Indian maid stands behind her and in the distance is the ship that will take her back to England for the last time.[20] For Shelley's portrait, he took his cue from the poet's overwritten description of himself in the Preface to *Prometheus Unbound* composing his drama 'upon the mountainous ruins of the Baths of Caracalla, among the flowery glades, and thickets of odoriferous blossoming trees, which are extended in ever winding labyrinths upon its immense platforms and dizzy arches suspended in the air'. It was an ideal subject for Severn, inspiring one of his most charming and memorable compositions as he relished his opportunity to paint again the gentle light and elegiac melancholy of 'dear old Rome'. Shelley, thoughtful but bright-eyed, pauses pen in hand, amongst the mossy ruins.

Mary Shelley was less concerned with atmospherics than the accuracy of her husband's features—and here she was far from satisfied: 'The nose is anything but right...The mouth is defective—& so is the face.' She begged the Hunts to see it, suggesting that Marianne cut a new silhouette of Shelley's features to help Severn out. Severn was as anxious as anyone to get his portrait right and himself invited Hunt to come and advise him. The adjustments he made earned the picture a warm welcome when it was installed in the Shelleys' dining room in Putney early in January 1845. 'The picture looks very well indeed in the place you have chosen & makes my dining room quite another thing...Percy & I are...thankful to you for the happy idea & execution', Mary Shelley wrote to Severn.[21] She was pleased, too, when a copy of the portrait was ordered after its showing at the RA Exhibition. And she obligingly told Severn of the opinions of others, including her two sisters-in-law, on how well he had caught Shelley's likeness, even if she forebore to tell him that they had last seen their brother in 1811 and 1814. But she never quite brought herself to say the same. She admired the figure, she said (overlooking its unnaturally long legs): but was silent about the face. Shelley's look was for her a private treasure no one could replicate.[22]

In his later years Severn wildly exaggerated his part in the writing of Milnes's *Life*—Keats's sister, Fanny, reflecting what Severn had told her, used to refer to the biography as 'yours' when writing to him.[23] Though he was not, and never could have been, the author of such a sophisticated work, Severn was Milnes's principal lieutenant and the kind of collaborator any biographer might want. He actively encouraged interest in the project, arranging for Haslam to show Milnes the originals of some of his letters from Rome. In 1845 he sent a further set of reminiscences, this time focusing on Keats's character as a young man and his developing love of painting and music. His long letter also contained the authoritative account, which now only he could give, of the depth of Keats's passion for Fanny Brawne at the end. He also talked to Milnes about his old friend. Alongside the tired old story of Keats's anger at hearing Severn traduced after his RA Gold Medal success, which Milnes duly incorporated, there were fresh insights, including an evocative vignette of Keats humming along for hours as Severn played at the keyboard ('following the air with a low kind of recitative' was how Milnes more decorously described this 'pleasing musical effect').[24]

Milnes had some awkward areas to cover, which Severn was happy to leave to his discretion. While Haslam was anxious that nothing should be said about Keats's lack of faith at the end, a point which had also troubled Dilke, Severn was not prescriptive, but conscientiously passed on Haslam's concerns. He was keen, too, that the contribution of others should be acknowledged, writing at a late stage to ensure that Dr Clark's medical skills and unselfish care were given their due. Milnes more than obliged: 'the attention he received was that of all the skill & knowledge that science could confer, and the sympathy was of the kind which discharges the weight of obligations for gratuitous service, and substitutes affection for benevolence and gratitude'.[25]

Above all, freed from Brown's constraining hand, Severn was determined to ensure two major corrections in the record: the importance of Fanny Brawne and the unimportance of the critics. 'The critique make of in its place but only a[s] the poor fellows least misfortune', Severn wrote to Milnes on 6 October 1845; the 'corroding care' which had 'hurried him to the grave' was his 'death-stricken marriage' to Fanny Brawne. It was a sensitive point and Severn was the first to insist on it. Though Brown's memoir had included Keats's three last desperate letters to him referring to the intolerable pain of her absence, he had given no clue to the lady's identity. Even this went too far in the judgement of Dilke, who kept in touch with Fanny far longer than anyone else in the Keats Circle. But Severn had seen what he had seen in Rome and now understood far more about the power of love. Innocently, he cared more for the truth than any pain that its publication might cause to Mrs Lindon, thinking only of the honour that it was to any young girl to have inspired such a passion. He gave her the best write-up he knew as a lady 'possessed of considerable property in addition to her beauty & youth & . . . devotedly attached to Keats & his fame'.[26] Milnes accepted what Severn told him, though by getting into a muddle over the identity of the object of Keats's affections, succeeded in putting all but those in the know off the scent.

On Keats and the critics, Severn was confronting what had become settled opinion. If Shelley, Byron, and Hunt were against him, as well as Brown's polemic, however, he had a strong ally in Charles Cowden Clarke. Both were anxious that Milnes should share their view. As Clarke eloquently put it: the reviewers 'hurt his heart' but they 'did not kill him'.[27] Milnes had no problem with this. As Keats's own letters showed, he was his own severest critic. Similarly, Severn's other concern that the emphasis on Keats's sufferings and early death had overlaid the essential image of the lively, fresh-eyed, companionable young man, was amply borne out by the reminiscences of his early friends as well as his own letters. Once again, Milnes followed Severn.

Truthful as he was on the essentials, Severn was less reliable elsewhere. He had already begun the habit of reimagining himself into key moments of Keats's life. He had read Brown's vivid account of Keats arriving home late and chilled one night and coughing up arterial blood. Now, for Milnes's benefit, Severn transplanted the scene to the following morning with he and Brown shaking their heads together over the awful portent.[28] He had his own version, too, of the composition of 'The Ode to a Nightingale', though in its artifice it was far less convincing than Brown's simple account of Keats taking a chair out one morning 'to the grass-plot under a plum-tree' in the garden at Wentworth Place, where a nightingale had built its nest, and, after two or three hours, coming back inside with the scraps of paper on which he had written his ode. Severn's account, as later told by his brother Charles, was far more consciously Romantic: 'one night, when Keats was spending the evening with friends at the large house then (as well as the familiar group of pine-trees) known as "The

Spaniards", he was missed. Joseph Severn, one of the company, went to look for him, and discovered him lying on the ground under the pines, and listening entranced to the song of the nightingale overhead; and either that night or the following morning he wrote the famous Ode.'[29] Severn even painted this alternative version in *John Keats Listening to the Nightingale at Hampstead Heath*, which was shown at the RA in 1851. It now hangs at Keats House, where it is a favourite with young visitors. It is not Severn at his best. Stiff and self-conscious, a gentlemanly-looking poet, book at his feet, looks upward from the Campagna-like wastes of Hampstead Heath, inspired by the song of a nightingale coyly profiled against the pale disc of the moon. This ponderous image has never effaced the one memorably conjured up in a few words by Brown.

Elsewhere, Severn had more success in imposing a distorted but influential version of a Keats moment on history. Animated by the new interest in Keats's life, he contributed a letter to the first number of *The Union* magazine in February 1846, describing the circumstances in which Keats composed 'The Bright Star' sonnet, sitting on deck as they sailed away to Italy writing down his poem in a volume of Shakespeare he gave to Severn. Severn knew, at the time, that Keats was writing out an earlier composition, not creating a new work. Twenty years later he went for a more dramatic effect: thanks to Severn's *Union* article 'Bright Star' was transformed into Keats's 'last poem' and placed at the end of collections of his work. Milnes followed Severn's testimony to the letter.[30]

'You and I have always agreed about him,' wrote Severn to Milnes in October 1845 'when nearly all his friends & admirers have been at variance, Keats' fame suffering meanwhile.'[31] It was a fair assessment in all but one respect, where Milnes showed a waywardness which mystified and irritated Keats's friends. For his description of Keats's appearance, he relied on the account of a woman, who, on her own admission, had only ever seen Keats twice, Anne Procter, wife of the poet 'Barry Cornwell'. But try as they might (Severn's portrait, *Keats and the Nightingale*, was, in part, designed to record Keats's colouring accurately), it took Keats's friends thirty years to persuade Milnes to expunge 'the blue eyes and auburn hair' Mrs Procter had imported. Severn had, at least, the satisfaction that Milnes chose to use his miniature for his frontispiece in 1848, stiff though the engraving of it was. He had been anxious on the point as William Smith's edition of Keats's poems in 1841 had used a portrait by William Hilton. This became a particular *bête noire* of Severn's, who complained to John Taylor in

1841 that it made Keats's eyes too small 'which takes from the resemblance . . . his openness & enthusiasm of mind'.[32]

By contrast, Severn was less proprietorial about what he had written about Keats. Despite Dilke's qualms over the appropriateness of publishing the letters from Rome with their references to Fanny Brawne and Keats's spiritual despair, Severn never thought of trying to suppress them. Indeed, he made sure that the letters he had written to Haslam were also seen by Milnes, who already knew Severn's letters to Brown. As the only account of Keats's last days, Severn knew they would play a big part in any biography. Coventry Patmore, who made transcriptions of them for Milnes, found them 'nothing short of frightful . . . I leave off copying them, with much the same impression as I awoke with, last night, after a very dreadful nightmare.'[33] But Severn was no longer the poorly educated, desperately insecure young man who had written the letters. Now he had a reputation to maintain. And deathbed scenes were important to nineteenth-century readers. He was anxious to appear at his literary best. Twice he wrote to Milnes begging him to correct 'any inaccuracy of language' or 'striking error' in his letters.[34] Milnes obliged with verbal smoothings and a sophistication of punctuation unknown to Severn. He made more substantive changes, too, omitting all references to Keats's intense sexual frustration as well as Severn's anxiety about Dr Clark's instructions to keep Keats on starvation rations. He also toned down (but without altogether excluding), the strength of Keats's suicidal determination and lack of conventional faith. Though Milnes's changes introduced an extraneous Olympian air to a grim scene and blunted some of the immediacy of Severn's letters, they still had an unforgettable impact. And when it came to Severn's lapidary account of Keats's final hours, Milnes was a good enough literary judge to confine his touching-up to the minimum.

Richard Monckton Milnes's *Life, Letters and Literary Remains of John Keats* was, for all its carelessness over details,[35] a skilful work. Its author used his own literary knowledge and insight to trace the influences on Keats's development as a poet, while moulding the reminiscences of his friends into a convincing portrait of Keats the man, robust and manly, spontaneous and passionate, and always dedicated to his craft. Though he included some unpublished work, most of Keats's best poetry was already available: the revelation of the biography came from its generous inclusion of his letters. They corrected many of the misconceptions of Keats which had developed. The idea of an ill-bred, undisciplined, sensual, over-sensitive, and depressive youth was replaced with that of the self-aware, articulate, committed artist, a young man always striving after greatness and developing at an extraordinary rate. Only in one respect did Milnes fail his subject. Like Shelley and Hunt before him, he looked not at Keats's absolute achievement in his twenty-five years on earth but at what it showed of his potential. So, what he had written was 'rather a promise than an achievement . . . When my imagination measured what he might have become by what he was it stood astonished at the result.' It led to an unnecessarily ambivalent assessment: 'they who will not allow him to have won his place in the first ranks of English poets will not deny the promise of his candidature', Milnes concluded, putting himself among the sceptics. Severn was, perhaps, one of those who had fostered his caution. 'His was a gigantic mind' he had written to Milnes, 'which would have required another 10 years to mature it.'[36] But though he could not rid himself of the thought that he was dealing with the life of a boy poet, Milnes brought much else into focus. Nor did he shy away from the major controversies, tackling head-on Shelley's potent if lachrymose image of the thin-skinned artist hounded to death by the critics, and judiciously placing Brown's polemics as 'the affectionate indignation' of a friend who 'out of an honest anger gave encouragement to the notion that [the critics'] brutality had a most injurious influence on the spirit and health of the poet'.[37]

Apart from Byron and the critics, everyone got a favourable mention in *The Life*. Even Hunt, who had declined an active cooperation (though he did agree to the inclusion of his fine letter to Severn at the time Keats was dying) was given a graceful reference. It could not, however, protect him from the pain of discovering criticisms of him in Keats's own letters, which later led him to block moves for a revised edition of *The Life*, which was not published till after Hunt's death. For the rest, one of Milnes's finest achievements, arising from the sureness with which he had found new sources and willing collaborators, was to reconstruct the Keats Circle and give a vivid sense of its individual members and their importance to the man at its centre. There was 'the invaluable worth' of Reynolds's friendship with Keats, 'the congeniality of tastes and benevolence of disposition' of Charles Brown, a tribute to Charles Cowden Clarke as Keats's early mentor, a warm acknowledgement of Haslam's helpfulness, and regrets at Haydon's sad demise. A generous construction was put on George Keats's financial dealings with his brother, which satisfied Dilke and Dilke himself, Rice, Woodhouse, Edward Holmes, and the publishers Taylor and Hessey 'who seem to have cordially appreciated his genius' were all given their rightful place in the Circle.[38]

The highest accolades of all were reserved for Severn. Everything he could have wanted to see in the biography was there: his influence on Keats's developing love of art; Keats's pleasure in making music with him; and Keats defending Severn against his enemies in the London arts establishment. Above all was the indelible image of Severn, the one selfless friend, devotedly easing Keats's dying agonies. Picking up on some of the language which Shelley had used in his Preface to *Adonais*, Milnes fixed Severn's place in the hearts of lovers of Keats for almost a century. 'Entirely regardless of his future prospects, and ready to abandon all the advantages of the position he had won, Mr Severn at once offered to accompany Keats to Italy. And there, as his letters of "energetic simplicity" described, he set about the "holy work of friendship and charity".'[39] Not only was Severn sanctified, he now became the one friend whose name was inseparable from Keats's. Milnes vividly recalled his first meetings in Rome in 1832 with 'the painter of City and Compagna . . . delighting all travellers who had the pleasure of his acquaintance by his talents and his worth. Nor was the self-devotion [*sic*] of his youth without its fruits in the estimation and respect of all those who loved the genius, revered the memory, and mourned the destiny of Keats.' Without Severn, Milnes wrote at the outset of his biography, 'I should probably never have thought of undertaking the task' of writing Keats's life. He sent him the first copy of his biography.[40]

Severn's standing as the best-known friend of Keats was not new. Shelley had eulogized him, Keats lovers had called on him in Rome and he was the only member of the Circle who had found his own way of keeping his name before the public. But now his status would be far more widely disseminated. With Reynolds out of London literary life and Brown dead in 1842 (remembering their happy bachelor times together in Florence and Rome, Severn felt that 'his sense of youth had gone ever'),[41] he now became the authority not only on Keats's last days but on his earlier life, too. He had moved from the edge of the Circle to its centre. The heart-breaking story of the desolate early death in Rome of a young poet of unequalled promise became perhaps the most romantic episode in nineteenth-century English literary history. Severn was an integral part of this: for the Victorians his loyalty transfigured the terrible last days in Piazza di Spagna. To love Keats was also to love Severn: in the annals of devoted male companionship he stood high, the surrogate for all the affection that Keats's admirers could no longer bestow on their idol. It was a tribute to Keats that he had inspired such selfless devotion and to Severn that he had offered it. The image, however misleading, was not one Severn was ever likely to deny. The myth-making had begun, willingly abetted by his enthusiastic recreation of the past.

As the unsurpassed Friend of Keats it would have been open to him to exploit his famous connection to further his artistic career. In 1850 Milnes put 'a Mr Robert Spence in North Shields' in touch with him. Spence had read the *Life* and was keen to own a picture of Keats from Severn's brush.[42] There might well have been others if he had wanted to confine his activities to turning out pictures of his increasingly illustrious friend, as he did in his later years. In 1850 it was too soon to narrow his artistic expectations. Furbishing Keats's reputation was still primarily a responsibility rather than a timely opportunity in the career of a declining artist.

Though not exploitative he could be officious, however. In 1840 Mary Shelley published Finch's egregious letter to John Gisborne of spring 1821 that described Keats's unbalanced mental and emotional state on his deathbed. It bolstered Shelley's reputation by explaining the feeling behind the preface to *Adonais*, but did a disservice to Keats. Fanny Lindon became aware of the letter only a few years later—and was appalled by it. At the time she was living in Heidelberg, where she had got to know Shelley's cousin, Thomas Medwin. In the teeth of fierce opposition from Mary Shelley he was endeavouring to put together a life of Shelley, digging out his material where he could and sometimes concocting it. He caught sight of Keats's signature in Fanny Lindon's copy of Shakespeare and began to sniff out a secret. At the time she would say nothing of her connection with Keats. Only her indignation at Finch's distorted record broke down some of her discretion. She showed Medwin Keats's letter from Naples and Severn's from Rome to her mother. He was keen to publish these finds.

Severn may have known of Mary Shelley's anxiety to get Medwin's biography suppressed, or been told of the affair by Hunt, who was also caught up in it. Though gossipy and inaccurate, the book proved to be less damaging than they had feared. Nonetheless, perhaps intending to champion Mary Shelley's cause, Severn complained to Medwin about the publication of his letter to Mrs Brawne, claiming in uncharacteristically legalistic fashion, that his copy-right had been breached. He might have done better to keep quiet. There could be little doubt of the source from which Medwin had obtained Severn's letter to Mrs Brawne. Equally, Finch's letter was obviously based on information from Severn. In so far as Severn's letter to Mrs Brawne contradicted Finch, it did nothing but good for Keats's reputation, and Severn's too.

So Fanny Lindon thought. Bewildered as she was by Severn's attitude—
'I wondered Mr Severn did not contradict' Finch's letter she innocently
commented—she did not want to fall out with him. Though his complaint to
Medwin was 'quite uncalled for', since the letter to Mrs Brawne 'only does
Mr Severn credit', she confessed to Maria Dilke 'I should be sorry for any ill
feeling to exist between myself & Mr Severn, whose kindness I have always
appreciated.' Could Mrs Dilke please let him know 'I am sorry I did not know
of his legal rights.'[43] The moral right to protect Keats's reputation was, as she
implied, a different matter. Fanny Brawne's dignified defence of the character of
her old lover made Severn's muddle look like self-importance.

However well or badly Severn pursued his responsibilities as 'The Friend
of Keats' and however gratifying the public recognition of his status, it could
not pay the bills. Throughout the 1840s the Severns' financial position steadily
deteriorated. He still touted for portrait commissions, though they came more
often now in the less remunerative form of drawings; he still tried to find a home
for *The Holy Sepulchre* and a way of making up the £250 outstanding on his costs
in producing it; in brighter moments he still made long lists in his sketchbook of
the grand pictures he hoped to paint; and he still hoped to secure election to the
Academy. In reality, however, he was obliged to make constant small economies
and press his patrons for early payment, ill concealing the desperation of his
and Eliza's finances.

On the face of it, they should have managed. When William Dyce gave his
evidence to the House of Commons select committee in 1841 on the prospects
for fresco, he suggested that an annual allowance of £700 a year would be
enough to tempt all but the most successful portrait painters to devote themselves to the new medium. Only Severn's ledgers for 1841–7, possibly his best
years in London, survive. They show that he managed to earn well over £500 in
most full years. Coupled with Eliza's annual allowance of £100 from the Earl of
Eglinton, the Severns' joint income was not far off Dyce's figure. But it was never
enough. There were six children to educate and support; Eliza maintained
expensive tastes; and though Severn could cut his costs and rather enjoyed
living economically, he was not good at increasing his income. It was not that the
market for paintings was in decline. In the 1840s and 1850s it expanded rapidly,
fuelled by the demands of a prosperous middle class for original work which
would complement their bright and busy décor. As G. D. Leslie recalled, 'artists
had a famous time of it', buying houses and gardens in St John's Wood, Kensington, and Hampstead and building large, luxuriously fitted studios which

they opened to the public on 'Show Sundays'.[44] What the public looked for was small, precise, sharply coloured pictures full of carefully painted details, which told stories, humorous or sentimental, dramatic or pathetic. But the precision of 'Dutch painting' was not Severn's style. Just as Haydon's grander, more declamatory manner with its gloomy chiaroscuro and elevated expression had gone out of fashion, so too had Severn's. Mid-century patrons were not looking to furnish their rooms with Italianate Magdalenes (let alone huge altarpieces) or poetic fancies. But Severn was reluctant to adapt to the new demands of the English market. As in Rome, where Penry Williams had steadily overtaken him, so in London William Dyce far surpassed him, in both popular and critical estimation, whether in sacred art, fresco, or literary painting. Nor, unlike Dyce, did Severn get any of the jobs in the art world which provided prominence and a steady income. As he plaintively wrote to Gladstone when soliciting his support in one of his bids to become the Surveyor of the Royal Collection, 'I am sinking under but for the want of a place of trust of this kind . . . the exercise of my Art here almost as a common trade must soon destroy me.'[45]

He did not often lose heart. At the end of his first decade in London, however, self-pity overcame him as he saw what he thought of as men of inferior talents getting ahead. His belief in his own artistic genius helped him survive the buffeting: he could still persuade himself that only his shortage of ready cash and the exigencies of trying to give his children a better education than his own were frustrating his career. To Eliza he even confided that Eastlake had got ahead only because of 'his ready money, in every way but this, he is my inferior'.[46] He was left with no option but to turn to his in-laws. It was time to see whether the high-spending Earl of Eglinton would, once again, bail his family out.

CHAPTER 15

An Interlude in Pimlico

WHATEVER his fame as the Friend of Keats or his artistic successes, Severn never doubted that his greatest achievement was the way he and Eliza brought up their children.[1] It was a victory against the odds. The Severns did not fit the roles laid down in Victorian marriage manuals where the husband was the master, engaged in the outside world at his office or counting house as his 'Angel' wife consoled him at home, educated his children, and concealed her domestic anxieties in return for his sustenance.[2] Eliza's unconventional childhood left her without maternal role models while, as an artist, Severn had no retreat outside the home. And though he was the 'Guvn'r' to Eliza's 'Mater', he increasingly failed to provide for his family. In the process, he lost his authority, conceding to Eliza, two of his children, and a son-in-law, mastery of the family finances and leaving them dependent on the sanctimonious charity of outsiders. Had he not married he would have struggled less. But he would also have missed out on the richest satisfaction of his life, his children.

All of them married well. Each made their mark: Claudia in marriage and motherhood; Walter as a respectable civil servant and distinguished water-colourist; Henry a successful engineer in the colonies; Mary surpassing her father in ability and achievement as an artist; Arthur the husband of Ruskin's indispensable 'Cos', Joan, and a bold landscape painter; and Eleanor blossoming as the wife of an eminent Oxford Classical scholar, Henry Furneaux, and mother of a family which would bring a distinction to Severn's descendants even he could hardly have imagined.[3]

In hard times, the Severn children pulled together, justifying their parents' overextended efforts to give them the best start in life. Sidelined as he was from the family finances, Severn was always involved in decisions on the children's education, while Walter, Mary, and Arthur, artistically the most gifted of his children, looked to him for approval of their work. In London he was the life and soul of their parties and encouraged their passion for amateur theatricals. Eliza, care-worn but still beautiful, patched up an old frock or wore a becoming shawl to cut an elegant figure at Eglinton Castle or her aunt's estate at Rozelle. In London it was she who dispensed the 'Tin', a scarce commodity much discussed in family letters. After a harsh decade, however, it was Severn who emerged with the best-paid position in his family as British Consul in Rome. His certainty that good times were always just round the corner was vindicated, his authority restored.

In 1850 his prospects had not looked promising. Eliza went for an extended stay with her aunt to sound out the Eglintons on helping her family. Initially, they offered only advice: Severn must make more efforts to sell his pictures.[4] He did his best, writing to his patrons with suggestions on what pictures might interest them. Gladstone he kept in reserve. The replies were slow in coming. Momentarily his confidence disappeared: 'People will not buy pictures this way . . . I have relied on a few old Patrons who have been (up to this moment) attach'd friends as I endeavoured to sustain the rank I had at Rome & never bore them.' In time, a few cheques arrived as Severn economized, swapping mutton for rabbit, a far cry from Eliza's overloaded tables in Ayrshire.[5]

As his circle of patrons narrowed, Severn went after the middle class market for portraits in the provinces.[6] In the following decade he and his wife were more often apart than together, he in pursuit of work, she staying, from time to time, with aristocratic friends as a respite from the calls of the duns, or educating the twins abroad. Desperately trying to hold the family together in a succession of cheap lodgings in Pimlico, Eliza learnt to ignore her husband's optimistic projections of future earnings, looking anxiously instead for £5 notes (sent in halves) in his letters. He accounted for every pair of socks he bought, compared prices for woollen vests, and sometimes travelled at night and always third class on the train, or left his hosts' houses early to cut his laundry bills and tips for servants. But though he could reduce his outgoings, he could not increase his earnings. The disillusionment began with his first visit to Manchester in 1851.

He went with high hopes and a portrait commission from his old friend James Cobbett. This quickly led to a further commission to paint the Dean of Manchester Cathedral, George Hull Bowers, who invited Severn to stay at his deanery in Salford. A photo of Bowers shows an exceptionally severe-looking cleric, with close-cropped white hair, lowering eyebrows, and furrowed chin.

One who knew him well, however, remarked that 'He generally had a sort of scowl on his face, but really was the kindest hearted man possible.'[7] He was hospitable too, passing his snuff box around the choir stalls during services and serving up the best port at the deanery. He owed his appointment to Lord John Russell, whose private tutor he had been. Their mutual connection with the Bedford family would have given the Dean and his guest much to talk about in the evenings, but at the back of Severn's mind, as he cultivated his new acquaintance, was the enticing prospect held out by Cobbett that Bowers would place *The Holy Sepulchre* in his cathedral and make up the £250 shortfall on the subscriptions. The relationship began well as the Dean introduced Severn around and offered some small family portrait commissions.

Manchester should have been fertile territory for an established London-based artist cultivating a new audience. There was no shortage of money or interest among its 'Millocrats'. Scientific and artistic societies flourished; there was an annual art show; Thomas Agnew, the London dealer, had a saleroom in Manchester; and there was no resident artist of standing to see off competition from newcomers. Grundy, a local printmaker, impressed with Severn's renown as a prize-winner in the 1843 cartoon competition, was keen to engrave some of his work and get him launched in a lucrative market he had until then barely explored. But, once again, Severn failed, relying on a small circle of patrons and concentrating on portraiture rather than the large narrative pictures loved by the prosperous Mancunians.[8]

He also saw himself as the victim of tense Church politics in the early 1850s. The drift towards Rome of several prominent Anglicans and the resurgence of the Catholic Church under Cardinal Wiseman strained relations between High and Low Churchmen in the Church of England, spilling over into highly charged disagreements about church furnishings and the organization of ecclesiastical space. In Manchester the tensions were particularly acute, with the Evangelical Bishop, James Prince Lee, at war with his High Church Dean and Chapter whose perks and privileges he was determined to cut back. The building, too, which had been designated as a cathedral as recently as 1847, was in a bad way. Such money as there was in the 1850s was mostly spent on shoring it up, though several stained-glass windows were installed, including some paid for by Dean Bowers. Ultimately, what defeated Severn in Manchester was not religious tensions nor the uncertain future of the cathedral building but a lack of enthusiasm for his altarpiece. Nor would the Dean allow his and his family's portraits to sit in Grundy's shop window. In the end Severn barely scraped together £100 in Manchester. Mary never forgot her mother's despair at the collapse of their hopes.[9]

Severn kept going. In May 1851 he was in Todmorden, working on a large portrait in oils of a local magistrate, John Crossley. He tried to fix his price at metropolitan levels, finding himself beaten down by the organizing committee of careful Yorkshiremen to £100. He produced a fine portrait, nonetheless, now in the Christ Church Art Gallery, New Zealand. Red-cheeked and firm-mouthed, every inch the Yorkshire gentleman, Crossley is shown against the mistily painted Pennine Moors with a gorgeous dog awaiting his command. A celebratory dinner was organized for the picture's unveiling.[10] That, together with his success in getting *The Holy Sepulchre* shown at the 1851 Great Exhibition, encouraged him to think of another 'flare up', 'a work from nature as I did in Italy to reinstate me in the minds of Artists & my friends'.[11] He was even willing to try 'the Pusey style', a wry reference to the Pre-Raphaelite Brotherhood's fondness for minutely detailed, laboriously painted landscapes which observed Ruskin's maxim of 'truth to nature'.

Had Ruskin liked the Brotherhood less, Severn might have appreciated them more. On the face of it he had much in common with them. Both loved Italian painting and rich colour; and they chose many of the same subjects. Millais made his name with *Isabella* in 1849 and Holman Hunt with a *Rienzi*, and both Severn and Millais painted *Ophelia* and scenes from *The Tempest*. Keats, too, was a major inspiration for the Brotherhood. For Severn, however, theirs was not 'honest' painting. The minuteness of their carefully observed landscapes was no more than photo realism while their symbolism and didactic intent aroused Severn's suspicions. Above all, devotee of the Nazarenes though he had been, he could follow neither Ruskin nor his acolytes in their admiration for the Italian Primitives. For him painting began with Raphael and Michelangelo. To paint like the Primitives was akin to putting Shakespeare into Latin.[12] Severn's hostility towards the PRB put him at odds with his children. Walter was keen to go with the latest fashion while Mary loved their choice of subjects and the care with which they painted. Ruskin's approval only sweetened her own. She read everything of his she could find and persuaded her father to get her and Arthur invited round. 'Take your time', Ruskin bade them as he set out his magnificent collection of Turners on his drawing room chairs.[13] But Severn never forgot the contrary young man he had known in Rome, the 'overgrown child' with 'his pretty butterfly existence in the gardens of literature & Art'. 'He dashes at everything regardless of truth, regardless of usefulness, & regardless of contradicting himself.'[14] Severn's critique of Ruskin and the PRB, scribbled down in a rush, was the closest he ever came to an artistic testament and showed how far he still clung to what he had learnt in the RA Schools. Painting, as Severn explained it, required not conceptualization but taste, imagination, and poetic feeling, alongside respect for the Great Masters. But he tried to please his children, taking more trouble over his major paintings and working at his landscape backgrounds. Mary gave her father's most important picture of the 1850s, *The Deserted Village*, her highest praise: it was 'beautiful, & so well finished, every part quite Pre-Raphaelite'.[15]

Severn's planned 'flare up' on the Pennine Moors was abandoned for more certain money-making ventures. In 1852 he was in Scotland cleaning and arranging the family pictures of Lady Lockhart of Lee and painting a commissioned portrait of Bishop Cameron. Alexander Lockhart had a hand in both these assignments. The third son of a Baronet, he had been MP for Lanarkshire from 1837 to 1841. Now he provided a London house for his mother at 'The Elms' on Brixton Hill, sharing it with his aunt and spinster sister. Distantly related to the Montgomeries,[16] he had known Eliza as a child in Scotland. 'The Elms' became a refuge for the Severns: when Eliza or her children needed fresh air they went to stay in what was then a salubrious South London village. The Lockharts also took a kind, if increasingly heavy-handed, interest in Severn family affairs. Severn often walked back to Pimlico at midnight after an evening discussing his deteriorating finances with them, while Eliza rarely took an important decision without Lockhart's say-so, particularly when Severn was away, as in the autumn of 1852 and early months of 1853. Helplessly, he watched from a distance as his family's fortunes crumbled: 'I know quite well all the bills & their dates & tremble at the trouble you & Walter have had', he wrote to his wife in November 1852. By January he could 'only pity' them '& hope & pray that you may be kept up so as to go safely to the end which must be near'.[17] The Severns had only one resource left, their children.

Walter, the eldest son, was already securely placed as a clerk at the Privy Council Office. Drudgery though it was, the light hours and long holidays left him free to pursue his bent for landscape painting and high society. The return to the family's dingy London lodgings was always a humiliation. Ruskin applauded his attempts to relieve their ugliness with embroidered 'curtains, chair & sofa covers—Tea clothes & fire screens'.[18] Hard-headed and worldly-wise, an indispensable counsellor to his mother, Walter was spared his father's fecklessness but lacked his geniality. There were rows as he tested the 'Govn'r's' authority, just as Severn had challenged his own father.

Claudia, the Severns' eldest child, comes across more pallidly only by comparison with her siblings. In 1851 she was engaged to a Wykehamist, Frederick Gale, who was mad about cricket: eventually, he would make his living writing about it. In the early years of the marriage, however, it was his training as a barrister which proved invaluable to the Severns. Claudia gave herself up to motherhood and charitable works, a gentle steadying presence in the Severn family. Stoically, she concealed her grief over the early death of a son; steadily, after frequent childbearing, she declined into invalidism. Her younger brother, Henry, the Severns' fourth child, was physically the least robust and so mostly educated at home. Though Severn can only have been one step ahead of his pupil on Euclid, he did his job well, encouraging his son's practical and scientific bent. Henry made toys for the twins and installed an electric cat deterrent in the garden. Even as his own prospects were deteriorating in Manchester, Severn went out of his way to secure an apprenticeship for him at the Fairing engineering works there. After further training in Birmingham, Henry secured a job helping to set up the new Australian Mint in 1853. In 1871 he moved to New Zealand, working as an assayer in the gold mines and developing a reputation as a leading amateur astronomer. The twins, Arthur and Eleanor, were protected from many of the family's humiliations, cosseted by their older siblings as only the youngest children in a large family can be. Arthur, with his puckish charm and happy-go-lucky self-confidence, had the makings of a man about town; Eleanor, not a beauty like her older sisters, had a quickness her twin lacked. Sharp-eyed and sharp-tongued, she was always a 'fearless' personality.[19]

At the heart of the Severn family was the luminous presence of Ann Mary, as Severn liked to say, 'my favourite and most gifted child'. From the time he rewarded her with a paint box for having read *The Ancient Mariner* at the age of twelve, she showed exceptional talent. Four years later she was admitted to the Antique School at the RA. Severn was more delighted than discomfited when soon after she won a portrait commission he had hoped to get himself.[20] In the early 1850s he arranged for her to study with Richmond, a stern, but expert taskmaster. It was a generous concession since Severn never quite liked to admit that Richmond was the better painter. In 1852, when just twenty, Mary showed a charming portrait of the twins at the Academy Exhibition. Of all the

Severns, she was the most loved and loveable. Like her mother, she had beauty and charm and a seriousness tempered by a sense of fun. Pure-hearted, devout but never prosy, a clear-eyed observer of human frailty, modest but aware of her great gifts, Mary was everyone's favourite sister. She could persuade Walter out of a temper; she knew her father's foibles but saw the best in him too; and she, as much as anyone, brought up Eleanor. Her sweetness of character still shines through the hundreds of her recently discovered letters, illustrated as they often are with line drawings and deft amusing caricatures. Though she had several girlfriends, particularly Mary Palliser who modelled for some of Severn's pictures, her 'greatest friend' was always her mother, whose Scottish accent she inherited.[21] Through the trials of the 1850s, Mary and Eliza held the Severn family together.

In May 1853 Severn exhibited a retouched version of *Mary Magdalene* at the RA Exhibition. It was the last of his pictures to attract wide attention and favourable comment in the press. The *Art-Journal* thought it an 'original subject, and a striking picture'; the *Spectator* 'a semi-mystic invention'; and the *Illustrated London News* 'an attempt in the highest walk of art'. But nobody bought it. In desperation, he put up some of his pictures, sketches and drawings for auction at Christie's on 17 June, selling only one for £3 15s. He could no longer brave it out with his creditors. While Mary and Walter took lodgings of their own as bolt-holes for family possessions, Severn disappeared on the night of the 20th, leaving Eliza to face the bailiffs. She took a succession of cheap rooms, irritating her landlords with the comings and goings of her boxes, desperate to remember where she had put the decent clothes she needed to approach friends for help. One of the first was Severn's old classmate, Edwin Landseer. Now immensely rich, he was tight-fisted, too. He recommended Mary to Colnaghi's, the engravers, for copying work, but would not bale out her father. Similarly, when Eliza fetched up in a hansom late at night outside the Eglintons' London residence, they refused her money. William Vaux, a Keeper at the British Museum and family friend, was more helpful, attending the enforced sale of the Severn family possessions and buying back a few antiques. The Lockharts were predictably ready with advice.[22]

Severn retreated to stay with the sister he knew least well, Charlotte Giles of Cross Street, Islington. She was ignorant of his financial problems and stood, overawed, as Eliza arrived for hurried consultations in Italian. Destitute though the Severns were, the gulf between them and the Giles's modest existence in working-class Islington was unbridgeable. Though Lockhart had warned

Severn he would be arrested if seen in daylight, he could not resist hearing the Bishops of London and Salisbury preach at St Leonard's Shoreditch, where he hid behind a curtain. He was troubled, however, by the memory that in all his recent attempts to raise cash, he had put Keats's watch in pawn. 'I enclose the ticket of my poor dear Keats's watch which, the sum being so small & the "article" so good—do send Ann & get over Westminster bridge—at once', he anxiously instructed Eliza. Sentiment and financial calculation coincided. Preoccupied though she was, Eliza rescued Keats's watch. 'I am obliged beyond what I can say', Severn told her.[23]

If he could still influence small things, he had lost all say on big ones. Lockhart and Gale worked up the settlement with creditors: 5*s* in the £ would be paid by regular instalments from Walter and Henry's salaries. Gale followed up on what Severn had told him was owing to him, discovering what a slap-dash business manager his father-in-law was. The Dean of Manchester made clear there was no hope of placing *The Holy Sepulchre* in his cathedral; he was still irritated by Severn's lackadaisical refusal to adjust the colouring in a portrait of his daughters. A Mr Hazeldine of Enfield, when applied to for the cost of some frames, explained, civilly enough, that he had paid for four portraits but received only two.[24]

Severn learnt of Gale's efforts from a distance. Lockhart had arranged for him to lodge with friends in Jersey, clear of British jurisdiction. He stayed there for over four months, painting portraits and giving art lessons in lieu of rent, and sketching landscapes as he ruefully considered his future. He was full of praise for the Mater's fortitude in holding things together, but felt his isolation. 'Do pray send me an empty envelope now & then addressed as above for I am afraid people may think you never write to me & that we don't care for each other', he begged Eliza after two and half months away. Vainly, he still hoped for jobs: Eliza was instructed to lobby for the Inspectorship of the School of Design and Gladstone solicited for support for the top job at the National Gallery. (Gladstone told Severn to be more realistic.)[25] Somehow, he also persuaded himself his time had come for election to the Royal Academy, encouraging both Walter and Mary to cultivate Leslie, who would 'do away with any injurious impression that might be against me'. But there were moments of despair, too. By the middle of August he had decided that Rome was the only place for him. He could do quick views for tourists there: 'Mind! I should never think of fame again or historical Art but only of plodding in a way that I shall be sure to excell as I have had so much practice.'[26] Eliza would not go, since Mary's prospects as a portrait painter came first. This was the lowest point of Severn's artistic career.

In November Lockhart told him he could safely return. Nervously, Severn came to the Lockharts' holiday home in Bognor and was delighted to find Henry there, preparing to take up his appointment in the Australian Mint. The Severns waved him off on the long journey from Portsmouth on 7 December. A Lockhart loan of £300 got Severn restarted in London but left him and Eliza increasingly reliant on their benefactors' self-important charity.[27] Mary deplored her family's dependence on Lockhart's goodwill. From the time of her father's flight to Jersey, it was she who provided a home for the Severns, working hard and putting up her prices. Walter wangled some cheques from old family friends, leading to a furious family row when Severn insisted on spending Lady Braye's £20 on violin lessons for Arthur.[28]

The 'renovating principle' was always strong in Severn.[29] He relaunched himself with a book of engravings, *Twelve Italian Scenes*, early in 1855. It was a way of reminding his public of his best pictures and the distinction of his patrons. Dedicated to Gladstone, it included work in the possession of the Queen, King Leopold of the Belgians, the Czar of Russia, Pope Pius IX, and a clutch of dukes and duchesses, marquesses and earls. He could still pull off a good sale, too. The Duke of Devonshire bought his *Juliet* for £55 in a transaction arranged by Joseph Paxton, whom he had got to know in Rome.[30] Sir Thomas Acland put him in touch with a Devon friend, the Reverend Walter Halliday. Halliday, with his rolling agricultural acres and picturesque estate at Glenthorne near Lynmouth was the epitome of the sporting Victorian parson.[31] Severn and he, both great talkers, got on famously. Halliday liked Severn's portraits of him and his wife so well he bought *The Ancient Mariner*, which had been on Severn's hands for more than fifteen years. Severn stayed at Glenthorne for three months in the autumn of 1855, painting a scene from Oliver Goldsmith's *The Deserted Village*. It was an attempt to move with the times, adopting the Pre-Raphaelite style and choosing the topical subject of enforced emigration and rural dislocation. In 1856 he returned to work on backgrounds for his picture.

He needed the company. In March 1855, Eliza solved the problem of the twins' education by taking them to France, where they could live more cheaply and prepare for Mary's arrival to study with the eminent teacher Ary Scheffer, in Paris. Severn missed them badly and was ticked off by Lockhart for his imprudence when he fitted in a quick weekend with them (including a 'cozey'

Papa keep off the
wind & rain inside Papa
M.S.'s study ! *M.S. never shut the*
window

12 Mary Newton's sketch of her father, Joseph Severn, shielding her from the rain as she paints in their shared lodgings in Pimlico *c.* 1858

dinner at the Café Royal) in November.[32] With Eliza away, he and Mary lived and worked companionably together at her lodgings, painting steadily, making do with beef tea at lunchtime and settling down in the evening before the fire, he deep in his newspapers and history books, she entranced by 'My beloved Keats' or a biography of Nelson. Once Severn took her to Glenthorne to meet Halliday and his nephew and heir, William Cosway.

With Severn staying at Glenthorne in the autumn of 1856, Mary went to join her mother and the twins in Paris, quickly winning a commission for a portrait of the elderly but still fascinating Lady Elgin and a command from the Empress Eugénie to paint the Prince Imperial. They were back in time for the unveiling of *The Deserted Village* at the RA Exhibition the following May. This is one of Severn's best works and now hangs in the Art Gallery of South Australia in Adelaide. A despairing group of men, women, and children console each other as they walk down a steep path carrying their heavy trunks and the tools of their trades away from their desolate hilltop village to where a boat waits for them in the bay. Severn took immense pains over this painting, filling his canvas with fine details and elaborating a careful composition infused with poetic melancholy. But it was poorly placed at the exhibition, attracted no notice, and failed to sell. He never again showed at the RA.

Though he got his *Mary Magdalene* included in the great Art Treasures exhibition in Manchester in 1857 and made a long list in his sketchbook of the grand paintings he would produce, including that ancient chimera *The Assassination of Lorenzo de Medici*,[33] the artistic fire had left him. In 1858 he and Mary worked side by side in the National Gallery, copying the same picture, she on commission as a wedding present for the Princess Royal, and he, less grandly, for a school. Mary, full of enthusiasm for Francesco Francia's touching *Pietà*, was appalled at her father's poor drawing and slapdash painting as well as his resistance to her suggestions for improving it. When his back was turned she did what she could to touch it up.[34] The torch had passed from father to daughter.

Her career was taking off. In 1857 she was taken up by the Royal Family. A portrait of the Queen's mother led to commissions for a sketch of the latest royal baby, a portrait of the Prince of Wales and drawings of some of the Queen's other children. Eliza could never get enough of Mary's triumphs: the Queen going through her portfolio with the Princess Royal and exclaiming 'how lovely, this is charming', Prince Albert standing beside her in his overtight, poorly made clothes, the Prince of Wales offering to come to her London lodgings to complete his sittings, Princess Alice resting her chin on her shoulder as Mary sketched. Briefly, Eliza came to Eton to join in the excitement: 'you were so <u>nice</u> to everybody here, so charming & all that ... & it made you look quite handsome again—& if you don't now & then rouse yourself & put on company manners, you wd. get quite old looking', Mary told her with her usual affectionate frankness.[35]

Perhaps Mary's advice influenced Eliza's decision to spend more time with her relations. In 1858 she was in Bath with Lady Jane and at Battle with Sir Charles and Lady Lamb. Her health was poor, she was still troubled about the education of the twins, life in London was drab and fretful, her bright confidence in her husband's gifts was gone. Somehow the Severns scraped together enough to send Arthur to Westminster School, while Eliza took Eleanor to Hanover for a year to add German to her already extensive linguistic repertoire. It was at this period, with Severn at loose ends in London, that Frederick Locker-Lampson, a literary man and shrewd observer of human nature, sought him out, discovering 'a jaunty, fresh-natured, irresponsible sort of elderly being leading a facile, slipshod, dressing-gowny, artistic existence in Pimlico ... he never seemed to be in want of anything, unless perhaps it might be a brush or comb'. Unkempt though Severn may have been, Locker warmed to him.

'Severn was especially amusing when he indulged in the melancholy looking-back vein. "Ah! Mr Locker, our youth! That was the time when Hope and Fruition went hand-in-hand—altri tempi, <u>altri tempi</u>. What is left to us? Vain anxieties, delusive hopes, unexpected issues." ' Severn took him to meet Hunt who 'discoursed about poetry as exhilaratingly as Ruskin does about art'.[36] But Severn and Hunt were both now out of the swim. When Hunt died a few months later, Severn was obliged to write to his son, Thornton, reminding him who he was and begging a ticket to the funeral.[37]

He began to plan the final phase of his life with Eliza: a quiet Derby and Joan existence in Rome. He had been reliving his triumphs there in the first set of memoirs he started writing in January 1857, 'Incidents of My Life'. He fiddled, too, with a novel he had started in 1839, 'The Dead Hand', about cloak-and-dagger adventures in the time of Titian and the dark manipulations of the Inquisition, racy but impossibly muddled. He also knocked off an atmospheric short story, 'The Pale Bride',[38] and, modelling himself on Walter Savage Landor, attempted some imaginary conversations between great men of the past. Thinking of Rome reminded him of his long failure to erect a monument commensurate with Keats's fame. He wrote to Gibson and consulted Dilke.

The inadequacy of Keats's epitaph rankled more than ever: 'now his fame is world-wide & his memory being cherished by every feeling man this stone has become a <u>downright anomaly</u> . . . he should have a tomb with some characteristic decorum about it & at least a true inscription <u>beyond ridicule</u>'. But Severn's suggested rewriting was both inaccurate and verbose: 'This grave / contains the Mortal remains of / John Keats / a young English Poet / Who died at Rome. Feb. 20, 1821, aged 23 years. His short life / was so embittered by discouragement and sickness / that he desired these words to mark his grave / 'Here lies one whose name was writ in water.' / Time / having reversed the sentence / His friends and admirers / Now inscribe his name / in Marble.' Dilke was no more willing than Brown had been to soften the harshness of Keats's epitaph: 'the unseemly stone tells the story of his life'. Though Milnes agreed with Dilke, Severn was undeterred. The grave might not survive much longer as it was. 'I do not think it would be honourable to Keats's friends to allow such a state of things,' he chided Dilke, 'certainly as regards myself I will not as far as I may chance to have the power.'[39] But would he ever have the power?

As he sat around in London dreaming of Rome he could still pull off the occasional coup and fetch a price far beyond anything Mary or Walter could command. In 1860 he sold an oil of *Ophelia* to the new Duke of Devonshire for 250 guineas, his best price since his Roman days, though far from his best picture. In May he welcomed two devoted Keatsians from Boston, the publisher James T. Fields and his wife, Annie. Happily he reminisced with them about 'poor, dear Keats'; genially he encouraged them to buy some of his paintings. They chose a dusty version of *Ariel* and a Gainsborough copy, and commissioned a drawing of Keats.[40] Prompted by the visit, Severn started to write down some reminiscences of Keats for publication in the new magazine that Fields was editing, *The Atlantic Monthly*. But though he still hoped to return to Rome, Eliza's uncertain health delayed their departure. Increasingly, their future now depended on Mary.

She was never short of admirers. There were love-lorn suitors amongst the Palliser and Richmond boys, a determined pursuit by Dugdale Astley, the son of one of her sitters, and an Eton schoolmaster, Coleridge, who got carried away during a sitting and jumped up and kissed her, much to her parents' consternation. Severn himself had always hoped she would marry 'the heir of Glenthorne', William Cosway. He was keen enough, but thrown into his company on a yachting holiday off Cowes, Mary could not wait to get back to London.[41] She would make her own choice. In 1859 she fell in love with a severe, egotistical, middle-aged bachelor, but a man of great distinction, Charles Newton, the close friend of Ruskin and Henry Wentworth Acland at Oxford. Though he was closer to her parents' generation of friends, Mary's chosen husband was a very different man from her father. A passionate archaeologist, he had worked as the British Museum's agent in the Aegean and joined the consular service. His greatest coup was his identification and investigation of the Mausoleum at Halicarnassus, whose spoils he brought back for display in the museum. Through William Vaux, a neighbour in Pimlico who worked at the British Museum, Mary was invited to prepare drawings of the relics to illustrate Newton's lectures. She welcomed the new challenge, which drew on what she had learnt in the Antique School at the RA. The romance of archaeology fascinated her as did the imagination and expertise of the man who had made such remarkable finds.[42]

In the face of her charm, intelligence, and passionate enthusiasm for his work, Newton's reserve broke down. There was a snag, however: he was about to take up an appointment as British Consul in Rome. For Mary, marriage and an absence from her portrait practice were out of the question as long as her family's finances remained uncertain. She put a brave face on it. In time all might be well: Newton had hopes of a Keepership at the British Museum. He was not

13 Mary Newton's sketch of Charles Newton, the great archaeologist, on his way to Rome to take up appointment as British Consul, 1858

happy in Rome. Fretting over his humdrum consular tasks, he kept an anxious eye on the ongoing reorganization at the British Museum and went for solitary walks to see the places where Mary had lived. Late in June he returned briefly to London, having determined to marry her. By the end of the year he was back for good to take up a new appointment as Keeper of the Greek and Roman Antiquities Department in Bloomsbury.

Severn did not hand over his best-loved child easily. A supper was arranged to celebrate the engagement. Mary primed her mother in advance, anxious that the family should be on its best behaviour: 'He does not wish me to <u>draw</u> for money—so when you see him you ought not to speak of this—He is so gentlemanlike, so refined, that I hope you will in speaking keep yr face <u>calm</u>, & not <u>rattle</u> out everything any how.' Unnaturally orderly and quiet, the Severns got through their meal. Newton was a man they respected but never warmed to. After supper there was a row. Newton was to take his fiancée to a party. Teasingly, Mary refused to tell her father where she was going on the arm of her chosen partner in life. 'Papa was very angry and behaved very oddly. He wd not see Mr Newton again', wrote the mystified young Eleanor in her diary.[43] Severn had lost his dearest child to another man. It hurt.

Newton's return to London offered Severn one last chance at the Holy Grail he had unsuccessfully pursued throughout the 1840s and 1850s, a secure position with a steady income. He had gone after everything that was going, however risible his claims. 'I cannot but think it hard that I am left the only one who has not been allowed to profit by that which I have rendered to others, in maintaining the solidity of Art . . . without profit, place Commission or anything but empty promise', he wrote feelingly to Gladstone in 1854. Though Gladstone had stopped buying his pictures he had not neglected his wider responsibilities as patron to the Severn family. He put in a word for Walter at the Privy Council Office, helped secure Henry's appointment at the Mint, and encouraged his wife and sister-in-law to give portrait commissions to Mary. He also did what he could for Severn, though even his patience ran out when Severn aspired to be Director at the National Gallery.[44]

The consulship in Rome was different. Severn's first tentative approach was well received: 'if you apply for it and think fit to refer to me it will give me sincere pleasure to bear testimony to your many good qualities', was Gladstone's reply. Newton provided hard-headed inside advice: 'Rome is a post much sought after . . . There are probably at least 50 names before Lord J. Russell [the Foreign Secretary] at this moment, so whatever interest you can command, you would do well to bring to bear at once. A Minister always likes to be asked to give an appointment by as many persons as he can.'[45] Severn determinedly set about marshalling his support. He had only a vague idea what the post might involve. He remembered the helpfulness of various consuls in the 1820s and 1830s, and sensed from Newton's experience that the ability to recover archaeological remains or spot artistic treasures going cheap might be a qualification. He set out his claims in a long letter to Russell: his familiarity with the Italian language and history, his services to his countrymen in the 1820s and 1830s, his friendship with Cardinal Weld and the history of the San Paolo altarpiece, his ability to acquire works of art for his country, and his wife's charitable services, not forgetting Lord William Russell's earlier patronage and Mary's portrait of Russell's wife and child.[46] While Mary wrote to her friends at Windsor, hoping for the Queen's approval, Severn contacted everyone he could think of (except Eastlake): Henry Wentworth Acland, now Professor of Medicine at Oxford, Bunsen, C. R. Cockerell the archaeologist, Monckton Milnes, Richard Redgrave at the South Kensington Museums, Ruskin, Lord Stanhope, the Chairman of the new National Portrait Gallery, Richard Chenevix-Trench, and his doctor, Quinn. Only with Milnes, Keats's biographer, did he hint at a further claim on the post:

'pardon all this trouble as 'tis for an old friend who never yet stinted his services to anyone as you know'.[47]

Most were helpful. Ruskin obligingly described him as 'a gleam of living sunshine ... I cannot fancy anything pleasanter for English people at Rome than to have you for Consul, so I can fancy nothing more profitable for English people at home than that your zeal and judgement should be on the watch for straying treasures.' Bunsen, who was terminally ill, rallied on his sickbed to dictate a testimonial to his daughter, remembering Severn in his Roman prime: 'he made himself universally useful and popular among the English residents', and outwitted 'jealous Italian artists and the clerical party' in getting his altarpiece into San Paolo. 'I never knew an artist possessing so much practical knowledge and ability as Mr Severn.'[48] Just over a month later Bunsen was dead. A man of European fame and firm Liberal credentials, he was much mourned, particularly in London, where for thirteen years he had been an influential Prussian Minister at the Court of St James. Severn believed that his appointment to Rome was a tribute to Bunsen's memory. Newton was probably nearer the mark: 'if Gladstone really asks for your appointment as a favour to himself, your chance is good ... No better supporter could be found in Cabinet.'[49]

There was only one problem. Severn was ineligible, and both Gladstone and Russell knew it. Though Gladstone took great pains over appointments and has gone down in history as the man who abolished patronage and place and opened the civil service to selection by merit, he sometimes filled other vacancies more in the spirit than the letter of the regulation.[50] He sent his Cabinet colleague, Russell, a judicious assessment of his client's qualifications for the post in Rome:

I have known Mr Severn since a period nearly thirty years back, when he resided in Rome as a distinguished English Artist and I have always entertained towards him sentiments of warm esteem and regard.

With respect to the technical duties of a Consul Mr Severn will doubtless bring evidence of his qualifications from those who have had opportunities of forming a judgement upon them:— All I need say is that I know no reason to presume unfavourably respecting them. With regard to his general intelligence and character, his temper, taste, and feeling, and his kindly and winning manners, I can speak of them in strong terms and with great confidence.[51]

Characteristically, he stated the problem only obliquely. First appointments in the consular service were reserved for those under fifty-one, and as Gladstone's reference to 'nearly thirty years back' made clear, Severn was too old to qualify.

Though he always took pains to conceal his true age, he was now sixty-seven, 'just on the wrong side' of the age bar as he put it to his doctor. The decision rested with the Foreign Secretary, Lord John Russell. The papers do not reveal how Gladstone persuaded him to break the rules. There is a chilliness to Russell's letter of appointment, however, which suggests that he resented Gladstone's insistence on a favour for his friend and client.[52]

The Severn family gloomily awaited the collapse of yet another of the Govn'r's 'Castels in the air'. 'I fear there is <u>no</u> chance of his getting it', young Eleanor wrote in her diary, reflecting what Mama had told her. They sat together on a drear January day. 'Suddenly Papa came into the room & said "You'll be glad to hear that I'm appointed Consul at Rome!" Oh we were so pleased we all danced for joy.'[53] Both Mary and her father had their mantras. For her it was the confidence that 'God will keep the good wine till the last': for Severn an injunction from Hume, 'Anticipate by your hopes and fancy future consolation which time infallibly brings to every affliction.'[54] At the end of the perilous 1850s, Mary found her reward in Newton, while Severn's indefatigability won him a fine position with a salary of £400 in the place where he most wanted to be. He wasted no time, setting off for Rome before the mandarins in the Foreign Office could object to his grey hairs. After a weekend with Eliza in Folkestone he boarded the Channel steamer, bearing his red diplomatic passport. It was a more astonishing transformation than anything Charles Dickens invented for Mr Micawber.

CHAPTER 16

British Consul

THROUGHOUT the 1860s Rome's future lay in the balance. While the king-doms, principalities, and dukedoms in the Italian peninsula and most of the papal estates came together in 1859 and 1860 under the leadership of Victor Emanuel of Piedmont and Sardinia, Rome and Venetia remained apart from the new Italy. In 1867 the Austrians were driven out of Venetia: Garibaldi's second attempt to march on Rome, however, was a failure. Nor did a series of attempts to negotiate a reduction in the pope's temporal power in return for a strengthening of his spiritual authority succeed. Rome, despite its inspiring connotations of past imperial grandeur and apparent rightness as the capital, stood aloof. But the pope's power there was precarious. For all the increasingly spectacular demonstrations of his spiritual command, Pius IX relied for his ability to control Rome on the French troops who had been stationed there since his return from exile in 1850.

'The Roman Question'—how king and pope could coexist when, as seemed inevitable, Rome became the Italian capital—fascinated the chanceries of Europe, and nowhere more so than in London. The British public, too, felt proprietorial about the progress of Italian unification, reading into it familiar elements from their own idealized island story: the thirst for liberty; the emer-gence of a constitutional monarchy and elected parliament; the fostering of national pride; and the struggle against a repressive Church. Throughout the 1860s they confidently awaited the final act in the drama, travelling in increasing numbers 'to gaze from the windows of their hotels on the fall of Troy and Rome'.[1] Their presence meant lots of work for the British Con-sul, distinguishing trouble-makers from tourists, contributing to the comfort of British travellers, and wheedling concessions out of the repressive Roman authorities.

Determined Evangelicals smuggled in forbidden Italian Bibles and tracts; English and Irish Catholics rallied to the pope in his hour of need; ladies, seduced by the glamour of Garibaldi, arrived to demonstrate their loyalty; oddballs, like the notorious medium Daniel Home, troubled the authorities: and, as always, there were those who got caught in difficulties of their own making, fell ill, went mad, or unexpectedly died in Rome. Severn was in a more exposed position than at any time in his life, mediating between a fractious resident community, where Protestants looked for the fearless assertion of the Englishman's rights and Catholics criticized any confrontation with the Vatican. Some of his scores of colourful dispatches on his travails were read by Queen and Cabinet; a few were published in Parliamentary Blue Books; his conduct was debated in Parliament and discussed in the press. Daily, the mandarins of the Foreign Office kept a watchful eye.

He loved the attention and was delighted to be back. For all his distrust of the cynical tyrannies of papal power and pride in representing a country on the side of progress and 'favouring liberty',[2] he was as fond as ever of 'dear old Rome'. Dark and dilapidated though the city was, the Church still exercised its picturesque pull. There were the great Easter festivals, the brilliant illuminations every April to mark the anniversary of the pope's return from exile, and the fortnightly excitements of the lottery draw in the Piazza Madama, where a young child picked out the winning tickets watched over by a Monsignor in full ecclesiastical fig. Sometimes Severn would happen on Pius IX taking his afternoon promenade on the Pincio, a figure of conspicuous piety (despite the snuff stains on his white cassock) in contrast to the splendour of his equipage. The crowds knelt reverently as he stopped to chat to friends and acquaintances.[3] It reminded Severn of old times. When he had finished his business at the Vatican there was nothing he liked better than to tuck his feet under his chair and reminisce with Antonelli, the Pope's Secretary of State, about the palmy days in Rome.[4]

Old friends like John Gibson, Cornelius, and Overbeck were still active. 'Health and longevity are, in truth, characteristic of life in Rome', Severn commented in his diary,[5] before remembering one who had died there far too young. He visited Keats's grave soon after his return. Now the path was well trodden, as admirers made their way to the edge of the cemetery to ponder the Romantic melancholy of the inscription and take a cutting as a souvenir. The custodian worried about the bareness of the grave. 'Sow and plant double'

Severn cheerfully advised.[6] The lack of a memorial at the site, however, continued to trouble him.

An elderly Spaniard came to the consulate, anxiously enquiring if he was 'Joseph Severn, the friend of Keats'. They had met only once before at Keats's bedside, and neither recognized the other, but Severn knew that Valentin de Llanos had gone on to marry Keats's only sister, Fanny, in 1826. Now she was in Rome, hoping to meet and thank the man who had nursed her dying brother. She came from distant Spain accompanying her son-in-law, Leopold Brockman, the chief consulting engineer on the Roman Railways, and curious to see the place where her brother had died. Severn's arrival in Rome within a few months seemed providential.[7]

A meeting was arranged for the Saturday morning after Easter.[8] For once, Severn was silent as he and Fanny clutched hands, tearfully remembering the bright genius of John Keats and his final sufferings. It was the start of a warm friendship that lasted until Severn's death. For Severn it always had the feeling of a family relationship. Her daughters, he wrote, 'met me reverently, as an elderly relation', while the young Louis de Llanos would always be his 'brother brush'.[9] For Fanny he became a proxy for the brother she had lost. In Spain she had learnt dignity and reserve. Frederick Locker Lampson tried to tempt her into talking about 'her wizard brother' but could get little response: 'she spoke [of him] as of a mystery—with a vague admiration but genuine affection'.[10] With Severn, however, she was much more open. As she relaxed, the 'same sweet vivacity which characterised the dear poet' emerged.[11]

He quickly recruited her to his campaign to replace Keats's tombstone, playing on her guilty awareness that she had had no part in erecting or maintaining it. She was happy to pay for a new stone with an epitaph more in keeping with her brother's eminence. While she mulled over the possibility of lines from *Adonais*, 'the broken lily lies—the storm is over past' or the words Trelawny had suggested as long ago as 1823, 'Whose master's hand is cold / Whose silver lyre unstrung', Severn worked on the draft he had shown Dilke in 1858. As so often before, however, nothing came of it. In the end Fanny did no more than plant out two bay trees at the grave before she left Rome in 1864.[12] Her confidence in Severn's judgement on everything to do with her brother, however, was unaffected.

In Rome she had consulted him on whether Keats's letters to her should be published. They are some of the freshest and most touching letters even Keats wrote, as he conscientiously tried to build an affectionate but responsible relationship with the young orphan sister he rarely saw. Funny, instructive, and a little awkward, they show Keats at his most loveable. Severn read them carefully but found nothing to enhance the poet's fame. As he later explained to Lord Houghton (as Monckton Milnes had now become): 'they are all addressed to a little girl & constrained in style'. Fanny accepted Severn's verdict, repeating it to Harry Buxton Forman in 1879.[13] Happily, this dogged editor persisted, including most of them in his new edition of Keats's letters in 1883 and throwing an attractive new light on the poet's character. Severn's failure to appreciate them was a measure of how conventional his idea of Keats had become. Having seen him undervalued for so long, he was anxious to avoid anything that would detract from Keats's image as a great Romantic poet. In the same spirit, he worked up a sanitized version of Keats's deathbed in his article for the *Atlantic Monthly*. He sent in his manuscript on 21 June 1862. Fields published a tidied-up version, 'On the Vicissitudes of Keats's Fame', in April 1863.[14]

'Vicissitudes', the only one of Severn's autobiographical pieces published in his lifetime, fills in some of the gaps left by Monckton Milnes's biography. Though Fanny Brawne remained anonymous, Severn presented her as the source of Keats's final unhappiness: 'a tender and enduring love' reciprocated by her, approved by her family and bolstered by 'fortune on her part & fame on his' as Severn fondly remembered, but all set at nought by Keats's last illness. He also touched on delicate terrain in writing far more fully than Milnes about Keats's suicidal determination. To counterbalance that, he introduced a deathbed conversion: 'I always think that he died a Christian, that Mercy was trembling on his dying lips, that his tortured soul was received by those blessed hands which could alone receive it.' These were the sort of pieties Keats's Victorian readers would have expected. Only Cowden Clarke took Severn to task for imagining he could fool the Evangelicals.[15] From the deathbed, Severn moved on to an eccentric collection of incidents designed to show how strong the feeling against Keats had been after his death, including Samuel Rogers's disobliging remarks in 1821 and Scott's guilt over the poet's death. He ended with a touching account of his most recent visit to the Protestant Cemetery and meeting with Fanny Keats de Llanos before finding room for a plug for a picture he was painting of a young shepherd asleep at Keats's grave.

'Vicissitudes' gives an idea of how Severn talked about Keats in his later years, discursive and often inaccurate, affectionate and amusing, but also with insights only he could now offer, as with his discussion of Keats's attitude to classical

Greece (which Fields cut from the published version). The article brought him new admirers and a letter from one of George Keats's daughters, Emma Speed of Louisville, Kentucky. He gave her a potted account of his career since he had first come to Rome in the 'dear company' of her uncle in 1820. All his own and his family's successes had turned on his association with Keats: 'the revered name of the Poet' had drawn his best patrons to him, chief among them Gladstone, he wrote, perpetuating yet another myth.[16]

Severn's famed association with Keats made him a figure of considerable interest in Rome but was of limited help in his new incarnation as British Consul. After two months he was confident that he was 'well in my saddle'. As others saw it, however, he had made a shaky start. Someone reported him to London for lighting up his house as part of the general illuminations in Rome on the anniversary of the pope's return from exile on 12 April 1850. This earned him the first of many reprimands from Edward Hammond, the Permanent Under Secretary in the Foreign Office: 'I regret to say that I entirely disapprove the illumination of your house on the occasion in question. I trust you will not again join in any demonstration of so political a significance.' It was a stiff put-down for an innocent beginner's mistake which Severn tried to shrug off as a courtesy to 'the Sovereign of the country'.[17]

An expert judge of Severn's conduct, Odo Russell, the British 'Agent' in Rome, shared the Foreign Office's concerns. The ablest and best-connected diplomat of his generation, Russell was appalled at Severn's appointment, complaining to his mother that he was

a good natured goose utterly unfit and unqualified for his post...sooner or later he will get into trouble and will have to be removed, for he is too old and too silly to learn his business. I can't understand how such an appointment could have been risked by the Foreign Office. I pity the poor man for he is so anxious to do well...The Consular Service requires training and experience as the Army and Navy do. Poor Mr Severn is a trouble instead of an assistance to me.[18]

Russell came of a distinguished Whig family and had the assurance and ability of his caste. Though diplomats were often snobbish about the consular service, however, Russell was more concerned with competence. Hard-working and ambitious, he had been in Rome since 1858. British Protestant sensitivities, enshrined in legislation, prevented his official accreditation to the papacy, but his apparently lowly status as 'Agent' officially attached to the British Mission in Turin from 1860 gave him a welcome freedom. Alongside his access to the pope and his ministers, he cultivated a range of less orthodox contacts. He was popular, too, with the British community, singing at evening parties; acting in amateur dramatics, and bringing in hats for the ladies in the diplomatic bag. Though he took long leaves every autumn, hobnobbing with emperors and princes and catching up with statesmen on both sides of the political spectrum in England, he was no slacker, doing 'twice as much work as most men, and with half the fuss'.[19] His Whiggish dispatches were avidly read in London: the Queen was a particular fan, the Foreign Office relied on them, and even as Prime Minister with a huge agenda of domestic reform, Gladstone would turn first to 'an Odo' in his red box.[20]

Russell's unorthodox status meant that, technically, the consul was outside his command. Initially, this had led to tussles with Charles Newton over the division of work, though Newton was judged a safe pair of hands and rewarded with a telegram of congratulation from the Foreign Secretary when he left Rome.[21] No two men could be more different than Newton and his father-in-law: the one rigorous, highly intellectual, and conscious of his gifts, the other instinctive, ill-educated, and unself-critical but big-hearted. While Newton's consular career ended in respectable esteem, Severn's did not, for all Russell's efforts to keep him straight.

The fact that the consular service could throw up two such different men as Newton and Severn was an indication of its amateurishness. Though appointments were keenly sought, there was no agreed recruitment standard, no progressive pay or career structure, inadequate leave and pension arrangements, and a bare minimum of training.[22] Severn spent just one afternoon in the Foreign Office being briefed on his duties. Nor were his written instructions much help. The standard injunction to apply himself to 'the protection and promotion of British trade' was beside the point in a place where there was no trade to promote and the routine returns he was 'required to furnish' fell to the able young Italian secretary, Alexander Franz, whom Newton had recruited to the consulate.[23]

It was not in Severn's nature, however, to be idle. With little guidance from the Foreign Office, he made up his job as he went along. On arrival in Rome he found in the consulate files a still extant instruction which appealed to him. In October 1860 the Piedmontese government had asked for help in their dealings with the Vatican and Lord John Russell had directed Newton to 'afford your Good Offices to Sardinian Subjects in Rome in such cases as may properly call for your intervention'.[24] It was a vague commission and did not extend to issuing passports. Severn, however, leapt at the charge to 'aid suffering Italians'. Here was a practical way of doing good and manifesting his government's hatred of repression, as well as its sympathy with the new Italian nation.

His first task, however, was to win the confidence of the Roman authorities. He went out of his way to publicize his success in persuading 'three mad Englishmen' who were going about Rome 'clad in Garibaldian costume' to leave before they were expelled. On the strength of that he then persuaded the Roman Governor to give passports to nineteen Italian railway men left high and dry when their work on the new railway was finished.[25] He also quickly established his credentials in the consulate office, stepping in to find a place under 'the great engineer Brockman' for Alexander Franz's brother, Francesco, who had been thrown into jail after an undergraduate prank, when he and a few friends released some racing pigeons with red, white, and green ribbons tied to their tail feathers at a concert in the great hall of Sapienza University. Severn's success in getting Francesco released and finding a job for him, earned him the undying loyalty of Alexander Franz, who looked after his chief's interests for the rest of his life, keeping the office running smoothly, taking on humdrum tasks, and, in later years, covering up for his master's absences and failing powers, all without upstaging him.[26]

Not only did Severn quickly establish good relations with the Governor of Rome, Monsignor Matteucci, he also relished his dealings in the Vatican with the Pope's Secretary of State, Cardinal Antonelli. Though a cardinal, Antonelli had never progressed beyond the order of sub-deacon. In his taste for palaces, pictures, pretty women, and family preferments, he was a throwback to the great Renaissance princes of the Church. But though he took little interest in doctrinal matters, Antonelli was a dominant influence in the Curia, a skilled diplomat and administrator, witty, discreet, and efficient. He fascinated foreigners in Rome. The stout east Prussian historian Gregorovius commented: 'The upper part of his face is clear-cut and almost handsome, the lower ends in the animal.'[27] Russell dealt warily with him. Severn was more incautious, finding him 'a remarkable man' with 'a fine countenance of the strong and yet refined old Italian type'.[28] For his part, Antonelli had immediately sized up his interlocutor, telling him that no one had more influence in Rome.

In his first autumn Severn's abilities were put to the test. With Russell on leave, it fell to him to handle the awkward case of Padre Passaglia. Passaglia, the most distinguished Jesuit theologian in Italy, who had worked closely with Pius on the development of the Doctrine of the Immaculate Conception in

1854 but had been driven out of his teaching appointments in Rome when he came under the spell of Cavour and put his keen intelligence to work in developing a case for enhancing the spiritual standing of the papacy through the abandonment of any claim to temporal power. He returned in October 1861 in the vain hope of persuading the Vatican to reach an accommodation with the new Italy. He and his hostess, a prominent English Catholic widow, Mrs Foljambe, who lived at the Palazzo Spada, soon found themselves harassed by the police. She appealed to Severn to get them called off. He dithered, anxious not to offend the Roman authorities. Passaglia, however, was a much-admired figure in London. Though he was not a British subject, the Foreign Office was prepared to grant him a passport to make his escape from Rome. As Severn continued to hesitate, Mrs Foljambe found her own way of spiriting Passaglia across the frontier, but not without complaining to the Foreign Office about the consul's irresolution. Though Severn failed the priest, he was quick to protect the lady, persuading Matteucci to call off the police watch, announcing that Mrs Foljambe was under his special protection, and arranging for her letters to England to go in the diplomatic bag. His self-congratulatory dispatch at the end of it all did not go down well in London. Matteucii's reported relief that 'there were two cool heads, his and mine to stop this affair in its serious tendency' irritated Hammond, who underlined the 'cool' and 'mine' before adding '!!' in the margin.[29]

It is a moot point whether Severn would have acted more decisively if he had had Eliza's 'Scotch head' to advise him.[30] In his anxiety to get to Rome, he had left her behind to get up her strength for Mary's wedding at the beginning of May and the long journey to Rome. Unfortunately, she was not well enough to see her daughter married and did not set off for the Continent with Eleanor until September. By 1861, thanks to French railways and the steamship service from Marseilles to Civita Vecchia, determined travellers could get from London to Rome in under five days. Eliza, by contrast, was eight months on the road and got no further than Marseilles, which she reached in December. There she took to her bed at the Hôtel des Bains. References in family letters to her symptoms, including lumbago, bilious attacks, neuralgia, and stomach pains, point to a possible diagnosis of cancer.

Severn wrote regularly, encouraging her to finish her journey. After the usual false start on accommodation, he had taken a splendid apartment high up above the Trevi Fountain in the Palazzo Poli. 'There is great doubt springing up if I have a Wife! at all!!', he wrote to her, 'people say my taking one large house

& now another is <u>all sham</u> & the Roman gossip is that these saloons are . . . for merchandise & commercial purposes.'[31] Though Walter, Mary, and Charles all travelled to Marseilles to see Eliza, Severn dared not leave his post and worried about the fare.[32] Eleanor did her best for her mother, bravely resisting the proselytizing attempts of the nuns who nursed her on her deathbed. 'Madame is a confirmed protestant and God willing will die in the religion that she has been brought up in' she announced as she showed the Reverend Mother the door.[33] Eliza had few possessions to leave. The silver spoons went to her absent husband and 'the head of Keats' to Mary, to go with her father's wedding present, the gold brooch he had originally had made in Rome for Fanny Brawne in the shape of a Greek lyre strung with Keats's hair.[34] On 13 April Eleanor summoned her father and brother-in-law, Frederick Gale, to Marseilles and made a pencil drawing of her dying mother. Eliza was just fifty-eight but, despite her fine features, had the toothless emaciated look of an old woman, her wispy hair bound in a cloth, her nose and sunken cheeks painfully thin.[35] Though Eleanor kept an anxious watch on every steamer coming into port as her mother lingered 'waiting for someone', the familiar figure of her father was not among the disembarking passengers.

Gale arrived shortly after Eliza's death at 3 o'clock in the morning on 17 April and arranged a hasty funeral.[36] By the time Severn reached them on the evening of the 18th his wife was already buried and Eleanor packed and ready to go to her sisters. Though he had been quick to notify the Foreign Office that he needed compassionate leave of absence,[37] there had been delays in getting a passport. Within twenty-four hours of arriving in Marseilles, he was back on his way, alone, to Rome. It had all been 'such a Sad mortification'. On Easter Sunday morning he sat on deck in calm seas writing down his memories of his wife, 'her great virtues and her faults which were of another tenor with her virtues'. Perhaps if these had survived, we would have a stronger sense of Severn's grief at the loss of his 'dear partner of 34 years'. When he came to praise her in family letters, it was as a mother rather than a wife. She had been 'a wonderfully good parent, so devoted to her children, untiring in her care'.[38] In the last decade they had spent more time apart than together. Did he feel that she had put her children's interests before his? Now he faced a crippling bill of £280, more than half a year's salary, for her expenses in Marseilles. He would be 'cramped' for a while. As always, he tried not to think about death: 'the intensity of my occupation drives me from brooding over my great loss', he reassured Tom. Once again, too, he took a long time to put up the grave stone.

Despite plaintive reminders from his children, it was over seven years before he replaced the simple wooden cross on Eliza's grave with a headstone.[39]

In Rome, there were consolations for the loss of Eliza. In June 1862 he received a letter from the Italian Foreign Minister thanking him for his help in securing the liberation of over fifty-five Italian prisoners and looking forward to further 'indulgent assistance'. He copied the letter to London.[40] The Foreign Office did not congratulate him. In September 1863 the Portuguese Consul, who had been officially acting for the Italians in Rome, was expelled. Severn seized his chance: 'it now occurs to me' he wrote to Lord John Russell 'that Your Lordship may please to honour me with some fresh instructions in the present extraordinary state of things where in all Consular protection is withdrawn from his Italian Majesty's subjects who may wish to visit Rome'. Grudgingly, the Foreign Office agreed: 'you may use your good offices for the protection of the subjects of the King of Italy at Rome in their lawful pursuits unless they prefer to have recourse to the protection of the Consul of some other Foreign Power'.[41] Technically, Severn's remit was still restricted. As time wore on, however, the dividing line between his duties as British and Italian Consul was often blurred.

Severn's daily contacts with Italians and his openness towards them were unusual for an Englishman in Rome. The British there normally kept to themselves, showering each other with visiting cards in the mornings or organizing picnics in the Campagna, private concerts, and dramatic readings and riding to hounds. Sociable and influential and now a widower Severn, by contrast, was as much in demand in Italian as British society. A little over a year after Eliza's death he became secretly engaged to Countess Lovatti, a cultured widow with her own palace in the Piazza del Populo. As unfriendly gossip got back to London, Severn's children were outraged. Russell, too, warned him that he would need a special dispensation from the pope for a 'mixed marriage'. Eleanor, who was about to join her father in Rome, anxiously demanded assurances: 'Is Madame Lovati to be mistress of our ménage or am I. I think certainly I ought to be ... We all know what the influence of Roman Catholics is', she concluded, thinking back to her painful time in Marseilles.[42]

By then both Severn and the Countess were having second thoughts. She had discovered that she would lose much of her property on remarriage and released him from his 'thraldom'.[43] He turned, instead, to Charlotte Cushman, the famous American actress who lived in Rome, resting between her periodic farewell tours. It seemed that this 'dear old lady ... of singular charm' was looking for rooms to rent. She would, Severn thought, unaware of the local speculation about her complicated female household, make an ideal chaperone for Eleanor.[44] In the end, Cushman did no more than rent a large studio from Severn as a private theatre, leaving Eleanor to the less charismatic (but unpredatory) chaperonage of a series of visiting English ladies.[45] Severn was far more alert to the danger of talk about his friendship with Countess Lovatti, trying to pass the whole thing off to the Foreign Office as a test case of the Vatican's weakening opposition to 'mixed marriages'. 'A Roman lady', he informed them, 'has most indulgently offered me the use of her name.'[46] Even for Severn this was steering extraordinarily close to the wind. Eleanor joined him in December 1863, putting her facility at languages to good use at the consulate and carefully keeping her father's fine piano under lock and key to prevent Franz Liszt breaking a few strings in his constant search for a good instrument on which to practise.[47] In just over a year Severn paid off the Marseilles debt. Now he began buying shares in the Acqua Marcia company, which was bringing a new water supply from Tivoli to Rome, as something for Eleanor to fall back on after he had gone.

With his domestic arrangements in good order, Severn settled into his singular consular prime. For all his lack of preparation for the job and the vagueness of his commission, his career, as recounted to his brothers and sister, Maria, in London was a story of adventurous feats and unqualified triumphs. 'No doubt Mr Gladstone knew well what talent I had, hidden, of which I did not know myself,' he wrote to Tom, 'for I am astonished at the things I do and how they become easy.'[48] His extraordinary emergence as British Consul at Rome brought out the worst, and the best, in Severn. His proud position played to his vanity but gave scope to his benevolence. When Severn overreached himself, as increasingly he did, it was not just because, as the Foreign Office complained, he was 'so impressed with the idea of his own importance',[49] but also because as 'the chosen representative of the British Empire ... to the Papal Dominion' he was in an unparalleled position to do good. Locker Lampson, who saw him in action at this time, remembered him as 'the most buoyant of Britons'. In Rome 'he had the opportunity of being, and was especially amiable and obliging'.[50] An instinctive Palmerstonian, Severn gloried in his nation's benevolence, its intolerance of injustice, its bulldog refusal to be ignored. Only the British, said Severn, could, like the Romans of old, proclaim Civis Romanus Sum and be respected anywhere in the world.[51]

Much of what he did in Rome was designed to make the lives of his fellow citizens more comfortable. He was equally alert to the needs of visitors. When

Christopher Wordsworth, nephew of the poet and later Bishop of Lincoln, returned to Rome in 1861, Severn set aside his preoccupation with Padre Passaglia to take his old friend on a tour of his favourite places, ending at San Pietro in Montorio.[52] Four years later he had the pleasure of welcoming Gladstone and his family for an extended stay, organizing their travel and accommodation, searching out art treasures going cheap and hosting evening parties in their honour. He was almost as obliging to the long-term British community in Rome, negotiating exemptions for them from Lenten restrictions which cramped their pleasures, helping to get the ban on hunting lifted, and offering to follow the American Minister's example of drawing up lists of visitors for presentation to the pope. The Foreign Office stepped in to prevent the latter initiative. They were no more enthusiastic about his hopes of preventing delays in the admission to Rome of the coffins of deceased Englishmen for burial at the Protestant Cemetery, or his planned approach to the French on keeping the city gates open for longer for the convenience of late travellers. When he dreamt up a scheme to enable the English to use the prohibited Rome–Naples railway and donate their fares to a Roman charity, the Foreign Office was stern: 'you would do well to abstain from interfering in such matters which do not strictly come within the sphere of your consular duties'.[53]

Severn had an increasingly assured hand, however, in relieving the Roman authorities of awkward British customers. The most controversial was Daniel Home, whose feats as a medium had brought him admirers all over Europe. Napoleon III and the Empress Eugénie, Thackeray, Bulwer Lytton, Monckton Milnes, Lady Shelley, and Elizabeth Barrett Browning (but not her husband), were all devotees. But there was trouble wherever he went and in 1855 the British Minister in Florence paid him to leave town. The Roman authorities were just as keen to be rid of him when he turned up in November 1863 demanding consular protection. Severn mediated as best he could, reminding Matteucci that Home had not broken any laws and getting a written undertaking that he would not hold séances in Rome. But soon the consul was hearing of suspicious private gatherings. He withdrew his protection, obliging Home to leave for Naples in a hurry.[54] There were complaints in the press and questions in the House. For once, the Foreign Office publicly supported Severn's actions.

Severn also showed a confident touch in dealing with the fervent Evangelical clergymen intent on bringing the Bible to the Roman people in their own language. The Society for the Propagation of Christian Knowledge produced its Italian translation in 1853. The British and Foreign Bible Society had one too, and there were specially commissioned editions of the New Testament. All were prohibited books in Rome. Even British visitors had to abandon their Bibles at the frontier if they had failed to arrange a *lascia passare* for them. Severn negotiated a helpful relaxation of this restriction, with Matteucci allowing travellers to bring in one copy of the Bible in English and another in Italian provided only that they wrote their names on the flyleaf.[55] The missionaries were another matter. They misdeclared themselves as Catholics at the frontiers in hopes that their luggage would not be searched, or secreted away the piles of Bibles and tracts they hoped to distribute in the Anti-Christ's lair. Severn had little sympathy for the Reverends Blood, Chester, and Brown who were all caught red-handed. But nor did he want to see them turned into Protestant martyrs. Monsignor Randi, Matteucci's successor, may have been bemused by a long explanation of the power of the Exeter Hall Evangelicals in British politics, but he took Severn's point and expelled the troublesome clerics rather than putting them in jail.[56] Their contaminating literature was returned to England in the secure diplomatic bag.

Severn was just as energetic in his interventions on behalf of vulnerable young English girls, especially when led astray by an alien Church. 'The priests are prowling about after the English young ladies, to make 'em papists, get their money and induce disastrous marriages', he warned his brother Tom whose daughter was thinking of coming out. An English lady whose nieces had been invited for lunch with Antonelli anxiously sought Severn's advice and was firmly advised against accepting the invitation.[57] In 1864 he tracked down a young English heiress, Ellen Larkworthy, at the Convent of the Sacred Heart in Rome, persuading her to abandon her suitor, a Knight of Malta, and return to her aunt in Frascati. Three years later, he put pressure on another girl who had moved to the Corso where she could 'accept calls from a Roman gentleman' to go back to her family. Though the Foreign Office disapproved of his chivalrous activism, Severn was unrepentant. He had rescued Miss Larkworthy 'from a cruel destiny of marriage without money and religion without truth'.[58] His efforts on behalf of other errant ladies were better received. In November 1862 a Mrs Schwarz was threatened with expulsion after giving Garibaldi a waterbed to use on his campaigns. Seven other ladies also came under suspicion just days before the arrival of the Prince and Princess of Wales. The crisis found Severn at his best. He adopted the light, humorous tone which made it easier for the authorities to back down. 'I explained that English ladies always have a fashionable hobby, sometimes physical sometimes moral, that now it was

Garibaldi of whom they were making a hero of Romance and aiding him with all kinds of invalid presents; but that these visits are simply romantic and never political.'[59] The expulsion orders were lifted and Severn rewarded with a seat at the Prince's right hand at dinner.[60]

Though Garibaldi's advance was stopped short of Rome in 1862, the authorities remained jumpy throughout the decade. In 1865 an innocent Scottish jockey came close to arrest. Napier Speir, riding in the red and green colours of Prince Doria, unwittingly attracted attention by wearing the customary white belt of the amateur rider. The wild enthusiasm of the crowds when he won his race took him by surprise, but the authorities refused to believe he had worn the Italian colours by accident, and so he was ordered out of the city. The British community was outraged. Lord Vaux of Harrowden pressed the consul to convene a protest meeting. Russell went to work on Antonelli while Severn played it as long as he could. Speir's expulsion was postponed for a fortnight, the meeting was deferred and, in the nick of time, the jockey left Rome of his own accord.[61] This and other incidents set Severn thinking about the difficulties under which the English operated in Rome without an accredited ambassador. Ought he to have taken Speir into his own house if the authorities had tried to arrest him? 'Every Englishman in Rome' would have expected it, he told the Foreign Office, although his apartments did not have diplomatic immunity. The Foreign Office attempted to clarify the position: 'if the life of a British subject was in danger he would be justified in so acting, in other cases he must use his discretion'. Hammond, who had little confidence in Severn's 'discretion', spelt out the position a little more fully: though the house of a consul was not inviolable the Roman government would be likely to respect it at least 'till explanations have been exchanged'.[62]

Severn would have done well to leave it at that. Instead, he raised his concerns with Matteucci, excitedly reporting back to London that the Governor was ready to confirm 'that as Consul I can now protect anyone I may deem worthy either within or without my house...the British Government not having a Minister at the Papal Court it was satisfactory to His Holiness and his Ministers that I should have the privileges of an Ambassador as regards my Consular asylum and that I may better carry out Your Lordship's instructions "to use my good offices for suffering Italians in Rome".' For the Foreign Office this was little more than ham-fisted consular self-aggrandizement. Murray, the Assistant Under Secretary responsible for the consular service, suggested that Severn be specifically prohibited from extending protection to foreigners. 'He will get us into difficulty some day with his so-called Ambassadorial right of asylum.' A weary Hammond cynically overruled him: 'Leave him alone—if he misuses his influence he must be disavowed.'[63]

As the historian of the British Consular Service has written, 'The members of the consular service suffered more than most from the snobberies of government service.'[64] The status gap between the elite diplomatic service and the far larger and more dispersed network of British consuls and vice-consuls was keenly felt on both sides. Severn, however, understood little of the fine and all-important social distinctions in the Foreign Office. So great was his pleasure in wearing his diplomatic uniform, it never troubled him that his braiding was only silver when Odo Russell's was gold. Tone-deaf to the attitudes of a reactionary hierarchy in the Foreign Office, he wrote to them with almost as much ebullience as to Tom and Maria. This style of self-congratulation was not to Foreign Office tastes. There, senior officials corrected his spelling and grammar or scribbled '!!!' in the margins of his dispatches; they ignored many of his requests for advice, told him 'not to interfere' or to refer to Russell rather than themselves. And they rarely lost an opportunity to complain over the late submission of commercial returns or to reprimand him for his misjudgements.

Severn was impervious to it all. He remembered the rare telegrams of approval from London and forgot the rest. Just occasionally, he was chastened, but never for long. Mostly he was baffled at London's failure to understand how well he was doing, and responded to complaints with detailed explanations of the situation on the ground. The more embattled he was, the louder he blew his own trumpet. His attempt to establish diplomatic immunity for his quarters in 1865 was the more astonishing given the crushing rebuke he had received from the Foreign Office the previous year in a case which raised the same issue.

The British had long chafed under the prohibition on Protestant places of worship within the walls of Rome. The Americans got round the ban by holding their services in the house of the US Minister. The English were obliged to trail out to a 'barn' beyond the Porta del Populo and complained that it was much too small. Severn came under pressure to allow services at his apartment at the Palazzo Poli, despite its lack of diplomatic immunity. He took the problem up with Cardinal Antonelli, who was delighted to get involved and came up with a solution so obvious that the British might have thought of it themselves. Why not hold two services every Sunday morning in the existing church? Severn reported the proposal to London as yet another of his triumphs. He was soon slapped down:

Lord Russell cannot but think it was rather imprudent to appeal to the Papal Government for permission to open a second British Chapel in Rome, when by the simple expedient of increasing the number of services in the existing Chapel as has now been done, full accommodation could be provided for the wants of the British Visitors ... though Lord Russell is willing to give you credit for having meant well, he thinks that you as Her Majesty's Consul should not interfere in future with the Papal Government in a matter in regard to which that Government is known to be very susceptible.[65]

Watching from the sidelines Odo Russell decided it was time to try to give Severn a more orthodox view of his duties. 'Your excellent heart and your generous nature lead you often to go beyond your instructions,—your anxious desire to do good prompts you to initiate plans before you even know whether they will meet with the approval of the Foreign Office.' Though Severn promised to 'do my best to be the dull consul you so judiciously suggest ... & never bore you again',[66] he was too old to learn new ways. His local knowledge was an asset and his ability to get favours out of the Roman authorities undeniable. For all his critics in London as well as Rome, his dual status representing the interests of both British and Italians gave him unique standing in the consular corps, while his literary and artistic associations attracted the reverence of the many visitors who sought him out in Rome. Over the decade Severn and Russell worked increasingly well together as Russell recognized that, with Severn, the carrot would always be more effective than the stick. 'I think you are quite right to be very careful and cautious in this Land of intrigue,' he wrote to Severn in an undated note, 'but they will have to get up very early before they can take you in, for you are up to their little ways and conspiracies.' 'Your charming note fills me with courage', Severn gratefully replied.[67] Though Russell's name was scarcely mentioned in Severn's triumphant letters home, he was always happiest when he could talk his problems over with him. In 1870 they collaborated on their last case together, that of Miss Dawkins and her friends Miss Cunliffe and Miss Greenstreet.

All three were suddenly ordered out of Rome in 1870 without explanation. This was an insult no British representative could accept. Severn immediately threw his cloak of consular protection over the ladies. But as he and Russell tried to get to the bottom of the business and the Vatican remained coy, alarming stories emerged of Miss Dawkins and her maid 'making acquaintances with priests in the Churches, Galleries and Museums and of inviting them to the house without even knowing their names'. An American family in the same building had complained, the resident British clergyman and his wife had stopped calling, and Miss Cunliffe and Miss Greenstreet, it now emerged, wanted no more to do with Miss Dawkins. The Foreign Office lagging well behind the game, demanded a 'searching inquiry' into the behaviour of the Roman authorities. Russell, acting on what Severn had discovered and fearful of what more might emerge, prevailed on them not to insist. Miss Dawkins, deprived of consular protection, was left to her own devices. Russell went out of his way to ensure that the Foreign Office appreciated Severn's shrewd part in the affair. Unusually, it telegraphed its approval.[68]

Severn's amazement at his good fortune in being British Consul never left him. 'What would our poor father have said had he known that his "little Joe" would one day be British Consul to the Papal Dominion?' He looked forward to seeing out his days, comfortable and respected, a force for good in Rome in his 'enviable position, so far beyond my poor merits & such as I could never dream of "To husband out life's taper at the close". I dare say even you are astonished as much as I am', he wrote complacently to Maria in 1868.[69] Once again and, as he thought, for the last time, he had successfully recreated himself.

CHAPTER 17

The New Rome

It tickled Severn's vanity to be taken by visitors to Rome as the son of the man who had nursed John Keats. He was confident he could still pass for fifty. Though a photograph taken in 1872 does not quite bear that out it still shows a man far younger than his seventy-nine years, a little grizzled and portly perhaps, but bright-eyed, upright and benign. William Howitt was reminded of Coleridge at the end of his life: both Coleridge and Severn wore black velvet waistcoats and threw their heads back when talking. But Coleridge was only sixty-three when he died while Severn was in his late seventies when Howitt first met him. His fine constitution and an early morning scrub with a horse brush and scalding hot water kept him fit. His only weakness was the rheumatism which 'stuck to him like a creditor'.[1] The crabbed hand of his despatches in 1867, and their infrequency, testify to the affliction which had made playing the piano a struggle and curtailed his daily walks. The attack was precipitated by the greatest grief of his life, the death of Mary on 2 January 1866.

Marriage to Charles Newton had given her a confidence and security she had never known in the hand-to-mouth Severn family life in Pimlico. The wife of a highly respected Keeper at the British Museum and herself a leading woman artist, she moved in cultured London society with grace and ease. At home in their tall dark house on Gower Street she could tease her husband out of his chilly absorption of an evening in his books and papers with funny but touching caricatures of their domestic life. She also drew the massive cartoons of antique remains which her husband used to illustrate his lectures and books. A new friend, Gertrude Jekyll, accompanied the Newtons on a tour of the Levant in 1863 where Mary drew her, engrossed in sketching a solemn group of Arabs as a curious crowd of onlookers peered over her shoulder. On the return journey they stayed with Severn and Eleanor in Rome. Now that he had settled to life as a widower, the old warmth in Mary's relationship with her father returned.

14 Group photograph including Joseph Severn (centre), Italy *c.* 1872, the only known photograph of Severn

In London she began again to paint children, perhaps as a consolation for the fact that she had none of her own.[2] Late in 1865 she caught measles from one of her subjects. Weakened by the infection, and in low spirits, she was traumatized by the suicide of a young girl who threw herself from the second-floor window of the opposite house on gloomy Gower Street. A brain fever developed. In just four days she was dead. The family's first concern was with how Severn and Eleanor would receive the shocking news, far away and unprepared as they were. Newton's peremptoriness barely concealed his anger at his loss: 'It has pleased God to take my dearest Mary back to himself', he informed Eleanor. Arthur and Claudia were much gentler.[3] The condolences flooded in. The Queen wrote through Lady Augusta Bruce. Wharton Marriott, the chaplain at Eton who conducted the funeral, aptly described 'a truly lovely spirit . . . Such a bright happy disposition in combination with such deep feeling, so much genius with such entire simplicity and humility unconscious of itself.'[4] Odo Russell's brother, Arthur, worried about the impact of Mary's death on her husband, but was breezily unconcerned about her father: 'Old Severn . . . is not a man who can feel much or long.'[5]

If he had seen Severn's brief tear-stained letter to Maria the morning he received the news, he might have been more compassionate. Mary's death affected Severn far more acutely than Eliza's had done. His wife, he consoled himself, had fulfilled her role as a mother, but with Mary, as with Keats, a huge potential had gone to waste. 'Mary was my greatest pride, she seemed to me the very perfection of human nature . . . I can scarce believe that I have lost her for ever', he was still lamenting a month later. After Eliza's death he had thrown himself into work as a distraction. Now, he told Tom, he went about ' "like a Roman flea" . . . you may chance to hear complaints of inattention on my part'.[6] Until then he had spent his summers painting at the Villa Rufinella in Frascati, which Victor Emanuel lent him as reward for his consular services. In future he went to the mountain village of Tolfa north of Rome hoping that the sulphur baths would ease his rheumatism. After Mary's death, Severn never quite recovered his old buoyancy.

In Rome the political climate darkened after the scares of 1867 when Garibaldi had once again marched on Rome. Severn fretted over the way that the privileges he had won for the comfort of British visitors were being eroded.[7] His enemies, too, were gathering. His principal accuser was a doctor, Thomas Small, whom he had engaged on his return to Rome but then replaced with an Italian physician. Small was a choleric Irishman, disappointed at not being consul himself. In December 1868 his irritation with Severn boiled over. He sent Odo Russell a minutely written ten-page letter of complaint, beginning with some generalized insults about the consul's 'bombastic vanity' and the fact that his appointment had been an inside job. Complicated charges followed about a lost sponge, an appropriated overcoat, and the personal effects of some of Small's patients. In the middle of the tirade was a poignant example of the jealousies which Severn's spectacular rise in Rome had fostered. William Ewing, who had helped him nurse Keats and then shared his quarters in the winter of 1823, was cited as a witness for the prosecution, having observed Severn wearing the disputed coat.[8] And on the complaints went: the consul had failed to pay his bills and set the Roman police on Small to keep him quiet.

Russell defended Severn in Rome and London, while quietly advising him to settle his account with Small.[9] Severn had an answer for everything, referring to the long-standing practice whereby consuls recommended a particular physician to English visitors in return for free medical attention. (Russell made enquiries and found the claim was true.) Franz backed up his chief, giving a taste of the obsequious respect which daily bolstered Severn's sense of himself in his consulate. The police had acted on their own initiative in silencing Small, wrote Franz, as 'they considered it most condemnable that he should insult with such gross offences a gentleman deserving all esteem and respect as the Consul is'.[10] London had no choice. They informed Small that after 'careful inquiry & investigation' they had concluded that his complaint 'appeared to be devoid of foundation'. For some, however, the incident confirmed their feeling that Severn was more trouble than he was worth. Hammond was particularly irritated by Severn's claims to be the 'protector' of British subjects in Rome as well as his willingness to bring in the Roman police against them. He scribbled a note to the Foreign Secretary to say so.[11]

Foreign Office disdain for their consul in Rome was nothing new. Now, however, Severn was losing credibility in a more crucial quarter. Gladstone was hearing criticism of him from a man whose opinion he respected. Among the flood of distinguished visitors who came to Rome for the Vatican Council in 1869 was Cardinal Manning, the Catholic Archbishop of Westminster and Gladstone's oldest surviving friend. The Prime Minister's appetite for news from the Council was insatiable. In addition to Russell's despatches, he also relied on reports from Liberal Catholics like Lord Acton and, on the conservative wing, Manning. Thirty years before, Manning had been delighted to go round the Vatican Galleries in the company of Gladstone and Severn. Now each mistrusted the other. While Severn blamed the Cardinal's influence over Pius IX for a hardening of attitudes in the Vatican towards mixed marriages,[12] Manning complained to Gladstone that Severn was a blundering meddler. He is 'well meaning', Gladstone replied 'but I fear not very efficient'. It was a judicious but damning verdict, which must have got out in Rome where Manning liked to show the Prime Minister's private letters around as a sign of his influence in high places.[13] Just as Severn shut his eyes to the manifest signs of the Foreign Office's lack of confidence in him, however, so too he remained unaware of his fall from grace with the Prime Minister: 'My Consulate has not been without good results & actual use & I may presume that it comes up to what Mr Gladstone expected of me', he smugly suggested to Walter in the spring of 1871.[14]

The heavy burden of reporting as the Vatican Council got under way led Russell to ask for reinforcements. An acting Second Secretary from the British delegation in Florence was assigned to help out at the beginning of 1870. Henry Samuel Cumming Clarke Jervoise had had a solid but unspectacular career serving as a junior clerk in the Foreign Office for fifteen years before private office and his first overseas posting to Florence, where he settled in comfortably under a experienced diplomat, Sir Augustus Paget. Jervoise was enough of a careerist, however, to welcome the chance of working alongside Odo Russell in Rome.[15] By the beginning of July it was clear that the Council was close to promulgating the doctrine of papal infallibility and Russell judged it safe to go on leave. He was anxious to be in London, close to the centre of British diplomatic activity as France and Prussia edged towards war. Left on his own, Jervoise trod carefully, labouring over his despatches and nervous about taking initiatives without specific Foreign Office instructions. He did not like the Italians and was wary of the Vatican.[16] In the middle of August he was horrified to read in the papers that Russell had been offered a new appointment in London. Anxiously he telegraphed the Foreign Office for clarification. They ordered him to remain where he was.[17] Reporting on sometimes opaque developments in Rome at an uncertain time was a daunting task, but one for which his Foreign Office training had equipped him. Nothing, however, had prepared him to manage Severn. Here was a consul who not only failed to play by the rules but scarcely seemed to know them. While Jervoise deliberately kept a low profile, Severn was raring to demonstrate an important British presence. As events moved towards their long anticipated climax in the final days of the pope's temporal power, the consul saw new opportunities. If Jervoise, as an unaccredited junior diplomat, chose not to seize the hour, it would fall to Severn to pursue a quasi-ambassadorial role in Rome. Without Russell to keep him straight, he quickly over-reached himself.

As the pope's assertion of spiritual authority culminated in the adoption of the dogma of papal infallibility on 18 July 1870, so his temporal power crumbled. The French garrison was withdrawn from Rome in preparation for the war with Prussia, which had been declared on 15 July. The French were quickly defeated and Napoleon III captured at Sedan on 3 September. It was now only a question of time before the Italians moved on Rome. At the Vatican, Antonelli initiated delicate conversations with Jervoise about whether, if necessary, the pope could take refuge in Malta, while the Italian Government waited in vain for a rising in Rome to justify the intervention of its troops. Negotiations between Victor Emanuel's envoy, Ponza di San Martino, and Pius IX to establish some basis on which pope and king could coexist in Rome foundered on the Vatican's intransigence. On 11 September the Italian troops crossed the frontier of the papal estates. The diplomatic community in Rome was horrified at the prospect of bloodshed.

As Severn saw it, his finest hour had arrived, the culmination of nearly a decade's work mediating between the Vatican and the Italian Government. A stray remark by Marini, the Pope's Under Secretary of State, encouraged him to put himself forward as intermediary between the opposing armies. He sent a note to Jervoise grandiloquently informing him that he had accepted 'the Papal appeal' and 'As I am Regent Consul for the King 'tis just possible that I may be able to do something.' A baffled Jervoise called on Severn to find out what was behind the Vatican invitation but was airily dismissed and left with no option but to seek instructions from London. Given the confusion in Rome, Severn's claims of unrivalled influence there, and London's desire to be a key player, a bemused Foreign Office could not ignore a serious invitation to mediate, however improbable the agent. Cautiously they telegraphed back: 'Mr Severn may agree to act as medium of communication between Papal and Italian Governments. Instruct him to act in full concurrence with you.'[18]

Difficulties in communication with Rome as it geared up for war delayed receipt of this authorization until 26 September. By then relations between Jervoise and Severn were so acrimonious that Jervoise chose to tell Severn only of the second, not the first sentence. Severn's initiative had, in any case, long since crashed. Toning down official Italian complaints to the Vatican as he had been doing throughout the 1860s was one thing. Finding a *modus vivendi* for Pius IX and Victor Emanuel in Rome was quite another, particularly in the absence of any British policy to guide him. The government was willing to offer the pope a safe haven away from Rome or even countenance his remaining there. Like the rest of the European powers, however, it was at a loss to work out what its relations should be with a pope who insisted on retaining his claim to sovereignty over the new capital of Italy. Severn ran out of diplomatic mileage almost as soon as he began, and had to look for reinforcement from Arnim, the Prussian Minister in Rome. Though an intrigued Arnim called round at the consulate at Severn's invitation, he could only say that he too had tried and failed at mediation and wish the consul luck.[19]

Even Severn recognized that he was now far out of his depth. On 16 September he sent Jervoise a note to tell him he had withdrawn from the mediation. Jervoise called at the consulate to find out more but was told only that 'A superior Power had stepped in and taken the matter out of his hands. It was a secret he was bound not to divulge.' When Severn then accused Jervoise of withholding essential information about British policy on the future of the papacy, the diplomat's patience with his uppity consul ran out: '[I told him] that I considered myself responsible to the F.O. to report what was taking place here, and that I imagined it was the first time a Consul had so addressed himself to either a Foreign Office or a Diplomatic Agent.' Jervoise drafted a stiff note setting out the ground rules for their future relations. The responsibility for all political reporting was to be his; contributions from Severn would be welcome but only if sent to the Foreign Office through him. 'I cannot receive half statements which are perfectly useless as far as enabling me to form an opinion or to furnish Lord Granville [the Foreign Secretary] with an intelligible report of what takes place ... Nor can I leave unnoticed the intemperate language and manner with which you addressed me on the occasion of my last visit.' While Jervoise was condescending, Severn was wilful: 'I regret exceedingly that I took the liberty to ask your advice and I now discover my mistake and apologise for so doing.' He would speak to Cardinal Bernardi about getting the posts out of Rome reopened just in case Jervoise was thinking of withholding his despatches from the diplomatic bag.[20] This was outright insubordination.

The Italians opened fire on Rome early in the morning of 20 September. Four hours later the white flag flew over St Peter's. By noon Victor Emanuel's troops were through the Porta Pia. On the following day the pope's flag was finally lowered from Castel Sant' Angelo. Severn, safely housed in the middle of the city, took events in his stride. The same crowds that had thronged around the pope two weeks earlier at the inauguration of the Acqua Marcia water supply in

Rome now came out to greet their new masters. The streets were thronged, houses illuminated and, as Severn jubilantly reported to the Foreign Office, there were noisy celebrations outside the Palazzo Poli in honour of the popular British Consul and his championship of 'suffering Italians'.[21]

Full as his hands were trying to keep London informed about the fast-changing situation in Rome, Jervoise still made time to put together a detailed complaint about Severn. The Foreign Office rallied to their embattled colleague, brimming over with not quite truthful indignation. A severe reprimand was drawn up. 'I have to acquaint you', Lord Granville wrote to Severn, 'that I entirely disapprove of the tone of your letters to that gentleman [Jervoise] and still more of your having undertaken without the slightest sanction on the part of Her Majesty's Government to interfere in matters which were wholly beyond your attributes as Her Majesty's Consul to deal with.'[22]

Severn was less concerned than he might have been about his 'trimming', complaining ruefully to Odo Russell about Jervoise's ungracious way of tripping him up and ineffectiveness in the new Rome.[23] With the Italians in charge there were opportunities to right long-standing grievances, not least, finding a place within the city walls where the British could worship at their ease. He had his eye on a disused church in the Piazza Navona and asked for it from Cadorna, who was now in charge in Rome. Cadorna, who had many more important things on his mind than the convenience of the English on Sunday mornings, wanted a written request from the Foreign Office. 'Desire him to keep quiet', was Hammond's response.[24] But Severn could not keep quiet. His next initiative was even more insensitive. With the pope having chosen to shut himself up in the Vatican, the museums there were closed, to the annoyance of the few visitors still in Rome. Severn took the matter up with Antonelli who shared Pius IX's bitter confinement in the Vatican. 'His Holiness has no other place to walk in but the Sculpture Galleries', was the reply. Undeterred, he tried to persuade Jervoise to make representations to the Italians. 'I am certainly not disposed to apply to the Italian authorities to ask favours from the Pope', an astonished Jervoise correctly replied. A week later the Vatican relented and agreed to open the galleries on Mondays. Severn thought he saw a way of getting back on civilized terms with Jervoise, affecting to believe that he had negotiated the relaxation. 'I am exceedingly obliged to you', he wrote, 'as I cannot finish my picture (*Marriage in Cana*) without a reference to the Etruscan museum.' The only response was a stiff note arranging a call. London had alerted Jervoise to yet more odd goings-on at the consulate.[25]

Not only had Severn been mixing up his roles as British and Italian Consul, he had also been communicating direct with a colonial official, the British Governor of Malta, without informing the Foreign Office. In the confused aftermath of the arrival of the Italians in Rome Severn worried that the small island of Malta in the southern Mediterranean was about to be overrun with refugees. There were Jesuits travelling there in the expectation that the pope would join them; young Romans anxious to avoid Italian conscription; and others with less respectable reasons for getting away from the newly installed Italian authorities. Though he never visited Malta, Severn had a fondness for it: 'I always hear of the Island that it is a Paradise in its government and institutions.' Now he proposed to help the governor sort the immigrant sheep from the goats by issuing or withholding what he called 'Letters of Protection'.[26] The governor, alarmed by Severn's concerns, was delighted with his proposal and asked the British consuls in Naples and Messina to follow suit.

Jervoise, by contrast, was appalled, as a search through the disorganized consulate records revealed how freely Severn had been issuing passports to Italians and drawing up impressive-looking 'Letters of Protection' on British Consulate notepaper signed by himself. He ordered Severn to stop the procedure while they sought instruction from London. Next morning he opened his copy of the *Roman Gazette* to find an official notice announcing that Italians travelling to Malta must have not only passports and visas but Severn's letters of protection. A nervous enquiry from the Vatican about whether the British Government was reneging on its offer of sanctuary in Malta for Pius IX inevitably followed. When Jervoise ordered Severn to cancel the official notice, Severn turned the tables: as a mere consul he could not countermand the orders of a governor.

He had become unmanageable. Jervoise appealed to the Foreign Office to free him from his tormentor. 'I cannot longer abstain from making a very strong representation to Your Lordship', he wrote to Lord Granville on 27 October 'with regard to the constant embarrassment which Mr Severn's proceedings have caused to myself. I cannot but feel that he is singularly deficient in tact and judgement, and though in conversation I have found him lend a very plausible attention . . . I have invariably found that he has acted in opposition to my advice.' 'The best portion of my time is occupied by Severn's vagaries', he privately complained to Hammond, 'he is a dangerous busybody & very unintelligible.' La Marmora, who had taken over from Cadorna as Roman Governor, and been treated to a rambling lecture from Severn on George IV, had discreetly enquired of Jervoise whether the 'old man' had started to drink.[27]

Astonishingly, Severn had no sense of the trouble he faced. While the mandarins worked out how to be rid of him, he looked for their help in securing recognition from the Italian Government of his services as their consul in Rome. He described his efforts for 'suffering Italians' in a long memorandum, sending it to the Italian Foreign Minister and copying it to Paget in Florence: 130 Italian political prisoners had been freed; official Italian communications with the papacy had been redrafted on an almost daily basis, preventing 'many serious conflicts' and using 'every possible fascination of words & patience'.[28] Severn could not have chosen a less sympathetic reader. Jervoise regularly fled to Florence to tell of his trials with his consul. Paget, who had been delighted by the 'proper jobation' administered to Severn in September[29] was nonplussed by Severn's 'long rigmarole'. Even Severn was none too sure what he might expect. 'I look forward to a reward in due course', he told his brother Tom. 'What shall I get? For I cannot accept a title of any kind, our Govt wont allow it! Will it be a picture? Or will it be money—or shall I get anything?'[30] Paget had no intention of helping Severn get anything. He passed the correspondence to London, with a complaint about the irregularity of Severn's direct contacts with the Italian Foreign Minister.[31] He had misjudged his quarry. Severn had no trouble turning back the snub. His 'long habit of communicating direct with the Italian Government' as their consul in Rome had misled him, he explained with apparent humility. He had, incidentally, had 'a most generous and elegant letter of thanks' written personally by the Italian Minister offering him a 'decorazione'.[32]

Though Severn could outwit Paget, he was in far deeper trouble with the Foreign Office than he realized. They had been looking for some time for a way to ease him out and now saw an opportunity. Franz's services at the consulate had always been paid for from Severn's emoluments as Italian Consul. Now that these had ended Russell was concerned that Franz might move on, essential though he was to the efficient working of the consulate when 'Mr Severn's great age and bad health' often kept him at the baths at Tolfa. Lord Granville, the Foreign Secretary, made the obvious suggestion that Franz should replace Severn. Russell pointed out that Severn would not be eligible for a pension until he had served ten years. Whilst he might be immediately retired 'with advantage to the Public' he would be left penniless.[33] And so Franz was made vice-consul, and Severn kept his post as consul.

Six weeks later, however, when Jervoise had set out his complaints, patience in London ran out. 'Severn ought to be ordered home at once, or he will proba-

bly do much mischief', Hammond recommended. 'At once' the compliant Lord
Granville scribbled.[34] This meant dismissal and a very public humiliation for
such a prominent figure. Knowing that there would be a fuss in Parliament and
the press, Hammond prudently sought Russell's agreement. Russell's measured
assessment of Severn's abilities implied a gentle but clear rebuke to Jervoise.
'Patiently listened to, judiciously advised, kindly treated and carefully managed,'
he wrote, 'Severn became a willing, useful and even energetic Agent during
the ten years we worked together in Rome and I regret a decision which must
lead the poor old man to the Workhouse.'[35] Hammond was obliged to allow
Russell to 'plead' for Severn with Lord Granville, knowing that the easy-going
Foreign Secretary would need little persuasion. Russell suggested a severe reprimand. He knew his man and kept the message simple. Severn had exceeded
his consular instructions in the affair of the Maltese Letters of Protection. 'I am
compelled to remind you that any further similar act of disobedience on your
part must necessarily lead to your dismissal from the Service. You will hence-
forward place yourself in communication with Mr Jervoise and follow his advice
whenever your opinion differs from his.' Granville signed the draft, excusing
himself to Hammond: 'I have done a wrong but pleasant thing.' Hammond took
it with ill grace, grumbling to Russell that Severn 'is such a fool: he will not
obey what you propose to say'. But Jervoise was jubilant: 'We shall have no
more trouble from Severn now.'[36]

It was the effective end of Consul Severn's career. Though he kept his post
until the beginning of 1872 there was little left for him to do and his steady
stream of despatches from Rome dried up. There were fewer British visitors and
trouble-makers, the Italians were no longer 'suffering' and with the pope shut up
in the Vatican there was little business to transact there. With Franz handling the
day-to-day work, Severn's post had become a 'sinecure'.[37] He was given a new
consular appointment early in 1871, accredited to the Italian government rather
than the papacy but with no guarantee that it would continue once the British
Embassy moved to Rome.[38] Comfortable in Florence, Paget put off his move
to the new capital for as long as could. He did not like the Romans, had great
difficulty finding a suitable house, and was as bemused as everyone else by the
prospect of working in a capital over which two sovereigns claimed authority.
On one thing, however, he was immovable: he would not have Severn in his
new mission. The post of consul would be abolished early in 1872.

By now Severn's relations with his Foreign Office 'colleagues' had broken
down. He took a grim delight in the inefficiency of the new British mission in

Rome. Bustling in at midday in December 1871, he found the First Secretary not yet in, and the Second still in bed.[39] Nor did he have any scruples about encouraging a petition against the abolition of his post. As Russell well knew, Severn was no ordinary consul. *The Times* thundered on 8 November 1871 over the 'great consideration' due to him for 'the tact and discretion' with which he had performed duties 'beyond those usually attached to the consular office'. Under the heading of 'SORDID ECONOMIES' the *Pall Mall Gazette* railed against the rumoured 'shabby treatment of a public servant' honoured by all those 'who value literary associations' or 'hold ancient services in respect'. Now, it appeared, 'he is to be dismissed upon a scanty pension'.[40]

The pension, which the Foreign Office negotiated with the Treasury, was even scantier than Severn had feared. He had counted on £240 a year: an indignant Walter discovered that he would get only £80. However exasperated at times, Walter was proud of the Pater's fame and unwilling to see him brought down in the world (or become a financial burden on his family). He approached Russell, warning him that without a better arrangement there would be trouble in Parliament.[41] Russell spoke to Hammond and Hammond to Granville. Though the Foreign Office establishment was hardly likely to do battle with the Treasury over its unloved consul, Lord Granville had a soft spot for Severn. He wrote to Gladstone who was 'grieved' to learn of his parlous financial future and offered a £60 annuity from the Special Service Fund of the Civil List. Gladstone's final act of patronage to his friend of forty years was just about enough to save face all round.[42] Nine months short of his eightieth birthday Severn was, at last, forced into retirement.

He had started to think about life as a pensioner in late 1870. 'How odd it will be ... but then I hope to do nothing but paint, shall I be like Titian who was painting at 99!!' he speculated to Maria.[43] The reality was more disheartening. Artistic life in the new Rome was not what it had been. Old colleagues, too, had gone: John Gibson in 1866, clutching in his dying hands an anxious telegram of enquiry from the Queen; Cornelius in 1867; and Overbeck in 1869, followed to his grave by half the dethroned royalties of Europe. Though the British Academy of Arts was still in being with Severn as one of its four trustees, it fell into neglect after Gibson's death.

Rome, too, was changing rapidly. Impatient though he had been under papal rule, Severn, like other long-standing residents, began to feel nostalgic for the old ways. He could never think of the 'poor old Pope' shut up in the Vatican without a pang.[44] The Church festivals were now less spectacular; carnival had lost its fun since the ban on the throwing of sugar plums; the Coliseum was weeded of its mossy greenery and the huge crucifix at its centre dismantled. Standing on his balcony high above the Trevi Fountain Severn saw everywhere signs that Rome was becoming more efficient. Slums were cleared, dunghills carted away, and new roads built. The air was purer but the romantic melancholy had gone as Rome rapidly modernized. Convents and monasteries were requisitioned to make way for the incoming army of politicians, diplomats, and civil servants, and cloistered communities forced onto the streets. Though food prices fell with the abolition of old customs duties, rents rocketed. He was relieved to have no official connection with this new Rome.[45]

He learnt to manage on his reduced income, sacking his manservant, and arranging for an Italian doctor and his family that he had got to know at Tolfa to join him in his Palazzo Poli apartment. Betta, his old cook, would not leave him even if he could not always pay her on time. Like the Franz brothers she was devoted. When he could, he still found something for his sister Maria in London. Though it was no longer £20 a quarter, he did produce the occasional £5 and persuaded Walter and Arthur to make up the difference. Walter handled the paperwork on his father's pensions in London, receiving, in return, sage advice about stopping smoking or looking up his widowed godmother, Lady Holland: 'she is very rich & alone . . . you were always a great favourite of her ladyship when you were a little boy.'[46] Father and son had settled into a wary but affectionate respect for each other: Severn still a little in awe of his son's worldliness and competence; Walter, though an impatient listener when he visited Rome, enjoying his father's tales of his famous friends.[47]

In December 1866, Walter married Mary Dalrymple Fergusson, who had property and was the daughter of a Scottish baronet. Severn liked the thought that his eldest son had married at the same age as him and, like him, chosen a Scotch bride. Eleanor's marriage prospects seemed less certain: perhaps, her father thought, she was too clever to marry. After Mary's death, she kept house for Charles Newton. Henry Furneaux, a middle-aged Classics don, spotted her as she stayed with some of Newton's friends in Oxford. He was about to take on his first parish and needed a wife. Behind her exotic connections and unusual accomplishments, he sensed her loneliness, warming towards her brave spirit, confident that she would make a good clergyman's wife. She had precious little money, but he was prepared to face down the expected disapproval of his solid Cornish gentry family.[48] In marriage Eleanor blossomed. In 1877 she took her husband to Rome to meet her father. As a successful wife and mother she could now manage him with ease. She cosseted him, sorted out his papers, burning thousands of old consular files, and made good the paltry furnishings in his bedroom. She moved with new confidence in Anglo-Roman society, but was just as much at home in the Ghetto bargaining over a carpet. The result gave Severn almost as much satisfaction as the six volumes of Plutarch's *Lives* she brought with her. They kept him happy for hours, curled up by the fire as absorbed in his reading as he had been as a boy in his attic bedroom in Mason's Court. 'I am rather pleased' he told Maria, 'that I forget it as soon as I read on, so read over and over again.'[49]

Arthur was the last of the Severn children to marry. His eye was caught at one of the Richmonds' parties in spring 1868 by 'a pretty good-natured-looking girl with frizzy hair and a complexion like a rose'.[50] She turned out to be Joan Agnew, Ruskin's 'Cos'. Ruskin was reluctant to let Joan go and doubted Arthur's steadiness, but the couple survived the three-year separation he imposed on them and were married on 20 April 1871. Severn, too, had been sceptical about his youngest son's early attempts to turn himself into a painter in Rome, doubting that he had 'the fag' for it. But though not naturally a persevering character, Arthur stuck to his painting, was helped by Walter and Mary, and had immediate success when all seven of the first watercolours he showed in London were sold. He was a more extravagant colourist than Walter and, though less ambitious than his father, more consistently successful with his eye-catching views of waves and clouds, moors and crags.

A year after the marriage, Ruskin and Arthur brought Joan to Rome to meet her father-in-law. It was an effort for Ruskin. He liked Rome no more than he had ever done. 'Setting out for Rome to my disgust', he grumbled in his diary on 11 May 1872. A visit to the Vatican galleries did not improve his temper: he found himself 'quarrelling with everything and everybody'. Only a 'glorious' Perugino and a 'little dog' of Botticelli offered some relief from the oppressive grandeur.[51] But one affectionate memory of his visit to Rome remained. In virtually the last of the many words he wrote for publication, he chose, for Joan's delight, to describe seeing her father-in-law, busying himself in his studio proud of his long-persisting creativity: 'the old man ... then eager in finishing his last picture of the Marriage in Cana, which he had caused to take place under a vine trellis, and delighted himself by painting the crystal and ruby glittering of the changing rivulet of water out of the Greek vase, glowing into wine'.[52] 'How things bind and blend themselves together!" Ruskin mused, thinking not just of the wine and water, but his own unexpected connection with the Severns.

Severn counted up his growing number of grandchildren, asking for their photographs and sending kisses to 'the chicks' he would never see. His children affectionately thought up activities to keep him busy. Claudia wanted a trio, words and music, for her three daughters; there was talk of a new edition of *Adonais*, with Walter and Arthur doing the illustrations and Severn adding reminiscences of Keats; Walter commissioned a self-portrait in consular uniform to hang over the fireplace in the dining room of his smart new house in Earls Court Square; Eleanor suggested he write pen portraits of the famous people he had known.[53] It was a tribute to Severn's artistic versatility that he could attempt them all.

He turned first to the self-portrait. For all his vanities, Severn was never much interested in painting himself. Even the photo he promised his sister and brothers in London never got taken. Only three fully worked self-portraits survive, a pencil drawing from around 1823, a study in chalks from 1840, and the final portrait in oils from 1875. Perhaps self-portraiture required a degree of introspection which he found uncomfortable: if nothing else, he saw it as a waste of his artistic time. As he explained to Vincent Novello in 1828, 'I never make portraits of myself, which in Painters, is like the Poets wanting the Park trees for their dinner—that is I've better to do.'[54] An official self-portrait, however, was a different matter. He donned his consular uniform again, dug out his ceremonial sword and pinned on his decoration as an Officer of the Order of the Crown of Italy with its eye-catching red ribbon.[55] But there is nothing grandiloquent about the result. This was not a portrait designed to hang in the corridors of power. Instead, he painted a touching souvenir for his family, a reminder for them of the honourable public position he had held, despite his enemies. There was both quiet pride and gentle benevolence in the image of himself which he wanted his descendants to retain.

In 1873 he returned to Tolfa for the first time since his retirement, taking Betta to cook his meals and a tin bath for his sulphur treatments. Though they eased his rheumatism he felt adrift. In 1870 he had been a popular figure there as a result of his successful efforts to persuade Cardinal Bernardi to install a piped water supply and save the local women a two-mile journey in the winter carrying water from a spring.[56] Now it was different. A row of chestnuts on his favourite walk had been cut down, the mountain children clamoured around him like beggars, and he was short of congenial company.[57] No longer were his stays interrupted by the arrival of important papers from Rome that only he could sign. He began work on the new edition of *Adonais* but then an admirer stole

15 Severn's self portrait in Consular uniform, 1875

his notes. He started, but did not finish, two lectures on the funeral customs of the Etruscans and ancient Romans. In September, in an unusually downbeat mood, he made a second attempt at writing his memoirs.

Wryly he called them 'My Tedious Life': 'As my life has been a dull long blank without the least interest except its length of 80 years & as I am now in these mountains passing a tedious time . . . It occurs to me to take this bleak waste of my long life & <u>make fun of it</u> . . . so will I try & be spicy picant & palatable . . . I may laugh at my follies & feel shame at my vanities.' Sensing that he needed to justify his tale still further, he even suggested that 'some lucky wight born with a genius like mine may thro' me turn it to account by seeing what I have so ill done or not done at all'. The loss of his proud position in Rome and the criticisms of his enemies still hurt, as did his failure to revive his artistic career. The act of writing, however, produced its usual invigorating effect. Soon he was rattling through a familiar collection of anecdotes. Far from telling a moralizing tale of defeat and disappointment, he produced a picaresque adventure story ending with his triumph over Camuccini in 1840 and the placing of the *Revelations* altarpiece in San Paolo. There he stopped.[58] He did not have the heart to write about his subsequent reverses.

Except in the damp, cold winter months back in Rome he kept up his painting, sometimes working for six or seven hours a day.[59] Ever since his return to Rome he had tried to keep his name as an artist before the public. In 1870 he showed two paintings in the international Exhibition of Sacred Art which Pius IX initiated to entertain the delegates at the Vatican Council. Though *The Holy Sepulchre* failed to please, he picked up a bronze medal for his *Mary Magdalene*. He tinkered with his collection of undiscovered 'Old Masters': a Guido, a Correggio, a 'Hannibal Scratchy' (Annibale Caracci), all picked up in junk shops for a few pounds and sure to be worth hundreds.[60] Cheekily, he tried to persuade Odo Russell of an outstanding commission from the Bedfords for a companion piece to *The Vintage*. It would only cost £250 he assured him, naming his top price.[61] Nothing came of it and he turned to painting portraits of Keats, mostly for the American market. He also began an affectionate *Isabella and the Pot of Basil*, telling Eleanor it was his 'most expressive' work yet.[62] There is some fine painting in it from a man well over eighty, but as with works done even in his prime, some surprisingly rough passages, too. Nor did he make progress with *The Marriage in Cana*. Tom suggested he give up painting altogether, but that was something he could not do. 'My pictures unfinished stand around me like starving children and reproach me with cruelty but I hope to pick up as the Spring advances', he assured Maria in 1875. The most tiring part of retirement, as he frequently complained, was learning to enjoy doing nothing (*dolce fa niente*). His other burden was having no one but himself to care for: 'the task is a novelty but irksome for I always feel a longing to have someone to bestow my good will upon' he complained to Fanny de Llanos.[63]

On good days he could still get out and never lost his liking for high places. Sixty years before, he had eagerly strode up the Highgate toll road to meet his friend John Keats and ramble together over Hampstead Heath with its distant views of a smoke-filled London beneath them. In old age, he still preferred the heights, cabbing it over to San Pietro in Montorio after his afternoon nap, to gaze down on Trastevere or across to the snow-capped Apennines far beyond Rome while he tried to walk the stiffness out of his legs. By 1877 he could only manage a daily 'trottata' on the arm of his doctor. In the winter he kept close to the fire. Nonetheless, as he liked to reassure himself, he was still 'The Most Respectable Antiquity in Rome without Mendings'.[64]

He had time on his hands to think back over his long life. Providence had been indulgent, saving him from his own impetuousness, or so he liked to believe in the calm of old age, forgetting that the most precipitate decision of his life had been the most fortunate. At other times, he was more conscious of having failed to live up to his promise. Though he did not doubt his genius, he could never put his finger on why he had not won the same success as his contemporaries at the RA. 'I always think I ought to have done more,' he confessed to Maria with whom he was more open about his failings than with his brothers, 'but I don't know how, for the present race of artists are very inferior to me and I don't see that they pick up as I did.'[65]

In his last decade he began, for the first time, to think about death with equanimity. He read George Dennis's trail-blazing study of the Etruscans and started comparing their burial rites with those of the ancient Romans. Quaint though his notions were, what caught his eye was the ease with which the Etruscans transited from life to the after-life and the companionable relations between the living and the dead in ancient Rome. He conjured up an image of them assembled round the urns of the ashes of the 'dear departed', chatting to them and recalling old times or with a small vase at each eye to catch their tears after 'a good cry'. Being Severn he also thought of the tears of enjoyment that mingled with their grieving as they 'died of laughing' at some congenial memory of their dead. It was, he wrote, a scene 'in every way adapted to encourage that endearing friendship which is the effort of our modern lives here above ground'.[66]

After many years of ill health Claudia died on 20 May 1874, the fourth of his children to predecease him. Severn kept the cutting recording her funeral in Mitcham, where her coffin was carried to church by relays of men from the local cricket club and the Working Men's Committee as 'the gentry of the immediate neighbourhood' looked on. ''Twas very sad, very sad the death of dear Claudia angel as she was', he philosophically wrote to Maria, before passing on to the astonishing news that a German prima donna (Verdi's late love, Theresa Stolz) was taking over at the Rome Opera.[67]

It was the deaths of his contemporaries that he marked most closely. He was not proud of outliving so many friends: his great age only increased his sense of loneliness. Just as his old artistic colleagues had gone, so had his sparring partners from his consular days. Antonelli died in 1876, leaving a vast fortune to which a young Italian, who said she was his daughter, laid claim. Even 'the dear old Pope' one year older than Severn but 'in brilliant old age', died in 1878 having outlived his enemy, Victor Emanuel, by a month.[68] Though Kirkup still flourished in Florence, sending ever quirkier letters, just one friend was left who had known Keats, Charles Cowden Clarke in Genoa. He and Severn kept in affectionate touch, sharing their memories and confessing to a growing disillusionment with Houghton's 'Life'. Now only they remained to tend the flame.

CHAPTER 18

Keeper of the Flame

FOR cultivated travellers coming to Rome in the 1860s and 1870s, a call on Joseph Severn was a high point of their visit.[1] Bearing their letters of introduction, they toiled up the difficult narrow staircase at the Scala Dante in the Palazzo Poli, propelled by the excitement of clasping the last hand that had held Keats's own. A few, like the young Oscar Browning, turned back, too shy to ring the bell.[2] Most waited expectantly as the elderly Betta shuffled to the door and then retreated into the vast apartment to see whether her master would receive them.

He greeted them in his dusty studio, piled high with the files from his consular days; his collection of engravings and 'Old Masters' could be dimly seen through the gloom; *The Marriage in Cana* sat forlornly on an easel, always tantalizingly in need of a few finishing touches, while others of his paintings lay rolled up in corners. On the wall hung his copy of Haydon's life mask of Keats. His table was cluttered with papers and books from which he would pull out one or two prize exhibits. There was Keats's 'last letter', written but never sent to Charles Brown off the Isle of Wight in September 1820, and the inscribed copy of *Adonais* received from Shelley in December 1821. Severn pointed out the bold ink markings in the margins and a number of heavily underlined passages. These were, he would explain, the work of Lord Byron, to whom he had lent the book when they met in Florence in 1823. There was the copy of Shakespeare's *Poems* which Keats had given him in Rome, a prompt for the story of the composition of Keats's last poem 'Bright Star'. There were other stirring tales of long ago times: Keats's anger when Hilton and his friends had attacked Severn's *Cave of Despair*; and the way that the poet had painfully but surely come to a simple but sustaining Christian faith in the last days of his life. Severn's eyes filled with tears as he remembered it all. Even Walter, a sometimes sceptical observer, was impressed by his father's powers of recall: 'His memory was wonderful—He would recount long conversations that took place in the days of Shelley, Keats & Leigh Hunt among others.'[3]

Severn's visitors were never disappointed. He would snip out a few lines from one of his Keats manuscripts until, belatedly, he discovered that they had a market value he had never imagined and guarded them more carefully. His privileged visitors left reluctantly as the old man tired, congratulating themselves on their good fortune in hearing authentic details about the life of the best loved of English poets from the man who had given up everything to be with Keats at the end. Keats's place in the pantheon now seemed secure. Severn's name, too, had become a byword for selfless friendship.

Yet nothing was as it seemed. Keats's unsent letter to Charles Brown, far from being his last, was followed by two more written from Italy; 'Bright Star' was not composed on the *Maria Crowther*; Severn had never met Lord Byron; Hilton had been a generous friend; and Keats's deathbed conversion was no more than a pious myth. In old age Severn became the source of misleading information which would keep Keats scholars busy for years as they set about cleaning up a confused record. Self-aggrandizing though some of the distortions were, they were less deliberate inventions than a refraction of memories through the prism of Severn's own 'daintily sentimental', expansive, uncritical viewpoint. As 'touched up' by Severn, the incidents of Keats's life made better, more poetic stories, or so he thought. He had always talked himself and his pictures up, half believing that both he and they were as good as he said. His reinventions of key moments in Keats's life shared the same spirit. Not everyone had liked Severn's brand of salesmanship. Now, unwittingly, he jeopardized his standing with posterity, laying down a reputation for gossipy unreliability and egomania.[4]

The many images of Keats which Severn produced in the last twenty years of his life were as affectionately misleading as his stories—and as warmly received. American admirers, in particular, were keen collectors of his portraits and scenes associated with Keats. The portraits fell into two groups: those, like the one commissioned for Annie Fields's birthday, done in the late 1850s and the 1860s; and a series from the 1870s which Severn described as 'memory' portraits.

The most striking thing about the images of Keats produced by his contemporaries is their variety. Just as his associates could never quite agree on descriptions of his appearance, so a uniform picture of him fails to emerge from their sketches and portraits. There is Charles Brown's engaging drawing of a humorous, chunky young blood done in 1819; Severn's intense, even feminine, image in the tiny but powerful sketch of 1816; Hilton's elegant Olympian, known only from an engraving of the original chalk drawing done for Taylor; Haydon's rough sketch of an ardent young man with the nose of a Greek god and the animated figure in the crowd in his *Christ's Entry into Jerusalem*. Most famous of all is Severn's 1819 miniature showing a broad-browed poet with inspiration in his eyes. The later portraits which Severn produced are different again. Those of the 1860s show a tranquil, kindly presence, head gracefully inclined, hair neatly parted, large eyes glowing. Here is the poet as gentleman, more Bunthorne than Adonais. Mary Newton loved them, producing her own versions, showing a yet more delicate, feminized Keats. Just as these tender images reflect the Severns' sense of Keats's benevolent influence over their lives, so some of the later ones give a more plaintive, troubled idea of the poet. In part this reflected the sources that Severn was by then relying on. Though he claimed to be painting from memory, he was also consulting his own, predominantly melancholy, collection of images of Keats.

Apart from the copy of the life mask, which Tom had acquired for him in 1869, there was the deathbed drawing and the death mask itself, too sacred a relic to be shown to visitors. His only version of the 1819 miniature was a copy in India ink which Charles Brown had given him in 1830. It gives a darker, more forceful sense of the poet than the original. Sadly, Severn had forgotten that amongst his papers was Brown's much livelier sketch of Keats.[5] He had also long since lost sight of his earliest drawing of Keats.

Keen though he was to refresh his memory of that, what he most wanted to see was the original of the miniature. Sir Charles Wentworth Dilke, grandson of the Dilke who had known Keats, inherited both the editorship of the *Athenaeum* and his grandfather's fascination with everything to do with the poet. By 1878 he owned three versions of the miniature, including the one which had belonged to Fanny Brawne. He was anxious to have Severn's opinion on whether it was the original. Severn, who had not laid hands on it for almost sixty years, leapt at the chance to see it again, suggesting that Dilke entrust his collection to a friend, Mrs Linder, who was visiting London.[6] But Dilke, who misread the name as Lindon (Fanny Brawne's married name) was not about to entrust his collection to anyone connected to the woman whose reputation he was busy vilifying. He was almost as sceptical about Severn's intentions and consulted Lord Houghton who agreed that 'as old Severn was very old and so poor that he was himself selling such Keats relics as he had, the chances are that, if they had not disappeared before they reached him, they would have made their way into a pawn shop or to an American collector'.[7] Severn was left to get by with what he had. In late 1877 he finished his first ever full-size portrait of Keats in oils based on Brown's copy of the miniature, proudly marking on the frame 'Painted by Joseph Severn in his 84th year'. It was followed a year later by what became known as 'the last portrait'. This shows a tentative, middle-aged figure, with none of the vivacity of Severn's early portraits. Fanny de Llanos who saw it in 1883, could only regret it 'had ever been painted'.[8] Those who had known Keats recognized how far Severn's pictures strayed from the original. Others, naturally enough, assumed authenticity.

Alongside the portraits, Severn painted or drew scenes associated with Keats. Some, like the picture of *Endymion Sleeping at Keats's Tomb*, were done for sale. Others were designed to make a point, like the portrait he planned of himself with Keats and Shelley, or his nice design for a statue of Keats. And there was his consoling image of an angel ministering to the dying Keats, drawn as Severn sensed his own end approaching.[9] As his other efforts went unrecognized, and even the charming *Isabella and the Pot of Basil* remained unsold, the demand for portraits of Keats came to Severn's rescue. In 1875 he discovered that the manuscripts were valuable, too. Walter became aware of Dilke's interest in acquiring Keatsiana, and mentioned it to his father and Aunt Maria. She unearthed a letter her brother had left behind when he rushed off to Italy. Dilke paid £5 for it. Severn was delighted to make the money over to his sister. Now she could buy some of the ' "fiddle faddel" that a lady is always in want of'.[10] A year later he discovered he had sold too cheaply and began to reassess his collection, hoping to raise yet more for himself and his sister.[11] In 1877 he sold Dilke one of his prize exhibits, Keats's 'last letter'; the following year he offered his incomplete manuscript of 'The Eve of St Agnes';[12] jokingly, he suggested to Maria that perhaps in a hundred years his own letters might be worth something. In fact, they already were. In 1878 a routine letter to an art patron and autograph collector, Thomas Wilkinson, sold for two shillings. Less happily, one of his more enterprising creditors from the 1850s was also selling an old note from Severn promising to pay off his debts.[13]

As he shrugged off his disappointments as an artist and the slights of his consular career, he clung to his unique position as 'the Friend of Keats'. His memories were rich and untroubled, the miseries of Keats's last weeks in Piazza di Spagna dulled in a romantic haze. Above all, Severn had lived long enough to see his own generous predictions about Keats's worth as a poet met and far exceeded. By the 1870s he had outstripped all others in the public's affection.

Keats was 'the pivot on which all my fortunes turn'd & still turn!!', 'the dear fellow' 'has been my stepping stone and is <u>even now</u>'. Lonely though he was in his old age, he could still find 'continued amusement' in the poet's works. 'I begin to live on them' he told Dilke in 1878.[14]

With gratitude came obligation. Severn was conscious of his responsibilities as 'the Friend of Keats'. Though his own memories had acquired a creative patina, he did his best to straighten out the mistakes of others. In 1864 he learnt that Lord Houghton, as Richard Monckton Milnes had become in 1863, was preparing a revised edition of his biography of Keats. Severn wrote to remind him of the corrections he needed to make: John, not George, was the eldest of the Keats brothers; and Keats had hazel eyes and light brown hair not, as Ann Procter had claimed, blue and auburn.[15] Houghton did not reply for nearly three years, when he sent a set of the unbound page proofs of his new work. Severn may have sensed something amiss. He dashed off a letter of congratulation promising to supply a fine Roman vellum binding for the book once he had seen the frontispiece. Two years later it had still not arrived.[16] By then Severn must have known that Houghton had chosen Hilton's image, in preference to the miniature. It had always been his particular bugbear. As he explained to Houghton: it was 'a very bad portrait ... It was not only not like Keats, but it made a sneaking fellow of him ... Keats himself thought that Hilton had some spite against him at this time.'[17] Not for nothing was Houghton known in Rome as 'Cool of the Evening'. He ignored Severn's anxieties, staying with the Hilton portrait in the companion volume of Keats's *Poems* published in 1871, and though, in his short memoir, he reinstated John as the eldest of the Keats brothers, he held to Ann Procter's description of the young poet's appearance. He had even dedicated the 1867 volume to her.

Though Severn and Cowden Clarke continued to correspond about making up for Houghton's errors by producing their own life of Keats,[18] Severn tolerated his insouciance. This was an influential friend whom he did not want to antagonize.[19] In 1876 he got his reward when Houghton, at last, settled to a memoir of Keats for the Aldine edition of the British Poets. Here was a new piece of writing, crisp and judicious. The idea of the wonderful boy poet of incomplete achievement now gave way to a portrait of 'a genius so real and character so strong', that the critics, however vile, could not touch him. For the first time, too, Fanny Brawne was named as Keats's great love, even if Houghton characteristically misspelt her name and still confused her with 'Charmian'. The contentious physical description of Keats was dropped and, most pleasing of all to Severn, Houghton placed at the front of his work a photo of the portrait he had done for the Fields in 1860.[20] He also had fine things to say about Severn, describing his letters from Rome about Keats as 'among the most interesting records in our literary history'. His account of Severn's motives for going to Rome with Keats, however, had changed. In 1871 he had written: 'Regardless of personal and professional advantages the painter devoted himself to the afflicted poet.' In 1876 he offered the more prosaic and not entirely accurate explanation that Severn 'was entitled to have his expenses paid for a visit to Italy and three years stay there'.[21] It is unlikely that Severn read Houghton's text closely. If he had, he would have been surprised to find in it quotations from Keats's letters to Fanny Brawne.

Severn's anxiety in his last years to ensure that his images of Keats determined posterity's sense of the poet's physical presence was of a piece with his increasing tendency in the 1870s to move himself centre stage in his reminiscences of Keats. He had, for example, convinced himself that the early drawing of Keats which Cowden Clarke had watched him dashing off dated, instead, from the occasion 'when I drew Keats's picture and Shelley read his essay on poetry'. Indeed, in 1879 he told one of his last visitors that Shelley had 'liked' the drawing 'very much'.[22] A new friend, Harry Buxton Forman, was also told of the association. Alert though he was to the more fanciful of Severn's reminiscences, this pioneering editor of Keats and Shelley found Severn's imagined connection irresistible. He reproduced the sketch as the frontispiece to the third volume of his edition of Keats describing it as 'Done in the presence of Shelley'.[23] So clear did the memory of the occasion become to Severn that he planned to immortalize it in a triple portrait of himself with Keats and Shelley.

This was not the only instance of Severn's way of overplaying his closeness to Shelley. Over the years, no doubt encouraged by his admirers, he had persuaded himself that he was the ministering friend eulogized in stanza 35 of *Adonais*: 'He, who gentlest of the wise, / Taught, soothed, loved, honoured the departed one.' It was a tempting, but incongruous claim. As Forman pointed out in asking for Severn's help in identifying the 'ministering friend', it could not be Severn since Shelley had said in his preface that, had he known him better, he would have included in the poem his own 'feeble tribute of applause'. Could it perhaps be Charles Cowden Clarke? Though Severn let slip in reply that Leigh Hunt had always assumed the honour, he was loathe to abandon his own claim.[24] Forman let the subject drop. As in his days as consul, however, Severn felt cheated of the glory that was his due.

For all his endeavours over the years to interest others in improving Keats's grave, the simple tombstone remained. It was, Severn felt, a standing reproach to him. Others were more concerned at its deterioration. The stone had sunk lopsidedly into the earth and the greenery in front was often trampled down by visitors pressing up close in their efforts to make out the famously desolate but now almost illegible epitaph. Mary Bartle Frere, the daughter of the general who had kept ruthless order in India during the Mutiny, was in Rome in 1867 and so troubled by the state of Keats's grave that she collected up money from her friends to do something about it. In America, Emma Speed was also concerned by reports of the condition of her uncle's last resting place and offered to pay towards its restoration. A friend who lived in Rome, Sarah Clarke, wrote to reassure her in 1875: thanks to Mary Frere's fundraising, the inscription had been re-cut and some of the overgrown foliage cut back.[25] The feeling remained, however, that more needed to be done—and an energetic campaigner was on hand.

Sir Vincent Eyre, a retired major general, regularly wintered in Rome where he was a popular member of the British community. His heroic feats in India where he had survived nine months as a prisoner of Afghan rebels in Kabul and acquitted himself bravely in the Mutiny in 1857 brought him a devoted circle of admirers. Eyre enjoyed organizing things and also amused himself writing verses—one of his poems was inspired by Severn's study of the dying Keats.[26] He was, it seemed, the ideal man to take charge of improving Keats's grave.

Severn was the first person to be consulted. He suggested that the time had finally come to put up a statue to Keats. He made a charming sketch, showing a well-dressed young poet, sitting in his habitual pose with one leg crossed over the other, looking manly and cheerful. Cowden Clarke thought it 'wonderfully well indicates his features and look as well as his favourite attitude'.[27] Others, who had never known Keats, were not so sure. Though Severn offered to lend the life mask, Sarah Clarke did her best to talk him out of the idea: 'a statue is such an uncertain thing even when the sculptor has the living figure to work from', she wrote to Emma Speed, 'that when he would have only a cast from the face & descriptions of the figure from the memories of Mr Severn of something known fifty years ago it would hardly be best to attempt it—It would also be very costly.' And so, Severn was cajoled into talking about other possibilities: perhaps the old stone could be incorporated in the side of a new pedestal with a medallion likeness on the opposite side and some new inscriptions 'that the friends might wish to add'. But this challenge was beyond them. As Sarah

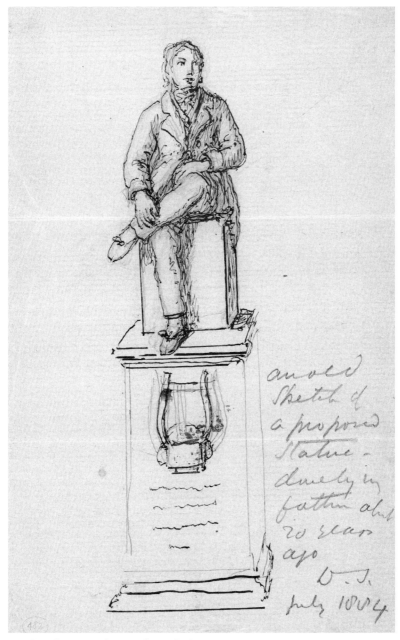

an old
Sketch of
a proposed
Statue -
done by my
father about
20 years
ago
J. S.
July 1884

16 Drawing of a proposed statue of Keats by Severn *c.* 1875

Clarke wrote, 'we shall all be sorry [to see] the old monument replaced by a new one—It is not very large or showy and is somewhat rude and quaint in Style—but it is so pathetic & so unique that everyone loves it.'²⁸ Only Severn failed to appreciate its melancholy charm. For everyone else in Rome the stone he had erected with so much hesitation was a poignant piece of history. It brought them closer to the poet and what was, for those who had not lived through it, the romance of his early death and slow rise to fame.

In March 1875 it was raised on a small marble plinth and a kerb set around the grave.²⁹ There was money left over and Eyre looked for a way to meet 'dear Mr Severn's' wish to have Keats's name and likeness recorded close to the grave. Warrington Wood, an American sculptor resident in Rome, volunteered his services in producing a portrait medallion based on Severn's copy of the life mask. Severn, who had nothing to fear from the competition of a sculptor, declared it a good likeness. The medallion was fixed to a wall close to the grave. Beneath it, Eyre placed a mawkish acrostic poem of his own devising, coyly spelling out the name of KEATS. The new ensemble was unveiled on 23 February 1876, the anniversary of Keats's death by English reckoning, before an elegant crowd of frock-coated gentlemen and fashionable ladies sheltering from the winter sunshine beneath their parasols. Severn had been invited to speak but felt unable to face the emotion of the occasion. Eyre read out a letter from him.³⁰

Not everyone approved of the new memorial but, though it was less than he had wanted, Severn was satisfied. A more determined man, like Trelawny, would have taken the opportunity of the discussions about Keats's grave in 1875 and 1876 to stake out his claim to a place next to his long-dead friend. But, though he sometimes talked wistfully about it, he made no preparations. Nor did it occur to him that by proposing a statue of Keats he might impoverish his own eventual resting place. Now he and Keats lie side by side on apparent terms of equality. Had Severn got his way in 1875 he would have condemned himself to lie in the shade cast by the bronzed splendour of the poet's monument.

Some funds from the Keats subscription remained. Eyre wanted to use them to link the two main sites on the pilgrims' route in Rome, the place where Keats was buried and the house where he had died. Though the civic authorities sucked their teeth over whether Keats was enough of a 'sublimity' to qualify for the honour of a plaque on the outside of 26 Piazza di Spagna,³¹ they gave permission early in 1879. On 28 February the plaque was unveiled beside the room looking on to the Spanish Steps where Keats had died. The *Daily*

News picturesquely described the occasion with 'some one hundred English, Americans and Germans of both sexes, surrounded by wondering groups of flower sellers and models', all standing around in the pouring rain until a shaft of bright sunshine lit up the memorial at the moment of its unveiling. Once again, Severn's 'age and infirmities' prevented him from attending, but Eyre was present to convey his greetings to the crowd.[32]

It was well for Severn that he was not there. Although the Italian version of the inscription was correct, the English text misstated Keats's age at death as twenty-six and said he had died on 24 February. The columns of the *Athenaeum* buzzed with affront. W. B. Scott, who had recently engraved Severn's deathbed drawing of Keats, quickly won editorial support from Charles Dilke for a correction. As they pointed out, Severn's letter of 27 February 1821 to Charles Brown had clearly established that Keats died at 11 p.m. on 23 February. Eyre, who knew nothing of the difference between English and Roman computations of time in 1821, tried to brush them off, claiming that there was little point in arguing over the difference of an hour. Cravenly, too, he fell back on laying the blame on the absent Severn. Not only was there his 'hurried letter' of 1821, but also 'on being questioned recently', he had 'referred to the date on the tombstone as "the most reliable" '.[33] Blaming Severn for a muddle over dates was, for anyone who knew him, entirely plausible. In this case, however, Eyre maligned him. Amongst Walter Severn's papers is the text of the proposed inscription in Italian in his father's hand. It clearly says that Keats died on 23 February 1821.[34] As the controversy raged in the *Athenaeum* Severn did not intervene. He was tired and had learnt painfully over the last year that keeping the flame could be a bitter experience.

Harry Buxton Forman (or Fuxton Boreman, as Swinburne liked to call him) was a civil servant whose official duties left ample time to pursue his own interests. Like the great novelist Anthony Trollope, he combined his literary work with a very respectable career in the Post Office, rising to be Second Secretary and Controller of Packet Services. He is now remembered, however, not for his services to the postal system but for his assiduity as the first scholarly editor of Shelley and Keats as well as his skilled literary forgeries. After his first meeting with Severn in Rome in 1872, a cordial correspondence developed as Forman sent a complementary copy of each volume of his new edition of Shelley. In return, Severn, showing a confidence in the postal services which Forman did not share, loaned him his prized copy of *Adonais*.[35] Though they had disagreed over the identity of the ministering angel in *Adonais*, Severn

17 Severn's portrait of Keats, commissioned by Annie and James T. Fields, 1860

was happy to cooperate when Forman turned from his first love, Shelley, to a new edition of Keats. Preparing his ground with characteristic thoroughness, Forman wrote to both Severn and Fanny de Llanos. Severn was much the more forthcoming, and it was to him alone that Forman confided his great secret.

Ahead of the 'complete library edition of everything, prose as well as verse', he would be publishing 'a very important addition . . . a volume consisting of thirty seven letters addressed to Miss Brawne from Keats . . . I never knew Keats till [I] read these letters', Forman wrote, 'and it is possible that even to you, who know that noble and hapless soul so well, there will be some added knowledge from these beautiful letters.'[36]

In his delight at this extraordinary news, Severn paid scant attention to Forman's conscientious warnings. Keats's letters, he wrote, contained 'lots of delightfully droll touches . . . but the general tone and keynote is the anguish as of one crucified'. Like Severn's drawing of the dying Keats, which Forman wanted as his frontispiece, the letters inspired a feeling of 'religious awe'. Briefly, he explained their origin. They had been kept by Fanny Brawne until her death and subsequently shown to Forman by her daughter. The postscript was mysterious: 'May I add that I have no other confidant in the matter, and that there are reasons for keeping it close till the book is ready?'[37] A less innocent man than Severn would have asked questions.

Instead, he eagerly set about answering Forman's detailed enquiries on the identity of Rice and 'Dilke senior', the location of Elm Cottage, the date of Keats's first breakdown in health, the card games they had played and who or what Sam Brawne's 'Bishop' might be. (A dog, Severn ventured.) It did not occur to him that there were others closer at hand who could have assisted Forman. Nor, given his pride as 'Keeper of the Flame', did it seem odd that only he was being consulted; and, despite the editor's warning about the sombre character of the letters, Severn never asked to see them. For good reason, Forman did not volunteer to show them. 'Your letter is a joy to me' Severn wrote by return of post, 'that you have received thirty seven letters of Keats to Fanny Brawne astonishes me with delight for they must be even superior to his poetry and will be a boon to the world quite unlooked for.'[38] Loyally, he kept Forman's secret, not even telling Maria until December. By then his own wistful hopes had hardened into a statement of fact: 'I am told', he wrote, that the letters 'are of a beauty beyond his poems.'[39]

Though Forman had disclosed the source of the letters, he had not told the full story. For most of her married life, Fanny Brawne kept quiet about her connection with Keats. In failing health in the early 1860s, however, and with a family in straitened circumstances, she had shown the love letters to her children explaining that 'they would some day be of considerable value'. She died in 1865, her husband, Louis Lindon, seven years later. By then Dilke was advertising his interest in acquiring Keats memorabilia in the *Athenaeum*. He happily bought from Herbert Lindon the Shakespeare which Keats had given to his mother. Lindon then showed Dilke the love letters. Dilke, who had his own motives for wanting the disordered intimate lives of public men kept under wraps, recognized the explosive nature of Keats's letters, buying them from the Lindon children, he said, to protect the poet's privacy. But as quotations from them began to appear in the *Athenaeum* and Houghton's 1876 memoir, Lindon felt cheated. As the legal owner of the copyright, he asked Dilke to return the letters. When Lord Houghton then declined to buy them, Margaret Lindon showed them to Forman.[40] He saw immediately that they cast an entirely new light on Keats's character and bought them on the understanding that he would publish them. 'The world had a claim to participate in them' as he boldly stated in his introduction. For its time, this was a brave declaration. The publication of Keats's letters to Fanny Brawne was a test case of the artist's right to keep his deepest emotions hidden. It was also the first of the three scandals about the private lives of famous authors which were to rock the late Victorian literary world.[41]

Severn was oblivious to the storm to come, his only concern his anxiety about whether his memory of events in Hampstead and Rome sixty years before would stand up to the test. On the whole he prided himself that he had come up to the mark.[42] He had even straightened out some of Forman's confusion about the layout of Wentworth Place and his obsessive interest (to which he devoted a long pedantic annex) with whether Keats could see Fanny Brawne from his sitting room. On factual points Severn gave the editor invaluable information which no one else could have offered: about the species of the trees in the garden at Wentworth Place; the colour of the cornelian Keats held in his hands on his sickbed in Rome; the character of the letters Fanny Brawne sent him there; whether Keats wore an engagement ring in Rome; the timing of his first attack in London and the speed of his recovery from it; and Fanny Brawne's appearance as a young woman. For a fair representation of this, he referred Forman to Titian's *Sacred and Profane Love*. 'Which of the two figures . . . is the likeness . . . the nude or the draped' the editor conscientiously enquired. '"Tis the lady in white . . . not the "nude" for shame!!", a scandalized Severn replied.[43] As usual, he fussed over Forman's choice of illustrations, encouraging him to track down his early sketch of Keats and even offering to send his precious copy of Shakespeare's *Poems* containing the 'Bright Star' sonnet. Conscientiously, Forman would not allow Severn to entrust it to the post, but was grateful

for the photograph of the poem Severn sent him. Eventually, Forman discovered the early sketch in the South Kensington Museums. It was, he wrote,
'exquisite'.[44]

Thinking back to the old days, Severn's 'vivacious' memory not only threw
up helpful practical information, it also warmly reimagined the past, recreating
himself as, indisputably, the Friend of Keats. A question from Forman about
the speed of Keats's recovery after his first attack, initiated a typically bold
flight of fancy. Here was Severn revealing himself as his admirers thought him
to be: here, too, was the young Severn as perhaps he ought to have been,
not hasty and largely self-concerned in his decision to go to Italy, but always
altruistic and devoted. 'We talked of his going to Italy', Severn told Forman,
'& as he was to go alone I then thought over in silence how I could possibly
accompany him, & the day after I had made up my mind & told him—he was
released from the very painful idea of dying alone although he could not express
it, but I saw the effect on [his] countenance—He arose from his bed during
the weekend Mr Brown showed me the ode to the Nightingale which had been
written & put among the books.'[45]

There was a germ of truth in Severn's suggestion that his decision to go to
Italy was less precipitous than it seemed. But the implication that it was
linked to a flare-up in Keats's creativity and the composition of perhaps his best-
known poem was not only wildly implausible but blatantly self-important. As a
witness to facts Severn was more reliable than many. Where he fell short was on
emotional truth. He did not, like Trelawny, who concocted ten different versions
of Shelley's death and cremation, deliberately set out to recreate the record.
Nor, like Dr Lord, who had been the Brawne family doctor in Hampstead in
the 1820s, did he come up with a string of inaccurate details about the distant
past.[46] The recreations of Severn's old age were exercises of a different sort,
compounding muddle with sentimentality. Expansively, in the warmth of his
debt to Keats, he reimagined himself as the friend he would have liked to be.
Most of his fictions were transparent. Only one—the attempt to pass off the
annotations in his copy of *Adonais* as Byron's—was calculated to mislead.[47]
Innocent though the rest of his inventions were, as Severn's memories of Keats
lost their freshness, they said more about his genial conventionality than Keats's
brave originality.

Forman was an experienced editor and proceeded judiciously. He used Severn's information selectively, throwing out the more self-serving statements and
softening others. At the same time, he was anxious to associate Severn closely

with his publication. Early on in the correspondence, he asked his permission to dedicate the volume to him. Severn accepted with alacrity.[48] Though he had not asked to see any of the letters, he wanted to see the dedication in draft, suggesting in a literal-minded way that Forman change the word 'ministration' to avoid any impression that he was a clergyman. Forman obliged, diplomatically assuring Severn that he 'had in my mind a public that know you well enough not to have fallen into that error'.[49] Whatever his eventual feelings about the rest of Forman's book, Severn had no reservations about the eloquent three-page dedication, repeating to friends and family in a breaking voice Forman's prediction that alongside the inextinguishable spirit of Keats 'whithersoever the name of "our Adonais" travels, there will yours also be found'.[50] By mid-December 1877, he was full of impatience: 'Your book I am most anxious to see & hope 'tis nearly got together for I think of it day & night.'[51]

Letters of John Keats to Fanny Brawne was published at the beginning of February 1878. Despite all Forman's efforts to put Fanny Brawne in a good light, it unfairly ruined her character for fifty years, and set back Keats's personal reputation for twenty. Though Forman kept a clutch of favourable reviews amongst his papers, the general reaction was one of outrage. Dilke led the attack over the violation of Keats's privacy: 'To publish the love-letters of a dead man who, if he were living, would cry out from the depths of his soul against it, seems to the common understanding of those to whom the affections are more than fame, a heinous offence.' He had already caricatured Fanny Brawne as heartless and mercenary in the selection of his grandfather's writings which he published in 1875.[52] Now he extended the indictment: the way in which she had encouraged her family to make money from Keats's letters was 'the greatest impeachment of a women's sense of womanly decency to be found in the history of literature'. Dilke had another target, too: 'Mr Forman's extraordinary preface', he added, 'is no less noticeable as a sign of the degradation to which the book maker has sunk.'[53]

Forman had been prepared for a hostile reaction. In time, he mended his fences with Fanny de Llanos, Severn, and even Dilke. But he did not soften his principles. Impenitently, he reprinted Keats's letters to Fanny Brawne in his new edition of Keats's works. Over the years they would come to be seen for what they were, an essential part of the Keats canon: in 1878, however, they dealt a devastating blow to all who had laboured to erase the image of the weak and oversensitive milk and water poet. They also revived the controversies of the 1820s about whether Keats was truly a gentleman. Matthew Arnold reverted to

Lockhart's tradition of snobbish invective in his complaint that 'Keats's love-letter is the love-letter of a surgeon's apprentice … the sort of thing one might hear read out in a breach of promise case.' Swinburne (of all people) went even further in his article on Keats in the *Encyclopaedia Britannica*: Keats's love letters 'ought never to have been written; … a manful kind of man or even a manly sort of boy, in his love-making or in his suffering, will not howl and snivel after such a lamentable fashion'.[54]

Well before the storm broke in the London press, far away in Rome Severn had been reading Keats's letters to Fanny Brawne. He was deeply upset by them. After a sixty-year silence he heard again the raw authentic voice of Keats, troubled, unreasonable, and needy. In the years since his death, he had cherished only the memory of his loveableness, the humour and generosity and the freshness of his vision. There were touching reminders of all these qualities, particularly in the early letters to Fanny Brawne, but as Keats grew sicker, his vulnerability and isolation made him mean-minded and suspicious. The unmistakable voice of the young poet, as Severn had heard it in Piazza di Spagna, cut through the sentimental accretions and distortions of the intervening years. 'I crave pardon for my bad writing', he wrote to Forman on 5 February, 'but I have been very much upset & altho' 'tis half a century since the disaster, yet I feel it most severely.'[55]

Naive though he was, Severn knew enough to recognize that the letters would shock a sentimental world. He may, too, have wondered if some of the criticism which Forman had to weather might fall on him. At best, the world might think him senile or gullible for collaborating in a dubious project. For once, however, Severn was not thinking about his own reputation. Benevolence overrode his vanity as it always had. His distress arose, as he explained to Forman, because now, at last, he had found the answer to the mystery which had always perplexed him, the suddenness of Keats's final collapse. It lay in his 'fatal passion' for Fanny Brawne, a passion so destructive that he had concealed it from Severn. Were it not for that, Keats 'might have lived many years'.[56]

It was a perverse conclusion. Severn had known how important Fanny Brawne was to Keats from Keats's confidences to him in Naples and his anguished reaction to the arrival of her letters in Rome. Indeed, it was Severn who insisted that Lord Houghton give Fanny her due in his biography. He also knew that, as Forman argued in his introduction to the *Letters*, Keats had been killed not by the reviewers, nor by love, but by consumption. Yet now he confused symptoms with causes, ignoring the fact that the obsessive nature of

Keats's passion for Fanny was a sign of his illness, unrealistically persuading himself that without her Keats would have prospered. For nearly a month he fretted away at the thought that he might have saved his friend's life. Of all his exercises in wish-fulfilment this was his most abject. By the beginning of March he was so overwrought that he suffered a stroke.[57]

Such was his fame that on 5 March *The Times* published a short announcement to prepare its readers: 'Mr J. Severn formerly British Consul in Rome, and well known as "The Friend of Keats", is announced to be dangerously ill in Rome.'[58] Walter rushed off to be with 'the dear old Pater'. Franz had already been called in to help Severn draw up his will on 2 March; the faithful Betta slept on a mattress at the foot of his bed; Dr Valeriani kept a watchful eye; and the local clergyman called frequently. He was well satisfied with Severn's spiritual preparation for the next world: 'He always expressed to me the deepest repentance for past sins and trust in the forgiveness of sins through Jesus Christ', Wasse later reported to Walter.[59] Encouraged by his son, Severn slowly recovered, sitting up in bed and chatting a little over breakfast, taking a few steps on the cherished carpet Eleanor had bought him and gradually regaining an interest in the world. But as his father slept, Walter did a clinically accurate watercolour sketch of him, noting the colours that would be needed to turn it into a deathbed portrait when the time came.[60] By the middle of March, however, he was able to inform the *Athenaeum* that his father was rather better.

Cherished by Betta and the Valerianis, Severn made a partial recovery. By the end of the month he was well enough to see Mary Cowden Clarke. Her husband, Charles had died in Genoa just a year before at the age of eighty-nine, having written his own sweetly accurate epitaph: 'Let not a bell be toll'd, or tear be shed / when I am dead / . . . In harmony I've lived—so let me die.' Though she kept up a cheerful correspondence with Severn after Charles's death, Mary had not seen him since the early 1840s. She and her sister, Sabilla, called at the Palazzo Poli finding Severn 'on a sick bed, arranged in his studio, and opposite to him, the portrait he was painting from memory when taken ill of Keats, still so dear to him. He spoke to us cheerily and with interest.' Mary's famous sister, Clara, who had long since given up her singing career to concentrate on the political ambitions of her husband, Count Gigliucci, wintered in Rome, calling regularly on Severn to take him for drives in her carriage. Nor did Mary Palliser, his daughter Mary's closest friend and a favourite model, neglect him when she was in Rome. And he enjoyed chatting about old times in Hampstead with a friend made in his consular days, the writer William Howitt. Howitt had first

18 Walter Severn's water colour and pencil portrait of Severn when ill in spring 1878 after the publication of *Letters of John Keats to Fanny Brawne*. Walter's indicated colourings suggest that he saw this as the basis for a deathbed portrait in oils

come to Severn in 1870 when he and his wife needed help with a difficult Roman landlord. 'It is best to cow such people who are generally poltroons', the consul robustly told him before launching into the old story of Keats's demonstration of how to get good dinners.[61] A new admirer, Mrs Linder, also paid court with bouquets of roses and bunches of violets, and Vincent Eyre, the Franz brothers, and Sarah Clarke called regularly. The Americans, too, kept on coming. Edmund Stedman first got to know Severn in May 1879, listening entranced to his reminiscences about sketching Keats 'when Shelley was present' or Allston's recognition of the genius of Keats's early poetry. All Severn's Roman callers remarked on his extraordinary cheerfulness.[62]

Left to himself he was more melancholy. Apart from rereading a few favourite books, he did not get beyond the English newspapers, sitting close to the fire, struggling to follow Gladstone's stance on the Eastern Question. Like the Irishwoman with the dictionary, he could not make out the story.[63] His greatest pleasure was in thinking back to his childhood, the flowers in the garden at Mason's Court, the games he had played, and his father's struggles to do the best for his children. He had no regrets as he looked back at his long life: 'a merciful Providence has gifted me with gravity, and the grace to reflect & review the many things I <u>did not do</u> withheld & protected by that indulgent Providence which now leaves me in calmness to nurse my old age'.[64]

Most of his time, as he picked up in the summer of 1878 and then struggled through a long damp winter, was spent with the Valerianis and Betta. They made much of him on his birthday and the Feast of St Joseph, ordering up a haunch of venison, bringing him posies of flowers, and toasting his longevity. In his later years, Severn took pride in remembering both the date of his birthday and his age. The doctor assured him he had many years to come. He was in two minds about the prospect. Even in 1876 he had confided to his diary on his birthday that he was living too long. By May 1879 he was 'quite prepared to die'.[65] He hated what he called the 'discrepancies' of old age, his feebleness and inability to get out on his own. He was now rather stooped and the rheumatism in his fingers made writing and drawing difficult. He had given up playing his fine old piano several years before, even for his own pleasure, irritated because he could no longer 'play true'.[66] Occasionally he added a touch or two to *The Marriage in Cana* but his enthusiasm for it had gone and though he had promised the English chaplain a painting on the improbable subject of *Cicero in Jerusalem*, he never made a start on it.[67] 'I get but few visitors, now and then, and am a little lonely, never speak any English.' But he did not give up on his British habits: 'I continue to drink tea in the morning' he reassured Maria in faraway London.[68] And he did what he could to make things easier for everyone after his death. Though he may have hoped to be buried next to Keats, he said nothing about it in his will and did not raise it with his executor, Alexander Franz. Nor, unlike his friends, Charles Cowden Clarke and Trelawny, who had long since reserved the grave next to Shelley and chosen a misleading inscription for it, did he attempt his own epitaph. At bottom, he was as uncertain as he had ever been of his intrinsic worth and place in history.

News of his family continued to cheer him. He had squirreled away a little money from his sales of Keats memorabilia and now was overjoyed to send £50 to Tom, who had fallen on hard times. His children he left to look after themselves. What little he had he gave to those with even less, just as he usually wrote to Maria rather than Tom or Charles 'as she is alone and so deserving'.[69] Betta was to inherit the reversionary interest in his pension while the Keats manuscripts were for Valeriani, who had been providing free medical attention for years. Walter bore it with what grace he could muster, while claiming the eldest son's right to his father's Order of Italy.[70] Severn prepared the way for Valeriani to make the most from the Keats bequest. On 27 May 1879 he took his handful of Keats letters over to the embassy where Franz witnessed his crabbed but authenticating signature and stamped them with a large vice-consulate seal.[71]

Apart from seizing the occasional opportunity for a benevolent gesture, Severn's flagging energies were devoted to shoring up his reputation as 'the Friend of Keats'. Though he offered to help Forman with his new edition of Keats, behind the editor's back he joined in the chorus of disapproval over the publication of the love letters. They would not 'add a jot' to Keats's fame he told James Fields. The 'fatal passion' should have remained as secret as Keats had kept it himself.[72] He also brooded over Forman's refusal to acknowledge him as the 'ministering friend' in *Adonais*, setting off on a wild goose chase to track down Shelley's letter to him of December 1821 which he had long since given away.[73] (It would not have helped his cause.)

Providence had reserved for him one last happiness. In the spring of 1879 he was delighted to hear that Henry, his second son, was returning to Europe with his family and planned to visit him in Rome. They had last met twenty-six years before, Severn shame-faced after his exile in Jersey, Henry setting off for Australia with high hopes. Since then Henry had acquired a reputation as an engineer and amateur astronomer as well as marrying and bringing up a family. Severn kept press cuttings of his son's public lectures in the Antipodes and Henry himself wrote to tell of his triumphs in the high-spirited way he learnt from his father. He inherited not just his father's ebullience but his humanity, too: it was his letter to his dying mother which had brought most comfort after Eliza's death. Now he was on his way to take up a new appointment in India, leaving his wife and children in London until he was settled.[74] Throughout the spring and early summer Severn waited anxiously in Rome. Late in July Henry arrived. In their two days together there was much to catch up on and a particular task which Severn had reserved for his technically proficient son. He took from its box the plaster copy of the mask of Keats which he had long had with him. With Valeriani watching, Henry set it up against a black velvet cloth and photographed it as Severn explained to them that they were seeing the only copy of Keats's death mask made from the wax original.[75] It was the last sad muddle of his old age. Not only were a number of copies of the death mask

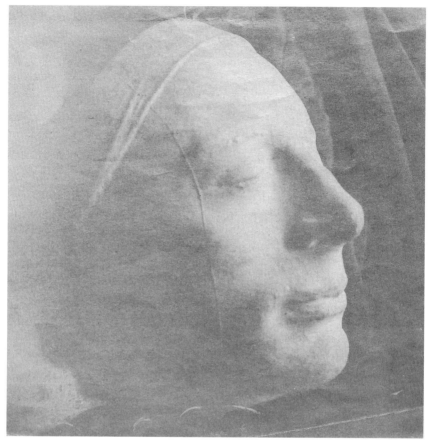

19 The photograph taken by Henry Severn in Rome a few days before his father's death of the mask of Keats which Severn owned and believed to be the first copy from the original death mask

in existence, including one owned by Browning, but, judging from Henry's photo, the precious relic he was photographing was a copy of the life, not the death mask.

Sixty years before, in the greatest crisis of his life as Keats lay dying, Severn cheered himself up by thinking of his eldest sister, Sarah, as 'the little cherub that sits up aloft—to keep watch for the life of poor Jack'. Now, in almost the last of his many letters to his youngest sister, Maria, he wrote again about 'the sweet little spirit' who had always looked out for 'poor Jack'.[76] For all his sorrows, his had been a lucky life. After his reunion with Henry there was nothing more he could want. He took to his bed with a fever. It had happened before and Valeriani was not unduly worried. Franz looked in on the Saturday morning but found no reason to put off his weekend in Tivoli. But that day and the next in the oppressive summer heat Severn's breathing grew weaker as he slipped into unconsciousness. He died at 8.15 on the Sunday evening with Betta and Valeriani beside him.[77]

There had been no time to alert the family. With Rome sweltering and many of the English out of town, Franz arranged a quick and quiet burial two days later. He chose a brick-lined vault. Though it was in an out-of-the-way corner of the new cemetery, it would be strong enough to support a statue. Like Keats's funeral, this one was a modest affair. The Valerianis and the Franz brothers saw him to his grave, joined by one stray Englishman, Arthur Glennie, a water-colourist and the nephew of Severn's old friend, the Reverend Walter Halliday. In 1821 it had been a cold February morning with the handful of mourners feeling only shocked despair at the blighted promise of Keats's young life. On 5 August 1879 in bright sunshine there was affectionate celebration of a very long life full of cheerful achievement. Franz was quietly pleased with the way he had organized this tribute from those who had been closest to Severn at the end. There would be time in the autumn when the English returned to think about a suitable monument in honour of the best-loved member of their community.

EPILOGUE: A FITTING PLACE

~

As word got round of Severn's death and quiet burial, a storm broke over Franz's head. The Rome correspondents of *The Times* and *Daily News* vied with each other in working up their indignation. The *Daily News* condemned 'the mean, almost furtive character' of the proceedings. *The Times* was shocked that Severn now lay 'at the furthest extremity of the burying ground, among absolute strangers of other lands'. Not even a daisy had been brought from Keats's grave to rest on Severn's 'mound'. The blame fell squarely on 'Mr Simon Franz', a 'capricious Italian official'.[1] An unseemly game of finger-pointing erupted in the correspondence columns of *The Times*. As in life, so in death, it must have seemed to Sir Augustus Paget that Severn was nothing but trouble. He quickly deflected the blame onto his vice-consul for failing to keep him informed, while Walter and Arthur clumsily explained their absence from their father's funeral.[2]

Hurt though he was,[3] Franz shouldered the burden of settling his old master's affairs and mediating between Walter and Valeriani in a row over the ownership of Keats's books which were advertised for sale, along with the manuscripts, in *The Times* just eleven days after Severn's death.[4] The inventory of his other possessions is a melancholy summation of his disappointments as an artist. In addition to the furniture, the 'old pianoforte', the consular sword and hat, and a clutch of copper and silver medals, were the unsold *Isabella* and *Mary Magdalene*, watercolours, pastels, and oil paintings, including a view of the Protestant Cemetery at night, a 'bello ritratto del poeta Keats' and more than one 'donna con bambino'. There was also a large Saint Gregory 'di Annibale Caracci' and a fine painting of Queen Esther, more cautiously listed as 'antico' rather than the Veronese Severn had always claimed. Number 28 on the inventory, *The Wedding in Cana* 'non terminato', was followed by the last item 'Cassa lunga continente un quadro arrotolato e relativo telaio', a large chest containing a rolled-up painting and its frame.[5] Here, mouldering in its travelling case, was *The Holy Sepulchre*, the altarpiece which had helped to bankrupt Severn in 1853, the massive canvas on which he had centred all his misguided ambition to replicate his Italian success back in England.

Even now it seemed no one wanted the painting. Walter offered it to the English Church, which had asked for a souvenir of Severn's art, but it was too big for their walls.[6] Nor did he follow up his father's testamentary wish that the *Mary Magdalene* be given to the National Gallery. He knew without trying them that they would not take it.[7] Ruskin, too, refused the offered *Isabella and the Pot of Basil*.[8] While Valeriani took the 'Caracci' as settlement for the rent that accrued in the months before Severn's rooms were cleared, Franz moved the rest of the pictures to his office. Eventually, Warrington Wood arranged to find room for them in the British Academy of Arts. (If they survived the Academy's move to via Margutta in 1895 they were then almost certainly lost when the Academy hastily closed in 1935 after months of Fascist harassment.)[9] In London Walter began an unhappy search for missing letters and memorabilia. Did Lord Houghton happen to have Byron's letter to Severn about *Adonais*, he politely, but unavailingly, enquired.[10] But short-changed though he felt by his father's will,[11] Walter knew that, as the eldest son, he had a responsibility to see his father more fittingly honoured in the Protestant Cemetery.

He proceeded cautiously, anxious to get things right this time and to carry the great and the good with him. Initially, he thought of a monument close to but not necessarily beside Keats, though he was also concerned to repair his father's long failure to mark the grave of his infant child, Arthur, who had died in 1837 and been hastily buried just behind Keats. The British in Rome had no doubts. Severn must be buried next to Keats with a suitable memorial to their friendship. Vincent Eyre took charge, advising Walter on how to frame the necessary petition to the municipal authorities for Severn's reburial in the old part of the cemetery.

Submitted in the names of Walter, Henry, and Arthur Severn, the petition made a persuasive case for granting the 'exceptional request' made by the sons whose father had 'always expressed a hope that he might be laid by his friend'. Not only that but 'their Father's old friends, and the public generally, always expected that he would be buried by the side of his illustrious friend who died in his arms, and with whose life his own name is so inseparably connected'. Severn's services as Italian Consul were also prayed in aid and a graceful reference included to 'the fact that the feelings and claims of Poets and painters have invariably been treated with more consideration in Italy than elsewhere'. The Commune di Roma wasted no time in granting the request, recognizing Severn's 'own merits' as well as 'his personal relations with the Poet Keats'.[12]

Fundraising now began in earnest. Eyre took the lead in Rome, putting Severn's last portrait of Keats up for sale and arranging for a photograph of it to be sent to all subscribers. John Field, an American who was often in Rome and had enjoyed taking Severn out in his later years, snapped it up for £40.[13] *The Marriage in Cana*, which went on sale at the same time, took longer to sell.[14] In the United States Richard Gilder of Scribners volunteered to organize the fundraising and in England, W. M. Rossetti helped Walter to approach potential subscribers.[15] The *Athenaeum*, too, joined in the fundraising, publishing an inspirational poem on 16 July 1881 by the bestselling author T. Hall Caine. It reads, in all its awfulness:

> Renouncing home and love and art and fame,
> His was the hand that nursed our Keats's youth,
> When Youth and life were leashed, and these with Ruth
> Ran for one good together: his the same
> Cool palm that laved the brow: the lips that came
> With tenderest tribute to the bruised breast—
> Ere o'er the bleeding heart the flowers found rest—
> And whispered first the awakened world's acclaim.
>
> And if the soul in sight of Darien
> Let fall some sign might not be heard of man,
> Be sure his anguish caught the vanishing breath.
> Full sixty years the voice is hushed that sung:
> Lay now the friend and friended, old and young,
> Brothers and lovers, side by side, in death.

Here was the apotheosis of Victorian sentiment about Severn's friendship with Keats, the maudlin image of a deathbed ennobled by Severn's reverent devotion and selfless renunciation, and a love so passionate that it verged on the homoerotic. The only accurate statement in this extravagant fancy was the fact that Keats had died some sixty years before.

A similar excess of sentiment fuelled Eyre's suggestion that a black and white marble medallion surmounted by a cross should be placed between the graves of Keats and Severn, showing the dying poet in the arms of his friend above the words 'In death not divided'. Other ideas, which Eyre passed on to Walter, were more felicitous. The grave stone itself, he suggested, should be 'as simple as possible, so as to correspond with that of Keats—only instead of a Greek lyre there might be a pallet [*sic*] & brushes to denote the Painter'. His proposed epitaph was less inspired: 'Here rests / Joseph Severn, The "Friend of Keats" He acquired fame as an Artist / and / was greatly honoured in Rome / where he filled the post of British Consul during Many Years / He died 3d August 1879— Aged 86— / This simple memorial is the affectionate tribute / Of a few of his friends & admirers.' (As with the Keats plaque, Eyre had got Severn's age at death wrong.)[16]

Judiciously, Walter consulted. Eleanor thought the proposed arrangement of the tombstone and the new medallion 'quite perfect', as did Mary Cowden Clarke.[17] And so a brochure for subscribers was sent out in June 1881 referring to the possibility of 'a monument or memorial tablet to perpetuate the resemblance of both poet and painter'. It was fortunate that the Rome correspondent of the *Daily News* did not get wind of the idea until after it had been abandoned. 'Happily', he wrote, 'this monstrous conception is to abide in the limbo of unfulfilled bad taste' as a warning of Keats's continuing vulnerability to 'the maudlin affectionateness of half-taught admirers'.[18] In the end, practical considerations prevailed. Putting up the medallion would have meant destroying the infant Arthur's grave,[19] as well as detracting from Keats's. As *The Times* commented 'the peculiar sanctity of time, to say no more, has attached to the simple headstone with the broken lyre'.

The idea of a matching stone for Severn, however, was widely welcomed. Walter trawled for ideas on an appropriate epitaph. Tennyson, Richard Chenevix-Trench, Dante Gabriel Rossetti, Sir Noel Paton, Francis Turner Palgrave, Vincent Eyre, and the family were all involved. Walter's own first preference was for a quotation from the Preface to *Adonais*; others wanted a reference to the love of Jonathan and David; while Tennyson's suggestions were surprisingly clumsy. Houghton's draft easily carried the day. For all his insensitivities, he was the acknowledged Victorian master of funerary eloquence. He spoke in 1869 at the unveiling of a monument to Leigh Hunt in Kensal Green Cemetery, a statue to Robert Burns in Glasgow in 1877, a bust of Coleridge in Westminster Abbey in 1885, and another of Thomas Gray at Pembroke College later that year. He also devised epitaphs, including the touching one for the young Scottish poet David Gray, who died of consumption at the age of twenty-three under the sad misapprehension that he had been a second Keats. Houghton immediately grasped the need for a read-across from the bare anonymity of Keats's stone to the pride of the friend who had gloried in his rise to fame. 'To the memory of JOSEPH SEVERN, Devoted Friend and Deathbed Companion of JOHN KEATS, whom he lived to see Numbered among the

Immortal Poets of England', Houghton suggested before going on to summarize Severn's other claims to fame: 'An Artist eminent for his Representations of Italian Life and Nature. British Consul at Rome from 1861 to 1872: And Officer of the Crown of Italy.' The epitaph concluded with a flourish: 'In recognition of his Services to Freedom and Humanity.' At the bottom of the stone is a cross.

Severn's remains were moved to lie next to Keats on 13 February 1882 at a private ceremony attended by Walter and three friends. At the same time a small stone was at last erected over Arthur's remains, recording with pride that Wordsworth had been present at his christening. A public unveiling of Severn's tombstone had been arranged in time for Houghton to get to Rome to give the oration, but he suffered a heart attack in Athens. His place was taken on 3 March by the American sculptor William Wetmore Story, and Thomas Trollope, now a prominent member of the English community in Rome. It became a festive occasion. The two graves were covered in garlands 'laid by loving hands'; the box hedge surrounding them was decked with flowers; and violet veils covered in jonquils and narcissus covered the tombstones. Once again, as at the unveiling of the Keats plaque in Piazza di Spagna, the sun broke through the clouds as two hundred British and American devotees assembled round the graves. The usual misleading pieties prevailed. Story recalled that at the time of their arrival in Rome Severn's artistic reputation was more secure than Keats's. Trollope, who planted what was humbly described as a 'fir tree', assured his audience that 'it might safely be asserted that among the thousands who...had come in contact with him [in Rome] he had never made an enemy'. Sir Augustus Paget was saved from hearing this nonsense by an unusually protracted bout of 'diplomatic 'flu'.[20] Vincent Eyre, who had died the previous September, was more missed.

Severn's reburial next to Keats coincided with the high watermark of Victorian sentiment about the virtues of close male friendship. The generation which insisted that he lie by his friend was one brought up on stirring tales in the Classics of the devotion of Nisus and Euryalus, Orestes and Pylades or, in the Bible, the companionship 'passing the love of women' of David and Jonathan. As a result, what had in practice been an agreeable but not especially close relationship until the last months of Keats's life, became transformed into the latest in a canonical line of noble, unselfish masculine fellowship.

Keats, who 'could not live without the love of my friends', would not have objected to lying in death beside a friend, surprised though he might have

20 The graves of Keats and Severn in the Protestant Cemetery, Rome

been by the identity of the man whom posterity identified as his inseparable companion. Nor, painfully aware as he always was of how little family he had of his own, would he have rejected the appearance which his grave now gives of being part of a family plot with himself as honorary uncle to young Arthur Severn. Severn himself had never quite had the courage to arrange all this, much though he desired it. To lie besides the famous was an honour the Victorians did not take lightly. Edward Trelawny, whose friendship with Shelley was a good deal less substantial than Severn's with Keats, left nothing to chance, booking his space next to Shelley more than sixty years before he died and later choosing an epitaph implying an illusory degree of closeness to the poet. 'Here', as Severn used to say looking at the empty grave, 'lies Trelawny'. On his sickbed in Athens, Lord Houghton also mused on the attractions of reserving a spot in the Protestant Cemetery where 'Keats would have lain very pleasantly between his friend and his biographer'.[21] But Houghton had made a bad name for himself in Rome in 1869 turning up at evening parties to which he had not been invited,[22] and there was no enthusiasm to find room for him next to Keats and Severn.

Joseph Severn: A Life

Today it is but a short trip on the metro from the small dark room where Keats died by the Spanish Steps to his and Severn's graves in the dappled sunlight of the Protestant Cemetery where two magnificent pines meet high overhead and shelter the site from the midday heat. For Severn it was a much longer journey. His was a chequered career. His achievements did not always match his ambitions and over-optimism led him astray more than once. But he had not been wrong about Keats. Nor, for all his frailties, had he failed him at the end. It was the delight of his life that the world came to recognize in Keats the genius which he had always known. In other ways, however, he miscalculated. For over fifty years he campaigned unsuccessfully to change Keats's grave into a place which reflected his growing fame. Never once did it occur to him that it would be his own reburial next to Keats which would turn a melancholy site into a fitting place of celebration. Now Keats and Severn lie side by side with the tragedy of Keats's anonymous epitaph counterpoised by the record of Severn's joy in his friend's posthumous triumph. Here, indeed, is a famous reminder of the rewards of friendship.

NOTES

Chapter 1 A Hazardous Childhood

1 St Leonard's Shoreditch Register of Baptisms 1785–1801, LMA, X094/035.

2 Guildhall Archive, Weavers Company Court Minutes 1775–85, MS 4655/17, Part II.

3 By 1802 Littel was living on a pension from the Weavers Company and in 1804 qualified for the free coat, shoes, and stockings given to the neediest in Norton Folgate. The £5 fee required to dissolve James Severn's uncompleted apprenticeship was never paid. Weavers Company Commonality Register, MS 4661/72; and Court Minutes, MS 4655/18, 2 October 1804.

4 LMA, St Luke's, Old Street, Register of Weddings X027/002.

5 R. Porter, *London: A Social History* (London: Hamish Hamilton, 1994), p. 260.

6 See the third edition of Richard Horwood's map (1813) in *The A–Z of Regency London*, Map 6Ac. The 1812 Poor Law assessment for St Leonard's Shoreditch shows twenty-nine householders paying rates in Mason's Court. Thomas Severn paid 4s 4¹/₂d; a few others had assessments five times as high. LMA, 991/LEN/137.

7 Severn to Maria Severn, 4 October 1824, *Letters and Memoirs*, p. 262.

8 'My Tedious Life' and 'Earliest Remembrances', *Letters and Memoirs*, pp. 626 and 583.

9 Though in his memoirs Severn described his father as a music master, his occupation, as recorded by his second daughter, Charlotte, at the time of their mother's death was 'piano tuner': 'Notes on the Severn Families', compiled by Major H. M. Severn, LMA, KPM/S 32.

10 Thomas Severn earned his own entry in the original *Grove Dictionary of Music and Musicians*, an entry perpetuated as far as the fifth edition, which notes his early struggles, his establishment of the City of London Classical Harmonists in 1831, and the fact that he wrote an opera, a cantata, a number of sacred settings, and some 'very popular' songs. Charles Severn was organist at the main Islington church, St Mary's, for fifty years and played for sixty in the Covent Garden orchestra during the Italian opera seasons.

11 Severn to Thomas Severn, 26 May 1827, LMA, KPM/S 492.

12 Rose Wild collection.

13 Houghton Library, Harvard bMS Eng 1434 (230), Thomas Severn to Severn, 24 July 1827.

14 Houghton Library, Harvard bMS Eng 1434 (303), Severn to Henry Severn, 22 March 1870.

15 'Earliest Remembrances', *Letters and Memoirs*, p. 584.

16 He described the episode in a separate reminiscence, 'The ten penny nail' in 'Incidents of my Life', Houghton Library, Harvard bMS Eng 1434 (493).

17 Houghton Library, Harvard MS Eng 1460, Severn scrapbook.

18 'My Tedious Life', *Letters and Memoirs*, p. 627.

19 Severn to James Severn, 4 December 1827, LMA, KPM/S 493.

20 'Earliest Remembrances', *Letters and Memoirs*, p. 582.

21 *Life and Letters*, p. 4.

Notes

Chapter 2 The Royal Academy Student

1 G. D. Leslie, *The Inner Life of the Royal Academy, with an Account of its Schools & Exhibitions Principally in the Reign of Queen Victoria* (London: John Murray, 1914), p. 4.

2 Fuseli quoted in the article on Northcote in the *Oxford DNB*, xxxxi, p. 137.

3 John Ruskin MS Diary 1840–1 additional entry for 2 January 1841 written in Naples on 15 January 1841, University of Lancaster, Ruskin Library.

4 H. Hoock, *The King's Artists: The Royal Academy of Arts as a 'National Institution' 1768–1820* (Oxford: Oxford University Press, 2000), p. 54.

5 W. T. Whitley, *Art in England 1800–1820* (Cambridge: Cambridge University Press, 1928), p. 85.

6 Hoock, *The King's Artists*, p. 56.

7 D. H. Solkin, ed, *Art on the Line: The Royal Academy Exhibitions at Somerset House 1780–1836* (New Haven and London: Yale University Press, 2001), pp. 1–9.

8 J. Barrell, *The Political Theory of Painting from Reynolds to Hazlitt: 'The Body of the Public'* (New Haven and London: Yale University Press, 1986), pp. 63–123.

9 Quoted in W. Vaughan, *British Painting: The Golden Age from Hogarth to Turner* (London: Thames & Hudson, 1999), p. 151.

10 A. M. W. Stirling, ed, *The Richmond Papers from the Correspondence and Manuscripts of George Richmond, R.A., and his Son Sir William Richmond, R.A., KCB* (London: Heinemann, 1926), p. 8.

11 J. Knowles, *The Life and Writings of Henry Fuseli Esq M.A. R.A.*, 3 vols (London: Henry Colburn, 1831), i, pp. 397 and 404, and Whitley, *Art in England 1800–1820*, p. 85.

12 Quoted in Whitley, *Art in England 1800–1820*, p. 84.

13 Knowles, *The Life and Writings of Henry Fuseli*, ii, pp. 341 and 367, and E. C. Mason, *The Mind of Henry Fuseli: Selections from his Writings with an Introductory Study* (London: Routledge & Kegan Paul, 1951), p. 285.

14 Quoted in Barrell, *The Political Theory of Painting*, p. 284.

15 Knowles, *The Life and Writings of Henry Fuseli*, i, p. 140.

16 C. R. Leslie, *Autobiographical Recollections*, ed. Tom Taylor, 2 vols (London: John Murray, 1860), i, p. 37.

17 Report on Conduct of RA Students in 1816. Fuseli Papers, RA Archive FU/414.

18 There is a rare copy in the British Library at 780.h.14.

19 RA Students Register 1769–1829, RA Archive.

20 *Life and Letters*, p. 22.

21 'My Tedious Life', *Letters and Memoirs*, p. 634. The coded reference to Severn's brothel-going is in Keats's letter to George and Georgiana Keats, 20 September 1819, *Letters*, ii, p. 205.

22 'My Tedious Life', *Letters and Memoirs*, p. 634.

23 *Annals of the Fine Arts*, iv, pp. 459–60.

24 Keats to George and Tom Keats, 5 January 1818, *Letters*, i, p. 200.

25 *Annals of the Fine Arts*, i, p. 360 and iii, p. 607.

26 J. B. Flagg, *The Life and Letters of Washington Allston* (London: R. Bentley, 1893), p. 111.

27 'On the Vicissitudes of Keats's Fame', *Atlantic Monthly*, 11 (April 1863), 402.

28 RA Council Minutes, 9 January 1813 and 24 November 1815, RA Archive.

29 Leslie, *Autobiographical Recollections*, ii, p. 52.

30 Leslie, *The Inner Life of the Royal Academy*, p. 14.

31 Unfortunately, the portrait which Leslie did of him at this time does not appear to have survived.

32 From 'The Life of Robert Seymour' in *Seymour's Sketches* (1867). 'My Tedious Life', *Letters and Memoirs*, p. 634.

33 One was reprinted in *Annals of the Fine Arts*, ii, 1818, p. 461: 'The Academy is like a microscope-/ For, by the magnifying power, are seen / Objects, that for attention ne'er could hope. No more, alas! than if they ne'er had been.' The reference to Severn's toast is in Keats to George and Tom Keats, 5 January, 1818, *Letters*, i, pp. 196-7.

34 *Life and Letters*, p. 10.

35 RA Council Minutes, 7 January 1817 f. 349, RA Archive.

36 For an interesting, but unreliable account of Catherwood's life see V. W. von Hagen, *Frederick Catherwood Architect* (New York: Oxford University Press, 1950).

37 See Keats's *Epistle to Charles Cowden Clarke* lines 109-14 and C. C. and M. Clarke, *Recollections of Writers* (London: Sampson, Low, 1878), p. 141.

38 Lamb to Leigh Hunt, 1825, in E. V. Lucas, ed., *Letters of Charles Lamb: To Which Are Added Those of His Sister Mary Lamb*, 3 vols (London: J. M. Dent & Sons, 1935), ii, p. 456.

39 Holmes to Severn, 23 February 1822, Houghton Library, Harvard MS Keats 4.15.27. Holmes to Severn, 17 December 1824 and 6 February 1828, Houghton Library, Harvard MS England 1460 (132) and (180).

40 R. D. Altick, *The Cowden Clarkes* (London: Oxford University Press, 1948), p. 49.

41 There was a persistent, but almost certainly misleading memory in Robert Seymour's family of Severn bringing Keats to supper at Holmes's father's house in Hoxton just before they left for Italy, *DNB* entry on Robert Seymour.

42 I am indebted for information on Seymour to Stephen Jarvis, who is writing a book about him.

43 This would explain Holmes's and C. C. Clarke's later belief that Severn met Keats through Holmes. Severn himself was always adamant that it was Haslam who made the introduction. See also Charles Brown to R. M. Milnes, 19 March 1841, and Edward Holmes to Charles Cowden Clarke, 19 December 1846, *Keats Circle*, ii, pp. 52 and 168.

44 *Life and Letters*, p. 12. In 'Incidents of My Life' Severn says that he went with 'a friend & fellow student'. Since Leslie also recorded very similar memories of the evening it seems likely that he and Severn went together.

45 'Incidents of My Life No 7', Houghton Library, Harvard bMS Eng 1434. Leslie, *Autobiographical Recollections*, ii, p. 49.

46 'Incidents of My Life No. 7', Houghton Library, Harvard bMS Eng 1434.

47 Houghton Library, Harvard bMS Eng 1434 (76). There is no date or address on this letter, suggesting it was left at the stage door for Severn to pick up.

48 *Life and Letters*, pp. 14-15.

Chapter 3 Painter and Poet

1 'My Tedious Life', *Letters and Memoirs*, p. 632 and Severn to Brown, 15 April 1830, *Letters of Charles Brown*, p. 316.

2 Bailey to Milnes, 7 May 1849, *Keats Circle*, ii, p. 268.

3 Keats to Fanny Brawne, 25 July 1819, *Letters*, ii, p. 133.

4 Quoted in D. Parson, *Portraits of Keats* (Cleveland: World Publishing Company, 1954), pp. 8 and 14-15.

5 *Life and Letters*, pp. 19-21.

6 C. and M. C. Clarke, *Recollections of Writers* (London: Sampson, Low, 1878), p. 154. Hunt to Severn 16 December 1822, *Life and Letters*, p. 131.

Notes

7 Keats to Severn, 1 November 1816, *Letters*, i, pp. 115–16.

8 So says Sharp in a typically irresponsible addition to what Severn actually wrote in 'My Tedious Life'. Compare *Life and Letters*, p. 30 with *Letters and Memoirs*, p. 632.

9 'My Tedious Life', *Letters and Memoirs*, p. 632.

10 The volume, now in the Houghton Library at Harvard, is in remarkably good condition.

11 Severn to Charles Brown, 15 April 1830, *Letters of Charles Brown*, p. 316.

12 *Life and Letters*, p. 18.

13 Charles Brown's 'Life of Keats', *Keats Circle*, ii, p. 57.

14 *Life and Letters*, pp. 17–18 and 30. Though it is obviously a follow-on from the earlier one (which W. J. Bate dated 22 May 1817), Sharp prints them ten pages apart and fails to make the connection. Neither of Severn's letters to George has survived.

15 Reynolds to Milnes, 22 December 1846, Bailey to Milnes, 7 May 1849, Severn to Milnes, 6 October 1845, *Keats Circle*, ii, pp. 274 and 132.

16 Keats to Reynolds, 9 April 1818, *Letters*, i, p. 267.

17 'My Tedious Life', *Letters and Memoirs*, p. 632.

18 *Life and Letters*, pp. 20–1. Severn's reminiscence on which Sharp's description is based was possibly No. 8 of 'Incidents of My Life', which is now, unfortunately, missing.

19 Clarke left two slightly different accounts of this occasion in *Recollections of Writers*, pp. 141–2 and 'Biographical Notes on Keats', 16 March 1846, *Keats Circle*, ii, p. 151.

20 Severn later misremembered that they had seen it at the National Gallery, which was not then open and where the picture did not arrive until 1826.

21 'Incidents of My Life', *Letters and Memoirs*, p. 591.

22 Severn to Brown, 15 April 1830, *Letters of Charles Brown*, p. 316.

23 Willard B. Pope, ed., *The Diary of Benjamin Robert Haydon*, 5 vols (Cambridge, MA: Harvard University Press, 1960, 1963) ii, pp. 198–9. Pope does not attempt to identify 'the noodle'.

24 'My Tedious Life', *Letters and Memoirs*, p. 637.

25 'My Tedious Life', *Letters and Memoirs*, pp. 636–7.

26 Pope, ed., *The Diary of Benjamin Robert Haydon*, ii, pp. 173–6 (28 December 1817).

27 *Life and Letters*, p. 31.

28 Ibid., pp. 116–17.

29 Keats to George and Georgiana Keats, 17 September 1817, *Letters*, ii, p. 187.

30 Tom Keats to John Taylor, 22 June 1818, *Letters*, i, p. 297.

31 Keats to Severn, 10 November 1819, *Letters*, ii, p. 228, *Life and Letters*, p. 32 and R. M. Milnes, *Life, Letters and Literary Remains of John Keats* (London: J. M. Dent, 1927), p. 208.

32 Keats to George and Georgiana Keats, 29 December 1818, *Letters*, ii, p. 17.

33 Introduction to L. Hunt, *The Autobiography of Leigh Hunt; with Reminiscences of Friends and Contemporaries* (Oxford: Oxford University Press [World's Classics series], 1928), p. 3. Hunt's wife also enjoyed showing it off to visitors (Hunt to Severn, 16 December, 1822, *Life and Letters*, p. 131).

34 Keats to James Rice, 24 November 1818, *Letters*, i, p. 407.

35 See D. Parson, *Portraits of Keats* (Cleveland: World Publishing Company, 1954), pp. 45–9.

36 'My Tedious Life', *Letters and Memoirs*, pp. 631–2.

37 *Life and Letters*, p. 31.

38 Severn to Brown, 15 April, 1830, *Letters of Charles Brown*, pp. 316–17.

39 Sonnet 'On the Elgin Marbles', line 5.

40 *Life and Letters*, p. 29.

41 Keats to George and Georgiana Keats, 3(?) March 1819, *Letters*, ii, p. 68.

42 See, for example, I. Jack, *Keats and the Mirror of Art* (Oxford: Clarendon Press, 1967).

43 Keats to George and Georgiana Keats, 14 October 1818, *Letters*, i, p. 395.

44 Bailey to Milnes, 15, 16 October 1848, *Keats Circle*, ii, p. 278.

45 Mary Cowden Clarke, *My Long Life: An Autobiographical Sketch* (London: Fisher Unwin, 1896), p. 12, Edward Holmes to Leigh Hunt, 1823, quoted in E. Blunden, *Shelley and Keats as They Struck Their Contemporaries: Notes Partly from Manuscript Sources* (London: C. W. Beaumont, 1925), p. 87.

46 Severn to R. M. Milnes, 6 October 1845, *Keats Circle*, ii, p. 133.

47 Keats to George and Georgiana Keats, 5 January 1818, *Letters*, i, p. 197.

48 Severn to R. M. Milnes, 6 October 1845, *Keats Circle*, ii, p. 133.

49 Severn to R. M. Milnes, 6 October 1845, *Keats Circle*, ii, p. 132.

50 *Life and Letters*, p. 31.

51 Ibid., p. 41.

52 Severn's 'Biographical Notes on Keats', 1845, *Keats Circle*, ii, p. 137.

53 Keats to George and Georgiana Keats, 17 December 1818, *Letters*, ii, p. 8.

54 Keats to George and Georgiana Keats, 14 October 1818, *Letters*, i, p. 393.

55 Keats to Severn, 29 March 1819, *Letters*, ii, p. 48.

56 *Annals of the Fine Arts*, iv, pp. 102–3.

57 Keats to Severn, 15 November 1819, *Letters*, ii, p. 232.

58 The current whereabouts of *The Cave of Despair* is unknown. There is, however, a black and white photograph of it in the Witt Collection at Somerset House. I am grateful to Elizabeth Carey for identifying the models for some of Severn's figures in the painting.

59 'My Tedious Life', *Letters and Memoirs*, p. 630.

60 Keats to George and Georgiana Keats, 20 September 1819, *Letters*, ii, p. 205.

61 Keats to Severn, 10 November 1819, *Letters*, ii, pp. 227–8. There is some doubt over the dating of this letter. William Sharp gives 27 October, which may well be more accurate.

62 *Annals of the Fine Arts*, ii, p. 366.

63 Keats to Severn, 15 November 1819, *Letters*, ii, p. 232.

64 This is, at least, what Sharp says in *Life and Letters*, pp. 26–7.

65 'My Tedious Life', *Letters and Memoirs*, p. 630.

66 RA Archive, RA General Assembly Minutes, 1 and 10 December 1819.

67 Unidentified press cutting in RA Archive.

68 G. D. Leslie, *The Inner Life of the Royal Academy: with an Account of its Schools & Exhibitions Principally in the Reign of Queen Victoria* (London: John Murray, 1914), p. 55, and Henry Stacey Marks, *Pen and Pencil Sketches*, 2 vols (London: Chatto & Windus, 1894), i, p. 225.

69 RA Archive, RA General Assembly Minutes, 10 December 1819.

70 *Annals of the Fine Arts*, iv, pp. 621–2.

71 'My Tedious Life', *Letters and Memoirs*, p. 631.

Chapter 4 The Warm South

1 Charles Brown to Henry Snook, 11 February 1820, *Letters of Charles Brown*, pp. 52–3.

2 'My Tedious Life', *Letters and Memoirs*, p. 631.

3 William Etty, a long-standing student in the RA Schools, fell foul of its envious atmosphere when he competed for a silver medal in the School of Painting in 1818 for a copy of Titian's *Ganymede*. His well-finished work was clearly far superior to that of the younger students around him. One of them, John Stevens, objected that Etty had removed his painting to apply the background at home. Etty was excluded and the medal awarded to Stevens. W. T. Whitley, *Art in England 1800–1820* (Cambridge: Cambridge University Press, 1928), p. 293.

4 An unidentified press cutting dated 19 December 1819 in the RA Archives. *The Annals of Fine Arts*, v, p. 398.

5 Brown's 'Life of Keats', *Keats Circle*, ii, pp. 73–4.

6 Keats to James Rice, 14, 16 February 1820, *Letters*, ii, p. 260.

7 'My Tedious Life', *Letters and Memoirs*, p. 637.

8 Severn to Haslam, July 1820, *Keats Circle*, i, pp. 121–3.

9 Ibid., pp. 122–3.

10 Shelley to Keats, 27 July 1820, *Letters*, ii, pp. 310–11.

11 Severn to Haslam, July 1820, *Keats Circle*, i, p. 121.

12 Severn to Haslam, July 1820, *Keats Circle*, i, pp. 121–2.

13 Keats to Fanny Brawne, 5 July 1820, *Letters*, ii, p. 303.

14 Keats to Fanny Brawne, August(?) 1820, *Letters*, ii, p. 312.

15 Keats to Fanny Keats, 13 August 1820, *Letters*, ii, p. 314.

16 Keats to John Taylor, 13 August 1820, *Letters*, ii, pp. 313–14 and 315.

17 Keats to Charles Brown, 13 August 1820, Brown's 'Life of Keats', *Keats Circle*, ii, pp. 77–8. Brown only ever allowed a heavily edited version of this letter to be published, leaving it unclear how specific was Keats's invitation to join him at this stage.

18 Keats to Brown, n.d., ibid., pp. 78–9. See also John Taylor to James Taylor, 23 August 1820: 'The Weather seems all at once quite altered, and for these three days I have had a fire': Nostrand, p. 168.

19 Fanny Brawne to Fanny Keats, 27 March 1821: F. Edgecumbe, *Letters of Fanny Brawne to Fanny Keats (1820–1824)* (London: Oxford University Press, 1936), p. 19.

20 'My Tedious Life', *Letters and Memoirs*, p. 638.

21 *Life and Letters*, p. 48. By Hyder Rollins's calculation Severn had five days to get ready (*Keats Circle*, i, p. 140 n. 1). Rollins has been followed in this by Jackson Bate, Andrew Motion, and Robert Gittings.

22 John Taylor to William Haslam, 13 September 1820, *Keats Circle*, i, p. 141. See also Fanny Brawne to Fanny Keats, 18 September 1821, reporting that the ship had 'waited a few days longer than we expected', *Letters of Fanny Brawne to Fanny Keats*, p. 2.

23 Severn to Haslam, 22 February 1821, *Keats Circle*, i, p. 221.

24 L. Hunt, *The Autobiography of Leigh Hunt; with Reminiscences of Friends and Contemporaries* (Oxford: Oxford University Press [World's Classics series] 1928), p. 333.

25 Severn to Brown, 19 September 1821, *Letters and Memoirs*, p. 173.

26 R. M. Milnes, *Life, Letters and Literary Remains of John Keats* (London: J. M. Dent, 1927), p. 209.

27 'My Tedious Life', *Letters and Memoirs*, p. 638. Dorothy Hewlett thought otherwise: 'He would have gone to Rome whether or not there had been anything in preparation for him there because Keats needed him' (*Adonais*, p. 336).

28 John Reynolds to John Taylor, 21 September 1821, *Keats Circle*, i, p. 157.

29 Taylor to Haslam, 13 September 1821, *Keats Circle*, i, p. 141.

30 'My Tedious Life', *Letters and Memoirs*, p. 638.

31 Quoted in *Life and Letters*, p. 48. In Rome Severn earned only eight guineas each for his miniatures. Severn to James Severn, 10 April 1821, LMA, KPM/S 461.

32 K. Garlick, *Sir Thomas Lawrence* (London: Routledge & Kegan Paul, 1954), p. 20.

33 'My Tedious Life', *Letters and Memoirs*, p. 639. Severn never named him and may not have followed up the letter of introduction even though it thoughtfully offered him a possible means of making money in Rome as a copyist.

34 'My Tedious Life', *Letters and Memoirs*, p. 639.

35 Severn to Maria Severn, 21 January 1821, *Letters and Memoirs*, p. 124. The miniature is now at Keats House.

36 'My Tedious Life', *Letters and Memoirs*, p. 639. Sharp's version is significantly embellished (*Life and Letters*, pp. 50–1).

37 Severn to Thomas Severn, 9 April 1837, *Letters and Memoirs*, p. 340.

38 'My Tedious Life', *Letters and Memoirs*, p. 640.

39 Severn to Haslam, [24] September 1820, *Keats Circle*, i, p. 149.

40 Taylor to Fanny Keats, 20 September 1820; M. Adami, *Fanny Keats* (New Haven and London: Yale University Press, 1938), p. 98; Fanny Brawne to Fanny Keats, 18 September 1821, *Letters of Fanny Brawne to Fanny Keats*, p. 3.

41 T. Landseer, ed., *Life and Letters of William Bewick (Artist)*, 2 vols (London, Hurst and Blackett, 1871), i, p. 280.

42 H. Mathews, *Diary of an Invalid being the Journal of a Tour in Pursuit of Health in Portugal Italy Switzerland and France in the Years 1817–1819*, 2 vols (2nd edn, London, 1820), p. 32.

43 Severn to Haslam, 18 September 1820, *Keats Circle*, i, p. 150. The pictures are now in Keats House. The self-portrait is reproduced in *Letters and Memoirs*, p. 101.

44 Severn's journal letter to Haslam, September 1820, *Keats Circle*, i, pp. 148–54.

45 Ibid., p. 153.

46 Haslam to Taylor and Hessey, 23 September 1820, *Keats Circle*, i, p. 158.

47 Severn's journal letter to Haslam, *Keats Circle*, i, p. 154.

48 'My Tedious Life', *Letters and Journals*, p. 640.

49 Severn to Haslam, 1 and 2 November 1820, *Keats Circle*, i, p. 166.

50 Keats to Brown, 28 September 1820, *Letters*, ii, p. 345. This letter was not, in fact, sent. Severn's drawing is in his scrapbook at Houghton Library, Harvard MS Eng 1460 f. 108.

51 Brown to Taylor, 5 October 1820, *Keats Circle*, i, p. 160.

52 Curiously, Severn kept it, though Brown later had a copy and included it in a censored version in his 'Life of Keats'.

53 Keats to Charles Brown, 30 September 1820, *Letters*, ii, pp. 344–6.

54 'My Tedious Life', *Letters and Memoirs*, p. 640.

55 'My Tedious Life', *Letters and Memoirs*, pp. 640–1. In February 1846 the *Union Magazine* published a facsimile of 'Bright Star' taken from the copy of Shakespeare's *Poems* which Keats gave Severn in January 1821, together with a letter from Severn claiming that he had seen Keats composing it on board the *Maria Crowther*. In *Life and Letters*, William Sharp wrote up the incident imagining details which Severn never claimed elsewhere (Keats writing hurriedly, reading his work over to Severn, Severn begging for a copy, etc.). This reinvention of an incident in which Severn was not an active participant brought the wrath of Keats biographers on his head. Robert Gittings, never a fan of Severn, threw out the whole story, claiming that all he had seen was Keats reading over the text of the poem which he had written out much earlier (R. Gittings, *John Keats* [Harmondsworth: Penguin, 1971], pp. 600–2). Jack Stillinger,

the editor of the definitive edition of Keats's *Poems*, takes a different view, accepting Severn's claim to have seen Keats writing out 'Bright Star'. As usual, it is Severn's early reminiscence, rather than his later invention, which is conclusive. In a letter to Brown, written seven months after Keats's death, he made clear he knew that earlier texts of the sonnet existed: 'Do you [know] "Bright Star—would I were stedfast as thou art"—he wrote this down in the ship— it is one of his most beautiful things. I will send it if you have it not': Severn to Brown, 19 September 1821, *Letters and Memoirs*, pp. 172–3.

56 Mathews, *Diary of an Invalid*, p. 6, and Landseer, *Life and Letters of William Bewick*, i, p. 287.

57 Severn 'Biographical Notes on Keats', October 1845, *Keats Circle*, ii, p. 134.

58 'Opium has been described as God's greatest gift to doctors . . . It is prescribed with benefit for all sorts of conditions—cough, sea-sickness, stomach and bowel complaints. Many travellers are never without it in their trunks': W. Hale-White, *Keats as Doctor and Patient* (London: Oxford University Press, 1938), p. 87.

59 Reproduced in *Letters and Memoirs*, p. 103.

60 'My Tedious Life', *Letters and Memoirs*, pp. 642–3.

61 On Keats's long-standing passion for Italy see R. Cavaliero, 'A Swoon to Death: Keats's Debt to Italy', *Keats-Shelley Review*, 11 (1997), 41–51.

62 Keats to Mrs Brawne, 24 October 1820, *Letters*, ii, p. 349, and Keats to Brown 1 and 2 November 1820, *Letters*, ii, p. 352. In *Life and Letters*, Sharp prints a long passage, purportedly by Severn, describing Keats inducting his travelling companions into an appreciation of the classical beauties and historical associations around them. Keats's letters tell a different story, and the elaborate prose of Sharp's concocted memoir was beyond Severn. Keats biographers generally follow Sharp's account, however.

63 Severn to Haslam, 1 and 2 November 1820, *Keats Circle*, i, p. 165 and Haslam to Severn, 4 December 1820, *Life and Letters*, p. 72

64 Severn to Haslam, 2 October 1820, *Keats Circle*, i, p. 163.

65 Keats to Mrs Brawne, 24 October 1821, *Letters*, ii, p. 350.

66 Keats to Brown, 1 November 1820, *Letters*, ii, pp. 351–2.

67 Severn to Haslam, 1 November 1820, *Keats Circle*, i, p. 165.

68 Keats to Mrs Brawne, 24 October 1820, *Letters*, ii, p. 349.

69 'On the Vicissitudes of Keats's Fame', *Atlantic Monthly*, 11 (1863), 602.

70 Severn to Haslam, 12 November 1820, *Keats Circle*, i, p. 165.

71 Severn to Maria Severn, 1 November 1820, *Letters and Memoirs*, pp. 105–6.

72 The precise dates of Severn and Keats's journey are difficult to establish. Keats's visas were issued by the British Legation on 6 November and the Papal Consul General the following day. On 15 November they made their first withdrawal from their bank account at Torlonia's in Rome. It seems probable therefore that they left Naples on 8 November arriving in Rome on the 14th.

73 Mathews, *Diary of an Invalid*, p. 286.

74 Severn quoted in *Life and Letters*, p. 64. The words may be William Sharp's, the experience that of all travellers from Naples to Rome in the 1820s.

75 Mathews, *Diary of an Invalid*, pp. 196–7; A. Jameson, *Diary of an Ennuye* (London: Henry Colburn, 1826), p. 268; Lady Morgan (Sydney Owenson), *Italy*, 3 vols (London: Henry Colburn, 1821), iii, p. 127.

76 Mathews, *Diary of an Invalid*, p. 286.

77 Lady Morgan, *Italy*, iii, p. 136, S. Martin, *Narrative of a Three Years Residence in Italy, 1819–1822* (Dublin, 1831), p. 109.

78 Thomas Medwin, *The Life of Percy Bysshe Shelley with an Introduction and Commentary by H. B. Forman* (London: Oxford University Press, 1913), p. 300. Though Medwin was often unreliable, he had a knack of picking up information others missed and was in Rome at the time of Keats's death.

79 'My Tedious Life', *Letters and Memoirs*, pp. 644–5.

80 M. Tapparelli d'Azeglio, *Things I Remember*, trans. and introd. E. R. Vincent (London: Oxford University Press, 1966), p. 208.

81 Jameson, *Diary of an Ennuyee*, p. 194; C. Eaton, *Rome in the Nineteenth Century*, 3 vols (Edinburgh: Hurst, Robinson, 1820), i, p. 132.

82 The record of Clark's wedding on 30 August 1820 has recently been discovered by Grant Scott (*Letters and Memoirs*, p. 114).

83 Dr Clark to unknown, 27 November 1821, *Keats Circle*, i, p. 172.

Chapter 5 Piazza di Spagna

1 J. R. Hale, ed., *The Italian Journal of Samuel Rogers* (London: Faber & Faber, 1956), p. 60, gives an estimate of 2,000 British in Rome in 1818. Severn's figure of 200 is in Severn to Maria Severn, 20 February 1821, *Letters and Memoirs*, p. 128.

2 H. Mathews, *The Diary of an Invalid, being the Journal of a Tour in Pursuit of Health in Portugal Italy Switzerland and France in the Years 1817–1819*, 2 vols (2nd edn, London, 1820), pp. 72–3, Lady Morgan (Sydney Owenson), *Italy*, 3 vols (London: Henry Colburn, 1821), ii. pp. 427–8 and C. Eaton, *Rome in the Nineteenth Century*, 3 vols (Edinburgh: Hurst, Robinson, 1820), ii, p. 264. (Mrs Eaton led a stirring rendition of 'God Save the King' at the top of the dome of St Peter's.)

3 'My Tedious Life', *Letters and Memoirs*, p. 647.

4 S. Brown, 'Suppose Me In Rome', in *Keats and Italy: A History of the Keats–Shelley House in Rome* (Rome, Il Labirinto, 2005), p. 23; and Eaton, *Rome in the Nineteenth Century*, iii, p. 298.

5 Finch is quoted in J. Richardson, *The Everlasting Spell: A Study of Keats and his Friends* (London: Jonathan Cape, 1963), p. 237. See too J. M. Colles, ed., *The Journal of John Mayne during a Tour on the Continent upon its Re-Opening after the Fall of Napoleon, 1814* (London: Lane, 1909), p. 162.

6 Lady Morgan, *Italy*, ii, pp. 426–7 and *The Italian Journal of Samuel Rogers: Edited with an Account of Roger's Life and of Travel in Italy in 1814–1821 by J. R. Hale* (London: Faber & Faber, 1956), p. 61. Angelletti to Finch is quoted in W. J. Bate, *John Keats* (Cambridge, MA: Harvard University Press, 1963), p. 674.

7 About the same time Henry Mathews and two friends paid £15 for six rooms and a kitchen, but these were off the Corso, on the fourth floor and they had to put up with two fish stalls below their windows and the constant sound of bagpipes: H. Mathews, *The Diary of an Invalid*, p. 73.

8 'Keats's Last Bank Account', *Keats–Shelley Memorial Bulletin*, 2 (1913), p. 95. Thackeray lampooned Torlonia as the Prince of Pollonia in his *Book of Snobs*. Stendhal commented, 'some say he should stay away from his parties because the wretched Jewish cast of his face puts a damper on things': M. H. B. Stendhal, *A Roman Journal*, ed. and trans. Haakon Chevalier (London: Orion Press, 1959), pp. 72–3.

9 There was not just Keats but Lady Flora Hastings, who was ostracized at court when a cancerous stomach tumour was misdiagnosed as a scandalous pregnancy. Nor did Clark, fearful of the effect on Queen Victoria and her husband, disclose Prince Albert's typhoid to them, a decision which fatally limited the nursing the Prince was given. Other well-known patients like John Stuart Mill found him insufficiently interventionist. Elizabeth Longford has suggested that Clark often concealed his diagnoses from his patients in an effort to cheer them. His real weakness was that he was 'too eager to please': 'Queen Victoria's Doctors' in M. Gilbert, ed., *A Century of Conflict 1850–1950: Essays for A J P Taylor* (London: Hamish Hamilton, 1966), p. 83. See too J. Premble, *The Mediterranean Passion: Victorians and Edwardians in the South* (London: Oxford University Press, 1988), p. 89.

10 Lord Brock, *John Keats and Joseph Severn: The Tragedy of the Last Illness* (London: The Keats–Shelley Memorial Association, 1973), p. 18.

11 J. Clark, *Medical Notes . . . The Effects of a Residence in the South of Europe* (London: T. & G. Underwood, 1820), p. 92.

12 Keats to Fanny Keats, 8 February 1820, *Letters*, ii, p. 253.

13 Mathews, *Diary of an Invalid*, p. 264, complaining that his doctor had stopped after taking only a thimble of blood.

14 Clark to unknown, November 1820, *Keats Circle*, i, p. 172.

15 It is tempting to think that Keats may have visited the Vatican. Dr Clark strongly recommended a visit in his book and Keats followed all the rest of his advice. While Severn certainly went, however, there is no record of a visit with Keats and it is hard to think that if he had gone, Severn would not have said so.

16 Severn to Haslam, 15 January 1821, *Keats Circle*, i, p. 198.

17 Sharp prints what he claims to be an amalgam of Severn's autobiographical memoranda of this time describing Keats's reaction to this statue: 'beautiful bad taste', 'an Aeolian harp'. This is almost certainly apocryphal since by 1820 access to the statue was extremely limited. Even Turner only gained admittance on his visit in 1819 because of his friendship with Canova. Mathews, *Diary of an Invalid*, p. 146, A. Jameson, *Diary of an Ennuyee* (London: Henry Colburn, 1826), p. 273. Keats to Fanny Brawne, February(?) 1820, *Letters*, ii, p. 256.

18 Eaton, *Rome in the Nineteenth Century*, p. 298.

19 'My Tedious Life', *Letters and Memoirs*, pp. 647–8.

20 'My Tedious Life', *Letters and Memoirs*, p. 647.

21 T. Mathews, *The Biography of John Gibson R.A., Sculptor Rome* (London: Heinemann, 1911), pp. 41 and 65.

22 'My Tedious Life', *Letters and Memoirs*, p. 645.

23 Keats to Haydon, 8 April 1818, *Letters*, i, p. 245.

24 Severn to Maria Severn, 21 January 1821, *Letters and Memoirs*, p. 125.

25 'My Tedious Life', *Letters and Memoirs*, p. 646.

26 Ibid., and Severn to Brown, 17 July 1821, *Letters of Charles Brown*, p. 79. See too *Keats Circle*, i, pp. xxxix–xl.

27 Severn to Maria Severn, 11 February 1821, *Letters and Memoirs*, p. 126.

28 Ibid., and Ewing to Severn, 29 September 1821, Houghton Library, Harvard bMS Eng 1434 (63).

29 Brown to Severn, 16 August 1828, *New Letters from Charles Brown to Joseph Severn*, (26).

30 Canova came to London late in 1815 to view the Elgin Marbles. Benjamin West introduced him to the student body who cheered him enthusiastically in the course of one of Sir

Anthony Carlisle's anatomy lectures. W. T. Whitley, *Art in England 1800–1820* (Cambridge: Cambridge University Press, 1928), pp. 251–2.

31 Lady Morgan, *Italy*, ii, p. 493.
32 Severn to Maria Severn, 19 February 1821, *Letters and Memoirs*, p. 127.
33 Haslam to Severn, [4] December 1820, *Letters and Memoirs*, pp. 110–11.
34 Severn to Haslam, 15 January 1821, *Letters and Memoirs*, p. 123.
35 The letter has not survived.
36 Severn to Brown, 17 December 1820, *Letters and Memoirs*, p. 113.
37 Severn to Haslam, 15 January 1821, *Letters and Memoirs*, p. 121.
38 Keats to Brown, 14 August 1820, Brown's 'Life of Keats', *Keats Circle*, ii, p. 78.
39 D. Lessing, *The Diaries of Jane Somers* (London: Flamingo, 2002), p. 227. In *On Death and Dying* (New York: Touchstone, 1997), Elizabeth Kubler-Ross suggests a more extended progression: denial, anger, bargaining, depression, and acceptance, which reflects more of the possibilities of current medical intervention than the simpler three-stage pattern.
40 Keats to Dilke, 21 September 1818, *Letters*, i, p. 369.
41 Fanny Brawne to Thomas Medwin, J. Richardson, *Fanny Brawne*, p. 165; and Brown's 'Life of Keats', *Keats Circle*, ii, p. 74.
42 Severn to Brown, 17 December 1820, *Letters and Memoirs*, p. 115.
43 Severn to Brown, 17 December 1820, *Letters and Memoirs*, p. 114.
44 Severn to Taylor, 24 December 1820, *Letters and Memoirs*, p. 116.
45 Severn to Taylor, 24 December 1820, *Letters and Memoirs*, p. 118.
46 This lovely copy, now in the possession of Ross Severn, was printed in Edinburgh in 1715 and bound in finely tooled leather with a delicate patterned design front and back of foliage and flowers, measuring 6 inches by 10. From the number of previous owners with their names, initials or dates written on the front cover, it looks like something Elton might have found in a second-hand bookshop in Rome. Severn's pencilled annotations are not dated. I have assumed they were made at the time he first read this Bible.

Chapter 6 'Thanks Joe'

1 Brown normally forwarded his letters from Severn to Taylor and Hessey, who then sent them on to Richard Woodhouse, Haslam, and Edward Holmes, who would return them for Brown to show to Thomas Richards. Similarly, Fanny Brawne was able to make copies of some of Severn's letters to Haslam for Fanny Keats to see, while Brown would look in on the Brawnes to read out chosen extracts from the letters he received.
2 Fanny Brawne to Fanny Keats, 27 March 1821: F. Edgecumbe, *Letters of Fanny Brawne to Fanny Keats (1820–1824)* (London: Oxford University Press, 1936), p. 19.
3 See Sue Brown, 'The Friend of Keats: The Reinvention of Joseph Severn', in Eugene Stelzig ed., *Romantic Autobiography* (Aldershot: Ashgate, 2009).
4 Isabella Jones to Taylor, 14 April 1821, *Letters and Memoirs*, pp. 149–51.
5 Thomas Dormandy, *The White Death: A History of Tuberculosis* (London: Hambledon & London, 1999), pp. 52–3.
6 J. Clark, *Medical Notes . . . The Effects of a Residence in the South of Europe* (London: T. & G. Underwood, 1820), p. 92.
7 *Life and Letters*, p. 37.
8 Severn to Taylor, 24 December 1820, *Letters and Memoirs*, p. 119.

Notes

9 Severn to Mrs Brawne, 11 January 1821, *Keats Circle*, i, pp. 187–91.

10 Severn to R. M. Milnes, 'Biographical Notes on Keats', *Keats Circle*, ii, p. 182.

11 Severn to Taylor, 24 December 1820, *Letters and Memoirs*, p. 117.

12 Keats to Jane Reynolds, September 1817, *Letters*, i, pp. 156–7.

13 Severn to Taylor, 25 and 26 January 1821, *Letters and Memoirs*, p. 134.

14 Severn to Haslam, 15 January 1821, *Letters and Memoirs*, pp. 120–1.

15 Severn to Haslam, 15 January 1821, *Letters and Memoirs*, pp. 120–3.

16 'My Tedious Life', *Letters and Memoirs*, p. 649.

17 The original is in the Keats–Shelley House in Rome.

18 Clark to ?Gray, 13 January 1821, *Keats Circle*, i, p. 194.

19 Severn to Haslam, 15 January 1821, *Letters and Memoirs*, p. 121.

20 Severn to Maria Severn, 21 January, 11, 14, 19, 20 February 1821, *Letters and Memoirs*, pp. 124–30.

21 Mrs Brawne to Severn, 6 February 1821 and Brown to Keats, 21 December 1820, *Letters*, ii, pp. 375 and 366. Haslam to Severn, 4 December 1820, *Life and Letters of Joseph Severn*, p. 73.

22 Brown to Severn, 15 January and 9 March 1821, *The Letters of Charles Brown*, pp. 67 and 73. Brown wrote to Severn on 15 January, 30 January, 9 March, and 23 March 1821.

23 Severn to Brown, 8 February 1821, Brown's 'Life of Keats', *Keats Circle*, ii, p. 91.

24 A. Hare, *The Life and Letters of Frances, Baroness Bunsen*, 2 vols (London: Smith, Elder, 1882), p. 171.

25 Severn to John Taylor, 5 January 1822, *Letters and Memoirs*, p. 190 and Severn to Brown, 8 February 1821, Brown's 'Life of Keats', *Keats Circle*, ii, p. 90.

26 Severn to Brown, 14 February 1821, Brown's 'Life of Keats', *Keats Circle*, ii, p. 91.

27 'My Tedious Life', *Letters and Memoirs*, p. 650.

28 Severn, 'On the Vicissitudes of Keats's Fame', *Atlantic Monthly*, 11 (April 1863), 404. Keats described violets to his sister in spring 1819 as 'the Princesses of flowers, and in a shower of rain almost as fine as barley sugar drops to a schoolboy's tongue' (Keats to Fanny Keats, 12 April 1819, *Letters*, ii, p. 55).

29 Severn to Brown, 14 February 1821, Brown's 'Life of Keats', *Keats Circle*, ii, p. 93.

30 Severn to Brown, 2 May 1821, '*The Keats Circle: Further Letters*', p. 197.

31 The first reference to de Llanos's visit comes in a letter from Gerald Griffin to his sister on 21 June 1825. Griffin, another literary man, was a good friend of de Llanos but an unreliable witness about Keats. His suggestion that de Llanos was intimate with Keats and saw him three days before his death was, however, broadly corroborated by Fanny Keats herself, even if the closeness of de Llanos's call to the time of Keats's death may have been exaggerated. D. Griffin, *Life of Gerald Griffin* (London: James Diffy, 1843), p. 190. See too H. E. Rollins, 'Fanny Keats: Biographical Notes', *Publications of the Modern Language Association of America* (March 1944), 203.

32 Severn to Brown, 14 February 1821, Brown's 'Life of Keats,' *Keats Circle*, ii, p. 93. S. Martin, *Narrative of a Three Years Residence in Italy, 1819–1822* (Dublin, 1831), p. 271.

33 Severn to Taylor, 6 March 1821, *Letters and Memoirs*, p. 138.

34 Severn to Haslam, 22 February 1821, *Letters and Memoirs*, pp. 135–7.

35 Severn to Haslam, 5 May 1821, *Letters and Memoirs*, p. 153.

36 Severn to Taylor, 6 March 1821, *Letters and Memoirs*, pp. 137–8.

37 Martin, *Three Years Residence in Italy*, pp. 260 and 271. Sir William died a year later, having been assured by Dr Clark that the only thing that ailed him was his attempt to suppress his grief at his daughter's death, out of consideration for his wife.

38 For a good description of carnival in 1821 see Lady Morgan, *Italy*, 3 vols (London: Henry Colburn, 1821), iii, pp. 87–98. The conjunction between Keats's funeral and carnival events in the Piazza di Spagna quarter has not previously been noticed by biographers of Severn and Keats.

39 Letter from Miss H. M. Poynter to Mrs Margaret McKail, 24 October 1921, LMA, KPM/K770 214. Severn named another mourner, Henderson, who has never been traced. It may well be that he misheard or misremembered Henry Parke's name as he did not include him among the mourners. There are, however, a number of inaccuracies in Poynter's account as transmitted by his daughter and recorded many years after the event. The paucity of the mourners is an indication of the haste with which the funeral was arranged as well as the fact that Severn took little part in the arrangements. Valentin de Llanos did not attend, nor did Lieutenant Elton, who fades from view after Keats's relapse in December.

40 'My Tedious Life', *Letters and Memoirs*, p. 650.

41 Severn exaggerated this success when writing home, claiming that the bill had been reduced to one-sixth of the initial charge.

42 'My Tedious Life', *Letters and Memoirs*, p. 650. In the first draft of his letter reporting Keats's death to Brown, Severn began to describe the visit of the police and then violently crossed out the passage before abandoning his letter. The original is in the Keats–Shelley House, Rome.

43 Severn to Brown, 27 February 1821, Brown's 'Life of Keats', *Keats Circle*, ii, p. 95.

44 Severn to Taylor, 6 March 1821, *Letters and Memoirs*, p. 138. See too R. Cavaliero, 'A Place Too Savage for an Invalid', *Keats–Shelley Review*, 6 (1991), 15.

45 Taylor to Severn, 6 February 1821, and James Hessey to Severn, 12 and 27 February 1821, *Keats Circle*, i, pp. 109–18. Taylor's fund was made up of £50 donated by Lord Fitzwilliam and £10 each from James Rice, the painters Hilton and De Wint, and two friends of Taylor and Hessey's.

46 Hunt to Severn, 8 March 1821, *Life and Letters*, pp. 86–7 which also includes a facsimile of the letter.

Chapter 7 'The Most Striking Year of My Life'

1 'Incidents of My Life', *Letters and Memoirs*, p. 586.

2 Quotations are from the Preface to *Prometheus Unbound*.

3 Severn to his mother, 'Spring 1821', *Letters and Memoirs*, p. 140.

4 Severn to Haslam, 5 May 1821, *Letters and Memoirs*, p. 153.

5 Finch left Rome around the time of Keats's death but was back there in late March and wrote to Gisborne on 7 April 1821. Gisborne did not send Finch's letter on to Shelley until 13 June. See Gisborne to Finch, 30 May 1821, Bodleian Library, Oxford, Finch Correspondence, d 8 f 234; and M. Shelley, ed., *Essays, Letters from Abroad by Percy Bysshe Shelley*, 2 vols (London: E. Moxon, 1840), ii, p. 296.

6 Finch to Gisborne 7 April 1821, in Shelley, *Essays, Letters from Abroad by Percy Bysshe Shelley*, ii, p. 296.

7 'My Tedious Life', *Letters and Memoirs*, p. 650.

8 Severn to Haslam 5 May 1821, *Letters and Memoirs*, p. 154.

9 Severn to Sarah Severn, 6 June 1821, *Letters and Memoirs*, p. 158. Though Severn never received a commission from the Duchess of Devonshire she thought well of him. See the Duchess of Devonshire to Sir Thomas Lawrence, 15 May 1823, RA Archive, LAW/4/130.

10 J. R. Hale, ed., *The Italian Journal of Samuel Rogers* (London: Faber & Faber, 1956), pp. 215, 217, 224, 232, 234, 237, and 244. C. Cockerell, *Travels in Southern Europe and the Levant 1810–17*, ed. J. P. Cockerell (London: Longman Green, 1903), p. 273.

11 Severn to Sarah Severn, 16 June 1821, *Letters and Memoirs*, p. 161 and Severn to Brown, 17 July 1821, *Letters of Charles Brown*, p. 80.

12 G. Blakiston, *Woburn and the Russells* (London: Constable, 1980), p. 188.

13 Severn to Haslam, 5 May 1821, *Letters and Memoirs*, p. 153.

14 'Incidents of My Life', *Letters and Memoirs*, p. 589. Severn kept his copy of *Romulus and Remus* to the end of his life, perhaps because of its associations with Beaumont.

15 Ibid., p. 590.

16 Quoted in T. Webb, 'City of the Soul: English Romantic Travellers in Rome', in M. Liversidge and C. Edwards, eds, *Imagining Rome: British Artists and Rome in the Nineteenth Century* (exhibition catalogue, Bristol City Museum and Art Gallery) (London: Merrell Holbarton, 1996), pp. 22–3.

17 'Incidents of My Life', *Letters and Memoirs*, p. 587.

18 C. Eastlake, *Contributions to the Literature of the Fine Arts Second Series with a Memoir Compiled by Lady Eastlake* (London: John Murray, 1870), pp. 89 and 90. See too the Duchess of Devonshire's comment to Sir Thomas Lawrence, 'Rome has had excellent society this year', 15 March 1823, RA Archive, LAW/4/104 RA.

19 'My Tedious Life', *Letters and Memoirs*, pp. 651–2 and 655.

20 Ewing to Severn, 29 September 1821, Houghton Library, Harvard bMS 1434 (63); Severn to Taylor, 16 May 1821, *Keats Circle*, i, p. 249; and Severn to Brown, 'early May' 1821, *Life and Letters*, p. 103.

21 Severn to Sarah Severn, 6 June 1821, *Letters and Memoirs*, p. 158.

22 Severn to James Severn, 10 April 1821, and Sarah Severn, 6 June and 9 July 1821, *Letters and Memoirs*, pp. 145–6, 158 and 162.

23 Severn to Brown, 'early May' 1821, *Life and Letters*, p. 107 and 'Incidents of My Life', *Letters and Memoirs*, p. 586.

24 Brown to Severn, 23 March 1821, *Life and Letters*, p. 98.

25 Taylor to Severn, 3 April 1821, *Letters and Memoirs*, pp. 142–4.

26 Severn to Taylor, 21 January 1825, *Keats–Shelley Journal*, 48 (1999), 20.

27 Severn to Taylor, 16 May 1821, *Keats Circle*, i, p. 249.

28 Severn to Brown, 17 July 1821, *Letters of Charles Brown*, p. 78.

29 Severn to Haslam, 5 May 1821, *Letters and Memoirs*, p. 156.

30 Brown to Severn, 13 August 1821, *Letters of Charles Brown*, p. 86.

31 Severn to Haslam, 5 May 1821, *Letters and Memoirs*, p. 153.

32 'Incidents of My Life', *Letters and Memoirs*, pp. 592–3. This sounds like one of Severn's later sentimentalizations of a more mundane incident, particularly as he described the shepherd in the autumn of 1821 as leaning against Keats's (non-existent) gravestone. Severn painted the scene which may have coloured his memory of it.

33 Severn to Brown, 17 July 1821, *Letters of Charles Brown*, p. 78.

Notes

34 This arrangement continues at Keats House. It was particularly admired by the great Anglo-German pianist Dame Myra Hess.

35 Severn to Brown, 1 January 1822, *Letters of Charles Brown*, p. 95 and Severn to Taylor, 5 January 1822, *Letters and Memoirs*, p. 191.

36 Taylor to Severn, 3 April 1821, *Letters and Memoirs*, p. 144.

37 Severn to James Severn 12 and 21 July 1821, *Letters and Memoirs*, pp. 163–6.

38 Severn to Brown, 17 July 1821, *Letters of Charles Brown*, p. 79. See, too, Severn to Haslam, 12 July 1821, *Keats Circle*, i, p. 251.

39 Brown to Severn, 13 August 1821, *New Letters of Charles Brown* (1). This was probably a confusion based on a hurried conversation with Taylor. See S. Brown, 'Fresh Light on the Friendship of Charles Brown and Joseph Severn', *Keats-Shelley Review*, 18 (2004), pp. 141–2. M. Pointon, 'Keats, Joseph Severn and William Hilton: Notes on a Dispute', *Notes and Queries*, 20 (Feb. 1973), 50–4 gives a critical view of Severn's suspicions of Hilton.

40 RA Archive, RA Council Minutes, 30 August 1821.

41 Severn to Sarah Severn, 29 October 1821, *Letters and Memoirs*, pp. 174–5. Howard's letter is referred to in *Life and Letters*, p. 104.

42 Raphael's *Transfiguration* was thought of at the time as the greatest of all paintings. Brown to Severn, 13 August 1821, *New Letters of Charles Brown* (1).

43 Severn to Sarah Severn, 29 October 1821, *Letters and Memoirs*, p. 175.

44 Severn to Brown, 19 September 1821, *Letters and Memoirs*, p. 173.

45 B. Magee, *Clouds of Glory: A Hoxton Childhood* (London: Jonathan Cape, 2003), p. 206.

46 In his letter of 29 October to Sarah complaining about the scolding she had given him, Severn says 'what with the one and the other I have had a walking about in my inside ever since', but 'the other' could as easily refer to the loss of his picture as to the discovery of young Henry's existence. No letters are extant between this one to Sarah at the end of October and Severn's letter to Maria on 26 December 1821, although Sharp refers to correspondence with Severn's family about the publication of *Adonais*.

47 V. W. von Hagen, *Frederick Catherwood Architect* (New York: Oxford University Press, 1950), p. 14.

48 Severn to Maria Severn, 15–19 September 1821, *Letters and Memoirs*, p. 167, Severn to Brown, 19 September 1821, *Life and Letters*, p. 111.

49 Severn to Maria Severn, 26 December 1821, *Letters and Memoirs*, p. 167. Catherwood's biographer, Victor Wolfgang von Hagen, suggests that he and Lady Westmorland were lovers. While this is possible, von Hagen is elsewhere extremely unreliable. Catherwood's letter of 10 May 1826 to Severn recounting a meeting with Lady Westmorland in London reads more like the letter of a concerned friend than a former lover: Houghton Library, Harvard bMS 1434 (28).

50 In later life he became a panoramist, moving to New York in 1838 and then travelling to Mexico and Guatemala with John Lloyd Stephens. There he produced some fine drawings in difficult jungle conditions of previously unknown Mayan remains. His next reincarnation was as a railway surveyor in Guyana and California. He drowned in 1850 when the boat in which he was returning to England to settle his affairs before permanent emigration to America sank.

51 *Life and Letters*, p. 113.

52 RA Archive, RA Council Minutes, 31 October 1821; Severn to Leslie 20 November 1821, *Letters and Memoirs*, p. 177; RA Archive, General Assembly Minutes, 1 December 1821.

53 Severn to Maria Severn, 26 December 1821, and Severn to Taylor, 5 January 1822, *Letters and Memoirs*, pp. 183 and 189.
54 Shelley to Severn, 29 November 1821, *Life and Letters*, pp. 118–19.
55 See Susan J. Wolfson, 'Keats Enters History: Autopsy, Adonais and the Fame of Keats', in N. Roe, ed., *Keats and History* (Cambridge: Cambridge University Press, 1995), pp. 17–45.
56 Severn to Brown, 1 January 1822, *Letters of Charles Brown*, p. 95.
57 *Life and Letters*, p. 120. Sharp claims to be quoting from a letter from Severn to his family.
58 Severn to Maria Severn, 26 December 1821, *Letters and Memoirs*, pp. 183–4.
59 Ibid., pp. 181–2.
60 'Incidents of My Life', *Letters and Memoirs*, p. 594.
61 Severn to John Taylor, 5 January 1822, *Letters and Memoirs*, p. 192.

Chapter 8 The RA Pensioner

1 Severn to Brown, 1 January 1822, *Letters of Charles Brown*, pp. 96–7.
2 W. Collins, *Memoirs of the Life of William Collins RA*, 2 vols (London: Longman, 1848), p. 101.
3 See K. Andrews, *The Nazarenes: A Brotherhood of German Painters in Rome* (Oxford: Clarendon Press, 1964).
4 Severn to C. R. Leslie, 20 November 1821, *Letters and Memoirs*, p. 179.
5 D. Robertson, *Sir Charles Eastlake and the Victorian Art World* (Princeton: Princeton University Press, 1978), p. 33; A. Cunningham, *Life of David Wilkie with his Journals, Tours and Critical Remarks on Works of Art*, 3 vols (London: John Murray, 1843), ii, pp. 199–200.
6 Severn to C. R. Leslie, 20 November 1821, and Severn to James Severn, 18 April 1821, *Letters and Memoirs*, pp. 178 and 147.
7 An unsourced article, probably by Richard Lane, quoted in K. Wells, 'The Return of the British Painters to Rome', p. 178.
8 C. Eaton, *Rome in the Nineteenth Century*, 3 vols (Edinburgh: Hurst, Robinson, 1820), iii, pp. 112–13.
9 Westmacott to Robert Finch, 8 December 1821, Bodleian Library, Oxford, Finch Papers, d17 f116.
10 Richard Evans to Thomas Lawrence, 25 April 1825, RA Archive, LAW/4/321.
11 Severn to James Severn, 24 March 1822, *Letters and Memoirs*, pp. 193–4.
12 Severn to Thomas Severn, 23 March 1823, *Letters and Memoirs*, p. 236.
13 Severn to James Severn, 24 March 1822, *Letters and Memoirs*, p. 193.
14 Severn to Sarah Severn, 27 June 1823, *Letters and Memoirs*, p. 246.
15 Severn to Maria Severn, 29 May 1822, and Severn to Thomas Severn, 24 March 1822, *Letters and Memoirs*, pp. 201 and 197.
16 Severn to Thomas Severn, 24 March 1822, *Letters and Memoirs*, p. 198.
17 See Robertson, *Sir Charles Eastlake*, pp. 25–8.
18 Eastlake to Sir Thomas Lawrence, 15 January 1823, RA Archive, LAW 14/87; and Severn to James Severn, 7 December 1822, LMA, KPMS 472. This Sir William is not to be confused with the more famous complaisant husband of Emma Hamilton.
19 Severn to Thomas Lawrence, 24 October 1822, *Letters and Memoirs*, pp. 212–13.
20 Lawrence to Severn, 23 December 1822, *Life and Letters*, p. 133.
21 Severn to Lawrence, 19 January 1823, *Letters and Memoirs*, pp. 224–6.

Notes

22 Eastlake to Lawrence, 15 January 1823, RA Archive, LAW/4/87.

23 Eastlake to Lawrence, 12 October 1823, RA Archive, LAW/4/164.

24 Lawrence to Eastlake, 19 November 1823, RA Archive LAW/4/167.

25 See S. Brown, 'Joseph Severn and the British Academy of Arts in Rome', *Journal of Anglo-Italian Studies*, 10 (2009), 63–72.

26 C. P. Brand, *Italy and the English Romantics: The Italianate Fashion in early Nineteenth-Century England* (Cambridge: Cambridge University Press, 1957), p. 11.

27 Severn to Thomas Severn, 24 March 1822, *Letters and Memoirs*, p. 198.

28 Severn to Thomas Severn, 5 July 1822, *Letters and Memoirs*, p. 205; Severn to John Taylor, 21 January 1825, *Keats–Shelley Journal*, 48 (1999), 20; and Severn to Haslam, 1 June 1823, *Letters and Memoirs*, p. 242. In 1822 the Roberts family asked for £20 for Henry's maintenance: Severn to Charles Brown, 26 October 1822, *Letters and Memoirs*, p. 217.

29 Kirkup's portrait is reproduced as the frontispiece to *Life and Letters*. The self-portrait sketch is in the London Metropolitan Archive.

30 Severn to Thomas Severn, 5 July 1822, *Letters and Memoirs*, pp. 205–6.

31 Robertson, *Sir Charles Eastlake*, p. 35, n. 53; and William Ewing to Severn, 29 September 1821, Houghton Library, Harvard bMS 1434 (63).

32 Severn to Thomas Severn, 5 July 1822, *Letters and Memoirs*, pp. 202–3.

33 'Incidents of My Life No 15', and Severn to Thomas Severn, 5 July 1822, *Letters and Memoirs*, pp. 595 and 203.

34 'Incidents of My Life No 15', *Letters and Memoirs*, pp. 596–7.

35 Severn to Thomas Severn, 5 July 1822, and Maria Severn, August [1822], *Letters and Memoirs*, pp. 203 and 209.

36 Severn to Maria Severn, August [1822], *Letters and Memoirs*, p. 211.

37 *Joseph Gott 1786–1860 Sculptor*, ed. Terry Friedman and Timothy Stevens (Leeds and Liverpool: exhibition catalogue, 1972), p. 41; and Severn to James Severn, 7 December 1822, LMA, KPM/S 472.

38 Severn to Sarah Severn, 23 March 1823, *Letters and Memoirs*, p. 234.

39 Hunt to Severn, 16 December 1822, *Letters and Memoirs*, p. 223.

40 Severn used this splendidly evocative phrase in his letters to both Hunt and Brown reporting on the proceedings: *Letters and Memoirs*, pp. 227 and 231.

41 Severn to Hunt, 21 January 1823, *Letters and Memoirs*, p. 231.

42 Severn to Brown, 9 April 1823, *Letters and Memoirs*, pp. 237–8.

43 Severn to Brown, 7 December 1822 and 21 January 1823, *Letters and Memoirs*, pp. 219 and 228.

44 Severn to Haslam, 1 June 1823, *Letters and Memoirs*, p. 242.

45 Taylor to John Clare, 9 March 1821, quoted in E. Blunden, *Keats's Publisher: A Memoir of John Taylor (1781–1864)* (London: Jonathan Cape, 1936), p. 88.

46 Severn to Haslam, 5 May, *Letters and Memoirs*, p. 156 and 12 July 1821, *Keats Circle*, i, p. 252.

47 Brown to Severn, 28 August 1821, *Letters of Charles Brown*, p. 91.

48 Severn to Brown, 1 January 1822, *Letters of Charles Brown*, p. 97.

49 Severn to Brown, 26 October 1822, *Letters and Memoirs*, p. 216.

50 Brown to Severn, 7 November 1822, *Letters of Charles Brown*, pp. 106–7.

51 W. St Clair, *Trelawny: The Incurable Romancer* (London: John Murray, 1977), p. 82.

52 Severn to Haslam, 12 July, *Keats Circle*, i, p. 252, and 5 May 1821, *Letters and Memoirs*, p. 156.

53 See J. C. Franklin, 'Once More the Poet: Keats, Severn and the Grecian Lyre', *Keats–Shelley Review*, 18 (2004), 104–22.

Chapter 9 'Searching for Fame and Fortune'

 1 Severn's unpublished manuscript 'The Appian Journey', Houghton Library, Harvard, Keats MS 4.16.5.
 2 Severn to Hunt, 26 June 1823, *Letters and Memoirs*, p. 244.
 3 Severn to Brown, 26 October 1822, *Letters and Memoirs*, p. 217.
 4 Brown to Thomas Richards, 11 January 1823, *Letters of Charles Brown*, p. 116.
 5 Bodleian Library, Oxford, Finch Papers d.15 t.4, Severn to Finch, 4 October 1824.
 6 Severn to Sarah Severn, 27 June 1823, *Letters and Memoirs*, p. 246. For Severn's subsequent revival of this falsehood see below pp. 318–19 and note 47 on p. 389.
 7 Brown's two articles about this expedition in the *New Monthly Magazine* in 1825 are reprinted in *Some Letters and Miscellanea of Charles Brown the Friend of Keats & Thomas Richards*, ed. M. B. Forman (London: Oxford University Press, 1937), pp. 59–81.
 8 Keats to George and Georgiana Keats, 31 December 1818, *Letters*, ii, p. 19; Brown to Thomas Richards, 22 August 1823, *Letters of Charles Brown*, p. 135; Houghton Library, Severn Scrapbook f.66 r, Harvard MS Eng 1460.
 9 Severn to Maria Severn, 23 August 1823, LMA, KPM/S 475.
10 A. Gilchrist, *The Life of William Etty R.A.*, 2 vols (London: David Bogne, 1855), pp. 118–19.
11 Severn to Hunt, 3 September 1823, and Brown and Severn to Finch, 3 September 1823, *Letters of Charles Brown*, pp. 139 and 137.
12 Brown to Finch, 22 September 1823, *Letters of Charles Brown*, p. 141.
13 Brown to Thomas Richards, 27 October 1823, in Forman, *Some Letters and Miscellanea*, p. 39.
14 E. Blunden, *Leigh Hunt: A Biography* (London: Cobden-Sanderson, 1930), p. 209.
15 Brown to Thomas Richards, 21 and 27 October 1823, in Forman, *Some Letters and Miscellanea*, pp. 39–40.
16 Severn to Sarah Severn, 11 January 1824, LMA, KPM/S 478.
17 Charles Brown, 'The Wishing Cap No. XVI', 'Actors and Artists at Rome', *The Examiner*, 3 October 1824, 626–8.
18 Severn to Thomas Severn, 11 January 1824, *Letters and Memoirs*, p. 249.
19 Richard Westmacott came across Johnnie in Florence in May 1824 and found him a little chastened: 'our old plague . . looked very ill . . altho' he tried to bolt up to me with his taking, innocent-sounding "Ah! how d'ye do, Sir?" I saw he made himself scarce as soon as possible': Westmacott to Severn, 20 May 1824, *Life and Letters*, p. 142. Predictably, John Hunt came to a bad end, pestering Leigh Hunt's grander friends for money as an adult, trading on the Hunt name in some controversial journalism, and dying of TB in 1846, leaving his wife and three children destitute. His parents did not mourn the loss of their most troublesome child. See E. M. Gates, ed., *Leigh Hunt: A Life in Letters together with some Correspondence of William Hazlitt* (Essex, CT: Falls River Press, 2000), p. 445.
20 Severn to Sarah Severn, 2 March 1824, LMA, KPM/S 479.
21 Severn to Thomas Severn, 15 December 1823, LMA, KPM/S 476.
22 Severn to Maria Severn, 10 April 1824, LMA, KPM/S 480.

23 There is a reference in Brown's letter to Severn of 17 March 1835 to having seen one of Severn's children, suggesting that, in addition to Brown's visit to Rome with Dilke in 1826 and Severn's journey to Florence in 1828, there was another meeting, most probably in Rome: *New Letters from Charles Brown* (39).

24 Brown to Severn, 18 June 1826, *New Letters from Charles Brown*. For details of this transaction see Sue Brown 'Fresh Light on the Friendship of Charles Brown and Joseph Severn', *Keats–Shelley Review*, 18 (2004), 145–6.

25 Quoted in C. Powell, *Turner in the South: Rome, Naples, Florence* (New Haven and London: Yale University Press, 1987), p. 72; Marquis d'Azeglio, *Things I Remember*, trans. and introd. E. R. P. Vincent (London: Oxford University Press, 1966), pp. 274–8; T. Landseer, ed., *Life and Letters of William Bewick (Artist)*, 2 vols (London, Hurst and Blackett, 1871), ii, p. 67.

26 D'Azeglio, *Things I Remember*, p. 226.

27 Lord William Russell to Severn, 23 January 1826, Houghton Library, Harvard bMS Eng 1434 (208).

28 L. Hunt, *The Autobiography of Leigh Hunt; with Reminiscences of Friends and Contemporaries* (Oxford: Oxford University Press [World's Classics series], 1923), p. 434.

29 Severn to Finch, 4 October 1824, Bodleian Library, Oxford, Finch Papers d.15 f.3.

30 'Incidents of My Life', *Letters and Memoirs*, p. 605.

31 In 'Incidents' Severn identifies his friend as Thomas Uwins but Uwins did not arrive in Rome until late October 1824. It may possibly have been Ewing who helped him out. For the portrait of Mrs Erskine, see the sketch dated 30 August 1824 in Houghton Library, Severn Scrapbook, Harvard MS Eng 1460 f 45 v.

32 Severn to Brown, 27 September 1824, *Letters and Memoirs*, p. 259; Brown to Severn, 5 November 1824, *New Letters from Charles Brown* (8); Severn to Maria Severn, 4 October 1824, *Letters and Memoirs*, p. 261; and Severn to Finch, 4 October 1824, Bodleian Library, Oxford, Finch Papers d.15 f.4.

33 Thomas Uwins to Zaccharia Uwins, 3 December 1824 and to D Uwins, 30 September 1826, in *Memoir of T. Uwins*, pp. 234 and 351.

34 Ibid., p. 191. Severn to Uwins, 4 August 1827, Severn to Uwins, 1 December 1825, and Uwins to Severn, 10 December 1825, ibid., pp. 212, 198–9 and 200–5.

35 Brown to Severn, 12 February 1825, *Letters of Charles Brown*, p. 214.

36 Lady Compton to Severn, 16 July 1827, Houghton Library, Harvard bMS Eng 1434 (39).

37 Brown to Severn, 23 February 1825, *New Letters from Charles Brown*.

38 W. Hazlitt, *Notes of a Journey through France and Italy [By W.H.]* (London: H Colborne, 1826), pp. 277–9.

39 See Brown to Severn, 18 and 27 June 1826, *Letters of Charles Brown*, and Crabb Robinson's account of a conversation with Severn on 1 June 1830: 'S knows Hazlitt by whom as might be expected he was ill treated': vol. 17 of Crabb Robinson's ms. diaries in Dr Williams Library. Robinson, an early fan of Hazlitt's later quarrelled with him and was always avid to hear ill of him.

40 Severn to Vincent Novello, 7 June 1830, *Letters and Memoirs*, pp. 308–10.

41 W. Hazlitt, *Complete Works*, vol. 17: *Uncollected Essays*, ed. P. P. Howe (London: J. M. Dent, 1933), pp. 134–42.

42 Brown to Severn, 2 January 1827, *New Letters from Charles Brown* (21).

43 Wilkie to his sister, 21 January 1826 and to Thomas Wilkie, 31 January 1826, in A. Cunningham, *The Life of Sir David Wilkie with his Journals, Tours and Critical Remarks on Works of Art*, 3 vols (London: John Murray, 1843), ii, pp. 225 and 231.

44 Severn to Thomas Severn, 21 November 1825 and Severn to Maria Severn, 4 October 1824, *Letters and Memoirs*, pp. 268 and 262.

45 Brown to Thomas Richards, 27 October 1823, *Letters of Charles Brown*, p. 145; and C. W. Dilke, *The Papers of a Critic Selected from the Writings of the Late Charles Wentworth Dilke, with a Biographical Sketch by his Grandson*, 2 vols (London: John Murray, 1875), i, p. 17.

46 David Wilkie to his sister 1 January 1827, in Cunningham, *The Life of Sir David Wilkie*, ii, p. 383.

47 William Bewick to W. Davison, 17 November 1850, in Landseer, *Life and Letters of William Bewick (Artist)*, ii, p. 150.

48 Wilkie to Sir James McGregor, 1826 and Wilkie to William Tait, 10 December 1826, in Cunningham, *The Life of Sir David Wilkie*, ii, pp. 217 and 381.

Chapter 10 Love, Marriage, and Persecution

1 Severn to Thomas Severn, 15 July 1827, *Letters and Memoirs*, p. 277 and Severn to Charles Severn, [1 January] 1827, LMA, KPM/S 491.

2 William Ewing to Severn, 29 September 1821 and 20 February 1823 and Thomas Severn to Severn, 24 June 1827, Houghton Library, Harvard bMS Eng 1434 (63), (64), and (230).

3 Severn to Maria Severn, 12 December 1825, *Letters and Memoirs*, p. 273.

4 Severn to Maria Severn, 14 January 1828 and to James Severn, 4 December 1827, LMA KPM/S 490 and 493.

5 Severn to Sarah Severn, 27 June 1823, *Letters and Memoirs*, p. 246. This statement attracted a highly critical assessment of Severn in an influential article by B. Ifor Evans, 'Keats and Joseph Severn: a Re-Estimate with Unpublished Letters', *London Mercury*, 30 (August 1934), 337–49. By omitting the underlinings and the last word, however, Evans gives a distorted view of the purpose of Severn's credo.

6 Thomas Severn to Severn, 24 June 1827, Houghton Library, Harvard bMS Eng 1434 (230).

7 Thomas Severn to Severn, 24 June 1827, Houghton Library, Harvard bMS Eng 1434 (230). Sarah Severn's married name is given in a pencilled note in an unknown hand tucked into the travelling case of the Severn family miniature at Keats House as Mrs Haynes Bailey. The IGI, however, offers no information on the date of her marriage or death, which may have resulted from a risky late pregnancy.

8 Severn to Thomas Uwins, 24 October 1829, *Letters and Memoirs*, p. 297.

9 Brown to Severn, 9 August 1825, *New Letters from Charles Brown* (11).

10 Severn to Thomas Severn, 21 November 1825, *Letters and Memoirs*, p. 270.

11 Severn to Thomas Severn, 26 May 1827 and to Maria Severn, 14 January 1828, LMA, KPM/S 492 and 490.

12 Severn to Sarah Severn, 9 December 1824, LMA, KPM/S 485; Severn to Thomas Severn, 15 July 1827, *Letters and Memoirs*, p. 282.

13 Brown to Severn, 18 June 1826, *New Letters from Charles Brown* (17).

14 Severn to Maria Severn, 12 December 1825, and to Thomas Severn, 15 July 1827, *Letters and Memoirs*, pp. 275 and 283; Brown to Severn, 2 February 1826, *New Letters from Charles Brown* (14).

15 G. Ticknor, *Life, Letters and Journals*, ed. G. S. Hillard, 2 vols (London: Sampson Low, 1876), ii, p. 68.

16 Severn to Thomas Severn, 15 July 1827, *Letters and Memoirs*, p. 282. Compare William Bewick's description of the typical quarters of English art students in Rome: 'his studio a comfortless room, with one window; the walls being coloured grey with soot and whiting, and as dirty as a workshop, with a cold brick floor, no better than our stables. His bedroom is without fire, without curtains, without carpet': Bewick to Bessy Bewick, 1 January 1828, in T. Landseer, ed., *Life and Letters of William Bewick (Artist)*, 2 vols (London: Hurst and Blackett, 1871), ii, p. 81.

17 Richard Westmacott to Severn, 20 May 1824, *Life and Letters*, p. 142.

18 A detailed account of her stay in Italy from 1827–8 is at the Bodleian Library, Oxford, MS Eng d. 2278.

19 Severn to Charles Severn, [1 January] 1827, LMA, KPM/S 491.

20 J. Pope-Hennessy, *Monckton Milnes: The Years of Promise* (London: Constable, 1949), p. 41.

21 Severn to Charles Severn, [1 January] 1827, LMA, KPM/S 491; Ilchester, ed., *The Journals of the Hon. H. E. Fox (afterwards fourth and last Lord Holland) 1818–1830* (London: Thornton Butterworth, 1923), pp. 273 and 312. Severn also described the scene in a letter to Vincent Novello on 8 March 1828, telling him that his music, whose performance Severn directed, 'produced a magical effect': BL Add. MS, Novello Papers, 11730 f 176. For descriptions of Lady Westmorland's tableaux see William Bewick to 'friends at home', 29 January 1827, in Landseer, ed., *Life and Letters of William Bewick*, ii, pp. 38–40; 'My Tedious Life', *Letters and Memoirs*, p. 657; and David Wilkie to his sister, 22 March 1827, in A. Cunningham, *The Life of Sir David Wilkie with his Journals, Tours and Critical Remarks on Works of Art*, 3 vols (London: John Murray, 1843), ii, p. 409.

22 This attractive picture now hangs in the Royal Palace, Brussels.

23 Severn to Thomas Severn, 26 May 1827, LMA, KPM/S 492; Ilchester, *The Journals of the Hon. H. E. Fox*, p. 244; 'My Tedious Life', *Letters and Memoirs*, pp. 655–6.

24 Severn to Sarah Severn, 9 December 1824, to Maria Severn, 14 January 1828, and to James Severn, 4 December 1824, LMA, KPM/S 485, 490, and 495; Ilchester, *The Journals of the Hon. H. E. Fox*, p. 248.

25 S. Birkenhead, *Against Oblivion: The Life of Joseph Severn* (London: Cassell and Company, 1943), p. 133.

26 For a fascinating account of the fortunes of the Eglinton family see I. Anstruther, *The Knight and the Umbrella: An Account of the Eglinton Tournament 1839* (London: Geoffrey Bles, 1963). Anstruther is, however, incorrect in giving Elizabeth Montgomerie's birth date as 1812 and saying that she was born in the same week as her legitimate half-brother Archie. In the 1851 census return her age is given as forty-seven.

27 *Life and Letters*, p. 151.

28 They still survive in the Charlton MS in an envelope ponderously marked by their youngest son, Arthur, 'Old Letters from the Mater and Pater!'.

29 Severn to Thomas Severn, 15 July 1827, *Letters and Memoirs*, p. 278.

30 'My Tedious Life', *Letters and Memoirs*, p. 658.

31 The marriage certificate is in the Rose Wild collection.

32 Kirkup to Severn, 6 November 1828, *Letters and Memoirs*, p. 290; Brown to Severn, 13 December 1828, *New Letters from Charles Brown* (28).

33 Lady Compton to Severn, 18 October 1828, Houghton Library, Harvard bMS Eng 1434 (179).

Notes

34 Eastlake to 'a friend at Liverpool', February 1829, W. T. Whitley, *Art in England 1820–37* (Cambridge: Cambridge University Press, 1930), p. 159.

35 Trelawny to Severn, 21 June 1829, *Life and Letters*, p. 158.

36 Kirkup to Severn, 6 November 1828, *Letters and Memoirs*, pp. 289–91.

37 'My Tedious Life', *Letters and Memoirs*, p. 658.

38 Severn to Brown n.d. but endorsed by Brown 'ansd. 29 March 1828', LMA, KPM/S 90. In his memoirs Severn misremembered that this happened after his marriage.

39 Brown to Severn, 5 September 1829, *New Letters from Charles Brown* (30).

40 Uwins to Severn, 13 August 1829, *Letters and Memoirs*, p. 294.

41 *Life and Letters*, p. 290.

42 J. Cobbett, *Journal of a Tour in Italy and also in Parts of France and Switzerland from October 1828 to September 1829* (London: Mills, 1830), pp. 270–1.

43 Severn got his medal back and listed it among his assets in 1840. It may well have fallen victim to his need for cash in the 1850s, however, as it was not among his possessions at the time of his death.

44 *Life and Letters*, pp. 153–5.

45 For information on Weld see 'My Tedious Life', *Letters and Memoirs*, pp. 658–9; Pope-Hennessey, *Richard Monckton Milnes: The Years of Promise*; Ilchester, *The Journals of the Hon. H. E. Fox*; and C. S. Isaacson, *The Story of the English Cardinals* (London: Elliot Stock, 1907).

46 'My Tedious Life', *Letters and Memoirs*, p. 661.

47 Severn to Mary Novello, 9 November 1833, *Letters and Memoirs*, p. 332; F. Bunsen, *A Memoir of Baron Bunsen*, 2 vols (London: Longmans, 1868), pp. 241–7.

48 Bunsen to Neibuhr, 17 February 1825, in Bunsen, *Memoir of Baron Bunsen*, i, p. 256.

49 See Finch's appointments diaries for 1829 and 1830, Bodlean Library, Oxford, Finch Papers; Kirkup to Severn, 26 October 1830, *Letters and Memoirs*, p. 312.

50 Or so he said in recalling that his friendship 'in great part arose from the delight she had in Keats's poetry'. There is, however, nothing in Lady Compton's surviving correspondence with Scott from Italy in the National Library of Scotland to support this, nor Severn's claim that he had 'been indirectly made well known' to Scott as a result of her monthly letters to him which 'often made mention of me': 'On the Adversities of Keats's Fame', *Letters and Memoirs*, pp. 618–19.

51 R. Pemberton Milnes, *Notes of a Tour by Mrs Milnes, Myself and Our Daughter from Milan to Naples, and by Rome and Florence to Milan AD 1831* (privately printed, n.d.), pp. 70–1: BL C.193.a.90.

52 'My Tedious Life', *Letters and Memoirs*, p. 601. When Maria Callcott fell ill in Rome 'dear Miss Leach' became a frequent caller: 'Journal of Italian Tour 1827–8', Bodleian Library, Oxford, MS Eng d. 2278.

53 Thomas Uwins to Zachary Uwins, July 1827, in S. Uwins, *A Memoir of Thomas Uwins R.A.*, 2 vols (London: Longman, Brown, 1858), ii, pp. 54–5.

54 Severn to Elizabeth Severn, 8 May 1833, *Letters and Memoirs*, p. 320 and Severn to Elizabeth Severn, 13 July 1838, Townsend MS. On Victorian marital reticence in sexual matters see J. Tosh, *A Man's Place: Masculinity and the Middle-Class Home in Victorian England* (New Haven and London: Yale University Press, 1999), p. 57.

55 Brown to Severn, 16 April 1831, *New Letters from Charles Brown* (33).

56 Severn to Brown, 15 April 1830, *Letters of Charles Brown*, p. 316.
57 Severn, quoted in *Life and Letters*, p. 168.

Chapter 11 'Everybody's Man and a Very Obliging Creature': Severn in his Roman Prime

1 Evans to Lawrence, 25 April 1825, RA Archive, LAW/41/321.
2 Kirkup to Lawrence, 20 December 1824, RA Archive, LAW/4/281.
3 Maria Callcott's unpublished diary of her visit to Rome in 1828–9 gives an example of a typical dinner party at which the guests were Kestner, the Hanoverian Minister, Mrs Bunsen, Havell, Severn, Wyatt, Williams, and Gibson. Bodleian Library, Oxford, MS Eng d. 2278, 40 (5 March 1828).
4 Severn to Kirkup, 20 August 1833, *Letters and Memoirs*, p. 326
5 Eastlake to Severn, 12 August [1831], Houghton Library, Harvard, bMS Eng 1434 (50).
6 Eastlake to Severn, 7 May 1834, MS: Houghton Library, Harvard, bMS Eng 1434 (52).
7 Uwins to Zachary Uwins, 3 December 1824, in *Memoir of Thomas Uwins*, i, p. 237.
8 It was eventually bought by Sir Charles Lamb, the Earl of Eglinton's stepfather. Westmacott to Severn, June 1832 and 27 September 1832, Houghton Library, Harvard, bMS Eng 1434 (258) and (259); and *Life and Letters*, p. 167.
9 Eastlake to Severn, 5 May 1828, [1832] and 7 May 1834. MS: Houghton Library, Harvard, bMS Eng 1434 (49), (51), and (52), and Severn to Kirkup, 20 August 1833, *Letters and Memoirs*, pp. 327–8.
10 Kathleen Wells, 'The Return of the British Painters to Rome after 1815', p. 124.
11 'Strictures on Pictures', *Fraser's Magazine*, 17 (June 1838), p. 762.
12 Uwins to Severn, 17 August 1831, *Memoir of Thomas Uwins*, ii, p. 257.
13 Brown to Severn, 17 September 1833, *New Letters from Charles Brown* (35); Westmacott to Severn, June [15] 1832, *Life and Letters*, p. 172; and Severn to Kirkup, 20 August 1833, *Letters and Memoirs*, p. 327.
14 Severn to Kirkup, 20 August 1833, *Letters and Memoirs*, p. 328.
15 Lord Ilchester, ed., *The Journal of the Hon. H.E. Fox (afterwards fourth and last Lord Holland) 1818–1830* (London: Thornton Butterworth, 1923), p. 347 (2 July 1829).
16 Severn to Uwins, 4 August 1827, in *Memoir of Thomas Uwins*, ii, pp. 212–13.
17 Severn to Uwins, 28 May 1829, ibid., ii, p. 233.
18 See the unpublished travel diary of Maria Callcott, Bodleian Library, Oxford, MS Eng d. 2278.
19 *Letters and Memoirs*, p. 19.
20 Eastlake to Severn, 5 January 1834, reporting a conversation between one of Severn's brothers and a banker from Naples, Houghton Library, Harvard bMS Eng 1434 (53).
21 Eastlake to Lawrence, 9 December 1828, RA Archive, LAW/5/287.
22 Uwins to Severn, 28 July 1829, *Memoir of Thomas Uwins*, ii, p. 242.
23 C. Powell, *Turner in the South: Rome, Naples, Florence* (New Haven and London: Yale University Press, 1987), p. 142.
24 Amongst his showings at the Royal Academy were *A Roman Peasant Girl Praying* (1828), *Sicilian Peasants Singing the Evening Hymn to the Virgin* (1830), and *The Roman Ave Maria* (1840).

25 'A Pictorial Rhapsody: Concluded' by Michael Angelo Titmarsh Esquire, *Fraser's Magazine*, July 1840.

26 Severn to Finch, 26 February 1830, E. Nitchie, *'The Reverend Colonel Finch'* (New York: Columbia University Press, 1940), p. 67.

27 'A Second Lecture on the Fine Arts' by Michael Angelo Titmarsh Esquire, *Fraser's Magazine*, June 1839.

28 *The Gladstone Diaries*, ed. M. R. D. Foot and H. C. G. Matthew (Oxford: Clarendon Press, 1968; vols. 1–2 ed. M. R. D. Foot), ii, p. 527 (15 December 1838).

29 'No epic work since the *Aeneid* had so great a cultural impact on Europe': R. Cavaliero, *Italia Romantica* (London: I.B.Tauris, 2005), p. 69.

30 *Life and Letters*, p. 182.

31 Severn to Elizabeth Severn, 8 January 1841, *Letters and Memoirs*, p. 396.

32 Severn to Elizabeth Severn, 12 January 1840, *Letters and Memoirs*, pp. 399–400.

33 *Gladstone Diaries*, i, pp. 474, 510, and 513 (16 April, and 2 and 4 June 1832).

34 Ibid., i, pp. 446 and 468 (? March and 2 April 1832).

35 He 'was a keen admirer of both facile and perfect manipulation of material. It pleased him to see difficulties overcome', W. Richmond, *George Richmond: The Richmond Papers, from the Correspondence and Manuscripts of G. Richmond R.A., and His Son, Sir William Richmond*, ed. A. M. W. Stirling (London: William Heinemann, 1926), p. 220. Richmond, the son of George Richmond and himself a painter, often accompanied Gladstone to the galleries in his later years and left an interesting account of his artistic tastes.

36 For an illuminating examination of Gladstone's development, see M. Pointon, 'W. E. Gladstone as an Art Patron and Collector', *Victorian Studies*, 19 (1975), 73–98.

37 *Gladstone Diaries*, i, p. 514 (2 June 1832). The reference to 'beauty and decay' is taken from line 55 of *Adonais*.

38 Nor did he include it in the list he drew up in 1878 of artists and sculptors for whom he had sat. Glynne-Gladstone Mss 2105, St Deiniol's Library Hawarden.

39 Though it is undated, Gladstone's age is given on the frame as twenty-four. In fact, he was only twenty-two at the time of his first visit to Rome. Severn's portrait predates the much better known oil sketch of Gladstone and his brothers by George Hayter done in preparation for the group portrait of the members of the 1833 Parliament.

40 Pointon, 'W. E. Gladstone as an Art Patron and Collector', 80–1.

41 *Gladstone Diaries*, ii, p. 524 (13 December 1838).

42 Ibid., ii, pp. 527 (15 December 1838), 548 (3 January 1839), and 556 (9 January 1839).

43 In fairness to Severn he does say in 'Incidents of My Life No 15', that it was Shelley's *Adonais* that drew Gladstone to him: *Letters and Memoirs*, p. 592. Though *Adonais* is not included in Gladstone's reading list his quotation from it in his diary entry for 2 June 1832 shows that he was aware of it when he first met Severn. Elsewhere, however, Severn states unequivocally that the attraction was Keats. See Severn to Mrs Philip Speed, 1 September 1863, *Keats Circle*, ii, pp. 324–5, and Severn to Maria Severn, 23 April 1875, *Letters and Memoirs*, p. 545.

44 *Gladstone Diaries*, i, pp. 470–1 (12 April 1832).

45 'On the Adversities of Keats's Fame', *Letters and Memoirs*, pp. 619–20.

46 Walter Scott, *The Journal of Sir Walter Scott*, ed. W. E. K. Anderson (Oxford: Clarendon Press, 1972), p. 693.

47 In 'On the Adversities of Keats's Fame', Severn compounded the error of his account of Scott's time in Rome by claiming that Scott himself had been editor of the *Quarterly Review*.

Notes

48 Maria Callcott, 'Journal of Italian Tour, 1827–8', Bodleian Library, Oxford, MS Eng d. 2278.

49 W. Allingham, *A Diary*, ed. H. Allingham and D. Radford (London: Macmillan & Co., 1907), p. 295.

50 A. and W. Galignani, with Cyrus Redding, *The Poetical Works of Coleridge Shelley and Keats* (Paris: Galignani, 1829), p. vi.

51 Fanny Brawne to Brown, 29 December 1829, in J. Richardson, *Fanny Brawne* (London: Vanguard Press, 1952), pp. 120–2.

52 Brown, quoted in C. Brown, *Life of John Keats*, ed. D. H. Bodurtha and W. B. Pope (London: Oxford University Press, 1937), p. 10.

53 Severn to Brown, 17 January 1830, and Brown to Severn, February 1830, *Life and Letters*, pp. 162 and 160–1.

54 Severn's designs for this bas-relief are reproduced in *Letters and Memoirs*, pp. 304–5.

55 Severn to Brown, 15 April 1830, *Letters and Memoirs*, pp. 303–6. Despite Severn's critical view of Hunt's impact on Keats, the two remained on amicable terms. In 1833 Severn was one of the initial subscribers to a limited edition of Leigh Hunt's poems designed to raise money for him: *The Times*, 1 February 1833.

56 See Brown to Severn, 17 September 1833, *New Letters from Charles Brown* (35).

57 Severn to Brown, 14 March 1834, *The Letters of Charles Brown*, p. 333.

58 J. Richardson, *The Everlasting Spell: A Study of Keats and his Friends* (London: Jonathan Cape, 1963), p. 79; Brown to Severn, 3 October 1832, *The Letters of Charles Brown*, p. 327.

59 Quoted in H. E. Rollins, *Keats' Reputation in America to 1848* (Cambridge, MA: Harvard University Press, 1946), p. 50.

60 Trench to William B. Donne, 18 February 1830, in R. C. Trench, *Letters and Memorials*, ed. C. Lowder, 2 vols (London: Kegan Paul, 1888), i, pp. 51 and 52.

61 Diary entry for 22 January 1831, in H. C. Robinson, *On Books and Their Writers*, ed. E. J. Morley, 3 vols (London: J. M. Dent, 1938), p. 390.

62 R. M. Milnes, *Life, Letters and Literary Remains of John Keats* (London: J. M. Dent, 1927), p. 3.

63 Severn to R. M. Milnes, 6 October 1845, *Keats Circle*, ii, p. 132.

64 Severn to Brown, 14 March 1834, *Letters and Memoirs*, pp. 333–4, and Brown to Severn (fragment), *New Letters from Charles Brown* (37).

65 It did not receive its first performance until 26 November 1951 in a fog-filled St Martin's Theatre London. The audience was enthusiastic, the critics less so: *Keats–Shelley Memorial Bulletin*, 4, p. 1.

66 Severn to Brown, 14 March 1834, *Letters and Memoirs*, p. 334.

67 A. Hallam, *The Writings of Arthur Hallam*, ed. T. H. Vail Motter (London: Oxford University Press, 1943), pp. 188 and 184.

68 Severn to Brown, 13 July 1836, *Letters and Memoirs*, p. 337.

69 Brown to Severn, 26 November 1836, *Life and Letters*, p. 178.

70 John Taylor took the same view as Brown, estimating in 1835 that if he brought out a new edition of Keats's poetry he would be lucky to sell 250 copies: E. Blunden, *Shelley and Keats as They Struck their Contemporaries: Notes Partly from Manuscript Sources* (London: C. W. Beaumont, 1925), p. 82.

71 Severn to Brown, 13 July 1836, *Letters and Memoirs*, p. 338.

72 Dyce to J. R. Hope-Scott, 17 September 1840, in M. Pointon, *William Dyce, 1806–1864: A Critical Biography* (Oxford: Clarendon Press, 1979), p. 14.

73 Trelawny to Severn, 21 June 1829, *Life and Letters*, pp. 158–9.

74 Eastlake to Severn, 2 September [1828], Houghton Library, Harvard bMS Eng 1434 (58).

75 Brown to Hunt, 1 January 1830, *The Letters of Charles Brown*, p. 320.

76 *Life and Letters*, p. 294.

77 Uwins to Severn, 20 November 1827, in *Memoir of Thomas Uwins*, ii, p. 221.

78 Richmond, *Richmond Papers*, p. 43.

79 R. Lister, *George Richmond: A Critical Biography* (London: Garton, 1981), p. 80.

80 Severn to Mary Novello, 9 November 1833, *Letters and Memoirs*, p. 332.

81 Severn to Brown, 13 July 1836, *Letters and Memoirs*, p. 336.

82 Elizabeth Severn to Mrs Elizabeth Severn, June 1834, LMA, KPM/S 495.

83 E. J. Morley, *The Life and Times of Henry Crabb Robinson* (London: Dent, 1935), p. 84.

84 Henry Crabb Robinson ms diaries, vol. 25 (30 April 1837), London, Dr Williams Library.

85 William Wordsworth to Dorothy Wordsworth, May 1837, in W. Wordsworth, *The Letters of William and Dorothy Wordworth: The Later Years (1821–1850)*, 3 vols, ed. Ernest de Selincourt (Oxford: Clarendon Press, 1939), ii, p. 856.

86 Now sadly lost.

87 Robinson, *Books and Writers*, ed. Morley, ii, p. 520.

88 Severn to Brown, 13 July 1836, *Letters and Memoirs*, p. 337.

89 Severn to Brown, 9 April 1837, *Letters and Memoirs*, p. 339.

Chapter 12 Going Home

1 Copy of Protestant Cemetery burial register, 1765–1841: information from Catherine Payling.

2 Mary Shelley's account of the cholera outbreak is in M. Shelley, *Rambles in Germany and Italy Part III 1842 and 1843*, repr. in Jeanne Moskal, ed., *The Novels and Selected Works of Mary Shelley*, vol. 8: *Travel Writing* (London: William Pickering, 1996), pp. 355–7 (Letter 20, May 3 [1843]). Severn's is in 'Incidents of My Life: The Roman Cholera', *Life and Letters*, pp. 179–83.

3 'My First Commission for a Picture', *Letters and Memoirs*, pp. 602–3.

4 'Incidents of My Life', *Life and Letters*, p. 180.

5 Severn to Brown, 21 November 1837, *Letters and Memoirs*, pp. 346–7.

6 *Joseph Gott 1786–1860 Sculptor*, ed. T. Friedman and T. Stevens (Leeds and Liverpool: exhibition catalogue, 1972), pp. 62–7.

7 Severn to Brown, 21 November 1837, and Severn to Thomas Severn, 9 April 1837, *Letters and Memoirs*, pp. 347 and 340.

8 Bunsen to Severn, 16 and 24 January 1837, Houghton Library, Harvard bMS Eng 1434 (20) and (21).

9 Severn to Brown, 17 January 1830, *Letters and Memoirs*, p. 299.

10 D. P. Webley, *Cast to the Winds: The Life and Work of Penry Williams (1802–1885)* (Aberystwyth: National Library of Wales, 1997), p. 4.

11 K. Wells, 'The Return of the British Artists to Rome' (University of Leicester PhD dissertation, 1984), pp. 114–21 and 127.

12 Collins to Wilkie, 9 March 1838, in W. Wilkie Collins, *Memoirs of the Life of William Collins RA*, 2 vols (London: Longman, 1848), ii, p. 133.

13 Severn to Kirkup, 20 August 1833, *Letters and Memoirs*, p. 326.

14 For an amusing account of the event, efficiently organized by the German artists in 1837, see J. Dafforne, *The Life and Works of Edward Matthew Ward R A* (London: Virtue & Co, [1879]), pp. 9–10.

15 Severn to Kirkup, 20 August 1833, *Letters and Memoirs*, pp. 326–7; Trench to F. D. Maurice, 20 February 1835, in R. C. Trench, *Letters and Memorials*, ed. Charles Lowder, 2 vols (London: Kegan Paul, 1888), i, p. 184.

16 Severn to Brown, 21 November 1837, *Letters and Memoirs*, p. 347, Severn to Elizabeth Severn, 6 August 1839, Townsend MS.

17 W. Richmond, *George Richmond: The Richmond Papers, from the Correspondence and Manuscripts of G. Richmond R.A., and His Son, Sir William Richmond*, ed. A. M. W. Stirling (London: William Heinemann, 1926) perpetuated the myth that Severn and Richmond were fellow-students at the Royal Academy. Richmond, who was sixteen years younger than Severn, did not arrive there until 1823. Severn did, however, have friends in common with both Richmond and Palmer, including Crabb Robinson and Linnell, who had engraved one of Severn's portraits of Keats.

18 J. B. Atlay, *Sir Henry Wentworth Acland, Bart. K.C.B., F.R.S. A Memoir* (London: Smith Elder, 1903), p. 57.

19 Palmer to Linnell, quoted in R. Lister, *Samuel Palmer: His Life and Art* (Cambridge: Cambridge University Press. 1987), p. 113.

20 RA Archive, George Richmond MS Diaries, 22 March, 10, 11, and 21 February and 10 March 1839. Ruskin is quoted in R. Lister, *George Richmond: A Critical Biography* (London: Garton, 1981), p. 62.

21 Thomas Severn to Severn, 20 January 1831, Houghton Library, Harvard bMS Eng 1460 (231).

22 Severn to Elizabeth Severn, 20 June 1838, *Letters and Memoirs*, p. 356.

23 Severn to Elizabeth Severn, 22 June 1838, *Letters and Memoirs*, pp. 356–9.

24 Severn to Elizabeth Severn, 22 June 1838, *Letters and Memoirs*, pp. 357–8, and 13 July 1838, MS Townsend.

25 Severn to Elizabeth Severn, 8 July 1838, *Letters and Memoirs*, p. 365.

26 Severn to Elizabeth Severn, 1 July 1838, *Letters and Memoirs*, p. 361.

27 Severn to Elizabeth Severn, 1 August 1838, MS Townsend.

28 Severn to Elizabeth Severn, 8 July 1838, *Letters and Memoirs*, p. 364, and 1 August 1838, MS Townsend.

29 Severn to Elizabeth Severn, 13 and 26 August 1838, MS Townsend.

30 Brown to Severn, 2 June 1838, *Life and Letters*, p. 186; Severn to Brown, 21 August 1838, *Letters and Memoirs*, p. 373; Brown to Severn, 23 August 1838, *Life and Letters*, pp. 186–7; Severn to Brown, 21 August 1838, *Letters and Memoirs*, p. 373.

31 Severn to Elizabeth Severn, 1 August 1838, MS Townsend; Severn to Gladstone, 3 August 1838, *Letters and Memoirs*, pp. 371–2. The sketch is now in Tate Britain.

32 Severn to Elizabeth Severn, 24 July, 9 June, 8 July, and 24 July 1838, MS Townsend.

33 Severn to Elizabeth Severn, 13 August 1838, MS Townsend.

34 Severn's ledgers for 1846 and 1847 show two payments from Lady Westmorland of £50 each for room decorations by Severn and there may have been subsequent commissions: *Letters and Memoirs*, pp. 688–9. Lady Westmorland's final years were sad. Acting in cahoots with her paid companion, Miss Doddemeale, her son attempted to have her committed for insanity. The plot was only foiled by her daughter, Lady Georgina Athill, who falsely accused Miss Doddemeale of stealing a ring as a way of securing her arrest. Lady Westmorland was then

smuggled out of the premises to her daughter's home, where she remained for the rest of her life. Miss Doddemeale successfully sued Lady Georgina for slander and was awarded £200. Lady Westmorland died in 1857 and was buried at the family seat at Apethorpe, Northamptonshire: Severn to Elizabeth Severn, 8 May 1855, MS Townsend; and C. Roberts, *The Remarkable Young Man* (London: Hodder & Stoughton, 1954), p. 268.

35 Severn to Elizabeth Severn, 8 July 1838, MS Townsend, 24 July 1838, *Letters and Memoirs*, p. 370, and 26 August 1838, MS Townsend.

36 Severn to Elizabeth Severn, 26 August 1838, MS Townsend.

37 Severn to Elizabeth Severn, 8 July 1838, *Letters and Memoirs*, p. 365; 13 July 1838, MS Townsend; 24 July 1838, *Letters and Memoirs*, p. 370; and 26 August 1838, MS Townsend.

38 Severn to Uwins, 12 March 1839, *Letters and Memoirs*, p. 378.

39 The picture has recently been restored and now hangs in the Hermitage Museum in St Petersburg.

40 Eastlake to Severn, 19 August 1839, *Life and Letters*, p. 189; Severn to Elizabeth Severn, 19 August 1839, *Letters and Memoirs*, p. 381; Uwins to Severn, 3 August 1839, *Memoir of Thomas Uwins*, ii, p. 280.

41 Severn to Elizabeth Severn, 16 August 1839, *Letters and Memoirs*, p. 381.

42 Severn to Elizabeth Severn, 9 and 10 December 1840, MS Townsend; and 18 November 1840, *Letters and Memoirs*, p. 388.

43 Julia to George Richmond, 30 December and 23 December 1840, *Letters and Memoirs*, p. 31.

44 Severn to Elizabeth Severn, 9 December 1840, MS Townsend.

45 Richmond to Julia Richmond 15 and 27 December 1840, George Richmond Papers, University of North Carolina.

46 Severn to Elizabeth Severn, 9 December 1840, MS Townsend.

47 J. Ruskin, *The Works of John Ruskin*, ed. E. T. Cook and A. Wedderburn, 39 vols (London: George Allen, 1903–12), xxxv: *Praeterita*, Pt. II, p. 274.

48 George Richmond Engagements Diary, 12 September 1840. RA Archive.

49 Ruskin, *The Works of John Ruskin*, iv: *Modern Painters*, Pt III, Ch. 7, p. 117.

50 Richmond to Julia Richmond, 15 December 1840, George Richmond Papers, University of North Carolina; and Richmond MS Diary, 16 December 1840, RA Archive.

51 J. Ruskin, *The Diaries of John Ruskin*, ed. J. Evans and J. H. Whitehouse, 3 vols (Oxford: Clarendon Press, 1956–59), pp. 116–17 and 121 (29 November and 6 December).

52 Ibid., p. 128 (28 December 1840).

53 Ruskin, *The Works of John Ruskin*, xxxv: *Praeterita*, Pt. II, p. 275.

54 Ruskin, *The Diaries*, pp. 123, 125, and 127 (12, 15, and 25 December 1840); and Richmond Diary, 26 December 1840, RA Archive. A misremembered reference in *Praeterita* to the Ruskin's spending Christmas Day with Severn and Richmond led to a misleading manuscript addition to Richmond's diary by his son William.

55 MS Diary of Mary Richardson 1840–1, 26 December 1840, Ruskin Library T49.

56 Ruskin, *The Diaries*, p. 134 (2 January 1841); and Mary Richardson MS Diary, 1 January 1841, Ruskin Library.

57 'The cockney . . . is the supreme type of Englishman in his sturdy optimism, in his unwavering determination not only to make the best of things as they are, but to make them seem actually better than they are by adapting his mood to the exigencies of the occasion, and in his supreme disdain of all outside influences': Edwin Pugh, quoted in R. Porter, *London: A Social History* (London: Hamish Hamilton, 1994), p. 303.

58 Ruskin to James Ruskin, 1852, in Ruskin, *The Works of John Ruskin*, xxxvi, p. 136; Ruskin to Severn, 23 January 1861, *Life and Letters*, p. 218.

59 Severn to Elizabeth Severn, 8 January 1841, *Letters and Memoirs*, pp. 395-404; Julia to George Richmond, 27 January 1841; and George to Julia Richmond, 22 January 1841, George Richmond Papers, University of North Carolina.

60 Severn to Elizabeth Severn, 7 January 1841, MS Townsend.

61 'Incidents of My Life. The Revelations Altarpiece', *Life and Letters*, p. 300. The altarpiece is now in the art gallery at San Paolo and has recently been restored.

62 Ibid., p. 300.

63 Grant Scott found them still there in 2002.

64 Ruskin, *The Works of John Ruskin*, xxxv: Praeterita, Pt II, p. 278.

Chapter 13 The Passion for Fresco

1 Severn to Elizabeth Severn, 8 May 1855, Townsend MS. Eleanor Severn, however, recalled Dante Gabriel Rossetti coming to the Severns' house in Buckingham Gate. Eliza was also firmly in the Millais camp after Ruskin's breach with his wife, Effie, who went on to marry Millais: Eleanor Severn, 'Autobiographical Notes', Charlton MS; and Walter Severn, 'Notes for a Memoir [of Severn]', Houghton Library, Harvard bMS Eng 1434 (514).

2 H. T. Ryall, ed., *Portraits of Eminent Conservatives and Statesmen with Genealogical and Historical Memoirs*, 2 vols (London: George Virtue, 1836-46).

3 Severn's Ledger 1841-7, *Letters and Memoirs*, p. 686.

4 Severn to Elizabeth Severn, 14 August 1853, Townsend MS; Uwins to Severn, 5 June 1832, *Memoir of Thomas Uwins*, ii, p. 261.

5 RA Archive, RA General Assembly Minutes, 1840.

6 H. S. Marks, *Pen and Pencil Sketches*, 2 vols (London: Chatto & Windus, 1894), i, p. 228.

7 Severn to William Haslam, 2 August 1842, *Letters and Memoirs*, p. 415.

8 Severn to Elizabeth Severn, 28 September [1843], 25 November [1851] and September 1844, Townsend MS.

9 W. E. Gladstone, *The Gladstone Diaries*, ed. M. R. D. Foot and H. C. G. Matthew (Oxford: Clarendon Press, 1968), iii, pp. 108 and 150 (18 May and 15 October 1841).

10 'Notes by W. E. Gladstone on his pictures and other works of Art', Flintshire Record Office, Gladstone-Glynne Mss 1473. Gladstone later passed the painting to John Duke Coleridge, who served as Attorney General in his first administration and would ultimately become Lord Chief Justice of England. Coleridge was a great admirer of Severn's work and also owned his *Ancient Mariner*, which was given to him in 1872 by the Revd Walter Halliday: *Notes and Queries*, 5th Series, vol. 6 (22 July 1876), 74-5. Both paintings remained in the possession of the Coleridge family until 2006.

11 Severn to Gladstone, 13 December [1843], BL Add. MS 44360 f. 380; Severn to Gladstone, 9 December [1843], *Letters and Memoirs*, p. 427; Gladstone to Severn, 21 June 1843, Houghton Library, Harvard bMS Eng 1434 (99).

12 Severn to Gladstone, 24 March 1846, BL Add. MS 44363 ff. 348-49.

13 Severn to Henry Acland, 28 August 1850, Bodleian Library, Oxford, MS Acland d. 81 ff. 181-2.

14 Gladstone to Severn, 22 July and 23 July 1850, Houghton Library, Harvard bMS Eng 1434 (114) and (115).

15 See M. Pointon, *William Dyce 1806–1864: A Critical Biography* (Oxford: Clarendon Press, 1979), pp. 58, 66–8, and 128–32.

16 This judgement is based on a photograph of the altarpiece in the Rose Wild collection.

17 R. and S. Redgrave, *A Century of British Painters* (London: Phaidon Press, 1947), p. 459.

18 For some lively accounts of the failed attempt to decorate the new Houses of Parliament in fresco see Redgrave and Redgrave, *A Century of British Painters*, pp. 458–68; M. H. Port, ed., *The Houses of Parliament* (London: Yale University Press, 1976), (especially the article by T. S. R. Boase, 'Painting'); and D. Robertson, *Sir Charles Eastlake and the Victorian Art World* (Princeton: Princeton University Press, 1978), pp. 58–77 and 324–44.

19 C. L. Eastlake, *Contributions to the Literature of the Fine Arts: Second Series with a Memoir Compiled by Lady Eastlake* (London: John Murray, 1870), p. 24.

20 Robertson, *Sir Charles Eastlake*, pp. 60–1.

21 Severn to Gladstone, 30 November 1841, *Letters and Memoirs*, p. 408.

22 *Athenaeum*, 9 April, 7 May, and 6 August 1842, pp. 314–17, 405–6, and 709–11.

23 Severn to Gladstone, 23 April 1842, *Letters and Memoirs*, pp. 409–10.

24 *Athenaeum*, 9 April 1842, pp. 754, 320.

25 *Athenaeum*, 6 August 1842, p. 711.

26 *Athenaeum*, 6 August 1842, p. 710. Dyce had tried to establish a different kind of studio system, the craft workshop, at the Government School of Design but with only limited success. See Pointon, *William Dyce*, p. 45.

27 Severn to Dilke, [April 1842], *Letters and Memoirs*, p. 411.

28 Ruskin to James Ruskin, 30 September [1845], in J. Ruskin, *Ruskin in Italy: Letters to his Parents 1845*, ed. H. I. Shapiro (Oxford: Clarendon Press, 1972), p. 217; Ruskin to Severn, 21 September [1845], *Life and Letters*, pp. 205–6.

29 Haydon to Dilke, 1841, in C. W. Dilke, *Papers of a Critic*, 2 vols (London: John Murray, 1875), p. 56.

30 Haydon to Kirkup, 16 August 1842 and Kirkup to Haydon, 6 August 1842, in T. Taylor, ed., *The Life of Benjamin Robert Haydon: Historical Painter from his Autobiography and Journals* (London: Longman, Brown, Green and Longmans, 1853), 3 vols, ii, pp. 189–90 and 192. Though Severn's name was excised, Haydon's readily recognizable comment on him was published in his lifetime.

31 Severn to Gladstone, 26 June [1843], BL Add. MS 44356 f. 195. Gladstone delightedly wrote to Severn late one night with advance news of his success, after quizzing Samuel Rogers, one of the judges, who had been to dinner with him. Gladstone to Severn, 4 June 1843, *Life and Letters*, p. 203.

32 *The Times*, 2 July 1845; Lady Holland to Edward Fox, 3 July 1843, in Ilchester, *Elizabeth, Lady Holland to her Son 1821–1845* (London: John Murray, 1946), p. 208; James Ruskin to Ruskin, 15/19 September 1845, in Shapiro, *Ruskin in Italy*, p. 248; *Britannia*, 13 September 1845, p. 587.

33 Redgrave and Redgrave, *A Century of British Art*, p. 401.

34 Severn to the Royal Commission on Fine Arts (draft) n.d. John Rylands Library.

35 Uwins to Severn, 26 July 1843, *Memoir of Thomas Uwins*, ii, p. 284.

36 Plate 12 in *The Decorations of the Garden-Pavilion in the Grounds of Buckingham Palace*, engraved under the superintendence of L. Gruner, introd. Mrs Jameson (London: 1846).

37 Eastlake to Severn, 26 August 1845, John Rylands Library.

38 Eastlake to Severn, 7 February, 16 and 20 May 1846, John Rylands Library.

39 Severn to Sir Robert Inglis, 22 May 1846, Eastlake to Severn, 11 June 1847, John Rylands Library.

40 Redgrave and Redgrave, *A Century of British Painting*, p. 465.

41 J. Dafferne, *The Life and Works of Edward Mathew Ward RA* (London: Virtue & Co [1879]), p. 39. L. Herrmann, *Nineteenth Century British Painting* (London: Giles de la Mare Publishers Limited, 2000), p. 297.

42 E. George, *The Life and Death of Benjamin Robert Haydon, Historical Painter 1786–1846* (London: Oxford University Press, 1948), p. 275. See too A. Hayter, *A Sultry Month Scenes of London Literary Life in 1846* (London: Faber & Faber, 1965).

43 Severn to Elizabeth Severn, 26 October 1847, Townsend MS.

44 Houghton Library, Harvard bMS Eng 1434 (489).

45 O. Millar, *The Victorian Pictures in the Collection of Her Majesty the Queen* (Cambridge: Cambridge University Press, 1992), p. xxxviii.

46 Arthur Severn to Joan Severn n.d., Houghton Library, Harvard bMS Eng 1434 (66).

47 Eastlake to Severn, 23 June 1850, Houghton Library, Harvard bMS Eng 1434 (55).

48 Eastlake to Severn, 27 July 1850, Houghton Library, Harvard bMS Eng 1434 (57).

49 Severn to Elizabeth Severn, 11 November 1850, Townsend MS.

50 Kirkup to Severn, 18 August and 30 October 1861, Houghton Library, Harvard bMS Eng 1434 (148) and (149).

51 Severn to Elizabeth Severn, 9 October 1846, Townsend MS.

52 For a superb description of this event, see I. Anstruther *The Knight and the Umbrella: An Account of the Eglinton Tournament 1839* (London: Geoffrey Bles, 1963).

53 Severn to Elizabeth Severn, 5 February [1845], Townsend MS.

Chapter 14 The Friend of Keats

1 Severn to Dilke, 3 February [1859], *Letters and Memoirs*, p. 469.

2 Brown to Milnes, 29 March 1841, *Keats Circle*, ii, p. 101.

3 Brown to Severn, 21 March 1841, *Letters of Charles Brown*, pp. 410–12.

4 Brown to Milnes, 29 March and 9 April 1841, *Keats Circle*, ii, pp. 100 and 102.

5 Brown to Milnes, 29 March 1841, *Letters of Charles Brown*, pp. 412–13.

6 Severn to Dilke, [April 1842], *Letters and Memoirs*, p. 412, and Severn to Dilke n.d. [1842], MS Churchill College, Cambridge; Dilke to Severn, [July 1842], *Keats Circle*, ii, p. 104.

7 Severn to Dilke, 2 May [1842], *Letters and Memoirs*, p. 413; Severn to Taylor, March [1841], *Keats Circle*, ii, pp. 97–8; Severn to Dilke, [April 1842], *Letters and Memoirs*, p. 412.

8 Mary to Elizabeth Severn, 1852, Charlton MS.

9 Fanny Brawne to Brown, 29 December 1829 (draft), in J. Richardson, *Fanny Brawne* (London: Vanguard Press, 1952), p. 121.

10 Mary to Elizabeth Severn n.d. but probably 1843, Charlton MS.

11 Severn to Haslam, 2 August 1842, *Letters and Memoirs*, p. 414.

12 Severn to Milnes, 27 July 1842, *Keats Circle*, ii, p. 112. The anecdotes printed in pp. 134–8 of *Keats Circle*, ii, are tentatively dated October 1845 but are more likely to date from 1842.

13 Quoted in *Keats Circle*, i, cxiv.

14 Severn to George Richmond, 28 April 1845, Grant Scott 'New Mary Shelley Letters to the Severns', *Keats–Shelley Journal*, 54 (2005), 77.

15 Arthur Severn 'Memoirs', Charlton MS; Walter Severn 'Notes for a Memoir of Mr Ruskin', Houghton Library, Harvard bMS Eng 1434 (573). Walter Severn remembered his father telling stories of visits to Turner's 'extraordinary house. How people went through the untidy rooms without seeing any sign of the Proprietor': J. Ruskin, *The Diaries of John Ruskin*, ed. Joan Evans and J. H. Whitehouse, 3 vols (Oxford: Clarendon Press, 1956–59), i, pp. 220 and 265; Eleanor Severn 'Autobiographical Notes', Charlton MS.

16 Browning to Elizabeth Barrett, 13 May 1846, in *The Brownings' Correspondence*, ed. Philip Kelley and Scott Lewis (London: Athlone Press, 1994), 14 vols, xii, January 1846–May 1846.

17 Mary Shelley to Elizabeth Severn, 7 May [1843], in G. Scott, 'New Mary Shelley Letters to the Severns', *Keats-Shelley Journal*, 54 (2005), 70–1. M. Shelley, *Rambles in Germany and Italy in 1840, 1842, and 1843*, ed. J. Moskal in *The Novels and Selected Works of Mary Shelley*, vol. 8: *Travel Writing* (London: William Pickering, 1996), p. 347.

18 S. Norman, *Flight of the Skylark: The Development of Shelley's Reputation* (London: Max Reinhardt,1954), p. 85.

19 Severn 'Adonais . . . with Notes', Houghton Library, Harvard Keats MS 4.16.3.

20 Somerset House, London, the Witt Collection.

21 Mary Shelley to Hunt, 23 December 1844, and to Leigh and Marianne Hunt, [27 December 1844], in M. Shelley, *The Letters of Mary Wollstonecroft Shelley*, ed. B. T. Bennett (London: Johns Hopkins University Press, 1988), vol. 3, pp. 170 and 173; Severn to Hunt, 6 January 1845, ibid., iii, p. 174 n. 1; Mary Shelley to Severn n.d., in Scott, 'New Mary Shelley Letters to the Severns', 73, where it is tentatively dated 10 January 1845.

22 Mary Shelley to Severn 16 July [1845] and ?10 January 1845, in Scott 'New Mary Shelley Letters to the Severns', 74 and 73.

23 Fanny de Llanos to Severn, 3 September 1877, *Life and Letters*, p. 256.

24 Severn to Milnes, 6 October 1845 and 5 May 1848, *Keats Circle*, ii, pp. 129–30 and 233; R. M. Milnes, *Life, Letters and Literary Remains of John Keats* (London: J. M. Dent, 1927), p. 208.

25 Severn to Milnes 13 July [1846] and 5 May 1848, *Keats Circle*, ii, pp. 159 and 232–3; Milnes, *Life, Letters and Literary Remains of John Keats*, p. 215.

26 Severn to Milnes, 6 October 1845, *Keats Circle*, ii, pp. 131 and 130; Dilke to Severn April [1842], ibid., ii, p. 104, (where it is misdated a year earlier); Severn to Milnes, 6 October 1845, ibid., ii, p. 130.

27 Charles Cowden Clarke to Milnes, 16 March 1846, *Keats Circle*, ii, p. 152.

28 Severn to Milnes, 6 October 1845, *Keats Circle*, ii, p. 130.

29 Charles Severn, quoted in *Life and Letters*, p. 40.

30 Sidney Colvin, a fine Keats biographer, spotted the error as early as 1915: Colvin to the Editor of *The Times*, 18 February 1915, pp. 55–6.

31 Severn to Milnes, 6 October 1845, *Keats Circle*, ii, p. 129.

32 Severn to Taylor, March 1841, *Keats Circle*, ii, p. 97.

33 Coventry Patmore to Milnes, 24 March 1847, *Keats Circle*, ii, p. 205.

34 Severn to Milnes, 6 October 1845 and 13 July 1846, *Keats Circle*, ii, pp. 131 and 159.

35 George was introduced as Keats's older brother, Fanny Brawne was confused with 'Charmian', the object of a brief Keats infatuation, Benjamin Bailey, by then Arch Deacon in Colombo, was assumed dead and Keats's appearance was misdescribed.

36 Milnes, *Life, Letters and Literary Remains of John Keats*, pp. 3 and 10; Severn to Milnes, [October 1845], *Keats Circle*, ii, p. 138.

37 Milnes *Life, Letters and Literary Remains of John Keats*, p. 126.

38 Ibid., p. 35.

39 Ibid., p. 225.

40 Ibid., pp. 226 and 4; J. Richardson, *The Everlasting Spell: A Study of Keats and his Friends* (London: Jonathan Cape, 1963), p. 174.

41 *Life and Letters*, p. 201.

42 Severn to Elizabeth Severn, 2 December 1850, Townsend MS. Severn asked £60 for 'Keats and the Nightingale'.

43 Fanny Lindon to [Mrs Dilke] n.d., in Richardson, *Fanny Brawne*, pp. 166–8.

44 G. D. Leslie, *The Inner Life of the Royal Academy with an Account of its Schools & Exhibitions Principally in the Reign of Queen Victoria* (London: John Murray, 1914), pp. 130–1.

45 Severn to Gladstone, 29 November 1844, *Letters and Memoirs*, p. 427.

46 Severn to Elizabeth Severn 20 November [1850], *Letters and Memoirs*, p. 438.

Chapter 15 An Interlude in Pimlico

1 See, for example, Severn to Elizabeth Severn, 28 October 1850, Townsend MS.

2 See J. Tosh, *A Man's Place: Masculinity and the Middle-Class Home in Victorian England* (New Haven and London: Yale University Press, 1999).

3 Her second daughter, Margaret, married F. E. Smith, 1st Lord Birkenhead, and her third, Sir Herbert Smith. The pattern was repeated in the next generation when the 2nd Lord Birkenhead, a noted biographer, married Sheila Berry, the daughter of the 1st Viscount Camrose, while his younger sister, Pam, married one of his wife's brothers, Michael Berry, later Lord Hartwell. Lady Juliet Townsend, the daughter of the 2nd Earl, is Lord Lieutenant of Northamptonshire and her cousin, Harriet Cullen, Chairman of the Keats–Shelley Society. Severn's other distinguished descendants include Walter's son, Claud, who was Acting Governor (in effect, Deputy Governor) of Hong Kong from 1912 to 1930, his daughter, Helen Christian, who married the Bishop of Newcastle and was a fine watercolourist and their son, John Herbert Wild, who was Master of University College, Oxford during the Second World War and later Dean of Durham Cathedral.

4 Severn to Elizabeth Severn, 15 November 1850, Townsend MS. The Eglintons did, eventually, buy *The Abdication of Mary Queen of Scots*, a finely finished history painting which recently sold for £115,000.

5 Severn to Elizabeth Severn, 15 November 1850, Townsend MS; Severn to Elizabeth Severn, 20 November [1850], *Letters and Memoirs*, pp. 438–9; Severn to Elizabeth Severn, 27 November and 30 October [1850], Townsend MS.

6 Severn to Elizabeth Severn, 11 December 1850, Townsend MS.

7 A. Boutflower, *Personal Reminiscences of Manchester Cathedral 1854–1912* (Manchester: Faith Press, 1913), p. 47.

8 See D. S. Macleod, *Art and the Victorian Middle Class: Money and the Making of Cultural Identity* (Cambridge: Cambridge University Press, 1996).

9 Mary Severn to Elizabeth Severn, 'Friday' [?1852], Charlton MS.

10 *Halifax Guardian*, 26 July 1851.

11 Severn to Elizabeth Severn, 2 July 1851, Townsend MS.

12 Severn, 'Ruskin's Modern Painters Vol. III, Part 4', Houghton Library, Harvard bMS Eng 1434 (490).

13 Arthur Severn, 'Memoirs', Charlton MS.

14 Severn, 'Ruskin's Modern Painters Vol. III, Part 4', Houghton Library, Harvard bMS Eng 1434 (490).

15 Mary Severn to Elizabeth Severn, 'Thursday' [1856], Charlton MS.

16 Severn to Elizabeth Severn, 23 September 1852, Townsend MS.

17 Severn to Elizabeth Severn, 23 November 1852 and 31 January 1853, Townsend MS.

18 Walter Severn 'Notes for a Memoir of Mr Ruskin', Houghton Library, Harvard bMS Eng 1434 (514).

19 Severn to Elizabeth Severn, 2 December 1856, Townsend MS.

20 Severn to Mary Severn, 4 October [1844] and to Elizabeth Severn, June 1849, Townsend MS.

21 Mary Severn to Elizabeth Severn, 18 January 1856, Charlton MS.

22 The travails of the Severns in the summer of 1853 are told in great detail in a manuscript diary which Mary kept at the time (Charlton MS). Much of it is reproduced in S. Birkenhead, *Against Oblivion: The Life of Joseph Severn* (London: Cassell and Company, 1943), pp. 178–88.

23 Severn to Elizabeth Severn, 25 and 23 June and 28 August 1853, Townsend MS.

24 Mary Severn, MS Diary, 19 July 1853, Charlton MS.

25 Severn to Elizabeth Severn, 24 July and 28 August and Severn to Walter Severn, 11 October 1853, Townsend MS. At this time the National Gallery was undergoing a major reorganization which would lead to the establishment of a new post of director, a position always intended for Eastlake.

26 Severn to Walter Severn, 11 October 1853 and to Elizabeth Severn, 14 August 1853, Townsend MS.

27 For an example of Lockhart's sanctimony, see his undated letter to Elizabeth Severn replying to one from her thanking him for his helpfulness: 'the thanks due, and due alone to the Highest Power may be, & I doubt not will be called forth & all thankful praises bestowed on the mighty & merciful Giver, not to secondary causes that may be employed', Townsend MS.

28 Mary Severn to Elizabeth Severn 28. February 1856, Charlton MS; Severn to Elizabeth Severn, 5 March 1856, *Letters and Memoirs*, p. 462.

29 Severn to Mary Severn, 29 January 1857, *Letters and Memoirs*, p. 464.

30 Severn to Elizabeth Severn, [6 November 1855] and 27 August 1856, Townsend MS.

31 J. B. Atlay, *Sir Henry Wentworth Acland, Bart. K.C.B., F.R.S. A Memoir* (London: Smith Elder, 1903), p. 51.

32 Severn to Elizabeth Severn, 1 December [1855], Townsend MS.

33 Mid-1850s sketchbook, Rose Wild collection.

34 Mary Severn to Elizabeth Severn, [30 April 1858], Charlton MS.

35 Mary Severn to Elizabeth Severn, 29 December, 5 November and [23 December] 1857. Further extracts from Mary's letters are printed in Birkenhead, *Against Oblivion*, pp. 192–5.

36 F. Locker-Lampson, *My Confidences: An Autobiographical Sketch Addressed to My Descendants*, ed. A. Birrell (London: Smith Elder, 1896), pp. 342–3 and 338.

37 *Letters and Memoirs*, p. 82.

38 Printed in *Life and Letters*, pp. 231–7.

39 Severn to Dilke 3 February [1859], *Letters and Memoirs*, pp. 468–70; Dilke to Milnes, 6 February 1859, Milnes to Dilke, 11 February 1859, Severn to Dilke, 13 February 1859, Nostrand, pp. 249–55 and 256–7.

40 J. T. Fields, *James T. Fields, Biographical Notes and Personal Sketches, with Unpublished Fragments and Tributes from Men and Women of Letters*, ed. Annie Adams Fields (London: Sampson, Low, 1881), p. 78; Severn to Fields, 21 and 31 May [1860] and 25 April 1871, *Letters and Memoirs*, pp. 470–3 and 530–1.

41 Mary Severn to Elizabeth Severn, n.d. Charlton MS.

42 Mary Severn to Eleanor Severn, 3 November 1859 (incomplete), Charlton MS.

43 Mary Severn to Elizabeth Severn, n.d., Houghton Library, Harvard bMS Eng 1434 (388); Eleanor Severn Diary, June 1860, Charlton MS.

44 Draft letter in mid-1850s sketchbook (Rose Wild collection); Gladstone to Severn, 31 August 1853 (Copy), BL Add. MS 44368.

45 Gladstone to Severn, 6 June 1860, Newton to Severn, 16 October 1860, Houghton Library, Harvard bMS Eng 1434 (115) and (178).

46 Severn to Lord John Russell, 9 October [1860] (Copy), Houghton Library, Harvard bMS Eng 1434 (294).

47 Severn to Milnes, 23 October 1860, Trinity College, Cambridge, Houghton Library, Houghton MS 22166.

48 Ruskin to Severn, 23 January 1861, Bunsen to Lord John Russell, 12 October 1860, *Life and Letters*, pp. 216–17 and 218.

49 Newton to Severn, 16 October 1860, Houghton Library, Harvard bMS Eng 1434 (178).

50 For a brilliant description of Gladstone's 'arrogant corner-cutting' on appointments see R. Jenkins, *Gladstone* (London: Macmillan, 1995), pp. 369–70.

51 Gladstone to Lord J Russell, 5 October 1860 (copy), Houghton Library, Harvard bMS Eng 1434 (455).

52 Severn to Dr Quinn, 4 June 1860, *Life and Letters*, p. 215; Severn to Gladstone, 23 October 1860 (copy), Houghton Library, Harvard bMS Eng 1434 (286); Lord John Russell to Charles Newton, 24 January 1861, and to Severn, 30 January 1861, Houghton Library, Harvard bMS Eng 1434 (465) and (201).

53 Eleanor Severn, MS Diary n.d., Charlton MS.

54 Mary Severn to Elizabeth Severn, 7 October 1857, Townsend MS; Joseph Severn 1850s sketchbook, Rose Wild collection.

Chapter 16 British Consul

1 F. Gregorovius, *The Roman Journals of Ferdinand Gregorovius 1852–74*, ed. Friedrich Althaus, trans. Mrs Gustavus W. Hamilton (London: George Bell, 1907), p. 263 (4 November 1866).

2 Severn's diary for 30 August 1862, printed in 'Severn's Roman Journals', *Atlantic Monthly*, 69 (May 1892), 638.

3 G. A. Sala, *Rome and Venice with Other Wanderings in Italy in 1866–7* (London: Tinsley, 1869), p. 374.

4 Severn to Odo Russell, 12 January 1864, TNA, FO 918/62.

5 'Severn's Roman Journals', *Atlantic Monthly*, 69 (May 1892), 633.

6 'On the Vicissitudes of Keats's Fame', *Atlantic Monthly*, 11 (April 1863), 407.

7 Severn dated this meeting to 1818 remembering that Fanny was then fifteen and her brother Tom still alive: 'Severn's Roman Journals', *Atlantic Monthly*, 69 (May 1892), 633.

8 It is unlikely that this was at the house in Piazza di Spagna where Keats died, though Severn's reference to meeting 'in the very place where her illustrious brother died' led Marie Adami to assume so: *Fanny Keats* (New Haven and London: Yale University Press, 1938), p. 154. More probably, he was referring to the coincidence of their meeting in Rome.

9 'Severn's Roman Journals', *Atlantic Monthly*, 69 (May 1892), 633.

10 F. Locker Lampson, *My Confidences: An Autobiographical Sketch Addressed to My Descendants*, ed. A. Birrell (London: Smith Elder, 1896), p. 343. The one photograph taken of her in Rome confirms the impression of bovine steadiness. Marie Adami who prints the photograph interprets it quite differently as showing 'Humour, shrewdness and an air of command' (*Fanny Keats*, p. 157).

11 'Severn's Roman Journals', *Atlantic Monthly*, 69 (May 1892), 633.

12 Severn's draft, which is printed in Adami, *Fanny Keats*, p. 164, shows that he hesitated between 24 and 26 February as the date of Keats's death. By English reckoning Keats died on the 23rd.

13 Severn to Lord Houghton, 28 September 1864, *Keats Circle*, ii, p. 327; Fanny de Llanos to H. B. Forman, 1 September 1879, in Adami, *Fanny Keats*, p. 196.

14 The original draft, titled 'On the Adversities of Keats's Fame', contains some interesting material omitted from the published version and is printed in *Letters and Memoirs*, pp. 609–21.

15 C. C. Clarke to Severn, 13 September 1864, *Life and Letters*, p. 257.

16 Severn to Mrs Philip Speed, 1 September 1863, *Keats Circle*, ii, p. 324.

17 Hammond to Severn, 18 May 1861 and Severn to Lord John Russell, 25 April 1861, TNA, FO 43/84.

18 Odo Russell to Lady William Russell, 27 April 1861, TNA, FO 918/85.

19 *The Times*, 26 August 1884.

20 N. Blakiston, *The Roman Question: Extracts from the Despatches of Odo Russell* (London: Chapman Hall, 1962), p. xxii.

21 Lord John Russell to Charles Newton, 6 February 1861, TNA, FO 43/994.

22 See D. C. M. Platt, *The Cinderella Service: British Consuls since 1825* (London: Longman, 1971).

23 Lord John Russell to Severn, 8 February 1861, TNA, FO 43/483; Severn to Odo Russell, 9 January 1864, *Letters and Memoirs*, p. 504.

24 Lord John Russell to Charles Newton, 20 October 1860, TNA, FO 43/79A.

25 Severn to FO, 4 April 1861 and 25 April 1861, TNA, FO 43/84.

26 Severn to Lord John Russell, 18 June, 4 July, and 23 September 1861, TNA, FO 43/84; Arthur Severn, 'Memoirs' (Typescript), p. 41, Charlton MS.

27 Gregorovius, *The Roman Journals of Ferdinand Gregorovius*, p. 202 (27 March 1864).

28 'Severn's Roman Journals' (undated entry), *Atlantic Monthly*, 69 (May 1892), 632.

29 Severn to Lord John Russell, 12 November 1861, TNA, FO 43/84.

30 Severn to Thomas Severn, 19 November 1861, LMA, KPM/S 510.

31 Severn to Elizabeth Severn, 23 October [1861], *Letters and Memoirs*, p. 483.

32 Severn to Elizabeth Severn, 25 February [1862], *Letters and Memoirs*, pp. 485–6.

33 Eleanor Severn to Claudia Gale, 14 April 1862, Charlton MS.

34 Mary Newton bequeathed the brooch to her closest friend, Mary Palliser. It is now at the Keats House in Hampstead. Elizabeth Severn's short list of bequests to her family is in the Charlton MS.

Notes

35 Charlton MS.

36 Acte du Décès, 17 April 1862. Archive Municipale, Marseilles.

37 Severn to FO, 15 April 1862, TNA, FO 43/87.

38 Severn to Thomas Severn, 2 May 1862, *Letters and Memoirs*, pp. 489–90.

39 The only surviving evidence for this is a typescript copy of a receipt for the costs of erecting a stone in 1869, Charlton MS.

40 Severn to FO, 21 June 1862, TNA, FO 43/87.

41 Severn to Lord John Russell, 12 September 1863 and FO to Severn, 21 September 1863, TNA, FO 43/90.

42 Eleanor Severn to Severn, 2 September 1863, *Letters and Memoirs*, pp. 499–501.

43 Severn to Odo Russell, 1 September 1863, *Letters and Memoirs*, p. 479.

44 'Severn's Roman Journals' (23 October 1861), *Atlantic Monthly*, 69 (May 1892), 633–4.

45 For a fascinating account of Charlotte Cushman and her circle see L. Merrill, *When Romeo was a Woman* (Ann Arbor: University of Michigan Press, 1999).

46 Severn to Lord John Russell, 20 June 1864, TNA, FO 43/92.

47 Eleanor Severn, MS Diary, Charlton MS.

48 Severn to Thomas Severn, 17 September 1861, LMA, KPM/S 508.

49 Murray's comments on Severn's dispatch of 5 December 1866 to Lord Stanley, TNA, FO 43/97.

50 F. Locker Lampson, *My Confidences*, p. 342.

51 Severn to FO, 3 December 1861, TNA, FO 43/84.

52 C. Wordsworth, DD, *Journal of a Tour in Italy*, 2 vols (London: Rivingtons, 1863), ii, pp. 23–34.

53 Severn to FO, 30 December 1861 and FO to Severn, 20 February 1862, TNA, FO 43/87; Severn to FO, 20 January 1864, FO 43/92; Severn to FO, 11 October 1862; and FO to Severn, 25 October 1862, FO 43/87.

54 Severn to Lord John Russell, 6 February 1864, TNA, FO 43/92.

55 Severn to Lord John Russell, 11 November 1864 and 27 March 1866, TNA, FO 43/92 and 43/97.

56 Severn to FO, 16 January and 21 May 1866, TNA, FO 43/97.

57 Severn to Thomas Severn, 8 April 1863, LMA, KPM/S 522.

58 Hammond's ms comment on Severn's dispatch of 7 September and Severn to Lord John Russell, 15 October 1864, TNA, FO 43/92.

59 Severn to Lord John Russell, 25 November 1862, TNA, FO 43/87. For an analysis of Garibaldi's appeal to his English female admirers see L. Riall, *Garibaldi: Invention of a Hero* (New Haven and London, Yale University Press, 2007), pp. 340–4.

60 Olivia Rossetti Agresti, however, records two instances of Severn's willingness to help prominent Garibaldians in her biography of the Italian artist Giovanni Costa, who fought with Garibaldi at Mentana. When he was forced out of Rome Severn protected his studio and its contents for three years until his return in 1870. Encouraged by William Richmond, George Richmond's son, Severn also issued passports to help the widow of an executed Garibaldi supporter escape with her baby, disguised as a wet nurse to the Richmonds: O. R. Agresti, *Giovanni Costa: His Life, Work and Times* (London: Grant Richards, 1904), pp. 141 and 163–6.

61 Severn to Lord John Russell, 12 April 1865, TNA, FO 43/95.

62 FO to Severn, 15 May 1865, TNA, FO 43/95.

63 Severn to FO, 27 May 1865 with Murray and Hammond's ms comments, TNA, FO 43/95. Severn was rather less obliging to the Presbyterian community in Rome who held services, which were widely advertised in hotels, banks, and reading rooms, in the private apartments of their pastor, Dr Lewis. Severn warned him in December 1866 that he risked being forced into exile if he did not desist. Dr Lewis and his flock rented the dining hall of an inn just outside the Porta del Populo from January 1867 to the beginning of 1871 when St Andrew's Church was opened, built just outside the city walls (article by Alison Sabetti in *St Andrew's Church Newsletter*, September 2008).

64 Platt, *The Cinderella Service*, p. ix.

65 Severn to Earl Russell, 15 January 1864 and FO to Severn, 29 January 1864, TNA, FO 43/92.

66 Odo Russell to Severn, 9 January 1864 and Severn to Odo Russell, 12 January [1864], Houghton Library, Harvard bMS Eng 1434 (7) and (278).

67 Odo Russell to Severn 'Thursday', Houghton Library, Harvard bMS Eng 1434 (10) and Severn to Odo Russell, 30 December 1866, TNA, FO 918/62.

68 See Blakiston, *The Roman Question*, pp. 421 and TNA, FO 43/107.

69 'Letter home'. n.d., *Life and Letters*, p. 249, Severn to Maria Severn, 8 July 1868, *Letters and Memoirs*, pp. 516–17.

Chapter 17 The New Rome

1 M. Howitt, ed., *Mary Howitt: An Autobiography*, 2 vols (London: William Isbister, 1889), ii, p. 212; Severn to Walter Severn, 19 April 1870, Houghton Library, Harvard bMS Eng 1434 (308); Severn to Thomas Severn, 8 July 1873, *Letters and Memoirs*, p. 536, Severn to Maria Severn, 1 December 1868, LMA, KPM/S 559.

2 There is a hint in a letter from her mother in 1862 that Mary may have had a miscarriage: 'I should be nearer to you all and you particularly at present': Elizabeth Severn to Mary Newton, 25 March 1862, Charlton MS.

3 Charles Newton to Eleanor Severn, 2 January 1866, Arthur Severn to Eleanor Severn, [2]January 1866, Claudia Gale to Severn and Eleanor Severn, 3 and 4 January 1866 and 9–10 January 1866, Charlton MS.

4 Wharton Marriott to Claudia Gale, 11 January 1866, Charlton MS.

5 Arthur Russell to Odo Russell, January, 1866, in N. Blakiston, *The Roman Question: Extracts from the Despatches of Odo Russell* (London: Chapman Hall, 1962), p. xxxii.

6 Severn to Maria Severn, 8 January 1866, LMA, KPM/S 543, and 8 February 1866, *Letters and Memoirs*, p. 513; Severn to Thomas Severn, 22 March 1866, LMA, KPM/S 545.

7 Severn to Lord Stanley, 24 March 1868, TNA, FO 43/102.

8 Dr Small to Odo Russell, 21 December 1868, TNA, FO 43/103B. As Ewing had died on 18 November, it is possible that Small was unfairly appropriating his name.

9 Odo Russell to Dr Small, 22 December 1868, and to Severn, 22 December 1868, TNA, FO 43/103B.

10 Alexander Franz to Odo Russell, 25 January 1869, TNA, FO 43/103B.

11 Hammond to Lord Clarendon, 8 February 1869, TNA, FO 43/103B.

12 Severn to FO, 4 November 1869, TNA, FO 43/104.

13 Gladstone to Manning, 14 August 1870, BL Add MS 44249 f 179 and Granville to Gladstone, 25 September 1870, *The Gladstone–Granville Correspondence*, ed. A. Ramm; with a

supplementary introduction by H. C. G. Matthew (Cambridge: For the Royal Historical Society by Cambridge University Press, 1998), p. 131 (309).

14 Severn to Walter Severn, 24 February 1871, Charlton MS.

15 Jervoise to Hammond, 1 July 1869, TNA, FO 391/23.

16 See Noel Blakiston, 'Joseph Severn, Consul in Rome, 1861–1871', *History Today*, 18 (May 1968), 332.

17 FO to Jervoise, 26 July 1870, TNA, FO 43/105.

18 Blakiston, *The Roman Question*, p. 332, Jervoise to Lord Granville, 14 September 1870, TNA, FO 43/170, FO to Jervoise, 19 September 1870, FO 43/105.

19 Jervoise to Lord Granville, 27 October 1870, TNA, FO 43/170.

20 Blakiston, *The Roman Question*, pp. 333–4.

21 Severn to FO, 28 September 1870, TNA, FO 43/111.

22 Lord Granville to Severn, 10 October 1870, TNA, FO 43/111.

23 Severn to Thomas Severn, 22 October 1870, *Letters and Memoirs*, p. 524, and Severn to Odo Russell, 2 November 1870, *Letters* and *Memoirs*, p. 527.

24 Hammond to Lord Granville, 4 October 1870, TNA, FO 43/111.

25 Severn to Foreign Office, 12 October 1870, Jervoise to Severn, 14 October 1870, Severn to Jervoise, 21 October 1870, and Jervoise to Severn, 22 October 1870, TNA, FO 43/111.

26 Severn to Governor of Malta, 15 October 1870, TNA, FO 43/111.

27 Jervoise to Lord Granville, 27 October 1870, TNA, FO 43/111, Jervoise to Hammond, 30 October 1870, FO 391/23.

28 Severn to Paget, 22 and 29 October 1870, TNA, FO 45/163.

29 Paget to Hammond, 27 October 1870, TNA, FO 391/23.

30 Severn to Thomas Severn, 22 October 1870, *Letters and Memoirs*, p. 524.

31 Paget to Severn, 1 November 1870, TNA, FO 45/167.

32 Severn to Paget, 2 November 1870, TNA, FO 45/167. Granville backed up Severn's view that his consular services for the Italians gave him the right to address the Italian Foreign Minister direct on the subject of his consulate. Granville ms note on Paget to FO, 2 November 1870, FO 45/167.

33 Russell to Lord Granville, 22 September 1870, TNA, FO 43/111.

34 Blakiston, *The Roman Question*, p. 334.

35 Odo Russell to Edward Hammond, 2 November 1870, TNA, FO 43/111.

36 Hammond to Odo Russell, 2 November 1870, Granville to Severn, 5 November 1870, Hammond to Russell, 3 November 1870, Granville to Jervoise, 5 November 1870, TNA, FO 43/111, Jervoise to Hammond, 22 November 1870, FO 391/23.

37 Severn to Maria Severn 7, 10 December 1870, *Letters and Memoirs*, p. 528.

38 Severn to Walter Severn, 1 March 1871, Charlton MS.

39 Severn to Walter Severn, 19 December 1871, *Letters and Memoirs*, p. 532.

40 *Pall Mall Gazette*, 21 November 1874, from Severn's scrapbook of press cuttings in the possession of David Severn.

41 Walter Severn to Odo Russell, 7 January, 1872, FO 918/62.

42 Gladstone to Lord Granville, and Granville to Gladstone, 24 January 1872, *The Gladstone–Granville Correspondence*, pp. 301–2 (639 and 640).

43 Severn to Maria Severn 7, 10 December 1870, *Letters and Memoirs*, p. 528.

44 Severn to Odo Russell, 2 November 1870, *Letters and Memoirs*, p. 526. See too F. Gregorovius, *The Roman Journals of Ferdinand Gregorovius 1852–74*, ed. F. Althaus, trans.

G. W. Hamilton (London: George Bell, 1907), pp. 389 and 437 (13 November 1870 and 12 January 1873).

45 Severn to Odo Russell, 26 August 1872, TNA, FO 918/62.
46 Severn to Walter Severn, 8 January 1875, Harvard bMS 1434 (313), to Maria Severn, 1 July 1873, LMA, KPM/S 604, to Walter Severn, 8 January 1872, *Letters and Memoirs*, p. 541.
47 Walter Severn 'Notes for a Memoir', Houghton Library, Harvard bMS Eng 1434 (514).
48 Henry Furneaux to Mrs T. Furneaux, 30 March 1870, Charlton MS.
49 Severn to Maria Severn, 9 December 1877, LMA, KPM/S 638.
50 A. Severn, *The Professor: Arthur Severn's Memoir of John Ruskin*, ed. James S. Dearelove (London: George Allen & Unwin, 1962), p. 27.
51 J. Ruskin, *The Diaries of John Ruskin*, ed. Joan Evans and J. H. Whitehouse, 3 vols (Oxford: Clarendon Press, 1956–9), iii, p. 725 (11–20 May 1872).
52 J. Ruskin, *The Works of John Ruskin*, ed. E. T. Cook and A. Wedderburn, 39 vols (London: George Allen, 1903–12), xxxv: *Praeterita*, Pt III, p. 561.
53 Claudia Gale to Severn, 25 December 1873, Charlton MS; Severn to Walter Severn, 29 October 1875, Houghton Library, Harvard bMS Eng 1434 (315); Severn to Eleanor Furneaux, 5 February 1878, LMA, KPM/S 43.
54 Severn to Vincent Novello, 8 March 1828, BL Add. MS, Novello Papers, 11730 f.172.
55 Venosta-Castelli to Severn, 9 March 1871, Charlton MS.
56 Severn to Cardinal Giuseppe Bernardi, 6 July 1870, Houghton Library, Harvard bMS Eng 1434 (279). Severn's efforts on behalf of the citizens of Tolfa are still acknowledged on the town's website (<http://www.latolfa.com/cultura/storia/severn>).
57 Severn to Thomas Severn, 10 August 1873, *Letters and Memoirs*, pp. 537–9.
58 'My Tedious Life' is printed in full in *Letters and Memoirs* pp. 625–64.
59 Severn to Thomas Severn, 8 July 1873, *Letters and Memoirs*, p. 536.
60 Severn to Walter Severn, n.d.[January 1869] and Severn to Elizabeth Severn, 3 January 1862, Houghton Library, Harvard bMS Eng 1434 (307) and (301).
61 Severn to Odo Russell, 26 August 1872, TNA, FO 918/62.
62 Severn to Charles Severn, Easter Sunday (1 April) 1877, LMA, KPM/S 636; Severn to Eleanor Furneaux, 24 March 1877 (copy), LMA, KPM/S 44.
63 Severn to Maria Severn, 21 March 1875, LMA, KPM/S 619; Severn to Fanny de Llanos, 8 December 1870, *More Letters*, p. 89.
64 Severn to Eleanor Furneaux, 26 March 1877, LMA, KPM/S 43; Severn to Maria Severn, 14 February 1875, *Letters and Memoirs*, p. 542; and Severn to Walter Severn, 11 March 1877, Houghton Library, Harvard bMS Eng 1434 (315).
65 Severn to Eleanor Furneaux, 14 December 1876, LMA, KPM/S 43; and to Maria Severn, 8 September 1875, LMA, KPM/S 623.
66 'Lecture on the Manners of the Ancients', Houghton Library, MS Harvard bMS Eng 1434 (487).
67 Severn to Maria Severn, 24 September 1874, LMA, KPM/S 616.
68 Severn to Maria Severn, 5 July 1875, LMA, KPM/S 622; and to Eleanor Furneaux, 26 March 1877, LMA KPM/S 43.

Chapter 18 Keeper of the Flame

1 Of the many published accounts of these occasions, one by W. S. Graham is a forgery, 'Meetings with Severn in Old Age', *The New Review*, 10/60 (May 1894), 593–606 (reprinted

in W. Graham, *Last Links with Byron, Shelley, and Keats* [London, 1898]). More reliable are E. Robertson, 'Reminiscences of Meeting Joseph Severn in Old Age', in *Life and Letters*, pp. 301–3; M. A. de Wolfe Howe, 'A Talk with Joseph Severn about John Keats', in *John Keats Memorial Volume February 1821*, ed. G. C. Williamson (London and New York: John Lane, 1921), pp. 105–6; Edmund C. Stedman's account of a call on Severn in May 1879 in *Century Magazine*, 27 (February 1884), p. 603; R. W. G., 'Meetings with Severn in Old Age', *Century Magazine*, 71 (February 1906), pp. 551–2; and J. T. Fields, *James T. Fields, Biographical Notes and Personal Sketches, with Unpublished Fragments and Tributes from Men and Women of Letters*, ed. A. Adams Fields (London: Sampson, Low, 1881), p. 78.

2 De Wolfe Howe, *John Keats Memorial Volume February 1921*, p. 57.

3 Walter Severn's 'Notes for a memoir of Joseph Severn', Houghton Library, Harvard bMS Eng 1434 (514).

4 For an illuminating account of the vicissitudes of Severn's fame see *Letters and Memoirs*, pp. 2–15.

5 He extracted it from the collection of Keats's letters which Fanny de Llanos lent him in 1862 and then appears to have forgotten all about it. See Fanny de Llanos to H. B. Forman, 15 October 1881 in Nostrand, p. 378 and p. 379, n. 4.

6 Severn to Dilke, 21 February 1878, BL Add. MS 43910 f. 204 (Dilke Papers 37). Dilke is, himself, responsible for some confusion over which is the original of the Keats miniature. He described it as 'far finer' than the copy made for his grandfather. 'It is more luminous and the hands are better painted.' Dilke also said that it was painted in watercolour. As a result, Richard Walker concluded that the original was the one now in the Fitzwilliam Museum, Cambridge. Though undoubtedly painted in watercolour, it is rather crudely done by comparison with the much more finished version in the National Portrait Gallery, and the hands, in particular, are poor. Though Walker thought that the version in the National Portrait Gallery had been painted in oils, the conservation report on it refers to watercolour and it is this version which Donald Parson judged the original: R. Walker, *Regency Portraits* (London: National Portrait Gallery, 1985), p. 288 and D. Parson, *Portraits of Keats* (Cleveland: World Publishing Company, 1954), pp. 45–9.

7 C. W. Dilke, BL Add. MS 43910 f. 199 and 43898 f. 279. Dilke was not the only one to confuse Mrs Linder with the Lindon family. Sharp and Joanna Richardson made the same mistake.

8 Fanny de Llanos to unnamed correspondent, quoted in M. Adami, *Fanny Keats* (New Haven and London: Yale University Press, 1938), p. 215.

9 Plate 37 in Parson, *Portraits of Keats*.

10 Severn to Maria Severn 23 April and 21 March 1875, LMA, KPM/S 619.

11 Severn to Maria Severn, 18 May 1876, LMA, KPM/S 630.

12 Severn to Dilke, 21 February 1878, BL Add. MS 43910 f. 204. Severn did not mention that the opening pages of the poem were missing. This, together with his advancing years, may explain his difficulty in remembering the poem's title. He first wrote it down as 'the Legend of St Agnes'.

13 Severn to Maria Severn, 23 April 1875, *Letters and Memoirs*, p. 545; Bodleian MS 41767 MS Eng.lett. d.338 ff. 6–9; and Houghton Library, Harvard MS bm S Am 1569.7 (577) *45M-183.

14 Severn to Maria Severn, 14 February 1875, *Letters and Memoirs*, p. 543, and 5 October, 1877, LMA, KPM/S 637, and Severn to Dilke n.d. (extract) LMA, KPM/B 055.

15 Severn to Lord Houghton, 28 September 1864, *Letters and Memoirs*, p. 509.

16 Severn to Lord Houghton, 26 October 1869, *Keats Circle*, ii, pp. 329–30.

17 Severn to Lord Houghton, 23 March 1868, *Keats Circle*, ii, p. 329. The original has now been lost. A posthumous oil painting showing a rather lugubrious, long-nosed Keats, based on Severn's miniature is in the National Portrait Gallery. By 1877 Severn had got confused and assumed that it was an engraving of this which Houghton had used: Severn to H. B. Forman, 20 October, 1877, in J. Severn, *John Keats: Letters of Joseph Severn to H. Buxton Forman* (Oxford: privately printed, 1933), p. 11.

18 C. C. Clarke to Severn, 11 February 1864 and 2 June 1875, *Life and Letters*, pp. 265 and 258.

19 See Severn to Arthur Severn, 18 February 1877: 'If you meet Lord Houghton, do address him as "my Son" for he is a dear friend of mine of many years standing & is an excellent good man', *Letters and Memoirs*, p. 548; and Severn to Lord Houghton, 26 October 1869 and 8 June 1873, *Keats Circle*, ii, pp. 329 and 333.

20 Severn had arranged with the Fields for them to send Houghton a photo of the portrait: Severn to J. T. Fields 25 April 1871, *Letters and Memoirs*, p. 530.

21 R. M. Milnes, *The Poetical Works of John Keats, with a memoir, by Lord Houghton: A New Revised and Enlarged Edition* (London: E. Moxon, Son & Co, 1871), p xi, and idem, *The Poetical Works of John Keats Chronologically Arranged and Edited, with a Memoir by Lord Houghton* (London: Aldine edition of the British Poets, 1876), p. xxix.

22 Severn to Thomas Severn, 10 August 1873 LMA, KPM/S 605, E. C. Stedman, *Century Magazine*, 27 (February 1884), p. 603.

23 Severn to H. B. Forman, 23 October, 1877, in Severn, *John Keats*, p. 13.

24 Severn to H. B. Forman, 15 November 1875, ibid., p. 1.

25 Sarah Clarke to Emma Speed, 3 February 1875, Keats–Shelley Memorial House MS 8.1.1.

26 Eyre to Lord Houghton, 23 March 1875, *Keats Circle*, ii, p. 341.

27 C. C. Clarke to Severn, 3 June 1875, *Life and Letters*, p. 258.

28 Sarah Clarke to Emma Speed, 3 February 1875, Keats–Shelley Memorial House MS 8.1.1.

29 *Illustrated Evening News*, 28 August 1875, p. 214.

30 *Illustrated London News*, 11 March 1876, p. 35.

31 Eyre to Lord Houghton, 4 February 1877, *Keats Circle*, ii, pp. 354–6.

32 *Daily News*, 3 March 1879, *The Times*, 1 March 1879.

33 Eyre to the Editor, *Athenaeum*, 2687, 26 April 1879, p. 536.

34 Houghton Library, Harvard bMS Eng 1434 (516). The plaque, as can now be seen, was recarved to show Keats's age at death as twenty-five. The date of death, however, remains the same as on the tombstone.

35 Severn to H. B. Forman, 10 January 1876 and 21 October 1877, in Severn, *John Keats*, pp. 3 and 4. Interestingly, in his correspondence with Forman, Severn did not claim that the annotations were by Byron.

36 H. B. Forman to Severn, 23 September 1877, Houghton Library, Harvard bMS Eng 1434 (78).

37 Ibid.

38 Severn to H. B. Forman, 26 September 1877, in Severn, *John Keats*, p. 9.

39 Severn to Maria Severn, 9 December 1877, LMA, KPM/S 638.

40 H. B. Forman to Severn, 23 September 1877, Houghton Library, Harvard bMS Eng 1434 (78).

41 The other two were Froude's *Life of Carlyle* published in 1882, which detailed the Carlyles' domestic misery, and John Cordy Jeaffreson's *The Real Shelley* published in 1885, which revealed the story of Shelley's first marriage and the suicide of his wife, Harriet. See R. Altick, *Lives and Letters: A History of Literary Biography in England and America* (New York: Alfred A. Knopf, 1966).

Notes

42 Severn to Maria Severn, 9 December 1877, LMA, KPM/S 638.

43 Severn to H. B. Forman, 28 October 1876, in Severn, *John Keats*. Ironically, the two figures are now thought to be representations of the same woman.

44 H. B. Forman to Severn, 15 September, 24 October, and 5 December 1878, Houghton Library, Harvard bMS Eng 1434 (80), (83) and (85).

45 Severn to H. B. Forman, 28 October 1877 and 20 October 1877, in Severn, *John Keats*, pp. 14 and 11.

46 See J. Richardson, *Fanny Brawne* (London: Vanguard Press, 1952), pp. 149 and 178 n. 11.

47 Severn's annotated copy of *Adonais* is now in the Pierpont Morgan Library, New York, (PML 20023). The side and under-linings are in a bold hand, quite unlike Severn's. The selection of marked passages is an idiosyncratic one with many of the most famous lines about Keats overlooked. The most heavily marked passage is in stanzas 36 and 37, which contain the words Trelawny wanted Severn to use for Keats's epitaph, 'Whose master's hand is cold, whose silver lyre unstrung'. That coincidence and the absence of any of Byron's usual depredations when borrowing books (the turned-down corners of which Leigh Hunt complained), suggest that the markings are Trevelyan's and possibly made when he was in Rome in spring 1823 overseeing the reburial of Shelley's ashes. Severn's claims that the annotations were Byron's were familiar within his family. See, for example, Eleanor Furneaux to Walter Severn, 20 January 1880: 'I have frequently heard from my father the story of his lending the "Adonais" to Lord Byron—who returned it to him with a note saying how fine he thought it all especially the passages he had marked with ink. My father showed us the Adonais again when we were in Rome last and particularly pointed out to us Byron's bold ink markings': Houghton Library, Harvard bMS Eng 1434 (389).

48 Severn to H. B. Forman, 20 October 1877, in Severn, *John Keats*, p. 11.

49 H. B. Forman to Severn, n.d., Houghton Library, Harvard bMSEng 1434 (82).

50 John Keats, *Letters of John Keats to Fanny Brawne, written in the years 1819 and 1820, and now given from the original manuscripts*, with introduction and notes by Harry Buxton Forman (London: Reeves & Turner, 1878), p. ix; *Life and Letters*, p. 272.

51 Severn to H. B. Forman, 10 December 1877, in Severn, *John Keats*, p. 18.

52 C. W. Dilke, ed., *The Papers of a Critic Selected from the Writings of the Late Charles Wentworth Dilke with a Biographical Sketch by his Grandson*, 2 vols (London: John Murray, 1875), i, pp. 7–11.

53 *Athenaeum*, 2625, 16 February 1878, p. 217.

54 Arnold and Swinburne are quoted in G. H. Ford, *Keats and the Victorians: A Study of His Influence and Rise to Fame 1821–1895* (New Haven and London: Yale University Press, 1944), pp. 71 and 169.

55 Severn to H. B. Forman, 5 February 1878, in Severn, *John Keats*, p. 20.

56 Ibid.

57 Walter Severn had no hesitation in connecting the stroke with Severn's distress over the publication of Keats's letters: Walter Severn to Eleanor Furneaux, 16 March 1878, Charlton MS.

58 *The Times*, 5 March 1878.

59 The Revd H. W. Wasse to Walter Severn, 6 August 1879, Keats–Shelley Memorial House MS Box 8 4.2 3.

60 Rose Wild collection.

61 M. Howitt, ed., *Mary Howitt: An Autobiography*, 2 vols (London: William Isbister, 1889), ii, p. 212.

62 E. C. Stedman, *Century Magazine*, 27 (February 1884), p. 603. 'RWG' also claimed to have met Severn for the first time that month, ibid., 71 (February 1906), pp. 55–2. See, too, Sarah Clarke to Emma Speed, 7 April, 1876: 'I don't know any one who seems to enjoy life more': Keats–Shelley Memorial House MS Box 8.2.

63 Severn to Walter Severn, 3 April 1877, Houghton Library, Harvard bMS Eng 1434 (317).

64 Severn to Maria Severn, 8 September 1875, LMA, KPM/S 623, and to Eleanor Furneaux, 14 December 1876 (copy), LMA, KPM/S 43.

65 *Life and Letters*, p. 278, and Severn to Eleanor Furneaux, 31 May 1879, Charlton MS.

66 Severn to Charles Severn, 'Easter Sunday' (1 April), 1877, LMA, KPM/S 636.

67 The Revd H. W. Wasse to Walter Severn, 6 August, 1879, Keats–Shelley Memorial House MS Box 8.4 23.

68 Severn to Maria Severn, 1 May 1879, LMA, KPM/S 645.

69 Severn to Maria Severn, 15 March, 1879, and to Charles Severn, 'Easter Sunday' (1 April), 1877, LMA, KPM/S 644 and 636.

70 Walter Severn to Eleanor Furneaux, 16 March 1878, Charlton MS.

71 See, for example, Keats to Severn, 29 March 1819, Houghton Library, Harvard MS Keats MS 1.50.

72 Severn to James T. Fields, 1 January 1879, *Letters and Memoirs*, p. 558.

73 Severn to Miss Haslam, 25 August 1878, New York, Pierpont Morgan MS, MA 790.

74 Twenty-three Severns got together in London to celebrate Henry's return. Severn to Maria Severn, 15 March 1879, LMA, KPMS 644.

75 'Very soon after [Keats] died my Father took a warm mould of the face, and then made a chalk cast, this is from the latter and has never been seen…don't let it be copied': Henry Severn to J. W. Guild, 23 June 1880, Charlton MS. Though copies of the death mask were very much scarcer than the life mask, Severn had forgotten that he had sent the original wax mask to Taylor. Lord Houghton bought it at a sale after Taylor's death and later copies, including that in the Keats–Shelley House, were probably made from this version. See Willard B. Pope, 'The Masks of Keats', *English Miscellany: A Symposium of History Literature and the Arts* (Rome, 1950), i, pp. 191–6. The mask of Keats which Henry photographed was willed to Valeriani. On his death in 1882 it passed to Henry Severn, who died shortly after, in 1883 in India, and may never have received it: Margharita Valeriani to Walter Severn, 23 February 1882, Houghton Library, Harvard bMS Eng 1434 (444). It seems likely that it then came to Eleanor Furneaux, whose children remembered seeing it in a box under the stairs in their early years: (Parson, *Portraits of Keats*, p. 77). A catalogue note for the sale of a copy of the death mask at Christies in 1996 suggests that Eleanor had this copy, with a note on the back by Severn identifying it as the death mask, destroyed. Severn was not the only one to confuse copies of the life and death masks. In the 1920s and 1930s the Victoria & Albert Museum casting service worked from a matrix described as the death mask which was identified in 1936 as a version of Haydon's life mask, probably made by the Brucciani firm of cast-makers: catalogue for Lot 461 in Christies sale 5718, 27 November 1996.

76 Severn to Maria Severn, 19 February 1821, *Letters and Memoirs*, p. 129 and 15 March 1879, LMA, KPM/S 644.

77 Alexander Franz to Walter Severn, 6 August 1879, Houghton Library, Harvard bMSEng 1434 (375).

Notes

Epilogue: A Fitting Place

1 *Daily News*, 11 August 1879, p. 5 and *The Times*, 11 August 1879.
2 *The Times*, 19 August 1879.
3 Alexander Franz to Walter Severn, 16 and 25 August 1879, Houghton Library, Harvard bMS Eng 1434 (376) and (377).
4 *The Times*, 14 August 1879, p. 11.
5 Inventory of Severn's possessions at death (in Italian), Houghton Library, Harvard bMS Eng 1434 (523).
6 The Revd H. W. Wasse to Walter Severn, 6 August 1879, Keats–Shelley House MS 8.4.23; Franz to Walter Severn, 22 October 1879 and 22 February 1880, Houghton Library, Harvard bMS Eng 1434 (378) and (382).
7 Walter Severn to Eleanor Furneaux, 16 March 1878, Charlton MS.
8 Ruskin to Walter Severn, 23 April [1880], Houghton Library, Harvard bMS 1434 (429).
9 See I. S. Monro, 'The British Academy of Arts in Rome', *Journal of the Royal Society of Arts*, 102, 42–56.
10 Walter Severn to Lord Houghton, 11 March 1880, Houghton Library, Harvard bMS 1434 (469).
11 Walter Severn to Eleanor Furneaux, 16 March 1878, Charlton MS.
12 Walter Severn's first draft of the petition is at LMA, KPM/S 68; a copy of the final text is in the Charlton MS. The official permission dated 30 March 1881 is at LMA, KPM/S 69.
13 J. W. Field to Walter Severn, 17 May 1881, Houghton Library, Harvard bMS Eng 1434 (371).
14 Vincent Eyre to Walter Severn, 27 April 1881, Houghton Library, Harvard bMS Eng 1434 (370).
15 R. W. Gilder to Walter Severn, n.d., and W. M. Rossetti to Walter Severn, 5 July 1881, Houghton Library, Harvard bMS Eng 1434 (391) and (416).
16 Eyre to Walter Severn, 4 April, 1881, Houghton Library, Harvard bMS 1434 (367).
17 E. Furneaux to Walter Severn, 14 April 1881, and Eyre to Walter Severn, 15 April 1881, Houghton Library, Harvard bMS 1434 (390) and (369).
18 *Daily News*, 18 February 1882, p. 5.
19 Franz to Walter Severn, 12 August 1881, Keats–Shelley House MS 8.9; Walter Severn to Lord Houghton, 14 July 1881, Houghton Library, Harvard bMS 1434 (470).
20 *The Times*, 4 March 1882, Augustus Paget to Walter Severn, 14 February and 3 March 1882, Houghton Library, Harvard bMS 1434 (413) and (412).
21 Lord Houghton to Walter Severn, n.d., J. Pope Hennessey, *Monckton Milnes: The Flight of Youth, 1851–1885* (London: Constable, 1951), p. 253.
22 Odo Russell to his mother, 30 March 1868, TNA, FO 918/85.

SELECT BIBLIOGRAPHY

Archival Sources

Private Collections

Charlton MS (in the possession of Lady Juliet Townsend), including Severn family correspondence, ms diaries of Eleanor Severn and Mary Newton and Mary Newton sketchbooks.

MS Townsend (in the possession of Lady Juliet Townsend, on temporary deposit in the Northamptonshire Record Office), including letters from Severn to his wife and correspondence of Mary Newton with the Severn family.

Severn's collections of press cuttings in the possession of David Severn.

Collection of Severn sketchbooks, drawings, and other memorabilia in the possession of Ross Severn.

Collection of Severn sketchbooks, commonplace books, portraits, drawings, photographs, and other memorabilia relating to Severn and Walter Severn in the possession of Rose Wild.

Severn family portraits in the possession of Mrs Katharine Mackenzie.

Public Collections

Archive Municipale, Marseille: record of Elizabeth Severn's death.

Bodleian Library: Finch Papers, Maria Callcott Diaries.

British Library: Dilke Papers, Gladstone Papers, Novello Papers.

Churchill College, Cambridge: Dilke–Roskill Papers.

Dr Williams Library, London: Henry Crabb Robinson diaries and correspondence.

Flintshire Record Office: Gladstone–Glynne Mss on deposit from St Deiniol's Library, Hawarden.

Guildhall Library, City of London: Weavers' Company Archive.

Houghton Library, Harvard: Joseph Severn Papers, at bMS Eng 1434, Severn Scrapbook at MS Eng 1460, MS Keats, Edmund Blunden Papers.

John Rylands University Library of Manchester: Papers of the Royal Fine Arts Commission (seen in photostat).

Keats–Shelley Memorial House, Rome: MS Box 8 relating to Severn's late years, death and burial.

London Metropolitan Archive: Keats House Papers including Severn's correspondence with his parents and siblings, Buxton Forman Papers, Records of births, marriages, and deaths, Poor Law rate registers.

National Archive, Kew: Russell Papers, Foreign Office Consular files.

National Art Library at the Victoria & Albert Museum: C. R. Leslie correspondence.

Carl H. Pforzheimer Collections of Shelley and His Circle at the New York Public Library: letters from Severn to Charles Brown.

Pierpont Morgan Library, New York: Severn's annotated copy of *Adonais*, Dilke's annotated copy of R. M. Milnes's *Life of Keats* and Severn correspondence.

Select Bibliography

Royal Academy Archive: RA Council and General Assembly minutes, RA students register 1769–1829, Fuseli Papers, Lawrence Papers, George Richmond Papers.

Ruskin Library, University of Lancaster: Mary Richardson ms diaries, John Ruskin ms diaries.

Trinity College, Cambridge: Houghton Papers.

General and Literary Manuscripts, Wilson Library, University of North Carolina at Chapel Hill: George Richmond Papers (seen in photostat).

The Witt Collection, Somerset House, London: photographs of some of Severn's artwork.

Secondary Sources

Abbott, Claude Colleer, *The Life and Letters of George Darley, Poet and Critic* (London: Oxford University Press, 1928).

Adami, Marie, *Fanny Keats* (New Haven and London: Yale University Press, 1938).

Agresti, Olivia Rossetti, *Giovanni Costa: His Life, Work and Times* (London: Grant Richards, 1904).

Allen, Peter, *The Cambridge Apostles: The Early Years* (Cambridge: Cambridge University Press, 1978).

Allingham, William, *A Diary*, ed. H. Allingham and D. Radford (London: Macmillan & Co., 1907).

Altick, Richard, *The Cowden Clarkes* (London: Oxford University Press, 1948).

——, *Lives and Letters: A History of Literary Biography in England and America* (New York: Alfred A Knopf, 1965).

Andrews, Keith, *The Nazarenes: A Brotherhood of German Painters in Rome* (Oxford: Clarendon Press, 1964).

Annals of the Fine Arts, ed., James Elmes, 5 vols (London: 1817–1821).

Anon., 'A Reminiscence of Joseph Severn', *Dublin University Review*, 91 (1880), 96–8.

The Art-Union, a Monthly Journal of the Fine Arts, Arts Decorative and Ornamental (London, 1839–46).

Anstruther, Ian, *The Knight and the Umbrella: An Account of the Eglinton Tournament 1839* (London: Geoffrey Bles, 1963).

Atlay, J. B., *Sir Henry Wentworth Acland, Bart. K.C.B., F.R.S.: A Memoir* (London: Smith Elder, 1903).

D'Azeglio, Tapparelli (Marchese Massimo), *Things I Remember*, trans. and introd. E. R. P. Vincent (London: Oxford University Press, 1966).

Barrell, John, *The Political Theory of Painting from Reynolds to Hazlitt: 'The Body of the Public'* (New Haven and London: Yale University Press, 1986).

Bate, Walter Jackson, *John Keats* (Cambridge, MA: Harvard University Press, 1963).

Beck-Friis, Johan, *The Protestant Cemetery in Rome: The Cemetery of Artists and Poets* (Malmo, Sweden: Allhems Forlag, 1995).

Bennett, Andrew, *Romantic Poets and the Culture of Posterity* (Cambridge: Cambridge University Press, 1999).

Birkenhead, Sheila, *Against Oblivion: The Life of Joseph Severn* (London: Cassell and Company, 1943).

——, *Illustrious Friends: The Story of Joseph Severn and His Son Arthur* (London: Hamish Hamilton, 1965).

Blainey, Ann, *Immortal Boy A Portrait of Leigh Hunt* (London: Croom Helm, 1985).

Blakiston, Georgiana, *Woburn and the Russells* (London: Constable, 1980).

Select Bibliography

Blakiston, Noel, *The Roman Question: Extracts from the Despatches of Odo Russell* (London: Chapman Hall, 1962).

——, 'Joseph Severn, Consul in Rome, 1861–1871', *History Today*, 18 (May 1968), 326–36.

Blunden, Edmund, *Shelley and Keats as they Struck their Contemporaries: Notes Partly from Manuscript Sources* (London: C. W. Beaumont, 1925).

——, *Leigh Hunt: A Biography* (London: Cobden-Sanderson, 1930).

——, *Keats's Publisher: A Memoir of John Taylor (1781–1864)* (London: Jonathan Cape, 1936).

Boutflower, Andrew, *Personal Reminiscences of Manchester Cathedral, 1854–1912* (Manchester: Faith Press, 1913).

Brand, C. P., *Italy and the English Romantics: The Italianate Fashion in Early Nineteenth-Century England* (Cambridge: Cambridge University Press, 1957).

Brock, Lord (Russell Claude), *John Keats and Joseph Severn: The Tragedy of the Last Illness* (London: The Keats–Shelley Memorial Association, 1973).

Bromley, J., *The Man of Ten Talents: A Portrait of Richard Chenevix Trench* (London: SPCK, 1959).

Brown, Charles, 'The Wishing Cap' No XVI 'Actors and Artists at Rome', *The Examiner*, 3 (October, 1824), 626–8.

——, *Life of John Keats*, ed. Dorothy Hyde Bodurtha and Willard Bissell Pope (London: Oxford University Press, 1937).

——, *Some Letters and Miscellanea of Charles Brown the Friend of Keats & Thomas Richards*, ed. Maurice Buxton Forman (London: Oxford University Press, 1937).

——, *The Letters of Charles Armitage Brown*, ed. Jack Stillinger (Cambridge, MA: Harvard University Press, 1966).

——, *New Letters from Charles Brown to Joseph Severn*, ed. Grant F. Scott and Sue Brown (University of Maryland Romantic Circles Electronic Edition, December 2007, <http:/www.rc.umd.edu/editions/brownsevern>).

Brown, Sally, 'Suppose Me In Rome', in *Keats and Italy: A History of the Keats–Shelley House in Rome* (Rome, Il Labirinto, 2005).

Brown, Sue, 'Fresh Light on the Friendship of Charles Brown and Joseph Severn', *Keats–Shelley Review*, 18 (2004), 138–48.

——, 'The Friend of Keats: the Reinvention of Joseph Severn' in Eugene Stelzig, ed., *Romantic Autobiography* (Aldershot: Ashgate, 2009).

——, 'Joseph Severn and the Establishment of the British Academy of Arts in Rome', *Journal of Anglo-Italian Studies*, 10 (2009) (University of Malta).

Browning, Robert and Elizabeth Barrett, *The Brownings' Correspondence*, ed. Philip Kelley and Scott Lewis, 14 vols (London: Athlone Press, 1994).

Bunsen, Frances, *A Memoir of Baron Bunsen*, 2 vols (London: Longmans, 1868).

Busco, Marie, *Sir Richard Westmacott Sculptor* (Cambridge: Cambridge University Press, 1994).

Cavaliero, Roderick, 'A Place too Savage for an Invalid', *Keats–Shelley Review*, 6, (1991), 1–17.

—— 'A Swoon to Death: Keats's Debt to Italy', *Keats–Shelley Review*, 11 (1997), 41–51.

——, *Italia Romantica* (London: I.B.Tauris, 2005).

Chadwick, Owen, *A History of the Popes 1830–1914* (Oxford: Clarendon Press, 1998).

Clark, James, *Medical Notes on Climate, Disease, Hospitals, and Medical Schools in France, Italy and Switzerland, comprising an Inquiry into the Effects of a Residence in the South of Europe in cases of Pulmonary Consumption, and illustrating the Present State of Medicine in Those Countries, London* (London: T. & G. Underwood, 1820).

Select Bibliography

Clarke, Charles Cowden, 'Recollections of Keats', *Atlantic Monthly*, 7 (1861), 86–100.

—— and Mary Cowden, *Recollections of Writers* (London: Sampson, Low, 1878).

Clarke, Mary Cowden, *My Long Life: An Autobiographic Sketch* (London: Fisher Unwin, 1896).

Cobbett, James P., *Journal of a Tour in Italy and also in Parts of France and Switzerland from October 1828 to September 1829* (London: Mills, 1830).

Cockerell, C. R., *Travels in Southern Europe and the Levant, 1810–1817*, ed. J. P. Cockerell (London: Longman Green, 1903).

Collins, John, *The Two Forgers: A Biography of Harry Buxton Forman & Thomas James Wise* (Aldershot: Scolar Press, 1992).

Collins, W. Wilkie, *Memoirs of the Life of William Collins RA*, 2 vols (London: Longman, 1848).

Colvin, Sydney, *John Keats: His Life and Poetry, His Friends Critics and After-Fame* (London: Macmillan, 1917).

Cunningham, Allan, *The Life of Sir David Wilkie with his Journals, Tours and Critical Remarks on Works of Art*, 3 vols (London: John Murray, 1843).

——, *The Lives of the Most Eminent British Painters, Sculptors & Architects*, 3 vols (London: George Bell, 1879–80).

Dafforne, James, *The Life and Works of Edward Matthew Ward R.A.* (London: Virtue & Co., [1879]).

De Cesare, Raffaele, *The Last Days of Papal Rome 1850–1870*, trans. Helen Zimmern (London: Archibald Constable, 1909).

De Wolfe Howe, M., 'A Talk with Joseph Severn about John Keats', in *Keats Memorial Volume February 1821*, ed. George C. Williamson (London and New York: John Lane, 1921), pp. 105–6.

Dicey, Edward, *Rome in 1860* (London: Macmillan, 1861).

Dictionary of National Biography, ed. Leslie Stephen and Sidney Lee, 22 vols (London: Oxford University Press, repr. 1921–2).

Dilke, Charles Wentworth, *The Papers of a Critic Selected from the Writings of the Late Charles Wentworth Dilke, with a Biographical Sketch by his Grandson*, 2 vols (London: John Murray, 1875).

Dormandy, Thomas, *The White Death: A History of Tuberculosis* (London: Hambledon & London, 1999).

Eastlake, Charles Locke, *Contributions to the Literature of the Fine Arts Second Series with a Memoir compiled by Lady Eastlake* (London: John Murray, 1870).

Eaton, Charlotte, *Rome in the Nineteenth Century*, 3 vols (Edinburgh: Hurst, Robinson, 1820).

Edgecumbe, Fred, ed., *Letters of Fanny Brawne to Fanny Keats (1820–1824)* (London: Oxford University Press, 1936).

Evans, B. Ifor, 'Keats and Joseph Severn: A Re-Estimate with Unpublished Letters', *London Mercury*, 30 (August 1934), 337–49.

Evans, Dorinda, *Benjamin West and his American Students* (London and Washington: Smithsonian Institution Press, 1980).

Fenton, James, *School of Genius: A History of the Royal Academy of Arts* (London: Royal Academy of Arts, 2006).

Select Bibliography

Fields, James T., *James T. Fields, Biographical Notes and Personal Sketches, with Unpublished Fragments and Tributes from Men and Women of Letters*, ed. Annie Adams Fields (London: Sampson, Low, 1881).

Flagg, Jared Bradley, *The Life and Letters of Washington Allston* (London: R. Bentley, 1893).

Ford, George H., *Keats and the Victorians: A Study of His Influence and Rise to Fame* (New Haven and London: Yale University Press, 1944).

Galignani, A. and W., with Cyrus Redding, *The Poetical Works of Coleridge, Shelley and Keats* (Paris: Galignani, 1829).

Galt, John, *The Life, Studies and Works of Benjamin West* (London: Cadell & Davies, 1820).

Garlick, Kenneth, *Sir Thomas Lawrence* (London: Routledge & Kegan Paul, 1954).

Gates, Eleanor M., ed., *Leigh Hunt: A Life in Letters Together with some Correspondence of William Hazlitt* (Essex, CT: Falls River Press, 2000).

Gay, H. Nelson, 'Keats Roman Piano' and 'Keats's Last Bank Account', *Bulletin & Review of the Keats–Shelley Memorial Rome*, 2 (1913), 95–9.

——, 'The Protestant Burial-Ground in Rome. A Historical Sketch. The Preservation of the graves of Keats and Shelley. A personal reminiscence. By Sir Rennell Rodd' (London: Macmillan & Co, 1913).

George, Eric, *The Life and Death of Benjamin Robert Haydon, Historical Painter 1786–1846* (London: Oxford University Press, 1948).

Gigliucci, Contessa Valeria, ed., *Clara Novello's Reminiscences* (London: Edward Arnold, 1910).

Gilbert, M., ed., *A Century of Conflict 1850–1950: Essays for A.J.P. Taylor* (London: Hamish Hamilton, 1966).

Gilchrist, Alexander, *Life of William Etty R.A.*, 2 vols (London: David Bogne, 1855).

Gittings, Robert, *John Keats: The Living Year* (London: Heinemann, 1954).

——, *The Mask of Keats: A Study of Problems* (London: Heinemann, 1956).

——, *John Keats* (Harmondsworth: Penguin, 1971).

——, ed., *Letters of John Keats: A New Selection* (London: Oxford University Press, 1970).

Gladstone, William Ewart, *The Gladstone Diaries*, ed. M. R. D. Foot and H. C. G. Matthew, 14 vols (vols 1–2 ed. M. R. D. Foot) (Oxford: Oxford University Press, 1968–94).

The Gladstone–Granville Correspondence, ed. Agatha Ramm; with a supplementary introduction by H. C. G. Matthew (Cambridge: For the Royal Historical Society by Cambridge University Press, 1998).

Gott, Joseph, *Joseph Gott 1786–1860 Sculptor*, ed. Terry Friedman and Timothy Stevens (Leeds and Liverpool: exhibition catalogue, 1972).

Graham, Maria, *Three Months passed in the Mountains East of Rome during the Year 1819* (London: 1821).

Graham, William, 'Meetings with Joseph Severn in Old Age', *New Review*, 10 (London, May 1894), 593–606.

Graves, Algernon, *A Dictionary of Artists Who Have Exhibited Works in the Principal London Exhibitions from 1760–1893*, 3 vols (London: H. Graves, 1901).

——, *The Royal Academy of Arts: A Complete Dictionary of Contributors & their Work from its Foundation in 1769 to 1904*, 8 vols (London: Graves and Bell, 1905–6).

——, *The British Institution 1806–1867: A Complete Dictionary of Contributors and their Work from the Foundation of the Institution* (London: George Bell, 1908).

——, *Art Sales from Early in Eighteenth Century to Early in Twentieth Century (mostly Old Masters and Early English Pictures)* (London: Graves, 1918).

Select Bibliography

Grayling, A. C., *The Quarrel of the Age: The Life and Times of William Hazlitt* (London: Weidenfeld & Nicolson, 2000).

Gregorovius, Ferdinand, *The Roman Journals of Ferdinand Gregorovius 1852–74*, ed. Friedrich Althaus, trans. Mrs Gustavus W. Hamilton (London: George Bell, 1907).

Griffin, Daniel, *Life of Gerald Griffin* (London: James Diffy, 1843).

Gruner, Ludwig, ed., *The Decorations of the Garden Pavilion in the Grounds of Buckingham Palace* (London: John Murray 1846).

Von Hagen, Victor Wolfgang, *Frederick Catherwood Architect* (New York: Oxford University Press, 1950).

Hale-White, William, *Keats as Doctor and Patient* (London: Oxford University Press, 1938).

Hallam, Arthur, *The Writings of Arthur Hallam*, ed. T. H. Vail Motter (London: Oxford University Press, 1943).

Hanna, William, ed., *Letters of Thomas Erskine of Winlathen* (New York: 1877).

Hare, Augustus, *The Life and Letters of Frances Baroness Bunsen*, 2 vols (London: Smith and Elder, 1882).

Haydon, Benjamin Robert, *Benjamin Robert Haydon Correspondence and Table-Talk with a Memoir by his Son Frederic Wordsworth Haydon*, 2 vols (London: Chatto & Windus, 1876).

——, *Autobiography with an Introduction and Epilogue by Edmund Blunden* (London: Oxford University Press World's Classics, 1927).

——*Neglected Genius: The Diaries of Benjamin Robert Haydon 1808–46*, ed. John Jolliffe (London: Hutchinson, 1990).

Hayter, Alethea, *A Sultry Month Scenes of London Literary Life in 1846* (London: Faber & Faber, 1965).

Hazlitt, William, *Notes of a Journey through France and Italy [By W.H.]* (London: H. Colborne, 1826).

——, *Complete Works*, vol. 17: *Uncollected Essays*, ed. P. P. Howe (London: J. M. Dent, 1933).

Hennell, Michael, *The Deans and Canons of Manchester Cathedral 1840–1948* (Manchester: privately printed [1987]).

Herrmann, Luke, *Nineteenth-Century British Painting* (London: Giles de la Mare Publishers, 2000).

Hewlett, Dorothy, *Adonais: A Life of John Keats* (London: Hurst and Blackett, 1937).

Hodgson, J. E. and Frederick A. Eaton, *The Royal Academy and its Members 1768–1830* (London: John Murray, 1905).

Holden, Anthony, *The Wit in the Dungeon: A Life of Leigh Hunt* (London: Little Brown, 2005).

Hoock, Holger, *The King's Artists: The Royal Academy of Arts as a 'National Institution' 1768–1820* (Oxford: Oxford University Press, 2000).

Horsley, John Callcott, *Recollections of a Royal Academician* (London: John Murray, 1903).

Horwood, Richard, *The A–Z of Regency London* (London: London Topographical Society, 1985).

Howitt, Margaret, ed., *Mary Howitt: An Autobiography*, 2 vols (London: Wm Isbister, 1889).

Hughes-Hallett, Penelope, *The Immortal Dinner* (London: Viking, 2000).

Hunt, Leigh, *The Autobiography of Leigh Hunt; with Reminiscences of Friends and Contemporaries* (Oxford: Oxford University Press [World's Classics series], 1923).

Hutchison, Sidney C., *The History of the Royal Academy 1768–1986* (London: Royce, 1986).

——, *The Homes of the Royal Academy* (London: Royal Academy of Arts, 1956).

Ilchester, the Earl of, *Elizabeth, Lady Holland to her Son 1821–1845* (London: John Murray, 1946).

———, ed., *The Journal of the Hon. H.E. Fox (afterwards fourth and last Lord Holland) 1818–1830* (London: Thornton Butterworth, 1923).

D'Ildeville, H. A., *Journal d'un diplomate en Italie 1862–66* (Paris: 1873).

Isaacson, Charles, *The Story of the English Cardinals* (London: Elliot Stock, 1907).

Jack, Ian, *Keats and the Mirror of Art* (Oxford: Clarendon Press, 1967).

[Jameson, Anna], *Diary of an Ennuyee* (London: Henry Colburn, 1826).

Jenkins, Elizabeth, 'Dr Gully, Severn and an Experiment in Psychometry', *Keats–Shelley Memorial Bulletin*, 21 (1970), 39–40.

Jenkins, Roy, *Gladstone* (London: Macmillan, 1995).

Keats, John, *Letters of John Keats to Fanny Brawne, written in the years 1819 and 1820, and now given from the original manuscripts*, with introduction and notes by Harry Buxton Forman (London: Reeves & Turner, 1878).

———, *The Letters of John Keats 1814–21*, ed. H. E. Rollins, 2 vols (Cambridge, MA: Harvard University Press, 1958).

———, *The Poems of John Keats*, ed. Jack Stillinger (London: Heinemann, 1978).

Knowles, John, *The Life and Writings of Henry Fuseli Esq M.A.R.A.*, 3 vols (London: Henry Colburn, 1831).

Kubler-Ross, Elizabeth, *On Death and Dying* (New York: Touchstone, 1997).

Landseer, Thomas, ed., *Life and Letters of William Bewick (Artist)*, 2 vols (London: Hurst and Blackett, 1871).

Lamert, B., *The History & Survey of London and Its Environs: From the Earliest Period to the Present Times*, 4 vols with atlas (London: T. Hughes, 1806).

Lehmann, Rudolf, *An Artist's Reminiscences* (London: Smith and Elder, 1894).

Leslie, Charles Robert, *Autobiographical Recollections*, ed. Tom Taylor, 2 vols (London: John Murray, 1860).

Leslie, George Dunlop, *The Inner Life of the Royal Academy with an Account of its Schools & Exhibitions Principally in the Reign of Queen Victoria* (London: John Murray, 1914).

Lessing, Doris, *The Diaries of Jane Somers* (London: Flamingo, 2002).

Lister, Raymond, *George Richmond: A Critical Biography* (London: Garton, 1981).

———, *Samuel Palmer: His Life and Art* (Cambridge: Cambridge University Press, 1987).

Liversidge, Michael and Catherine Edwards, eds, *Imagining Rome: British Artists and Rome in the Nineteenth Century* (exhibition catalogue, Bristol City Museum and Art Gallery) (London: Merrell Holbarton, 1996).

Locker Lampson, Frederick, *My Confidences: An Autobiographical Sketch Addressed to My Descendants*, ed. Augustine Birrell (London: Smith Elder, 1896).

Lucas, Edward Verrall, ed., *Letters of Charles Lamb: To Which Are Added Those of His Sister Mary Lamb*, 3 vols (London: J. M. Dent & Sons, 1935).

MacFarlane, Charles, *Reminiscences of a Literary Life* (London: John Murray, 1917).

MacGillivray, J. R., *Keats: A Bibliography and Reference Guide with an Essay on Keats's Reputation* (Toronto: University of Toronto Press, 1949).

Macleod, D. S., *Art and the Victorian Middle Class Money and the Making of Cultural Identity* (Cambridge: Cambridge University Press, 1996).

McCormick, E. H., *The Friend of Keats: A Life of Charles Armitage Brown* (Wellington, New Zealand: Victoria University Press, 1989).

McIntyre, C. T., *England against the Papacy 1858–61* (Cambridge: Cambridge University Press, 1983).

Select Bibliography

Magee, Bryan, *Clouds of Glory: A Hoxton Childhood* (London: Jonathan Cape, 2003).

Malins, Edward, *Samuel Palmer's Italian Honeymoon* (London: Oxford University Press, 1968).

Marks, Henry Stacey, *Pen and Pencil Sketches*, 2 vols (London: Chatto & Windus, 1894).

Mander, David, *More Light than Power: An Illustrated History of Shoreditch* (London: 1996).

Marquess, William Henry, *Lives of the Poet: The First Century of Keats Biography* (Pennsylvania: Pennsylvania State University Press, 1985).

Martin, R. B., *Tennyson: The Unquiet Heart* (London: Faber & Faber, 1983).

[Martin, Selma], *Narrative of a Three Years Residence in Italy, 1819–1822* (Dublin, 1831).

Mason, Eudo C., *The Mind of Henry Fuseli: Selections from his Writings with an Introductory Study* (London: Routledge & Kegan Paul, 1951).

Matthews, Geoffrey M., ed., *Keats: The Critical Heritage* (London: Routledge & Kegan Paul, 1971).

Matthews, Henry, *The Diary of an Invalid being the Journal of a Tour in Pursuit of Health in Portugal Italy Switzerland and France in the Years 1817–1819*, 2 vols (2nd edn, London, 1820).

Matthews, Samantha, *Poetical Remains Poets' Graves, Bodies, and Books in the Nineteenth Century* (Oxford: Oxford University Press, 2004).

Matthews, T., ed, *The Biography of John Gibson RA., Sculptor Rome* (London: Heinemann, 1911).

Mayne, John, *The Journal of John Mayne during a Tour on the Continent upon its Reopening after the Fall of Napoleon, 1816*, ed. J. M. Colles (London: Lane, 1909).

Medwin, Thomas, *The Life of Percy Byshhe Shelley with an Introduction and Commentary by H. B. Forman* (London: Oxford University Press, 1913).

Merrill, Lisa, *When Romeo was a Woman* (Ann Arbor: University of Michigan Press, 1999).

Millar, Oliver, *The Victorian Pictures in the Collection of Her Majesty the Queen* (Cambridge: Cambridge University Press, 1992).

Milnes, Robert Pemberton, *Notes of a Tour by Mrs Milnes, Myself and Our Daughter from Milan to Naples and by Rome and Florence to Milan AD 1831* (privately printed, n.d.), BL, C.193.a.90.

Milnes, Richard Monckton, *The Poetical Works of John Keats, with a memoir, by Lord Houghton: A New Revised and Enlarged Edition* (London: E. Moxon, Son & Co, 1871).

——, *The Poetical Works of John Keats, Chronologically Arranged and Edited, with a Memoir by Lord Houghton* (London: Aldine edition of the British Poets, 1876).

——, *Life, Letters and Literary Remains of John Keats* (London: J. M. Dent, 1927).

Monkhouse, Cosmo, *Life of Leigh Hunt* (London: Henry Colburn, 1893).

Monro, Ian S., 'The British Academy of Arts in Rome', *Journal of the Royal Society of Arts*, 102 (1952) 42–56.

Morgan, Lady (Sydney Owenson), *Italy*, 3 vols (London: Henry Colburn, 1821).

Motion, Andrew, *Keats* (London: Faber & Faber, 1997).

——, *Salt Water* (London: Faber & Faber, 1997).

Morley, Edith J., *The Life and Times of Henry Crabb Robinson* (London: Dent, 1935).

Murray, John, *Handbook for Travellers in Central Italy* (London: John Murray, 1843).

Najarian, James, *Victorian Keats: Manliness, Sexuality and Desire* (Basingstoke: Palgrave, 2002).

Newton, Charles T., *Travels and Discoveries in the Levant*, 2 vols (London: 1865).

Nitchie, E., *The Reverend Colonel Finch* (New York: Columbia University Press, 1940).

Norman, Sylvia, *Flight of the Skylark: The Development of Shelley's Reputation* (London: Max Reinhardt, 1954).

Nostrand, Sudie, 'The Keats Circle: Further Letters' (New York: New York University doctoral dissertation, 1973).

Select Bibliography

O'Connor, Maura, *The Romance of Italy and the English Imagination* (London: Macmillan, 1998).

Ormond, Richard and Malcolm Rogers, *Dictionary of British Portraiture*, vol. 3, (London: Batsford, 1981).

Oxford Dictionary of National Biography, ed. H.C.G. Matthew and Brian Harrison, 61 vols (Oxford: Oxford University Press, 2004).

Parson, Donald, *Portraits of Keats* (Cleveland: World Publishing Company, 1954).

Pevsner, Nicholas, *Academies of Art, Past and Present* (Cambridge: Cambridge University Press, 1990).

Platt, D. C. M., *The Cinderella Service: British Consuls since 1825* (London: Longman, 1971).

Pointon, Marcia, 'Keats, Joseph Severn and William Hilton: Notes on a Dispute', *Notes and Queries*, 20 (Feb. 1973), 50–4.

——, 'W. E. Gladstone as an Art Patron and Collector', *Victorian Studies*, 19 (1975), 73–98.

——, *William Dyce, 1806–1864: A Critical Biography* (Oxford: Clarendon Press, 1979).

Pope, Willard B., 'The Mask of Keats', in *English Miscellany: A Symposium of History Literature and the Arts* (Rome: 1950).

——, ed., *The Diary of Benjamin Robert Haydon*, 5 vols (Cambridge, MA: Harvard University Press, 1960, 1963).

Pope-Hennessy, James, *Monckton Milnes: The Years of Promise* (London: Constable, 1949).

——, *Monckton Milnes: The Flight of Youth, 1851–1885* (London: Constable, 1951).

Port, M. H., ed., *The Houses of Parliament* (London: Yale University Press, 1976).

Porter, Roy, *London: A Social History* (London: Hamish Hamilton, 1994).

Powell, Cecilia, *Turner in the South: Rome, Naples, Florence* (New Haven and London: Yale University Press, 1987).

——, *Italy in the Age of Turner 'The Garden of the World'* (Dulwich Picture Gallery exhibition catalogue) (London: 1998).

Premble, John, *The Mediterranean Passion: Victorians and Edwardians in the South* (London: Oxford University Press, 1988).

Raimbach, M. T. S., ed., *Memoirs and Recollections of Abraham Raimbach, Including a Memoir of Sir David Wilkie* (London: F. Shobeel, 1843).

Redgrave, Richard and Samuel Redgrave, *A Century of British Painters* (London: Phaidon Press, 1947).

Riall, Lucy, *Garibaldi: Invention of a Hero* (New Haven and London: Yale University Press, 2007).

Richardson, Joanna, *Fanny Brawne* (London: Vanguard Press, 1952).

——, *The Everlasting Spell: A Study of Keats and his Friends* (London: Jonathan Cape, 1963).

Richmond, William, *George Richmond: The Richmond Papers, from the Correspondence and Manuscripts of G. Richmond R.A., and His Son, Sir William Richmond*, ed. A. M. W. Stirling (London: William Heinemann, 1926).

Roberts, Cecil, *The Remarkable Young Man* (London: Hodder & Stoughton, 1954).

Robertson, David, *Sir Charles Eastlake and the Victorian Art World* (Princeton: Princeton University Press, 1978).

Robinson, Henry Crabb, *Diary, Reminiscences & Correspondence*, ed. Thomas Sadler, 3 vols (London: Macmillan, 1869).

——, *On Books and Their Writers*, ed. Edith J. Morley, 3 vols (London: J. M. Dent, 1938).

Roe, Nicholas, ed., *Keats and History* (Cambridge: Cambridge University Press, 1995).

——, *Fiery Heart: The First Life of Leigh Hunt* (London: Pimlico, 2005).

Rogers, Neville, ed., *Keats, Shelley and Rome: An Illustrated Miscellany* (London: Keats Shelley Memorial Association, 1949).

Rogers, Samuel, *The Italian Journal of Samuel Rogers, Edited with an Account of Roger's Life and of Travel in Italy in 1814-1821*, by J. R. Hale (London: Faber & Faber, 1956).

Rollins, Hyder Edward, *Keats Reputation in America to 1848* (Cambridge, MA: Harvard University Press, 1946).

——, ed., *The Keats Circle: Letters and Papers and More Letters and Poems of the Keats Circle, 1811-1878*, 2 vols (2nd edn, Cambridge, MA: Harvard University Press, 1965).

Rossetti, William Michael, *Life of John Keats* (London: Walter Scott, 1887).

Ruskin, John, *The Works of John Ruskin*, ed. E. T. Cook and Alexander Wedderburn, 39 vols (London: George Allen, 1903-12).

——, *The Diaries of John Ruskin*, ed. Joan Evans and J. H. Whitehouse, 3 vols (Oxford: Clarendon Press, 1956-9).

——, *Ruskin in Italy: Letters to his Parents 1845*, ed. Harold I. Shapiro (Oxford: Clarendon Press, 1972).

Ryall, H. T., ed., *Portraits of Eminent Conservatives and Statesmen with Genealogical and Historical Memoirs*, 2 vols (London: George Virtue, 1836-46).

Sala, George Augustus, *Rome and Venice with Other Wanderings in Italy in 1866* (London: Tinsley, 1869).

Sandby, W., *The History of the Royal Academy*, 2 vols (London: Longmans Green, 1862).

Scott, Grant F., 'Writing Keats's Last Days: Severn, Sharp and Romantic Biography', *Studies in Romanticism*, 42 (2003), 3-26.

——, 'New Mary Shelley Letters to the Severns', *Keats-Shelley Journal*, 54 (2005), 62-77.

——, 'New Severn Letters and Paintings: An Update with Corrections', *Keats-Shelley Journal* (2009).

Scott, Walter, *The Journal of Sir Walter Scott*, ed. W. E. K. Anderson (Oxford: Clarendon Press, 1972).

Severn, Arthur, *The Professor: Arthur Severn's Memoir of John Ruskin*, ed. James S. Dearelove (London: George Allen & Unwin, 1962).

Severn, Joseph, 'On the Vicissitudes of Keats's Fame', *Atlantic Monthly*, (April 1863), 401-7.

——, *John Keats: Letters of Joseph Severn to H. Buxton Forman* (Oxford: privately printed, 1933).

——, *Joseph Severn: Letters and Memoirs*, ed. Grant F. Scott, (Aldershot: Ashgate, 2005).

Sharp, William, *The Life and Letters of Joseph Severn* (London: Sampson Low, Marston & Company, 1892).

——, 'Joseph Severn and His Correspondents', *Atlantic Monthly*, 68 (December 1891), 736-49.

——, 'The Portraits of Keats', *Century Magazine*, (February 1906), 535-51.

——, 'Severn's Roman Journals', *Atlantic Monthly*, 69 (May 1892), 631-44.

Sharpe, J. B., *Elements of Anatomy Designed for the Use of Students in Fine Arts* (London: 1818).

Shelley, Mary, ed., *Essays, Letters from Abroad by Percy Bysshe Shelley*, 2 vols (London: E. Moxon, 1840).

——, *Rambles in Germany and Italy. Part III 1842 and 1843*, repr. in Jeanne Moskal, ed., *The Novels and Selected Works of Mary Shelley*, vol. 8: *Travel Writing* (London: William Pickering, 1996).

——, *The Letters of Mary Wollstonecroft Shelley*, ed. Betty T. Bennett, vol. 3 (London: Johns Hopkins University Press, 1988).

Select Bibliography

Siegel, Jonah, *Desire and Excess: The Nineteenth Century Culture of Art* (Princeton, NJ: Princeton University Press, 2000).

Smith, Charles Eastlake, ed., *Journals and Correspondence of Lady Eastlake*, 2 vols (London: John Murray, 1895).

Smith, Denis Mack, *Modern Italy: A Political History* (New Haven and London: Yale University Press, rev. edn, 1997).

Smith, Hillas, *Keats and Medicine* (Newport, IOW: Cross, 1995).

Solkin, David H., ed., *Art on the Line: The Royal Academy Exhibitions at Somerset House 1780–1836* (New Haven and London: Yale University Press, 2001).

St Clair, William, *Trelawny: The Incurable Romancer* (London: John Murray, 1977).

Stedman, E. C., 'A Call on Joseph Severn', *Century Magazine*, 27 (February 1884), 603.

Steegman, John, *Victorian Taste: A Study of the Arts and Architecture from 1830 to 1870* (London: Nelson, 1970).

Stendhal, Marie Henri Beyle, *A Roman Journal*, ed. and trans. Haakon Chevalier (London: Orion Press, 1959).

Sugano, Michael, 'Was "Keats's Last Sonnet" Really Written on the Maria Crowther?', *Studies in Romanticism*, 34 (1995), 413–40.

Taylor, Tom, ed., *The Life of Benjamin Robert Haydon: Historical Painter from his Autobiography and Journals* (London: Longman, Brown, Green and Longmans, 1853), 3 vols.

Thackeray, William Makepeace, 'Strictures on Pictures', 'A Second Lecture on the Fine Arts by Micheal Angelo Titmarsh Esquire', and 'A Pictorial Rhapsody: Concluded', *Fraser's Magazine*, 102 (June 1838), 758–64; 114 (June 1839), 743–50; and 121 (July 1840), 720–32.

Ticknor, George, *Life, Letters and Journals*, ed. G. S. Hillard, 2 vols (London: Sampson Low, 1876).

Tosh, John, *A Man's Place: Masculinity and the Middle-Class Home in Victorian England* (New Haven and London: Yale University Press, 1999).

Trench, Richard Chenevix, *Letters and Memorials*, ed. Charles Lowder, 2 vols (London: Kegan Paul, 1888).

Treves, Guiliana Artom, *The Golden Ring: The Anglo Florentines 1847–1862* (London: Longman Green, 1956).

Uwins, Sarah, *Memoir of Thomas Uwins R.A.*, 2 vols (London: Longman, Brown, 1858).

Ward, Aileen, *John Keats: The Making of a Poet* (London: Secker & Warburg, 1963).

Vaughan, William, *British Painting: The Golden Age from Hogarth to Turner* (London: Thames & Hudson, 1999).

Walker, Richard, *Regency Portraits* (London: National Portrait Gallery, 1985).

Wallace-Hadrill, Andrew, *The British School at Rome: One Hundred Years* (Rome: British School at Rome, 2006).

Webley, Derrick Pritchard, *Cast to the Winds: The Life and Work of Penry Williams (1802–1885)* (Aberystwyth: National Library of Wales, 1997).

Weld, Charles Richard, *Last Winter in Rome* (London: Longmans Green, 1865).

Wells, Kathleen M., 'The Return of the British Artists to Rome after 1815' (University of Leicester: PhD dissertation, 1984).

Whitley, William T., *Art in England, 1800–1820* (Cambridge: Cambridge University Press, 1928).

——, *Art in England, 1821–1837* (Cambridge: Cambridge University Press, 1930).

Williamson, George C., *The Keats Letters, Papers and Other Relics, forming the Dilke Bequest and an Account of the Portraits of Keats with 14 reproductions* (introd. H. Buxton Forman) (London: John Lane, 1914).

Williams, D. E., *The Life and Correspondence of Sir Thomas Lawrence*, 2 vols (London: Colburn & Bentley, 1831).

Wolfson, Susan J., 'Keats Enters History: Autopsy, Adonais and the Fame of Keats', in Nicholas Roe, ed., *Keats and History* (1995).

Wordsworth, Christopher, DD, *Journal of a Tour in Italy*, 2 vols (London: Rivingtons, 1863).

Wordsworth, William, *The Letters of William and Dorothy Wordsworth: The Later Years (1821–1850)*, ed. Ernest de Selincourt, 3 vols (Oxford: Clarendon Press, 1939).

Wu, Duncan, *William Hazlitt: The First Modern Man* (Oxford: Oxford University Press, 2008).

INDEX

Index

Fuseli, Heinrich 17, 19, 21, 25, 27, 35, 39, 41, 50, 55, 135, 138, 184
  artistic practice 22–3, 28
  artistic theory 23–4, 46
  favours Severn 52–3, 56

Gainsborough, Thomas 120, 277
Gale, Frederick 270, 272, 290
Garibaldi, Giuseppe 282, 283, 294, 295, 301
Genzano 161–2, 166
George III 18, 20
George IV 65, 142
Gibbon, Edward 166, 207
Gibson, John 88, 141, 144, 147, 165, 173, 175, 189, 196, 199, 202, 205, 209, 219, 254, 276, 283
  artistic training 86
  love of Rome 86–7
  generosity to other artists 86, 190, 195, 214, 221
  leads artistic community in Rome 117, 169, 193
  death 310
Gilder, Richard 342
Girometti, Guiseppe 203, 206
Gisborne, John and Maria 59, 116, 262
Gittings, Robert 2
Gladstone, William Ewart 4, 215, 220, 237, 253, 273, 287, 292, 335
  in Rome 195–9, 293
  enthusiasm for Severn's work 195, 197, 234
  as Severn's patron 221, 234–5, 246, 264, 266, 272, 279–81, 286, 310
  portraits by Severn 196–7, 232
  loses confidence in Severn 302–3
Gladstone, John 195
Glennie, Arthur 339
Gluck, Christoph Wilibald 29, 47
Glynne, Sir Stephen 197
Glynne, Catherine (Mrs Gladstone) 197–9
Goswell Street 13, 16, 30, 52, 128

Gott, Joseph 142, 144, 147, 173, 189, 212
  designs for Keats's and Shelley's tombstones 149, 152
Grant, Francis 232
Granville, Lord, see Leveson-Gower
Gray, David 343
Gray, Thomas 343
Gregorovius, Ferdinand 288
Greenstreet, Miss 297–8

Hallam, Arthur 196, 201, 203, 205
Halliday, Reverend Walter 273–4, 339
Hamilton, Duke of 169, see Douglas
Hamilton, Lady Emma 126
Hamilton, Lady Jane 176
Hamilton, Sir William 140
Hamlet, Thomas 25, 234
Hammond, Edward Sir 286, 289, 295–6, 302, 306–7, 309–10
Hanmer, Sir John 233
Hare, Augustus 209
Haslam, William 49, 59–60, 66, 67, 68, 73, 74, 75, 96, 102–3, 125, 126, 149, 150–1, 202, 219, 250, 256, 259, 260
  friendship with Severn 30–1, 100–1, 105, 108, 251–3
  introduces Severn to Keats 33–4
  suggests Severn go with Keats to Rome 61–4, 89–90
  maintenance of Severn's illegitimate child 62, 128, 143
Havell, William 189, 193–4
Hawes, Sir Benjamin 236
Haydn, Joseph 2, 29, 85, 163
Haydon, Benjamin Robert 19, 21, 24, 26, 34–5, 39–40, 41–2, 44, 57, 60, 118, 126, 156, 209, 246, 260, 264, 318
  influence on Keats 40, 46
  contempt for Severn 41, 56, 239–40
  suicide 243
  Christ's Entry into Jerusalem 58, 136, 320
Hayter, George 164, 218
Hazlitt, William 18, 23, 29, 58, 169
  in Rome 165
  The English Students at Rome 165–7
Herbert, J. R. 242

Index

Index

Index

Index

Index

Index